■ Praise for Telecommunications Essentials

"In *Telecommunications Essentials*, Goleniewski guides us through the ever-changing world of telecommunications with much sense and a great deal of style. Her wide ranging and in-depth study into this complex field is superbly researched and written. Its emphasis on learning and technology is thought-provoking and never fails to be relevant to the field today. It is essential reading."

—Chris Barclay, Director, Strategy & Planning, Retail, Telstra

"Lillian Goleniewski has a gift in presenting the complexity of telecommunications to her audiences. The careers of countless people in Australia have benefited from their contact with her. Her material is now captured in this book, which should rightfully grace any self-respecting technical collection."

—Dr. Bob Horton, Deputy Chairman, Australian Communications Authority

"If you need one good reference book on telecom, this is it. It's comprehensive, easy to understand, and up-to-date on latest technology—definitely a must-have for both beginners and professionals."

—To Chee Eng, Principal Analyst, Telecoms and Internet, Gartner Group

"Lili Goleniewski is a gifted communicator and educator who combines clear explanation of complex technologies with a firm grasp of the dynamic commercial environment in which those technologies are being deployed. The author's extensive international experience in communicating to an audience drawn from diverse cultures and differing levels of familiarity with technical concepts and the English language enables her to enliven subject matter that otherwise can be dauntingly unapproachable. I commend this book to anyone seeking to develop their understanding of developing communications technologies, regardless of their technical background."

—Peter Leonard, Managing Partner, Technology and Communications,
Gilbert & Tobin Lawyers

"*Telecommunications Essentials* provides a thorough overview of all aspects of the telecommunications network. Whether you are new to telecom or have years of experience, this well-organized and detailed reference will help you learn what you need to know or remember what you have forgotten."

—David West, Executive Vice President, Equinox Information Systems

"Here is a book that demystifies a technical world. Lili applies a matter-of-fact style and laces this with humor and the occasional wonder to weave all the complex building blocks of the telecommunications industry into a readable book. The book will be a permanent fixture on my 'go to find an answer' reference list."

—Kiron Chatterjee CEO, Koshen Holdings and former CEO of Asia Online

"*Telecommunication Essentials* is an excellent high-level view of telecom. It provides interesting examples of actual and potential applications in telecom. This is an extraordinarily useful and timely book."

—Natasha K. Zaslove, Lawyer

"Reviewing Lili's book was a joy. *Telecommunications Essentials* approaches the subject unlike typical academic or reference texts—instead, it tells stories, effectively and engagingly explaining the new culture evolving around telecommunications, with just the right amount of relevant technical details. *Telecommunications Essentials* traces the evolution of public networks from simple voice conduits to the life-changing multiservice information universe of the near future, intriguingly and provocatively predicting how we, as humans, might radically change our interactions—with each other and with machines—as a result.

I recommend Lili's book to anyone seeking an informative, enjoyable ride through today's telecommunications landscape."

—Steven Riley, Microsoft Telecommunications Consulting

Telecommunications Essentials

The Complete Global Source for Communications Fundamentals, Data Networking and the Internet, and Next-Generation Networks

Lillian Goleniewski

✦ Addison-Wesley

Boston • San Francisco • New York • Toronto • Montreal
London • Munich • Paris • Madrid
Capetown • Sydney • Tokyo • Singapore • Mexico City

The publisher offers discounts on this book when ordered in quantity for special sales. For more information, please contact:

Pearson Education Corporate Sales Division
201 W. 103rd Street
Indianapolis, IN 46290
(800) 428-5331
corpsales@pearsoned.com

Visit AW on the Web: www.aw.com/cseng/

Library of Congress Cataloging-in-Publication Data

Goleniewski, Lillian.
    Telecommunications essentials : the complete global source for communications
    fundamentals, data networking and the Internet, and next-generation networks / Lillian Goleniewski.
        p. cm.
    Includes bibliographical references and index.
    ISBN 0-201-76032-0
    1. Telecommunication. I. Title.
TK5101 G598 2002
    621.382—dc21   2001053752

ISBN 0-201-76032-0
Text printed on recycled paper

1 2 3 4 5 6 7 8 9 10—CRS—0504030201
First printing, December 2001

To all students of telecom worldwide, who continue to inspire me with their desire to learn about the industry and reward me with their genuine enthusiasm about the subject when they understand it!

Contents

Introduction

I love telecommunications. It is powerful and it empowers, with far-reaching consequences. It has demonstrated the potential to transform society and business, and the revolution has only just begun. With the invention of the telephone, human communications and commerce were forever changed: Time and distance began to melt away as a barrier to doing business, keeping in touch with loved ones, and being able to immediately respond to major world events. Through the use of computers and telecommunications networks, humans have been able to extend their powers of thinking, influence, and productivity, just as those in the Industrial Age were able to extend the power of their muscles, or physical self, through use of heavy machinery. Today, new inventions and developments are again poising telecommunications as a force to be reckoned with, forever changing human communications and commerce, and introducing machines as members of the networked society. This is an exciting era, and we face a host of new telecommunications technologies and applications that bring breathtaking new opportunities, particularly in the industries of entertainment, education, health care, government, advertising, lifestyle, and, sadly, warfare.

I have a favorite quote, from Eric Hoffer's *Vanguard Management*: "In a time of drastic change, it is the learners who inherit the future. The learned find themselves equipped to live in a world that no longer exists." That you are reading this book shows that you are aware of the monumental changes taking place in telecommunications infrastructures and usage and that you are eager to learn what those are—as well you should be! This book provides a thorough foundation for understanding a wide range of telecommunications principles and technologies.

If you are new to the communications and information industry, or if you simply want an understandable, yet comprehensive overview of telecommunications, this book is for you. *Telecommunications Essentials* will equip you with a blueprint on which you can build. The telecommunications landscape is vast; for a newcomer, it is treacherous terrain to navigate. This book provides you with a logical progression in gluing together all the pieces of the telecommunications puzzle. This book helps you to master the basic building blocks of key technologies, from the principles of telecommunications transmission and networking to the current and evolving nature of the Internet, broadband architecture, and optical networking, addressing both wired and wireless alternatives.

■ What This Book Covers

This book provides a concentrated, high-level overview of the terminology and issues that comprise telecommunications, and it discusses the major telecommunications infrastructures, including the PSTN, the Internet, cable TV, and wireless.

The book is divided into three parts. Part I, "Telecommunications Fundamentals," explains the basics, the arts and sciences of telecommunications. It begins by explaining the factors that are contributing to the telecommunications revolution and talks about some of the exciting new technologies that are on the horizon. Part I gives you a good grounding in the basics of telecommunications technology and terminology, covering communications fundamentals, and including the characteristics and uses of the various transmission media. Part I also discusses the processes involved in establishing communications channels, examining the differences between circuit-switched and packet-switched networks, and it explores the nature of the public switched telephone network (PSTN).

Part II, "Data Networking Basics," introduces the basics of data communications and networking. It discusses today's wide area and local area networking alternatives, as well as how the public Internet is structured. It also explores next-generation network services, such as virtual private networks (VPNs), Voice over IP, and streaming media.

Part III, "Next-Generation Networks," explores the realm of broadband networking and emerging technologies, including the near and distant future of communications and its convergence with related infotech industries. Part III covers next-generation network architectures, optical networking, broadband access alternatives, home area networking, and the realm of wireless communications.

In almost every aspect of life, it's important to put and keep things in context. A good idea in one situation might be a terrible idea in another situation. This is often the case with telecommunications; there is no one-size-fits-all be-all and end-all telecommunications solution. In assessing telecommunications needs, it is important to think about the prevailing conditions, so that you can choose the best transmission media, the best network architecture, and so on for the situation. It's also important to remember that prevailing conditions change. So what's right for you today may change six months down the road. As you plan a telecommunications strategy, it is important to look as far into the future as you can, to make your network as adaptable to future innovations as possible.

Online Tools That Supplement the Book

As founder and president of the LIDO Organization (www.telecomessentials.com), I have been involved in providing educational and advisory services to developers, suppliers, regulators, investors, consultants, and users of telecommunications technologies and networks since 1984. I want to share my knowledge of telecommunications with people in the format that best fits their learning styles. Some learn best in a classroom situation, where they can make eye contact with the instructor, view graphics while the instructor is explaining concepts, and ask questions in person. LIDO has been providing seminars for these learners for 17 years. Some people prefer to learn at their own pace, and they like the convenience and ability to track down further information that online learning affords. For these people, LIDO has provided e-learning programs (Web-delivered or via software license) since 1999. Yet other people learn best from books—when they can carry their learning tool with them anywhere and read and reread as time and circumstances allow. Therefore, I decided to write this book, to provide a comprehensive source on telecommunications essentials.

A 1775 quote from Samuel Johnson summarizes LIDO's approach to knowledge solutions in telecommunications: "Knowledge is of two kinds: We know a subject or we know where we can find information upon it." LIDO presents this book to help you learn, and it offers the Telecom Essentials Learning Center (www.telecomessentials.com/learningcenter) to help you keep learning. The Telecom Essentials Learning Center offers a number of helpful resources to help reinforce your telecommunications knowledge:

- **Online quizzes**—The online quizzes allow you to test your knowledge after reading each chapter. The quizzes are designed to reinforce what you have learned and assess those areas where you might wish to review the chapter.
- **Online telecommunications glossary**—The telecommunications vocabulary seems to grow daily. You can use the online glossary to search thousands of terms to find definitions quickly.

- **Student discussion forums**—These forums are your place to meet other individuals interested in the telecom field. You will find groups where you can discuss course materials and current events in telecom and where you can make valuable connections with individuals around the world to help advance your telecom knowledge and contact bases.

- **Links to thousands of related Web sites**—Each chapter is supported with links to recommended books, recommended magazines, and a comprehensive list of key sites to visit. This portal includes more than 6,000 links to important destinations in the world of telecom.

The Telecom Essentials Learning Center will help you to keep learning long after you have mastered the essentials of telecommunications.

As a LIDO student, you can also enjoy full access to Telecom WebCentral (www.telecomwebcentral.com). At Telecom WebCentral, you will have at your fingertips up-to-the-moment information on the latest applications and financial and legal news, as well as connections to telecom career groups and newsgroups.

Whether in seminar, book, or e-learning format, LIDO explains telecommunications technologies very clearly and in an entertaining and interesting fashion to a very diverse professional audience. It also supports ongoing learning by providing knowledge exchanges and e-business opportunities in a Web-based knowledge center and community. LIDO seminars are offered worldwide, and the perspectives you gain from this book, or by attending LIDO seminars, or from e-learning programs are not U.S.-centric. They provide knowledge and understanding of telecommunications environments on a global basis.

About the Author

Lillian Goleniewski is founder and president of the LIDO Organization, Inc., the leading provider of education, information, and advisory services in the area of telecommunications technologies, services, and networks. The LIDO Organization, established in 1984, is internationally recognized for providing expert educational programs and building telecommunications knowledge. Since its inception, LIDO has focused on the development and delivery of high-quality education and effective knowledge transfer. Recognizing that learning is life-long, LIDO's educational programs are Web-powered via LIDO Telecom WebCentral (www.telecomwebcentral.com), a globally recognized telecom knowledge portal that offers more than 6,000 resources to help enforce and build telecom knowledge.

Ms. Goleniewski lectures extensively on various telecommunications technology and management topics throughout the world. She is the author and creator of LIDO Telecommunications Essentials, offered in both seminar and e-learning formats. LIDO Telecommunications Essentials seminars have been conducted on an international basis since 1984 and are currently offered in Asia, Australia, Europe, the Middle East, New Zealand, North America, and South America. More than 20,000 people worldwide have attended LIDO's Telecommunications Essentials seminar series.

Ms. Goleniewski has been active in the design, development, and program participation of several major industry conferences since 1991. She is an Industry Advisory Board member of the Key3Media Comdex Forums & Conferences, IDG's ComNet Washington DC, and EJ Krause Expocomm conferences worldwide.

Ms. Goleniewski's diverse industry participation includes serving as a judge for the Global Information Infrastructure Awards from 1995 to 1999, as well as serving as a member of the Michigan Information Network (MIN) technical committee. Ms. Goleniewski has served as an instructor with the San Francisco State University College of Extended Learning, and she has acted as a mentor for the GirlGeeks.com community. She is a member of and contributor to the Advanced Networked Cities and Regions Association (ANCARA), as well as a member of the Technology Empowerment Network (www.techempower.net), a global initiative of the Technology Pioneers.

Prior to forming the LIDO Organization, Ms. Goleniewski held the position of Telecommunications Operations Manager at the Electric Power Research Institute (EPRI), the research and development arm of the U.S. utility industry. Before joining EPRI, Ms. Goleniewski was vice president of operations of a San Francisco-based telecommunications consulting firm.

Ms. Goleniewski graduated Phi Beta Kappa and summa cum laude from Wayne State University in Detroit, Michigan. She holds a bachelor's degree in psychology and has completed numerous postgraduate studies in information technologies, as well as in psychology. Ms. Goleniewski was the recipient of a National Science Foundation Award to conduct research in the area of human perception and information processing.

Ms. Goleniewski is fluent in Polish and has conversational skills in both Russian and French.

Acknowledgments

My many and heartfelt thanks to all the people involved with this book. First, Stephane Thomas (associate editor, Addison-Wesley) is the brilliant young woman at Addison-Wesley who came after me to write this book, and then worked with me to make it a reality, not the least of which meant finding a talented editor. That editor, Kitty Jarrett, had to work with some nontraditional approaches, timetables, and my globe-trotting calendar, but despite all, was able to capture my voice throughout the book to create a very special mix of technology, delivered with a human touch. I'm hoping to see Kitty become a permanent part of LIDO Telecom Essentials Learning Center.

I'd like to extend special thanks to my key reviewers, whose comments were extremely helpful (and sometimes just extreme). Their combined thoughts are represented throughout the book. Some are old friends, some are new friends, and some I've never met, but all of them are involved with the industry in one way or another, and as a group they represent the kind of audience this book is intended for. They represent professionals in IT&T, marketing, sales, business development, education, government, finance, and law, and they come from various corners of the world. Thank you, Dr. Richard Horton (senior program manager, Market Development, ODTR, Ireland) for providing three views in one: those of scientist, a regulator with global experience, and a European. Along with providing technical commentary, his voice ensured that we provided you with at least an understanding of the significance of the regulatory environment to the telecom industry. Big thanks to Mr. Steve Riley (telecommunications consultant, Microsoft), for his dedication in providing a technical voice, ensuring that you would never be misled by my simplification of a complex subject, and for his encouraging notes about some of my more controversial comments. I'd like to thank Mr. Craig Mathias (principal, Farpoint Group), my favorite wireless guru, for sharing his vast wireless knowledge with me over the years, as well as for his ongoing contributions to LIDO's seminar programs on wireless and mobile essentials. My gratitude to Mr. Reb Forte (chief financial officer, Portarius); Mr. David West (executive vice president, Equinox Information Systems); Ms. Natasha Zaslove (lawyer and technology marketing consultant); Mr. Peter Leonard (partner, Gilbert & Tobin); and Ms. Valerie Forte (vice president, business development, LIDO), who offered a mélange of marketing, sales, finance, business, and legal perspectives. Many thanks for the time and feedback you all contributed to the successful completion of this book. To the colleagues I've known over the years (and you know who you are), a really special thank-you for your friendship and constant encouragement—you're simply the best!

I'd like to also acknowledge and express gratitude to Mr. Blake Webster, LIDO's Web master, for the design and implementation of the Telecom Essentials Learning Center, the Web-based learning resource that accompanies this book. I've always appreciated his ability to visually manifest my ideas, and never more so than in the design of the artwork for the cover of this book. His creative interpretation emphasizes our belief that telecommunications is a universe unto itself, where there's heaps to explore! And I'm grateful to Ms. Melanie Buck of Addison-Wesley for designing the perfect book cover out of it! I'd also like to thank one of LIDO's interns, Ms. Judy Starcevich, for her diligent work on Telecom WebCentral and the Telecom Essentials Learning Center; keeping up with telecom resources on the Web is an awesome task, and not one many take on so bravely.

I'm delighted to be fortunate enough to acknowledge and thank a family that can be counted on to do whatever it takes. Their support has always been a blessing, and their help in taking care of my home and me, while I sat chained to my computer, was no small sacrifice—Mom, Dad, and Richard, and Alcatraz, I appreciate you greatly!

Finally, my sincere and hearty thanks to all those behind the scenes at Addison-Wesley, who have always expressed great enthusiasm for the project, from the artists in the art department, to the marketing team, to the production staff: You've all been an absolute pleasure to work with!

Part I

Telecommunications Fundamentals

Understanding the Telecommunications Revolution

In recent years, the word *telecommunications* has been used so often, and applied in so many situations, that it has become part of our daily lexicon, yet its definition remains elusive. So, let's start with a definition. The word *telecommunications* has its roots in Greek: *tele* means "over a distance," and *communicara* means "the ability to share." Hence, *telecommunications* literally means "the sharing of information over a distance." Telecommunications is more than a set of technologies, it's more than an enormous global industry (estimated to be US$2.5 trillion), it's more than twenty-first-century business and law that is being re-created to accommodate a virtual world, and it's more than a creator and destroyer of the state of the economy. Telecommunications is a way of life. Telecommunications affects how and where you do everything—live, work, play, socialize, entertain, serve, study, teach, rest, heal, and protect. Telecommunications has served a critical role in shaping society and culture, as well as in shaping business and economics.

It is important to examine telecommunications from the broadest perspective possible to truly appreciate the depth and complexity of this field and thereby understand the opportunities it affords. The best way to learn to "think telecom" is to quickly examine how it is changing both business and lifestyle.

Throughout the 1980s and 1990s, much of the IT&T (information technologies and telecommunications) industry's focus was on how to reengineer the likes of financial institutions, manufacturing, retail, service, and government. These technology deployments were largely pursued and justified on the grounds of reducing costs and enhancing competitiveness by speeding communications.

Today, we are shifting our focus to another set of objectives: Our technology deployments are targeted at supporting not just the needs of a business enterprise, but also those of the consumers. The revolution in integrated media is transforming all aspects of human activity related to communication and information. We are moving to computer-based environments that support the creation, sharing, and distribution of multimodal information. Whereas traditional telecommunications networks have allowed us to cross barriers associated with time and distance, the new multimedia realm is allowing us to include vital physical cues in the information stream, introducing a physical reality into the world of electronic communications, goods, and services. Not surprisingly, some of the industries that are being most radically revolutionized are those that deal with the human senses, including entertainment, health care, education, advertising, and, sadly, warfare. In each of these key sectors, there are telecommunications solutions that address the business need, reduce costs, or enhance operations by speeding business processes and aiding communications. These industries are also examining how to virtualize their products and/or services—that is, how to apply telecommunications to support electronic services targeted at the consumers of that industry's products. Not surprisingly, changing the way you attend a class, see a doctor, watch a movie, get a date, shop for software, take a cruise, and stay in touch creates significant changes in how you use your time and money. Simply put, technology changes your way and pace of life.

This chapter presents the big picture of the telecommunications revolution, and the rest of the book gives greater detail about the specific technologies and applications that will comprise the telecommunications future.

■ Changes in Telecommunications

A quick orientation of how emerging technologies are affecting industries and lifestyle highlights the importance of understanding the principles of telecommunications, and, hopefully, to inspire you to "think telecom." The changes discussed here are ultimately very important to how telecommunications networks will evolve and to where the growth areas will be.

An enormous amount of the activity driving telecommunications has to do with the emergence of advanced applications; likewise, advances in telecommunications capabilities spur developments in computing platforms and capabilities. The two are intimately and forever intertwined. The following sections discuss some of the changes that are occurring in both telecommunications and in computing platforms and applications, as well as some of the changes expected in the next several years.

Incorporating Human Senses in Telecommunications

Telecommunications has allowed a virtual world to emerge—one in which time and distance no longer represent a barrier to doing business or communicating—but we're still lacking something that is a critical part of the human information-processing realm. The human mind acts on physical sensations in the course of its information processing; the senses of sight, sound, touch, and motion are key to our perception and decision making. Developments in sensory technologies and networks will allow a new genre of sensory reality to emerge, bridging the gap between humans and machines. One of the most significant evolutions occurring in computing and communications is the introduction of the human senses into electronic information streams. The following are a few of the key developments in support of this more intuitive collaborative human–machine environment:

- Computers are now capable of hearing and speaking, as demonstrated by Tellme, a popular U.S. voice-activated service that responds to defined voice prompts and provides free stock quotes, weather information, and entertainment guides to 35,000 U.S. cities.

- The capability to produce three-dimensional sound through digital mastery—a technology called "virtual miking"—is being developed at the University of Southern California's Integrated Media Systems Center.

- Virtual touch, or *haptics*, enables a user to reach in and physically interact with simulated computer content, such as feeling the weight of the Hope diamond in your hand or feeling the fur of a lion. Two companies producing technology in this area are SensAble Technologies and Immersion Corporation. They are producing state-of-the-art force feedback, whole-hand sensing, and real-time 3D interaction technologies, and these hardware and software products have a wide range of applications for the manufacturing and consumer markets, including virtual-reality job training, computer-aided design, remote handling of hazardous materials, and "touch" museums.

- The seduction of smell is also beginning to find its way into computers, allowing marketers to capitalize on the many subtle psychological states that smell can induce. Studies show that aromas can be used to trigger fear, excitement, and many other emotions. Smell can be used to attract visitors to Web sites, to make them linger longer and buy more, to help them assimilate and retain information, or to instill the most satisfying or terrifying of emotional states (now that's an interactive game!). Three companies providing this technology today are Aromajet, DigiScents, and TriSenx. Aromajet, for example, creates products that address video games, entertainment, medical, market research, personal and home products, and marketing and point of sales applications.

■ The visual information stream provides the most rapid infusion of information, and a large portion of the human brain is devoted to processing visual information. To help humans process visual information, computers today can see; equipped with video cameras, computers can capture and send images, and can display high-quality entertainment programming. The visual stream is incredibly demanding in terms of network performance; thus, networks today are rapidly preparing to enable this most meaningful of information streams to be easily distributed.

The Emergence of Wearables

How we engage in computing and communications will change dramatically in the next decade. Portable computing devices have changed our notion of what and where a workplace is and emphasized our desire for mobility and wireless communication; they are beginning to redefine the phrase *dressed for success*. But the portable devices we know today are just a stepping stone on the way to wearables. Context-aware wearable computing will be the ultimate in light, ergonomic, reliable, flexible, and scalable platforms. Products that are available for use in industrial environments today will soon lead to inexpensive, easy-to-use wearables appearing at your neighborhood electronics store:

■ Xybernaut's Mobile Assistant IV (MA-IV), a wearable computer, provides its wearer with a full-fledged PC that has a 233MHz Pentium chip, 32MB memory, and upward of 3GB storage. A wrist keyboard sports 60 keys. Headgear suspended in front of the eye provides a full-color VGA screen, the size of a postage stamp but so close to the eye that images appear as on a 15-inch monitor. A miniature video camera fits snugly in a shirt pocket. Bell Canada workers use MA-IVs in the field; they replace the need to carry manuals and provide the ability to send images and video back to confer with supervisors. The MA-IV is rather bulky, weighing in at 4.4 pounds (2 kilograms), but the soon-to-be-released MA-V will be the first mass-market version, and it promises to be lightweight.

■ MIThril is the next-generation wearables research platform currently in development at MIT's Media Lab. It is a functional, operational body-worn computing architecture for context-aware human-computer interaction research and general-purpose wearable computing applications. The MIThril architecture combines a multiprotocol body bus and body network, integrating a range of sensors, interfaces, and computing cores. It is designed to be integrated into everyday clothing, and it is both ergonomic and flexible. It combines small, light-weight RISC processors (including the StrongARM), a single-cable power/data "body bus," and high-bandwidth wireless networking in a package that is nearly as light, comfortable, and unobtrusive as ordinary street clothing.

Bandwidth

A term that you hear often when discussing telecommunications is *bandwidth*. Bandwidth is a critical commodity. Historically, bandwidth has been very expensive, as it was based on the sharing of limited physical resources, such as twisted-pair copper cables and coax. *Bandwidth* is largely used today to refer to the capacity of a network or a telecom link, and it is generally measured in bits per second (bps). *Bandwidth* actually refers to the range of frequencies involved—that is, the difference between the lowest and highest frequencies supported—and the greater the range of frequencies, the greater the bandwidth, and hence the greater the number of bits per second, or information carried.

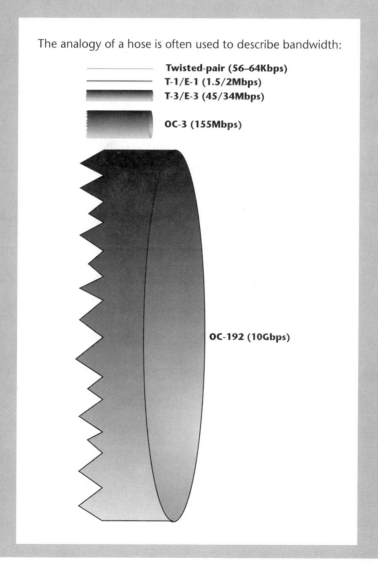

The analogy of a hose is often used to describe bandwidth:

Twisted-pair (56–64Kbps)
T-1/E-1 (1.5/2Mbps)
T-3/E-3 (45/34Mbps)

OC-3 (155Mbps)

OC-192 (10Gbps)

To be truly useful, wearables will need to be aware of where you are and what you're doing. Armed with this info, they will be able to give you information accordingly. (Location-based services are discussed in Chapter 14, "Wireless Communications.")

Moving Toward Pervasive Computing

As we distribute intelligence across a wider range of devices, we are experiencing *pervasive computing,* also called *ubiquitous computing.* We are taking computers out of stand-alone boxes to which we are tied and putting them into ordinary things, in everyday objects around us. These new things, because they are smart, have a sense of self-awareness and are able to take care of themselves. When we embed intelligence into a device, we create an interesting new opportunity for business. That device has to have a reason for being, and it has to have a reason to continue evolving so that you will spend more money and time on it. To address this challenge, device manufacturers are beginning to bundle content and applications with their products. The result is smart refrigerators, smart washing machines, smart ovens, smart cabinets, smart furniture, smart beds, smart televisions, smart toothbrushes, and an endless list of other smart devices. (These smart devices are discussed in detail in Chapter 15, "The Broadband Home and HANs.")

Devices are becoming smaller and more powerful all the time, and they're getting physically closer to our bodies, as well. The growing amount of intelligence distributed throughout the network is causing changes in user profiles.

Moving Toward Machine-to-Machine Communications

We are moving away from human-to-human communications to an era of machine-to-machine communications. Today, there are just over 6 billion human beings on the planet, yet the number of microprocessors is reported to be more than 15 billion. Devices have become increasingly intelligent, and one characteristic of an intelligent system is that it can communicate. As the universe of communications-enabled devices grows, so does the traffic volume between them. As these smart things begin to take on many of the tasks and communications that humans traditionally exchanged, they will change the very fabric of our society. For example, your smart washing machine will initiate a call to the service center to report a problem and schedule resolution with the help of an intelligent Web agent long before you even realize that something is wrong! These developments are predicted to result in the majority of traffic—up to 95% of it—being exchanged between machines, with traditional human-to-human communications representing only 5% of the network traffic by 2010.

Adapting to New Traffic Patterns

Sharing of information can occur in a number of ways—via smoke signals, by letters sent through the postal service, or as transmissions through electrical or optical media, for example. Before we get into the technical details of the technologies in the industry, it's important to understand the driving forces behind computing and communications. You need to understand the impact these forces have on network traffic and therefore on network infrastructure. In today's environment, telecommunications embodies four main traffic types, each of which has different requirements in terms of network capacity, tolerance for delays—and particularly variations in the delay—in the network, and tolerance for potential congestion and therefore losses in the network:

- **Voice**—Voice traffic has been strong in the developed world for years, and more subscriber lines are being deployed all the time. However, some three billion people in the world haven't even used a basic telephone yet, so there is yet a huge market to be served. Voice communications are typically referred to as being *narrowband*, meaning that they don't require a large amount of network capacity. For voice services to be intelligible and easy to use, delays must be kept to a minimum, however, so the delay factors in moving information from Point A to Point B have to be tightly controlled in order to support real-time voice streams. (Concepts such as delay, latency, and error control are discussed in Chapter 6, "Data Communications Basics.")

- **Data**—Data communications refers to the exchange of digitized information between two machines. Depending on the application supported, the bandwidth or capacity requirements can range from medium to high. As more objects that are visual in nature (such as images and video) are included with the data, that capacity demand increases. Depending again on the type of application, data may be more or less tolerant of delays. Text-based exchanges are generally quite tolerant of delays. But again, the more real-time nature there is to the information type, as in video, the tighter the control you need over the latencies. Data traffic is growing much faster than voice traffic; it has grown at an average rate of about 30% to 40% per year for the past decade. To accommodate data communication, network services have been developed to address the need for greater capacity, cleaner transmission facilities, and smarter network management tools. Data encompasses many different information types. In the past, we saw these different types as being separate entities (for example, video and voice in a videoconference), but in the future, we must be careful not to separate things this way because, after all, in the digital age, all data is represented as ones and zeros.

■ **Image**—Image communications requires medium to high bandwidth—the greater the resolution required, the greater the bandwidth required. For example, many of the images taken in medical diagnostics require very high resolution. Image traffic tolerates some delay because it includes no motion artifacts that would be affected by any distortions in the network.

■ **Video**—Video communications, which are becoming increasingly popular and are requiring ever-greater bandwidth, are extremely sensitive to delay. The future is about visual communications. We need to figure out how to make video available over a network infrastructure that can support it and at a price point that consumers are willing to pay. When our infrastructures are capable of supporting the capacities and the delay limitations required by real-time applications, video will grow by leaps and bounds.

All this new voice, data, and video traffic means that there is growth in backbone traffic levels as well. This is discussed further later in the chapter, in the section "Increasing Backbone Bandwidth."

The telecommunications revolution has spawned great growth in the amount and types of traffic, and we'll see even more types of traffic as we begin to incorporate human senses as part of the network. The coming chapters talk in detail about what a network needs in order to handle the various traffic types.

Handling New Types of Applications

The new traffic patterns imply that the network will also be host to a new set of applications—not just simple voice or text-based data, but to new genres of applications that combine the various media types.

The ability to handle digital entertainment applications in a network is crucial. In some parts of the world, such as Asia, education may have primary focus, and that should tell us where we can expect greater success going forward. But throughout much of the world, entertainment is where people are willing to spend the limited numbers of dollars that they have to spend on electronic goods and services. The digital entertainment realm will include video editing, digital content creation, digital imaging, 3D gaming, and virtual reality applications, and all these will drive the evolution of the network. It's the chicken and the egg story: What comes first, the network or the applications? Why would you want a fiber-optic broadband connection if there's nothing good to draw over that connection? Why would you want to create a 3D virtual reality application when there's no way to distribute it? The bottom line is that the applications and the infrastructures have to evolve hand-in-hand to manifest the benefits and the dollars we associate with their future.

Another form of application that will be increasingly important is in the realm of streaming media. A great focus is put on the real-time delivery of information, as in entertainment, education, training, customer presentations, IPO trade shows, and telemedicine consultations. (Streaming media is discussed in detail in Chapter 11, "Next-Generation Network Services.")

E-commerce (electronic commerce) and m-commerce (mobile commerce) introduce several new requirements for content management, transaction platforms, and privacy and security tools, so they affect the types of information that have to be encoded into the basic data stream and how the network deals with knowledge of what's contained within those packets. (Security is discussed in detail in Chapter 11.)

Increasing Backbone Bandwidth

Many of the changes discussed so far, but primarily the changes in traffic patterns and applications, will require immense amounts of backbone bandwidth. Table 1.1 lists a number of the requirements that emerging applications are likely to make on backbone bandwidth.

Table 1.1 Backbone Bandwidth Requirements for Advanced Applications

Application	Bandwidth Needed	Examples
Online virtual reality	1,000–70,000 terabits per second	Life-size 3D holography; telepresence
Machine communications	50,000–200,000 terabits per second	Smart things; Web agents; robots
Meta-computing	50,000–200,000 terabits per second	Weather prediction; warfare modeling

In addition, advances in broadband access technologies will drive a demand for additional capacity in network backbones. Once 100Gbps broadband residential access becomes available—and there are developments on the horizon—the core networks will require capacities measured in exabits per second (that is, 1 billion Gbps). These backbone bandwidth demands make the revolutionary forces of optical networking critical to our future. (Optical networking is discussed in detail in Chapter 12, "Optical Networking.")

Responding to Political and Regulatory Forces

New developments always bring with them politics. Different groups vie for money, power, the ability to bring new products to market first and alone, and the

Metric Prefixes and Equivalents

The following table defines commonly used metric prefixes:

Prefix	Abbreviation	Meaning
Deca	da	10 (10)
Hecto	h	10^2 (100)
Kilo	K	10^3 (1,000)
Mega	M	10^6 (1,000,000)
Giga	G	10^9 (1,000,000,000)
Tera	T	10^{12} (1,000,000,000,000)
Peta	P	10^{15} (1,000,000,000,000,000)
Exa	E	10^{18} (1,000,000,000,000,000,000)
Deci	d	10^{-1} (0.1)
Centi	c	10^{-2} (0.01)
Milli	m	10^{-3} (0.001)
Micro	μ	10^{-6} (0.000001)
Nano	n	10^{-9} (0.000000001)
Pico	p	10^{-12} (0.000000000001)
Femto	f	10^{-15} (0.000000000000001)
Atto	a	10^{-18} (0.000000000000000001)

For example, 10Gbps = 10,000,000,000bps, and 4KHz = 4,000Hz (that is, cycles per second).

The following shows the relationships of commonly used units of measure to one another:

1Kbps = 1,000bps

1Gbps = 1,000Mbps

1Tbps = 1,000Gbps

1Pbps = 1,000Tbps

1Ebps = 1,000Pbps

right to squash others' new ideas. A prominent characteristic of the telecommunications sector is the extent to which it is influenced by government policy and regulation. The forces these exert on the sector are inextricably tied to technological and market forces.

Because of the pervasive nature of information and communication technologies and the services that derive from them, coupled with the large prizes to be won, the telecommunications sector is subjected to a lot of attention from policymakers. Particularly over the past 20 years or so, telecommunications policy and regulation have been prominent on the agendas of governments around the world. This reflects the global trend toward liberalization, including, in many countries, privatization of the former monopoly telcos. However, interest from policymakers in telecommunications goes much deeper than this. A great deal of this interest stems from the extended reach and wide impact that information and communication technologies have. Here are some examples:

- Telephony, e-mail, and information services permit contact between friends and families and offer convenience to people in running their day-to-day lives. Thus, they have major economic and social implications.

- In the business arena, information and communication technologies offer business efficiency and enable the creation of new business activities. Thus, they have major employment and economic implications.

- Multimedia and the Internet offer new audio, video, and data services that affect entertainment and education, among other areas. These new services are overlapping with traditional radio and television broadcasting, and major cultural implications are appearing.

- News delivery influences peoples' perceptions of governments and their own well-being, thereby influencing voter attitudes. Telecommunications brings attention to cultural trends. Therefore, telecommunications has major political as well as cultural implications.

- Government applications of information and communication technologies affect the efficiency of government. Defense, national security, and crimefighting applications are bringing with them major political implications.

Given this background of the pervasive impact that information and communication technologies have, it is hardly surprising they get heavy policy attention.

Regulatory Background

Although many national regulatory authorities today are separate from central government, they are, nevertheless, built on foundations of government policy. Indeed, the very act of creating an independent regulatory body is a key policy decision. Historically, before telecommunications privatization and liberalization came to the fore, regulation was often carried out within central government, which also controlled the state-run telcos. That has changed in recent years in many, but not all, countries.

Given their policy foundation, and the fact that government policies vary from country to country and from time to time, it is not surprising that regulatory environments evolve and differ from country to country. These evolutions and international variations sometimes pose planning problems for the industry, and these problems can lead to frustrations and tensions between companies and regulatory agencies. They can also lead to disagreements between countries (for example, over trade issues). Although moves to encourage international harmonization of regulatory regimes (for example, by the International Telecommunications Union [ITU] and by the European Commission) have been partially successful, differences remain in the ways in which countries interpret laws and recommendations. Moreover, given that regulations need to reflect changing market conditions and changing technological capabilities, it is inevitable that over time regulatory environments will change, too. So regulation is best viewed as another of the variables, such as technological change, that the telecommunications industry needs to take into account.

The Policy and Regulatory Players

At the global level, there are a number of international bodies that govern or make recommendations about telecommunications policy and regulation. In addition to the ITU and the European Commission, there are various standards bodies (for example, Institute of Electrical and Electronics Engineers [IEEE], European Telecommunications Standards Institute [ETSI], American National Standards Institute [ANSI], the Telecommunication Technology Committee [TTC]) and industry associations (for example, the European Competitive Telecommunications Association [ECTA], the Telecommunications Industry Association [TIA]). Representatives of national governments and regulatory authorities meet formally (for example, ITU World Radio Conferences, where many countries are represented) and informally (for example, Europe's National Regulatory Authorities [NRAs] exchange views at Independent Regulators Group [IRG] meetings). Other organizations, such as the World Trade Organization (WTO) and regional bodies, also influence telecommunications policy and regulation at the international level.

At the national level, several parts of central government are generally involved, and there can sometimes be more than one regulatory body for a nation. Some of these organizations are major players; others play less prominent, but nevertheless influential, roles. In the United States, for example, the Federal Communications Commission (FCC) is the national regulatory body, and public utility commissions regulate at the state level. The U.S. State Department coordinates policy regarding international bodies such as the ITU. The White House, the Department of Commerce, largely through the National Telecommunications and Information Administration (NTIA), the Justice Department, the Trade Representative, and the Department of Defense are among the various parts of the administration that set or contribute to telecommunications policy. The U.S. Congress and the U.S. government's legislative branch also play important roles. In addition, industry associations, policy "think tanks," regulatory affairs departments within companies, telecommunications lawyers, and lobbyists all contribute to policy debates and influence the shape of the regulatory environment.

Other countries organize their policy and regulatory activities differently from the United States. For example, in the United Kingdom, the Office of Telecommunications (OFTEL) mainly regulates what in the United States would be known as "common carrier" matters, whereas the Radiocommunications Agency (RA) deals with radio and spectrum matters. However, at the time of writing, it has been proposed that OFTEL and RA be combined into a new Office of Communications (OFCOM). In Hong Kong, telecommunications regulation was previously dealt with by the post office, but now the Office of the Telecommunications Authority (OFTA) is the regulatory body. So, not only do regulatory environments change, but so, too, do the regulatory players.

The Main Regulatory Issues

Let's look briefly at what regulators do. Again, this varies somewhat from country to country and over time. In the early years of liberalization, much time would typically be spent in licensing new entrants and in putting in place regulations designed to keep a former monopoly telco from abusing its position by, for example, stifling its new competitors or by charging inappropriately high prices to its customers. Here the regulator is acting as a proxy for market forces. As effective competition takes root, the role of the regulator changes somewhat. Much of the work then typically involves ensuring that all licensed operators or service providers meet their license obligations and taking steps to encourage the development of the market such that consumers benefit.

The focus of most regulatory bodies is, or should be, primarily on looking after the interests of the various end users of telecommunications. However, most regulators would recognize that this can be achieved only if there is a healthy and vibrant industry to deliver the products and services. So while there are often natural tensions between a regulator and the companies being regulated, it is at the same time important for cooperation between the regulator and the industry to take place. In Ireland, for example, the role of the regulator is encapsulated by the following mission statement: "The purpose of the Office of the Director of Telecommunications Regulation is to regulate with integrity, impartiality, and expertise to facilitate rapid development of a competitive leading-edge telecommunications sector that provides the best in price, choice, and quality to the end user, attracts business investment, and supports ongoing social and economic growth."

Flowing from regulators' high-level objectives are a range of activities such as licensing, price control, service-level agreements, interconnection, radio spectrum management, and access to infrastructure. Often, regulatory bodies consult formally with the industry, consumers, and other interested parties on major issues before introducing regulatory changes. A more detailed appreciation of what telecommunications regulators do and what their priorities are can be obtained by looking at the various reports, consultation papers, and speeches at regulatory bodies' Web sites.

■ The New Public Network

Given the revolutionary changes in telecommunications, it is clear that we are moving toward a new public network. The new public network needs to have end-to-end digitalization. We began implementing digital technology in the early 1960s, and we've done quite well at getting it deployed throughout the various backbone networks. Worldwide, probably some 80% of backbones are now digitalized. However, the local loop—that is, the last mile between the subscriber and the network—is still largely analog. Only around 7% of the subscriber lines today are digital, so the vast majority of users are functionally limited to analog usage.

We face an incredible modernization task to digitalize the local loop and to truly make the network digital from end-to-end. However, the even greater challenge rests in the "last mile" economics and politics. The regulatory and political issues are critical indeed. Without broadband access, the Internet can't grow, advanced applications can't take off, revenues can't be realized, and we can't progress. The local loop is largely in the control of the incumbent telephone companies worldwide, and they do not seem to have the political and economic incentive to make end-to-end digitalization happen. There's lots of discussion on how to resolve this—by regulation, by enforcement, by market forces. When we find some resolution, the telecommunications industry will blossom like never before. (See Chapter 2, "Telecommunications Technology Fundamentals," and Chapter 13, "Broadband Access Solutions.")

Another factor that affects the new public network is that we are now in the last years of the electronic era and in the first years of a new generation of optical, or photonic, networking. Conversions between electrical and optical signals reduce the data rates and introduce the potential for distortion; hence, they affect the data stream. To eliminate these conversions, we need to work toward achieving an end-to-end optical networking scenario. (See Chapter 12.)

The new public network must also be an intelligent programmable network. That is, we want to distribute service logic via databases on a networkwide basis so that anywhere in the world, you can access any service or feature you want, regardless of the network provider or network platform that you are connected to. This intelligent programmable network requires some form of communication between the network elements. In the public switched telephone network (PSTN), this communication is done through the use of high-speed common-channel signaling systems that allow real-time communications between the network elements. In essence, it's like a private subnetwork. No voice, data, or image traffic is carried on these channels—only the signaling information that dictates who's calling, what rights they have, what features and services they want to use, and so on. Because there are many manufacturers and providers of network platforms, it's important that the programmable platforms use open application programming interfaces. (See Chapter 5, "The PSTN," and Chapter 10, "Next-Generation Networks.")

The new public network requires a new broadband infrastructure that has very high capacities and offers multichannel service (that is, one physical medium can carry multiple conversations). The two dominant media types in the broadband arena are high-speed fiber (run as close as possible to the customer) and broadband wireless (over the last few feet or meters to the customer, if needed). (See Chapter 13.)

It is very important that the new public network be a low-latency network. Humans cannot suffer much delay—on the order of 650 milliseconds—in receiving information before it becomes unintelligible. To give you some perspective on this, on a satellite call, the delay between the time you say hi to the time you hear the response is annoying, but it lasts only 500 milliseconds. Current infrastructures, such as the Internet, may impart as much as 1,000 or 2,000 milliseconds of delay. They therefore play havoc with any type of traffic that is delay sensitive—and voice, video, and multimedia are all very delay sensitive. So when we say we want to build low-latency networks for the future, we mean networks that impose no delays that result from congestion points. (See Chapter 10.)

Another characteristic of the new public network is that, in contrast to today's world, where we have separate platforms for each of the traffic types, the platforms need to be multiservice—they have to accommodate voice, data, and video streams, as well as any streams invented in the future. (See Chapter 10.)

The new public network should also be agnostic. That is, it should not follow only one protocol, but it should understand that the universe truly is multiprotocol and we will always have multiple protocols to deal with. The best way to create an agnostic network is to have a box that enables interfaces for the most prevalent of the data protocols. (See Chapter 9, "The Internet: Infrastructure and Service Providers.")

The new public network also needs to include a new generation of telephony services, one that makes use of packet-switching technologies to derive transmission efficiencies, while also allowing voice to be bundled in with more standard data applications, to provide for more robust environments. (See Chapter 11.)

Quality of Service (QoS) guarantees are an absolute prerequisite for the new public network. The network must be able to distinguish between the various traffic types so that it can apply the appropriate network resources and ensure that the latency requirements are being met, that the loss requirements are being met, and that the bandwidth required is being allocated. (See Chapter 10.)

Finally, encryption and security services are necessary in telecommunications devices and networks. Once upon a time, this was a separate function within the company, but now it is an essential element of telecom service. (See Chapter 11.)

■ Convergence

In the new public network, we are moving from a narrowband to a broadband world, meaning we are going from single-channel to multichannel arrangements, and we are also moving from low bandwidth to high bandwidth. We're also shifting from a circuit-switched environment to a packet-switched environment. Circuit switching implies the use of an exclusive channel—one channel, one conversation for the duration of that call—whereas packet switching allows multiple conversations to share one channel. (Circuit switching and packet switching are discussed in detail in Chapter 4, "Establishing Communications Channels.")

We're also quickly departing from an era in which we try to force data to run over a network that was largely built for voice. We're moving toward a network where we're applying voice to data applications so that they can run over the higher-quality digital networks. We're shifting from electronic networks to all-optical networking. This transition will take some time, perhaps three to five years.

Another shift is from single media to multimedia (that is, multiple media types and personal control over what you view, when you view it, and in what combination). The shift continues, from just voice to multimodal combinations (that is, combinations in which you have further control in selecting exactly what appeals to your cognitive map). For example, some people would rather see the movie than read the book, and others prefer the book, so not everybody responds to things the same way. People think in different ways, and we need to provide all the modalities that enable individual choice over the various media formats.

We're also shifting from a fixed environment to a mobile environment, and that will have a dramatic impact on the types of applications we want served over wireless networks. (See Chapter 14.) This shift goes a step further: from portable computers to wearable computers, from unresponsive stand-alone devices to affective, wearable friends.

Because of all these forces, convergence is occurring in many different areas.

Convergence occurs in networks, where the PSTN, the Internet, wireless alternatives, broadcast networks, and cable TV, as well as the back-office functions that support them, are all coming together to service the same sets of traffic and to deliver the same types of features and services. Network services are converging because customers prefer bundled services. They want one bill, one provider for local, long distance, wireless, Internet access, hosting, applications partnering, security features, firewall protection, conversions from legacy systems, and settlement processes.

Convergence also occurs in devices, such as televisions, telephones, computers, smart appliances, intelligent clothing and jewelry, and smart tattoos. (See Chapter 15.)

Convergence occurs in applications as well. Communications, information services, entertainment, e-commerce and m-commerce, and affective computing are all overlapping and blending with one another to create new generations of traditional applications such as edutainment and infotainment. Going forward, we're relying on the bright young minds that have been born into a digital economy to fantasize about brilliant new applications that are beyond the traditional forms.

Convergence happens in industries. Today industries share digital technology as a common denominator, so biotechnology, computing, consumer electronics, entertainment, publishing, power utilities, and telecommunications are all coming together and finding reasons and synergies for why they should work together or become one.

Finally, convergence occurs in humans and machines. Today we have artificial limbs and organs, and we have intelligent implants. Tomorrow, we may see neural interfaces and artificial life.

As you can see, telecommunications is much more than just a set of technologies or business plans, and it's more than an industry in which you can guarantee success and early retirement. It's a way of life—and the more you understand that, the more fun you'll have learning the technical details.

For more learning resources, quizzes, and discussion forums on concepts related to this chapter, see www.telecomessentials.com/learningcenter.

Chapter 2

Telecommunications Technology Fundamentals

This chapter talks about the types of transmission lines and network connections, the electromagnetic spectrum, and what bandwidth is all about in this emerging broadband era. It looks at the differences between analog and digital signals, and it discusses multiplexing. Finally, this chapter describes the various standards bodies and their roles in shaping aspects of telecommunications.

■ Transmission Lines

Two prerequisites must be satisfied to have successful communication. The first prerequisite is understandability. The transmitter and receiver must speak the same language. It doesn't matter how big or how clean a pipe you have between the two endpoints. If they're not speaking the same language, you will not be able to understand the message. In the case of data communications, we've resolved these issues quite elegantly: We have software and hardware translation devices that can convert between the different languages that individual computing systems speak. In the realm of human communications, we're about to embark on that exciting journey as well. Through the use of advanced voice-processing systems, in the next five to seven years we should have the ability to do real-time foreign language translation as part of the network service.

The second prerequisite is the capability to detect errors as they occur and to have some procedure for resolving those errors. In the case of human communications, intelligent terminals at either end—human beings—can detect noise that may have affected a transmission and request a retransmission, thereby correcting for that error. In the case of data devices, similar logic has to be built in to end devices so that they can detect errors and request a retransmission in order to correct for the errors.

If these two prerequisites—understandability and error control—are met, then communication can occur. We communicate by using data devices over what is generically termed a *transmission line*. There are five main types of transmission lines—circuits, channels, lines, trunks, and virtual circuits—each of which has a specific meaning. The following sections describe each of these types of transmission lines in detail.

Circuits

A *circuit* is the physical path that runs between two or more points. It terminates on a *port* (that is, a point of electrical or optical interface), and that port can be in a host computer (that is, a switching device used to establish connections), on a multiplexer, or in another device, as discussed later in this chapter.

In and of itself, a circuit does not define the number of simultaneous conversations that can be carried; that is a function of the type of circuit it is. For example, a simple, traditional telephone circuit is designed to carry just one conversation over one physical pathway. However, converting that to a digital circuit gives you the ability to extract or derive multiple channels over that circuit, subsequently facilitating multiple simultaneous conversations. So, the circuit is the measure of the physical entity.

There are two types of circuits: two-wire circuits and four-wire circuits.

Two-Wire Circuits

A two-wire circuit has two insulated electrical conductors. One wire is used for transmission of the information. The other wire acts as the return path to complete the electrical circuit. Two-wire circuits are generally deployed in the analog local loop, which is the last mile between the subscriber and the subscriber's first point of access into the network. Figure 2.1 shows an example of a two-wire circuit.

Two-Wire and Four-Wire Versus Two-Pair and Four-Pair

Don't confuse the terms *two-wire circuit* and *four-wire circuit* with the terms *two-pair* and *four-pair*. *Two-pair* and *four-pair* refer to the number of wires in the internal cabling plan. *Two-wire* and *four-wire* have to do with the number of electrical conductors associated with a transmission line.

Figure 2.1 A two-wire circuit

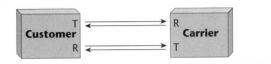

Figure 2.2 A four-wire circuit

Four-Wire Circuits

A four-wire circuit has two pairs of conductors. That is, it has two sets of one-way transmission paths: one path for each direction and a complementary path to complete the electrical circuit (see Figure 2.2). Four-wire circuits are used where there is distance between the termination points which requires that the signal be strengthened periodically. So, for example, four-wire circuits connect the various switches that make up the public switched telephone network (PSTN). Four-wire circuits are also used with leased lines, where a customer may be connecting locations of its own that are separated by distance. Also, all digital circuits are provisioned on a four-wire basis.

There are two types of four-wire circuits: physical four-wire and logical four-wire. In *physical four-wire* you can actually count four wires. In *logical four-wire*, physically there are only two wires, but you derive the four individual paths by splitting the frequency. Half of the frequency band carries the transmit signal, and the other half carries the receive signal. So you can't always tell just by looking what kind of circuit you're dealing with; the application dictates the type of circuit it is.

Using Two-Wire and Four-Wire Circuits

Whenever you release energy into space, it loses power as it's traveling over a distance. So, because networks were designed to carry communications over a distance, we need tools to augment signals that have been losing power as they have traveled across the network, which are called *attenuated signals*. These tools are called amplifiers and repeaters. An *amplifier* boosts an attenuated signal back up to its original power level so it can continue to make its way across the network. The PSTN traditionally used copper wires. Based on how quickly the signals flow through the copper wires, there's a certain distance requirement between amplifiers. The distance requirement between amplifiers is relatively short on copper wires—generally about 6,000 feet (1,800 meters). As networks were built, these distance considerations were kept in mind. (Repeaters are discussed later in this chapter, in the section "Digital Transmission.")

Network builders had to give some thought to another aspect of amplifiers: First-generation amplifiers were unidirectional. They could only amplify a signal moving in one direction, so any time you needed to provision a circuit that was going to be crossing a distance, you had to literally provision two circuits—one to amplify the information in the transmit direction and a second to amplify the information in the receive direction. Therefore, whenever a network was crossing a distance, it needed to use a four-wire circuit. But in building out the millions of local loops for subscribers, it was seen as being cost-effective to have to pull only two wires into every home rather than four. Therefore, the local loops were intentionally engineered to be very short; some 70% to 80% of the local loops worldwide are less than 2 miles (3.2 kilometers) long. Because the local loops are short, they don't need amplifiers, and therefore the subscriber access service can be provisioned over a two-wire circuit. However, the local loop is increasingly being digitalized, so as we migrate to an end-to-end digital environment, everything becomes four-wire. Figure 2.3 shows an example of a segment of a network in which two- and four-wire circuits are traditionally used.

Channels

A *channel* defines a logical coversation path. It is the frequency band, time slot, or wavelength (also referred to as *lambda*) over which a single conversation flows. A channel is a child of the digital age because digital facilities enable multiple channels. The number of channels on a transmission line determines the number of

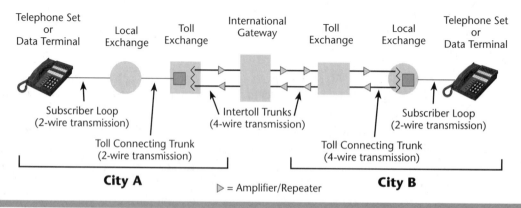

Figure 2.3   Using two-wire and four-wire circuits

simultaneous conversations that can be supported. Because we are becoming more digitalized all the time, you often hear people refer to the number of channels rather than the number of circuits.

Lines and Trunks

Lines and trunks are basically the same thing, but they're used in different situations. A *line* is a connection that is configured to support a normal calling load generated by one individual. A *trunk* is a circuit that is configured to support the calling loads generated by a group of users; it is the transmission facility that ties together switching systems. A *switching system* is a device that connects two transmission lines together. There are two major categories of switching systems:

- **CPE switches**—The most prevalent form of switch in the customer premises equipment (CPE) environment is the private branch exchange (PBX), which is called a private automatic branch exchange (PABX) in some parts of the world. A PBX is used to establish connections between two points. It establishes connections between telephones that are internal to the organization, and it establishes connections between internal extensions and the outside world (that is, the PSTN).

- **Network switches**—A hierarchy of network switches has evolved over time, and the appropriate switch is called into action, depending on which two points the switches are connecting together. For example, in Figure 2.4 the CPE is on the left-hand side. Each individual single-line instrument represents a subscriber line. (Again, the fact that it's called a *line* means that it's a circuit configured to carry the calling load of just one user.) Above the single-line instrument is a business enterprise with a PBX. The connection from this PBX to the PSTN occurs over a trunk that is specifically configured to carry the calling load of multiple users. Beyond the PBX are multiple end users that are attached to that PBX. Each end user's connection would be referred to as a *station line,* again emphasizing that the line is carrying the calling load of one user.

The customer environment attaches to the PSTN, and the first point of access is the *local exchange,* which is also referred to as a *Class 5 office* (and in North America, as a *central office*). The traditional local exchange switch can handle one or more exchanges, with each exchange capable of handling up to 10,000 subscriber lines, numbered 0000 to 9999. The only kind of call that a local exchange can complete on its own, without touching any of the other switches in the network, is to another number in that same local exchange. Local exchanges are discussed in detail in Chapter 5, "The PSTN."

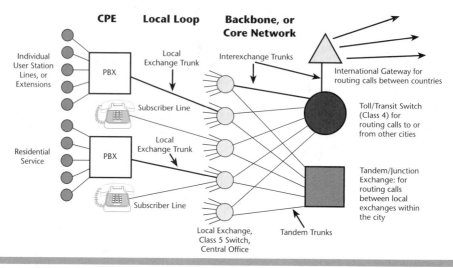

Figure 2.4 Lines, trunks, and switches

For a local exchange to call a neighbor that resides 10 miles (16 kilometers) away and who draws a dial tone from a different local exchange, the connection between those two different exchanges is accomplished through the second part of the hierarchy—a *tandem switch* (also called a *junction exchange*). The tandem switch is used to connect local exchanges throughout the metropolitan area. When it's time to make a toll call, one that is long-distance in nature, another switching center is called into action—the *toll center* (also called the *Class 4 office, transit switch,* or *trunk exchange*). The toll center is responsible for establishing and completing national, long-distance communications.

The top of the hierarchy is the *international gateway,* whose exchanges are specifically designed to connect calls between different countries.

A trunk supplies the connections between the numerous switches within the PSTN, between customer-owned switches such as the PBX, and between the PBXs and the PSTN. On the other hand, a line supports a single user in the form of a subscriber line in the PSTN or an extension provisioned from the PBX. (Chapter 5 describes in detail the entities involved in managing local, tandem, and toll exchanges.)

Virtual Circuits

Today, because of the great interest in and increased use of packet switching, most networks use virtual circuits. Unlike a physical circuit, which terminates on specific physical ports, a *virtual circuit* is a series of logical connections between sending and receiving devices (see Figure 2.5). The virtual circuit is a connection between two devices that acts as though it's a direct connection, but it may, in fact, be composed of a variety of different routes. These connections are defined by table entries inside the switch. A connection is established after both devices exchange agreement on communications parameters that are important to establishing and maintaining the connection and on providing the proper performance for the application they are supporting. The types of communication parameters that could be included are message size, the path to be taken, how to deal with acknowledgements in the event of errors, flow-control procedures, and error-control procedures. The term *virtual circuit* is largely used to describe connections between two hosts in a packet-switching network, where the two hosts can communicate as though they have a dedicated connection, although the packets may be taking very different routes to arrive at their destination.

There are two types of virtual circuits: permanent virtual circuits (PVCs) and switched virtual circuits (SVCs). The vast majority of implementations today involve PVCs. PVCs and SVCs are commonly used in packet-switching networks (for example, X.25, Frame Relay, ATM).

PVCs

A *PVC* is a virtual circuit that is permanently available; that is, the connection always exists between the two locations or two devices in question. A PVC is manually configured by a network management system, and it remains in place until

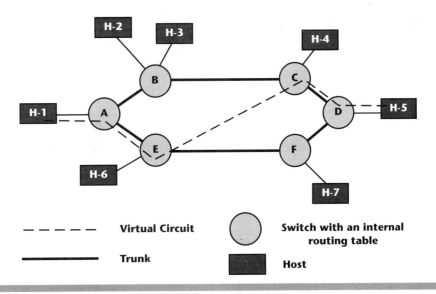

Figure 2.5 A virtual circuit

the user reconfigures the network. Its use is analogous to the use of a dedicated private line because it provides an always-on condition between two locations or two devices.

SVCs

In contrast to PVCs, SVCs are set up on demand. They are provisioned dynamically by using signaling techniques. An SVC must be reestablished each time data is to be sent, and after the data has been sent, the SVC disappears. An SVC is therefore analogous to a dialup connection in the PSTN. The main benefit of an SVC is that you can use it to access the network from anyplace. The predominant application for SVCs is to accommodate people who are working at home, in a hotel, at an airport, or otherwise outside the physical location of the enterprise network.

■ Types of Network Connections

Three major types of networks connections can be made:

- **Switched network connections**—A switched connection is referred to as a *dialup* connection. This implies that you're using a series of network switches to establish the connection between the parties.

- **Leased-line network connections**—A leased line is also referred to as a private line. With a leased line, the same locations or the same devices are always connected, and transmission between those locations or devices always occurs on the same path.

- **Dedicated network connections**—In essence, a dedicated line works exactly like a leased line. It is always connected and it always uses the same path for transmission. However, the end user may own the transmission facility (rather than lease it) such that it is exclusive to that user.

■ The Electromagnetic Spectrum and Bandwidth

This section talks about bandwidth and about where the various transmission media lie within the electromagnetic spectrum.

The Electromagnetic Spectrum

When electrons move, they create electromagnetic waves that can propagate through free space. This phenomenon was first predicted to exist by James Maxwell, in 1865, and it was first produced and observed by Heinrich Hertz in 1887.

All modern communication depends on manipulating and controlling signals within the electromagnetic spectrum.

The electromagnetic spectrum ranges from extremely low-frequency radio waves of 30Hz, with wavelengths of nearly the earth's diameter, to high-frequency cosmic rays of more than 10 million trillion Hz, with wavelengths smaller than the nucleus of an atom. The electromagnetic spectrum is depicted as a logarithmic progression: The scale increases by multiples of 10, so the higher regions encompass a greater span of frequencies than do the lower regions.

Although the electromagnetic spectrum represents an enormous range of frequencies, not all the frequencies are suitable to purposes of human communications. At the very low end of the spectrum are signals that would be traveling at 30Hz (that is, at 30 cycles per second). One of the benefits of a very low frequency is that it can travel much farther than a high frequency before it loses power (that is, attenuates). So a 30Hz signal provides the benefit of being able to travel halfway around the world before it requires some form of amplification. For example, one defense agency uses 30Hz to communicate with its submarines by using telemetry (for example, a message that says "We're still here. We're still here" is sent, and the subs know that if they don't get that message, they better see what's going on). Again, the benefit of very-low-frequency signals is that they can travel a very long distance before they attenuate.

At the high end of the electromagnetic spectrum, signals travel over a band of 10 million trillion Hz (that is, 10^{22}Hz). This end of the spectrum has phenomenal bandwidth, but it has its own set of problems. The wave forms are so miniscule that they're highly distorted by any type of interference, particularly environmental interference such as precipitation. Furthermore, higher-frequency wave forms such

Infrasound and the Animal World

The universe is full of *infrasound*—the frequencies below the range of human hearing. Earthquakes, wind, thunder, volcanoes, and ocean storms—massive movements of earth, air, fire, and water—generate infrasound. In the past, very-low-frequency sound has not been thought to play much of a role in animals' lives. However, we know now that sound at the lowest frequencies of elephant rumbles (14Hz to 35Hz) has remarkable properties. It is little affected by passage through forests and grasslands, and male and female elephants use it to find one another for reproduction. It seems that elephants communicate with one another by using calls that are too low-pitched for human beings to hear, and because of the properties of the infrasound range, these communications can take place over very long distances. Intense infrasonic calls have also been recorded from finback whales.

as x-rays, gamma rays, and cosmic rays are not very good to human physiology and therefore aren't available for us to use for communication at this point.

Because of the problems with very low and very high frequencies, we primarily use the middle of the electromagnetic spectrum for communication—the radio, microwave, infrared, and visible light portions of the spectrum. We do this by modulating the amplitudes, the frequencies, and the phases of the electromagnetic waves. Bandwidth is actually a measure of the difference between the lowest and highest frequencies being carried. Each of these communications bands offers differing amounts of bandwidth, based on the range of frequencies they cover. The higher up in the spectrum you go, the greater the range of frequencies involved.

Figure 2.6 shows the electromagnetic spectrum and where some of the various transmission media operate. Along the right-hand side is the terminology that the International Telecommunication Union (ITU) applies to the various bands: Extremely low, very low, low, medium, high, very high (VHF), ultrahigh (UHF), superhigh (SHF), extremely high (EHF), and tremendously high frequencies

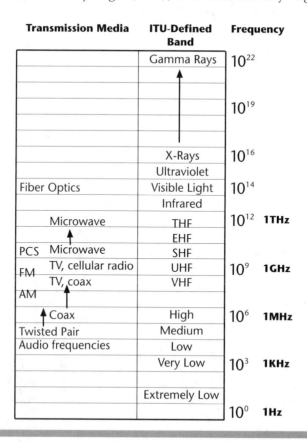

Figure 2.6 The electromagnetic spectrum

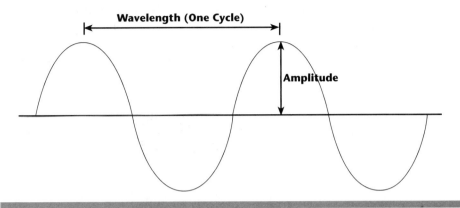

Figure 2.7 An electromagnetic wave

(THF) are all various forms of radio bands. And then we move into the light range, with infrared and visible light. You can see just by the placement of the various transmission media that not all are prepared to face the high-bandwidth future that demanding advanced applications (such as streaming media, e-learning, networked interactive games, interactive TV, telemedicine, metacomputing, and Web agents) will require.

The radio, microwave, infrared, and visible light portions of the spectrum can all be used for transmitting information by modulating various measurements related to electromagnetic waves (see Figure 2.7):

- **Frequency**—The number of oscillations per second of an electromagnetic wave is called its *frequency*.
- **Hertz**—Frequency is measured in *Hertz (Hz)*, in honor of Heinrich Hertz.
- **Wavelength**—The *wavelength* is the distance between two consecutive maxima or minima of the wave form.
- **Amplitude**—*Amplitude* is a measure of the height of the wave, which indicates the strength of the signal.
- **Phase**—*Phase* refers to the angle of the wave form at any given moment.
- **Bandwidth**—The range of frequencies (that is, the difference between the lowest and highest frequencies carried) that make up a signal is called *bandwidth*.

You can manipulate frequency, amplitude, and phase in order to distinguish between a one and a zero. Hence, you can represent digital information over the electromagnetic spectrum. One way to manipulate frequency is by sending ones at a high frequency and zeros at a low frequency. Devices that do this are called *frequency-modulated devices*. You can also modulate amplitude by sending ones at a high amplitude or voltage and zeros at a low amplitude. A complementary receiving device could then determine whether a one or a zero is being sent. As yet another example, because the phase of the wave form refers to shifting where the signal begins, you could have ones begin at 90 degrees and zeros begin at 270 degrees. The receiving device could discriminate between these two bit states (zero versus one) based on the phase of the wave as compared to a reference wave.

Twisted-pair, which was the original foundation of the telecommunications network, has a maximum usable bandwidth of about 1MHz. Coax, on the other hand, has greater capacity, offering a total of 1GHz of frequency spectrum. The radio range, particularly microwave, is the workhorse of the radio spectrum. It gives us 100GHz to operate with. In comparison, fiber optics operates over a band of more than 200THz (terahertz). So, as we see increasingly more bandwidth-hungry applications, we'll need to use fiber optics to carry the amount of traffic those applications generate. Twisted-pair will see little use with the future application set. Figure 2.8 plots various telecommunications devices on the electromagnetic spectrum.

Bandwidth

As mentioned earlier, *bandwidth* is the range of frequencies that make up a signal. There are three major classes of bandwidth that we refer to in telecommunications networks: narrowband, wideband, and broadband.

Narrowband

Narrowband means that you can accommodate up to 64Kbps, which is also known as the DS-0 (Digital Signal level 0) channel. This is the fundamental increment on which digital networks were built. Initially, this metric of 64Kbps was derived based on our understanding of what it would take to carry voice in a digital manner through the network. If we combine these 64Kbps channels together, we can achieve wideband transmission rates.

Wideband

Wideband is defined as being $n \times$ 64Kbps, up to approximately 45Mbps. A range of services are provisioned to support wideband capabilities, including T-carrier, E-carrier, and J-carrier services. These are the services on which the first generation of digital hierarchy was built.

T-1 offers 1.544Mbps, and because the T-carrier system is a North American standard, T-1 is used in the United States. It is also used in some overseas territories, such as South Korea and Hong Kong. E-1, which provides a total of 2.048Mbps, is

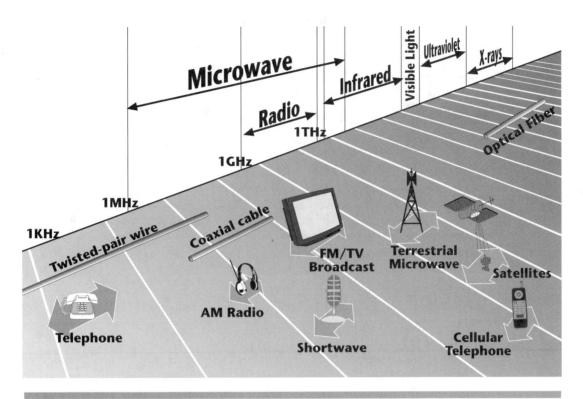

Figure 2.8 Telecommunications devices and the electromagnetic spectrum

specified by the ITU. It is the international standard used throughout Europe, Africa, most of Asia-Pacific, the Middle East, and Latin America. J-carrier is the Japanese standard, and J-1 offers 1.544Mbps.

Not every office or application requires the total capacity of T-1, E-1, or J-1, so you can subscribe to *fractional services*, which means you subscribe to bundles of channels that offer less than the full rate. Fractional services are normally provided in bundles of 4, so you can subscribe to 4 channels, 8 channels, 12 channels, and so on. Fractional services are also referred as $n \times 56Kbps/64Kbps$ in the T-carrier system and $n \times 64Kbps$ under E-carrier. High-bandwidth facilities include T-3, E-3, and J-3. T-3 offers 45Mbps, E-3 offers 34Mbps, and J-3 supports 32Mbps. (T-, E-, and J-carrier services are discussed in more detail in Chapter 5.)

Broadband

The future hierarchy, of course, rests on broadband capacities, and *broadband* can be defined in different ways, depending on what part of the industry you're talking

The Impact of Fiber Optics on Bandwidth

So far this chapter has used a lot of bits-per-second measurements. It can be difficult to grasp what these measurements really mean. So, here's a real-world example. Today, fiber optics very easily accommodates 10Gbps (that is, 10 billion bits per second). But what does that really mean? At 10Gbps you'd be able to transmit all 32 volumes of the *Encyclopedia Britannica* in 1/10 second—the blink of an eye. That is an incredible speed. Not many people have a computer capable of capturing 10Gbps.

Keep in mind that underlying all the various changes in telecommunications technologies and infrastructures, a larger shift is also occurring—the shift from the electronic to the optical, or photonic, era. To extract and make use of the inherent capacity that fiber optics affords, we will need an entire new generation of devices that are optical at heart. Otherwise, we'll need to stop a signal, convert it back into an electrical form to process it through the network node, and then convert it back into optics to pass it along, and this will not allow us to exercise the high data rates that we're beginning to envision.

about. Technically speaking, the ITU has defined broadband as being anything over 2Mbps. But this definition was created in the 1970s, when 2Mbps seemed like a remarkable capacity.

Given today's environment, for wireline facilities, it may be more appropriate to think of broadband as starting where the optical network infrastructure starts. Synchronous Digital Hierarchy (SDH) and Synchronous Optical Network (SONET) are part of the second generation of digital hierarchy, which is based on fiber optics as the physical infrastructure. (SDH and SONET are discussed in detail in Chapter 5.) The starting rate (that is, the lowest data rate supported) on SDH/SONET is roughly 51Mbps. So, for the wireline technologies—those used in the core or backbone network—51Mbps is considered the starting point for broadband. In the wireless realm, though, if we could get 2Mbps to a handheld today, we'd be extremely happy and would be willing to call it broadband. So, remember that the definition of broadband really depends on the situation. But we can pretty easily say that broadband is always a multichannel facility that affords higher capacities than the traditional voice channel, and in the local loop, 2Mbps is a major improvement.

▪ Analog and Digital Transmission

There are a number of differences between analog and digital transmission, and it is important to understand how conversions between analog and digital occur. Let's look first at the older form of transmission, analog.

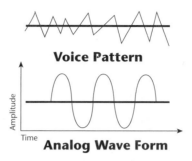

Figure 2.9 Analog transmission

Analog Transmission

An analog wave form (or signal) is characterized by being continuously variable along amplitude and frequency. In the case of telephony, for instance, when you speak into a handset, there are changes in the air pressure around your mouth. Those changes in air pressure fall onto the handset, where they are amplified and then converted into current, or voltage fluctuations. Those fluctuations in current are an analog of the actual voice pattern—hence the use of the term *analog* to describe these signals (see Figure 2.9).

When it comes to an analog circuit—what we also refer to as a voice-grade line—we need to also define the frequency band in which it operates. The human voice, for example, can typically generate frequencies from 100Hz to 10,000Hz, for a bandwidth of 9,900Hz. But the ear does not require a vast range of frequencies to elicit meaning from ordinary speech; the vast majority of sounds we make that constitute intelligible speech fall between 250Hz and 3,400Hz. So, the phone company typically allotted a total bandwidth of 4,000Hz for voice transmission. Remember that the total frequency spectrum of twisted-pair is 1MHz. To provision a voice-grade analog circuit, bandwidth-limiting filters are put on that circuit to filter out all frequencies above 4,000Hz. That's why analog circuits can conduct only fairly low-speed data communications. The maximum data rate over an analog facility is 33.6Kbps when there are analog loops at either end.

How 56Kbps Modems Break the 33.6Kbps Barrier

With 56Kbps modems, only one end of the loop can be analog. The other end of the connection has to be digital. So, in other words, if you're using a 56Kbps modem to access your Internet service provider (ISP), you have an analog connection from your home to the local exchange. But the ISP has a digital subscriber line (DSL) or a digital termination facility from its location to its exchange.

Analog facilities have limited bandwidth, which means they cannot support high-speed data. Another characteristic of analog is that noise is accumulated as the signal traverses the network. As the signal moves across the distance, it loses power and becomes impaired by factors such as moisture in the cable, dirt on a contact, and critters chewing on the cable somewhere in the network. By the time the signal arrives at the amplifier, it is not only attenuated, it is also impaired and noisy. One of the problems with a basic amplifier is that it is a dumb device. All it knows how to do is to add power, so it takes a weak and impaired signal, adds power to it, and brings it back up to its original power level. But along with an increased signal, the amplifier passes along an increased noise level. So in an analog network, each time a signal goes through an amplifier, it accumulates noise. After you mix together coffee and cream, you can no longer separate them. The same concept applies in analog networks: After you mix the signal and the noise, you can no longer separate the two, and, as a result, you end up with very high error rates.

Digital Transmission

Digital transmission is quite different from analog transmission. For one thing, the signal is much simpler. Rather than being a continuously variable wave form, it is a series of discrete pulses, representing one bits and zero bits (see Figure 2.10). Each computer uses a coding scheme that defines what combinations of ones and zeros constitute all the characters in a character set (that is, lowercase letters, uppercase letters, punctuation marks, digits, keyboard control functions).

How the ones and zeros are physically carried through the network depends on whether the network is electrical or optical. In electrical networks, one bits are represented as high voltage, and zero bits are represented as null, or low voltage. In optical networks, one bits are represented by the presence of light, and zero bits are

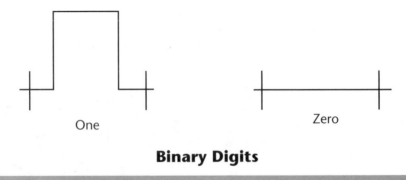

Binary Digits

Figure 2.10 Digital transmission

represented by the absence of light. The ones and zeros—the on/off conditions—are carried through the network, and the receiving device repackages the ones and zeros to determine what character is being represented. Because a digital signal is easier to reproduce than an analog signal, we can treat it with a little less care in the network. Rather than use dumb amplifiers, digital networks use *regenerative repeaters*, also referred to as *signal regenerators*. As a strong, clean, digital pulse travels over a distance, it loses power, similar to an analog signal. The digital pulse, like an analog signal, is eroded by impairments in the network. But the weakened and impaired signal enters the regenerative repeater, where the repeater examines the signal to determine what was supposed to be a one and what was supposed to be a zero. The repeater regenerates a new signal to pass on to the next point in the network, in essence eliminating noise and thus vastly improving the error rate.

Analog Versus Digital Transmission

Table 2.1 summarizes the characteristics of analog and digital networks.

Table 2.1 Characteristics of Analog and Digital Networks

Feature	Analog Characteristics	Digital Characteristics
Signal	Continuously variable, in both amplitude and frequency	Discrete signal, represented as either changes in voltage or changes in light levels
Traffic measurement	Hz (for example, a telephone channel is 4KHz)	Bits per second (for example, a T-1 line carries 1.544Mbps, and an E-1 line transports 2.048Mbps)
Bandwidth	Low bandwidth (4KHz), which means low data transmission rates (up to 33.6Kbps) because of limited channel bandwidth	High bandwidth that can support high-speed data and emerging applications that involve video and multimedia
Network capacity	Low; one conversation per telephone channel	High; multiplexers enable multiple conversations to share a communications channel and hence to achieve greater transmission efficiencies
Network manageability	Poor; a lot of labor is needed for network maintenance and control because dumb analog devices do not provide management information streams that allow the device to be remotely managed	Good; smart devices produce alerts, alarms, traffic statistics, and performance measurements, and technicians at a network control center (NCC) or network operations center (NOC) can remotely monitor and manage the various network elements

Table 2.1 Characteristics of Analog and Digital Networks *(continued)*

Feature	Analog Characteristics	Digital Characteristics
Power requirement	High because the signal contains a wide range of frequencies and amplitudes	Low because only two discrete signals—the one and the zero—need to be transmitted
Security	Poor; when you tap into an analog circuit, you hear the voice stream in its native form, and it is difficult to detect an intrusion	Good; encryption can be used
Error rates	High; 10^{-5} bits (that is, 1 in 100,000 bits) is guaranteed to have an error	Low; with twisted-pair, 10^{-7} (that, is 1 in 10 million bits per second) will have an error, with satellite, 10^{-9} (that is, 1 in 1 billion per second) will have an error, and with fiber, 10^{-11} (that is only 1 in 10 trillion bits per second) will have an error

Conversion: Codecs and Modems

The fact is that today we don't have all-digital or all-analog networks; we have a mix of the two. Therefore, at various points in a network, it is necessary to convert between the two signal types. The devices that handle these conversions are codecs and modems (see Figure 2.11).

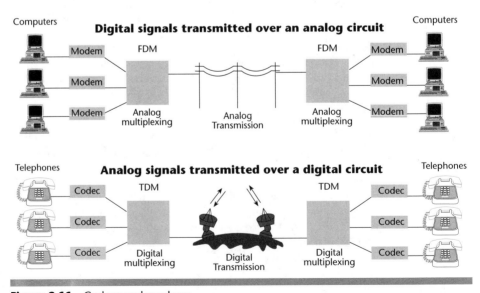

Figure 2.11 Codecs and modems

A *codec* (which is a contraction of *coder-decoder*) converts analog signals into digital signals. There are different codecs for different purposes. For the PSTN, for example, there are codecs that minimize the number of bits per second required to carry voice digitally through the PSTN. In cellular networks, because of the constraints and available spectrum, a codec needs to compress the voice further, to get the most efficient use of the spectrum. Codecs applied to video communication also require very specific compression techniques to be able to move those high-bandwidth signals over what may be somewhat limited channels today.

A *modem* (which is a contraction of *modulator-demodulator*) is used to infuse digital data onto transmission facilities. Some modems are designed specifically to work with analog voice-grade lines. There are also modems that are designed to work specifically with digital facilities (for example, ISDN modems, ADSL modems). A modem manipulates the variables of the electromagnetic wave to differentiate between the ones and zeros.

Although it is possible to convert between analog and digital networks, in general, conversions are a weak link in a network. A conversion is a point at which network troubles can occur, an opportunity for errors and distortions to be introduced. Therefore, ideally, we want to move toward an end-to-end digital and end-to-end optical environment. This means that nowhere between the transmitter and the receiver do signal conversions need to be done.

Multiplexing

Multiplexers, often called *muxes*, are extremely important to telecommunications. Their main reason for being is to reduce network costs by minimizing the number of communications links needed between two points. As with all other computing systems, multiplexers have evolved. Each new generation has additional intelligence, and additional intelligence brings more benefits. The types of benefits that have accrued, for example, include the following:

- The capability to do data compression so that you can encode certain characters with fewer bits than normally required and free up that additional capacity for the movement of other information.

- The capability to do error detection and correction between the two points that are being connected to ensure that data integrity and accuracy are being maintained.

- The capability to manage transmission resources on a dynamic basis, with such things as priority levels. If you have only one 64Kbps channel left, who gets it? Or what happens when the link between San Francisco and Hong Kong goes down? How else can you reroute traffic to get the high-priority information where it needs to go? Multiplexers help solve such problems.

The more intelligent the multiplexer, the more actively and intelligently it can work on your behalf to dynamically make use of the transmission resources you have.

When you're working with network design and telecommunications, you need to consider line cost versus device cost. You can provide extremely high levels of service by ensuring that everybody always has a live and available communications link. But you must pay for those services on an ongoing basis, and their costs become extremely high. You can offset the costs associated with providing large numbers of lines by instead using devices such as multiplexers that help you make more intelligent use of a smaller group of lines.

Figure 2.12 illustrates a network without multiplexers. Let's say this network is for Bob's department stores. The CPU is at Location A, a data center that's in New York that manages all the credit authorization functions for all the Bob's stores. Location B, the San Francisco area, has five different Bob's stores in different locations. Many customers will want to make purchases using their Bob's credit cards, so we need to have a communications link back to the New York credit authorization center so that the proper approvals and validations can be made. Given that it's a sales transaction, the most likely choice of communications link is the use of a leased line from each of the locations in San Francisco back to the main headquarters in New York.

Remember that the use of leased lines is a very expensive type of network connection. Because this network resource has been reserved for one company's usage only, nobody else has access to that bandwidth, and providers can't make use of it in the evenings or the weekends to carry residential traffic, so the company pays a

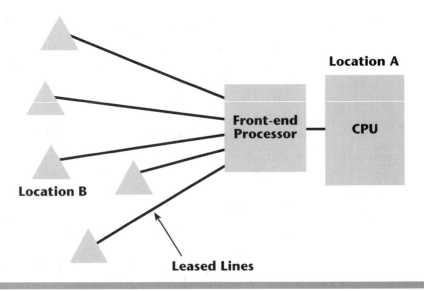

Figure 2.12   A network without multiplexers

premium. Even though it is the most expensive approach to networking, the vast majority of data networking today still takes place using leased lines, because they make the network manager feel very much in control of the network's destiny. With leased lines, the bandwidth is not affected by sudden shifts of traffic elsewhere in the network, the company can apply its own sophisticated network management tools, and the network manager feels a sense of security in knowing who the user communities are at either end of that link. But leased lines have another negative attribute: They are mileage sensitive, so the longer the communications link, the higher the cost. And in a network that doesn't efficiently make use of that communication's link all day long, leased lines become overkill and an expensive proposition.

The astute network manager at Bob's tries to think about ways to make the network less expensive. One solution, shown in Figure 2.13, is to put in multiplexers. Multiplexers always come in pairs, so if you have one at one end, you must have one at the other end. They are also symmetrical, so if there are five outputs available in San Francisco, there must also be five inputs in the New York location. The key savings in this scenario comes from using only one leased line between New York and California. In San Francisco, short leased lines, referred to as *tail circuits,* run from the centrally placed multiplexer to each of the individual locations. Thus, five locations are sharing one high-cost leased line, rather than each having its own leased line. Intelligence embedded in the multiplexers allows the network manager to manage access to that bandwidth and to allocate network services to the endpoints.

Various techniques—including Frequency Division Multiplexing (FDM), Time Division Multiplexing (TDM), Statistical Time Division Multiplexing (STDM), intelligent multiplexing, inverse multiplexing, and Wavelength Division Multiplexing (WDM)/Dense Wavelength Division Multiplexing (DWDM)—enable multiple channels to coexist on one link. The following sections examine each of these techniques.

FDM

FDM is an environment in which the entire frequency band available on the communications link is divided into smaller individual bands or channels (see Figure 2.14). Each user is assigned to a different frequency. The signals all travel in parallel over the same communications link, but they are divided by frequency—that is, each signal rides on a different portion of the frequency spectrum. Frequency, which is an analog parameter, implies that the type of link you see with FDM is usually an analog facility. A disadvantage of frequency division muxes is that they can be difficult to reconfigure in an environment in which there's a great deal of dynamic change. For instance, to increase the capacity of Channel 1

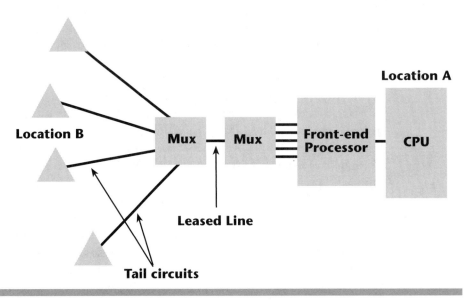

Figure 2.13 A network with multiplexers

in Figure 2.14, you would also have to tweak Channels 2, 3, and 4 to accommodate that change.

If an enterprise has a high degree of moves, additions, and changes, FDM would be an expensive system to maintain because it would require the additional expertise of frequency engineering and reconfiguration. Given the environment today, we don't make great use of FDM, but it is still used extensively in cable TV and in radio. In cable TV, multiple channels of programming all coexist on the coax coming into your home, and they are separated based on the frequency band in which they travel. When you enter a channel number on your set-top box or cable-ready TV, you're essentially indicating to the network what portion of the frequency band it's traveling on.

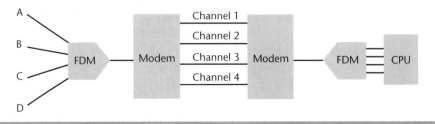

Figure 2.14 FDM

Figure 2.15 TDM

TDM

The second muxing technique to be delivered to the marketplace was TDM. There are various levels of TDM. In the plain-vanilla TDM model, as shown in Figure 2.15, a dedicated time slot is provided for each port or point of interface on the system. Each device in a predetermined sequence is allotted a time slot during which it can transmit. That time slot would enable one character of data, or 8 bits of digitized voice, to be placed on the communications link. The allocated time slots have to be framed in order for the individual channels to be separated out. A problem with a standard time-division mux is that there is a one-to-one correlation between each port and time slot, so if the device attached to Port 2 is out for the day, nobody else can make use of Time Slot 2. Hence, there is a tendency to waste bandwidth when vacant slots occur because of idle stations. However, this type of TDM is more efficient than standard FDM because more subchannels can be derived.

FDM and TDM can be combined. For example, you could use FDM to carve out individual channels and then within each of those channels apply TDM to carry multiple conversations on each channel. In fact, this is the way that some digital cellular systems work (for example, Global Systems for Mobile Communications [GSM]). Digital cellular systems are discussed in Chapter 14, "Wireless Communications."

STDM

STDM was introduced to overcome the limitation of standard TDM, in which stations cannot use each other's time slots. Statistical time-division multiplexers, sometimes called *statistical muxes* or *stat muxes*, dynamically allocate the time slots among the active terminals, which means that you can actually have more terminals than you have time slots (see Figure 2.16).

A stat mux is a smarter mux and it has more memory than other muxes, so if all the time slots are busy, excess data goes into a buffer. If the buffer fills up, the additional access data gets lost, so it's important to think about how much traffic to

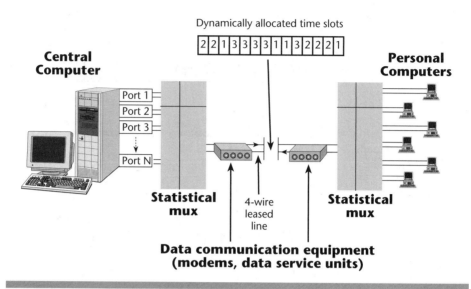

Figure 2.16 STDM

put through the stat mux to ensure that performance variables are maintained. By dynamically allocating the time slots, you get the most efficient use of bandwidth. Additionally, because these are smarter muxes, they have the additional intelligence mentioned earlier in terms of compression and error-control features. Because of the dynamic allocation of time slots, a stat mux is able to carry two to five times more traffic than a traditional time-division mux. But, again, as you load the stat mux with traffic, you run the risk of delays and data loss occurring.

Stat muxes are extremely important because they are the basis on which packet-switching technologies (for example, X.25, IP, Frame Relay, ATM) are built. The main benefit of a stat mux is the efficient use of bandwidth, which leads to transmission efficiencies.

Intelligent Multiplexing

An intelligent multiplexer is often referred to as a *concentrator*, particularly in the telecom world. Rather than being a device used in pairs, it is used as a singular device, a line-sharing device whose purpose is to concentrate large numbers of low-speed lines to be carried over a high-speed line to a further point in the network. A good example of a concentrator is in a device called the *digital loop carrier* (DLC), which is also referred to as a *remote concentrator* or *remote terminal*. In Figure 2.17, twisted-pairs go from the local exchange to the neighborhood. Before the advent of DLCs, you needed a twisted-pair for each household. If the demand

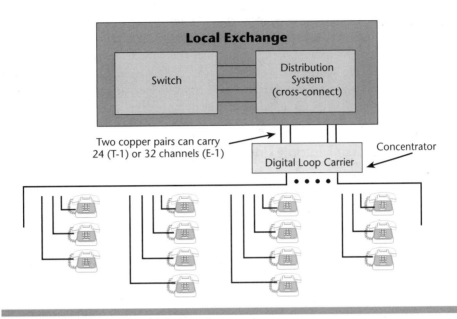

Figure 2.17 Intelligent multiplexing: Concentrators

increased beyond the number of pairs you had available out of that local exchange, you were out of luck until a new local exchange was added.

With digital technology, you can make better use of the existing pairs. Instead of using each pair individually per subscriber from the local exchange to the subscriber, you can put a DLC in the center. You use a series of either fiber-optic pairs or microwave beams to connect the local exchange to this intermediate DLC, and those facilities then carry multiplexed traffic. When you get to the DLC, you break out the individual twisted-pairs to the household. This allows you to eliminate much of what used to be an analog plant leading up to the local exchange. It also allows you to provide service to customers who are outside the distance specifications between a subscriber and the local exchange. So, in effect, that DLC can be used to reduce the loop length.

Traditional DLCs are not interoperable with some of the new DSL offerings, including ADSL and SDSL. For example, about 30% to 40% of the U.S. population is serviced through DLCs. And in general, globally, the more rural or remote a city or neighborhood, the more likely that it is serviced via a DLC. For those people to be able to subscribe to the new high-bandwidth DSL services, the carrier will have to replace the DLC with a newer generation of device. Lucent's xDSL Access Gateway, for example, is such a device; it offers a multiservice access system that provides Lite and full-rate ADSL, Integrated Services Digital Network (ISDN), Asynchronous Transfer Mode (ATM), and plain old telephone service

(POTS)/analog over twisted-pair lines or fiber. Or, the carrier may simply determine that the market area doesn't promise enough revenue and leave cable modems or broadband wireless as the only available broadband access technique. But the nature of a concentrator is that it enables you to aggregate numerous low-speed residential lines and to multiplex them onto high-bandwidth facilities to pass off to the local exchange.

Inverse Multiplexing

The inverse multiplexer arrived on the scene in the 1990s. It does the opposite of what the multiplexers described so far do. Rather than combine lots of low-bit-rate streams to ride over a high-bit-rate pipe, an inverse multiplexer breaks down a high-bandwidth signal into a group of smaller-data-rate signals that can be dispersed over a range of channels to be carried over the network. A primary application for inverse multiplexers is to support of high-bandwidth applications such as videoconferencing.

In Figure 2.18, a videoconference is to occur at 1.5Mbps. For a good-quality, full-motion, long-session video, you need substantial bandwidth. It's one thing to tolerate pixelation or artifacts in motion for a 15-minute meeting that saves you the time of driving to meet your colleague. However, for a two-hour meeting to evaluate a new advertising campaign, the quality needs to parallel what most of us use as a reference point: television. The company policy is to hold a two-hour

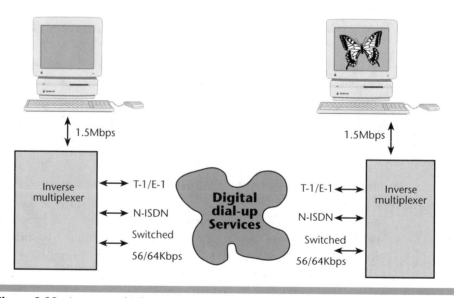

Figure 2.18 Inverse multiplexing

videoconferenced meeting twice each month. Very few customers are willing to pay for a 1.5Mbps to 2Mbps connection for an application that they're using just four hours each month. Instead, they want to be able to make use of their existing digital facilities to carry that traffic. An inverse mux allows them to do so. In Figure 2.18, the 1.5Mbps video stream is introduced into the inverse multiplexer, the inverse mux splits that up into twenty-four 64Kbps channels, and each of these twenty-four channels occupies a separate channel on an existing T-1/E-1 facility or PRI ISDN. (PRI ISDN is discussed in Chapter 3, "Transmission Media: Characteristics and Applications.") The channels are carried across the network separately. At the destination point, a complementary inverse mux again reaggregates, resynchronizes, and reproduces that high-bandwidth signal so that it can be projected on the destination video monitor.

Inverse multiplexing therefore allows you to experience a bit of elastic bandwidth. You can allocate existing capacity to a high-bandwidth application without having to subscribe to a separate link just for that purpose.

WDM/DWDM

WDM was specifically developed for use with fiber optics. In the past, we could use only a fraction of the available bandwidth of a fiber-optic system. This was mainly because we had to convert the optical pulses into electrical signals to regenerate them as they moved through the fiber network. And because repeaters were originally electronic, data rates were limited to about 2.5Gbps. In 1994, something very important happened: optical amplifiers called *erbium-doped fiber amplifiers* (EDFAs) were introduced. Erbium is a chemical that's injected into the fiber. As a light pulse passes through the erbium, the light is amplified and continues on its merry way, without having to be stopped and processed as an electrical signal. The introduction of EDFAs immediately opened up the opportunity to make use of fiber-optic systems operating at 10Gbps.

EDFAs also paved the way to developing wavelength division multiplexers. Before the advent of WDM, we were using only one wavelength of light within each fiber, whereas the visible light spectrum engages a large number of different wavelengths. WDM takes advantage of the fact that multiple colors or frequencies of light can be transmitted simultaneously down a single optical fiber. The data rate that's supported by each of the wavelengths depends on the type of light source. Today, we have light sources that operate at a rate of OC-48, which is shorthand for 2.5Gbps. We have light sources that operate at OC-192, which is equivalent to 10Gbps. And there are systems in trial that operate at OC-768, offering 40Gbps per wavelength. In the future, we'll go beyond that. Part of the evolution of WDM is that every year we double the number of bits per second that can be carried on a wavelength, and every year we double the number of wavelengths that can be carried over a single fiber. But we have just begun. Soon light sources should be able to pulse in the terabits per second range, and in five years, light sources should pulse in the petabits per second (1,000Tbps) range.

One thing to clarify about the first use of WDM is that unlike with the other types of multiplexing, where the goal is to aggregate smaller channels into one larger channel, WDM is meant to furnish separate channels for each service, at the full data rate. Increasingly, enterprises are making use of new high-capacity switches and routers that are equipped with 2.5Gbps interfaces, so there's a great deal of desire within the user community to be able to plug in to a channel of sufficient size to carry that high-bandwidth signal end-to-end, without having to break it down into smaller increments only to build them back out at the destination.

WDM furnishes a separate channel for each service at the full rate; you cannot aggregate smaller channels into one large channel. Systems that support more than 16 wavelengths are referred to as DWDM (see Figure 2.19). Systems at the OC-48 or 2.5Gbps level today can support upward of 128 channels or wavelengths. Systems at OC-192 or 10Gbps support more than 32 wavelengths. New systems that operate at 40Gbps (OC-768) are emerging, and Bell Labs is working on a technique that it says might enable us to extract up to 15,000 channels or wavelengths on a single fiber. So the revolution truly has just begun. The progress in this area is so great that each year we're approximately doubling performance while halving costs. Again, great emphasis is being placed on the optical sector, so many companies—traditional telecom providers, data networking providers, and new start-ups—are focusing attention on the optical revolution. (WDM, DWDM, and EDFAs are discussed in more detail in Chapter 12, "Optical Networking.")

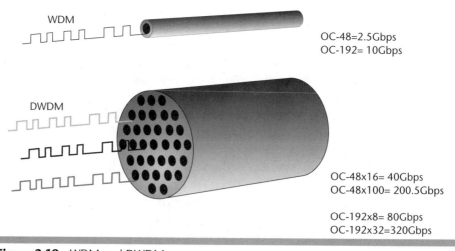

Figure 2.19   WDM and DWDM

■ Standards Organizations

Telecommunications is a major industry sector for two main reasons: First, it generates vast amounts of revenue every year, and second, it touches every aspect of life and business. Networking is an international phenomenon, and recommendations have to be made on how systems and networks should interoperate. Standardization within the industry is intended to perform three basic functions:

- Facilitate interconnection between different users.
- Facilitate the portability of equipment within different regions and applications, with the intent of increasing market size, resulting in reduced costs for all.
- Ensure equipment interoperability, so that different vendors' products work with each other.

Standards bodies that make such recommendations have traditionally been active in Europe, North America, and Japan. In recent years, the Internet Society (ISOC) has also become an increasingly important organization.

The ITU is a body of the United Nations that includes members from around the world. Three specific groups within the ITU are relevant to telecommunications. The ITU-T, the telecommunications standardization sector, develops recommendations for wireline networks. ITU-R, the radio communications standardization sector,

Standards Organization Time Line

The following time line shows some of the important dates in the history of standards organizations:

1865　The ITU was established by 20 European states at the first International Telegraph Convention.

1923　The CCIF was established in Paris, for the study of long-distance telephony.

1925　The CCITT (now the ITU-T) was established for the technical study of telephony problems. The CCIF and CCITT both became part of the ITU.

1927　The CCIR was formed in Washington, with the objective of concentrating on technical issues surrounding radio communications.

1947　The ITU was recognized as an agency of the United Nations, specializing in telecommunications.

1959　The CCIF and the CCITT were combined and became known simply as the CCITT, now called the ITU-T.

deals with the wireless arena. The ITU-D sector works on standards for developing nations. The ITU standards are followed throughout most of the world, including Africa, most of Asia-Pacific, Europe, Latin America, and the Middle East.

The second major standards body is the America National Standards Institute (ANSI), whose recommendations are followed throughout North America, as well as in some Asian countries.

The third major body is the Telecommunications Technology Committee, which is followed in Japan.

ISOC has an agreement to work with the ITU to ensure that developments do not take place separately in evolving the PSTN versus the Internet. These organizations are working toward converging networks on the same sets of requirements and functions.

In order to make room for the many—often conflicting—interests, the international standards-making organizations concentrate on producing what are known as *base standards*. These base standards contain allowable variants or options, which are defined by the implementer. By adopting any of the variants, or options, the implementer is compliant with the standard, but there is no guarantee that the equipment will interoperate with the equipment of other vendors. This problem of interoperability and internetworking is addressed by regional and national standards bodies, often involving trade organizations and users groups. These groups adapt the international base standards as functional standards, which contain a limited amount of agreed-upon allowable options. These groups also develop test specifications and methods, and independent test houses then perform the necessary conformance testing and certify products that meet the requirements. (See Figures 2.20 and 2.21.)

Table 2.2 lists some of the key standards organizations throughout the world.

Table 2.2 Standards Organizations

Region	Standards Organizations
International	ITU, ITU-T, ITU-R, ITU-D, IEC, ISO
Australia	ACA, ACC, AIIA, ATUG
Europe	AFNOR (France), CEN and CENLEC, CEPT, DIN (Germany), DTI (UK), ETSI, European Community (EU)
Japanese	JISC, TTC
New Zealand	ITANZ
North America	ANSI (USA), EIA, FCC (USA), IEEE, NIST, SCC (Canadian)

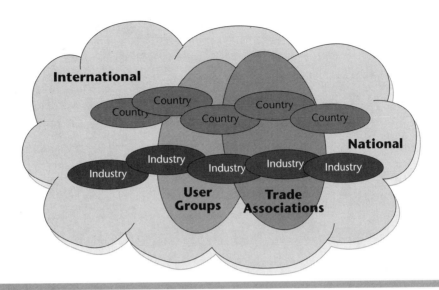

Figure 2.20 Standards-making groups

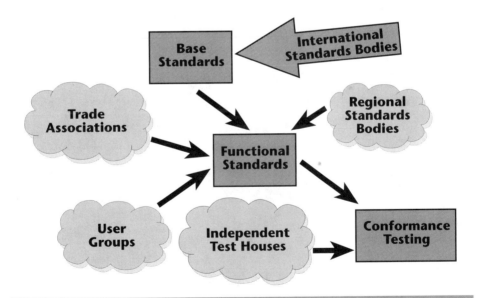

Figure 2.21 The standards-making process

For more learning resources, quizzes, and discussion forums on concepts related to this chapter, see www.telecomessentials.com/learningcenter.

Chapter 3

Transmission Media: Characteristics and Applications

Transmission media are the physical pathways that connect computers, other devices, and people on a network—the highways and byways that comprise the information superhighway. Each transmission medium requires specialized network hardware that has to be compatible with that medium. You have probably heard terms such as Layer 1, Layer 2, and so on. These terms are used to refer to the OSI reference model, which defines network hardware and services in terms of the functions they perform. (The OSI reference model is discussed in detail in Chapter 6, "Data Communications Basics.") Transmission media operate at Layer 1 of the OSI model: They encompass the physical entity and describe the types of highways on which the voice and data can travel.

It would be convenient if we could construct a network of only one medium. But that's impractical for anything but an extremely small network. So, in general, we use combinations of media types. There are three main categories of media types:

- **Cable**—Types of cable include unshielded twisted-pair (UTP), shielded twisted-pair (STP), and coaxial cable. Cable is inexpensive compared to the other media types, but as you'll learn when we get into the specifics, a major disadvantage of cable is that it offers a rather limited spectrum that will not be able to handle the truly advanced applications of the future.

- **Wireless**—Wireless media include radio frequencies, microwave, satellite, and infrared. Deployment of wireless media is faster and less costly than deployment of cable, particularly where there is little or no existing infrastructure (for example, Asia Pacific, Latin America, eastern and central

Prevailing Conditions and Network Diversity

No one of the three categories of media types can be considered best. Each is useful in different situations, and often you need to take advantage of a number of media types. When you are building a new network or upgrading an old one, your choice of media type should be based on the prevailing conditions.

The saying "don't put all your eggs in one basket" can be applied to networking. Having multiple pathways of fibers in and out of a building is not always enough. You need diversity—terrestrial and nonterrestrial facilities combined—because in disastrous events such as earthquakes, floods, and fires, if one alternative is completely disabled, you may be able to rely on another medium.

Europe). Wireless is also useful where environmental circumstances make it impossible or cost-prohibitive to use cable (for example, the Amazon, the Empty Quarter in Saudi Arabia, oil rigs). The disadvantage of wireless is that it provides slow data rates.

- ▪ **Fiber optics**—Fiber offers enormous bandwidth and immunity to many types of interferences and noise. Therefore, fiber provides very clear communications and a relatively noise-free environment. The downside of fiber is that it is costly to purchase and deploy because it requires specialized equipment and techniques.

You can assess various parameters to determine which media type is most appropriate for a given application. This chapter focuses on the five most commonly used transmission media formats: twisted-copper pair, coaxial cable, microwave, satellite, and fiber optics. Table 3.1 provides a quick comparison of some of the important characteristics of these five media types.

The frequency spectrum in which the medium operates directly relates to the bit rate you can obtain with the medium. You can see in Table 3.1 that twisted-pair affords the lowest frequency spectrum, a maximum of 1MHz, whereas fiber optics affords 75THz.

Another important characteristic is a medium's susceptibility to noise and the subsequent error rate. Again, twisted-pair suffers from many impairments. Coax and fiber suffer fewer impairments than twisted-pair because of how the cable is constructed, and fiber suffers the least because it is not affected by electrical interference. The error rate of wireless depends on the prevailing conditions.

Yet another characteristic that you need to evaluate is the distance required between the repeaters. This is a major cost issue for those constructing and operating the networks. In the case of twisted-pair deployed as an analog telephone chan-

Table 3.1 Transmission Media Characteristics

Media Type	Frequency Spectrum	Performance Error Rate	Distance Between Repeaters	Security	Cost
Twisted-pair	1MHz	Poor to fair (10^{-5})	Short (1.2 miles/2 km)	Poor	Low
Coaxial	1GHz	Good (10^{-7} to 10^{-9})	Short (1.5 miles/2.5 km)	Good	Moderate
Microwave	100GHz	Good (10^{-9})	Medium (up to 45 miles/72 km)	Poor	Moderate
Satellite	100GHz	Good (10^{-9})	Long (up to 22,3000 miles/36,000 km)	Poor	Moderate to high
Fiber	75THz	Great (10^{-11} to 10^{-13})	Long (up to 4,000 miles/6,400 km)	Good	Moderate to high

nel, the distance between the amplifiers is roughly 1.1 miles (1.8 kilometers). When twisted-pair is used in digital mode, the repeater spacing drops to about 1,800 feet (550 meters). With twisted-pair, a great many network elements must be installed and subsequently maintained over their lifetime, and they can be a potential source of trouble in the network. Coax offers about a 25% increase in the distance between repeaters over twisted-pair. With microwave and satellite, the distance between repeaters depends on the frequency bands in which you're operating and the orbits in which the satellites travel. In the area of fiber, we see new innovations every three to four months, and as discussed later in this chapter, some new developments promise distances as great as 4,000 miles (6,400 kilometers) between the repeaters or amplifiers in the network.

Security is another important characteristic. There is no such thing as complete security, and no transmission medium in and of itself can provide security. But using encryption and authentication helps ensure security. Also, different media types have different characteristics that enable rapid intrusion as well as characteristics that enable better detection of intrusion. For example, with fiber, an optical time domain reflectometer (OTDR) can be used to detect potential leaks that could be the result of unwanted intrusion.

Finally, you need to consider the costs associated with the media types. You need to look at three types of costs: acquisition cost (for example, the costs of the cable per foot/meter, of the transceiver and laser diode, and of the microwave tower), installation and maintenance costs (for example, the costs of parts as a result of wear and tear and environmental conditions), and internal premises costs for enterprises (for example, the costs of moves, adds, and changes, and of relocating workers as they change office spaces).

The following sections examine twisted-pair, coaxial cable, microwave, satellite, and fiber optics in detail.

■ Twisted-pair

The historical foundation of the public switched telephone network (PSTN) lies in the twisted-pair, and even today most people who have access to networks access those networks through a local loop built on twisted-pair. So, although twisted-pair has contributed a great deal to the evolution of communications, advanced applications on the horizon require larger amounts of bandwidth than twisted-pair can deliver, so the future of twisted-pair is diminishing. Figure 3.1 shows an example of four-pair UTP.

The total usable frequency spectrum of twisted-pair copper cable is about 1MHz (that is, one million cycles per second). Loosely translated into bits per second (bps)—a measurement of the amount of information being transported over a distance—you see about 2Mbps to 3Mbps over 1MHz of spectrum. But there's an inverse relationship between distance and loop length, and hence the available bandwidth, so as you shorten the distances, you can actually exercise higher data rates over twisted copper pairs. For instance, in local area networks (LANs), you can use Ethernet, which offers 100Mbps over twisted-pair, but the distance end-to-end on that network can be no more than 330 feet (100 meters). New develop-

Figure 3.1 Twisted-pair

ments will likely allow more efficient use of twisted-pair and enable the higher data rates that are needed for Web surfing and Internet access, but it will be important to limit the distance of the twisted-pair from the access point.

Another characteristic of twisted-pair is that it requires short distances between repeaters. Again, this means that more components need to be maintained and there are more points where trouble can arise, which leads to higher costs in terms of long-term operation.

Twisted-pair is also highly susceptible to interference and distortion, including electromagnetic interference (EMI), radio frequency interference (RFI), and the effects of moisture and corrosion. Therefore, the age and health of twisted-pair cable are important factors.

The greatest use of twisted-pair in the future is likely to be in the enterprise premises, for desktop wiring. Eventually enterprise premises will migrate to fiber and forms of wireless, but in the near future, they will continue to use twisted-pair internally.

Categories of Twisted-pair

There are two types of twisted-pair: UTP and STP. In STP, a metallic shield around the wire pairs minimizes the impact of the outside interference. Most implementations today use UTP. Twisted-pair is also divided into categories that specify the maximum data rate possible. In general, the cable category term refers to the ANSI/TIA/EIA 568-A Commercial Building Telecommunications Cabling Standards. Other standards bodies—including ISO/IEC, NEMA, and ICEA—are also working on specifying Category 6 and above cable.

The following are the cable types specified in the ANSI/TIA/EIA Cabling Standards:

- **Category 1**—Cat 1 cable is for voice telephony only; it does not support data.
- **Category 2**—Cat 2 cable can accommodate up to 4Mbps and is associated with Token Ring LANs.
- **Category 3**—Cat 3 cable operates over 16MHz on UTP and supports up to 10Mbps over a range of 330 feet (100 meters). Key LAN applications include 10Mbps Ethernet and 4Mbps Token Ring LANs.
- **Category 4**—Cat 4 cable operates over 20MHz on UTP and can carry up to 16Mbps over a range of 330 feet (100 meters). The key LAN application is 16Mbps Token Ring.
- **Category 5**—Cat 5 cable operates over 100MHz on UTP and can handle up to 100Mbps over a range of 330 feet (100 meters). Key LAN applications include 100BaseTX, ATM, CDDI, and 1000BaseT.
- **Category 5E**—Cat 5E (enhanced) operates over 100MHz on UTP, with a range of 330 feet (100 meters). The key LAN application is 1000BaseT.

Advanced cable types, such as the following, are being developed all the time:

- **Category 6**—Cat 6 cable operates over 250MHz on UTP, over a range of 330 feet (100 meters). Category 6 is expected to support 1Gbps, but only over short distances. There are currently no applications for Cat 6.

- **Category 7**—Cat 7 cable will operate over 600MHz over a range of 330 feet (100 meters) and will use STP or screened twisted-pair (ScTP).

The predominant cable categories in use today are Cat 3 and Cat 5E. Cat 4 and Cat 5 are largely defunct, and Cat 6 and Cat 7 are not yet standards in the United States.

Applications of Twisted-pair

The primary applications of twisted-pair are in premises distribution systems, telephony, private branch exchanges (PBXs) between the telephone sets and the switching cabinets, LANs, and local loops.

Analog and Digital Twisted-pair

Twisted-pair is used in traditional analog subscriber lines, also known as the telephony channel, or 4KHz channel. Digital twisted-pair takes the form of Integrated Services Digital Network (ISDN) and the new-generation family of Digital Subscriber Line (DSL) standards, collectively referred to as xDSL.

ISDN

Narrowband ISDN (N-ISDN) was introduced in 1983 as a network architecture and set of standards for an all-digital network. It was intended to provide end-to-end digital service using the public telephone networks worldwide and, therefore, to provide high-quality, error-free transmission. N-ISDN entails two different specifications:

- **Basic Rate Interface (BRI)**—Also referred to as Basic Rate Access (BRA), BRI includes two B-channels and one D-channel (often called 2B+D). The B channels are the bearer channels, which, for example, carry voice, data, or fax transmissions. The D channel is the delta channel, which is where signaling takes place. Because signaling doesn't occur over long periods of time, where allowed by the service provider, the D channel can also be used to carry low-speed packet-switched data. Each B channel offers 64Kbps, and the D channel provides 16Kbps. So, in total, 2B+D offers 144Kbps, delivered over a single twisted-pair with a maximum loop length of about 3.5 miles (5.5 kilometers). BRI is used in residences, in small businesses that need only a couple lines, and for centrex customers. (A *centrex customer* leases extensions from the local exchange rather than acquiring its own PBX for the customer premise. Thus, the local exchange pretends to be a private PBX that performs connections among the internal extensions and between the internal extensions and the outside network.)

- **Primary Rate Interface (PRI)**—Also referred to as Primary Rate Access (PRA), PRI is used for business systems. It terminates on an intelligent system (that is, a PBX, a multiplexer, an automatic call distribution system such as the sequencers you encounter when you dial an airline). There are two different PRI standards, each deployed over two twisted-pairs: The North American and Japanese infrastructure uses 23B+D, and other countries use 30B+D. As with BRI, in PRI each of the B channels is 64Kbps. With PRI, the D channel is 64Kbps. So, 23B+D provides twenty-three 64Kbps B-channels for information and one 64Kbps D-channel for signaling and additional packet data. And 30B+D provides thirty 64Kbps channels and one 64Kbps D-channel.

Given today's interest in Internet access and Web surfing, BRI is no longer the most appropriate specification. We all want quicker download times. Most people are willing to tolerate an eight-second download of a Web page, and just one second can make a difference in customer loyalty. As we experience more rapid information access, our brains become somewhat synchronized to that, and we want it faster and faster and faster. Therefore, N-ISDN has seen better days, and other broadband access solutions are gaining ground. (ISDN is discussed further in Chapter 7, "Wide Area Networking.")

xDSL
The DSL family includes the following:

- High-Bit-Rate DSL (HDSL)
- Asymmetrical DSL (ADSL)
- ISDN DSL (IDSL)
- Symmetrical (or Single-Line) DSL (SDSL)
- Rate Adaptive DSL (RADSL)
- Very-High-Bit-Rate DSL (VDSL)

As in many other areas of telecommunications, with xDSL there is not one perfect solution. One of the main considerations with xDSL is that not every form of xDSL is available in every location from all carriers. The solution also depends on the environment and the prevailing conditions. For example, the amount of bandwidth needed at the endpoint of a network—and therefore the DSL family member you choose—is determined by the applications in use. If the goal is to surf the Web, you want to be able to download quickly in one direction, but you need only a small channel on the return path to handle mouse clicks. In this case, you can get by with an asymmetrical service. On the other hand, if you're working from home and you want to transfer images or other files, or if you want to engage in videoconferencing, then you need substantial bandwidth in the upstream direction as well as in the downstream direction. In this case, you need a symmetrical service. Some of the members of the DSL family are symmetrical and some are asymmetrical, and each member has other unique characteristics. The following sections briefly describe each of these DSL family members, and Chapter 13, "Broadband Access Solutions," covers xDSL in more detail.

HDSL   Carriers use HDSL to provision T-1 or E-1 capacities because HDSL deployment costs less than other alternatives when you need to think about customers who are otherwise outside the permitted loop lengths. HDSL is a symmetrical service that can be deployed over a distance of about 2.2 miles (3.6 kilometers). HDSL is deployed over two twisted-pairs, and it affords equal bandwidth in both directions (that is, it is symmetrical).

HDSL is deployed as two twisted-pairs, but some homes have only a single pair of wiring running through the walls. Therefore, a form of HDSL called HDSL2 is being promoted for consumer/residential action. HDSL2 provides symmetrical capacities of up to 1.5Mbps or 2Mbps over a single twisted-pair. The projections for deployment of HDSL2 do not suggest large numbers.

ADSL   ADSL is an asymmetrical service that is deployed over one twisted-pair. With ADSL, the majority of bandwidth is devoted to the downstream direction, from the network to the user, with a small return path that is generally sufficient to enable telephony or simple commands. ADSL is limited to a distance of about 3.5 miles (5.5 kilometers) from the exchange point. New developments allow the distance to be extended because remote terminals can be placed closer to the customer.

There are two ADSL standards: ADSL1 and ADSL2. The vast majority of the ADSL that is currently deployed and available is ADSL1. ADSL1 supports 1.5Mbps (North American standards) to 2Mbps (International Telecommunication Union [ITU] standards) downstream and 16Kbps to 64Kbps upstream. This type of bandwidth is sufficient to provide good Web surfing, to carry a low grade of entertainment video, and to conduct upstream activities that don't command a great deal of bandwidth. However, ADSL1 is not sufficient for things such as the digital TV or interactive services that are likely to be available in the near future. For these activities, ADSL2 is preferred. ADSL2 supports 6Mbps (North American standards) to 8Mbps (ITU standards) downstream and 640Kbps to 840Kbps upstream.

We are continuously trying to deploy ADSL over longer distances. We'd like to get up to 7.5 miles (12 kilometers) or so, but predominantly today ADSL operates over distances up to 2.3 miles (3.7 kilometers). Again, the greater the distance, the lower the data rate, and the shorter the distance, the better the throughput.

IDSL   IDSL has a maximum loop length of 3.5 miles (5.5 kilometers), and it is deployed as a single twisted-pair that offers 128Kbps in each direction. It is basically ISDN without the voice service. As discussed previously, this data rate is too low to be pursued in the future, but if there are no broadband solutions available, you can use IDSL to get double the rate of a 56Kbps analog connection.

SDSL   SDSL is a symmetrical service that has a maximum loop length of 3.5 miles (5.5 kilometers) and is deployed as a single twisted-pair. It is a good solution in businesses, residences, small offices, and home offices, and for remote access into corporate facilities. You can deploy variable capacities for SDSL, in multiples of 64Kbps, up to a maximum of 2Mbps in each direction.

RADSL   RADSL has a maximum loop length of 3.5 miles (5.5 kilometers) and is deployed as a single twisted-pair. It adapts the data rate dynamically, based on any changes that may be occurring in the line conditions and based on the loop length. With RADSL, the rates can vary widely, from 600Kbps to 7Mbps downstream and from 128Kbps to 1Mbps upstream. RADSL can be configured to be a symmetrical or an asymmetrical service.

VDSL   VDSL provides a maximum span of about 1 mile (1.5 kilometers) over a single twisted-pair. Over this distance, you can get up to a rate of 13Mbps downstream. But if you shorten the distance to 1,000 feet (300 meters), you can get up to 52Mbps downstream, which would be enough capacity to facilitate tomorrow's digital TVs. With VDSL you can get up to 1.5Mbps to 2.3Mbps upstream.

Advantages and Disadvantages of Twisted-pair

Twisted-pair has several key advantages:

- **High availability**—More than one billion telephone subscriber lines based on twisted-pair have been deployed, and if it's there, we're going to use it. You may have heard the argument that telcos are trapped in their copper cages, and rather than build out an infrastructure that's truly designed for tomorrow's applications, they hang on to protecting their existing investment. It is a huge investment: More than US$250 billion in terms of book value is associated with the twisted-pair deployed worldwide. This can be construed as both an advantage and a disadvantage.

■ **Low cost of installation on premises**—The actual cost of installing twisted-pair on premises is very low.

■ **Low cost for local moves, adds, and changes in places**—An individual can simply pull out the twisted-pair terminating on a modular plug and replace it in another jack in the enterprise, without requiring the intervention of a technician. Of course, this assumes that the wiring is already in place; otherwise, there is the additional cost of a new installation.

The following are the disadvantages of twisted-pair:

■ **Limited frequency spectrum**—The total usable frequency spectrum of twisted-pair copper cable is about 1MHz.

■ **Limited data rates**—The longer a signal has to travel over twisted-pair, the lower the data rate. At 30 feet (100 meters), twisted-pair can carry 100Mbps, but at 3.5 miles (5.5 kilometers), the data rate drops to 2Mbps or less.

■ **Short distances required between repeaters**—More components need to be maintained and where trouble can arise, and this leads to higher long-term operational costs.

■ **High error rate**—Twisted-pair is highly susceptibility to signal interference such as EMI and RFI.

Although twisted-pair has been deployed widely and been adapted to some new applications, better media are coming down the pike for tomorrow's broadband world.

■ Coaxial Cable

The second transmission medium to be introduced was coaxial cable (often called *coax*), which began being deployed in telephony networks around the mid-1920s. Figure 3.2 shows the components of coax. In the center of a coaxial cable is a copper wire that acts as the conductor, where the information travels. The copper wire in coax is thicker than that in twisted-pair, and it's also unaffected by surrounding wires that contribute to EMI, so it can provide a higher transmission rate than twisted-pair. The center conductor is surrounded by plastic insulation, which helps filter out extraneous interference. The insulation is covered by the return path, which is usually braided-copper shielding or aluminum foil-type covering. Outer jackets form a protective outer covering for coax; how many outer jackets there are and what type they are depend on the intended use of the cable (for

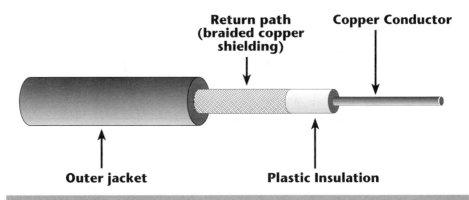

Figure 3.2 Coaxial cable

example, whether the cable is meant to be strung in the air or underground, whether rodent protection is required).

Characteristics of Coaxial

Coax affords a great deal more frequency spectrum than does twisted-pair. Traditional coaxial cable networks generally support 370MHz. Newer deployments, such as hybrid fiber coax (HFC) architectures, support 750MHz or 1,000MHz systems. (HFC is discussed in detail in Chapter 13.) Therefore, coax provides from 370 to 1,000 times more capacity than single twisted-pair. With this additional capacity, you can carve out individual channels, which makes coax a broadband facility. Multiplexing techniques can be applied to coax to derive multiple channels. Coax offers slightly better performance than twisted-pair, because the metallic shielding protects the center conductor from outside interferences; hence the performance of coax is on the order of 10^{-9} (that is, 1 in 1 billion) bps received in error. Amplifiers need to be spaced every 1.5 miles (2.5 kilometers), which is another improvement over twisted-pair, but it still means you need a substantial number of amplifiers deployed throughout the network.

Cable TV operators, like the telephony network providers, have been prevalent users of coax, but in the past decade they have been reengineering their backbone networks so that they are fiber based, thereby eliminating many amplifiers and subsequently improving performance. Remember from Chapter 2, "Telecommunications Technology Fundamentals," that amplifiers accumulate noise over a distance. So, in a large franchise area for a cable TV operator, as you get toward the outer fringes, greater noise accumulates and a lower service level is provided than is provided to some of the neighbors upstream. By reengineering their backbones to be fiber based, cable providers can also limit how many amplifiers have to be deployed.

One problem with coax has to do with the deployment architecture. Coaxial cable and HFC architectures are deployed in bus topologies. In a bus topology, the bandwidth is shared, which means congestion levels increase as more users in the neighborhood avail themselves of these features and services. A bus topology also presents security risks. It's sort of like going back to the party line in telephony. You do not have your own dedicated twisted-pair that's yours and only yours. Instead, several channels are devoted to accommodating voice telephony and are shared by everyone in the neighborhood, which makes encryption important. Also, there are some problems with noise in bus topologies. The points where the coax connects into set-top boxes or cable-ready TV sets tend to collect noise, so the cable tends to pick up extraneous noise from vacuum cleaners or hair dryers or passing motorcycles. Thus, if every household on the network is running a hair dryer at 6:30 AM, the upstream paths are subjected to this noise, with the result that there will be some performance degradations. (Bus topologies are discussed in more detail in Chapter 8, "Local Area Networking.")

Applications of Coaxial

In the mid-1920s, coax was applied to telephony networks as interoffice trunks. Rather than having to add more copper cable bundles with 1,500 or 3,000 pairs of copper wires in them, you could displace those big cables (which are very difficult to install cost-effectively) with a much smaller coaxial cable.

The next major use of coax in telecom occurred in the 1950s, when it was deployed as submarine cable to carry international traffic. Then it was also introduced into the data processing realm in the mid- to late 1960s. Early computer architectures required coax as the media type from the terminal to the host. LANs were predominantly based on coax from 1980 to about 1987.

Coax has also been used in community antenna TV (CATV, or cable TV) and in the local loop, in the form of HFC architectures. In HFC, you bring fiber as close as possible to the neighborhood; then on a neighborhood node, you terminate that fiber, and from that node you fan the coax out to the home service by that particular node. (This is described in detail in Chapter 13.)

Advantages and Disadvantages of Coaxial

The advantages of coax include the following:

- **Broadband system**—On coax there is a sufficient frequency range to support multiple channels, which allows for much greater throughput.

- **Greater channel capacity**—Each of the multiple channels offers substantial capacity. The capacity depends on where you are in the world. In the North

American system, each channel in the cable television system is 6MHz wide (according to the National Television Systems Committee [NTSC] standard). In Europe, with the Phase Alternate Line (PAL) standard, the channels are 8MHz wide. Within one of these channels, you can provision high-speed Internet access—that's how cable modems operate. But remember that one channel now is being shared by everybody who is using that coax from that neighborhood node, and that can range from 200 to 2,000 homes.

- **Greater bandwidth**—With coax, you have greater bandwidth system-wide, and you also have greater bandwidth for each channel. Because you have greater bandwidth per channel, you can support a mixed range of services. Voice, data, and even video and multimedia can benefit from the enhanced capacity.

- **Lower error rates**—Because of its insulation, coax has lower error rates and therefore slightly better performance than twisted-pair. The error rate is generally 10^{-9} (that is, 1 in 1 billion) bps.

- **Greater spacing between amplifiers**—Coax's cable shielding reduces noise and crosstalk, which means amplifiers can be spaced farther apart than with twisted-pair.

The main disadvantages of coax are as follows:

- **Problems with the deployment architecture**—The bus topology in which coax is deployed is susceptible to congestion, noise, and security risks.

- **Bidirectional upgrade required**—In countries in which there is a history of CATV, these cable systems were designed for broadcasting, not interactive communications. So, before they can offer to the subscriber any form of two-way services, those networks have to be upgraded to bidirectional systems.

- **Great noise**—The return path has some noise problems, so you have to deploy added intelligence into the end equipment to ensure that error control is being taken care of.

- **High installation costs**—Installation costs in the local environment are high.

- **High costs for local moves, adds, and changes**—You can't easily do away with the termination of a coax cable. You basically have to pull in a whole new cable to a new locale; it's not a simple modular plug environment.

- **Susceptible to damage from lightening strikes**—Coax is susceptible to damage from lightening strikes, so if you live in an area with a lot of lightening strikes, you must be wary because if that lightening is conducted by your coax, it could very well fry the equipment at the end of it.

■ Microwave

Microwave was used during World War II in military applications, and because it was successful in that environment, it was introduced into commercial communications. Microwave was deployed in the PSTN as a replacement for coaxial cable in the late 1940s.

As mentioned earlier, twisted-pair and coax both face limitations because of the frequency spectrum and the manner in which they are deployed. But microwave promises to have a much brighter future than twisted-pair on coax. Many locations cannot be cost-effectively cabled by using wires (for example, the Sahara, the Amazon, places where buildings are on mountaintops, and villages separated by valleys), and this is where microwave can shine.

Characteristics of Microwave

Microwave is defined as falling in the 1GHz to 100GHz frequency band. But systems today do not operate across this full range of frequencies. In fact, current microwave systems largely operate up to the 50GHz range. At the 60GHz level, we encounter the *oxygen layer,* where the microwave is absorbed by the surrounding oxygen. At this point we haven't developed a cost-effective approach to building radios that operate in those higher-frequency bands, but that is very much the intention and the direction wireless communications will take in the future. In fact, when we look forward to exercising more spectrum in order to deliver things such as interactive video to a palmtop, we'll be looking at techniques that use those higher portions of the frequency band, the 60GHz to 100GHz part of the spectrum.

The amount of bandwidth that you can realize out of the very large microwave spectrum is often limited by regulations as much as by technology. Before you can deploy a microwave system, you have to be licensed to operate that system, in all environments except your own private campus. In your own private territory, you can use unlicensed bands, but if you want to cross the public domain using licensed spectrum, you must first be granted approval by your spectrum management agency to operate within a given frequency allocation.

Some communities are very concerned about the potential health hazards of microwave and create legislation or council laws that prohibit placement of such systems. Some communities are very sensitive to the unsightliness of towers and argue that the value of real estate will drop if they are constructed. Therefore, several companies specialize in building camouflaged towers. When you see a tall tree, a church steeple, a light post, or a chimney, it could be a wireless tower disguised to protect your aesthetic balance.

Microwave is generally allocated in chunks of 30MHz to 45MHz channels, so it makes available a substantial amount of bandwidth to end users and operators of telecommunications networks.

Microwave is subject to the uncertainties of the physical environment. Metals in the area, precipitation, fog, rainfall, and a number of other factors can cause reflections, and therefore degradations and echoes. The higher (in elevation) we move away from land-based systems, the better the performance will be because there will be less intrusion from other land-based systems, such as television, radio, and police and military systems.

Repeater spacing with microwave varies depending on the frequency you are transmitting. Remember from Chapter 2 that lower frequencies can travel farther than higher frequencies before they attenuate. Higher frequencies lose power more rapidly. So, in microwave systems that operate in the 2GHz, 4GHz, and 6GHz bands, towers can be separated by 45 miles (72 kilometers). When you get into the higher frequency allocations, such as 18GHz, 23GHz, and 45GHz, the spacing needs to be much shorter, in the range of 1 to 5 miles (1.6 to 8 kilometers). This is an important issue in network design and, depending on the scope over which you want to deploy these facilities, it can have a significant impact on the investment needed.

Another important design criterion is that microwave requires line of sight and is a highly directional beam. Microwave requires a clear, unobstructed view, and it can't move through any obstacles, even things you wouldn't think would be obstacles, such as leaves on a tree. Technologies that depend on line of sight may work brilliantly where you have the appropriate terrain and climate, and they may not perform very well where you have many obstacles or much precipitation. Furthermore, line of sight is restricted by the curvature of the earth, and the curvature of the earth causes you to lose line of sight at about 90 miles (144 kilometers).

The impact of precipitation on microwave can be great. Microwave beams are small, and as you go up into the higher bands, the wave forms get smaller and smaller. Pretty soon they're smaller than a raindrop, and they can be absorbed by a raindrop and then scattered in a million directions. Therefore, in wet atmospheric conditions, there is a great potential for problems with microwave. As a result, practicing network diversity—using both terrestrial and nonterrestrial alternatives—is critical.

Applications of Microwave

One application associated with microwave is to replace the use of leased lines in a private network. Figure 3.3 shows a simple voice environment that initially made use of dedicated leased lines, also known as tie trunks, to link together two PBXs in

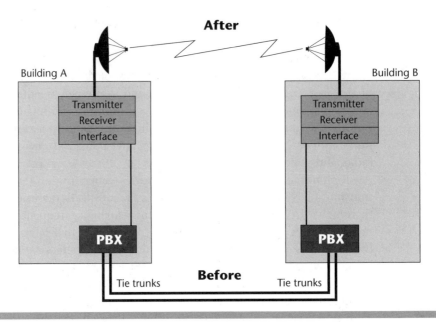

Figure 3.3 Connecting multiple PBXs with microwave

two different buildings across town from one another. Because these tie trunks were billed on a monthly basis and they were mileage sensitive, they were going to be a cost factor forever. Instead, a digital microwave system could be purchased to replace the tie trunks. This system would provide capacity between the buildings and do away with the monthly cost associated with the leased lines. This setup is commonly used by multinode or multilocation customers (for example, a health care facility with clinics and hospitals scattered throughout a state or territory, a university with multiple campuses, a retail location with multiple branches, or a bank with multiple branches).

Another key application of microwave is *bypassing*, which can be interpreted in multiple ways. Initially—and this is really how microwave came into the life of the end user—this technique was used to bypass the local telecommunications company. With the introduction of competition in the long-distance marketplace, end users in the United States initially had choices about who would be their primary long-distance carrier (that is, interexchange carrier). But to get to that carrier to transport the long-distance portion of the call, we still needed to get special local access trunks that led through the local operator to the competing interexchange provider. That meant paying an additional monthly fee for these local access trunks, and in an attempt to bypass those additional costs, businesses began to bypass the local telephone company by simply putting up a digital microwave system—a microwave tower with a shot directly to the interexchange carrier's point of presence.

Bypassing can also be used to circumvent construction. Say that a pharmaceutical company on a large campus has a public thoroughfare, and across the street there's a lovely park where the employees take their lunch and otherwise relax during the day. No one foresaw the fame and fortune the company would achieve with its latest migraine medicine, so it had not planned to build another facility to house the 300 people it now needed to add. Nobody ever provisioned conduit leading to that park across the street. The cost and time to get permission to break ground, lay conduit, pull cable, repave, and relandscape would be cost-prohibitive and time-prohibitive. To bypass that entire operation, microwave could be used between the main campus and the remote park (see Figure 3.4). This is essentially the same strategy that wireless local loop is pursuing. Rather than take the time and money to build out a wireline facility, you can do it much more rapidly and much more cost-effectively on a wireless basis. For instance, provisioning a twisted-pair or coaxial cable costs roughly US$1,200 to US$1,500 per subscriber and requires a 12- to 18-month deployment time. Wireless costs US$700 to US$800 per subscriber and requires 3 to 6 months of deployment time. There could always be something that delays the process (for example, contractual problems with the building developer), but, generally, you can deploy a microwave system much more rapidly at a much lower price point. Therefore, these

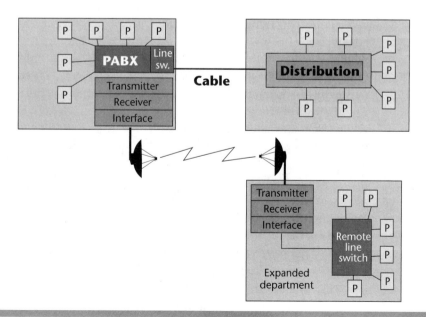

Figure 3.4   A bypassing construction that uses microwave

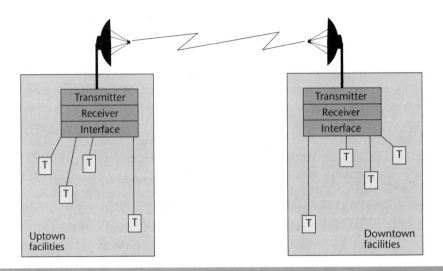

Figure 3.5 A LAN interconnect using microwave

systems are very popular in parts of the world where there is not already a local loop infrastructure.

Another application for microwave is in the data realm. Say that in your company the buildings that have telephone systems today are going to have LANs as well, and you want to unite the disparate LANs to create a virtual whole. You can use microwave technology as a bridge between two different LANs, giving it the appearance of being one LAN (see Figure 3.5). The main thing that inhibits or potentially slows down the growth of microwave is that only so many people can be operating on the same frequencies in the same area. Therefore, a big limitation of microwave is potential congestion in key metropolitan areas.

Microwave has a disaster-recovery application as well. Because microwave is relatively inexpensive and quick to deploy, it is a good candidate for use after a disaster damages wireline media, systems, or structures.

Advantages and Disadvantages of Microwave

The advantages of microwave are as follows:

- **Cost savings**—Using microwave is less expensive than using leased lines.

- **Portability and reconfiguration flexibility**—You can pick up microwave and carry it to a new building. You can't do that with cables.

- **Substantial bandwidth**—A substantial amount of microwave bandwidth is allocated, so high-speed data, video, and multimedia can be supported.

The the main disadvantages of microwave are as follows:

- **Line-of-sight requirement**—You need to ensure that there are no obstacles between towers.

- **Susceptibility to environmentally caused distortions**—Because the environment (for example, heavy rainstorms) can cause distortion, you need to have backups.

- **Regulatory licensing requirement**—The requirement for regulatory licensing means that you must have time and flexibility to deal with the spectrum agency.

- **Potential environmental restrictions**—Some communities do not allow microwave towers or require that they be camouflaged.

Emerging Applications and Developments in Microwave

A number of microwave applications are emerging. Wireless local loop is one application that is already being used to speed deployment and reduce the cost of bringing in subscriber access. There are also two techniques for supplying broadband access via point-to-point microwave—Multichannel Multipoint Distribution Service (MMDS) and Local Multipoint Distribution Service (LMDS)—which are introduced here and discussed in more detail in Chapter 13.

MMDS

MMDS essentially started as a digital TV system, and because it is digital, it provides great capacity—it enables more than 150 channels. This system operates in the 2GHz to 3GHz band, so it can cover a fairly large area (approximately 30 miles [48 kilometers]). But, again, if the terrain is hostile or environmental conditions are not favorable, the performance you experience may not be comparable to what you would see with wireline approaches. And, of course, the capacity is being shared among all the users receiving service via a given base station. At the moment MMDS has fallen out of favor with most carriers, but remember that its usability depends on the prevailing conditions. With developments in smart antenna design and nonline-of-sight systems, many of MMDS's shortcomings will be addressed in the future (see Chapter 13).

LMDS

LMDS is also referred to as Multipoint Video Distribution service in Europe. It operates over a very large frequency allocation, a 1.3GHz band that's generally located somewhere in the range of 28GHz to 45GHz, depending on the country you're in (some systems in the United Kingdom operate in the 10GHz range).

Because it operates at high frequencies, it attenuates rather rapidly compared to MMDS, and it operates over a much smaller area, a *microcell,* which is 0.5 to 3 miles (1 to 5 kilometers) in range. LMDS is a very popular technique for delivering wireless local loop, particularly in Asia Pacific, Africa, Latin America, and parts of eastern Europe.

■ Satellite

In 1947, Arthur C. Clarke (well known for his science fiction, particularly *2001: A Space Odyssey*) presented a paper to the scientific community in Washington, DC. Clarke suggested that if we explored orbits in higher elevations above the earth, we might achieve an orbit at which a satellite would be able to serve as a communications broadcast tool. Until that point, we were beginning early explorations of satellites, but they were what we today would call low-earth-orbiting satellites, which means they were at relatively low altitudes over the earth and revolved around the earth much faster than the earth rotates on its own axis. Clarke theorized that if we sent a satellite into a higher orbit, it would encounter a geosynchronous orbit, meaning that the satellite would rotate around the earth at exactly the same rate at which the earth rotates on its axis; the orbiting device would appear to hang stationary over a given point on earth. Clarke's hypotheses were supported and thus began the development of the communications sector for the space industry.

NASA launched the first experimental satellite in 1963. The first commercial satellite was launched in 1965, so 1965 marked the beginning of the use of satellite communications to support public telephony as well as television, particularly international television. Since then, large numbers of satellites have been launched. At this point, there are more than 250 communications-based satellites in space, as well as hundreds of other specialized satellites that are used for meteorological purposes, defense, remote sensing, geological exploration, and so on, for a total of more than 700 satellites orbiting the earth. And it seems that many more satellites will be launched in the future.

There are still approximately three billion people who are not served by even basic communications services, and we can't possibly deploy enough wireline facilities in a short enough time frame to equalize the situation worldwide. Therefore, satellites are very important in bringing infrastructure into areas of the world that have previously not enjoyed that luxury. Satellites are beginning to see increased investment and, in fact, other facilities in space are as well. According to *US News & World Report* ("The New Space Race," November 8, 1999), U.S. companies are expected to invest as much as US$500 billion in space by the year 2010, and this is causing some military analysts to believe that the military will be called on to defend U.S. interests in space, much as navies were formed to protect sea commerce in the 1700s.

In descriptions of satellite services, you'll encounter three abbreviations that relate to the applications that are supported:

- **FSS**—Fixed satellite services (FSS) refers to the conventional fixed services. They are offered in both the C-band and the Ku-band allocations.

- **BSS**—The second set of services is broadcast satellite services (BSS). BSS includes standard television and direct broadcast. These largely operate in the Ku-band, at 18GHz. Because the general application of television so far has been one way, 18GHz shows just the downlink frequency allocation. As we begin to move toward interactive TV, we'll start to see the use of two different bands in BSS.

- **MSS**—Mobile satellite services (MSS) accommodates mobility. MSS makes use of either Ka-band satellites or L-band satellites.

The satellite's *footprint* refers to the area of earth that the satellite's beams cover. Much of the progress in satellite developments has been in new generations of antennas that can provide more spot beams that can deliver higher-quality service to targeted areas, rather than simply one big beam with which users at the fringes of the footprint begin to see a degradation in service.

Another thing that's very important about and unique to satellites is the broadcast property. After you send data uplink to the satellite, it comes back downlink over the entire footprint. So you can achieve point-to-multipoint communications very cost-effectively. This had a dramatic impact on the media business. Take a big newspaper that has seven regional printing presses within the United States. Before satellites, the paper would have had to send a separate transmission to each of those printing locations so local ads could be inserted and such, but with a satellite you beam it up once, and when it comes down, it rains over the entire footprint of the United States. If each of the printing presses has a satellite station properly focused on the satellite and knows what frequency to receive on, it will get the information instantaneously.

An interesting design parameter associated with satellites is that as you increase the number of locations, the economic benefit of using satellites increases. With leased lines, logic dictates that the more locations you have and the greater the distances between them, the more expensive the network will become. But when using satellite technology, the more locations you have that are sharing the hub station and transponder, the cheaper the network becomes for all concerned. Thus, satellite technology presents a very attractive networking solution for many customers.

Remember that there are 700 or so satellites in space. On top of those 700 satellites, there are about 250,000 pieces of debris that have been cataloged by the space agencies. Furthermore, we are seeing an increase in comet and solar flare activity. A solar flare can decommission an entire satellite in one pulse, and a little speck of comet dust can put a baseball-size crater into a solar panel. Because of all these hazards, strategies have to be put in place to protect the satellites that are currently there.

We often don't recognize what great capabilities satellite can provide. But if we set our sights on more than just the planet earth and realize that there is a great frontier to explore, we realize that although fiber may be the best solution on the planet, when we want to advance in space, satellite communication is extremely important.

Frequency Allocations of Satellite

The frequency spectrum in which satellites operate is the microwave frequency spectrum. Therefore, microwave and satellite signals are really the same thing. The difference is that with satellite, the repeaters for augmenting the signals are placed on platforms that reside in high orbit rather than on terrestrial towers. And, of course, this means that the power levels associated with satellite communications are greater than those of terrestrial microwave networks. The actual power required depends on the orbit the satellites operate in (geosynchronous orbit satellites require the most power and low-earth-orbit satellites require the least). A number of factors are involved in the bandwidth availability of satellite. First, it depends on what spectrum the regulatory agencies have allocated for use within the nation. Second, it depends on the portion of the frequency spectrum in which you're actually operating. Finally, it depends on the number of transponders you have on the satellite. The *transponder* is the key communications component in satellite. It accepts the signal coming from the earth station and then shifts that signal to another frequency. When the signal is on the new frequency, it is amplified and rebroadcast downlink.

In satellite communications, the frequency allocations always specify two different bands: one is used for the uplink from earth station to satellite and one for the downlink from satellite to earth station. Many different bands are specified in the various satellite standards, but the most dominant frequency bands used for purposes of communications are C-band, Ku-band, Ka-band, and L-band.

C-Band

With C-band, you transmit uplink around the 6GHz range and downlink around the 4GHz range. The advantage of C-band, as compared to other bands, is that because it operates in the lower frequency bands, it is fairly tolerant of adverse weather conditions. It has larger wave forms, so it doesn't suffer as much distur-bance as do smaller wave forms in the presence of precipitation, for instance.

The disadvantage of C-band is that its allocation of frequencies is also shared by terrestrial systems. So selecting sites can take time because you have to contend with what your neighbors have installed and are operating. Licensing can take time, as well.

Ku-Band

Ku-band was introduced in the early 1980s and revolutionized how we use satellite communications. First, it operates on the uplink at around 14GHz and on the downlink at around 11GHz. The key advantage of Ku-band is that this frequency band allocation is usually reserved specifically for satellite use, so there are no con-flicts from terrestrial systems. Therefore, site selection and licensing can take place much more rapidly. Second, because it doesn't interfere with terrestrial systems, it offers portability. Therefore, a Ku-band dish can be placed on top of a news van or inside a briefcase, and a news reporter can go to the story as it is breaking to broad-cast it live and without conflict with surrounding systems.

The disadvantage of Ku-band is that it's a slightly higher frequency allocation than C-band, so you can experience distortions under bad climactic conditions (for example, humidity, fog, rain).

Ka-Band

The new generation of satellite—the broadband satellites—will operate in the Ka-band. The key advantage of Ka-band is that it offers a wide frequency band: about 30GHz uplink and about 20GHz downlink. The difference between 20GHz and 30GHz for Ka-band is much greater than the difference between 4GHz and 6GHz for C-band. This expanded bandwidth means that Ka-band satellites are better pre-pared than satellites operating at other bands to accommodate telemedicine, tele-education, telesurveillance, and networked interactive games.

A disadvantage of Ka-band is that it's even higher up in the frequency band than the other bands, so rain fade (that is, degradation of signal because of rain) can be a more severe issue. Thus, more intelligent technologies have to be embed-ded at the terminal points to be able to cost-effectively deal with error detection and correction.

L-Band

L-band operates in the 390MHz to 1550MHz range, supporting various mobile and fixed applications. Because L-band operates in the lower frequencies, L-band systems are more tolerant of adverse weather conditions than are other systems. It is largely used to support very-small-aperture terminal (VSAT) networks and mobile communi-cations, including handheld terminals, vehicular devices, and maritime applications.

Satellite Network Segments

Satellite networks have three major segments:

- **Space segment**—The space segment is the actual design of the satellite and the orbit in which it operates. Most satellites have one of two designs: a barrel-shaped satellite that is normally used to accommodate standard communications or a satellite with a very wide wingspan that is generally used for television. Satellites are launched into specific orbits to cover the parts of earth for which coverage is desired.

- **Control segment**—The control segment defines the frequency spectrum over which satellites operate and the types of signaling techniques used between the ground station and the satellite to control those communications.

- **Ground segment**—The ground segment is the earth station—the antenna designs and the access techniques used to enable multiple conversations to share the links up to the satellite. The ground segment of satellites continues to change as new technologies are introduced.

Satellite Orbits

Another important thing that affects the use and application of satellites are the orbits in which they operate. As shown in Figure 3.6, there are three major orbits: geosynchronous orbit (GEO), middle earth orbit (MEO), and low earth orbit (LEO). We have traditionally used GEOs. MEOs and LEOs are relatively new developments that offer possibilities for supporting advanced applications.

Shrinking Earth Stations

We've progressed very quickly in satellite history. The first earth station that accompanied the Early Bird satellite in 1965 had a massive facility. The dome on the building was 18 stories high, the antenna weighed 380 tons, and the entire building had liquid helium running through it to keep it cool. This was not something an end user could wheel into a parking lot or place on top of a building. But we have continued to shrink the sizes of earth stations, and today many businesses use VSATs, in which the dish diameter is 2 feet (0.6 meters) or less. You can literally hang a VSAT outside your window and have a network up and running within four hours (assuming that you have your frequency bands allocated and licensed).

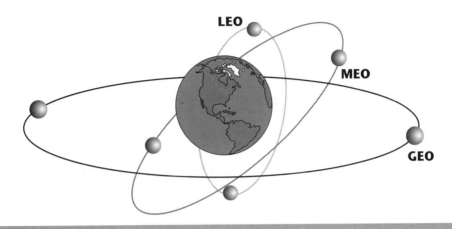

Figure 3.6 Satellite orbits

Unusable Satellite Bands

The bands between about 1,000 miles and 6,250 miles (about 1,600 kilometers and 10,000 kilometers) cannot be used for satellites because the Van Allen radiation belts act negatively on satellites.

GEO Satellites

A GEO satellite is launched to 22,300 miles (36,000 kilometers) above the equator. A signal from such a satellite must travel quite a distance; as a result, there is a delay. It's a 0.25-second delay in each direction, so from the time you say "Hello, how are you?" to the time that you hear the person's response, "Fine," there is a 0.5-second delay, and that results in somewhat of a stilted conversation. Many data applications, especially those that involve entertainment such as games, cannot perform with a delay this great.

GEO satellites have the benefit of providing the largest footprint of the satellite types. You can cover the entire world with just three GEO satellites, but the delay factor in getting to that orbit inhibits its use with the continuously growing range of real-time applications that are very sensitive to delay.

The fact that it is launched at such a high orbit also means that a GEO satellite requires the most power of all the satellite systems. And because the trend in satellites has been to deliver more data as well as interactive services (which are very delay sensitive) directly to the user, we are now seeing more satellites launched at the lower orbits.

We are beginning to see data rates of up to 155Mbps with GEO systems, particularly in the Ka-band. That data rate is not commonly available today, but it is feasible with the new generation of broadband satellites. Going to higher data rates, however, necessitates larger antennas, more so for GEO systems than for satellites in other orbits. Parabolic satellite antennas 33 feet (10 meters) in diameter can now be built, and it should soon be possible to extend them to 66 feet (20 meters) or 98 feet (30 meters).

The main applications of GEO systems are one-way broadcast, VSAT systems, and point-to-multipoint links. With GEO systems, there are no delay factors to worry about with one-way broadcasts. As a result, international television is largely distributed over these satellite networks today.

VSATs Business enterprises use VSAT networks as a means of private networking, essentially setting up point-to-point links or connections between two locales. A VSAT station is so compact that it can be put outside a window in an office environment. VSATs are commonly deployed to reduce the costs associated with the leased lines, and depending on how large the network is, they can reduce those costs by as much as 50%. Most users of VSATs are enterprises that have 100 or more nodes or locations (for example, banks that have many branches, gas stations that have many locations, convenience stores). VSATs elegantly and economically help these types of enterprises do things such as transport information relevant to a sale made from a remote location to a central point, remotely process information, and process reservations and transactions. (See Figure 3.7.)

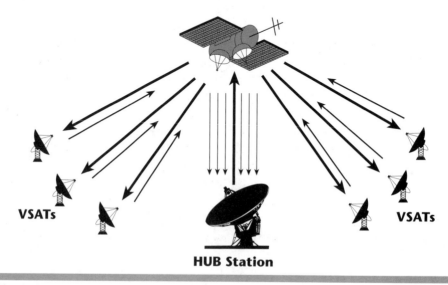

HUB Station

Figure 3.7 A VSAT system

Another use for VSATs is business video. Before about 1994, the only way to do point-to-multipoint video was by satellite. No terrestrial conference bridges would allow it. So, if you wanted to have a CEO provide his state-of-the-company address to all employees at different locations, the easiest way to get that footprint was by satellite.

VSATs are also useful as disaster-recovery tools. Because you can set up a VSAT system very quickly, it can be very useful in the event of a major disaster, when land-based facilities are entirely disabled.

VSATs are also useful in vehicle tracking systems, to communicate with drivers, arrange for payload drop-offs and pickups, and handle standard messaging without disrupting drivers' transportation schedules.

An emerging application for VSAT is broadband Internet access. Products such as Hughes DirecPC provide Internet downloads at up to 2Mbps. Similarly, intranets (that is, site-to-site connections between company locations) could be based on VSATs.

The following are the key advantages of VSATs:

■ **Easily accesses remote locations**—Where it would be difficult to facilitate a wireline arrangement, such as on an oil rig, a VSAT can easily be set up.

■ **Rapid deployment**—A VSAT system can be installed in two to four hours (as long as you have already secured the license to operate within an allocated spectrum).

■ **Scalable**—A VSAT system can grow to facilitate more bandwidth, with the addition of more interfaces.

■ **Platform agnostic**—A VSAT can support a variety of data networking protocols.

■ **Distance-insensitive to transmission costs**—The transmission cost is the same whether your locations are 100 miles (161 kilometers) apart or 3,000 miles (4,828 kilometers) apart. As long as the locations are within the footprint of the satellite, the costs are distance-insensitive. (This does not necessarily translate to distance-insensitive pricing.)

■ **Cost reductions via shared-hub facilities**—The more you share the system, the more your costs are reduced.

■ **Flexible network configuration**—You can be flexible with your network configurations. As with a microwave system, you can pick it up and move it.

Disadvantages of VSATs include the following:

■ **Transmission quality subject to weather conditions**—Stormy weather can cause disruptions. Most large users of VSAT networks have some leased lines available to use as backup when disruptions occur.

■ **Local zoning restrictions**—City councils may not want to see VSAT equipment protruding from buildings.

■ **Potentially high startup costs for small installations**—A small company could face a high startup cost if it does not have many nodes. (On the other hand, if it's the only available recourse—if there is no way to communicate without it—then the installation cost is a moot point.)

MEO Satellites

MEO satellites orbit at an elevation of about 6,200 to 9,400 miles (10,000 to 15,000 kilometers). MEO satellites are closer to the earth than GEO satellites, so they move across the sky much more rapidly—in about one to two hours. As a result, to get global coverage, you need more satellites (about five times more) than you would with GEO systems. But because the altitude is lower, the delay is also reduced, so instead of a 0.5-second delay, you see a 0.1-second delay.

The main applications for MEOs are in regional networks, to support mobile voice and low-speed data, in the range of 9.6Kbps to 38Kbps. The companies that use MEOs tend to have their movement within a region rather than over the entire globe, so they want a larger footprint over, for example, the Asia-Pacific region, to support mobility of mainly voice communications.

LEO Satellites

LEOs are a lot like cellular networks, except that in the case of LEOs, the cells rather than the users are moving. With LEOs a provider could bypass the global PSTN. Because LEOs are in such low orbits, they greatly reduce the transit times, so the delays are comparable to what you'd experience on the PSTN, and therefore delay-sensitive applications can survive. Their low orbits also mean that power consumption is much lower than with a higher-orbiting satellite, so you can direct it into a user's handheld. Also, LEOs offer greatly increased network capacity overall on a global basis.

LEOs orbit at about 400 to 1,000 miles (640 to 1,600 kilometers). LEOs can be used with smaller terminals than can the other satellites because they are much closer to the earth (40 times closer). But, again, because they are closer to earth, you need many more LEOs than other satellites to get the same coverage (about 20 times more LEOs than GEOs and 5 times more LEOs than MEOs). A user must always be able to see at least one LEO satellite that is well clear of the horizon.

As mentioned earlier, the early satellites rotated around the earth so fast that we couldn't use them for communications. But we've added switching into the satellite platform. So, as a LEO satellite begins to go out of view, a call is switched—that is, handed over—to the next satellite coming in. Therefore, it works very much like the cellular system, where you are handed off to different frequencies during a conversation. Of course, a benefit of being lower in the sky means that the delay with LEOs is reduced—only about 0.05 seconds—and this makes LEOs very appealing for interactive services.

The key applications planned for LEOs are support for mobile voice, low-speed data, and high-speed data. There are three categories of LEOs, and each category is optimized for certain applications:

- **Little LEOs**—Little LEOs offer 2.4Kbps to 300Kbps and operate in the 800MHz range. They are ideal for delivering messaging, paging, and vehicle location services.

- **Big LEOs**—Big LEOs offer 2.4Kbps to 9.6Kbps and operate in the 2GHz range. They provide rather low data rates and are largely designed to provide voice services to areas that aren't currently served by any form of terrestrial or cellular architecture.

- **Broadband LEOs**—Broadband LEOs offer 16Kbps to 155Mbps. They operate in the Ka-band, at 20GHz to 30GHz, and they support data and multimedia files at up to 155Mbps.

Applications of Satellite

The traditional applications for satellites have been to serve remote areas where terrestrial facilities were not available; to provide the capability for point-to-multipoint communications for cost-efficiencies; to provide disaster-recovery support; to provide remote monitoring and control; to facilitate two-way data messaging, vehicle tracking, mobile communications, and maritime and air navigation; to distribute TV, video, and multimedia; and to provide for defense communications.

HALEs

A slightly different orbit is being introduced: *high-altitude, long-endurance (HALE) satellites*, which the ITU also calls *high-altitude platform stations* (HAPS). HALEs are in extremely low orbit. They're about 11 miles (17.8 kilometers) overhead, and they operate at about 47GHz, although the ITU has also designated other bands of operation, including 3G bands. The main applications are Internet access, resource monitoring, and data networking in metropolitan areas. In essence, they are aircraft that hover over a city area, providing network capacity for metropolitan area networking. Some may be dirigibles, and others may have wings and fly like conventional aircraft.

The key advantage associated with HALEs is a very moderate launch cost, compared to the cost associated with traditional satellites. By applying what we are learning to do with phased-array antennas (discussed later in this chapter) to HALEs, we can provide a wide capacity: some 3,500 beams could enable mobile two-way communications and video distribution in an area about 300 miles (about 500 kilometers) across.

Advantages and Disadvantages of Satellite

The advantages of satellite include the following:

- Access to remote areas
- Coverage of large geographical areas
- Insensitivity to topology
- Distance-insensitive costs
- High bandwidth

The disadvantages of satellite include the following:

- High initial cost
- Propagation delay with GEO systems
- Environmental interference problems
- Licensing requirements
- Regulatory constraints in some regions
- Danger posed by space debris, solar flare activity, and meteor showers

Emerging Applications and Innovations in Satellite

Satellite is being used in a number of emerging applications. Two emerging applications of satellite are automotive navigation and digital audio radio, such as the SIRIUS system, with which you can receive more than 100 radio stations throughout the footprint of the satellite. Not only do you receive the music or programming you want, but you can immediately determine who the artist is and what CD it is from, and you can even compile a customized version for yourself. Use of satellite in Internet backbones is another emerging application, because of the huge growth in traffic levels. Terrestrial facilities can't handle all this traffic alone, so we have to rely on some satellite backbones, especially to reach into places such as Africa and Latin America. Additional emerging applications include Internet access, satellite caching, and multimedia. The farther you are from the point at which an application resides, the worse the experience you have. So, if we put applications on a satellite, everybody within the footprint is always only one hop away, thereby greatly reducing the latencies or delays encountered in ultimately drawing on the content. Again, what may make a difference here is whether it's an interactive application and what orbit that satellite is in, but this is one application that merges the ISP and satellite industry together. Other emerging applications of satellites include telemedicine, distance learning, remote imaging, and weather information.

Satellites have seen a number of innovations and are facing yet more in the future. The most significant change in the coming years is that satellites will increasingly deliver information directly to the consumer rather than to a commercial data hub. This might mean that aerospace corporations become major competitors of traditional telecom carriers.

Another key innovation will be phased-array antennas (see Figure 3.8). A phased-array antenna consists of multiple transmitting elements, arranged in a fixed geometric array. These small flat antennas are steered electronically, and they provide great agility and fast tracking. In addition, they have the capability to form multiple antenna beams simultaneously. That is, these phased arrays achieve directional selectivity by electronically imposing minute delays on the signals that are moving from or to different parts of the array. The beam is electrically pointed by adjusting the phases of the individual transmitters. This enables very fast and precise steering of the communications beam, which is very important for high-bandwidth communication because the data rate is inversely proportional to the angular offset. The arrays can be programmed to send a grid of electronically formed radio beams to track moving targets or to receive signals from only certain directions. This enables 100-fold spectrum reuse and may allow us to reach 1,000-fold spectrum reuse. Phased arrays have the additional advantage of being flat, which makes them more suitable than other antennas for many applications, particularly mobile installations.

Key challenges for satellites today are related to power and offering mobile services. Because the small antennas now used in portable transceivers intercept only a

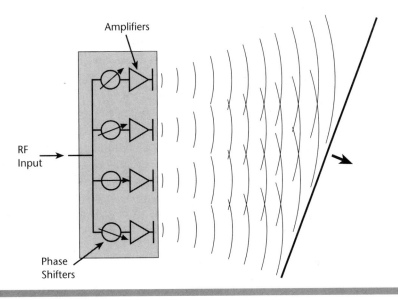

Figure 3.8 Phased-array antennas

tiny fraction of the satellite signal, satellites must have a lot of power and sensitivity; a typical solar array on a GEO satellite increased in power from 2kW to more than 10kW in just several years. Another innovation involves moving further up the frequency spectrum, to make use of extremely high frequencies (EHF). The highest-frequency satellite systems today use wavelengths that are comparable to the size of a raindrop. Consequently, a raindrop can act as a lens, bending the waves and distorting the signals. But these ill effects can be mitigated by using error-correction techniques, by applying more power when necessary, or by using more ground terminals so data can follow diverse paths. When wavelengths are smaller than a millimeter, there are yet more obstacles. Infrared and optical beams are easily absorbed in the atmosphere. So, in the near future, they may very well be restricted to use within buildings, but there have been some new developments on Free Space Optics, which are discussed in Chapter 13.

▪ Fiber Optics

In the late 1950s and early 1960s, a number of people were working in the realm of fiber optics simultaneously. Charles Kao, who was a scientist with ITT, is often acknowledged as being one of the fathers of fiber optics. Kao theorized that if we could develop a procedure for manufacturing ultrapure, ultrathin filaments of glass, we could use this as a revolutionary new communications pipeline. Thus began the move toward researching and developing optical technology.

In 1970, we first had the developments that today allow us to deploy the large amounts of fiber we have. The first development was a procedure for manufacturing ultrapure filaments of glass, a procedure called "broomsticking," that was introduced by Corning Glassworks. Glass that has an inner core etched into it is melted at extremely high temperatures, and as the glass is melting and dropping down the tube, it begins to cool and form a strand. By the time it gets to the bottom of the tube, it is a fiber-optic thread. Being able to create the fiber cable itself solved half the equation, but because the fiber's diameter is minuscule (measured in micrometers, or microns, abbreviated μ), the light source that will pulse energy on this tiny fiber also has to be minuscule. In 1970, Bell Labs completed the equation by introducing the first laser diode small enough to fit through the eye of a needle. So the two things that determine the performance characteristics of a given fiber implementation are the type of cable used and the type of light source used.

Characteristics of Fiber Optics

Fiber optics operates in the visible light spectrum, in the range from 10^{14}Hz to 10^{15}Hz. Wavelength is a measure of the width of the waves being transmitted.

Different fiber-optic materials are optimized for different wavelengths. The EIA/TIA standards currently support three wavelengths for fiber-optic transmission: 850, 1,300, and 1,550 nanometers (nm). Each of these bands is about 200nm wide and offers about 25THz of capacity, which means there is a total of some 75THz of capacity on a fiber cable. The bandwidth of fiber is also determined by the number of wavelengths that it can carry, as well as by the number of bits per second that each wavelength supports. (As discussed in Chapter 2, each year, wavelength division multiplexers are enabling us to derive twice as many wavelengths as the year before, and hence they enable us to exploit the underlying capacity of the fiber cables.)

With fiber, today we can space repeaters about 500 miles (800 kilometers) apart, but new developments promise that, in the very near future, new techniques will stretch that spacing. Trials have been successfully completed at distances of 2,500 miles (4,000 kilometers) by Xros (now Nortel) and, more recently, at a distance of 4,000 miles (6,400 kilometers) by Williams Communications (using Corvis).

Components of Fiber Optics

As mentioned earlier, the two things that determine the performance characteristics of a given fiber implementation are the type of cable used and the type of light source used. Let's look at the components of each.

Fiber-Optic Cable

Figure 3.9 shows the basic components of fiber-optic cable. Fiber-optic cable is available in many sizes. It can have as few as a couple pairs of fiber or it can have bundles that contain upward of 400 or 500 fiber pairs. Each of the fibers is protected with cladding, which ensures that the light energy remains within the fiber rather than bouncing out into the exterior. The cladding is surrounded by plastic shielding, which, among others things, ensures that you can't bend the fiber to the point at which it would break; the plastic shielding therefore limits how much stress you can put on a given fiber. That plastic shielding is then further reinforced with Kevlar reinforcing material—very strong material that is five times stronger than steel—to prevent other intrusions. Outer jackets cover the Kevlar reinforcing material, and the number and type of outer jackets depend on the environment where the cable is meant to be deployed (for example, buried underground, used in the ocean, strung through the air).

There are two major categories of fiber: multimode and monomode (also known as single mode). Fiber size is a measure of the core diameter and cladding (outside) diameter. It is expressed in the format *xx/zz*, where *xx* is the core diameter and *zz* is the outside diameter of the cladding. For example, a 62.5/125-micron fiber has a core

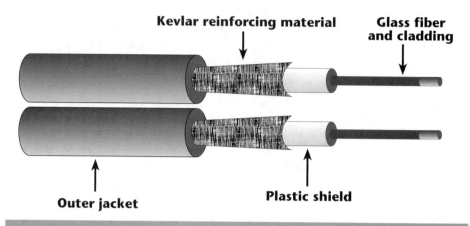

Figure 3.9 Fiber-optic cable

diameter of 62.5 microns and a total diameter of 125 microns. The 62.5/125-micron fiber is the only size currently supported by the EIA/TIA standard.

The core diameter of the fiber in multimode ranges from 50 microns to 62.5 microns, which is large relative to the wavelength of the light passing through it; as a result, multimode fiber suffers from modal dispersion (that is, the tendency of light to travel in a wave-like motion rather than in a straight line), and repeaters need to be spaced fairly close together (about 10 to 40 miles [16 to 64 kilometers] apart). The diameter of multimode also has a benefit: It makes the fiber more tolerant of errors related to fitting the fiber to transmitter or receiver attachments, so termination of multimode is rather easy.

The more high-performance mode of fiber, single-mode fiber, has a fiber diameter that is almost the same as the wavelength of light passing through it—from 8 microns to 12 microns. Therefore, the light can use only one path—it must travel straight down the center of the fiber. As a result, single-mode fiber does not suffer from modal dispersions and it maintains very good signal quality over longer distances. Therefore, with single-mode fiber, repeaters can be spaced farther apart (as mentioned earlier, they are currently about 500 miles [804 kilometers] apart, with the distances getting greater rapidly). But because single-mode fiber has such a smaller diameter, it is difficult to terminate, so experienced technical support may be needed to perform splices and other work with single-mode fiber.

The bottom line is that multimode fiber is less expensive than single-mode fiber but offers lower performance than single-mode fiber. Single-mode fiber is more expensive and offers higher performance, and it has been used in most of the long-distance networks that use fiber.

Light Sources

In the realm of light sources, there are also two categories: light-emitting diodes (LEDs) and laser diodes. The cheaper, lower-performer category is LEDs. LEDs are relatively inexpensive, they have a long life, and they are rather tolerant of extreme temperatures. However, they couple only about 3% of light into the fiber, so their data rates are low, currently about 500Mbps.

Laser diodes are capable of much higher transmission speeds than LEDs. They are a pure light source that provides coherent energy that has little distortion. Laser diodes, therefore, are commonly used for long-haul and high-speed transmission. Laser diodes offer better performance than LEDs, and they are more expensive, although the cost of these components has been dropping about 40% per year. As the costs drop, performance is also improving; in the very near future, we should see the introduction of light sources that pulse one trillion bits per second.

So, when you want to carry traffic over the long haul, the best combination is single-mode fiber with laser diodes. For very short implementations, such as in a campus network environment, the cost-efficiencies of multimode and LEDs may make this combination a more appropriate solution. But in general, as we look forward to the new developments in optical equipment—such as wavelength division multiplexers, optical cross-connects, and optical switches—we will need higher-quality fiber to interface to. It appears that roughly 95% of the world's fiber plant is not prepared to operate at the high speed that we are evolving to with optical equipment. So, even though we have been actively deploying fiber for years, not all of it is compatible with the next generation of optical equipment. This means that we will see new companies laying new highways and using the latest and greatest in fiber, as well as older companies having to upgrade their plants if they want to take advantage of what the optical equipment has to offer.

How Fiber-Optic Transmission Works

As shown in Figure 3.10, in fiber-optic transmission, the digital bit stream enters the light source, in this case the laser diode. If a one bit is present, the light source pulses light in that time slot, but if there is a zero bit, there is no light pulse. The absence or presence of light therefore represents the discrete ones and zeros. Light energy, like other forms of energy, attenuates as it moves over a distance, so it has to run though an amplification or repeating process. As mentioned earlier, until about 1994, electronic repeaters were used with fiber, so the optical signal would have to stop; be converted into electrical energy; be resynchronized, retimed, and regenerated; and then be converted back into optical energy to be passed to the next point in the network. This was a major problem because it limited the data rate to 2.5Gbps. But some developments were introduced in the early 1990s that

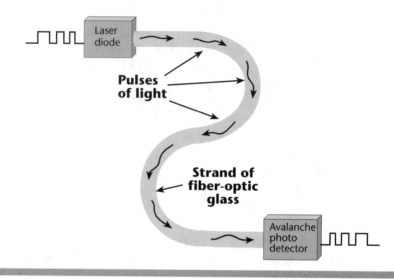

Figure 3.10   Fiber-optic transmission

dramatically changed long-distance communications over fiber. The next section of this chapter talks about these innovations.

Innovations in Fiber Optics: EDFAs, WDM, and DWDM

As mentioned in Chapter 2, erbium-doped fiber amplifiers (EDFAs) are optical repeaters that are made of fiber doped with erbium metal at periodic intervals (normally every 30 to 60 miles [50 to 100 kilometers]). The introduction of EDFAs made it possible for fiber-optic systems to operate at 10Gbps. EDFAs also opened the way for Wavelength Division Multiplexing (WDM), the process of dividing up the optical transmission spectrum into a number of nonoverlapping wavelengths, with each wavelength supporting a single high-speed communications channel. Today, undersea cables need to be designed with WDM in mind, and until recently, most were not, which means they have inappropriate repeater spacing. So, again, for the next generation of fiber communications over undersea cables, many systems will have to be replaced or upgraded.

An optical multiplexing hierarchy was the predecessor to WDM: Synchronous Digital Hierarchy (SDH) and Synchronous Optical Network (SONET). SDH/SONET is a time-division multiplexed system, and within SDH/SONET fiber cables, you can carry energy over just one wavelength. (SDH/SONET is discussed in detail in Chapter 5, "The PSTN.") With Dense WDM (DWDM), you can operate over 16 or more wavelengths. Products that are currently shipping

Forecasting Optical Developments

The basic equation in assessing the development of optics is that every year the data rate that can be supported on a wavelength doubles and every year the number of wavelengths that can be supported on a fiber doubles as well.

support anywhere from 80 wavelengths to 128 wavelengths and operate at data rates of 2.5Gbps to 10Gbps. New systems are emerging that operate at 40Gbps. Meanwhile, research is also under way with dense wavelength division multi-plexers that will be capable of supporting as many as 15,000 wavelengths. These developments are just the tip of the iceberg with what we can expect in coming years. (WDM and DWDM are discussed in more detail in Chapter 12, "Optical Networking.")

Applications of Fiber Optics

Fiber has a number of key applications. It is used in both public and private net-work backbones, so the vast majority of the backbones of the PSTNs worldwide have been upgraded to fiber. The backbones of the Internet providers are fiber. Cable TV systems and power utilities have reengineered and upgraded their back-bones as well.

Surprisingly, electric power utilities are the second largest network operator after the telcos. They have vast infrastructures for generating and transmitting elec-tricity; these infrastructures rely on fiber-optic communications systems to direct and control power distribution. After they have put in fiber, they have often found themselves with excess capacity and in a position to resell *dark fiber* to interested parties. When you lease dark fiber, you're basically leasing a pair of fibers, but you don't have the active electronics and photonics included with it, so you are respon-sible for acquiring that equipment and adding it to the network. But with dark fiber, you're not paying for bandwidth—you're paying for the physical facility—and if you want to upgrade your systems to laser diodes that pulse more bits per second, or if you want to add a wavelength division multiplexer to access more wavelengths, these changes will not affect your monthly cost for the fiber pair itself. Power utilities have been big players in the deployment of fiber throughout the world.

Another application of fiber is in the local loop. There are numerous arrange-ments of fiber in the local loop, including HFC (that is, fiber to a neighborhood node and then coax on to the subscribers); fiber to the curb with a twisted-pair solution to the home; fiber to the home that terminates on its own individual optical unit; and passive optical networking, which promises to greatly reduce the cost of bringing fiber to the home. Chapter 15 covers the details of these various arrangements.

Another application for fiber is in LANs. Fiber Distributed Data Interface (FDDI) was the first optical LAN backbone that offered 100Mbps backbone capacity, but today it has largely been displaced by the use of 100Mbps and Gigabit Ethernet, both of which can be accommodated over fiber.

Another application of fiber involves the use of imagery or video when extremely high resolution is critical (for example, in telemedicine). Consider an application that involves the transmission of images between an imaging center and a doctor's office. Say you went to the imaging center to have an x-ray of your lungs, and in the transmission of your lung x-ray, a little bit of noise in the network put a big black spot on your lung. If that happened, you would likely be scheduled for radical surgery. So, for this type of application, you want a network which ensures that very little noise can affect the resolution and hence the outcome of the analysis. A lot of this use of fiber occurs in early-adopter environments where there are applications for imaging, such as universities, health care environments, and entertainment environments.

Another frontier where fiber is now being investigated is in home area networks (HANs). This is a very interesting area because when broadband access comes into your home, you see a shift in where the bottleneck resides, from the local loop to inside the home. Broadband access into the home requires a broadband network within the home to properly distribute the entertainment, data, and voice services that are collectively being transported over that broadband access into the home. So, there are ways to wire a new home with fiber or to retrofit an older home so that you can enjoy really high-quality entertainment and data networks within the home. (HANs are discussed in more detail in Chapter 15, "The Broadband Home and HANs.")

Advantages and Disadvantages of Fiber Optics

The advantages of fiber optics are as follows:

- **Extremely high bandwidth**—Fiber offers far more bandwidth than any other cable-based medium.

- **Elastic traffic-carrying capacity**—Without having to change the fiber, assuming that it's the correct generation of fiber, you can add equipment that provides additional capacity over the original fiber alone. This, along with DWDM's capability to turn various wavelengths on and off at will, enables dynamic network bandwidth provisioning to accommodate fluctuations in traffic.

- **Not susceptible to electromagnetic impairments or interference**—Because fiber is not susceptible to electromagnetic impairments or interference, it has a very low bit error rate, 10^{-13}, which means fiber-optic transmissions are virtually noise free.

- **Secure transmission and early detection**—By constantly monitoring the optical network, you can detect when the light pulse diminishes, enabling you to detect leaks.

- **Low in weight and mass**—Because fiber is low in weight and mass, much less human installation power is needed than with traditional copper cable or coax bundles.

The disadvantages of fiber optics include the following:

- **High installation costs, but dropping**—Fiber installation is still relatively costly, although the cost has been dropping by about 60% per year, depending on the components. So the price keeps getting better, although it can still mean a fairly impressive investment. For example, the capital cost of bringing fiber to the home, including the construction efforts, is about US$2,500 per subscriber. But it is also anticipated to be down to about US$1,200 to US$1,500 per subscriber by around 2003.

- **Special test equipment required**—When you start putting in fiber, you have to acquire specialized test equipment because none of the test equipment you use on an electrical network will work with fiber. You need an optical time-domain reflectometer (OTDR), and when you get into more sophisticated optical networks, you need highly specialized optical probes that can cost US$1 million—and you need one at each location.

- **Shortage of components and manufacturing sites**—We currently have a shortage of components and a shortage of manufacturing sites to make more fiber. Those that don't already have contracts negotiated for the delivery of fiber may have a very hard time getting more over the next year, until we ramp up the manufacturing facilities to take on the growing demand. This is also the case with the production of optical components, such as optical switches and optical wavelength routers.

- **Vulnerability to physical damage**—Fiber is a small medium, so it can very easily be cut or otherwise damaged (for example, in a railroad car derailment, in the midst of construction activities). When you choose fiber as the primary medium, you have to address backup, restoration, and survivability from the start because the likelihood of damage is great.

▪ **Vulnerability to damage caused by wildlife**—A number of flora and fauna cause damage to fiber. A number of birds really like the Kevlar reinforcing material and think it makes lovely nests for their babies, so they peck away at fiber-optic cables to get at that Kevlar material. At least five different types of ants seem to enjoy the plastic shielding in their diet, so they nibble at the underground fibers. Sharks have been known to chomp on cable near the repeating points. A plant called the Christmas tree plant thinks that fiber-optic cable is a tree root and wraps itself around it very tightly and chokes it off.

Wiring for Tomorrow: Undersea Fiber Cables

The first undersea cable, which was laid for telegraph, was laid in 1851 between England and France. In 1956 the first coax cable—called transatlantic link (TAT-1)—went in. TAT-1 had the capacity to carry 35 conversations over 64Kbps channels.

The first fiber undersea cable, laid in 1988, was called TAT-8 and could support 4,000 voice channels. But undersea use of fiber didn't take off until 1994, when optical amplifiers were introduced. By the end of 1998, some 23 million miles of fiber-optic cable had been laid throughout the world, by dozens of companies, at tremendous cost. By mid-1999 the total transatlantic bandwidth was 3Tbps, compared to just 100Gbps in 1998. By the end of 2001, we are likely to reach 6Tbps. Between Asia and Europe, in 1997, we had bandwidth of 11Gbps; by 1999, we had 21Gbps; and by 2003, we should have 321Gbps. You can see that a great deal of spending has been done on fiber-optic cable, all over the world.

Fiber technology breakthroughs are having a profound impact on service providers, and that's witnessed by the constantly changing prices for intercontinental capacity. The construction cost of 64Kbps circuits has dropped from almost US$1,500 in 1988, to US$300 in 1995, to just a couple dollars per line today. When operators purchase undersea capacity, they pay two charges. The first is a one-time charge for the bandwidth—the *indefeasible right of use*. The second is an ongoing operations, administration, and maintenance charge that's recurring for the maintenance vessels that service the cable, and this is typically 3% to 5% of the total purchase cost.

The economic shifts look like this for a capacity of 155Mbps: At the start of 1997, it would have cost US$20 million; in 1998, it was down to US$10 million; in early 2000, it was down to US$2 to US$3 million; and in 2001, it's expected to be at US$1 million. The operations, administration, and maintenance charges have remained the same because the contracts originally called for the calculation of those charges based on the cable length as well as the bandwidth, so as you increased your bandwidth, your operations, administration, and maintenance charges increased. Those agreements were recently changed so that you are only charged the operations, administration, and maintenance costs for the length of the cable. Hence, as you expand capacity, the maintenance charge is dropped.

As you can see, there's a great deal of excitement about wiring the world with fiber in preparation for accommodating tomorrow's advanced applications. Chapter 12 elaborates on the range of equipment that's being introduced to allow us to take advantage of the vast potential of the fiber-optic spectrum.

For more learning resources, quizzes, and discussion forums on concepts related to this chapter, see www.telecomessentials.com/learningcenter.

Chapter 4

Establishing Communications Channels

This chapter discusses the key definitions and characteristics that are associated with the processes involved in establishing communications channels. It covers networking modes and switching modes, including the differences between routing and switching. It also covers the details of circuit switching and its particular applications, where it shines and where it's fallen short in the past. This chapter also looks at packet switching—why it has become such a darling in recent years, what it's potential prospects are, and what challenges it faces the future. The chapter ends with a quick comparison between the public switched telephone network (PSTN) and the Internet, because they are both related to the topics at hand.

■ Establishing Connections: Switching Modes and Networking Modes

For messages to travel across a network, a transmission path must be established to either switch or route the messages to their final destinations. Therefore, network providers need a mechanism that allows them to deliver the proper connections when and where a customer requests them. *When*, as you can imagine, is ideally now or bandwidth on demand. *Where* has two components: path calculation, which entails establishing the proper physical or logical connection to the ultimate destination, and forwarding, which is concerned with how to actually guide the traffic across the backbone so that it uses that physical and logical connection to best advantage.

The networking techniques that evolved over time to handle the *when* and *where* came about because traditionally, relatively few high-capacity backbone cables existed. Those few backbone cables had to be manipulated to meet the needs of many individual customers, all of whom had varied bandwidth needs. Two networking techniques arose:

■ **Networking modes**—There are two networking modes: connection oriented and connectionless.

■ **Switching modes**—There are also two switching modes: circuit switching and packet switching. Both of these switching modes offer forms of bandwidth on demand. (But remember that the connection speed can never be greater than the speed of the customer's access line; the fastest connection you can get into the network is what your access line supports.) As you'll learn later in this chapter, circuit switching and packet switching have different ways of performing path calculations and forwarding functions.

The following sections describe networking modes and switching modes in detail.

Networking Modes

When most people are evaluating a network, they concentrate on circuit switching versus packet switching. But it's also very important to consider the networking mode, which can be either connection oriented or connectionless.

Connection-Oriented Networking

As time-sensitive applications become more important, connection-oriented networks are becoming increasingly desirable. In a connection-oriented network, the connection setup is performed before information transfer occurs. Information about the connections in the networks helps to provide service guarantees and makes it possible to most efficiently use network bandwidth by switching transmissions to appropriate connections as the connections are set up. In other words, the path is conceived at the outset, and after the path is determined, all the subsequent information follows the same path to the destination. In a connection-oriented network, there can be some delay up front while the connection is being set up; but because the path is predetermined, there is no delay at intermediate nodes in this type of network after the connection is set up.

Connection-oriented networks can actually operate in either switching mode: They can be either circuit switched or packet switched. Connection-oriented circuit-switched networks include the PSTN (covered later in this chapter and in detail in Chapter 5, "The PSTN"), SDH/SONET (covered in more detail in Chapter 5), and DWDM (covered in detail in Chapter 12, "Optical Networking") networks. Connection-oriented packet-switched networks (covered later in this chapter and in detail in Chapter 7, "Wide Area Networking") include X.25, Frame Relay, and ATM networks.

Connection-oriented networks can be operated in two modes:

- **Provisioned**—In provisioned networks, the connections can be set up ahead of time based on expected traffic. These connections are known as permanent virtual circuits (PVCs).
- **Switched**—In switched networks, the connections are set up on demand and released after the data exchange is complete. These connections are known as switched virtual circuits (SVCs).

Connectionless Networking

In a connectionless network, no explicit connection setup is performed before data is transmitted. Instead, each data packet is routed to its destination based on information contained in the header. In other words, there is no preconceived path. Rather, each fragment (that is, packet) of the overall traffic stream is individually addressed and individually routed. In a connectionless network, the delay in the overall transit time is increased because each packet has to be individually routed at each intermediate node. Applications that are time sensitive would suffer on a connectionless network because the path is not guaranteed, and therefore it is impossible to calculate the potential delays or latencies that might be encountered.

Connectionless networks imply the use of packet switches, so only packet-switched networks are connectionless. An example of a connectionless packet-switched network is the public Internet—that wild and woolly place over which absolutely no one has any control. It's a virtual network that consists of more than 150,000 separate subnetworks and some 10,000 Internet service providers (ISPs), so being able to guarantee performance is nearly impossible at this time. One solution is to use private internets (that is, Internet Protocol [IP] backbones), which achieve cost-efficiencies but, because they are private, provide the ability to control their performance and thereby serve business-class services. For example, a large carrier (such as AT&T or British Telecom) might own its own internet infrastructure, over a very wide geographic area. Because it owns and controls those networks end to end, it can provision and engineer the networks so that business customers can get the proper service-level agreements and can guarantee the performance of their virtual private networks and streaming media networks. The downside in this situation is reliance on one vendor for the entire network.

Switching Modes

Let's start our discussion of switching modes by talking about switching and routing. Switching is the process of physically moving bits through a network node, from an input port to an output port. (A *network node* is any point on the network where communications lines interface. So a network node might be a PBX, a local exchange, a multiplexer, a modem, a host computer, or one of a number of other devices.) Switching elements are specialized computers that are used to connect two or more transmission lines. The switching process is based on information that's gathered through a routing process. A switching element might consult a table to determine, based on number dialed, the most cost-effective trunk over which to forward a call. This switching process is relatively straightforward compared to the type of path determination that IP routers in the Internet might use, which can be very complex.

Routing, on the other hand, involves moving information from a source to a destination across an internetwork, which means moving information across networks. In general, routing involves at least one intermediate node along the way, and it usually involves numerous intermediate nodes and networks. Routing involves two basic activities: determining the optimal path and transporting information through an internetwork. Routing algorithms are necessary to initialize and maintain routing tables. Routing algorithms work with a whole slew of information, called *metrics,* which they use to determine the best path to the destination. Some examples of the metrics that a routing algorithm might use are path length, destination, next-hop associations, reliability, delay, bandwidth, load, and communication cost. A router could use several variables to calculate the best path for a packet, to get it to a node that's one step closer to its destination. The route information varies depending on the algorithm used, and the algorithms vary depending on the routing protocol chosen. Most manufacturers today support the key standards, including Routing Information Protocol (RIP), Open Shortest Path First (OSPF), and Intermediate System to Intermediate System (IS-IS). Network engineers generally decide which of these protocols to use. Routing protocols can also be designed to automatically detect and respond to network changes. (Protocols and metrics are discussed in detail in Chapter 9, "The Internet: Infrastructure and Service Providers.")

There are two types of routers that you should be familiar with: static routers and dynamic routers. A *static router* knows only its own table; it has no idea what the routing tables of its upstream neighbors look like, and it does not have the capability of communicating with its upstream neighbors. If a link goes down in a network that uses static routers, the network administrator has to manually reconfigure the static routers' routing tables to take the downed trunk out of service. This reconfiguration would not affect any change in the upstream routers, so technicians at those locations would then also have to include or accommodate the change. A *dynamic router,* on the other hand, can communicate with its upstream neighbors, so if a change occurred to its routing table, it would forward that change so that the upstream routers could also adjust their routing tables. Furthermore, a dynamic router not only has a view of its own routing table, but it can also see those of its neighbors, or the entire network or routing area, depending on the protocol. It therefore works much better in addressing the dynamic traffic patterns that are common in today's networks.

As noted earlier in the chapter, there are two switching modes: circuit switching and packet switching. Circuit switches are position based; that is, bits arrive in a certain position and are switched to a different position. The position to which bits are switched is determined by a combination of one or more of three dimensions: space (that is, the interface or port number), time, and wavelength. Packet switching is based on labels; addressing information in the packet headers, or labels, helps to determine how to switch or forward a packet through the network node.

Circuit Switching

Circuit switching has been the basis of voice networks worldwide for many years. You can apply three terms to the nature of a circuit-switched call to help remember what this is: continuous, exclusive, and temporary. One of the key attributes of a circuit-switched connection is that it is a reserved network resource that is yours and only yours for the full duration of a conversation. But when that conversation is over, the connection is released. A circuit-switched environment requires that an end-to-end circuit be set up before a call can begin. A fixed share of network resources is reserved for the call, and no other call can use those resources until the original connection is closed. A call request signal must travel to the destination and be acknowledged before any transmission can actually begin. As Figure 4.1 illustrates, you can trace the path from one end of the call to the other end; that path would not vary for the full duration of the call, and the capacity provisioned on that path would be yours and yours alone.

Advantages and Disadvantages of Circuit Switching   Circuit switching uses many lines to economize on switching and routing computation. When a call is set up, a line is dedicated to it, so no further routing calculations are needed.

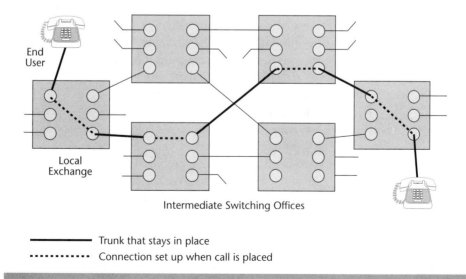

────────── Trunk that stays in place

············ Connection set up when call is placed

Figure 4.1   A circuit-switched call

Since they were introduced in the mid-1980s, digital cross-connect systems (DCSs) have greatly eased the process of reconfiguring circuit-switched networks and responding to conditions such as congestion and failure. DCSs create predefined circuit capacity, and then voice switches are used to route calls over circuits that are set up by these DCSs. DCSs are analogous to the old patch panels. You may have seen a main distribution frame (MDF) on which twisted-pair wiring is terminated. The MDF is a manual patch panel, and before DCSs were introduced, when it was necessary to reconfigure a network based on outage, congestion, or customer demand as a result of shifting traffic patterns, technicians had to spend days or even weeks, manually making changes at the MDF. The DCS is a software patch panel, and within the software are databases that define alternate routes—alternate connections that can be activated in the event that the network encounters a condition that requires some form of manipulation. DACSs are one of the elements of the PSTN that contribute to its reliability: When network conditions change, in a matter of minutes, a DCS can reconfigure the network around those changes. With such tools, the PSTN is able to offer five 9s reliability—in other words, 99.999% guaranteed uptime. (DCSs are discussed in more detail in Chapter 5.)

Circuit switching offers the benefits of low latency and minimal delays because the routing calculation on the path is made only once, at the beginning of the call, and there are no more delays incurred subsequently in calculating the next hop that should be taken. Traditionally, this was sometimes seen as a disadvantage because it meant that the circuits might not be used as efficiently as possible. Around half of most voice calls is silence. Most people breathe and occasionally pause in their speech. So, when voice communications are conducted over a circuit that's being continuously held, and half the time nothing is being transmitted, the circuit is not being used very efficiently. But remember that this is an issue that is important when bandwidth is constrained. And as mentioned earlier in the book, through the optical revolution, bandwidth is being released at an astounding rate, so the efficient use of circuits because of bandwidth constraints will not present the same sort of issue in the future that it once did. Hence, the low latencies or delays that circuit switching guarantees are more important than its potential drawbacks in bandwidth efficiency.

Circuit switching has been optimized for real-time voice traffic for which Quality of Service (QoS) is needed. Because it involves path calculation at the front end, you know how many switches and cables you're going to go through, so you can use a pricing mechanism that's based on distance and time. The more resources you use, either over time or over distance, the greater the cost. Again, developments in fiber economics are changing some of the old rules, and distance is no longer necessarily an added cost element. (QoS is discussed in more detail in Chapter 10, "Next-Generation Networks.")

Generations of Circuit Switches   Circuit switches have been around for quite some time. We've already been through three basic generations, and we're beginning to see a fourth generation.

The History of the Strowger Switch

The Strowger switch has a rather amusing history, and as it's so rare that we have really amusing stories in telecommunications, I'll share it with you. Once upon a time in the wild west, there was a young man named Alman B. Strowger who wasn't a telecommunications engineer by trade. He was a mortician. As life would have it, he had a competitor in town. During this period, there were no dial pads to use when making a telephone call. Instead, you had to talk with the town telephone operator, and she would extend the connection on your behalf. Mr. Strowger's competitor's wife was the town telephone operator. So, needless to say, anytime there was gossip about a gun battle about to brew on Main Street, she let her husband know, and he was there to collect the bodies before Mr. Strowger got a chance. Mr. Strowger decided to use technology to get a competitive advantage, and he invented the Strowger switch. The new switch meant that you could dial a number directly from your phone and thereby bypass the town telephone operator.

The first generation of circuit switches was introduced in 1888. It was referred to as the step relay switch, the step-by-step switch, or the Strowger switch, in honor of the man who invented it (see Figure 4.2).

In 1935 the second generation of circuit switches was introduced: crossbar switches (see Figure 4.3). Crossbar switches were electromechanical, but each one could service a larger number of subscribers. Both step relay and crossbar switches

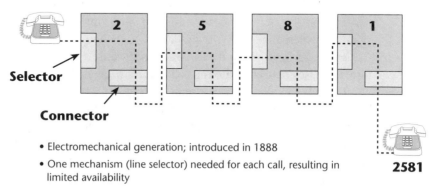

Selector

Connector

- Electromechanical generation; introduced in 1888
- One mechanism (line selector) needed for each call, resulting in limited availability
- Line selector listens for each digit and sets a separate selector and connector for each digit
- The four-part switch is occupied during the entire call
- Electromechanical is very labor intensive and requires a large amount of space

2581

Figure 4.2   A step relay switch

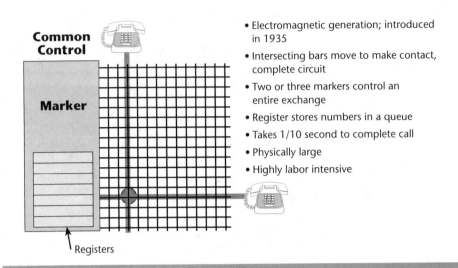

- Electromagnetic generation; introduced in 1935
- Intersecting bars move to make contact, complete circuit
- Two or three markers control an entire exchange
- Register stores numbers in a queue
- Takes 1/10 second to complete call
- Physically large
- Highly labor intensive

Figure 4.3 A crossbar switch

still exist in the world. Of course, they are generally in underdeveloped areas, but they're not all relegated to museums quite yet. Every year you hear about one or two being decommissioned somewhere in the world.

The third generation of circuit switches—stored program control (also referred to as electronic common control)—was introduced in 1968. A stored program control is a computer-driven software-controlled switch. Because this type of switch is electronic, there are no moving parts, and the switch has a longer life than earlier generations of switches. Because it is software controlled, it offers more guarantees against obsolescence, easier upgradability to enhanced feature sets, and better control over user features and cost features because everything can be programmed into databases that facilitate the call control process (see Figure 4.4).

The three generations of circuit switches are in place and operating at various levels of activity. With each new generation of switches, we've basically added more connection-oriented features, features that somehow help in making connections (for example, customer features such as call forwarding and call waiting). Circuit switches in the future will likely be able to define connections based on a requested service class. Examples of variables that define a service class are the amount of delay that can be tolerated end-to-end, as well as between components, and the maximum loss that can be tolerated before the transmission is greatly hampered. Hence, we will be able to build connections to meet a particular service class and thereby aid in ensuring the proper performance of an application.

Customer premises equipment (CPE) circuit switches include PBXs. In the PSTN, circuit switches include the local exchanges with which subscribers access

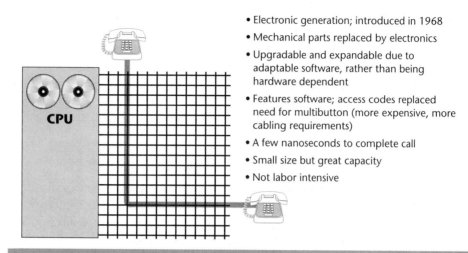

- Electronic generation; introduced in 1968
- Mechanical parts replaced by electronics
- Upgradable and expandable due to adaptable software, rather than being hardware dependent
- Features software; access codes replaced need for multibutton (more expensive, more cabling requirements)
- A few nanoseconds to complete call
- Small size but great capacity
- Not labor intensive

Figure 4.4   A stored program control switch

the network, the tandem or junction switches that interconnect numbers of local exchanges throughout a metro area, the toll or transit switches used for national long-distance communications, and international gateways used for cross-country communications. A large number of vendors sell these circuit switches, as well as more specialized niche products.

A fourth generation of switches—optical networking switches—is emerging now (see Chapter 13, "Broadband Access Solutions"). Often, these optical networking elements are referred to as *wavelength routers* or *optical switches*. The idea is to be able to provision a very high-speed path, at OC-48 (that is 2.5Gbps), to provision a path end-to-end across a network of dense wavelength division multiplexers. This will be increasingly important in providing communications interfaces to the high-speed switches that have become available.

Circuit switches double their performance: cost ratio approximately every 80 months to 40 months (that is, normally the performance improves every 80 months, although sometimes new generations are created more rapidly—every 40 months). Major architectural changes in circuit switches occur relatively infrequently. Network switches are responsible for doing all the work of setting up and tearing down calls, as well as for addressing and providing the features that are requested. They provide a very high level of functionality on a very centralized basis within the network, and that enables the end stations to be very cheap and very dumb (for example, a single-line telephone). Again, when intelligence was extremely expensive, there was something to be gained by centralizing it in a monolithic switch because that allowed consumers to access the network and to participate as users with a very low entry point. Until recently, if you wanted to spend time on the Internet, you had to have a PC, and that costs considerably more than a single-line telephone. On the other hand, costs are dropping in electronics and appliances all the time, so this is also becoming less of an issue, and perhaps in this way, too, distributing the intelligence makes sense. This is the age-old argument about smart core/dumb edge versus dumb core/ smart edge, and it speaks to the differences in philosophies between classic telecommunications engineers (affectionately referred to as "bell heads") and modern-day data communications engineers ("net heads"). Chapter 11 talks more about the evolution of the intelligent edge.

Packet Switching

Whereas circuit switching was invented to facilitate voice telephony, packet switching has its origin in data communications. In fact, packet switching was developed specifically as a solution for the communications implications of a form of data processing called *interactive processing*.

The first generation of data processing was batch processing, in which a data entry clerk would sit down at a job entry terminal and key a volume of data onto an intermediate medium—initially key punch cards, and later tape or disk. The data were then preaccumulated on an intermediate medium, and at some later point a job would be scheduled and a link would be established to the host that would be responsible for processing the data. When you began to transmit this preaccumulated volume, you had a steady stream of continuous high-volume data, so batch processing made quite effective use of a circuit-switched environment.

In contrast to batch processing, in interactive processing, data entry occurs online, so, in essence, data is transmitted only when you press the Enter key, but when you're looking at the screen or filling in a spreadsheet, nothing is being transmitted. Thus, interactive processing involves a traffic stream that's described as being *bursty* in nature, and bursty implies that you have long connect times but low data volumes. Therefore, interactive processing does not make efficient use of circuit-switched links: The connection would be established and held for a long period of time, with only little data passed. Packet switching was developed to increase the efficiencies associated with bursty transmission. Packet switching involves the multiplexing of multiple packets over one virtual circuit (that is, the end-to-end logical connection that creates a complete path across the network from source to destination node; see Chapter 2, "Telecommunications Technology Fundamentals"). It also involves decentralizing the network intelligence—not only the intelligence for maintaining and tearing down the connections in centralized switches but also the endpoints that participate in the control of the end-to-end session.

Packets   A *packet* is a basically a container for bits. We also use terms such as *blocks* and *frames* and *cells* and *datagrams* to depict the same concept. A packet can be a number of sizes, contain different numbers of bits, and have varying amounts of navigational control that the network nodes can use to navigate and route the packet. (Chapter 7 discusses some of the different types of packets and the techniques that use them.) In general, the features of the packet depend on the considerations. Each protocol, as it's developed over time, makes certain assumptions about whether bandwidth is available, or whether there's too much noise, and therefore too much retransmission needed, or whether the key issue is latency. Packets of different sizes may therefore perform differently in different environments.

A packet is, in essence, a store-and-forward mechanism for transmitting information. Packets are forwarded through a series of packet switches, also known as routers, that ultimately lead to the destination. Information is divided into packets that contain two very important messages: the destination address and the sequence number. The original forms of packet switching (developed in the late 1960s and early 1970s) were connectionless infrastructures. In a connectionless environment, each packet is routed individually, and the packets might not all take the same path to the destination point, and hence they may arrive out of sequence. Therefore, the sequence number is very important; the terminating point needs it to be able to reassemble the message in its proper order.

Generally, in packet switching, packets from many different sources are statistically multiplexed and sent on to their destinations over virtual circuits. Multiple connections share transmission lines, which means the packet switches or routers must do many more routing calculations. Figure 4.5 illustrates a packet-switched network that uses virtual circuits. You can see that packets are queued up at the various nodes, based on availability of the virtual circuits, and that this queuing can impose delays. The first generation of packet-switched networks could support only data; it could not support voice or video at all because there was so much delay associated with those networks. As packet-switched environments are evolving, we are developing techniques to be able to separate and prioritize those traffic types. (Chapter 10 talks about those issues in depth.)

Connectionless Versus Connection-Oriented Packet-Switched Networks   There are two forms of packet-switched networks: connectionless and connection oriented.

Connectionless Packet-Switched Networks   You can picture connectionless networks by using a postal service metaphor: I write a letter, I put it in an envelope, and I address the envelope. My carrier does not care in the least what it says on my envelope because she knows where she is taking that envelope. It's going to the next point of presence, which is the local post office. The local post office will be concerned with the destination zip code, but it isn't concerned at all about the

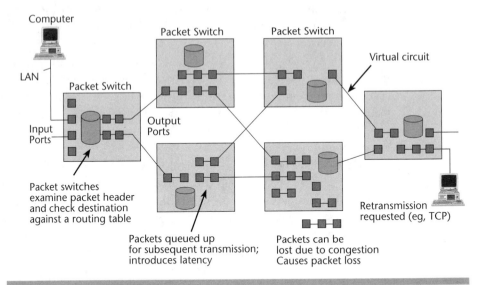

Figure 4.5 A packet-switched network

name or street address on the envelope. It simply wants to know what regional center to route it to. The regional center cares about the destination city, and the destination local post office cares about the actual street address because it needs to assign the letter to the right carrier. The carrier needs to care about the name so that the letter finds its way into the right mailbox. If you end up with someone else's letter in your box, the ultimate responsibility for error control is yours because you are the endpoint.

A connectionless environment worries about getting a packet one step closer to the destination (see Figure 4.6). It doesn't worry about having an end-to-end view of the path over which the message will flow; this is the fundamental difference between connection-oriented and connectionless environments, and, hence, between infrastructures such as the Internet and the PSTN. Examples of connectionless packet-switched networks include the public Internet, private IP backbones or networks, Internet-based VPNs, and LANs. Again, each packet (referred to as a *datagram transmission*) is an independent unit that contains the source and destination address, which increases the overhead. That's one of the issues with connectionless packet-switched networks: If we have to address each packet, then the overall percentage of control information relevant to the actual data being transported rises.

Each router performs a path calculation function independently, and each relies on its own type of routing protocols (for example, Open Shortest Path First [OSPF], Intermediate System to Intermediate System [IS-IS], or Border Gateway

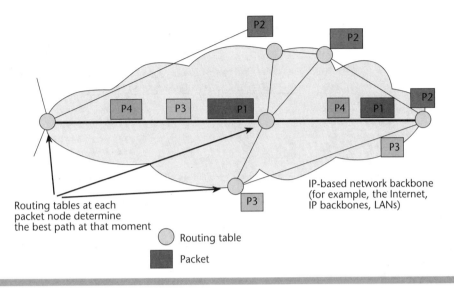

Figure 4.6 A connectionless network

Protocol [BGP]). Each router calculates the appropriate next hop for each destination, which is generally based on the smallest number of hops (although some routing protocols use an abstract notion of "cost," as defined by the network administrator, in making their decisions). Packets are forwarded, then, on a hop-by-hop basis rather than as part of an end-to-end connection. Each packet must be individually routed, which increases delays, and the more hops, the greater the delay. Therefore, connectionless environments provide less control over ensuring QoS because of unknown latencies, unknown retransmissions, and unknown sequences in which the packets will arrive.

Connectionless Packet-Switched Networks   The connection-oriented packet-switched environment is something like a telephone network, in which a call setup is performed end-to-end. X.25, Frame Relay, ATM, and Multiprotocol Label Switching (MPLS) are all connection-oriented techniques. In a connection-oriented packet-switched network, only one call request packet contains the source and destination address (see Figure 4.7). Therefore, the subsequent packets don't have to contain the address information, which reduces the overall overhead. The call request packet establishes the virtual circuit. Each individual switch along each path, then, forwards traffic to the appropriate next switch until packets all arrive at the destination. With connection-oriented networks, we do not need to route each individual packet. Instead, each packet is marked as belonging to some specific flow that identifies which virtual circuit it belongs to. Thus, the switch

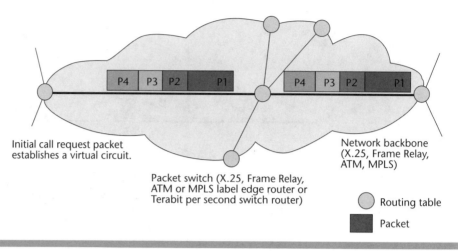

Figure 4.7 A connection-oriented network

needs only to look at the mark and forward the packet to the correct interface because the flow is already set up in the switch's table. No repeated per-packet computation is required; consequently, connection-oriented networks reduce latencies, or delays.

In the connection-oriented environment, the entry node contains the routing table, where the path is calculated and determined, and all packets follow that same path on to the destination node, thereby offering a better guarantee of service.

Advantages and Disadvantages of Packet Switching   Packet-switching techniques have a number of limitations, including the following:

- Latencies occur because connection-oriented packet switching is a store-and-forward mechanism.

- *Jitter* (that is, variable delay, or delay in moving the bits between any two switches) occurs. There are two main types of delay: jitter and entry-to-exit-point delay. Say that your end-to-end delay might meet the desired minimum of 150 milliseconds, but between Switches 1 and 2, the delay is 20 milliseconds and between Switches 2 and 3, it's 130 milliseconds. That variation in delay, or jitter, will hamper some applications, so it needs to be controlled so that the network can support demanding applications.

- Packet loss occurs as congestion occurs at the packet switches or routers, and it can considerably degrade real-time applications. For example, if a few packets of a voice call are lost, then you'll hear pops and clicks, but if the loss climbs into the 30% to 40% range, the voice might sound like "ye ah ng ng ah mm mm ah." This is the experience that many people today find at times when using the public Internet for telephony, where at peak periods of day, packet loss can be as great as 40%.

Given these drawbacks and the way packet-switched networks evolved, packet-switched networks originally gave no QoS guarantees—they offered only best-effort QoS. But they guaranteed high reliability because you would be able to route packets through alternate nodes or pathways if they encountered link-resistant failures along the way; thus, you were guaranteed that information would be transported, but not within metrics such as latency and packet loss. Currently, protocols are being developed that will enable real-time applications such as voice, video, audio, and interactive multimedia to perform properly on packet-switched networks.

The pricing mechanism that evolved with packet-switched networks was a bit different from that used for circuit-switched networks. It was not based on time and distance but on usage. You're either billed based on the volume of packets or the amount of bandwidth that you subscribe to. Distance insensitivity is a part of the packet-switched networking environment.

Generations of Packet Switches   Similar to circuit switches, packet switches have gone through three basic generations: X.25 switches (first generation), routers (second generation), and Frame Relay and cell switches (third generation). Each generation of packet switching has increased the efficiency of packet processing and in the speed of the interfaces that it supports. In effect, the size of the pipes and the size of the interfaces dictate how effectively the packet-switched network performs. In packet switching, the processing is being pushed outside the network to the end nodes, so you need to have more intelligent software at the end nodes that get involved in the session setup, maintenance, and teardown, as well as flow control from end to end.

Besides X.25 switches, routers, and Frame Relay switches, packet switches include ATM switches and a new breed, called Tbps (terabits per second) switch routers. A large number of vendors sell these packet switches, and it seems that more companies jump on the bandwagon each day.

Packet switches are doubling their performance: cost ratio every 20 to 10 months, so we see the evolution of new entries in the product line much more rapidly in this environment than in the circuit-switched world. However, again we rely on expensive end stations—PCs or other computers—to finish the job of communication in packet switching. These end stations have to rely on protocols such as Transmission Control Protocol/Internet Protocol (TCP/IP), an open standard for internetworking that performs the equivalent of call setup/teardown and correct receipt of data. (TCP/IP is discussed in Chapter 9.) These end stations also have to ensure that all the data has been received and that it has been received correctly.

Comparing Circuit Switching and Packet Switching

What does the future hold for circuit switching and packet switching? Circuit switching is superior to packet switching in terms of eliminating queuing delays, which results in completely predictable latency and jitter in the backbone. Given the trend toward real-time visual and sensory communication streams, this seems to be the most important characteristic for us to strive toward. With the large capacities that are afforded with the new DWDM systems and other optical network elements, minimizing latency becomes more important than optimizing bandwidth via statistical multiplexing. (DWDM and other forms of multiplexing are discussed in Chapter 2.) We're likely to see the use of statistical multiplexing continue to increase at the edge and at the customer premises, as a means of economically integrating and aggregating traffic from the enterprise to present it over the access link to the network. In the core, fiber-based and circuit-switched networks are likely to prevail.

Table 4.1 is a brief comparison of circuit switching and packet switching. As you look at the table, keep in mind that as we get more bandwidth, circuit-switched networks do not have to be so concerned with bandwidth efficiency. And as QoS is added to packet-switched networks, these networks are able to support real-time applications. Again, the prevailing conditions have a lot to do with what is best in a given network.

Table 4.1 Circuit Switching Versus Packet Switching

Characteristic	Circuit Switching	Packet Switching
Origin	Voice telephony	Data networking
Connectionless or connection oriented	Connection oriented	Both
Key applications	Real-time voice, streaming media, videoconferencing, video-on-demand, and other delay- and loss-sensitive traffic applications	Bursty data traffic that has long connect times but low data volumes; applications that are delay and loss tolerant
Latency/delay/jitter	Low latency and minimal delays	Subject to latency, delay, and jitter because of its store-and-forward nature
Network intelligence	Centralized	Decentralized
Bandwidth efficiency	Low	High
Packet loss	Low	High

▓ The PSTN Versus the Internet

In one very important fashion, the PSTN and the public Internet are one and the same thing: they both exist on the same physical infrastructure. There would be no Internet without the PSTN. The communications links, or backbones, that ISPs run on are delivered over the PSTN, and the access lines for entry into the Internet are all subscriber lines that are part of the PSTN. But what differentiates the PSTN and the Internet is the equipment that's attached to each network, its use, and how it formats the information it carries.

PSTN Characteristics

The PSTN basically includes telephones, fax machines, and circuit switches that set up continuous but temporary connections. In a PSTN environment, the circuit is established between two subscribers: The PSTN connects together two subscribers. But in the PSTN, a circuit is established between two subscribers and kept open for the duration of the call, including periods of silence. This provides guaranteed QoS and minimal latencies, and it means that the PSTN is optimized for voice and other real-time applications. It also means that the PSTN uses bandwidth inefficiently, making services more expensive. But we are constantly finding ourselves able to release more bandwidth and derive more channels over that bandwidth.

Internet Characteristics

The Internet basically includes clients, which are the user interface and the input/output device for information; the servers, which are the centralized repositories of wisdom that you are seeking; and the packet switches, which route and relay the packets of information between the clients and servers. Whereas the PSTN connects together two subscribers, the Internet connects together networks. As on the PSTN, messages on the Internet are routed to specific end devices. These messages take various forms, such as e-mail, instant messaging, and real-time audio/video communications. Unlike the PSTN, however, the Internet breaks down the messages into packets of data, which contain the routing information, which will then lead them to their destination. Individual packets may take different routes, but they'll be reassembled in the proper order at the destination. This system is optimal for the most efficient of transmission facilities, particularly when you're supporting bursty traffic that involves long periods of silence. In turn, this results in less expensive services. However, the tradeoff is that you get only best-effort QoS. Significant progress is being made on introducing QoS to the Internet, though, and in the next two or three years, this will change a great deal.

What Is Meant by Next-Generation Network?

At this point, we need to apply a definition to the term *next-generation network* because throughout this book it is used with a very specific meaning. The decreasing cost of bandwidth, combined with the availability of low-cost and powerful chip technology, favorably highlights the economies of statistical multiplexing and packet switching, as long as latencies and loss can be controlled. From that standpoint, next-generation networks embody two fundamental concepts. First, a next-generation network is a high-speed packet- or cell-based network that's capable of transporting and routing a multitude of services, including voice, data, video, and multimedia while supporting QoS. Second, a next-generation network is a common platform for applications and services that the customer can access across the entire network as well as outside the network.

Converging Networks: The Next Generation

Networks are evolving so that they can address the growing demand for QoS. The two different infrastructures—circuit switching and packet switching—are not trying to replace each other. Instead, they are converging. This marriage is required between the existing legacy environment (the circuit-switched network) and the new and unique IP marketplace (the packet-switched network). To address this convergence, a number of devices have emerged that have a number of names, including Voice over IP gateways, media gateways, next-generation switches, and softswitches. These are all elements that are discussed in Chapter 11, "Next-Generation Network Services." These new devices in essence allow interoperability to exist seamlessly between the PSTN and packet-switched networks, whether IP or ATM or MPLS.

For more learning resources, quizzes, and discussion forums on concepts related to this chapter, see www.telecomessentials.com/learningcenter.

Chapter 5

The PSTN

This chapter talks about the public switched telephone network (PSTN). It talks about what comprises the PSTN, what sorts of technologies have been used to complete the connections, how the signaling systems operate, and what the basic backbone architectures entail in terms of components and transmission capacities. This chapter also discusses intelligent networks (INs) and what they promise in terms of service logic and feature availability. Finally, this chapter describes some of the trends in the evolution of the PSTN that will support the new generation of applications.

■ The PSTN Infrastructure

Our views about what a network should be designed to support and what the infrastructure should be comprised of have changed quite a bit over the years, as applications and technology have changed. Before discussing what is needed in a network today, this chapter takes a look at how the PSTN infrastructure evolved and where it is today.

The traditional PSTN infrastructure was specifically designed to support only voice communications. At the time this infrastructure was being designed, we had no notion of data communications. Initially the traffic type the PSTN was designed to support was continuous real-time voice.

Another variable that's important to the design of the PSTN has to do with the length of calls. Most voice calls are quite short, so the circuit switches in the PSTN are engineered for call durations of three minutes or less. The average Internet session, on the other hand, lasts around an hour. This means that increased Internet access through the PSTN has, in some locales, put a strain on the local exchanges. If a circuit switch is blocked because it is carrying a long Internet session, people may not be able to get a dial tone. There are several solutions to this problem. For example, as discussed in Chapter 10, "Next-Generation Networks," we can apply intelligence in front of some exchanges so that calls destined for ISPs can be diverted over a packet-switched network to the ISP rather than being completed on a circuit-switched basis through the local exchange.

Yet another variable that's important to the design of the PSTN has to do with what it was designed to support. The capacities of the channels in the PSTN are of the narrowband generation—they are based on 64Kbps channels. The worldwide infrastructure to accommodate voice communications evolved to include a series of circuit switches. Different switches are used based on the locations to which they're connecting. The switches have a high degree of intelligence built into them, both for establishing the communications channels and for delivering the service logic to activate a growing array of features. In the traditional framework, the monolithic switches in the network had all the smarts. The switch manufacturer and the carrier worked together very closely, and the carrier was not able to introduce new features and services into a particular area until a software release was available for the switch platform through which the neighborhood was being serviced. Thus, carriers were often unable to roll out new services and features because they hadn't yet received the new software releases from the switch manufacturers. Over time, we have separated the functions of switching and connection establishment from the functions involved in the intelligence that enables various services and features to be activated.

The traditional PSTN is associated with highly developed, although not necessarily integrated, operational support systems (such as billing systems, provisioning systems, network management systems, customer contact systems, and security systems). These systems have very well-developed business processes and techniques for managing their environments. But the various systems' databases cannot yet all speak to one another to give one comprehensive view. (But at least those systems exist, unlike in the public Internet, where the operational support systems are only now beginning to emerge to help manage that environment.)

The backbone of the traditional PSTN was largely based on a generation that we call the Plesiochronous Digital Hierarchy (PDH), which includes the T-carrier, E-carrier, and J-carrier standards. The local loop of the PSTN was provisioned as a twisted-copper-pair analog subscriber line.

Service Providers

Many abbreviations and acronyms are used to define the various players and the parts of the network in which they play. Some telcos can and do fulfill more than one of these functions; the extent to which they can or do fulfill more than one of these functions partly depends on the policy, regulatory, and licensing conditions that prevail in different countries. The following terms are largely used in the United States, but they are important to the discussion in this chapter because they illustrate the functions service providers are addressing:

- **PTO**—PTO stands for *public telecommunications operator*, which is the name for an incumbent carrier in places other than the United States.

- **VAN**—VAN stands for *value-added network provider*. This term originated around 1970 and was applied to companies that were competing to provide telecommunications services, specifically with offerings focused on data communications and data networking. VANs provided more than a simple pipe from Point A to Point B. They provided some additional intelligence in the network, to, for example, perform error detection and correction, or to convert protocols or languages that different computers speak so that you could have interoperability across the network.

- **LEC**—In the local environment we use the acronym LEC for *local exchange carrier*. There was originally no competition among LECs, but as soon as competition in the local loop picked up, LECs were segmented into ILECs, CLECs, and DCLECs.

- **ILEC**—The ILEC is the *incumbent local exchange carrier*, the original common carrier that either once had, or in some countries still has, monopoly rights in the local loop. For most residents in the United States, this would be one of the four "baby Bells"—Qwest Communications International, SBC Communications, BellSouth Corporation, and Verizon Communications.

- **CLEC**—The CLEC is the *competitive local exchange carrier*. CLECs came about as a result of the Telecommunications Act of 1996, which opened up competition in the local loop. The CLEC is the competitor to the ILEC. Although the decline of the telecommunications economy in 2000 and 2001 forced several CLECs out of business, there are still some CLECs in the United States, and they currently focus on delivering dial tone to business customers.

- **DCLEC (or DLEC)**—DCLEC stands for *data competitive local exchange carrier*. The DCLEC is a company that is specifically focused on supporting data services (for example, providers that offer DSL services to end users).

- **ELEC**—ELEC stands for *Ethernet local exchange carrier*. The ELEC specializes in providing Ethernet solutions in the local loop and metro area.

- **IXC**—The *interexchange carrier* (IXC) is the carrier for long-distance and international communications. AT&T Corporation, WorldCom, Sprint, Qwest, and Verizon are the primary IXCs in the United States. Unless certain stringent requirements imposed by the Federal Communications Commission are met, an IXC cannot offer long-distance services in the areas where it is also the ILEC.

- ■ SP—Because so many lines are being blurred today by bundled services and bundled territories of operation, the basic term *service provider* (SP) is commonly used to refer generically to providers of different types of services.

Network Access

Figure 5.1 is a simple diagram of network access. On the left-hand side is the customer environment, which includes residences (single-line instruments being served by an access line) and business premises (with onsite telephone systems such as private branch exchange [PBXs] or key telephone systems—smaller site systems for installations where there are 50 or fewer employees). Those in the customer environment are connected to the PSTN via access lines. The *access network,* or the *local loop* we so often talk about, includes whatever equipment resides at the customer premise (that is, the customer premises equipment [CPE]), the access line leading to the local exchange, the components at the local exchange on which those access lines terminate (that is, the distribution cross-connects), and the logic used to help control the flow of traffic over the access lines. In the United States, competition is allowed in the local loop, and a myriad of players are interested in owning the local loop (for example, Internet service providers [ISPs], wireless operators, cable TV companies, power utilities). However, worldwide, the incumbent local providers continue to dominate the local loop, and, as usual, politics and economics are principal factors in delaying the mass deployment of high-speed residential access.

The local exchange, in the center of Figure 5.1, is the backbone, or the core, of the network. From the local exchange, we can establish connections into the other providers, such as IXCs for long distance, international carriers for overseas calls, cellular providers, and ISPs.

Services Beyond the Local Loop

Traditionally, we have thought of the local loop as leading to the home or to the business and ending there. But the need for additional bandwidth and capability is now shifting: We need these things within the premise, as well as on the local loop. It is therefore a logical extension for the service provider to not only give you access lines and termination, but also to provide you with the home area networking facilities you need in order to have an end-to-end broadband package. Chapter 15, "The Broadband Home and HANs," talks more about this.

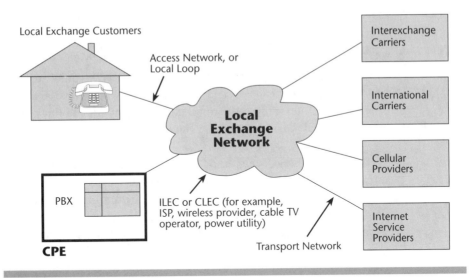

Figure 5.1 Network access

The underlying network access facilities can be either analog or digital loops, and they connect the exchanges to the customer premises. At the customer premises there are the network interfaces, CPE, premises distribution systems where wiring is cross-connected, and network interfaces. The equipment for providing switch access services includes line-termination cards, carrier and multiplexer equipment, and local exchange switching capabilities that support addressing, supervisory alerting, call progress, and other signaling functions.

Access Services

The main categories of access services are trunks, business lines for key telephone systems, centrex service, leased lines, and residential subscriber lines.

Trunks are used to provide connections into the PBX environment. There are three subcategories of trunks:

- **Two-way local exchange trunks**—On these trunks, traffic flows in both the incoming and outgoing directions.
- **DID trunks**—Direct inward dialing (DID) trunks are designed for only incoming calls. A benefit of DID trunks is that they enable the dialed number to ring directly on a user's phone rather than having to go through a centralized attendant. If the population knows whom they want to call directly, and if you want to ease the process of connecting the call, this can be a very useful feature. Another benefit of DID trunks is that they make it

seem like a private line goes directly to the user, but with DID you can support perhaps 100 different numbers with a group of only 25 to 35 trunks (traffic engineering is used to determine the proper number of trunks).

■ **DOD trunks**—Direct outward dialing (DOD) trunks are used specifically for outgoing calls. DOD trunks are used when you dial an access code such as the number 9 or the number 8 to get an outside-line dial tone before you can dial the actual number that you want to reach.

To service the key telephone systems, business lines connect the network termination at the user to the local exchange. Users that want to use the local exchange as if it were their PBX rent centrex trunks on a monthly basis. Large companies often access the network via leased lines, which can be a very expensive solution, and home users access the network via residential subscriber lines.

Access lines can either be in analog facilities or they can be digital carrier services. Analog transmission is often called *plain old telephone service* (POTS for short). Three main types of digital services are offered by using twisted-pair cable. The first type of digital services involves T-1 access (at 1.5Mbps), E-1 access (at 2. 048Mbps), and J-1 access (at 1.544Mbps). The second type of digital services is narrowband ISDN (N-ISDN) services, including Basic Rate Interface (BRI) for residences and small businesses and Primary Rate Interface (PRI) for larger businesses. The third type of digital services is the xDSL subscriber lines and high-speed digital subscriber lines that enable the all-important applications of Internet access and multimedia exploration. (Chapter 3, "Transmission Media: Characteristics and Applications," describes the digital services in more detail.)

Transport Services

Transport services are the network switching, transmission, and related services that support information transfer between the originating and terminating access facilities. The underlying facilities include local exchanges and tandem switches, toll and transit switches, international gateways, and interoffice transmission equipment. Transport services include switched services, nonswitched services, and virtual private networks (VPNs).

Switched Services

There are two main types of switched services: public and private.

Switched public services include local calling, long-distance calling, toll-free calling, international calling, directory assistance, operator assistance, and emergency services.

Switched private services can be switchable either because they are deployed within the CPE or because they are deployed on a carrier basis. With CPE-based services, you can add capabilities to the telephone systems onsite in the PBXs—a feature called *electronic tandem networking*. For example, you can use electronic tandem networking to gain some flexibility in routing around congestion points: If the preferred leased line from Switch A to Switch B is occupied or not available, the switch can decide how to reroute that traffic to still reach Switch B, but through a different series of leased lines. However, because leased lines (also referred to as *tie trunks*) are mileage sensitive and dedicated to individual customers, they are very expensive; thus, not much private voice networking is done over tie trunks because there are several more attractive solutions, such as VPNs, which are discussed shortly.

With carrier-based switched private services, a centrex customer could partition and implement extensions across multiple local exchanges and in this way be able to switch traffic between those locations.

Nonswitched Services

Nonswitched services include leased lines, foreign exchange (FX) lines, and off-premises exchanges (OPXs). With leased lines, two locations or two devices are always on, using the same transmission path.

FX lines allow you to make a toll call appear to be a local call. For example, you might have a dedicated leased line that runs from your customer premise to a local exchange in a distant area where you call large numbers of customers. When anyone behind your PBX dials a number associated with that foreign local exchange, the PBX automatically selects the FX line. The dial tone the caller receives is actually coming from the distant local exchange, and the call proceeds as if it were a local call. The tradeoff with FX lines is that although you are not charged per call for your long-distance calls to the specified exchange, you pay a flat monthly fee for the leased line and you have to apply some traffic engineering to ensure that you're not making people wait for the FX line to become available. So with FX lines, you need to find the right balance point between reducing costs and ensuring a high level of service.

OPXs are used in distributed environments, such as a city government. Say that the city government has public works stations, libraries, fire stations, and parks and recreation facilities that are too far from the PBX to be served by the normal cabling. The city uses an OPX setup: It leases a circuit from the PBX to the off-premise location and ties it in as if it were part of that PBX. City government employees can then call one another, using their normal extension plan, their call accounting information can be accumulated so that cost allocations can be performed, and the employees can have access to the full suite of features that a business PBX offers.

VPNs

Although you might think that VPNs are related to the Internet or to Internet Protocol (IP) and are a somewhat new development, they actually originated in the circuit-

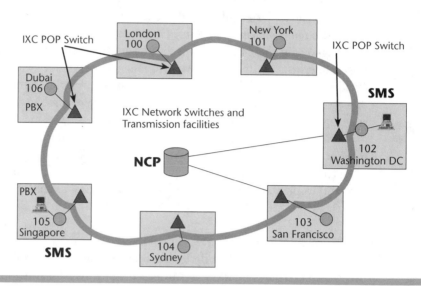

Figure 5.2   An example of a VPN

switched network environment, with AT&T's software-defined network (SDN) in the early 1980s. A VPN is a concept, not a technology platform or a set of networking techniques. A VPN defines a network in which customer traffic is isolated over shared-service provider facilities, so as more customers share the same facilities, their costs go down. The purpose of a VPN, then, is to reduce the high cost of leased lines, while still providing high quality of service and guaranteeing that private traffic has capacity between locations. Figure 5.2 shows an example of a VPN.

The underlying facilities of a VPN include the carrier public network, augmented by network control points and service management systems. Under computer control, the traffic is then routed through the public network in a manner that makes the VPN service seem like a facilities-based private network. Access to the VPN can occur via dedicated access, leased lines, or carrier-switched access, using either an analog or a digital carrier.

The network control point represents a centralized database that stores a subscriber's unique VPN information. The network control point screens every call and then applies call processing in accordance with the customer-defined requirements. A common-channel signaling network connects the various network elements so that they can exchange information with each other in real-time. (Common-channel signaling is discussed later in this chapter, in the section "Signaling Systems.")

A service management system is used to build and maintain the VPN database. It allows customers to program specific functions to accommodate their particular business applications. It transmits information to the network control points, with important instructions on a customer-by-customer basis. Thus, VPNs introduce to the realm of the PSTN a lower-cost alternative to building a private voice network.

PSTN Architecture

The PSTN includes a number of transmission links and nodes. There are basically four types of nodes: CPE nodes, switching nodes, transmission nodes, and service nodes.

CPE Nodes

CPE nodes generally refer to the equipment that's located at the customer site. The main function of CPE nodes is to transmit and receive user information. The other key function is to exchange control information with the network. In the traditional realm, this equipment includes PBXs, key telephone systems, and single-line telephones.

Switching Nodes

Switching nodes interconnect transmission facilities at various locations and route traffic through a network. They set up the circuit connections for a signal path, based on the number dialed. To facilitate this type of switching, the ITU standardized a worldwide numbering plan (based on ITU E.164) that essentially acts as the routing instructions for how to complete a call through the PSTN. The switching nodes include the local exchanges, tandem exchanges (for routing calls between local exchanges within a city), toll offices (for routing calls to or from other cities), and international gateways (for routing calls to or from other countries). Primary network intelligence is contained in the Class 4 switches (that is, toll offices switches) and Class 5 switches (that is, local exchange switches). The Class 4 toll switches provide long-distance switching and network features, and the Class 5 switches provide the local switching and telephony features that subscribers subscribe to. Figure 5.3 shows where the types of telephone exchanges are located.

The Local Exchange   The local exchange (also called the Class 5 office or central office) is where communications common carriers terminate customer lines and locate the switching equipment that interconnects those lines. This class office represents the local network. Every subscriber line location in a local exchange is assigned a number, generally seven or eight digits. The first three (or four) digits represent the exchange and identify the local exchange switch that serves a particular telephone. The last four digits identify the individual line number, which is a circuit that is physically connected from the local exchange to the subscriber. The traditional local exchange switch can handle one or more exchanges, with each

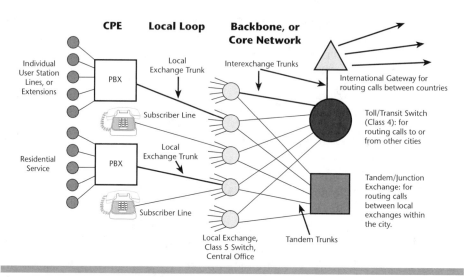

Figure 5.3 Types of telephone exchanges

exchange capable of handling up to 10,000 subscriber lines, numbered 0000 to 9999. In large metropolitan areas, it is common to find one local exchange building housing more than one local exchange switch and for each switch to handle five or more exchanges. These offices are sometimes referred to as *multi-entity buildings*.

The Tandem Office The tandem office, or junction network, is an exchange that is used primarily as a switching point for traffic between local exchanges in a metropolitan area. It is an office that is used to interconnect the local end offices over tandem trunks in a densely settled exchange area where it is not economical for a telephone company to provide direct interconnection between all end offices. The tandem office completes all calls between the end offices but is not directly connected to subscribers.

The Toll Office The toll office (also called the trunk exchange or transit switch) is a telephone company switching center where channels and toll message circuits terminate—in other words, where national long-distance connections are made. This is usually one particular exchange in a city, but larger cities may have several exchanges where toll message circuits terminate.

The International Gateway An international gateway is the point to and from which international services are available in each country. Protocol conversion may take place in the gateway; in ITU terminology, this is called a *centre de transit* (CT). C1 and C2 international exchanges connect only international circuits. CT2 exchanges switch traffic between regional groups of countries, and CT1 exchanges switch traffic between continents. CT3 exchanges connect switch traffic between the national PSTN and the international gateway.

Transmission Nodes

Transmission nodes are part of the transport infrastructure, and they provide communication paths that carry user traffic and network control information between the nodes in a network. The transmission nodes include the transmission media discussed in Chapter 3, as well as transport equipment, including amplifiers and/or repeaters, multiplexers, digital cross-connects, and digital loop carriers.

Service Nodes

Service nodes handle *signaling*, which is the transmission of information to control the setup, holding, charging, and releasing of connections, as well as the transmission of information to control network operations and billing. A very important area related to service nodes is the ITU standard specification Signaling System 7 (SS7), which is covered later in this chapter.

■ The Transport Network Infrastructure

The transport network includes two main infrastructures. The first is the PDH, also known as T-carrier, E-carrier, and J-carrier wideband transmission standards. This infrastructure was first introduced in the early 1960s. The second infrastructure of the transport network is the Synchronous Digital Hierarchy (SDH; ITU terminology), also known as Synchronous Optical Network (SONET; ANSI terminology), which was first formalized and standardized in 1988. SDH/SONET is the second generation of digital hierarchy, and it is based on a physical infrastructure of optical fibers.

PDH and SDH/SONET are voice-centric circuit-switched network models that switch millions of 64Kbps circuits between various switching points. Each circuit is multiplexed numerous times for aggregation onto transmission facilities. Aggregation occurs at many points in the network: in the access network, within the local exchange, and throughout the interexchanges. Hence, a significant portion of the cost of a network goes to the equipment that performs this aggregation—the multiplexers and cross-connects in both the PDH and SDH/SONET environments.

The PDH Infrastructure

The term *Plesiochronous* makes PDH sound like a dinosaur, and in a way, it is—it's an outdated architecture from the standpoint of the data rates it offers. But the word *Plesiochronous* means "minute variations in timing," and that refers to the fact that the PDH is an *asynchronous infrastructure*. Each network element—that is, each exchange, multiplexer, cross-connect, repeater, and so on—gets its clocking pulse from a different clocking source, and even though those clocking sources are synchronized, there are minute fluctuations in timing. To differentiate the beginning and the end of a conversation, we have to channelize conversations.

PDH was the first system designed to use digitized voice transmission. It was born of the telcos' desire to better use their cable facilities and to enhance the quality of calls. PDH was first used by telcos as a means of aggregating multiple voice channels into a single high-speed digital backbone. Standards that are used today for all-digital switching and transmission come from the original PDH specifications.

PDH defines several things: First, it's an integrated digital network, so it can carry a range of traffic, as long as that traffic is being presented in a digital manner. Therefore, PDH represented the first opportunity for users and carriers to combine voice and data traffic over the same pipes. Second, it specifies the different transmission levels or data rates, some of which are available for customers to subscribe to and others of which are used by operators internally within the backbones. Third, it defines within each of the transmission levels how many channels can be made available.

The T-, E-, and J-Carrier Standards

T-carrier, E-carrier, and J-carrier are PDH standards that are followed in different regions of the world: J-carrier is followed throughout Japan; T-carrier is followed throughout North America; and E-carrier is followed throughout Europe and the majority of other locations throughout the world, including large parts of Asia, Latin America, and Africa. Figure 5.4 compares these three standards. They all share one increment as a common denominator: 64Kbps. But each of the three standards multiplexes together a different number of these 64Kbps channels to derive higher transmission rates.

Having three separate standards—T-, E-, and J-carrier—means that we have to cross between systems that use different standards, and in doing so, we incur additional overhead.

Elements of the PDH Infrastructure

As shown in Figure 5.5, the following are the key elements of the PDH infrastructure:

- Transmission media
- Repeaters
- Channel service units (CSUs)
- Multiplexers
- Digital loop carriers (DLCs)
- Digital cross-connect systems (DCSs)

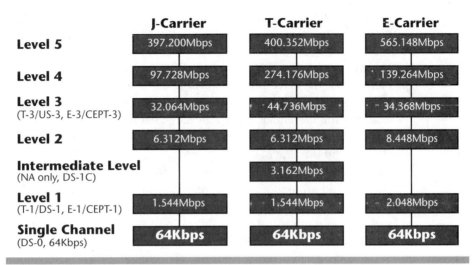

Figure 5.4 T-carrier, E-carrier, and J-carrier standards

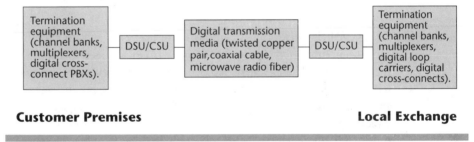

Figure 5.5 PDH components

Transmission media PDH can include a wide variety of transmission media, and the type you use is contingent on the bandwidth you want to be able to support. You could use copper pairs to provision T-1, E-1, or J-1 services, but if you wanted to get into the higher-bandwidth capacities afforded under T-3, E-3, or J-3, you would deploy a higher-bandwidth medium, such as coax, microwave, or fiber. PDH operates on four-wire circuits, which means it operates in full-duplex and you can communicate in both directions simultaneously.

CSUs A CSU terminates each end of a T-, E-, or J-carrier facility. It equalizes the received signal, filters the transmitted and received wave forms, and interacts with customers' and carriers' test facilities. You use a CSU to perform diagnostic tests on span lines and to set up a T-1, E-1, or J-1 line with a PBX, a channel bank, a multi-plexer, or any other compliant data terminal equipment.

Multiplexers A series of time-division multiplexers enables us to move up the hierarchy of the PDH infrastructure. The first in the series of multiplexers is gener-ally referred to as *channel banks*. A channel bank has several purposes. First, it con-solidates the individual voice and data channels so that they can travel over the higher-speed transmission line. In the case of a T-1, a channel bank consolidates 24 channels; in the case of an E-1, a channel bank consolidates 32 channels. Channel banks can accept analog inputs, which means they can digitize analog voice. So, if you're using an analog switch—either a local exchange or a PBX—the channel bank should be equipped with the codecs that run an analog voice stream through a process of digitization called Pulse Code Modulation (PCM) to convert the ana-log voice into a digital bitstream that can be transported over the digital carrier. (Codecs are discussed in Chapter 2, "Telecommunications Technology Fundamen-tals," and PCM is discussed later in this chapter.)

Beyond the channel bank, the multiplexing hierarchy steps through the indi-vidual transmission levels. In the case of T-carrier, the levels are T-1 through T-4; for E-carrier, they are E-1 through E-5; and for J-carrier, they are J-1 through J-5.

DLCs DLCs—also called remote terminals, concentrators, or remote concentra-tors—were introduced in the mid-1970s, specifically as a way to economically expand the telco network. They were deployed to improve efficiency and to lower costs. DLCs reduced analog facilities by up to 80%, and they led to building, real estate liquidation, and maintenance efficiencies as well. They also eliminated the need for load coils, which are used to improve transmission on wire pairs for distances greater than 3.4 miles (5.5 kilometers). DLCs also reduced the number of pairs of copper wires required between the local exchange and the subscriber; they did this by sharing pairs or transmission facilities among many multiplexed conversations. Essentially, the DLC architecture, shown in Figure 5.6, reduces the loop lengths and makes more effective use of high-capacity trunks from a neighborhood into the local exchange.

DLCs continue to evolve, and as they do so, they become smaller systems. The original DLCs were built so that an individual system could service around 600 subscribers, but these boxes achieved only about a 50% fill ratio, which meant that half of the capacity was not being used. Now, given the distribution and density of neighborhoods and populations, smaller DLCs are being created. These systems service up to about 96 subscribers, and utilization is at around a 90% level. These smaller DLCs allow for faster service rollout and a shorter pay-back period for the deployment. They also facilitate quick response to growth in services and competition.

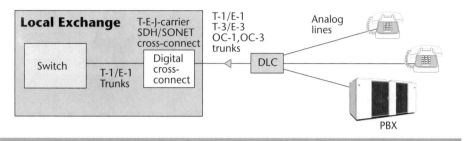

Figure 5.6 DLC architecture

With ever-increasing interest in high-speed broadband access, DLCs could be a tool for shortening loop length, thereby bringing more bandwidth to the customer. Consequently, some of the additional changes that have occurred with the newer generations of DLCs also provide interfaces for SDH/SONET or optical fibers. However, bear in mind that the vast majority of DLCs deployed are incompatible with the xDSL services. It is imperative that the proper generation of DLC be deployed in order to meet the customer's demand for broadband residential access via twisted-pair.

DCSs DCSs were developed in 1981 and officially introduced in 1985. They basically automated the process of circuit provisioning and replaced the use of manual patch panels. The key feature of DCSs is called drop and insert. This refers to the capability of the cross-connect to exchange channels from one facility to another. It is used to implement appropriate routing of traffic, to reroute around congestion or failure, and to allow customers to dynamically reconfigure their own networks. Generally it keeps communications paths in place for continuous use over a period of months, or sometimes even years, but it does allow change as demand warrants.

Essentially, a DCS is a computer system with a variety of software databases that describe first-choice routes and alternate routes (see Figure 5.7). If Channel 7 normally goes out over Line 1 and then goes out over Trunk 1, but Trunk 1 fails, the digital cross-connect can consult its alternate routing table, which might say to reroute that particular line over Trunk 2. A reconfiguration can take place in a matter of minutes.

Digital cross-connects provide for four levels of switching. You can switch between DS-3s and DS-3s or between E-3s and E-3s. You can switch between DS-1s and DS-1s or between E-1s and E-1s. You can switch between DS-0s and E-0s, and you can also potentially switch below that level by using submultiplexed data streams within the DS-0 channel. Some of the individual intelligent multiplexers, such as T-1/E-1 muxes and T-3/E-3 muxes, also offer this capability.

The fact that reconfigurations can be implemented in a matter of minutes—and that customers can implement this capability on their own private networks—is the most

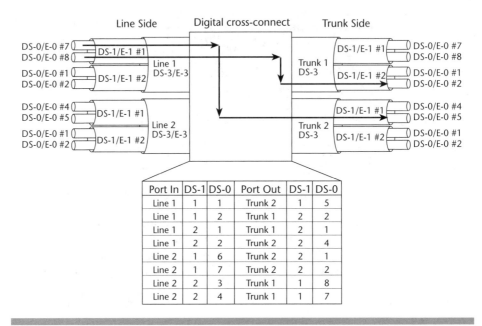

Figure 5.7 The DCS

important and favorable characteristic of the DCS. The main applications for cross-connects are to provide disaster recovery, to bypass a system during maintenance without affecting traffic flows, to reconfigure the network to address peak traffic demands, and to implement a temporary application that can be reconfigured as needed.

Voice Compression Standards
Let me take a moment to talk about how voice was digitalized to carry over the PSTN under the original sampling theorem.

PCM   When PCM was developed, we lived in an environment that was largely analog. Therefore, in designing a digitization scheme, it was important to consider that voice would have to undergo many conversions between analog and digital as it was transmitted through the numerous switching nodes and components of a network. And if it had to go through a number of conversions, it could withstand only so many conversions before it began to lose toll quality. Therefore, the sampling theorem that was developed suggested that in order to reproduce voice in toll-quality manner, you have to sample that voice at twice the rate of the highest frequency carried. The highest frequency being carried in the telephone channel was 4,000Hz, so we needed a sampling rate of 8,000 samples per second. Every time we take a sample, we're measuring the amplitude, or voltage, of the signal at that point. Say that the amplitude of the signal is +1.25 volts. We would take that amplitude value and convert it into a binary expression, an 8-bit word. Now we have 8,000 samples per second and 8 bits per sample, resulting in 64Kbps required to carry voice in a digital manner. This is how the 64Kbps channel was derived as the basic building block of PDH.

ADPCM   As networks have become more digitalized, fewer conversions take place, and voice can be carried at a higher quality over fewer bits per second. Another standard that is used in the PSTN is Adaptive Differential PCM (ADPCM), which essentially carries digital voice at 32Kbps. ADPCM does something wonderful for an end user. Say you have a traditional T-1 line with PCM channel banks. Over that one T-1, you can extract 24 channels, each of which carries 64Kbps. But your traffic increases, and you need more channels to carry voice traffic. You have two options: You can add another T-1 line, which means a substantial monthly investment, or you can put ADPCM channel banks on the T-1 that you already have, which gives you 48 channels of 64Kbps each. In essence, you can double the capacity of the network without having to add more subscriber lines.

Needless to say, voice compression continues to be applied, and not just in the PSTN. For instance, in wireless networks such as cellular networks, where spectrum is at a premium, we compress voice down to 8Kbps so that we can support more callers within each of the cells.

T-Carrier and E-Carrier Signal Hierarchy

Because competition has entered the marketplace, different operators in an area have often bought equipment from different manufacturers, which means there are a number of standards to deal with. Even if a country once followed ITU standards, new companies may have entered the country with North American–standard

DS-*x* Versus TX-*x* and CEPT-*x* Versus E-*x*

Technically, the DS-*x* and CEPT-*x* terminology (DS-1, DS-3, CEPT-1, CEPT-3, and so on) indicates a specific signal level (and thus usable bandwidth), as well as the electrical interface specification. T-*x* and E-*x* terminology (T-1, T-3, E-1, E-3, and so on) indicates the type of carrier—a specific physical implementation of a DS-*x*/CEPT-*x*. Today, however, the terms DS-*x* and T-*x* are often used interchangeably. For example, someone might use the term DS-1 and another person might use the term T-1 to refer to the same thing—a digital transport that can carry 1.544Mbps over a total of 24 channels. The same applies to the use of the European designation: E-1 is the same as CEPT-1, and so on.

equipment and interfaced with the existing ITU-based equipment. Thus, you really need to be familiar with all the standards. This section covers the signal hierarchy for both T-carrier and E-carrier standards.

The T-Carrier Digital Signal Hierarchy   Table 5.1 lists the levels in the T-carrier digital signal hierarchy, the basic building block of which, DS-0, is the 64Kbps channel.

Table 5.1   The T-Carrier Digital Signal Hierarchy

Digital Signal Level	Bit Rate	DS-0 Channel	Number of T-1 Lines
DS-0 (T-0)	64Kbps	1	—
DS-1 (T-1)	1.544Mbps	24	1
DS-2 (T-2)	6.312Mbps	96	4
DS-3 (T-3)	44.736Mbps	672	28
DS-4 (T-4)	274.176Mbps	4,032	168

The first subscriber level, Digital Signal Level 1 (DS-1), provides 1.544Mbps and a total of 24 channels. The DS-2 level is not a subscriber level, nor is it used very frequently in the PSTN. You might see it installed on some campus networks, or perhaps to bundle some DS-1s out of a tandem exchange to a toll exchange.

DS-3 is a high-bandwidth alternative for subscribers, and it is used for interexchange trunks. Both users and carriers get 44.736Mbps with DS-3, which is a total of 672 channels that can carry combined voice, data, fax, and image traffic.

T-Carrier and J-Carrier: Stealing Bits for Signaling

In the T-carrier and J-carrier system, the signaling for each conversation flows in the same channel as the conversation. Thus, for voice purposes, we have the full 64Kbps channel, and every now and then we steal one of the bits of digital voice and replace it with the proper signaling bit. This does not affect the understandability or voice quality of the message. However, if a data stream were traveling through that channel and we went about stealing bits, we would obviously be changing the meaning of the content. Therefore, we accommodate 56Kbps of data within each channel, leaving a little bit of room for the signaling bits to be inserted as needed.

The DS-4 level is used only within the telco, again on interexchange trunks. DS-4 offers roughly 274Mbps and 4,032 channels.

With each of these levels, you must go through a separate multiplexing level. Remember that each of the muxes is driven by a different clocking source, so they each bundle their channels in a slightly different framework. In building the 64Kbps channels up to a T-1 and then building those T-1s up to T-2s and those T-2s up to T-3s, everything is fine unless somewhere along the way one customer decides to extract some capacity to drop off that allocation midway. Say, for example, that you're in Washington, DC, and you need to connect to San Francisco. In Washington, DC, you'd have a T-1 coming into the local exchange, along with multiple other customers in the neighborhood. The local exchange might bundle those T-1s onto a T-2 to pass off to the tandem, and the tandem would bundle them up into T-3s to send to the toll center. The toll center would bundle them up for T-4s to pass across the long haul to San Francisco. This works great, but then you need to add an office in Kansas City. So you need to add a T-4 mux to break it down to all the respective T-3s. Then you need to break down the T-3s into their T-2s, and then break down the T-2s into all their T-1s, and then find your T-1 so that you can extract the channels you want to drop off. Then you need to bundle them all back up onto the T-1 and go back up the scale again. This strict hierarchy requires you to go through all the changes—you can't jump steps as you bundle and unbundle traffic. Therefore, the PDH hierarchy is characterized by a lot of back-to-back multiplexing and demultiplexing in order to drop and add payload. That is one of the highest-cost components of this generation of the PSTN.

The E-Carrier Digital Signal Hierarchy   As shown in Table 5.2, E-carrier signals are often called CEPT levels (for Common European Postal and Telegraphy); 64Kbps is the basic increment in E-carrier. CEPT-1 (or E-1) operates at 2.048Mbps and is delivered over 32 channels.

CEPT-2, like T-2, is not used much. CEPT-3, the high-bandwidth alternative, offers 34Mbps and 512 channels. CEPT-4 and CEPT-5 are largely used within telco

E-Carrier: Separate Signaling Channels

The E-carrier system is different from the T-carrier and J-carrier systems in an important way: In the E-carrier system, the signaling information travels in separate channels from the voice and data traffic. Two of the 32 channels are devoted to carrying signaling and control information, and the other 30 channels are available to carry customer payload at 64Kbps. In T-carrier and J-carrier, because the signaling information flows in the conversation channel, voice channels are 64Kbps, but data channels are 56Kbps, with the remaining capacity reserved for signaling.

Table 5.2 The E-Carrier Digital Signal Hierarchy

CEPT Signal Level	Bit Rate	E-0 Channel	Number of E-1 Lines
CEPT-0 (E-0)	64Kbps	—	—
CEPT-1 (E-1)	2.048Mbps	32	1
CEPT-2 (E-2)	8.488Mbps	128	4
CEPT-3 (E-3)	34.368Mbps	512	16
CEPT-4 (E-4)	139.246Mbps	2,048	64
CEPT-5 (E-5)	565.148Mbps	8,192	256

networks, again for their interexchange trunks. Like T-carrier, E-carrier has a strict hierarchy of multiplexers.

The SDH/SONET Infrastructure

SDH/SONET, created in the mid-1980s, is the second generation of digital hierarchy. Whereas PDH involves a lot of overhead because it includes three standards throughout the worldwide, SDH/SONET uses one common standard that applies to networks worldwide. SDH is the ITU standard and followed throughout the parts of the world where ITU standards dominate; SONET is the ANSI standard, which is part of SDH, and it is used in North America and Japan. SDH/SONET was created to be an industry standard for high-speed transmission over optical fiber. It was actually part of a much bigger standard in the works at that time—Broadband ISDN. Broadband ISDN was envisioned for use with advanced applications (for example, tele-education, telesurveillance, telegambling, the ability to collaborate, HDTV). Two technologies were required in order to support such applications—a transport infrastructure that had the significant bandwidth needed to support them (SDH/SONET) and a switching technology (ATM) that could ensure that latencies could be controlled and kept very low. Consequently, SDH/SONET and ATM, as modern broadband technologies, were both born out of the Broadband ISDN standard and a desire to be able to deliver advanced applications.

SDH/SONET is a family of transmission standards designed to achieve compatibility between different fiber-optic transport products, as well as to provide compatibility with the existing digital hierarchy, PDH. A lot of fiber-optic systems have been deployed in the past 16 or more years, but they're not all compatible with one another. They use different forms of cables with different diameters, and they use different types of light sources. And where there are physical incompatibilities, you can't achieve *midspan meet*—where two carrier services have to come together. A railroad analogy can be used here. Think back to when people had just begun to build railroads. Oftentimes, one provider was building tracks going east to west that were a certain width and another provider was building tracks going west to east that were a different width. When the providers met in the middle, their cars couldn't cross each other's tracks. The same thing happens when there's a lack of physical compatibility in fiber-optic transport, and that means you lose the ability to carry network management information on an end-to-end basis. You may not be able to do end-to-end monitoring and control of a network that is multivendor or multicarrier in nature if the vendors or carriers use incompatible physical fiber-optic equipment.

It's always important to develop and have available very strong network management tools. The goal of network management is not to *eliminate* downtime—because we know that would be impractical; rather, it is to *minimize* the resolution time. So the ability to do end-to-end testing remotely is very critical to quick recoverability. SDH/SONET provides the physical layer (that is, Layer 1) framework for broadband applications. It provides a standardized list of optical parameters that define the types of cables and light sources that are allowed. It defines a new table of data rates that are much higher than older transmission rates. It redefines how the multiplexing process occurs as you move within the different transmission levels. It also affords very robust operations capabilities, such as service restoration.

The SDH/SONET specifications define a *frame format*—that is, how the bits are packaged together to be transported over the fiber. As mentioned earlier, they define the nature of the physical interfaces (for example, couplers, light sources). They define the optical carrier line rates, or transmission levels, and they define the sorts of messages that are exchanged in order to support operations, administration, maintenance, and provisioning.

An important aspect of SDH/SONET is that it introduced the notion of a ring operation to address network survivability by handling rapid restoration. With SDH/SONET, we use a dual-counter-rotating ring. Imagine that you have four network nodes. As shown in Figure 5.8, with a dual-counter-rotating ring, you link each of these four network nodes together by using one pair of fibers; that pair of fibers becomes the primary fiber, and information will flow over it in a clockwise manner. You run another pair of fibers, which may actually be housed in the same cable as the first pair of fibers, to join the four nodes together. The second pair of fibers become the protect fiber, which is designed to carry information in a counter-clockwise manner. In theory, if a cable is cut between Node A and Node B, you can still move a message from A to B by reversing the information flow and going from A to D to C to B. This enables you to recover immediately—within 50 milliseconds—from outages that occur, for example, because a construction crew

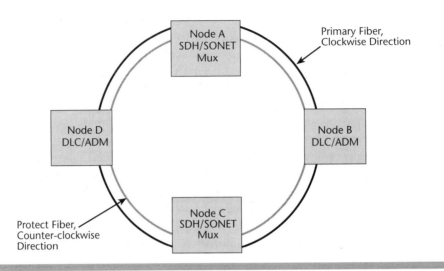

Figure 5.8 SDH/SONET ring architecture

has cut a cable. Obviously, if a major earthquake hit and all the streets were broken up, a counter-rotating ring wouldn't necessarily ensure survivability, but for smaller-scale problems, it can very adequately handle a backup. This is one of the greatest strengths of SDH/SONET and will likely keep it operational in networks for another 10 to 20 years. But these types of capabilities are also being introduced in the new generations of standards, such as WDM, and when that occurs, we will start to move away from SDH/SONET because SDH/SONET is a TDM system that does not take advantage of the fact that light can be spatially multiplexed, allowing multiple wavelengths to be carried over one fiber pair.

SDH/SONET is also important because it grooms and routes traffic. *Grooming* means that SDH/SONET selectively removes channels from a digital facility for routing to a designated remote location via another digital facility; basically, it enables you to drop and add payload flexibly. SDH/SONET also provides for performance monitoring so that you can understand the performance of the network, its components, and the congestion levels.

The SDH/SONET Signal Hierarchy

The SDH/SONET signal hierarchy deals with *optical carrier levels*, which refer to the optical aspect of the transmission—the optical pulse as it travels through the fibers. These optical pulses go through electronic muxes, and when the signal is going through these network elements, the bits are packaged in a frame for transport across the fiber. In the case of SONET, this frame is called the Synchronous Transport Signal (STS), and in SDH, the frame is called Synchronous Transport

Module (STM). Two types of rates are important in the realm of SDH/SONET: The *payload rate* refers to the capacity available to carry customer content, and the *data rate* refers to the total capacity available for customer content as well as network management information.

Table 5.3 shows the SDH/SONET signal hierarchy. You don't have to memorize all these levels, but you'll consistently encounter four or five of them in your readings that you should commit to memory.

Table 5.3   The SDH/SONET Signal Hierarchy

OC Level	SONET	SDH	Data Rate (Mbps)	Payload Rate (Mbps)
OC-1	STS-1	STM-0	51.48	50.840
OC-3	STS-3	STM-1	155.52	150.336
OC-9	STS-9	STM-3	466.56	451.008
OC-12	STS-12	STM-4	622.08	601.344
OC-18	STS-18	STM-6	933.12	902.016
OC-24	STS-24	STM-8	1,244.16	1,202.688
OC-36	STS-36	STM-12	1,866.00	1,804.032
OC-48	STS-48	STM-16	2,488.32	2,405.376
OC-96	STS-96	STM-32	4,876.64	4,810.752
OC-192	STS-192	STM-64	9,953.28	9,621.504

The levels of the SDH/SONET signal hierarchy that are most important to be familiar with are OC-1, OC-3, OC-12, OC-48, and OC-192:

- **OC-1**—OC-1 offers about 51Mbps and is generally used as customer access lines. Early adopter types of customers—such as universities, airports, financial institutions, large government agencies, and ISPs—would use OC-1.

- **OC-3**—OC-3 provides about 155Mbps. End users such as companies in the aerospace industry and high-tier ISPs would need this extensive level.

- **OC-12**—OC-12 provides about 622Mbps. It is another capacity toward which high-tier ISPs are moving. It was originally deployed for the metropolitan area fiber rings built out across cities worldwide, although those rings are now moving to OC-48.

■ **OC-48**—OC-48 offers about 2.5Gbps. This capacity has been deployed for backbone, or core, networks. Today the metropolitan area rings are moving from OC-12 to OC-48, and the backbone links are moving from OC-48 to OC-192.

■ **OC-192**—OC-192 supports about 10Gbps and is being used for backbone networks.

There are more levels in the SDH/SONET signal hierarchy, but the ones discussed here are the ones for which equipment is currently being manufactured. We are in early stages of building new muxes that can also operate at OC-768 and that will support 40Gbps. Some people feel that electronic muxes really are not suitable for the higher data rates and that we should concentrate on moving to all-optical muxes and switches.

How do the high optical-carrier levels relate to all the lower-level signals out there—such as those from a 1.5Mbps T-1 or a 2Mbps E-1? There are mechanisms that enable us to map signal levels below DS-3 (that is, below 45Mbps) into what SDH calls *virtual containers* or what SONET calls *virtual tributaries*. A virtual container or tributary basically defines the data structure for the transport and switching of sub-51Mbps network services such as DS-1, E-1, DS-2, and E-3. Table 5.4 shows the various line rates that are supported and what existing standard each refers to. For most people, this type of detail won't make or break success in the industry, but it's important to know that a virtual tributary or virtual container can provide a highway for lower-rate data signals to coexist in high-speed optical pipes.

Table 5.4 Virtual Container/Virtual Tributary Line Rates and Standards

Virtual Container/ Virtual Tributary Level	Line Rate	Standard
VC-11/VT-1.5	1.728Mbps	DS-1/E-1
VC-2/VT-2	2.304Mbps	E-1
VT-3	3.456Mbps	DS-1C
VC-2/VT-6	6.912Mbps	DS-2
VT-6-N	$n \times 6.9$Mbps	(future)
async DS-3/VC-3	44.736/34.368Mbps	DS-3/E-3
VC-4	139.264Mbps	DS-4/E-4

In contrast to PDH, SDH/SONET is a *synchronous* infrastructure. This means that each of the network elements draws its clocking pulse from one clocking source—so everybody is marching to the beat of the same drummer. Instead of using special framing bits to delineate channels, SDH/SONET uses a special pointer bit in front of each conversation that essentially says "start of a new conversation." When it's time to drop that channel off at a customer premise, we can identify it by its pointer bit and extract it without having to disturb any of the other traffic. This reduces the overhead associated with multiplexers by a factor of 10.

SDH/SONET Muxes and Cross-Connects

SDH/SONET was built for and largely relies on fiber-optic transmission media. It also includes a variety of multiplexers and cross-connects, as well as equipment that could be placed at the customer premise. There are two main categories of SDH/SONET multiplexers (see Figure 5.9):

- **Terminal muxes**—Terminal muxes enable signals to move through the hierarchy of optical carrier levels. They act as access nodes and support current services by accepting electrical interfaces and lower-level signals, including DS-1/E-1, DS-2, and DS-3/E-3. They concentrate one or more optical carrier signals and represent one of the optical carrier levels.

- **Add/drop muxes (ADMs)**—ADMs facilitate easy dropping and adding of payload and are therefore the building blocks of the SDH/SONET network.

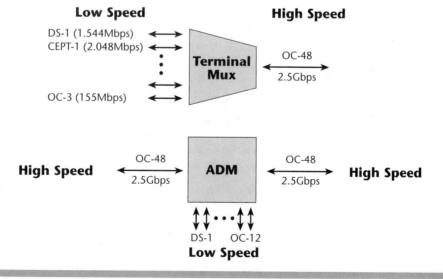

Figure 5.9 Terminal muxes versus ADMs

An add/drop mux converts one or more lower-level signals, such as T-1 or E-1 signals, into and from one of the optical carrier levels. It can drop lower-rate signals to be transported on different facilities, or it can add lower-rate signals into the higher-rate optical carrier levels, and basically it allows telcos to add and drop traffic easily and conveniently all along the network.

There are also two categories of SDH/SONET cross-connects:

- **Wideband digital cross-connects**—These terminate SDH/SONET and DS-3/E-3 signals. Switching occurs at the DS-0, DS-1/E-1, and VT/VC levels.

- **Broadband digital cross-connects**—Broadband digital cross-connects interface at the various SDH/SONET signal levels as well as the legacy DS-3/E-3 levels, but they then switch at the optical carrier levels. They can make cross-connections at DS-3/E-3, OC-1, and concatenated levels (that is, where you combine several frames of an OC-1 together). Generally, a broadband digital cross-connect is used as an SDH/SONET hub that grooms the optical carrier levels for broadband restoration purposes or for routing traffic.

▪ Signaling Systems

This section discusses the nervous system of the network: the signaling system. A great deal of information needs to be passed back and forth between the network elements in the completion of a call and also in the servicing of specialized features. Four main types of signals handle this passing of information:

- **Supervisory signals**—Supervisory signals handle the on-hook/off-hook condition. For instance, when you lift a telephone handset (that is, go off-hook), a signal tells the local exchange that you want a dial tone, and if you exist in the database as an authenticated user, you are then delivered that service; when you hang up (that is, go back on-hook), you send a notice that says you want to remove the service. A network is always monitoring for these supervisory signals to determine when someone needs to activate or deactivate service.

- **Address signals**—Address signals have to do with the number dialed, which essentially consists of country codes, city codes, area codes, prefixes, and the subscriber number. This string of digits, which we refer to as the telephone number, is, in effect, a routing instruction to the network hierarchy.

- **Information signals**—Information signals are associated with activating and delivering various enhanced features. For instance, a call-waiting tone

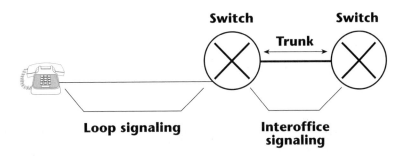

Figure 5.10 Customer loop and interoffice signaling

is an information signal, and pressing *72 on your phone might send an information signal that tells your local exchange to forward your calls.

- **Alerting signals**—Alerting signals are the ringing tones, the busy tones, and any specific busy alerts that are used to indicate network congestion or unavailability.

Signaling takes place in two key parts of the network: in the access network, where it's called *loop signaling*, and in the core, where it's called *interoffice signaling* (see Figure 5.10).

With analog loop signaling, two types of starts exist:

- **Ground start**—*Ground start* means that when you seize that line, it's immediately grounded so that no other call can potentially conflict with it. Ground start is used with a contentious system, perhaps a PBX at a corporate enterprise, to avoid collisions. For example, say you seize a trunk and place a call, and now you're in the ringing state. There are short periods of silence between ringing tones. The local exchange could mistake one of these periods of silence to mean that that trunk is available and try to send a call in over that same trunk that you're trying to place a call out over; this would cause a collision (referred to as *glare*). Consequently, when you're dealing with systems and contention for the resource, grounding the trunk up front is the most efficient procedure.
- **Loop start**—Pay telephones and residential phones use *loop start,* which means that the circuit is grounded when the connection is completed.

There are various start standards for digital subscriber signaling, and they are defined in accordance with the service being provided.

Interoffice signaling has been through several generations of signaling approaches. In the first generation, called per-trunk signaling, the complete path—

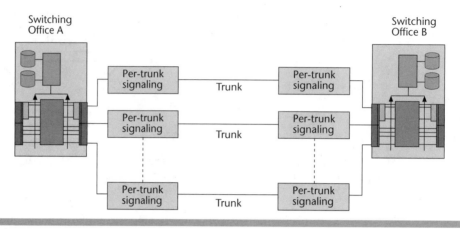

Figure 5.11 Per-trunk signaling

all the way to the destination point—is set up in order to just carry the signaling information in the first place (see Figure 5.11). This method uses trunks very inefficiently; trunks may be put into place to carry 20 or 30 ringing tones, but if nobody is on the other end to take that call, the network trunk is being used but not generating any revenue. Also, when a call is initiated and begins to progress, you can no longer send any other signaling information over that trunk; being able to pass a call-waiting tone, for instance, would not be feasible.

We have moved away from the per-trunk signaling environment to what we use today—common-channel signaling (see Figure 5.12). You can think of common-channel signaling as being a separate subnetwork over which the signaling message flows between intelligent networking components that assist in the call completion and assist in the delivery of the service logic needed to deliver the requested feature. Today, we predominantly use the ITU-T standard for common-channel signaling: SS7.

SS7 Architecture

SS7 is critical to the functioning and operation of the modern network. With SS7, a packet data network overlays and controls the operation of the underlying voice networks; signaling information is carried on an entirely different path than voice and data traffic. Signaling doesn't take a great deal of time, so we can multiplex many signaling messages over one channel, and that's why the signaling system is a packet network. The signaling system takes advantage of the efficiencies of statistical multiplexing for what is essentially bursty data. The SS7 signaling data link is a full-duplex digital transmission channel that operates at

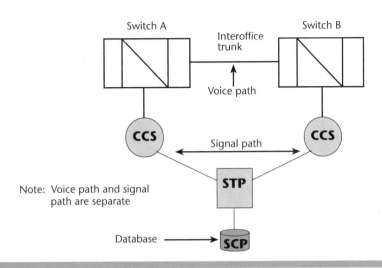

Figure 5.12 Common-channel signaling

either 56Kbps or 64Kbps, depending on the standards under which the network is operating (for example, T-carrier and J-carrier operate at 56Kbps, E-carrier operates at 64Kbps).

SS7 is an entire architecture that performs out-of-band signaling (that is, signaling in which the conversation and the signaling take place over different paths) in support of the information-exchange functions that are necessary in the PSTN, such as call establishment, billing, and routing. Database access messages convey information between toll centers and centralized databases to permit real-time access to billing-related information and other services. The SS7 architecture defines the procedures for the setup, ongoing management, and clearing of a call, and it allows you to pass along customer-related information (for example, the identity of the caller, the primary carrier chosen) that helps in routing calls. The efficiency of the network also results in faster call setup times and provides for more efficient use of the circuits when carrying the voice or data traffic. In addition, SS7 supports services that require signaling during a call as it is occurring—not in the same band as the conversation.

SS7 permits the telephone company to offer one database to several switches, thereby freeing up switch capacity for other functions, and this is what makes SS7 the foundation for INs and advanced intelligent networks (AINs). It is also the foundation for network interconnection and enhanced services. Without SS7, we would not be able to enjoy the level of interoperability we have today. SS7 is also a key to the development of new generations of services on the Internet, particularly those that support traditional telephony services. To be able to accommodate

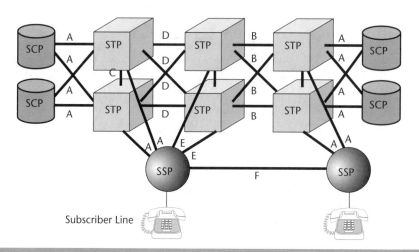

Figure 5.13 An SS7 network

features such as call forwarding, call waiting, and conference calling, you must be able to tap into the service logic that delivers those features. Until quite recently, the Internet has not been able to do this, but the year 2000 saw the introduction of SS7 gateways, which allow an interface between circuit-switched networks (with their powerful SS7 infrastructure) and the emerging packet-switched networks that need to be capable of handling the more traditional type of voice communications on a more cost-effective basis.

As Figure 5.13 shows, there are the three prerequisite components in the SS7 network: service switching points (SSPs), service control points (SCPs), and signal transfer points (STPs).

SSPs

SSPs are the switches that originate and terminate calls. They receive signals from the CPE and perform call processing on behalf of a user. The user, by dialing particular digits, triggers the network to request certain services. For instance, if you preface a number with a toll-free prefix, that toll-free arrangement triggers the local exchange, or SSP, to initiate a database lookup to determine the physical address of that toll-free number (that is, where it resides in the network). The SSP reaches into the network to find the database that can translate the toll-free number into a physical address in order to then complete the toll-free call. The SSP does this by interacting with a device called the SCP, which is discussed shortly.

SSPs are typically implemented at local exchanges, access tandem offices, or toll centers that contain the network-signaling protocols. The SSP serves as the source and destination point for the SS7 messages.

SCPs

The second key component of SS7 is SCP. This is the network element that interfaces with the SSP as well as the STP. Most importantly, the SCP is the network element that contains the network configuration and call-completion database; in other words, it contains the service logic to act on the types of calls and features the users are requesting. SCPs are centralized nodes that contain service logic— basically software and databases—for the management of the call. They provide functions such as digit translation, call routing, and verification of credit cards. The SCPs receive traffic from the SSP via the STP and return responses, based on that query, via the STP.

STPs

The STP is responsible for translating the SS7 messages and then routing those messages between the appropriate network nodes and databases. Notice in Figure 5.13 that the SCPs and the STPs are both redundant, and that the links running between them are also redundant.

SS7 and the Internet

If a network loses its signaling system, it loses the capability to complete calls, as well as to do any form of billing or passing along of management information. This makes SS7 critical. The SS7 signaling data link, as mentioned earlier in the chapter, is a full-duplex digital transmission channel that operates at either 56Kbps or 64Kbps. A variety of other SS7 links are defined as well, and each has specific uses within the signaling network:

- **A (access) links**—An A link interconnects an STP with either an SSP or an SCP. The SSP and SCP, collectively, are referred to as the *signaling endpoints*. A message sent to and from the SSPs or SCPs first goes to its home STP, which, in turn, processes or routes the message.

- **B (bridge) links, D (diagonal) links, and B/D links**—A B link connects an STP to another STP. Typically, a quad of B links interconnect peer (or primary) STPs (for example, the STPs from one network to the STPs of another network). The distinction between a B link and a D link is rather arbitrary, and such links may be referred to as *B/D links*.

- **C (cross) links**—C links interconnect mated STPs.

- **E (extended) links**—E links provide enhanced reliability by providing a set of links from the SSP to a second STP pair.

- **F (fully associated) links**—F links are links that directly connect to signaling endpoints.

■ Intelligent Networks

The ITU's standardization of SS7, in 1980, began the evolution toward the concept of intelligent networking. An IN includes a set of nodes that rely on widespread distribution of call-handling functions and capabilities (see Figure 5.14). Before the advent of INs, customers could have only the services and features available from their local exchanges. Their ability to demand and achieve new services from the operator was very much tied to the generation of software in the local exchange and whether it had yet incorporated the feature of interest. With INs, you can centrally place this type of service and feature logic on a node (such as an SCP), and then any switch can reach it and make use of that feature. The objective of the IN initially was to ease the introduction of new services into the network. It also provided a foundation for complex services that would be required and desirable on a networkwide basis, such as the automation of the operator-assistance function. Because of the IN and specialized peripherals—again, computing systems loaded with specific software—we no longer have to use operators to place a credit card call or a collect call.

Intelligent networking gives carriers the capability to directly develop network functionality on outboard processors connected to the switches, instead of having to be tied to their switch manufacturer and having to rely on the internal software. A main feature developed for the IN during the early and mid-1980s was *digit translation*, which was applied to toll-free number translation and VPNs. Customers could develop a unique calling plan that identified their location. They could invent their own numbering plan so that they could dial numbers that were easy

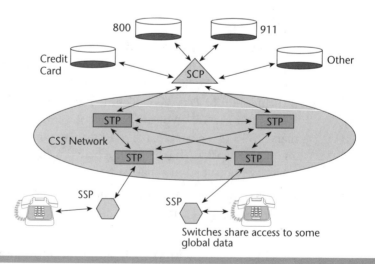

Figure 5.14 An IN

for them to remember, and in the network, the IN infrastructure would translate these private numbers into network physical addresses (for example, country code, city code, area code).

The IN also enables operator-assistance features such as eliminating credit card calling and collect calling as manual fulfillment processes. The IN also enables the identification of primary carriers (where competition exists), so that customers can select their primary carriers. *Local number portability*—which allows you to keep your own telephone number when you move to a new location—is a rather new concept that can be delivered thanks to the sophistication of this IN infrastructure. With local number portability, although your physical address will be different at your new location, you may want to keep your old phone number so your friends and colleagues can easily recall it. But for calls made with your old number to reach your new physical address, there must be translation tables in the network that can identify your correct physical address and properly route incoming calls to you.

AINs

Around the mid-1980s, Bellcore (which is now Telcordia) pioneered the second generation of INs, which we call AINs (see Figure 5.15). AINs move the service logic outside the switch and onto an independent SCP. An AIN is a service-independent network architecture that allows carriers to create and uniformly support telecom services and features via a common architectural platform, with the objective of allowing for rapid creation of customizable telecommunication services.

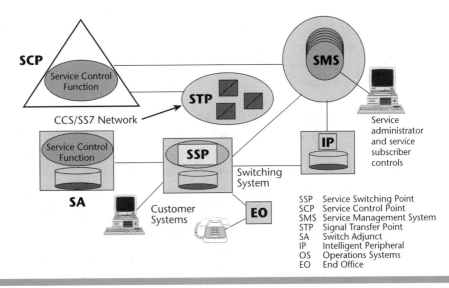

Figure 5.15 AIN architecture

An AIN is composed of intelligent nodes that are linked via SS7 to support a variety of services and advanced call-handling features across multiple vendor domains. With the introduction of the AIN architecture, a few additional components were needed. First, the service management system is a service-creation environment that facilitates the technical and customer service representatives' interface with the provisioning and network management systems. Second, intelligent peripherals are computing platforms that serve a very specific purpose but have a very widespread demand across the network (for example, voice recognition and voice synthesis capabilities to process third-party-assisted calls).

AINs can be used for a number of applications, including intelligent call routing, visitor location registration, virtual number service, voice-activated dialing, voice response, speech recognition, and text-to-speech conversion. The AIN infrastructure is critical in mobile communications. The reason you can roam across cellular networks is that IN databases are able to log whether you are present in your home network or in a visitor network, and they can identify whether you're authenticated to use the network. If you are authenticated to use the network, IN databases can identify which services should be made available to you. Virtual number services are also an important application of AINs; for example, a 700 number can identify and locate you within a footprint, rather than requiring you to be at a specific telephone to receive a call.

Next-Generation Networks

The SS7 network acts as the backbone for the AIN—it provides access to the AIN features, allows for efficient call setup and teardown, and interconnects thousands of service providers under one common signaling network. The capability to communicate with SS7 networks is essential for all service providers because SS7 networks give next-generation local exchange carriers access to an existing base of service features.

Next-Generation Network Equipment

SS7 uses new genres of equipment to ensure that packet-based telephony switching gateways can in fact support key legacy services and signaling features. For example, the next-generation gateway switch supports the traditional Class 4, or toll switch, services and the Class 5, or local exchange switch, services. It is designed to support a wide variety of traffic—data, voice, fax, multimedia, and other emerging sensory forms—over a data backbone. The next-generation gateway switch provides seamless interoperability between the circuits that network the PSTN and packet-switching networks, such as IP backbones, ATM networks, Frame Relay networks, and emerging MPLS networks. We can use these gateway switches to connect with the SS7 network and to handle the IP services that are so popular

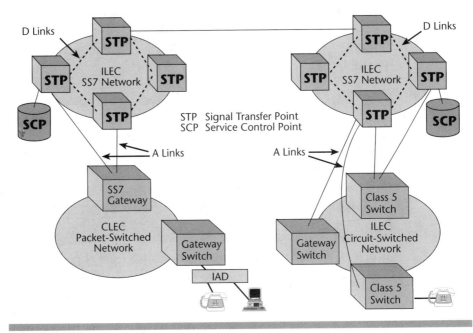

Figure 5.16 Next-generation gateway switches

Telephony Signaling Protocols and SS7

A number of telephony signaling protocols are currently used, and we don't know yet which will become the standard. Today, H.323 is found most frequently and offers the greatest range of vendor interoperability. Session Initiation Protocol (SIP), which is an Internet Engineering Task Force (IETF) standard, has a lot of support from the Internet community, and it is being included on more devices all the time. Over the next few years, we will be better able to determine which will be the dominant protocols, although IETF's SIP protocol is gaining popularity and supplanting H.323. (Signaling protocols are discussed in detail in Chapter 11, "Next-Generation Network Services.")

today. These gateway switches support a variety of telephony signaling protocols (for example, H.323, Session Initiation Protocol [SIP], Media Gateway Control Protocol [MGCP]) for communicating with the underlying SS7 architecture.

As shown in Figure 5.16, there are different forms of these next-generation gateway switches for different purposes. In the bottom right of Figure 5.16 is an ILEC and its resident circuit-switched network, which is a series of Class 5 offices at the perimeter. These Class 5 offices are connected to the SS7 network or the

STPs via A links. These Class 5 offices then connect into a CLEC's packet-switched network, and their first point of interface is a gateway switch. Among other things, this gateway switch is responsible for digitalizing and packetizing the voice to prepare it for transport over the packet-switched network. The CLEC's packet-switched network also has an SS7 gateway, which is capable of communicating with the underlying ILEC's SS7 network so that it can map the appropriate IP addresses associated with the destination telephone number, which is served by a given destination media gateway. The next-generation gateway switch, therefore, provides a means to seamlessly interoperate between two very important and existing infrastructures.

Figure 5.17 is an end-to-end view of a next-generation network. It shows an interconnected environment between the legacy circuit-switched network and the emerging packet-based networks. A subscriber at the customer premise (for example, a residence, a business site) is connected to the local exchange, known as the end office, by access lines. From there, trunks link to a media gateway switch, which, through SS7 interfaces, can reach into the underlying intelligence within the SS7 network and further add the necessary information to process the call as it's been requested. The call then goes out on a packet basis throughout a series of switches or routers (depending on what the provider is using as the backbone) and reaches a destination media gateway switch that unpackages the voice, undigitalizes it, and delivers it to the destination phone.

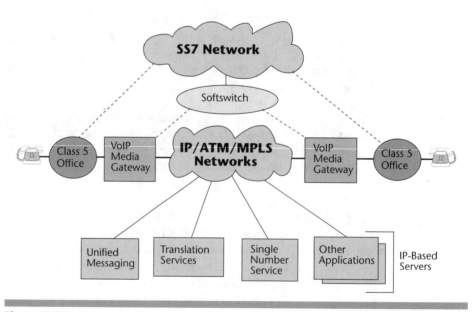

Figure 5.17   Next-generation networks

Although tremendous amounts of time and money have been spent in developing the intelligence that provides the telephony features we know today, there are still many new applications to be developed. These new applications, which are increasingly being developed for IP, include unified messaging, single-number service, and a network-type Rolodex that houses all kinds of contact and other information about people. We will be able to use databases to service calls when we have an integration or an interconnection between two networks. We will be able to provide traditional voice telephony features and introduce new generations of IP-based services.

Next-Generation Networks Versus the PSTN

The characteristics of next-generation networks are very different from what the traditional PSTN was aiming at. Next-generation networks are not being designed for just voice, data, or video. They're being designed for multimedia, and this requires capacities that are broadband in nature, networks that are engineered for extremely low and controllable latencies, and infrastructures that provide the ability to administer quality of service on a very granular level.

This book has talked about the explosion of bandwidth that's occurring because of developments in optics. As you have more and more bandwidth, it becomes cheaper and cheaper. When bandwidth becomes very inexpensive or free, a carrier needs to find other ways to generate revenue, such as by offering a large variety of value-added services (for example, reliability, priority, customer service, and encryption or security). But to administer all these services and to provide differentiated pricing, which can result in handsome revenue streams, there must be mechanisms for controlling, monitoring, and billing.

The following are important features of the next-generation network infrastructure that are covered in detail in later chapters:

- It has very fast packet switching, with capacities that we're beginning to need to measure in terabits per second (Tbps) and soon in petabits per second (1Pbps =1,000Tbps), and on its heels, in exabits per second (1Ebps = 1 billion Gbps). (See Chapter 10.)

- It places great emphasis on optical networking elements, to take advantage of the abundant bandwidth that's inherent in the visible light spectrum. (See Chapter 12, "Optical Networking.")

- Multiservice access is being created, so we will not have separate devices for voice and data as we do today, but we'll have nodes that can accommodate any traffic type. We are also creating intelligent edges; we're displacing the smarts for processing service requests, delivering features, and accommodating advanced applications by deploying them at the edge. This allows for more rapid introduction, as well as more customization of the feature sets. The core also has to be multiservice, but it also needs to be able to differentiate between the requirements of the different traffic streams. (See Chapter 10.)

- Next-generation telephony is very important for new entrants, particularly because of the costs of deploying normal local exchanges. A regular local exchange costs in the neighborhood of US$3 million to US$5 million, whereas a media gateway will be on the order of US$100,000. For those seeking to become competitors in the local loop environment, next-generation telephony offers a very cost-effective means of gaining entry. (See Chapter 11.)

- Intelligent networking is being applied to the public data infrastructure as well as the Internet. (See Chapter 10.)

- Network operators are introducing video and multimedia elements, video servers, media farms, video compression, and decompression devices, all of which become part of what constitutes the entire communications network. (See Chapter 10.)

- Access is moving toward the broadband realm on both a wired and a wireless basis. (See Chapter 13, "Broadband Access Solutions.")

For more learning resources, quizzes, and discussion forums on concepts related to this chapter, see www.telecomessentials.com/learningcenter.

Part II

Data Networking Basics

Chapter 6

Data Communications Basics

This chapter explores some of the basics of data communications. It starts with a discussion of the evolution of data communication and then discusses the terminology used to describe different aspects of data networking. It's important to have a good grasp of these basics before wading into deeper waters.

■ The Evolution of Data Communication

Data communication, or *data networking,* is the exchange of digital information between computers and other digital devices via telecommunications nodes and wired or wireless links. To understand the evolution of networking services, it is important to first understand the general computing architectures and traffic types, both of which have changed over time.

Data Communication Architectures

In the rather brief history of data networking, a variety of architectures have arisen, and each has had unique impacts on network variables. Table 6.1 shows a basic time line of the architectures that have prevailed during different periods. Each architecture has slightly different traffic characteristics, has slightly different requirements in terms of security and access control, and has presented a different volume and consistency of traffic to the network. With each new computing architecture, there has been a demand for new generations of network services.

Table 6.1 Time Line of Data Networking Architectures

Time	Architecture
1970s	Stand-alone mainframes
Early 1980s	Networked mainframes
Early 1980s	Stand-alone workstations
Early to late 1980s	Local area networking
Mid-1980s to mid-1990s	LAN internetworking
Mid-1990s	Internet commercialization
Mid- to late 1990s	Application-driven networks
Late 1990s	Remote-access workers
Early 2000s	Home area networking

Stand-alone Mainframes

The 1970s was the era of stand-alone mainframes. These were very hierarchical networks, where certain paths needed to be taken. It was a time of terminal-to-host connectivity. At the bottom of the heap we had smart terminals, and a group of these terminals would report to an upper-level manager, often referred to as a *cluster controller.*

The cluster controller was responsible for managing the traffic flows in and out of its underlying terminals and for scheduling resources upstream from those terminals. In turn, a number of cluster controllers would be managed by yet another level of manager, called the *front-end processor,* which served as the interface between the underlying communications network and the applications stored in the host. That front-end processor ultimately led to the host, where the users' applications resided. In this era, a given terminal could only have access to the host that was upstream from it. If you wanted to make use of applications that resided on another host, you either needed a different terminal or had the pleasure of working with a variety of cables under your desk, changing the connections as needed.

Networked Mainframes

A major change occurred in the early 1980s: People began networking the mainframes. This was called *multidomain networking,* and it enabled one terminal device on a desktop to access numerous hosts that were networked together.

Stand-alone Workstations

Also in the early 1980s, stand-alone workstations began to appear in the enterprise. This did not generally happen because the data processing department had decided that it would move to workstations; rather, it happened because technically astute users began to bring their own workstations into the firm, and then they would ask the data processing or MIS (Management Information Services) department to allow connectivity into the corporate resources from their workstations.

LANs

As independent workstations began to penetrate the corporate environment, we started to study how data was actually being used. We found that 80% of the information being used within a business was coming from within that location, and only 20% was being exchanged with other locations or other entities. This let businesses know that for the majority of their communications, they needed networks that had a limited geographical span, and hence evolved the local area network (LAN). LANs were defined as serving a business address—a given building or at most a campus environment.

A shift began to occur in how the network needed to accommodate data. In the mainframe environment, with its single-terminal-to-host communications, traffic volumes were predictable. The traffic levels between a given terminal and its host were known, so it was possible to make some fairly adequate assumptions about the amount of capacity to provision between those two points. However, in the LAN environment, the traffic patterns were very unpredictable. For example, in a business with 100 PCs on one LAN and 50 PCs on another LAN, the level of traffic on each LAN might change throughout the day. Sometimes it was extremely high volume, sometimes there was nothing going on, and sometimes it was a steady, average stream. This unpredictability introduced a requirement for network services that could be flexible in how they addressed bandwidth requirements (that is, services that could introduce bandwidth on demand). Frame Relay, which is discussed in Chapter 7, "Wide Area Networking," is one such network service. Frame Relay provides the capability to actually provide more bandwidth than you subscribe to, but because the traffic patterns fluctuate, the overall usage should balance out at the end of the day.

So throughout the mid- to late 1980s, the major design emphasis was on deploying LANs, which help to speed up corporate communications, to make the workforce more productive, and to reduce costs associated with the sharing of software and hardware resources.

LAN Internetworking

As LANs were popping up in enterprises all over, it became necessary to come up with a tool for internetworking them. Otherwise, islands of knowledge existed on a given LAN, but these islands couldn't communicate with other departments, clusters, or divisions located elsewhere in the enterprise. LAN internetworking therefore took place throughout the late 1980s and early to mid-1990s, bringing with it the evolution, introduction, and rapid penetration of interconnection devices such as hubs, bridges, routers, and brouters, whose purpose is to internetwork between separate networks.

Internet Commercialization

In the mid-1990s, yet another alternative for data networking came about, with the commercialization of the Internet. Before about 1995, the Internet was mainly available to the academic, research, and government communities. Because it presented a very cost-effective means for data networking, particularly with text-based, bursty data flows, it held a significant appeal for the academic and research community. However, until the introduction of the World Wide Web, the Internet remained largely an academic platform. The intuitive graphical interfaces and navigational controls of the WWW made it of interest to those without UNIX skills. The Internet was particularly useful for applications such as e-mail, for which there was finally one standard that was open enough to enable messaging exchanges between various businesses that used different systems.

Application-Driven Networks

Toward the mid- to late 1990s, we began to see the development of advanced applications, such as videoconferencing, collaboration, multimedia, and media conferencing. This caused another shift in how we thought about deploying networks. In the days of hierarchical networks, decisions about network resources were based on how many devices there were and how far they were away from one another. But when advanced applications—which had great capacity demands and could not tolerate delays or congestion—began to be developed, these applications began to dictate the type of network needed. Therefore, the architecture shifted from being device driven to being application driven.

Remote-Access Workers

In the late 1990s, with the downsizing of information technology (IT) departments, both in terms of physical size and cost, it became much easier to deploy IT resources to the worker than to require the worker to come to the IT resources. Remote access, or teleworking, become a frequently used personnel approach that had advantages in terms of enhanced employee productivity, better morale, and savings in transportation costs. Also, as many large corporations downsized, workers became self-employed and worked from small offices/home offices. This architecture featuring remote-access workers focused on providing appropriate data networking capabilities to people in their homes, in hotels, in airports, and in any other place where they might need to access the network. Facilities were designed specifically to authenticate and authorize remote users and to allow them access to corporate LANs and their underlying resources.

HANs

Today, individuals are increasingly using their residences as places to carry out professional functions, and they increasingly need to network intelligent devices that are used for work, educational, or leisure activities. Therefore, home area networks (HANs) are becoming a new network domain that needs to be addressed; these days we don't need to think about just the last mile, but about the last 328 feet (100 meters)!

Data Communication Traffic

As the architecture of data networks has changed, so have the applications people use, and as applications have changed, so has the traffic on the network. This section talks about some of the most commonly used applications today and how much bandwidth they need, how sensitive they are to delay, where the error control needs to be performed, and how well they can tolerate loss.

The most pervasive, frequently used application is e-mail. Today, it's possible to append an entire family vacation photo album to an e-mail message, and this massive file would require a lot of bandwidth. But e-mail in its generic text-based form is a low-bandwidth application that is delay insensitive. If an e-mail message gets trapped somewhere in the Net for several seconds, its understandability will not be affected because by the time you view it, it will have all been put on the server where your e-mail resides, waiting for you to pick it up. Another issue you have to consider with e-mail is error control. Networks today rarely perform error control because it slows down the traffic too much, so error control and recovery need to be handled at the endpoints. Instead, internetworking protocols deployed at the end node, such as Transmission Control Protocol (TCP), detect errors and request retransmissions to fix them.

Another prevalent data networking application is transaction processing. Examples of transaction processing include a store getting approval for a credit card purchase and a police officer checking a database for your driver's license number to see whether you have any outstanding tickets. Transaction processing is characterized by many short inputs and short outputs, which means it is generally a fairly low-bandwidth application, assuming that it involves text-based messages. Remember that if you add images or video, the bandwidth requirements grow substantially. Thus, if a police officer downloads a photo from your license, the bandwidth required will rise. Transaction processing is very delay sensitive because with transactions you generally have a person waiting for something to be completed (for example, for a reservation to be made, for a sales transaction to be approved, for a seat to be assigned by an airline). Users want subsecond response time, so with transaction processing, delays are very important, and increased traffic contributes to delay. For example, say you're at an airport and your flight is canceled. Everyone queues up to get on another flight. The agents work as quickly as they can, but because of the increased level of traffic as more people all try to get on the one available flight, everything backs up, and you have to wait a long time for a response to get back to you. With transaction processing, you have to be aware of delay, and error control is the responsibility of the endpoints. Transaction processing is fairly tolerant of losses because the applications ensure that all the elements and records associated with a particular transaction have been properly sent and received before committing the transaction to the underlying database.

Another type of application is file transfer, which involves getting a large bulk of data moved from one computer to another. File transfer is generally a high-bandwidth application because it deals with a bulk of data. File transfer is machine-to-machine communication, and the machines can work around delay factors, as long as they're not trying to perform a real-time function based on the information being delivered. So file transfer is a passive activity—it's not driving process control—and it can tolerate delay. File transfer can also tolerate losses. With file transfer, error control can be performed at the endpoints.

Two other important applications are interactive computing and information retrieval. Here bandwidth is dependent on the objects that you are retrieving: If it's text, it's low bandwidth; if it's pictures, good luck in today's environment. Interactive computing and information retrieval are delay sensitive when it comes to downloads, so higher speeds are preferred. Real-time voice is a low-bandwidth application but is extremely delay sensitive. Real-time audio and video require medium, high, and even very high bandwidth, and are extremely delay sensitive. Multimedia traffic and interactive services require very high bandwidth, and they are extremely delay sensitive and extremely loss sensitive.

Anything that is text-based—such as e-mail, transaction processing, file transfer, and even the ability to access a database for text-based information—is fairly tolerant of losses. But in real-time traffic, such as voice, audio, or video, losses cause severe degradation in the application. Going forward for the new generation of networks, the ITU suggests that a network should have no less than 1% packet loss (see www.itu.org), and that's far from the case in today's networks. The public Internet experiences something like 40% packet loss during some times of day.

■ Data Flow

This section discusses some of the important issues that affect data flow in a network:

- ■ The parts of the data circuit that comprises every network, including data terminal equipment (DTE), the data communications (or channel) equipment (DCE), the transmission channel, and the physical interface
- ■ Modems and modulation
- ■ Simplex, half-duplex, and full-duplex data transmission
- ■ Coding schemes
- ■ Asynchronous and synchronous transmission modes
- ■ Error control

The DTE, the DCE, the Transmission Channel, and the Physical Interface

Every data network is a seven-part data circuit: the originating DTE, its physical interface, the originating DCE, the transmission channel, the receiving DCE, its physical interface, and the receiving DTE (see Figure 6.1). The transmission channel is the network service that the user subscribes to with a carrier (for example, a dialup connection with an ISP).

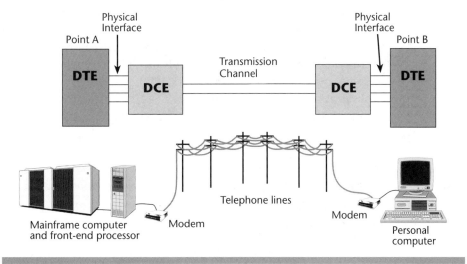

Figure 6.1 The DTE, DCE, transmission channel, and physical interface

The DTE transmits data between two points without error; its main responsibilities are to transmit and receive information and to perform error control. The DTE generally supports the end-user applications program, data files, and databases. The DTE includes any type of computer terminal, including PCs, as well as printers, hosts, front-end processors, multiplexers, and LAN interconnection devices such as routers.

The DCE, on the other hand, provides an interface between the DTE and the transmission channel (that is, between the carrier's networks). The DCE establishes, maintains, and terminates a connection between the DTE and the transmission channel. It is responsible for ensuring that the signal that comes out of the DTE is compatible with the requirements of the transmission channel. So, for instance, with an analog voice-grade line, the DCE would be responsible for translating the digital data coming from the PC into an analog form that could be transmitted over that voice-grade line. A variety of different conversions (for example, digital-to-analog conversion, conversion in voltage levels) might need to take place in a network, depending on the network service. The DCE contains the signal coding that makes these conversions possible. For example, a DCE might have to determine what type of voltage level to attribute to the one bit versus the zero bit. There are rules about how many of one type of bit you can send in a row, and if too many of them are sent in sequence, the network can lose synchronization, and then transmission errors might be introduced. The DCE applies such rules and performs the needed signal conversions. Examples of DCEs include channel service units (CSUs), data service units (DSUs), network termination units, PBX data terminal interfaces, and modems. DCEs all perform essentially the same generic function, but the names differ, depending on the type of network service to which they're attached.

Another part of a data network is the physical interface, which defines how many pins are in the connector, how many wires are in the cable, and what signal is being carried over which of the pins and over which of the wires, to ensure that the information is being viewed compatibly. In Figure 6.1, the lines that join the DTE and DCE together represent the physical interface. There are many different forms of physical interfaces; for example, an RS-232 is used frequently for asynchronous communications and a V.35 is often used with synchronous communications.

Modems and Modulation

No discussion of data communications is complete without a discussion of modulation. As mentioned in Chapter 2, "Telecommunications Technology Fundamentals," the term *modem* is a contraction of the terms *modulate* and *demodulate,* and these terms refer to the fact that a modem alters a carrier signal based on whether it is transmitting a one or a zero. Digital transmission requires the use of modulation schemes, which are sometimes also called *line-coding techniques.* Modulation schemes infuse the digital information onto the transmission medium (see Figure 6.2). Over time, many modulation schemes have been developed, and they vary in the speed at which they operate, the quality of wire they require, their immunity to noise, and their complexity. The variety of modulation schemes means that incompatibilities exist.

Components of Modulation Schemes
Modems can permute any of the three main characteristics of analog wave forms—amplitude, frequency, and phase—to encode information (see Figure 6.3):

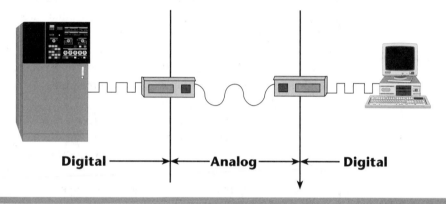

Figure 6.2 Modems

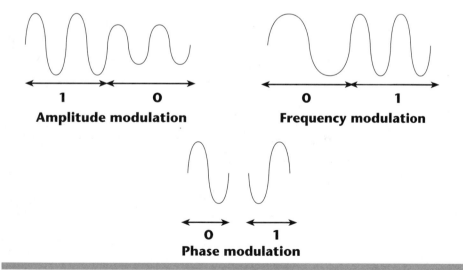

Figure 6.3 Amplitude, frequency, and phase modulation

- **Amplitude modulation**—A modem that relies on amplitude modulation might associate ones with a high amplitude and zeros with a low amplitude. A compatible receiving modem can discriminate between the two bits and properly interpret them so that the receiving device can reproduce the message correctly.

- **Frequency modulation**—A frequency modulation-based modem alters the frequency value, so in Figure 6.3, zero represents a low frequency and one represents a high frequency; a complementary modem discriminates based on the frequency at which it receives the signal.

- **Phase modulation**—Phase modulation refers to the position of the wave form at a particular instant in time, so we could have a 90-degree phase, a 180-degree phase, or a 270-degree phase. A phase modulation-based modem uses the phases to differentiate between ones and zeros, so, for example, zeros can be transmitted beginning at a 90-degree phase and ones may be transmitted beginning at a 270-degree phase.

Thus, by using the three characteristics of a wave form, a modem can encode multiple bits within a single cycle of the wave form (see Figure 6.4). The more of these variables the modem can detect, the greater the bit rate it can produce.

Modulation schemes also vary in their *spectral efficiency,* which is a measure of the number of digital bits that can be encoded in a single cycle of a wave form. The duration of a single cycle of a wave form is called the *symbol time.* To get more bits

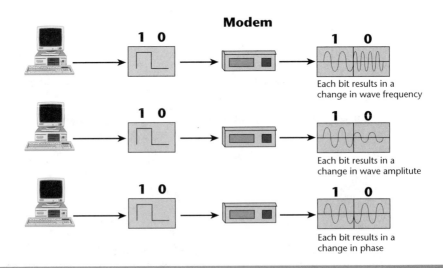

Figure 6.4 Signal modulation

per Hertz, many modulation techniques provide more voltage levels. To encode k bits in the same symbol time, 2^k voltage levels are required. It becomes more difficult for the receiver to discriminate among many voltage levels with consistent precision as the speed increases. So it becomes a challenge to discriminate at a very high data rate. (Chapter 14, "Wireless Communications," talks more about spectrum reuse.)

Categories of Modulation Schemes

There are several different categories of modulation schemes. The first one is called the *single-carrier modulation scheme*, in which a single channel occupies the entire bandwidth. The second category is the *multicarrier modulation scheme*, which uses and aggregates a certain amount of bandwidth and then subdivides it into subbands. Each subband is encoded by using a single-carrier technique, and bit streams from the subbands are bonded together at the receiver. This allows us to avoid placing any bits on portions of the frequency band that may be subject to noise and might result in distortion. Multicarrier techniques became possible with the development of digital signal processing (DSP). Table 6.2 lists some of the most commonly used modulation schemes, and the following sections describe them in more detail.

Table 6.2   Single-Carrier and Multicarrier Modulation Schemes

Scheme	Description
Single-Carrier	
2B1Q	Used with ISDN, IDSL, and HDSL.
QAM 64	Used with North American and European digital cable for forward (that is, downstream) channels.
QAM 256	Used with North American digital cable for forward (that is, downstream) channels.
QAM 16	Used with U.S. digital cable for reverse (that is, upstream) channels.
QPSK	Used in U.S. digital cable for reverse (that is, upstream) channels, as well as in direct broadcast satellite.
CAP	Used in some ADSL deployments.
Multicarrier	
DMT	Used within ADSL and is a preferred technique because it provides good quality.
OFDM	Used in European digital over-the-air broadcast.

Single-Carrier Modulation Schemes   The single-carrier scheme Quadrature Amplitude Modulation (QAM) modulates both the amplitude and phase. Because it uses both amplitude and phase, QAM yields a higher spectral efficiency than does 2B1Q, which means it provides more bits per second. The number of levels of amplitude and the number of phase angles are a function of line quality. Cleaner lines translate into more spectral efficiency or more bits per Hz. Various levels of QAM exist, and they are referred to as QAM *nn*, where *nn* indicates the number of states per Hertz. The number of bits per symbol time is *k*, where $2^k = nn$. So, 4 bits/Hz is equivalent to QAM 16, 6 bits/Hz is equivalent to QAM 64, and 8 bits/Hz is equivalent to QAM 256. As you can see, QAM has vastly improved throughput as compared to earlier techniques such as 2B1Q, which provided only 2 bits/Hz.

Quadrature Phase Shift Keying (QPSK) is another single-carrier scheme. It is equivalent to QAM 4, with which you get 2 bits per symbol time. QPSK is designed to operate in harsh environments, such as over-the-air transmission and cable TV return paths. Because of its robustness and relatively low complexity, QPSK is widely used in cases such as direct broadcast satellite. Although QPSK does not provide as many bits per second as some other schemes, it ensures quality in implementations where interference could be a problem.

Carrierless Amplitude Modulation/Phase Modulation (CAP) is another single-carrier scheme. CAP combines amplitude and phase modulation, and it is one of the early techniques used for ADSL. However, we have found that portions of the band over which ADSL operates conduct noise from exterior devices such as ham radios and CB radios, so if these devices are operating while you're on a call over an ADSL line, you experience static in the voice call or corrupted bits in a data session. Consequently, CAP is no longer the preferred technique with ADSL because it provides a rather low quality of service. (ADSL is discussed in Chapter 3, "Transmission Media: Characteristics and Applications," and in Chapter 13, "Broadband Access Solutions.")

Multicarrier Modulation Schemes   Discrete Multitone (DMT) is a multicarrier scheme that allows variable spectral efficiency among the subbands it creates. Therefore, it is used in wireline media, where noise characteristics of each wire might differ, as in the wires used to carry xDSL facilities.Because spectral efficiency can be optimized for each individual wire with DMT, DMT has become the preferred choice for use with ADSL.

Orthogonal Frequency Division Multiplexing (OFDM) is another multicarrier technique, and it uses a common modulation technique for each subband. OFDM is generally used in over-the-air broadcast, where all subbands are presumed to have uniform noise characteristics, and it is predominantly used in Europe, although some emerging techniques in the United States plan to make use of OFDM.

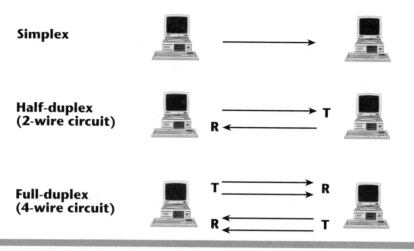

Figure 6.5 Simplex, half-duplex, and full-duplex data transmission

Simplex, Half-Duplex, and Full-Duplex Data Transmission

The direction of information flow takes three forms: simplex, half-duplex, and full-duplex (see Figure 6.5).

Simplex means that you can transmit information in one direction only. Of course simplex does not have great appeal to today's business communications, which involve a two-way exchange. Nonetheless, there are many applications of simplex circuits, such as a doorbell at your home. When someone presses the button, a signal goes to the chimes, and nothing returns over that pair of wires. Another example of a simplex application is an alarm circuit. If someone opens a door he's not authorized to open, a signal is sent out over the wires to the security desk, but nothing comes back over the wires.

Half-duplex means you can transmit information in two directions, but in only one direction at a time (for example, with a pair of walkie-talkies). Half-duplex is associated with two-wire circuits, which have one path to carry information and a second wire or path to complete the electrical loop. In half-duplex we can communicate in both directions, but we can use only one direction at a time. As a result, there has to be a procedure for manipulating who's seen as the transmitter and who's seen as the receiver, and there has to be a way to reverse who acts as the receiver and who acts as the transmitter. Line turnarounds handle these reversals, but they add overhead to a session because the devices undertake a dialog to determine who is the transmitter and who is the receiver. For communication that involves much back-and-forth exchange of data, half-duplex is an inefficient way of communicating.

Full-duplex, also referred to simply as *duplex*, involves a four-wire circuit, and it provides the capability to communicate in two directions simultaneously. There's an individual transmit and receive path for each end of the conversation. Therefore, no line turnarounds are required, which means full-duplex offers the most efficient form of data communication. All digital services are provisioned on a four-wire circuit and hence provide full-duplex capabilities.

Coding Schemes: ASCII, EBCDIC, Unicode, and Beyond

A *coding scheme* is a pattern of bits that are used to represent the characters in a character set, as well as carriage returns and other keyboard functions. Over time, different computer manufacturers and consortiums have introduced different coding schemes. The most commonly used coding schemes are ASCII, EBCDIC, and Unicode.

The American Standard Code for Information Interchange (ASCII) is probably the most familiar coding scheme. ASCII has seven information bits per character, and it has one additional bit that's a control bit, called a *parity bit,* that is used for purposes of error detection. In ASCII, seven ones or zeros are bundled together to represent each character. A total of 128 characters (that is, 2^7, for the *seven* bits of information per character and the two possible values of each character) can be represented in ASCII coding.

At about the same time that the whole world agreed on ASCII as a common coding scheme, IBM introduced its own proprietary scheme, called Extended Binary Coded Decimal Interchange Code (EBCDIC). EBCDIC involves eight bits of information per character and no control bits. Therefore, you can represent 256 possible characters (that is, 2^8) with EBCDIC. This sounds like a lot of characters, but it's not enough to handle all the characters needed in the languages throughout the world. Complex Asian languages, for instance, can include up to 60,000 characters.

In Table 6.3, you can see that the uppercase letter A in ASCII coding looks quite different than it does in EBCDIC. This could be a source of incompatibility. If your workstation is coded in ASCII and you're trying to communicate with a host that's looking for EBCDIC, you will end up with garbage on your screen because your machine will not be able to understand the alphabet that the host is using.

Table 6.3   ASCII Versus EBCDIC

Character or Symbol	ASCII	EBCDIC
A	1000001	11000001
K	1001011	11010010
M	1001101	11010100
2	0110010	11110010
Carriage return	0001101	00010101

In the mid-1980s, a coding scheme called Unicode was formed. Unicode assigns 16 bits per character (that is, 2^{16}), which translates to more than 65,000 possible characters. But can you imagine a terminal with 60,000 keys to press? Despite its breadth, Unicode has not become an overriding standard for those who use complex languages.

Most people now believe that the best way to handle coding is to use natural language interfaces, such as voice recognition. By 2008 or 2009, natural language interfaces are expected to be the most common form of data entry. But until we get there, you should know that there are different coding schemes because they could be a potential source of incompatibility in a network and you therefore need to consider conversion between schemes. Conversion could be performed by a network element on the customer premise, or it could be a function that a network provider offers. In fact, the early packet-switched X.25 networks provided code conversion as a value-added feature.

Transmission Modes: Asynchronous and Synchronous Transmission

Another concept to be familiar with is the distinction between transmission modes. To appreciate the distinction, let's look at the historical time line again. The first type of terminals that were introduced were dumb terminals. They had no processing capabilities and no memories. They had no clocking references, so the only way they could determine where to find the beginning or the end of a character was by framing the character with start and stop bits. These systems used *asynchronous transmission,* in which one character is transmitted at a time, at a variable speed (that is, the speed depends on things such as how quickly you type or whether you stop to answer the phone). Asynchronous transmission uses a start bit and a stop bit with each character. In addition, asynchronous communication typically deals with ASCII-encoded information, which means a third control bit, a parity bit, needs to be accounted for. These extra control bits add up to fairly significant overhead. In essence, asynchronous transmission has 30% inefficiency because for every seven bits of information, there are three bits of control. Another disadvantage of asynchronous transmission is that it operates at comparatively low speeds; today, in general, it operates at about 115,000bps.

Synchronous transmission emerged in the late 1960s, when IBM introduced its interactive processing line, which included smart terminals. These smart terminals could process information and use algorithms; for example, a terminal could use an algorithm on a message block to determine what it was composed of and in that way very succinctly detect and check for errors. Smart terminals were also smart in the sense that they had buffers, so they could accumulate the characters that you were typing in until they had a big block of them that they could send all at one time. Smart terminals also had clocking devices, whereby on one pair of wires, a clocking pulse could be sent from the transmitter to the receiver. The receiver would lock in on that clocking pulse, and it could determine that with every clocking pulse it saw on one wire, it would have a bit of information present on the other wire. Therefore, the receiver could use the clocking pulse to simply count off the bits to determine where the beginning and the end of the character were, rather than actually having to frame each character with a start and a stop bit. Synchronous transmission, in classic data communications, implied that you were sending information a block at a time at a fixed speed.

Another benefit of synchronous transmission is very tight error control. As mentioned earlier, smart terminals have processors and can apply mathematical algorithms to a block. By calculating the contents of that block, the terminal comes up with a 16- or 32-bit code that identifies the structure of the block's contents. The terminal adds this code to the end of the block and sends it to the receiver. The receiver performs the same map on the block, and it comes up with its own 16- or 32-bit code. The receiver then compares its code with the one the terminal sent, and if they match, the receiver sends an ACK, a positive acknowledgment that everything's okay, and it moves on to sending the next block. If the two codes don't match, the receiver sends a NACK, a negative acknowledgment, which says there was an error in transmission and the previous block needs to be resent before anything else can happen. If that error is not corrected within some number of attempts that the user specifies, the receiver will disengage the session. This ensures that errors are not introduced. Yet another benefit of synchronous transmission is that it operates at higher speeds than asynchronous transmission, and today you commonly see it performing at 2Mbps.

These two types of transmission make sense in different applications. For machine-to-machine communications where you want to take advantage of high speeds and you want to guarantee accuracy in the data flow—such as electronic funds transfer—synchronous communication is best. On the other hand, in a situation in which a human is accessing a database or reading today's horoscope, speed may not be of the essence and error control may not be critical, so the lower-cost asynchronous method would be appropriate.

Keep in mind that things are never simple in telecom, and you rarely deal with simple alternatives; rather, you deal with layers and combinations of issues. Consider the following human example. You can think of an escalator as being a synchronous network. The steps are presented at the same rate consistently, and they all travel up the ramp at the same speed. Passengers alight on steps, and all passengers are carried through that network at the same speed; therefore, the network is synchronous. However, each passenger alights on the escalator at a different rate, which makes the access to the network asynchronous. For example, an eight-year-old child might run up to the escalator at high speed and jump straight onto the third step. Behind that child might be an injured athlete with a cane, who cautiously waits while several stair pass, until he feels confident that he's going to step on the center of the stair. So people get on the escalator at varying rates and in different places; there is not consistent timing that determines their presence, and therefore the access onto the escalator is asynchronous.

Now let's put this human analogy into telecommunications terms. The escalator scenario describes the modern broadband network. SDH/SONET is a synchronous network infrastructure. When bits get into an SDH/SONET frame, they all travel at OC-3 or OC-12 or one of the other line rates that SDH/SONET supports. But access onto that network might be asynchronous, through an ATM switch, where a movie might be coming in like a fire hose of information through one interface and next to it a dribble of text-based e-mail is slowly coming in. One stream of bits comes in quickly and one comes in slowly, but when they get packaged together into a frame for transport over the fiber, they're all transported at the same rate.

Error Control

Error control, which is a process of detecting and correcting errors, takes a number of forms, the two most common of which are parity checking and cyclical redundancy checking.

In ASCII-based terminals, which use asynchronous transmission, most often the error control is parity checking. *Parity checking* is a simple process of adding up the bit values to come up with a common value, either even or odd. It doesn't matter which one, but once you've selected either even or odd, every terminal must be set to that value. Let's say we're using odd parity. If you look at Character #1 in Figure 6.6, and add up the bits for it, you see that they equal 2, which is an even number. We need odd parity, so the terminal inserts a 1 bit to make that a 3, which is an odd number. For Character #2 the bits add up to 3, so the terminal

Bit Position	Information Character					
	#1	#2	#3	#4	#5	#6
1	0	1	0	0	1	0
2	1	0	0	0	0	1
3	0	0	1	1	0	1
4	0	1	1	1	1	0
5	0	0	0	0	1	1
6	1	1	1	1	1	0
7	0	0	0	1	1	0
Parity bit	**1**	**0**	**0**	**1**	**0**	**0**

Figure 6.6 Parity checking

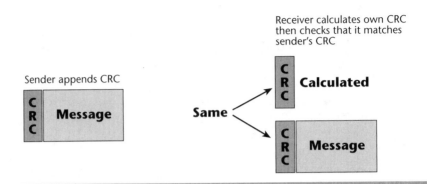

Figure 6.7 Cyclical redundancy checking

inserts a 0 as a parity bit to maintain the odd value. The terminal follows this pattern with each of the six characters, and then it sends all the bits across the network to the receiver. The receiver then adds up the bits the same way the terminal did, and if they equal an odd number, the receiver assumes that everything has arrived correctly. If they don't equal an odd number, the receiver knows that there is a problem but cannot correct the problem—and this is the trouble with parity checking. To determine that an error had occurred, you would have to look at the output report, and therefore errors can easily go unnoticed. Thus, parity checking is not the best technique when it comes to ensuring the correctness of information.

Synchronous terminals and transmission uses a type of error control called *cyclical redundancy checking* (see Figure 6.7). This is the method mentioned earlier in the chapter, whereby the entire message block is run through a mathematical algorithm. A cyclical redundancy check (CRC) code is appended to the message, and the message is sent to the receiver. The receiver recalculates the message block and compares the two CRCs. If they match, the communication continues, and if they don't match, the receiver either requests retransmissions until the problem is fixed or it disengages the session if it is not capable of being fixed within some predetermined timeframe.

■ The OSI Reference Model and Protocols

Before two computers or network devices can exchange information, they must establish communication, and this is where protocols come in. A network protocol enables two devices to communicate by using one set of rules. The OSI model and protocol standards help to ensure that networking devices are capable of working together over a network.

The OSI Reference Model

In the early 1970s, a problem was brewing. There were many different computer manufacturers, and there were many incompatibilities among them. Furthermore, each manufacturer created different product lines, and even within one company there were often incompatibilities between their product lines. So the International Standards Organization got involved and created the Open Systems Interconnection (OSI) reference model, which is a reference blueprint for device manufacturers and software developers to use when creating products.

The OSI model, shown in Figure 6.8, has seven layers that describe the tasks that must be performed to transfer information on a network. When data is being transferred over a network, it must pass through each layer of the OSI model. As the data passes through each layer, information is added to that data. At the destination, the additional information is removed. Layers 4 through 7 occur at the end node, and Layers 1 through 3 are the most important to telecommunications networks.

It's important to understand that this model is exactly that—a model. It's a conceptual framework that is useful for describing the necessary functions required of a network device or member. No actual networking product implements the model precisely as described.

Layer 7, the application layer, is responsible for exchanging information between the programs that are running on a computer and other services on a network. This

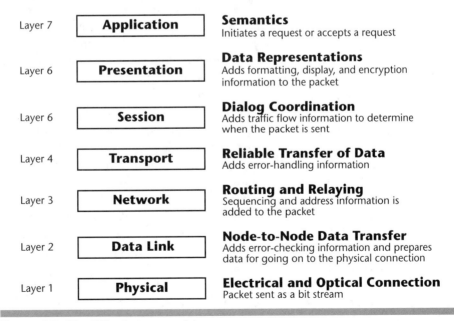

Figure 6.8 The OSI reference model

layer supports application and end-user processes. It acts as a window for applications to access network services. It handles general network access, flow control, error recovery, and file transfer. Examples of application layer protocols include File Transfer Protocol (FTP), Telnet, Simple Mail Transfer Protocol (SMTP), and Hypertext Transfer Protocol (HTTP).

Layer 6, the presentation layer, formats information so that a software application can read it. It performs transformations on the data to provide a standardized application interface and common communication services. It offers services such as encryption, compression, and reformatting. The presentation layer adds a field in each packet that tells how the information within the packet is encoded. It indicates whether any compression has been performed and, if it has, it indicates what type of compression, so that the receiver can decompress it properly. It also indicates whether there has been any encryption, and if there has, it indicates what type, so that the receiver can properly decrypt it. The presentation layer ensures that the transmitter and receiver are seeing the information in the same format.

Layer 5, the session layer, supports connections between sessions and handles administrative tasks and security. It establishes and monitors connections between computers, and it provides the control structure for communication between applications. Examples of session layer protocols include NetBIOS, DSN, and Lightweight Directory Access Protocol (LDAP).

Layer 4, the transport layer, corrects transmission errors and ensures that the information is delivered reliably. It provides an end-to-end error recovery and flow control capability. It deals with packet handling, repackaging of messages, division of messages into smaller packets, and error handling. Examples of transport layer protocols include Transmission Control Protocol (TCP), User Datagram Protocol (UDP), and Sequenced Packet Exchange (SPX).

Layer 3, the networking layer, identifies computers on a network and determines how to direct information transfer over that network. In other words, it is a routing and relaying layer. It defines how to move information between networks as well as between devices. The key responsibility of this layer is to add the addressing information and the control functions needed to move the data through the network and its intermediate nodes. It is involved in establishing, maintaining, and terminating connections, including packet switching, routing, data congestion, reassembly of data, and translation of logical addresses to physical addresses. Examples of networking layer protocols are X.25, Internet Protocol (IP), Internetwork Packet Exchange (IPX), and Message Transform Program 3 (MTP3).

Layer 2, the data-link layer, groups data into containers to prepare that data for transfer over a network. It puts the ones and zeros into a container that allows the movement of information between two devices on this same network. The protocols at this layer specify the rules that must be followed in transmitting a single frame between one device and another over a single data link. Bits are packaged into frames of data, and they include the necessary synchronization, error control, and flow control information. Examples of data link layer protocols in a LAN environment include Ethernet, Token Ring, and Fiber Distributed Data Interface (FDDI). Examples of data-link layer protocols in a WAN environment include Frame Relay and ATM. Examples of data-link layer protocols within the PSTN are Signaling System 7 and MTP2.

Layer 1, the physical layer, defines how a transmission medium connects to a computer, as well as how electrical or optical information is transferred on the transmission medium. The physical layer defines the types of cables or wireless interfaces that are allowed, the voltage levels used to represent the bits or the optical levels, the types of connectors that are allowed, and the types of transmission rates that can be supported. Every network service and every network device has definitions at the physical layer in terms of what it can physically interface with. For example, the physical layer deals with unshielded twisted-pair (UTP) and shielded twisted-pair (STP), coax, 10BaseT (an Ethernet standard that allows the use of twisted-pair to support 10Mbps to the desktop), multimode fiber and single-mode fiber, xDSL, ISDN, and the various capacities in the PDH (for example, DS-1/DS-3, E-1/E-3) and SDH/SONET (for example, OC-1 through OC-192) networks.

Protocols and Protocol Stacks

Protocols are the hardware or software components that carry out the OSI model guidelines for transferring information on a network. A protocol may be one component or a collection of components that carry out a task. A protocol stack, or protocol suite, is made up of multiple protocols that are used to exchange information between computers. One protocol in the stack might be used to specify how network interface cards (NICs) communicate, and another might specify how a computer reads information from the NIC. Figure 6.9 shows the TCP protocol stack and how it relates to the OSI model.

For More Protocol Information

The Web site www.protocols.com provides easy-to-understand information about protocols.

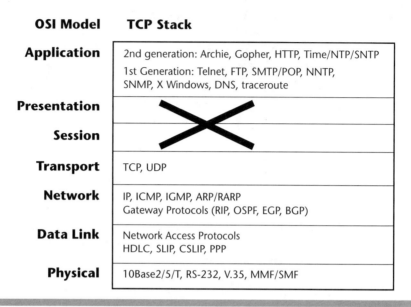

Figure 6.9 The OSI model versus the TCP/IP stack

A *layer* is a section of a protocol stack that is responsible for performing one particular aspect of information transfer. Because some protocols are capable of performing one function, one layer in a protocol stack may not necessarily correspond to one layer in the OSI model. *Tunneling* describes the process of using a protocol to transfer information through a network, using a different type of protocol.

For more learning resources, quizzes, and discussion forums on concepts related to this chapter, see www.telecomessentials.com/learningcenter.

Chapter 7

Wide Area Networking

A *wide area network* (WAN) is a group of computer networks that are connected over long distances by telecommunications links, which can be either wireline or wireless. A number of WAN links can be used, each of which was developed to address specific requirements in data communications. To meet specific network and application needs, a number of WAN techniques (whether deployed over public or private networks) have been developed and become popular over the years. Leased lines offer the greatest network management control. With leased lines, a known amount of bandwidth is provisioned, and no one else has access to it; also, you know who the users are. The disadvantage is that leased lines are very costly, you pay a premium for the comfort of having control over your own destiny.

To reduce the costs associated with leased lines, many customers migrate to Frame Relay services. Frame Relay was introduced in the early 1990s and was largely designed as an application for LAN-to-LAN interconnection. Because numerous subscribers share its virtual circuits, Frame Relay offers great cost-efficiency as compared to leased lines. Another WAN alternative to leased lines is Asynchronous Transfer Mode (ATM), which is perhaps the best solution, especially in environments that have intensive multimedia applications or other high-bandwidth applications. Virtual private networks (VPNs) are increasingly being used in WANs as well.

A *data service* is a digital service offered for data communications at subscriber locations. Remember that data communication was essentially an add-on to the public switched telephone network (PSTN). As we began to introduce options designed for data, we needed to introduce into networks specialized equipment that was meant for such service (see Figure 7.1). The end user needed data terminal

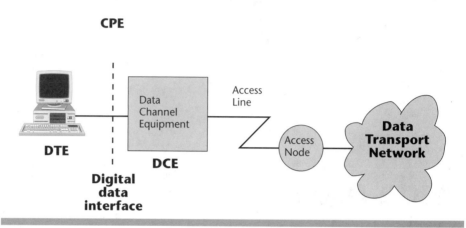

Figure 7.1 Data service components

equipment (DTE) at the customer premise, as well as a physical interface to data communications, or data channel, equipment (DCE). From that DCE there would be an access link into a specific access node, designed to facilitate the data service in question (for example, a digital switching hub for a digital data service [DDS] over leased lines, a unique X.25 packet switch for X.25 services).

Despite the fact that there are numerous WAN options, all of which can offer various cost-efficiencies or performance improvements, the many separate networks in use translate into high costs associated with the overall infrastructure—for both the end user and the operator. One goal of WANs today is to integrate voice, data, and video traffic so that it runs through a common platform (in terms of access nodes) and through a common core network (in terms of the transport infrastructure). For example, the goal of ATM is to provide an integrated broadband infrastructure that minimizes the range of required equipment that needs to be maintained on an ongoing basis.

All the various WAN options can be put into two major categories of data networks: circuit-switched and packet-switched networks. This chapter discusses the categories and characteristics of WANs. It covers the use of circuit-switched WAN options—leased lines and Integrated Services Digital Network (ISDN)—as well as packet-switching WAN options—X.25, Frame Relay, and ATM.

■ Circuit-Switched Networks

There are two main types of circuit-switched WANs: those based on leased lines and customer premises equipment (CPE) to manage the leased lines, and those based on ISDN, including both Basic Rate Interface (BRI) and Primary Rate Interface (PRI).

Leased Lines

Leased lines can be configured in one of two ways. The first approach uses point-to-point leased lines, as shown in Figure 7.2. In this approach, a communications link joins two nodes—and only two nodes. The good thing about this setup, of course, is that there is no contention. The two devices always have an available communications path. The disadvantage becomes pronounced when the network starts to grow, either in the number of devices or in the distance between the locations. Because leased lines are calculated on a mileage-sensitive basis, the cost increases as the network scope increases.

To increase the cost-efficiency of a leased-line network, you can use a multipoint leased-line network, in which you have a shared communications facility where multiple nodes vie for access to the communications link. The advantage of this configuration is that it combines mileage, so the overall monthly cost associated with the leased line is reduced. The disadvantage is that you must introduce some type of intelligent scheme that allows you to determine which device gets to use the communications pathway at what time. Figure 7.3 shows a multipoint leased-line network.

Leased lines, then, are configured on a point-to-point or on a multipoint basis. This can be accomplished by using a number of approaches, including these:

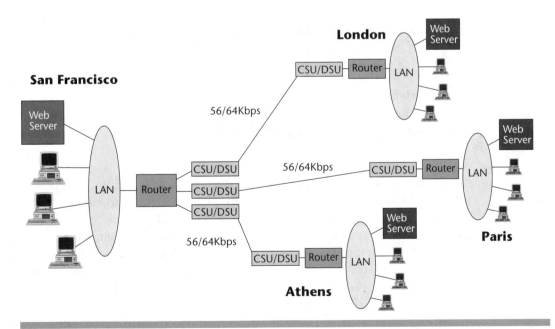

Figure 7.2   Point-to-point leased lines

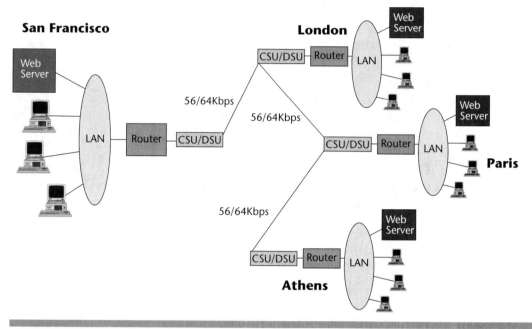

Figure 7.3 Multipoint leased-line network

- DDSs, which essentially use 56Kbps or 64Kbps leased lines
- T-, E-, or J-carrier backbone
- SDH/SONET backbone
- Dark fiber backbone

The following sections describe these approaches.

DDSs

A DDS uses leased lines that operate at either 56Kbps or 64Kbps, depending on whether you are being served over a T-, E-, or J-carrier infrastructure. Figure 7.4 illustrates the equipment associated with a DDS network. Two pieces of equipment are located at the customer site: the DTE (for example, host computers, routers) and DCE (for example, the data service unit [DSU]), which are connected to one another via a physical interface (for example, an RS-232, a V.35). The data access line (that is, the 56Kbps or 64Kbps facility) runs from the DCE to a specialized DDS hub that is a digital circuit switch. (Remember that when this service was introduced, local exchanges were analog, so in order to introduce DDS into a metropolitan area, the telcos had to put into the exchange environment a specific digital circuit-switched hub for those services.) The DDS hubs connect into the digital

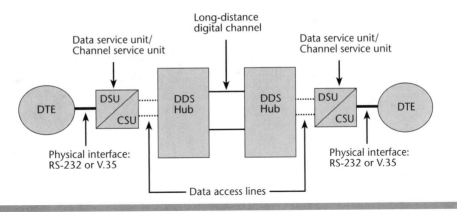

Figure 7.4 DDS equipment

transport network; destination cities attach to the network the same way, using the same equipment configurations.

The DSU is a device that connects various DTE together via RS-232 or V.35 interfaces with the digital services that offer 56Kbps or 64Kbps access. DSUs can be used to accommodate DDS, Frame Relay, and ATM facilities. When the DSU is combined with a channel service unit (CSU), it interfaces with services at the 64Kbps level, as well as $n \times 64$Kbps, up to either T-1, E-1, or J-1 capacities. (These levels are described in detail in Chapter 5, "The PSTN.") The DSU converts the binary data pulse it receives from the DTE to the bipolar format required by the network. Within the computer, the one bits are positive voltages, and the zero bits are no voltages or low-level voltages. The *ones density rule* says that if you transmit more than 15 zeros in a row, the network may lose synchronization, which means transmission errors could occur. Therefore, the DSU performs a bipolar variation—it alternates the one bits as positive and as negative voltages. The DSU also supplies the transmit and receive logic, as well as the timing. The CSU provides a means to perform diagnostics.

DDS facilities can be used for LAN interconnection, access to the Internet, and remote PC access to local hosts. One thing to bear in mind with a traditional DDS approach is that it is a leased-line service. If the leased line goes down, the network is out of service, and recovering the service can be a lengthy process, depending on how many network providers are associated with the link end-to-end. The mere process of troubleshooting and identifying within whose network the problem lies can often lead to resolution times of 24 to 48 hours—or even more, if network managers do not cooperate with one another. If you rely on the DDS network for critical applications, you need a backup in the event that the leased line fails at some point, and the best backup option is generally *switched digital access,* which is a dialup option in which facilities are allocated based on demand rather than being associated with a specific customer all the time. Switched digital access supports

Videoconferencing Data Rates

Switched 384Kbps data rate can support full-motion videoconferencing, which requires a frame rate of 30 frames per second. Below a 384Kbps data rate, the frame rate begins to drop to only 10 to 15 frames per second, and jerky video results. Therefore, enterprises that require applications such as full-motion videoconferencing are often interested in services that offer 384Kbps.

transmission rates of 56Kbps, 64Kbps, 384Kbps, and 1,536Kbps. Another potential backup is ISDN, which is described later in this chapter.

T-, E-, and J-Carrier Backbone

In the 1980s, as networks, traffic, and applications were evolving and growing, customers saw a rise in the amount of data traffic they were carrying, and they began to institute various data services to address those, but this resulted in a hodgepodge of single-purpose networks based on leased lines that included unique universes of equipment or specific applications.

For example, Figure 7.5 shows that you have a variety of networks under operation: Both point-to-point and multipoint leased lines are being used to provide

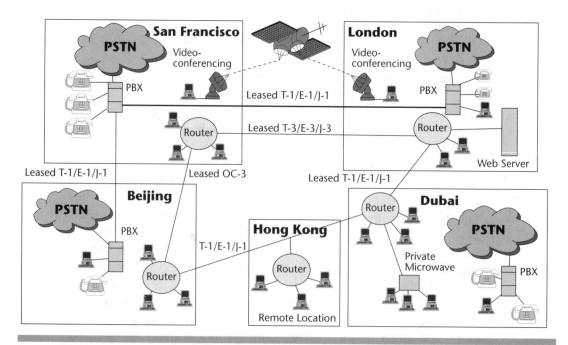

Figure 7.5   Single-purpose leased-line networks

Fractional Services

Some locations may be too small to justify a full T-1 or E-1 facility. In those cases, fractional services can be used; they allow you to subscribe to capacity in small bundles of 56Kbps or 64Kbps channels, which are generally provided in increments of four channels. These are referred to as fractional T-1 (FT-1) and fractional E-1 (FE-1) services.

connectivity between LANs in various cities around the world. The PBXs for the most part are relying on the PSTN, but there is a leased line between San Francisco and London because of the volume of traffic and security requirements. The video-conferencing systems between San Francisco and London make use of a specially provisioned satellite link. In essence, there are four separate networks, you're paying for four different infrastructures, and you don't have complete connectivity between all the locations, users, and resources. You therefore want to build an enterprise backbone network that ties together everybody with one common infrastructure and that provides for more fluid connectivity between the various locations and applications. This requires intelligent equipment at each location, to manage the transmission resource and to properly allocate the capacity to voice, data, image, video, fax, or other forms of transmissions.

The facilities used to transport the information on this revised network can be combinations of privately owned and leased facilities, but the equipment to manage those transmission facilities is owned and managed by the customer. You might be leasing a T-1 or an E-1 from a network operator, or you might be leasing dark fiber from a railroad company. Between some locations, you might deploy a privately owned digital microwave system. You can integrate what used to be four separate networks into one cohesive backbone (see Figure 7.6). In terms of the capacities and components that would then be used within that backbone, the majority of customers today would rely on the dimensions that are deliverable from the T-, E-, and J-carrier infrastructure, although early adopters, and those with high levels of visual information processing, are already migrating to the optical carrier levels of the SDH/SONET hierarchy.

The customer needs the following equipment to manage the transmission facilities (refer to Figure 5.5 in Chapter 5):

- **Transmission media**—The customer might be using copper twisted-pairs with T-1 or E-1 and might be using higher-bandwidth media such as coax, microwave, or fiber with T-3 or E-3 capacities. These are four-wire circuits operating in full-duplex, which means that you can communicate in both directions simultaneously.

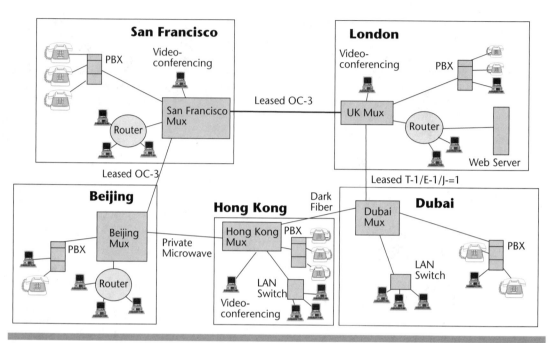

Figure 7.6 An enterprise backbone network

■ **CSU**—The CSU terminates each end of the T-1/E-1 or J-1 carrier facility. The CSU equalizes the received signal, filters the transmitted and received wave forms, and interacts with the customer's, as well as the carrier's, test facility so that diagnostics can be performed. Essentially, the CSU is used to set up the T-1/E-1/J-1 line with a customer-owned PBX, channel banks as stand-alone devices, intelligent multiplexers (for example, T-, E-, or J-carrier multiplexers), and any other DS-*x*/CEPT-*x*–compliant DTE, such as digital cross-connects.

■ **Time-Division Multiplexers**—One type of mux, channel banks, consolidate the individual channels: 24 channels are associated with T-1, and 32 channels are associated with E-1. These voice and data channels are 64Kbps each, and they can be aggregated onto a higher-speed transmission line. Channel banks were designed to accept analog input, so if there is an analog switch either at the PBX or at the local exchange, that analog signal can be digitized, using Pulse Code Modulation (PCM), as described in Chapter 5. The channel banks provide a first level of aggregation. Beyond that, the customer might want to migrate to higher bandwidth, which would involve using T-1/T-3, E-1/E-3 multiplexers. (Refer to Chapter 5 for a description of the rates associated with the various digital signal levels.)

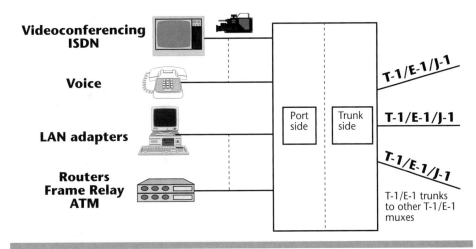

Figure 7.7 T-1/T-3 and E-1/E-3 muxes

The most important piece of equipment in building out the enterprise backbone network is the intelligent multiplexers because they act dynamically to manage transmission resources. They allow you to make on-the-fly decisions about who is allocated the capacity, how much capacity needs to be allocated to each user, and whether individual users have rights to access the resource they want to access. As shown in Figure 7.7, the intelligent muxes basically form a smart computer. An intelligent mux has a port side to which you interface the universe of information resources, which could be the videoconferencing systems, or the voice systems, or the variety of data universe that you have. On the trunk side, you terminate the T-1s/E-1s or T-3s/E-3s.

Inside the muxes are databases that allow you to make decisions in real-time. One of the greatest benefits of managing your own bandwidth between locations is that you can use that bandwidth as you need it. There are two ways you can use T-, E-, or J-carrier facilities. First, you can use them as an access pipe. For example, you can use a T-1 to access the local exchange and to replace combined voice and data trunks. When you are using it to access the PSTN, you have to work within the subscribed standards. For example, with T-1 you get 24 channels at 64Kbps per channel, so if you have only a little bit of data to send, you can't reallocate your extra bandwidth to another application. You are stuck with static bandwidth allocation (see Figure 7.8), either twenty-four 64Kbps channels or one 1,536Kbps channel.

A second way in which you can use T-, E-, or J-carrier facilities is to build a private network. For example, if you use a T-1/E-1 to tie together two of your own locations, then basically you can do as you wish with that pipe. You're in control of it, and you have the intelligent equipment at either end that can manage it on your

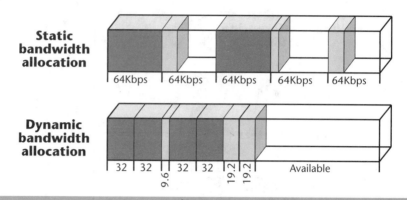

Figure 7.8 Static versus dynamic bandwidth allocation

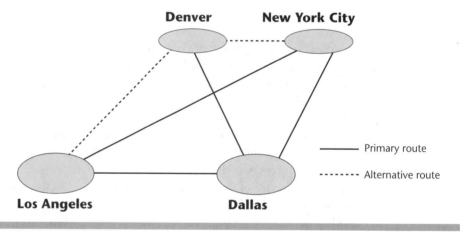

Figure 7.9 Dynamic alternative routing

behalf. For example, you can dynamically assign bandwidth; you can allocate only as much capacity as is necessary for an application, which more efficiently uses the capacity available on the digital facility. When you use the T-1/E-1 to build a private network, you can also perform dynamic alternative routing. Figure 7.9 shows an example of dynamic alternative routing. The primary route between Los Angeles and New York City is the direct diagonal line between them. But say there is a problem and that link fails. The multiplexer in Los Angeles will be smart enough to know to reroute its highest-priority traffic through Denver to get it to New York. And in Denver, it may take the second-priority traffic and reduce it to priority three in order to make room for the incoming high-priority traffic from Los Angeles. When the primary link is recovered, the network will revert to the original routing mechanisms. Dynamic alternative routing is useful in the face of congestion, failure, and when a customer needs to reconfigure capacities based on activities and personnel at given locations at random times.

Another element that a customer can use in creating a comprehensive enterprise backbone is the digital cross-connect. This device was introduced in 1985, with the purpose of automating the process of provisioning circuits—in essence, replacing the use of manual patch panels. The key feature of the digital cross-connect system (DCS) is its capability to "drop an insert," which means the cross-connect can exchange channels from one facility to another (refer to Figure 5.7 in Chapter 5). It is used to implement appropriate routing of traffic, to reroute around congestion or failure, or to allow customers to dynamically reconfigure their networks. With digital cross-connects, network configurations are defined entirely in software, and this gives the customer great control and allows reconfigurations to be implemented in a matter of minutes rather than hours or days. The levels at which switching can be performed are at the DS-3/CEPT-3 level, DS-1/CEPT-1 level, and DS-0/CEPT-0 level. Sub-DS-O and sub-CEPT-0 levels are also possible. This capability is also offered by some of the intelligent multiplexers—the T-1/E-1 and T-3/E-3 multiplexers—so the functionality can be bundled.

The main applications for the digital access cross-connects are disaster recovery, bypassing systems during scheduled maintenance, addressing peak traffic demand, and implementing temporary applications. For customers that need to support even more advanced applications—such as computer-aided design, three-dimensional modeling and simulation, visualization, and multimedia—the capacities of the T-, E-, and J-carrier infrastructure may not suffice, so the next step is to migrate to the SDH/SONET signal hierarchy.

SDH/SONET Backbone

As discussed in Chapter 5, SDH/SONET is the second generation of digital infrastructure, based on the use of fiber optics. With SDH/SONET, an enterprise might today subscribe to OC-1 and OC-3 in order to build an enterprise backbone. Remember from Chapter 5 that the OC-1 level provides roughly 51Mbps, 50Mbps of which are available for payload. OC-3 provides a total data rate of 155Mbps, with a little over 150Mbps for the customer payload. In today's environment, given the high cost of such leased lines, the customers that use the SDH/SONET levels are still considered early adopters. They include airports, aerospace companies, universities that have medical campuses or significant art schools, large government agencies such as the U.S. Internal Revenue Service, and the military. These early adopters typically have a rather minor presence in the marketplace at this time, but as we move toward greater use of visual and sensory applications, more users will require this type of bandwidth.

To build out a private SDH/SONET network, a customer would need two types of multiplexers: terminal muxes and add/drop muxes (ADMs). A customer would also need two types of cross-connects to build out a private SDH/SONET network: wideband cross-connects and broadband cross-connects. (Chapter 5 describes these muxes and cross-connects.)

Dark Fiber

With dark fiber, the customer leases the fiber itself and buys the necessary equipment to actually activate the fiber. The customer pays for the physical media, not for bandwidth, and as the customer adds equipment that can either pulse more bits per second or extract more wavelengths out of the underlying fiber, the bandwidth essentially becomes cheaper and cheaper.

ISDN

Another circuit-switched WAN option is ISDN. The International Telecommunication Union Telecommunications Standardization sector (ITU-T) formalized the ISDN standard in 1983. According to the ITU-T (www.itu.org), ISDN is "a network evolved from the telephony integrated digital network that provides end-to-end connectivity to support a wide range of services, including voice and nonvoice services, to which users have access by a limited set or standard multipurpose customer interfaces." One of the ideas behind narrowband ISDN (N-ISDN), as the first generation of ISDN was called, was to give customers one access into the network, from which they could then engage in circuit-switched, leased-line, or packet-switched options. Although all these options were available before ISDN, each one generally required its own special access line and device, which meant extra costs and administrative responsibilities because of the large number of options. The goal of ISDN was to provide one plug into the network, from which you could then go out over multiple alternatives.

ISDN Networks

A couple of key elements are required to form an ISDN network (see Figure 7.10). First, you must have a digital local exchange, and that digital exchange must be loaded with ISDN software. This is not an inexpensive proposition. The ISDN software alone costs around US$1 million, and each exchange costs in the neighborhood of US$3 million to US$5 million. Not all exchanges today are digital; a fairly significant number of exchanges—some 30% to 40% in the United States, for example—are analog, so not every locale can get ISDN services. But if you do have an exchange and the proper ISDN software, you also need a Signaling System 7 (SS7) network and a CPE that is compatible with the ISDN network. (SS7 is discussed in detail in Chapter 5.)

As discussed in Chapter 3, "Transmission Media: Characteristics and Applications," N-ISDN has two interfaces (see Figure 7.11): BRI and PRI.

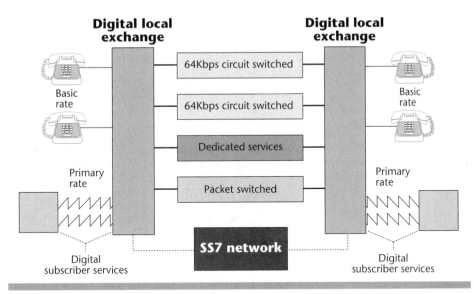

Figure 7.10   ISDN components

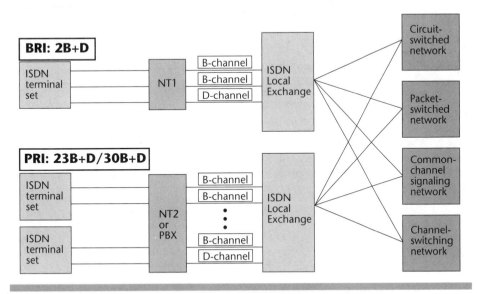

Figure 7.11   N-ISDN network interfaces

BRI is primarily used for residential service, small businesses, and centrex environments. BRI is offered only by local telcos, and how they offer it varies greatly. It can be configured as either 1B, 2B, 1B+D, or the full 2B+D; 128Kbps transmission requires that two B-channels be used. One application for this is Internet access, so you might have a BRI device, such as an ISDN modem, that would bond together two B-channels to provide the 128Kbps access to the ISP.

PRI is primarily used for business applications, and both local and interexchange carriers offer it. In support of the voice environment, PRI applications would include access to PBX and call center networks, replacement of existing analog trunk groups, and configuration of PBX tie-lines. Q-Sig, a standard that's an enhanced version of the D-channel signaling protocol, supports feature transparency between different vendors' PBXs. A key data application of PRI is LAN/WAN integration.

ISDN Applications

The following are the main applications for N-ISDN:

- **Internet access**—You would use N-ISDN to increase the speeds otherwise supported by your analog voice-grade line, when you do not have available other broadband access options, such as DSL, cable modems, or broadband wireless, available.

- **Remote access**—You would use N-ISDN to give teleworkers or telecommuters access to corporate resources.

- **LAN/WAN connections**—As mentioned earlier, N-ISDN is a technique for LAN interconnection, so bridging multiple LANs across a WAN could be done over ISDN connections.

- **High-capacity access**—You could use N-ISDN if you needed to increase your capacity for things such as graphics, file transfer, video, and multimedia networking. Keep in mind that N-ISDN will not provide motion as good as you would get with the higher-capacity services, but it will be much better than what you get with an analog facility.

- **Private line backup**—You could use N-ISDN as a backup to the private line services discussed earlier (for example, DDS).

- **Dial-up Frame Relay access**—Frame Relay is a very popular data networking option, particularly for LAN-to-LAN interconnection. You can use ISDN to provide measured-use dialup access to Frame Relay services in which the user dials in to a remote access port on the carrier's Frame Relay switch at either 64Kbps or 128Kbps connections. This can be used at smaller sites and for remote access (for example, for telecommuters).

- **BRI 0B+D for packet data**—One 16Kbps D-channel can be shared by up to eight devices. BRI 0B+D makes use of 9.6Kbps of D-channel capacity to support low-speed data terminals. This requires a terminal adapter that encapsulates the user data in D-channel frames. Applications for BRI 0B+D include credit card terminals and automatic teller machines.

- **ISDN DSL (IDSL)**—IDSL delivers full-duplex, dedicated data services; it does not support voice services. It is provided either on a 1B or a 2B configuration (that is, 64Kbps or 128Kbps). IDSL is compatible with existing digital loop carrier systems, which, as mentioned previously, serve 30% to 40% of the U.S. population. Digital loop carriers are especially common in remote rural areas. Some of the new DSL services (which are discussed in Chapter 13, "Broadband Access Solutions") are incompatible with these older-generation digital loop carriers. IDSL, however, is compatible with them, so it can be used to deliver digital private line service at speeds up to 128Kbps. In today's environment, 128Kbps is not what we strive for, so even though IDSL can facilitate some speedier communications, it is not as fast as some other broadband access options, making its future rather short.

■ Packet-Switched Networks

Packet switching was developed as a solution for the communications implications of interactive processing—it was designed to support bursty data traffic, which has long connect times but low data volumes. Packet switching involves the application of statistical multiplexing, whereby numerous conversations can make use of one common communications channel, which significantly increases transmission efficiency. (Chapter 2, "Telecommunications Technology Fundamentals," discusses statistical multiplexing in more detail.) However, sharing a communications link introduces latency. A key issue that we have to address in the future is how packet-switched networks can support latency-sensitive traffic such as real-time streams.

With packet switching, packets are routed through a series of intermediate nodes, often involving multiple networks; they are routed in a store-and-forward manner through a series of packet switches (that is, routers) that ultimately lead to the destination. Information is divided into packets that include a destination address and a sequence number. Let's look at an analogy. Think about telecommunications as a transportation network in which the physical roadway is a gravelly, potholed, single-lane alley. This is the traditional voice channel—twisted-pair deployed in a limited spectrum to support voice. We can pave that alleyway and make it a slicker surface, which equates to DSL. The road can now accommodate some additional information and move traffic along at a faster rate. We could then build a street with four lanes, the equivalent of coaxial cable. We could even build a much more sophisticated interstate turnpike, with eight lanes in each direction, that we could say is equivalent to fiber, which gives us increased capacities over traditional roadways. And we even have vehicles that travel through the air—and that would be the wireless realm.

Over these roadways travel vehicles—that is, packets, such as X.25, Frame Relay, Internet Protocol (IP), and ATM. The vehicles can carry different numbers of passengers, and the sophistication of their navigation controls also varies. The vehicles vary in how quickly they can accelerate and move through the transportation grid. So, for instance, IP is like a bus. What's the advantage of a bus over, say, a Ferrari (that is, packets that don't want to end up queued up behind a busload of tourists or slick multimedia versus unpredictable bursty data)? The bus can hold a large number of passengers, and it needs only one driver to carry those passengers between their stops. However, the bus takes longer than the Ferrari to maneuver through the intersections, or switching points. Whereas the Ferrari can zip through an intersection, the bus lumbers through, in what equates to latency. Smaller vehicles can move through the intersections more quickly, and they reduce latency, but larger vehicles reduce the number of drivers that you need. You can move more passengers using a smaller number of controls, but at the cost of higher latencies. Also, if there's congestion at an intersection, the Ferrari would be able to move onto the shoulder of the road to move around that congestion and continue on its way, whereas the bus would be forced to wait because it can't navigate as easily.

The secret to understanding the various packet formulas is realizing where their strengths and weaknesses lie. They vary as to the number of bits they contain, how much control they give you over delays or losses, and the rules they use to address the highways and the destination points.

Remember from Chapter 2 that packet switching deals with containerized, labeled entities we generically call packets, which vary in size. These packets come from different sources—from different users at one customer site or from different users at different customers. All these different packets are statistically multiplexed and sent on to their destinations over virtual circuits. Also remember from Chapter 2 that a virtual circuit is a set of *logical* connections that create a pathway between two points; they are not a *physical* connection that you can trace end-to-end that belongs to just one conversation. So, a virtual circuit is a shared communications link that is set up on demand based on negotiated communications parameters.

Because packet switching is a store-and-forward process of relaying through a series of intermediate nodes, latency and packet loss can considerably degrade real-time applications. In fact, the first generation of packet switching, X.25, dealt with data only. It could not handle voice or video. As discussed later in this chapter, newer generations can handle data because we have found ways to tweak the network.

In general, in the traditional mode, packet switching offered no Quality of Service (QoS) guarantees. It did, however, offer the knowledge that packets would make it to their destination point because they could be rerouted around trouble points. But because they could be rerouted around trouble points, which might mean congestion points or failed points, there could be no guarantees about the latencies or losses that you would experience. Therefore, it's a relatively new concept to try to build in QoS as a metric in packet-switched networks.

A packet-switched network is a data-centric environment, and instead of switching millions of physical circuits, as happens in the circuit-switched environment, the data-centric network switches packets, packet switches, or switched virtual circuits. Aggregation of these physical packets tends to happen at the edge of the carrier network. The first packet switch in the network immediately converts the physical circuit to a virtual circuit, or a stream of packets. As you can see in Figure 7.12, multiple packets are being statistically multiplexed as they come in through the packet switch, a routing table is consulted, an appropriate path is selected, and the packets are sent over the correct virtual circuit, leading to the next most logical stop in the network.

The speed of the transmission facilities between the switches directly affects the performance of packet-switched networks; this is why many new-generation packet switches—IP and ATM switches, for instance—are now shipping with high-speed interfaces, such as OC-48 (that is, 2.5Gbps) interfaces. OC-48 interfaces on a switch could potentially eliminate the need for an entire layer of aggregation that we currently do according to the traditional model of 64Kbps channels. By eliminating that layer of aggregation, we can actually allow direct connection to an optical network by using DWDM at the full rate of the service and interface.

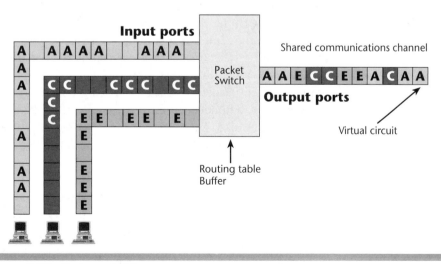

Figure 7.12 Packet switching

(See Chapter 2 for information on DWDM.) With data traffic growing monthly, transport networks will increasingly rely on data switches to manage and aggregate the traffic, and the transport network will be providing low-cost and reliable connections between these switches.

Remember from Chapter 4, "Establishing Communications Channels," that there are two main types of packet-switched networks: connection-oriented and connectionless networks. In a connection-oriented environment (such as X.25, Frame Relay, ATM, and VPNs that are based on Frame Relay or ATM networks), a call is set up end-to-end at the onset of the communication. Only one call request packet that contains the source and destination address is necessary. That initial call request packet establishes a virtual circuit to the destination so that subsequent packets need only be read for the marking information that defines the virtual circuit to be taken. The intermediate nodes do not need to look at the addressing information in order to calculate a path for each packet independently. This reduces delay because routing decisions do not have to be made at the intermediate nodes. Where the error control is performed depends on the generation of the network. With X.25, error detection and correction was a value-added feature of the network. A provision of X.25 was to detect and correct for errors while they were in transport, hence improving data communications. But as networks became more digital and fiber based, noise became less of a problem; thus, the subsequent generations of packet switching—Frame Relay and ATM, for instance—give the endpoints the responsibility for error detection and correction. Not having to stop packets and investigate them in the throes of transmission greatly decreases the delays that would otherwise be encountered. So in a connection-oriented environment, a virtual circuit defines the path end-to-end, and all packets follow the same path throughout the course of the session.

As discussed in Chapter 4, the connectionless environment (which includes X.25 networks, the public Internet, private IP-based backbones, and LANs) can be likened to the postal service, in which a message is relayed from point to point, with each relay getting one step closer to its ultimate destination. In a connectionless environment, each packet of a message is an independent unit that contains the source and destination address. Each packet is independently routed at each intermediate node it crosses. The more hops it goes through, the greater the delays that are accumulated, which greatly affects delay-sensitive applications, including any form of real-time voice, real-time audio, real-time video, video-on-demand, and streaming media. But connectionless environments can work around problems, which is why they were so strong in the early days, when there were frequent system failures and links that were too noisy to perform correctly. Connectionless packets could circumvent these system failures or noisy conditions and still meet at the destination point with high integrity. The connectionless environment offered the flexibility of routing around problem areas, but at the risk of greater overhead associated with the overall transmission, because addressing had to be included in each packet, and also at the risk of greater delays because each packet had to be independently routed.

X.25

In 1970 Tymnet introduced X.25, which was the first generation of packet switching. X.25 packet-switching networks evolved as an option for data communications and therefore did not compete directly with the telephony providers. The providers of such networks were put in a special category, called value-added network (VAN) providers.

The X.25 packet-switching technique emerged out of a need to address the characteristics of interactive processing, which had been introduced in the late 1960s. As mentioned earlier in the chapter, interactive processing is a bursty data flow that implies long connect times but low data volumes. X.25 provided a technique for many conversations to share a communications channel.

X.25 Networks

Because of when X.25 was created, it was based on an analog network infrastructure. A big problem with analog networks is the accumulation of noise through the amplification points, which leads to the very high error rate associated with analog networks. So, one of the value-added services provided by X.25 networks was error control as a function within the network. Because packet switching is a store-and-forward technique, at every intermediate node at which an X.25 packet would be halted the packet would undergo an error check. If everything in the packet was correct, the intermediate node would return an acknowledgment to the original transmitting node, requesting it to forward the next packet. If the packet the node received was not correct, the node would send a message requesting a retransmission. Thus, at any point in the routing and relaying of those packets, if noise contributed to errors, the errors could be resolved, which resulted in a much more accurate data flow.

Remember that what is beneficial or not beneficial about a particular network depends on the prevailing conditions, so in an analog infrastructure, where noise was an issue, error control was a highly desirable feature. But performing that error control procedure on every packet at every node in addition to developing routing instructions at each intermediate node for the next point to which to relay the packet increased the delays that were encountered end-to-end in the transmission of information. Because X.25 packet-switching networks were for data only, it was not important to be able to tightly control delays or losses.

Another early attribute of X.25 was the size of its packet. It used relatively small packets, generally 128 bytes or 256 bytes long. This is another issue that changes according to the times. Small packets were desirable in the X.25 generation because

Packet Size in X.25, Frame Relay, and ATM

The next generation of packet-switched networks after X.25 is Frame Relay. In Frame Relay, the packet sizes are variable, but they can be up to 4,096 bytes. Frame Relay operates over a digital network, where noise is not much of an issue because regenerative repeaters eliminate the noise that may accumulate on the signal during transmission. As a result, all the error control procedures are removed from Frame Relay networks in order to make them faster. Furthermore, in Frame Relay we're not very concerned about having to retransmit information. There's less likelihood that errors or noise in the network will cause the need for retransmission. Thus, Frame Relay uses a larger packet size than X.25, and the result is bandwidth efficiency. A Frame Relay packet contains less control information for a larger group of bytes of information, and this means the packet makes better use of the available bandwidth.

If we jump ahead one more generation, to ATM switching, we find that packets are called *cells*. They're small—only 53 bytes—which gives them the capability to cross intersections quickly. They can transition through network nodes very quickly, but because they are so small, control information is applied to very small cells. This means that there's an underlying assumption that bandwidth isn't an issue, that you're not trying to conserve on bandwidth, and that the prevailing condition that you're trying to satisfy is low latencies.

You can see that the optimum size of the packets really depends on a number of factors, such as the performance of the network, the cost of the bandwidth, and the demand of the applications it's serving.

of the noise factor. If there was noise in the network, there would be errors, and hence fairly frequent retransmissions were necessary. Retransmitting a smaller packet is more efficient than retransmitting very long blocks of information, so X.25 was specifically designed to use small packets. Again, X.25 was designed in an older generation, so it tends to operate over comparatively slow links, largely in the 56Kbps to 2Mbps range.

Like the PSTN, the X.25 packet-switched network has a hierarchy. There are two main categories of packet switches. Some packet switches (such as the square packet switches in Figure 7.13) are close to the customer—in fact, they are at the points where the customers access the network. These packet switches are involved with routing and relaying packets and with error detection and correction. This is also where added intelligence would reside in order to be able to convert between different protocols being used by different computers, or to convert between different operating speeds or between different coding schemes. In other words, this is another value-added piece of the equation. One benefit of X.25 was that it allowed you to create a network that provided connectivity between unlike equipment because it could perform the necessary conversions on your behalf, as

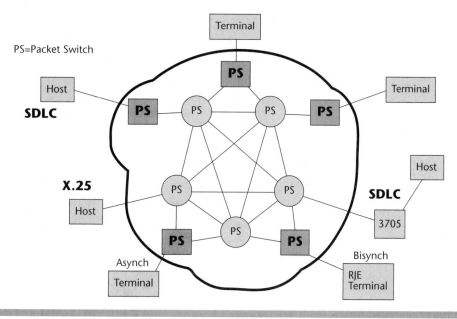

Figure 7.13 An X.25 packet-switched network

part of the network service. The packet switches in the second category—the inner tier of packet switches (such as the round packet switches in Figure 7.13)—do not provide those sorts of high-level value-added features. They are involved strictly with the routing and relaying of packets and with error control and detection.

Again, the links that join the packet switches throughout the network could be combinations of analog and digital facilities. In advanced network infrastructures, they would be digital, but there are still infrastructures around the world that have not yet been reengineered or upgraded, and this is where X.25 still has an application. If you're only concerned with networking locations that are served over advanced digital infrastructures, you're probably not very interested in X.25. You'll get much better performance from Frame Relay. But if you have a global network and you have locations in areas that don't have sophisticated Frame Relay services—or even digital networks—in place, then X.25 will suit your data networking needs very well, on a cost-effective basis, albeit accommodating slower data rates. But if you're only trying to accommodate an automatic teller machine in a banking environment, for example, you don't need broadband capacity to the kiosk. Applications for X.25 continue to prevail, but this is a quickly aging technology, and many successors improve on its performance.

Another of the original benefits of X.25 was that it could handle alternative routing. X.25 was built with the intention of being able to circumvent failed nodes or failed links.

To connect to an X.25 network, you need a packet assembler/disassembler (PAD) to interface non-X.25 devices to an X.25 network. PADs convert protocols into packets, as prescribed by the X.25 standard, so that the data can travel across an X.25 packet network. These PADs may reside either at the customer premise or in the network.

X.25 is essentially the ITU-T's standard access protocol between user devices and a packet-switching network. It defines the interface for terminals operating in the packet mode, connected to public data networks by dedicated circuits. Some additional X protocols are commonly used:

- X.28 is the standard protocol between the terminal and the PAD.

- X.29 is the standard protocol between the PAD and the network.

- X.75 is the gateway protocol that defines how to interconnect two or more packet-switched data networks. One could be a private packet data network and the other a public packet data network, or they could be two different network operators' networks, and so on. (Gateway protocols, which imply a means by which you can cross into other people's backyards, are discussed in Chapter 9, "The Internet: Infrastructure and Service Providers.")

Advantages and Disadvantages of X.25

The advantages of X.25 are as follows:

- Powerful addressing facilities, because X.25 is the first approach to providing Layer 3 networking address information to enable routing and relaying through a series of intermediate nodes and networks

- Better bandwidth utilization, thanks to statistical multiplexing

- Improved congestion control because it enables packets to circumvent congested nodes and be rerouted via other links and nodes

- Improved error control that is done continually in the network at each intermediate node and in the face of all sorts of failures

- High availability in the face of node and line failures because rerouting is possible

The disadvantages of X.25 are as follows:

- Queuing delays

- Lower-speed communications links

- Smaller packet sizes, which means it doesn't make use of bandwidth as well as some of the newer protocols that involve larger frames

- No QoS guarantees, so delay-sensitive applications will likely suffer

- For data only, and today we are striving for integrated solutions

Frame Relay

The second generation of packet switching, Frame Relay, was introduced in 1991. Frame Relay assumes that there's a digital infrastructure in place and that few errors will result from network noise. Therefore, the entire error detection and correction process has been removed from the Frame Relay network, and error control is done entirely in the endpoints. This means that traffic is not delayed by being stopped and checked, which translates to much faster throughput over Frame Relay networks than over X.25 networks.

The lack of error control in the network also means that it is possible to carry voice and video over a Frame Relay network. However, Frame Relay is not innately designed to do that. The packet sizes enabled under Frame Relay are large—up to 4,096 bytes—and variable, which means that there could be a 100-byte packet going through a network node, with a 4,000-byte packet right behind it. When you have packets of varying sizes, you can't predict the delay in processing those packets through the network, and when you can't predict the delay, you can't properly address the latency requirements of real-time voice or video. Yet we do, in fact, run voice and video over Frame Relay networks, by tweaking the system in one of several ways. For example, we could provision separate links to carry the voice and the data traffic, and thus some excess data bursting wouldn't affect any real-time telephony, for instance, that is under way. We could prioritize traffic by application and in that way enable access to bandwidth, based on priority. In public Frame Relay networks, we often convert frames to equal-sized cells. At the core of the Frame Relay network is ATM because ATM, at the moment, offers the strongest suite of tools for traffic management. Thus, many networks, including IP backbones, the Internet, and Frame Relay have ATM at their core. You can trick the system in order to get added utility out of Frame Relay networks, but keep in mind that when you do this, you lose a little bit of the cost-efficiencies you would otherwise have by running all your traffic in the same manner over the same link.

The types of links that connect the Frame Relay switching points operate at high speeds—they run the full range of the wide band of the PDH hierarchy. Where a Frame Relay network is running over a T-carrier infrastructure, the links can operate at 1.5Mbps to 45Mbps; for networks being served by E-carrier platforms, the links can operate at 2Mbps to 34Mbps.

The standards for Frame Relay come from the ITU-T, which defines Frame Relay as "a conversational communication service provided by a subnetwork for high-speed bursty data." This definition implies that we have a two-way capability (it is "conversational") and that Frame Relay is not an end-to-end solution (it is a "subnetwork"). So we don't look for a Frame Relay device such as a Frame Relay telephone; instead, we look at Frame Relay to serve as the cloud—that is, the WAN solution that links together computer networks that are distributed across a country or across the world. And "high-speed bursty data" suggests that Frame Relay's preliminary application is in support of data and, specifically, LAN-to-LAN internetworking.

Frame Relay Applications

What type of an environment might be a candidate for Frame Relay? One such environment is a hub-and-spoke network, in which traffic from remote locations travels through a central site. This is similar to the airline system, in which key airports serve as main hubs; the largest of the 777s travel between the main hubs, and to get to a smaller city, you go through a hub to get on a smaller aircraft that then takes you to your destination. Frame Relay is also used where you are seeking to replace the use of the very expensive leased lines. Depending on the network topology, Frame Relay could potentially reduce costs up to 50% as compared to using leased lines.

Frame Relay is also used to give a network some bandwidth flexibility—that is, bandwidth on demand. Because the main application of Frame Relay is LAN internetworking, and because LANs produce highly unpredictable traffic flows, paying for a subscribed set of bandwidth whether you're using it or not may not be very cost-effective. Frame Relay provides the capability to burst above what you've committed to financially. (This is discussed later in this chapter, in the section "Frame Relay Networks.")

Frame Relay is also useful in a multiprotocol environment. Although IP seems to rule the world, it is not the only protocol in use. It is a multiprotocol world. There are SNA networks in place, still making use of IBM's Synchronous Data Link Control (SDLC). The largest legacy networks today are some of the billing systems run by the world's telco operators. Frame Relay is used by more than 60,000 enterprises worldwide, and those that are highly focused on multimedia applications use ATM. Few customers use only one protocol. They have multiple protocols in their networks, and Frame Relay can handle them all because it simply encapsulates another protocol into a Frame Relay envelope and carries it through the network—it doesn't care what's inside the envelope.

Closed user groups—where you want to know who has access in and out of your network—can be achieved with Frame Relay, unlike with the public Internet, where you have no idea who's on there at any point in time. Frame Relay also allows you to predict the level of the network's performance, so it enables you to set metrics. This makes it an especially attractive solution if you are operating with countries where there are good carrier infrastructures.

Frame Relay Networks

Frame Relay is an interface specification that defines how information must be packaged in order for the Frame Relay network to act on it and to deliver it to its destination. Therefore, it is not necessarily associated with a specific piece of

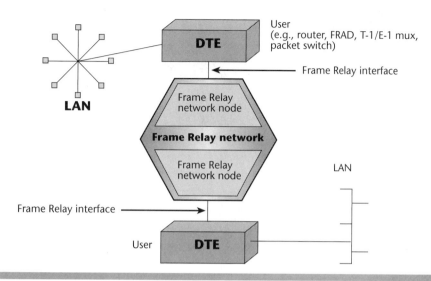

Figure 7.14   Frame Relay interface definitions

equipment. The Frame Relay interface could reside on multiple platforms. As shown in Figure 7.14, the Frame Relay interface resides on DTE, which is most likely a router but could also be a Frame Relay access device (FRAD), used to provide access for Voice over Frame Relay (VoFR). It could be a T-1 or an E-1 multiplexer with a Frame Relay interface. One of the things that is so valuable about Frame Relay is that it doesn't represent an investment in altogether new technology. You can upgrade existing platforms, which can make a lot of economic sense. Frame Relay can be deployed on a wide range of platforms, and predominantly it is seen today on routers.

The Frame Relay interface takes the native data stream, no matter what the protocol (for example, TCP/IP, SDLC, X.25), and puts it inside a Frame Relay envelope. Essentially, Frame Relay puts the native data into an encapsulated form, using Link Access Protocol D (LAPD), that the Frame Relay switches can act on.

The Frame Relay header format, LAPD, is shown in Figure 7.15. A beginning flag essentially starts the communication. A Frame Relay header is the very important part of the envelope that contains the addressing information. The user data is the native block of information. Next, the frame-check sequence performs a cyclical redundancy check, and an ending flag closes the frame. An expanded view of the Frame Relay header includes the data link connection identifier (DLCI), which is the addressing scheme that defines the source and destination addresses. A few fields can be used for purposes of managing a minimal amount of QoS. The forward explicit congestion notifier (FECN) and backward explicit congestion notifier

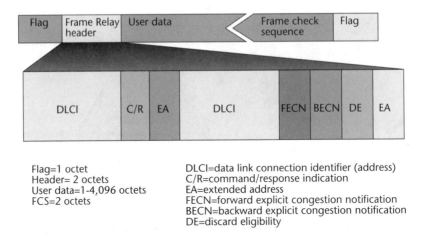

Flag=1 octet
Header= 2 octets
User data=1-4,096 octets
FCS=2 octets

DLCI=data link connection identifier (address)
C/R=command/response indication
EA=extended address
FECN=forward explicit congestion notification
BECN=backward explicit congestion notification
DE=discard eligibility

Figure 7.15   Frame Relay frame format (LAPD)

(BECN) fields are used to manage the traffic flow. The FECN tells the receiver, "I'm experiencing delays getting to you, so anticipate those delays. Don't time-out the session." BECN tells the transmitter, "Whoa! We've got delays ahead. Throttle back or slow down on your introduction of data, or we'll end up losing those frames because of congestion." You use the discard eligibility field to mark a frame as being either discard eligible or not and to control what occurs between voice and data in, for instance, a period of congestion. Frame Relay enables you to control the traffic flow a bit and you can determine whether to drop a frame. But notice that there is no place in the frame for defining latency requirements or loss tolerances—the stricter QoS traffic measurements. Nonetheless, the switches will read the DLCIs to determine how to properly forward the frame.

In a Frame Relay network, the customer environment includes the full complement of information resources that the customer wants to use on this network. Next, the CPE—which could be a router, bridge, FRAD, mux, or switch—contains the interface that formats packets into the Frame Relay frames. From the CPE, an access line (called a user network interface [UNI]) connects to the Frame Relay provider switch. That UNI could be a leased line, such as 56Kbps/64Kbps, or T-1/E-1, an ISDN line, or an analog dialup line.

The UNI then leads to the Frame Relay switch, which is basically a statistical multiplexer. Based on the type of subscription in place, the traffic is either sent out over a permanent virtual circuit (PVC) or over a switched virtual circuit (SVC). Recall from Chapter 2 that a PVC is analogous to a leased line. It is predetermined, and it is manually configured and entered into a network management system so that it stays between two locations until it is reprogrammed. SVCs, on the other

The Frame Relay Forum

If you want to know the latest on what standards are mature, available, and deliverable, consult the Frame Relay Forum (www.frforum.com). The Frame Relay Forum is a pseudostandards body that produces the recommendations to which most of these devices are built and whose recommendations are largely observed throughout the operator community. You can get a full list of the UNIs from the Frame Relay Forum, along with all the published and draft standards associated with Frame Relay.

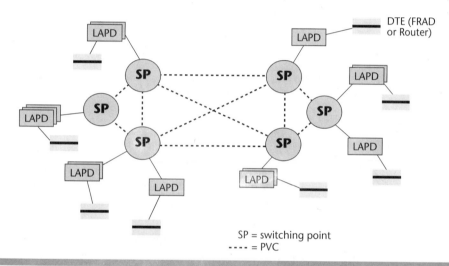

Figure 7.16 PVCs in a Frame Relay network

hand, are like the dialup scenario; they are dynamically provisioned via signaling on an as-needed basis. Figure 7.16 illustrates the use of PVCs. When a packet goes through the interface in the DTE (probably a router or a FRAD), it is put into the LAPD format, and then the LAPD frame is passed to the switching point. The switching point looks at the DLCI and then looks it up in its table to determine over which particular circuit or virtual circuit to send the message.

Subscribers specify the port speed and the committed information rate (CIR) in a Frame Relay network. Port prices are based on bandwidth, which determines the speed of the interface into the network. The PVC charges are based on the CIR and the distance. The CIR generally refers to the PVC's minimum bandwidth under normal conditions. Generally, the CIR is less than the access rate into the network, and the access rate into the network determines the maximum amount of bandwidth that you can use.

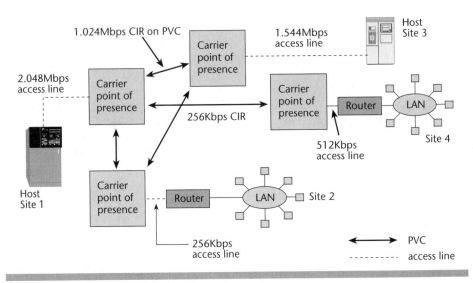

Figure 7.17   Frame Relay bandwidth-on-demand

Figure 7.17 illustrates the bandwidth-on-demand flexibility mentioned earlier in this chapter. Say you have an access line that allows 2.048Mbps, an E-1, to your carrier's switching point. Between these two locations of the network, you have contracted for a PVC that is essentially 1Mbps. In this environment, bandwidth-on-demand works like this: You are allowed to burst above your PVC's CIR of 1Mbps, up to the rate of your access line, or port speed, which is 2Mbps. In other words, you are paying for 1Mbps, but you're actually allowed to transmit at 2Mbps for short periods of time.

If you try to keep transmitting at your burst rate over a sustained period, the network will do one of two things. It might start dropping frames, which is another reason voice and video might suffer over Frame Relay. Or there might be a software mechanism that allows the excess traffic to be captured so that you can be billed for overtime. But the carrier is banking on the fact that not everybody is making use of the CIR at all times. Again, LAN traffic is quite unpredictable, so there are lulls in the day when you're not transmitting anything and other times when you need twice your CIR, and ideally, at the end of the day it all balances out. But the carrier is playing the same gamble, assuming that not everybody is going to try to exercise their CIR at the same time. If they do, whether you still experience your CIR will depend on the integrity of engineering of the Frame Relay provider. In other words, if the provider oversubscribes this PVC and if everyone attempts to burst at the same time, somebody is not going to have capacity available. This is a big issue in terms of vendor selection. Frame Relay networks are much less expensive than other options because the operators are also saving on how they're carrying that traffic.

With SVCs, the connections are established on demand, so the routing tables do not store path identifiers—just the address of each site. Users can connect to any site, as long as the address is programmed into the router and SVC capacity is available. Subscribers control call setup via their own routers or FRADs. The router programming, then, controls allocation of the aggregate bandwidth. SVCs share bandwidth, and they do so either on a first-come, first-served basis or on a custom basis, where chosen SVCs are disconnected when a higher-priority application needs bandwidth.

Frame Relay Performance Issues

You need to consider a number of performance issues with Frame Relay:

- **Likelihood of bottlenecks**—This depends on whether the operator has oversubscribed the backbone.
- **Ability to handle bursts**—Does the operator let you burst above your CIR for sufficient periods, or are the bursts so limited that you really don't get bandwidth-on-demand?
- **Level of network delay**—Operators commit to different maximum delays on different routes, so if you are going to be handling delay-sensitive traffic, you especially need to address this issue.
- **Network availability guarantees**—You need to determine to what level you can get a service-level agreement (SLA) that guarantees network availability. This depends on the vendor, not on technology.

As far as Frame Relay QoS goes, you can expect to be able to have classes of service (CoSs), where you specify your CIR and your maximum burst rate, as well as some minor traffic parameters, such as the discard eligibility bits and the congestion notifiers. Otherwise, Frame Relay has no provisions for the control of latencies and losses.

VoFR

VoFR has been gaining interest among both carriers and users in the past few years. A main driver behind VoFR is more efficient use of Frame Relay bandwidth. The average full-duplex voice conversation consists of about half silence, which indicates that voice has a bursty quality. Data networks have been sharing bandwidth for many years. Voice is just another protocol, so why not let it also share bandwidth, as it is a rather bursty stream, and in this way achieve better use of the Frame Relay resource? The goal of VoFR is not to replace existing voice networks, but rather to make use of what you have available in Frame Relay to carry overflow traffic or additional voice traffic. Voice is compressed in Frame Relay, and then encapsulated into the Frame Relay protocol via a FRAD. Again, the main advantage of this is better use of a single data network and the cost savings derived from this efficiency. But remember that if you run everything over a single network, voice quality may suffer, and, even worse, data performance may suffer.

The Frame Relay Forum has specified the FRF.11 standard for how to deploy VoFR. It provides bandwidth-efficient networking of digital voice and Group 3 fax communications over Frame Relay. It defines multiplexed virtual connections, up to 255 subchannels on a single Frame Relay DLCI, and it defines support of data subchannels on a multiplexed Frame Relay DLCI.

The ITU has defined some VoFR compression standards:

- **ITU G.711 PCM**—Regular PCM is the compression standard that was part and parcel of the PDH hierarchy, which carried voice at 64Kbps. That's a very high rate, given what we can achieve today.

- **ITU G.726/G.727 ADPCM**—In the PSTN, we also went to Adaptive Differential PCM (ADPCM), which reduced the data rate to 32Kbps.

- **ITU G.723.1 MP-MLQ**—With Frame Relay networks we can apply Multipulse-Maximum Likelihood Quantization (MP-MLQ), which reduces voice to 4.8Kbps and can permit up to 10 voice channels on a single 64Kbps connection.

Another feature of VoFR that is important is *voice activity detection* (VAD). VAD algorithms reduce the amount of information needed to re-create the voice at the destination end by removing silent periods and redundant information found in human speech; this also helps with compression.

Jitter is another quality issue related to VoFR. *Jitter* is the variation in delays on the receive side of the transmission from one packet to the next. Delay varies, depending on the traffic in the switch, and severe jitter can make conversations very difficult to understand. Dropped packets can cause clicks or pops, and a great deal of packet loss would result in altogether unintelligible conversation.

FRF.12 addresses the fragmentation of both data frames and VoFR frames. It reduces delay variation, segments voice signals into smaller data bundles, and, ultimately, provides better performance. Because bundles are smaller, when some get lost, the network feels less impact.

Another VoFR consideration is the ability to prioritize voice traffic, which, of course, is very delay sensitive. The need for echo cancellation that's caused by round-trip delay is another consideration. Echo cancellation is required on voice circuits over 500 miles (800 kilometers) long. A final consideration is voice interpolation. Equipment is needed to re-create lost voice information so that retransmissions don't need to be performed, because voice retransmissions would be ineffective. Voice, unlike data, cannot wait for retransmissions to occur.

Advantages and Disadvantages of Frame Relay
The advantages of Frame Relay are as follows:

- Provides cost savings compared to leased lines
- Runs on multiprotocol networks
- Provides control over the user community
- Gives predictable performance and reliability
- Provides minimum guaranteed throughput
- Provides network management and control
- Provides greater bandwidth flexibility
- Currently used by some 60,000 companies and provided about US$8 billion in revenue in 2000

Disadvantages of Frame Relay include the following:

- Provides weak network management ability
- Inherently unsuitable for delay-sensitive traffic, such as voice and video
- Requires high-quality digital circuits, so it does not work everywhere
- Not entirely standardized

Overall, Frame Relay represents a viable and cost-effective solution for data networking, particularly where LAN-to-LAN interconnection is the main goal.

ATM

ATM is a series of standards that was first introduced by the ITU-T, in 1988, as part of a larger vision for the future of networks called Broadband ISDN. Broadband ISDN defined a new genre of applications, and most of those applications, not surprisingly, involved video or multimedia content, and this is where ATM shines. ATM was designed to be a master integrator: one platform, one infrastructure over which voice, data, video, multimedia, images, and other forms of traffic that we may have not thought of yet can all coexist and all be assigned the appropriate network resources based on their needs. ATM wasn't designed to be a technique for voice; it wasn't designed as a new solution for data. It was designed for multimedia, but it hasn't yet had a chance to really demonstrate its greatest strengths in today's environment.

A huge number of networks—roughly 80% to 85% of all Internet backbones and Frame Relay networks—have ATM at their core. Today, ATM is still the only WAN approach that provides an architected QoS, which then gives network operators the opportunity to manage the traffic inside the network, which is a prerequisite to being able to offer business-class services, such as virtual private networks (VPNs), VoFR, Voice over IP, and Voice over ATM. ATM has the capability to provide the appropriate guarantees to delay-sensitive traffic. ATM is working on your behalf more than may be evident in what you read and hear, especially as IP is the public's current darling. (Chapter 11, "Next-Generation Network Services," discusses the possibility and benefits of marrying ATM and IP.)

By definition ATM is a high-bandwidth, fast packet-switching and multiplexing technique that enables the seamless end-to-end transmission of voice, data, image, and video traffic. It's a high-capacity, low-latency switching fabric that's adaptable for multiservice and multirate connections. The capacities it affords, including low latency, are absolutely prerequisite to the support of advanced applications for which this switching technology was designed.

ATM switches characteristically have large capacities. They range from 10Gbps to 160Gbps, and new products are emerging in the Tbps range. (In comparison, IP routers typically offer capacities ranging from 4Gbps to 60Gbps, although there are also new Tbps switch routers emerging.)

The best advantages of ATM include the robust QoS and high-speed interfaces. ATM was the first networking approach that supported high-speed interfaces, both 155Mbps and 622Mbps. Therefore, as an enterprise wanted to reengineer its campus network to higher bandwidth, ATM presented a viable solution. The 1997 introduction of Gigabit Ethernet presented a more economical approach, and today, ATM is implemented in the enterprise because it offers the capability to administer QoS for multimedia and real-time traffic. Of course, over time other solutions and architectures also begin to incorporate the features that people seek, so new-generation IP routers and switches accommodate the same high-speed interfaces that ATM does. Both ATM and IP today ship with 2.5Gbps (that is, OC-48) interfaces. Today, ATM can administer QoS, and IP is getting close. (QoS and ATM's service classes are discussed in detail in Chapter 10, "Next-Generation Networks.")

ATM enables access bandwidth to be shared among multiple sources and it enables network resources to be shared among multiple users. It allows different services to be combined within a single access channel (see Figure 7.18).

ATM Applications

There are many key applications for ATM. The ATM standard began in the carrier community, as a means of reengineering the PSTN to meet the demands of future applications. As Frame Relay networks began to see the demand to accommodate voice and video, they also began to institute ATM in their core in order to be able to administrate service guarantees. The same goes for the Internet backbone, especially where there's an interest in providing more than just consumer Internet

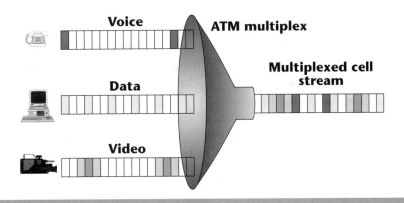

Figure 7.18 Mapping services into ATM

access, but also in providing business-class services, where the customer wants some SLAs tied to QoS and network performance.

There's also a need for ATM in VPNs that need to carry multimedia traffic, and where you want to reengineer the network environment to be integrated—for example, replacing individual PBXs for voice and LAN switches for data with an enterprise network switch that can integrate all your traffic into one point at the customer edge.

Finally, ATM can be used to enhance or expand campus and workgroup networks; that is, it can be used to upgrade LANs. In the early days of ATM, one of the first marketplaces where it saw adoption was in the LAN community. If you wanted to make a move to a campus network that could support 155Mbps or 622Mbps, the only solution was to go to an ATM environment. However, at the end of 1997, the standards for Gigabit Ethernet were formalized and introduced, and that is a much cheaper technology and transition path than ATM. To go from 100Mbps Ethernet to ATM means going to an entirely new technology. It's an investment in an entirely new generation of equipment and a requirement for an entirely new set of technical skills. A great many more programmers are knowledgeable in other techniques, such as IP, than in ATM. However, Gigabit Ethernet doesn't require learning a new protocol, which is a benefit for network engineers. Gigabit Ethernet also has a much lower cost in terms of the actual components and boards. Therefore, with the formalization of Gigabit Ethernet, people turned away from ATM in the LAN and decided they would simply throw bandwidth at the problem in the campus network. But remember that Ethernet does not within itself address QoS, so we can't continue to throw bandwidth at this problem much longer because when applications truly turn to the visual and multimedia realm, Gigabit Ethernet will not suffice, and QoS will need to be included.

Early adopters, such as the U.S. Navy, universities, and health care campuses, today are deploying ATM. ISPs are the biggest customers of ATM, followed by financial institutions, manufacturers, health care, government, education, research labs, and other enterprises that use broadband applications.

ATM drivers include the capability to consolidate multiple data, voice, and video applications onto a common transport network with specified QoS on a per-application basis. It is also being used to replace multiple point-to-point leased lines, which were used to support individual applications' networks. In addition, Frame Relay is being extended to speeds above T-1 and E-1.

The major inhibitor of ATM is the high service cost. Remember that one of the benefits of Frame Relay is that it is an upgrade of existing technology, so it doesn't require an entirely new set of skills and an investment in new equipment. With ATM you do have an entirely new generation of equipment that needs to be acquired and skill sets that must be built to properly implement and manage ATM, which may have a big financial impact on the overall picture.

ATM Interfaces

ATM is a very high-bandwidth, high-performance system that uses a uniform 53-byte cell: 5 bytes of addressing information and 48 bytes of payload. The benefit of the small cell size is reduced latency in transmitting through the network nodes. The disadvantage of the small cell size, however, is that it means increased overhead. But remember that ATM was built in support of the vision of Broadband ISDN, and the second set of standards in support of Broadband ISDN was SDH/SONET. In other words, ATM was created with an eye toward the deployment of fiber, which offers tremendous capacities and hence makes bandwidth less of an issue.

ATM is a connection-oriented network, which for purposes of real-time, multimedia, and time-sensitive traffic is very important because it allows controlled latencies. It operates over a virtual circuit path, which leads to great efficiency in terms of network management. Payload error control is done at the endpoints, and some limited error control procedures are performed on the headers of the cells within the network itself. ATM supports asynchronous information access: Some applications consume a high percentage of capacity (for instance, video-on-demand) and others consume much less (for example, e-mail); thus, ATM allows multirate connections. Finally, ATM has a highly defined and structured set of QoS definitions.

The ATM Layers

As discussed in the following sections, ATM has three main layers (see Figure 7.19): the physical layer, the ATM layer, and the ATM adaptation layer.

The Physical Layer The physical layer basically defines what transmission media are supported, what transmission rates are supported, what physical inter-

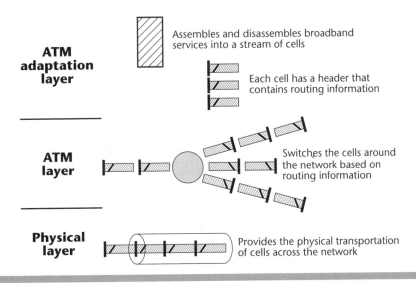

ATM adaptation layer — Assembles and disassembles broadband services into a stream of cells

Each cell has a header that contains routing information

ATM layer — Switches the cells around the network based on routing information

Physical layer — Provides the physical transportation of cells across the network

Figure 7.19 ATM layers

faces are supported, and what the electrical and optical coding schemes are for the ones and zeros. Like the OSI physical layer, it's a definition of the physical elements of getting the ones and zeros over the network.

The ATM Layer   The ATM switch performs activities at the ATM layer. It performs four main functions: switching, routing, congestion management, and multiplexing.

The ATM Adaptation Layer   The ATM adaptation layer (AAL) is the segmentation and reassembly layer. The native stream (whether it's real-time, analog, voice, MPEG-2 compressed video, or TCP/IP) goes through the adaptation layer, where it is segmented into 48-byte cells. Those 48-byte cells are then passed up to the first ATM switch in the network, which applies the header information that defines on which path and which channel the conversation is to take place. (This speaks, again, to the connection-orientation of ATM.)

   At the onset of the call, there is a negotiation phase, and each switch that's required to complete the call to the destination gets involved with determining whether it has a path and channel of the proper QoS to deliver on the requested call. If it does, at that time it makes a table entry that identifies what path and channel the call will take between the two switches. If along the way one of the switches can't guarantee the QoS being requested, the session is denied. ATM provides an end-to-end view of the network and an assurance that all along the way, the proper QoS can be met. Again, the adaptation layer segments the information into the 48-byte cells, and each switch, in turn, applies the headers that contain the routing information, and at the receiving end, the adaptation layer again reassembles the cells into the native stream that is understood by the end device. There are adaptation layers for various traffic types—for real-time traffic, for connection-oriented data, for connectionless data, for compressed video, and so on.

Within the AAL are a number of options:

- **AAL 0**—When a customer's network equipment takes care of all the AAL-related functions, the network uses a Null AAL (also known as AAL 0). This means that no services are performed and that cells are transferred between the service interface and the ATM network transparently.

- **AAL 1**—AAL 1 is designed to meet the needs of isochronous, constant bit rate (CBR) services, such as digital voice and video, and is used for applications that are sensitive to both cell loss and delay and to emulate conventional leased lines. It requires an additional byte of header information for sequence numbering, leaving 47 bytes for payload. This adaptation layer corresponds to fractional and full T-1/E-1 and T-3/E-3. AAL Type 1 provides a timing recovery functional to maintain the bit timing across the ATM network and to avoid buffer overflow/underflow at the receiver.

- **AAL 2**—AAL 2 is for isochronous variable-bit-rate (VBR) services such as packetized video. It allows ATM cells to be transmitted before the payload is full to accommodate an application's timing requirements.

- **AAL 3/4**—AAL 3/4 supports VBR data, such as LAN applications, or bursty connection-oriented traffic, such as error messages. It is designed for traffic that can tolerate delay but not cell loss. This type performs error detection on each cell by using a sophisticated error-checking mechanism that consumes 4 bytes of each 48-byte payload. AAL 3/4 allows ATM cells to be multiplexed, and it supports the process of segmentation and reassembly required to carry variable length frames over the ATM network. It also provides a per-cell cyclical redundancy check (CRC) to detect transmission errors and a per-frame length check to detect loss of cells in a frame.

- **AAL 5**—AAL 5 is intended to accommodate bursty LAN data traffic with less overhead than AAL 3/4. It is also known as SEAL (simple and efficient adaptation layer). Its major feature is that it uses information in the cell header to identify the first and last cells of a frame, so that it doesn't need to consume any of the cell payload to perform this function. AAL 5 uses a per-frame CRC to detect both transmission and cell-loss errors, and it is expected to be required by ITU-T for the support of call-control signaling and Frame Relay interworking.

The ATM Forum

For the latest information on which ATM standards are supported, are in the works, and are completely formalized, the ATM Forum (www.atmforum.com) is the best resource.

The ATM Transmission Path

I've mentioned several times the virtual path and the virtual channel, and Figure 7. 20 gives them a bit more context. Think of the virtual channel as an individual conversation, so that each voice, video, data, and image transmission has its own unique virtual channel. The number of that channel will change between any two switches, depending on what was assigned at the time the session was negotiated.

All similar virtual channels—that is, all those that have the same QoS request—are bundled into a common virtual path. Virtual Path 1 might be all real-time voice that has a very low tolerance for delay and loss; Virtual Path 2 might be for streaming media, which requires continuous bandwidth, minimum delay, and no loss; and Virtual Path 3 might be for non-mission-critical data, so best-effort service is fine. ATM is very elastic in terms of its tolerance of any losses and delays and allocation of bandwidth. It provides an easy means for the network operator to

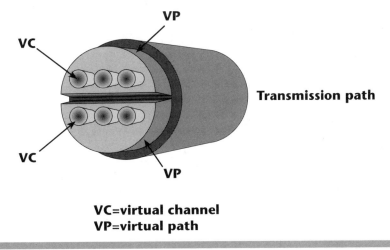

VC=virtual channel
VP=virtual path

Figure 7.20   The relationship of VP, VC, and transmission path

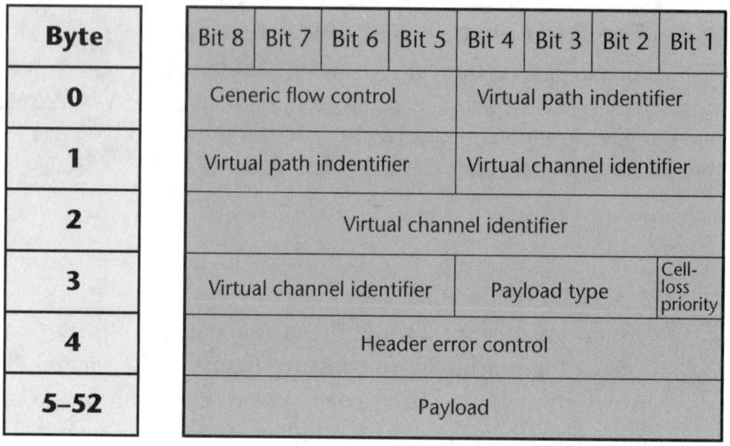

Byte	Bit 8	Bit 7	Bit 6	Bit 5	Bit 4	Bit 3	Bit 2	Bit 1
0	Generic flow control				Virtual path indentifier			
1	Virtual path indentifier				Virtual channel identifier			
2	Virtual channel identifier							
3	Virtual channel identifier			Payload type			Cell-loss priority	
4	Header error control							
5–52	Payload							

Figure 7.21 ATM cell structure

administrate QoS. Instead of having to manage each channel individually in order to guarantee the service class requested, the manager can do it on a path basis, thereby easing the network management process.

To illustrate how we identify what paths and channels need to be taken within the cell, Figure 7.21 shows an ATM cell structure. The header information includes information on the virtual path between Switch A and Switch B. It also shows the channel assignment, the type of payload, and the loss tolerance. In essence, the header provides the QoS metric, and the payload makes up the other 48 bytes of that cell. QoS is one of the great strengths of ATM, and ATM defines a series of specific QoS parameters that tailor cells to fit the video, data, voice, and mixed-media traffic.

Where ATM Fits in the Network

When does ATM fit into the network, and in what part does it fit? The way technologies seem to evolve is that they find their first placement in the core network, where there are high traffic volumes, to justify the investments required for the new technologies. Therefore, much of today's ATM equipment is in core networks—either ISPs, telcos, or other network operators. ATM then filters into the access network and into the metropolitan area network. Typically, you find it first where there are concentrations of early adopter-type customers. Ultimately, a new technology makes its way into the LAN, where you must reengineer the local enterprise to provide QoS, not just high bandwidth (see Figure 7.22).

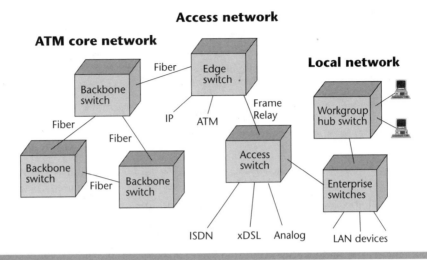

Figure 7.22 The ATM infrastructure

ATM Markets

According to Vertical Systems Consulting (www.verticalsystems.com), by 2002 the global market for equipment and services is expected to be roughly US$13 billion, with about half of that, US$6.9 billion, outside the United States. Equipment revenues by 2002 are expected to be around US$9.4 billion, and service revenues around US$3.9 billion. The United States today accounts for 75% of the worldwide revenues. Europe is the second largest market, and the United Kingdom accounts for most of the ATM ports. Canada is next biggest, and Asia Pacific is the fastest growing. Some 50 providers currently offer ATM UNI services.

Advantages and Disadvantages of ATM

ATM's benefits can be summarized as follows:

- Provides hardware switching, which results in high performance
- Allows dynamic bandwidth for bursty data
- Provides CoS and QoS support for multimedia
- Scales in speed and network size
- Provides a common LAN/WAN architecture
- Provides opportunities for simplification via its virtual circuit architecture
- Has strong traffic engineering and network management capabilities
- Currently used by some 1,500 U.S. enterprises

The following are disadvantages of ATM:

- Has small cell size
- Has high overhead
- Has high service costs
- Requires new equipment
- Requires new technical expertise

Another disadvantage of ATM is that confusion arises when some of the capabilities of ATM begin to be offered by other approaches, such as Multiprotocol Label Switching (MPLS), as discussed in Chapter 10.

For more learning resources, quizzes, and discussion forums on concepts related to this chapter, see www.telecomessentials.com/learningcenter.

Chapter 8

Local Area Networking

This entire book uses terminology that comes from the domain of local area networking, and in this chapter, you'll become familiar with the basics of local area network (LAN) components—the history of LANs, the key issues in the various architectures, issues related to LAN interconnection and internetworking, and trends in enterprise networks.

▪ LAN Basics

In the early 1980s, when most businesses were still using networked mainframes, two changes took place in computing infrastructures. First, there was a general growth in the number of devices in the organization, which created traffic growth. Second, skilled, engineering-oriented users began sneaking their own workstations in to work, and they would ask the company's MIS department to provide networking to the host computer; this created additional challenges for enterprise networking.

The increased traffic made companies step back to figure out how all the information that was creating all the traffic was being used. They found that about 80% of the information used by people within a given business address also came from within that address. Only 20% was being exchanged with a location outside the enterprise's physical perimeters. This was a clue that a networking option was needed to focus on a more limited geographical span, and the solution that emerged became known as the LAN.

LAN Concepts and Benefits

Given that in the 1980s up to 80% of the data used within a business address also came from that address, one key concept associated with the traditional LAN is that it acts as a common data highway that allows the linking of internal information resources. This common highway provides a great economic advantage because it allows resources—both software and hardware—to be shared.

Another key concept associated with local area networking is that the LAN is responsible for connecting the senders and the receivers, and it discriminates between all the nodes on the network. Traditionally, LANs relied on a shared medium (see Figure 8.1). Everyone was basically connected to the same cable (until about 1987, the medium was generally coax cable, and then other media were built into the recommendations, as well). Because there's an increasing demand for bandwidth to the desktop to support multimedia applications, we are moving away from these shared-media environments to configurations that use hubs or switches. These devices enable each workstation to have its own dedicated connection, increasing the bandwidth available to the workstation.

Finally, LANs can be deployed to serve either peer-to-peer arrangements, where essentially every node is equal (that is, capable of processing and storing in its own right), or server-based networks, in which one computer is the repository (that is, the *server*) and the other computers request information from and store information on the server.

There are four benefits associated with creating these internal LAN infrastructures:

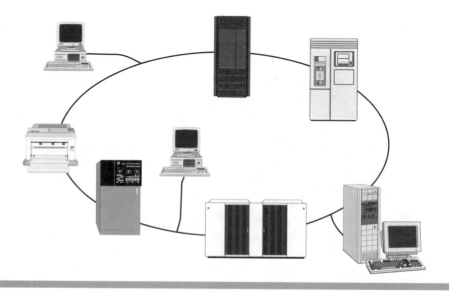

Figure 8.1   An example of a shared-medium LAN

- They allow very timely access to data. Knowledge is a competitive edge, so the faster you have access to the newest and latest information, the better off you will be in servicing customers and developing products.

- They allow standardization of applications. Over time, departments acquire different computing platforms, depending on the cycles between centralized and decentralized management. So, instead of having to go through the labor hours and cost of porting applications to reside in different platforms, you can use LANs to enable sharing of an application over the common data highway, resulting in savings and convenience.

- Because of the resource sharing, they provide great cost reductions.

- They promote speedy and functional communication within an organization.

LAN Components

Typically, a LAN is made up of several key elements:

- **Network nodes**—A network node is not a specific device; it is a single, addressable entity. It is an element to which a communications line interfaces, so a node could be a personal computer, a multiplexer, a modem, and so on. In the context of a LAN, a unique address is associated with each network node.

- **NICs**—The network interface card (NIC), sometimes referred to as a network adapter card, fits inside a computer and connects it to the underlying physical transport.

- **Cabling system**—The cabling system (which can be either wired or wireless media) performs the actual connection.

- **Software**—Software moves from computer to computer and packages bits into known containers with proper navigational controls.

- **User interface**—The user interface provides a way for the user to operate the software.

- **Operating system**—The operating system services the users' needs for files and devices such as printers, and it provides network management functions.

LAN Characteristics

LANs are grouped according to four key characteristics:

- The types of transmission media over which they can operate

- The transport technique they use to transmit data over the network (that is, broadband or baseband)

■ The access method, which is involved in determining who gets to use the network and when they get to use it

■ The topology, or mapping, of the network (that is, the physical and logical connections between the nodes on the network)

The following sections describe each of these four characteristics in detail.

LAN Transmission Media

Chapter 3, "Transmission Media: Characteristics and Applications," describes the advantages and disadvantages of the media types, and this section talks specifically about the considerations in selecting the appropriate media for a LAN.

First and foremost, as with selecting transmission media for metropolitan area network (MAN) or wide area network (WAN) environments, you need to think about bandwidth. You need to evaluate the kind of capacity you need: How much do you need per client? How much do you need per server? Typically servers require more capacity than clients because they service multiple simultaneous sessions, but some clients in an organization might use applications such as three-dimensional modeling and simulation and therefore require as much capacity as some of the shared servers. You should also evaluate the bandwidth based on traffic inside workgroups and traffic over the backbone between workgroups. Clusters or workgroups are made up of people who have the greatest community of interest, and therefore the majority of traffic sharing occurs within each cluster. However, there are reasons to have interdepartmental or interworkgroup communications as well, and therefore you need the backbone to provide connectivity between all the distinct clusters. So, the backbone should be engineered for great future capacity, and the workgroups should be set up so that they can easily be adjusted in the cases of moves, adds, and other changes.

The second consideration regarding LAN transmission media has to do with cost and ease of connectivity, and that speaks specifically to the installation, as well as to moves, adds, and other changes. In the average, rather stable, environment, at least 60% to 75% of the employees are relocated at least once a year, so equipment, features, and services must move along with them. And, of course, some environments have many reorganizations and require yet more consideration in this area. For example, in an enterprise where reorganization is common, a wireless LAN is probably the easiest way to support such a dynamic environment. The tradeoff is that wireless media provide less bandwidth than, say, fiber, and with a wireless LAN, you have to create smaller clusters. Again, what media you choose depends greatly on the application.

The third consideration regarding LAN transmission media is sensitivity to interference and noise. If a LAN is being deployed in a manufacturing plant where other equipment emits interfering levels of noise, the noise could play havoc with a twisted-pair or a wireless LAN, whereas coax and fiber would be much less susceptible to the interference.

Finally, of course, you need to consider security requirements. Again, there is no such thing as complete security, and each situation needs a different amount of security. You need to add encryption and other security mechanisms in almost any environment, but in some cases, you need to take the extra step of choosing a medium that's more difficult to tap into, such as coax or fiber.

Most of the LAN standards today support the full range of media types. They vary in terms of things such as the distances allowed between the devices and their backbones, so you need to choose the media that are appropriate given your situation.

LAN Transport Techniques

An important feature of a LAN is its transport technique: whether it is broadband or baseband (see Figure 8.2). *Broadband* means multichannel, so a broadband LAN implies that, through Frequency Division Multiplexing (FDM), multiple independent channels can carry analog or digital information, depending on the interfaces. This is essentially the way cable TV operates: There are multiple channels of programming, and each one runs over a different portion of the frequency band. When you request a particular channel from the interface device, the set-top box, the device selects the frequency band on which that channel is allocated. Cable TV is a multichannel coaxial system. The vast majority of LANs (probably 85% or so), however, are baseband LANs that use the Ethernet standard.

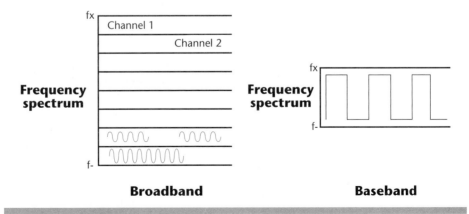

Figure 8.2 Broadband versus baseband

Table 8.1 Traditional LAN Standards

Characteristic	Ethernet	Token Ring	FDDI
Standard	IEEE 802.3	IEEE 802.5	ANSI X3T9.5
Logical topology	Bus	Ring	Ring
Physical topology	Bus, star	Ring, star	Dual ring, dual bus
Media	Coax, UTP/STP, fiber	Coax, UTP, STP	Fiber
Transmission mode	Baseband	Baseband	Baseband
Bandwidth	10Mbps, 100Mbps, 1000Mbps	4Mbps, 16Mbps, 100Mbps	100Mbps
Media access	Nondeterministic	Deterministic	Deterministic
Control	CSMA/CD, CSMA/CA	Token passing	Token passing

Baseband implies a single-channel digital system, and this single channel carries information in containers—that is, packets or frames—that are specified by the LAN standard in use. The traditional LAN standards are Ethernet, Token Ring, and Fiber Distributed Data Interface (FDDI). Table 8.1 compares these three standards.

The most widely used of the baseband standards is Ethernet, which, as mentioned earlier, accounts for about 85% of the installed LAN base. IEEE 802.3 is the working group that creates the Ethernet standards. IEEE 802.3 defines the first generation of Ethernet (that is, 10Mbps); 802.3u defines Fast Ethernet (that is, 100Mbps); and 802.3z, which appeared at the end of 1997, defines Gigabit Ethernet (that is, 1Gbps). We're now awaiting 10Gbps Ethernet. Ethernet technology in general, but particularly Gigabit and 10Gbps Ethernet, is being considered as a very plausible solution for broadband in the local loop. You will increasingly see announcements about neighborhoods that will be testing this approach to creating what is essentially a high-bandwidth shared system. Token Ring originated in the IBM environment. It's specified under IEEE 802.5, and it appears as 4Mbps, 16Mbps, and 100Mbps. (The 100Mbps specification, called High-speed Token Ring, never gained acceptance in the marketplace.) Table 8.2 lists some of the most commonly used Ethernet LAN technologies and the cabling requirements for each.

Despite the fact that FDDI was the first LAN standard to provide 100Mbps for use in a backbone application, it did not capture a major market share. The transition to a higher grade of Ethernet is much simpler for companies than is a transition to an entirely new protocol.

Table 8.2 LAN Technologies and Cabling Requirements

Technology	Type of Cable
Ethernet (10Mbps)	
10Base5	Thick coax
10Base2	Thin coax
10BaseT	2-pair UTP
10BaseFL	2 strands of multimode optical fiber
Fast Ethernet (100Mbps)	
100BaseTX	2-pair Cat 5 UTP
100BaseT4	4-pair Cat 3 UTP
100BaseT2	2-pair Cat 3 UTP
100BaseFX	2 strands of multimode optical fiber
Gigabit Ethernet (1Gbps)	
1000BaseSX	Short-wavelength multimode optical fiber
1000BaseLX	Long-wavelength single-mode optical fiber
1000BaseCX	Coax patch cable
1000BaseT	4-pair Cat 5 or Cat 5e UTP
1000BaseTX	2-pair Cat 6 (currently a TIA draft proposal)

The prevailing standard in the world is Ethernet. It generally appears as Fast Ethernet or Gigabit Ethernet in the backbone, connecting together individual Fast Ethernet or 10Mbps Ethernet LAN segments (see Figure 8.3).

LAN Access Methods

The third main LAN characteristic is the access methods, which are involved in determining who gets to use the network and when they get to use it. There are two main approaches: token passing and carrier-sense multiple-access/collision detect (CSMA/CD).

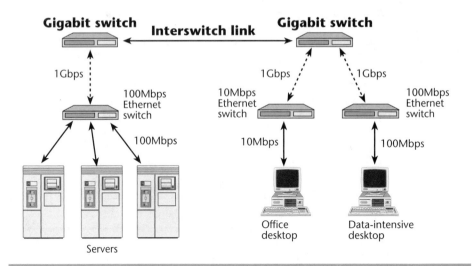

Figure 8.3   An example of Gigabit Ethernet

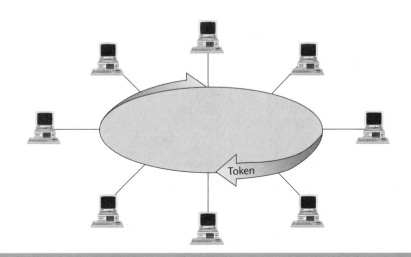

Figure 8.4   Token passing

Token Passing

Token passing is used with the Token Ring and FDDI architectures (see Figure 8.4).
Here is how Token Ring works:

1. The active master, chosen through a process called *beaconing,* inserts a
   token (that is, specially formatted packet) into the ring.

2. The token circulates the ring and is regenerated by each workstation it passes. (In Token Ring networks, a workstation obtains data only from its upstream neighbor, regenerates it, and sends it to its downstream neighbor.)

3. When a workstation has data to send, it waits for the token to pass by and grabs it off the wire. The station then injects its data packets onto the wire.

4. The packets circulate the ring and are examined and regenerated by each workstation. Once the receiving workstation receives the packets, it marks them as received when it regenerates and reinjects them. This marking notifies the sender that the data was in fact received when it finally returns to the sender. The sender then generates a new token and injects it into the ring.

To prevent any particular workstation from hogging the ring, a transmitting station can hold the token (and thus transmit data packets) for a specific interval, called the *token hold time*. If the time expires before the station has transmitted all its information, it must stop transmitting and put a new token back on the ring so that other stations have a chance to communicate. When the token gets back to the waiting workstation, it can resume transmitting.

A benefit of token passing is that it is a *deterministic* technique: You can always calculate the maximum delay that you'll encounter in moving information between any two points on that network, and this is especially important for applications with defined response times, such as process control. For example, an oil pipeline may have sensors in the pipelines to detect minute leakage. The oil company wants to know exactly how long it will take for the alarm from the sensor to reach the control station to shut off the valve, in order to avoid leaking oil into the community. In a LAN where there's a need to determine the delay, token passing works very well. The disadvantage of token passing is that it occurs in a unidirectional ring, so it takes time to pass the tokens. A device has to wait until it receives a token before it can send it, and if the ring is broken because a device goes down, the ring is then unable to send tokens until the ring is recovered (that is, the failed device is either taken out of commission or reinitiated). Today, almost all Token Ring interfaces have an electrical shunt present to prevent this from happening.

CSMA/CD

CSMA/CD is used with the Ethernet standard. CSMA/CD is a *nondeterministic* access method, meaning that any device can send whenever it determines that the network is clear. However, each device must listen to the network at all times because there is the potential for a collision to occur. If a collision occurs, both sending devices back off the network and wait a random number of nanoseconds or milliseconds before attempting to retransmit.

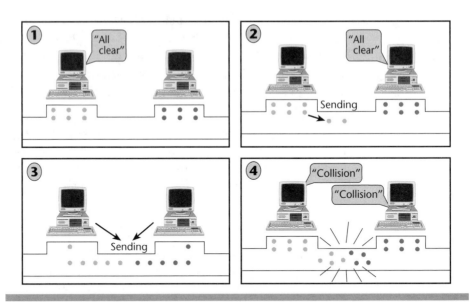

Figure 8.5 CSMA/CD

Figure 8.5 shows an example of how CSMA/CD works:

1. The terminals listen to the network.

2. Both of the terminals assume that the network is clear. They both start sending, but they continue listening because they know there's a chance that their messages will collide.

3. The messages do collide, so both terminals stop sending.

4. One terminal waits 20 milliseconds, and the other waits 50 milliseconds, and then they again attempt to transmit, assuming that their messages won't bump into each other. Because the terminals waited different amounts of time, most likely the messages don't collide and therefore get transmitted. However, if the messages collide again, the terminals repeat the back-off and random-wait procedure up to 16 times before the frames are dropped.

In this type of environment, the more devices you add and the greater the traffic volumes, the more likely collisions will occur. When collisions start to exceed the available throughput, you need to start segmenting the LAN into smaller clusters, called *collision domains* in Ethernet parlance, or consider making the move to switched Ethernet LANs.

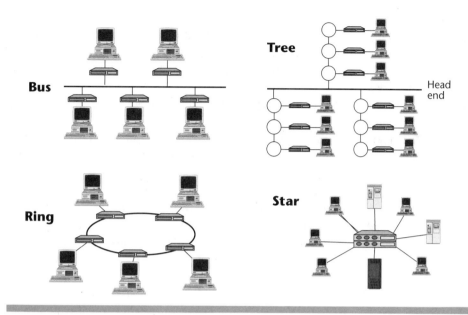

Figure 8.6 LAN topologies

LAN Topologies

The final characteristic of a LAN has to do with *topologies*—the physical and logical mapping of the network. The most common LAN topologies are the tree, bus, ring, and star topologies, which are illustrated in Figure 8.6. The tree topology is commonly used in broadband LANs, and the bus, ring, and star topologies are used in baseband LANs. In today's environment, the most common physical topology is the star, and the most common logical topology—that is, how the signals are exchanged between stations—is the bus.

Tree Topology

In the tree topology, the root of the tree is the headend, or the central retransmission facility. The trunk cable is attached to this root. Various branch cables are attached to the trunk cable. From there, user devices can be connected. Although most broadband networks use a single cable, some use a dual-cable system—one cable for each direction to and from the headend. All transmissions must pass through the headend because each device transmits on one frequency and receives on another. The headend is responsible for translating the device's transmit frequency to the receive frequency of another device, and this frequency translation is called *remodulation*.

Bus Topology

The bus topology, which is the oldest topology, functions like a multipoint circuit. All stations are attached via cable taps or connections to a single length of cable—a wire with two open ends. The single cable is referred to as a *trunk, backbone,* or *segment.*

Each station can detect and place signals on the bus according to the access method. Only one computer at a time can send data on a bus network. Signals travel in both directions along the bus, from the point of insertion. Any other station on the network can receive a transmission from the station. Because the data is sent to the entire network, it travels from one end of the cable to the other. If the signal were to be allowed to continue uninterrupted, it would keep bouncing back and forth along the cable, preventing other computers from sending signals. Therefore, the signal must be stopped after it's had a chance to reach the proper destination address. A component called a *terminator* is placed at each end of the cable to absorb free signals and to clear the cable so that other computers can send data.

The bus topology is a *passive* topology. Computers only listen for data being sent on the network; they are not responsible for moving data from one computer to the next. An advantage of the bus topology is that it uses short cable lengths, and therefore it uses cable economically. Because the transmission media are inexpensive and easy to work with, the network is easy to extend. A disadvantage of the bus topology is that problems are difficult to isolate. A cable break can affect many users, and the network can become slow when traffic is heavy.

Ring Topology

In the ring topology, the nodes are connected by point-to-point links that are arranged to form an unbroken loop configuration. At each station the signal is received, regenerated, and transmitted to the next station on the ring, and data is transmitted in one direction around the ring. The ring is an *active* topology. That is, each computer acts like a repeater to boost the signal and send it on to the next computer. Because the signal passes through each computer, the failure of one computer can affect the entire network—but in practice this rarely occurs, because the ring interfaces contain passive electrical shunts that allow the ring to remain intact in case a station is down or malfunctioning.

An advantage of the ring topology is that it can spread over long distances because each station regenerates the signal. Another advantage is ease of implementing distributed control and checking facilities; all computers have equal access, and the performance is even, despite the fact that there are many users. A potential disadvantage is sensitivity to station failures (that is, one failed station might break the ring). Also, problems in a ring network are difficult to isolate, and network reconfiguration disrupts the operation of the entire network.

Star Topology

In the star topology, all stations are connected by cable segments to a centralized component called a *hub*. Devices can communicate with each other only through the hub. The star topology offers centralized resources and management. The advantages of the star topology include ease of fault isolation, ease of bypassing and repairing faulty stations, and high cost-efficiencies. Also, it's much easier to modify or add new computers in a star network than to do so in other topologies. Disadvantages include the need for a lot of cable to interconnect all the stations and the potential for total network disruption if the central hub facility fails.

There are a number of variations on star networks. The star bus, for instance, is a combination of the bus and star topologies. It involves several star networks linked together with linear bus trunks. The star ring, sometimes referred to as the star-wired ring, looks similar to a star bus, except that the hubs in the star ring are connected in a star pattern and the main hub contains the actual ring.

■ LAN Interconnection and Internetworking

The realm of LAN interconnection devices offers a number of options. This section discusses the nature of hubs, LAN switches, virtual LANs (VLANs), bridges, routers, and IP switches.

Hubs

Hubs interconnect the wiring that's connected to workstations. They are a building block of most networks. There are three major types of hubs:

- **Active**—Active hubs regenerate and retransmit signals, just as a repeater does. Because hubs typically have 8 to 12 ports for network computers to connect to, they are sometimes called *multiport repeaters*. Active hubs require electrical power to run (that's why they're called active).

- **Passive**—Passive hubs serve as connection points and do not regenerate the signal; the signal simply passes through the hub. They do not require electrical power to run. Wiring panels and punchdown blocks are examples of passive hubs.

- **Hybrid**—Hybrid hubs accommodate several different types of cables.

You can connect hubs together to expand a hub network. The advantages of hubs are that they make it easy to change or expand wiring systems, they use different ports to accommodate different cabling types, and they centralize the monitoring of network activity and traffic. Hubs, which are sometimes called *concentrators* or *multistation access units* (MSAUs), can also eliminate the need for NICs with onboard transceivers at each node or personal computer.

A group of transceivers can all be located in and managed by an *intelligent hub*. Intelligent hubs are modular and chassis based, with slots that accommodate the user's choice of interface modules—such at Ethernet, Token Ring, or FDDI—for connectivity to LANs, WANs, or other network devices. The number of ports on the NIC determines the number of users in the particular star. Intelligent hubs often provide integrated management and internetworking capabilities, as well as Simple Network Management Protocol (SNMP)-based network management. New generations also offer bridging, routing, and switching functions.

Figure 8.7 shows a network that uses a combination of interconnection devices. Intelligent hubs provide connectivity between workstations that comprise a given cluster. An internal backbone is used to internetwork the intelligent hubs to move between different clusters. Those intelligent hubs then connect into a backbone router for purposes of WAN, or campuswide, connectivity.

LAN Switches

LAN switches are a very cost-effective solution to the need for increased bandwidth in workgroups. Each port on the switch delivers a dedicated channel to the device or devices attached to that port, thereby increasing the workgroup's total bandwidth and also increasing the bandwidth available to individual users.

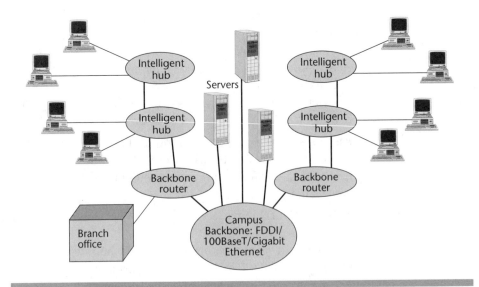

Figure 8.7 Using interconnection devices

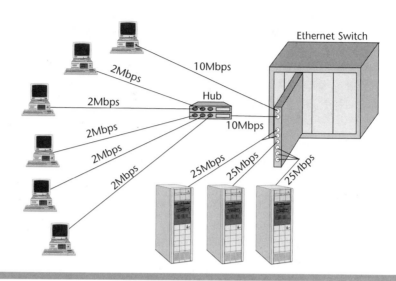

Figure 8.8 An example of a switched Ethernet configuration

Figure 8.8 shows a simple example of a switched Ethernet configuration. One workstation requires 10Mbps on its own, so it has the full services of a 10Mbps port on the switched Ethernet card. Five workstations, on the other hand, each need 2Mbps, so one 10Mbps port serves all five workstations. These five workstations connect into a hub, and that hub connects into the actual port. Servers have extra bandwidth requirements—the ones in Figure 8.8 require 25Mbps—so they are each served by a bonding of several 10Mbps ports.

The key applications for LAN switches are to interconnect the elements of a distributed computing system, to provide high-speed connections to campus backbones and servers, and to provide high bandwidth to individual users who need it. Instead of sharing a 10Mbps LAN among a number of terminals in a workgroup, a LAN switch can be used, and an individual workstation can get the entire 10Mbps. LAN switches provide great scalability because they enable the network to increase in bandwidth with the fairly simple addition of more switched ports. Thus, LAN switches have many benefits, including scalability in terms of bandwidth, flexibility, and high performance.

Figure 8.9 shows how an Ethernet switch can be used to connect devices that are on the same segment, some of which are served by one shelf of the Ethernet switch and others of which are served by connecting shelves together. On the backplane, you can provide internetworking between the Ethernet segments, so you can provide internetworking on a campuswide basis.

As the amount of traffic has grown in the enterprise and as the nature of applications has become more sophisticated, we have been increasing the

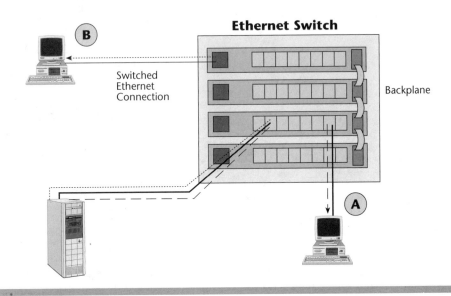

Figure 8.9   An Ethernet switch

bandwidth associated with LANs. Today, it is common to see 10Mbps being delivered to an individual desktop and 100Mbps serving as the cluster capacity. To facilitate internetworking between these high-capacity desktops and Fast Ethernet clusters, Gigabit Ethernet is increasingly being used in the backbone. As shown in Figure 8.3 earlier in the chapter, Gigabit Ethernet switches can connect underlying 100Mbps or 10Mbps LAN segments, and the 10Mbps or 100Mbps LAN switches can deliver 10Mbps to the desktop and 100Mbps to the segment.

VLANs

Switched LANs enable us to create VLANs, which don't completely fit the earlier definition of a LAN as being limited in geographical scope. With a VLAN, geography has no meaning. You could have two people in a Singapore office, three in New York, one in London, and four in Cairo, and they could all be part of the same LAN, a VLAN, because the LAN is defined by software rather than by hardware and location. Figure 8.10 shows an example of a VLAN.

A switched VLAN is a high-speed, low-latency broadcast group that unites an arbitrary collection of endstations on multiple LAN segments. Switched virtual networking eliminates the bottlenecks that are normally associated with a physical LAN topology by creating high-speed switched connections between endstations on different LAN segments. Users who want to belong to a particular broadcast domain do not have to be physically located on that LAN segment.

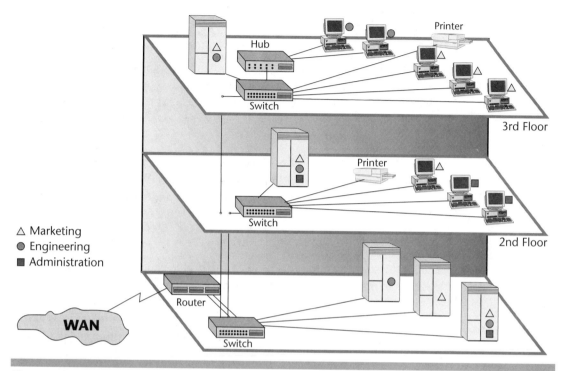

Figure 8.10 A VLAN

VLANs provide a software-based, value-added function by enabling the creation of a virtual broadcast domain, a shared LAN segment within a switched environment. Switching latencies on VLANs are typically one-tenth those of fast routers. However, routers are still required for inter-VLAN communications.

Bridges

Bridges entered the networking scene before routers. Applications for bridges include connecting network segments (for example, by taking 5 to 10 individual clusters and creating the appearance of a single logical VLAN). A bridge can also be used to increase the number of computers on a network or to extend the distance of a segment beyond what the specifications allow. Similarly, a bridge can be used for network segmentation in order to reduce traffic bottlenecks, or to control the flow of network traffic. Bridges can connect similar as well as dissimilar networks.

Bridges have several important functions:

- **Learning**—When the bridge is first connected to the network, it sends an announcement that says, "Hello. I'm your new bridge. What's your address?" All the other devices respond with, "Hello. Welcome to the neighborhood," along with their addresses. The bridge builds a table of local addresses, called the *Media Access Control sublayer addresses*. The MAC sublayer (which is equivalent to OSI Layer 2) controls access to the shared transmission medium. It is responsible for making the data frames and putting bits in fields that make sense, and it works with the physical layer, Layer 1. MAC standards, including IEEE 802.3, 802.4, and 802.5, define unique frame formats. Every NIC ever made has a globally unique burned-in MAC address.

- **Performing packet routing**—Bridges either filter, ignore, or forward packets.

- **Using the Spanning Tree Algorithm**—Bridges use the Spanning Tree Algorithm to select the most efficient network path and to disable all the other potential routes.

Figure 8.11 illustrates a local bridge installed between two LAN segments that are located at the same local premise. When the bridge is plugged in, it sends out a hello message to its community; the devices answer, and the bridge builds an addressing table. Say that PC A wants to send a document to Printer 1. The bridge realizes that that printer resides within its community. It knows the address and it therefore does not do anything except filter the packet. On the other hand, if PC A is attempting to communicate with Server Z, the bridge says, "Well, I don't know where that server is. It's not part of my local community, so it must be somewhere else on the other side of this bridge." The bridge then broadcasts that information

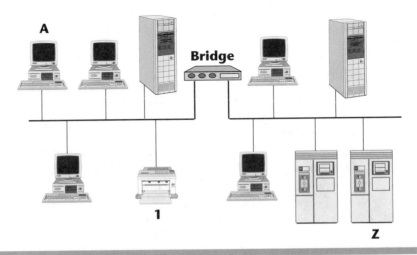

Figure 8.11 An example of a local bridge

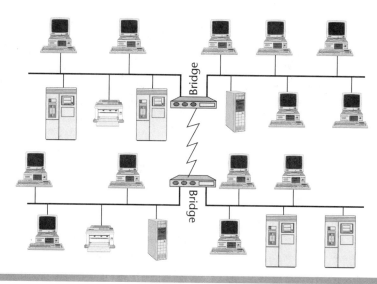

Figure 8.12   An example of remote bridges

out to as many LAN segments as are connected to the other side of the bridge. In essence, the bridge creates broadcast storms.

Bridges are not networkable devices; they can't target a destination network. All they can determine is whether a destination is or is not on its segment, and if the destination is somewhere else, the bridge sends a message to every somewhere else that it knows about. This can be an especially big problem if you use a bridge in a remote mode, as shown in Figure 8.12, because, in essence, you are trying to connect together remote locations by using a WAN link, which is expensive in terms of bandwidth. You pay for every bit sent, so sending messages to LAN segments that don't need to see them across a WAN link that doesn't need to be congested is inefficient.

Although bridges can operate in local and remote areas, today they are mostly used in the local environment. They operate at OSI Layer 2 and they are point-to-point—they do not understand networking or routing and relaying through a series of nodes. Bridges are protocol independent (Layer 3 and up), which keeps the software simple and inexpensive. Bridges cannot translate between different Layer 2 protocols (for example, between Ethernet and Token Ring). Bridges are primarily used to isolate traffic loads in the local environment because they offer fast throughput; a bridge doesn't have to do intelligent routing, which makes it faster and less expensive than a traditional router. Over time we've merged together the best features of bridges and routers so that some of the problems with each have begun to disappear.

Flat Networks

Flat networks are constructed by using bridges or Layer 2 LAN switches. This type of network is easy to configure, and it promises better performance than hierarchical networks; it offers higher throughput with lower latencies. However, the scalability of a flat network is limited, and a flat network is subject to broadcast storms.

Routers

The most popular internetworking device today is the router (see Figure 8.13). The applications for routers are quite similar to those for bridges. You use them for network segmentation and connection; that is, you use them either to segment larger networks into smaller ones or to connect smaller networks into a larger virtual whole. You can use a router to switch and route packets across multiple communications paths and disparate Layer 2 network types, and because it is a Layer 3 device, a router is networkable—it understands how to read network addresses and how to select the destination or target network, so it prohibits broadcast storms. This capability allows routers to act as firewalls between LAN segments. Routers can be associated with traffic filtering and isolation, and because they can read information about the network and transport protocols used, they can make forwarding decisions.

Routers can make linking and rerouting decisions, which makes possible selective routing of individual packets over multiple communication paths. Remember that bridges have to disable all but one path, whereas a router can decide on the fly between numerous communications paths. The path a router selects depends on the user's requirements, including cost, speed, and priority.

Routers are protocol specific, but they can support multiple protocols, such as TCP/IP or Novell's IPX/SPX. The key is that each of the protocols a router supports for internetworking requires its own separate routing table, so the more protocols the router supports, the more complex it is, the more memory intensive it is, and the more expensive it is. Routers can be used as bridges to connect similar and dissimilar networks, and again, they are often applied as firewalls.

The functions of a router are as follows:

- **Learning**—A router learns who its neighbors are and builds an addressing table based on their addresses.
- **Filtering**—A router filters packets based on the addressing information it has gathered.

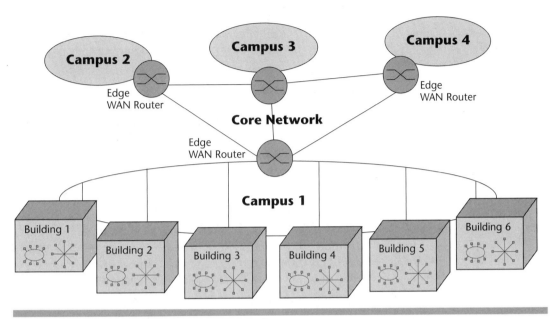

Figure 8.13 An example of routers in a network

- **Routing and switching**—A router selects the best destinations based on the network addresses, distance, cost, and availability.
- **Adapting to network conditions**—A router adapts to network conditions by changing what it considers to be the best or optimum paths, depending on the network traffic status.

How do routers actually work? A router has input ports for receiving packets and output ports for sending those packets toward their destination. When the packet comes to the input port, the router examines the packet header and checks the destination against a *routing table* (that is, a database that tells the router how to send packets to various destinations). Based on the information in the routing table, the packet is sent to a particular output port, and the output port sends the packets to a router that is one step closer to that packet's destination. Packets are delivered from node to node (that is, router to router) because, at each node, the router modifies the MAC address to be that of the next node. The destination network address does not change, of course, but the destination MAC changes at each node—this is the only way that the packet can travel from one node to the next.

If packets come to the input port more quickly than the router can process them, they are sent to a holding area called an *input queue*. The router then processes packets from the queue in the order in which were received. If the number of packets received exceeds the length of the queue, packets may be lost. When this happens, an error control mechanism (such as TCP) that is housed on the sending and receiving computers will have the packets resent. (You'll learn more about TCP in Chapter 9, "The Internet: Infrastructure and Service Providers.") There are two types of routing tables:

- **Static**—The simpler kind of routing table is the static routing table. In a static routing table, there are specific ways of routing data to other networks, and only those paths can be used. New routes can be added to the routing table, but they have to be manually programmed. Static routing can't adjust routes as network traffic changes, so it isn't an optimal option for many applications today. A static router knows only its own routing table and does not communicate changes to any of its neighbors.

- **Dynamic**—Dynamic routing is much more useful than static routing. It allows a packet to take multiple routes to reach its final destination. Dynamic routing also allows routers to change the way they route information, based on the amount of network traffic on some paths and routers. In dynamic routing, the routing table is a dynamic routing table that changes as network conditions change. A dynamic router talks with other routers so that they can all update their tables to reflect any changes.

There are two broad types of routing protocols: interior and exterior. Interior routing protocols are typically used only in the routers of an enterprise's intranet (that is, its internal network). Interior routing protocols include Routing Information Protocol (RIP) and Open Shortest Path First (OSPF). Exterior protocols are typically used for routers that are located in the Internet. Whereas there may be many different interior routing schemes, a single exterior routing system manages

Hierarchical Networks

Routers, when built into an enterprise internetwork, create a hierarchical network (that is, subnetworks interconnected by routers). They control traffic flow through segmentation, but this can degrade network performance because of delays, and it adds complexity to the overall network configuration. Hierarchical networks are typically used at the edge of a network to interconnect LANs or to provide WAN connectivity to remote LANs. Again, within the customer premises, the simpler bridge-based flat networks are used. As has been mentioned several times, however, traffic levels keep growing, and LANs keep getting busier, so both the edge and the core network are becoming loaded, resulting in network slowness and unacceptable delays.

the whole global Internet, and it's based on Border Gateway Protocol 4 (BGP-4). (Routing protocols are discussed in detail in Chapter 9.)

Routers use a hierarchical addressing scheme, whereby the address includes both the network address and the node address. Routers operate at Layer 3, so they are networkable—you can route and relay traffic through a series of routers. Routers are protocol sensitive, so the more internetworking protocols they support, the more complex the software and the greater the number of routing tables and algorithms required to support those protocols.

IP Switches

The network core is responsible for providing interconnectivity, server access, and network management to the edge devices on the network periphery. At the edge of a LAN, a shortage of network capacity, coupled with proliferation of broadcasts and multicasts, can create significant network problems. When the edge demand exceeds the capacity of the core, buffer overruns create capacity overload and lead to lost packets, reducing the availability and reliability of the network. As a result, users today are suffering from congestion, inadequate server access, and slow response times. People want to see information in a matter of a few seconds, so these problems are increasingly frustrating.

The solution to the problem of these increases in traffic in the core and at the edge is the IP switch. The IP switch was designed to speed up increasingly choked networks. An IP switch replaces the slower, more processing-intensive routers. Routers, in general, are slower than switches because they must examine multiple packet fields, make substitutions in the packet headers, and then compute the routes on a packet-by-packet basis. All this activity introduces congestion and latency. The idea behind IP switching was to find a way to make what is essentially a connectionless data technology behave like the more reliable circuit-switched network. The goal is to make networks—intranets, extranets, and the Internet—faster, as well as to enable the deployment of new genres of applications, including voice, video, and other streaming traffic.

IP switching has two major objectives. One is to add Quality of Service (QoS) support to IP. If we can make a network behave in a connection-oriented fashion, we can allocate resources end-to-end that promise to meet the required service level. (QoS is discussed in detail in Chapter 10, "Next-Generation Networks.") The second objective of IP switching is to provide a way to scale economically because we know that data traffic is growing at a substantial rate (about 30% to 40% per year). IP switching basically replaces a network that consists entirely of Layer 3 hop-by-hop routing and the subsequent associated delays with a route once/switch everything else scenario. That is, the first packet is routed, and then all the subsequent packets are switched on a Layer 2 basis to the

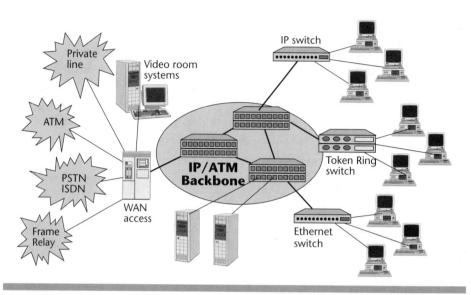

Figure 8.14 A switched LAN infrastructure with an IP/ATM backbone

destination over the selected virtual circuit. So IP switches vastly improve the performance at LAN/WAN integration points.

Figure 8.14 shows a switched LAN infrastructure that makes use of a high-speed packet backbone, which could be IP, ATM, or MPLS. An Ethernet switch serves a cluster, and a Token Ring switch serves another cluster. An IP switch serves a high-demand cluster. The infrastructure also includes individual servers as well as WAN access devices, all connected to the WAN edge devices, which in this case are the IP switches that help connect or establish a connection-oriented link end-to-end and thereby guarantee latencies and improve the performance associated with the internetwork.

■ Enterprise Network Trends

This chapter has mentioned some of the many trends in enterprise networks; they are summarized here. First, today there is more intelligence in the environment. We are moving to an era of ubiquitous, or pervasive, computing, which means that intelligence is being embedded into everyday objects. As these objects become intelligent, they communicate with each other, and hence they need network access points. Network intelligence is increasingly moving toward the edge, so policy management, proper QoS mapping, and aggregation of packets is increasingly occurring at the edge of the network. The current trend is for the core to become fast but dumb. However, the debate over the pros and cons of intelligence at the edge versus intelligence in the core has swung back and forth over the years. The reigning trend ultimately depends on what forces (technological, market, policy, regulatory, legal) are at work and which players dominate at any point in time.

We continue to see the emergence of very high-bandwidth, low-latency multimedia applications, and the bandwidth explosion that's under way will make it possible for content developers to create interesting new applications. We're also seeing more reliance on personal computing and communications, although the network touch points will change with personal digital assistants, intelligent appliances, and wearables.

We're also seeing a growing base of high-end routing systems as the old 80/20 scenario is reversing: Today 80% of information exchange is not occurring within locations but between different companies that work together either as allies or partners or that serve one another in some way. User devices are becoming increasingly smart, running with higher-level protocols, and everyone wants to be networked. The new applications, especially those in multimedia, video, and other streaming environments, are more bandwidth intensive, and they are also extremely delay sensitive.

The emerging enterprise network is characterized as being one that provides high capacity and most campus networks are reengineering to the Gigabit Ethernet standard. They will migrate to even higher rates, but at the moment, this migration means simply throwing bandwidth at the problem. You can support high-bandwidth applications with additional bandwidth, but remember that Ethernet does not offer good QoS. Therefore, when multimedia applications are the most dominant application type, we may have to shift to a different architecture—to one that supports QoS. Low delay is also necessary to support real-time flows, as is efficient support for bursty traffic, so the benefits of statistical multiplexing are needed. Networks need cost-effective end-to-end connectivity to handle the growing range of touch points, and we need a way to easily manage, reassign, and reallocate networks through standardized interfaces. In the not-too-distant future, we should see incredible advances on these fronts.

For more learning resources, quizzes, and discussion forums on concepts related to this chapter, see www.telecomessentials.com/learningcenter.

Chapter 9

The Internet: Infrastructure and Service Providers

This chapter explores the Internet, including how the Internet actually works, the structure of the Internet in terms of the various levels of service providers, and the organization and characteristics of the growing variety of service providers.

■ Internet Basics

Figure 9.1 is an astounding graph that speaks to the pace of Internet development. It shows the number of years it took a number of technologies to reach 50 million users worldwide. As you can see, whereas it took 74 years for the telephone to reach 50 million users, it took the World Wide Web only 4.

What forces are propelling our interest in the Internet? One main force is that usage is increasing dramatically; today some 250 million people worldwide have Internet access, and that number is growing by leaps and bounds. The Internet is very useful and easy to use, and for a growing number of people in the developed world, it is now the first place to look for information. As one colleague recently told me, in the past week, besides the numerous times he had used the Internet to get information for my work, he'd used the Internet to look up hotels for a weekend break, to determine what concerts are on in Dublin, to check the specification of a car, to transfer funds between bank accounts, to find the address of an old friend, and to obtain sheet music. Electronic commerce (e-commerce) is also growing, in both the business-to-consumer and business-to-business sectors. Another

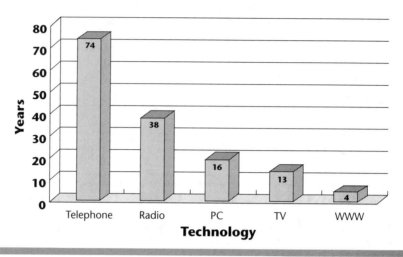

Figure 9.1   Internet pace: Years to reach 50 million users worldwide

contributor is the major shift toward the use of advanced applications, including pervasive computing, which introduces a wide range of intelligent appliances that are ready to communicate through the Internet, as well as applications that include the more captivating visual and sensory streams. Finally, the availability of broadband, or high-speed access technologies, further drives our interest in and our ability to interact with Web sites that involve the use of these advanced applications and offer e-commerce capabilities.

A Brief History of the Internet

To help understand the factors that contributed to the creation of the Internet, let's look very briefly at the history of the Internet. In 1969 the Advanced Research Projects Agency (ARPA) of the U.S. Department of Defense initiated a project to develop a distributed network. There were several reasons for doing this. First, the project was launched during the Cold War era, when there was an interest in building a network that had no single point of failure, and that could sustain an attack yet continue to function. Second, four supercomputer centers were located in four universities throughout the United States, and we wanted to connect them together so that we could engage in some more intensive processing feats. So, the Internet started as a wide area, packet-switching network called the ARPANET.

Toward the mid-1970s, ARPA was renamed the Defense Advanced Research Projects Agency (DARPA), and while it was working on the distributed, or packet-switched, network, it was also working on local area networks (LANs), paging networks, and satellite networks. DARPA recognized that there was a need for some form of internetworking protocol that would allow open communications between

Jonathan Postel and the Internet

Jonathan Postel played a pivotal role in creating and administering the Internet. He was one of a small group of computer scientists who created the ARPANET, the precursor to the Internet. For more than 30 years he served as editor of the Request for Comments (RFC) series of technical notes that began with the earliest days of the ARPANET and continued into the Internet. Although intended to be informal, RFCs often laid the foundation for technical standards governing the Internet's operation. Nearly 2,500 RFCs have been produced.

Also for 30 years, Postel handled the administrative end of Internet addresses, under the auspices of the Internet Assigned Numbers Authority (IANA), a U.S. government—financed entity. As part of the effort to hand over administration of the Internet to an international private corporation, Postel delivered a proposal to the government for transforming IANA into a nonprofit corporation with broad representation from the commercial and academic sectors. That organization is today known as the Internet Corporation for Assigned Names and Numbers (ICANN).

disparate networks. So, Internet Protocol (IP) was created to support an open-architecture network that could link multiple disparate networks via gateways—what we today refer to as *routers*.

In 1980, Transmission Control Protocol/Internet Protocol (TCP/IP) began to be implemented on an experimental basis, and by 1983, it was required in order for a subnetwork to participate in the larger virtual Internet.

The original Internet model was not based on the telephone network model. It involved distributed control rather than centralized control, and it relied on cooperation among its users, which initially were largely academicians and researchers. With the original Internet, there's no regulation, no monopoly, and no universal service mandate (although these issues are being considered seriously now).

Today, no one agency is in charge of the Internet, although the Internet Society (ISOC) is a nonprofit, nongovernmental, international organization that focuses on Internet standards, education, and policy issues. ISOC is an organization for Internet professionals that serves as the organizational home of the Internet Engineering Task Force (IETF), which oversees various organizational and coordinating tasks. ISOC is composed of a board of trustees, the Internet Architecture Board, the IETF, the Internet Research Task Force, the Internet Engineering Steering Group, and the Internet Research Steering Group.

The IETF is an international community of network designers, operators, vendors, and researchers, whose job is to evolve the Internet and smooth its operation by creating technical standards through consensus. Other organizations that are critical to the functioning of the Internet include American Registry for Internet Numbers (ARIN) in the United States, Asia Pacific Network Information Center

Prevailing Conditions and Exchange Points

Since the beginning of the Internet's history, we've been trying to prevent having a single point of failure. We have distributed nodes throughout the network so that if one node goes down or a series of links goes down, there can still be movement between the other devices, based on a wide variety of alternative nodes and links.

But we're doing a turnaround now because these very interconnection points that provide interconnection between ISPs can also act as vulnerable points for the network and even for a nation. If the exchange points are taken down within a given country, the Internet activity within that country may cease or fail altogether, with great economic consequences. Always remember that, in the end, the prevailing conditions dictate whether an architecture is truly good, reliable, and high performance.

(APNIC) in Asia-Pacific, and RIPE NCC (Reseaux IP Europeens Network Coordination Center) in Europe. These organizations manage and sell IP addresses and autonomous system numbers. IANA manages and assigns protocol and port number, and ICANN (formed in 1998) is responsible for managing top-level domain names and the root name servers. ICANN also delegates control for domain name registry below the top-level domains. (Domain names and the role of IP addresses are discussed later in this chapter.)

What the Internet Is and How It Works

To understand the Internet, it's important to first understand the concept of a computer network (see Figure 9.2). A network is formed by interconnecting a set of computers, typically referred to as *hosts,* in such a way that they can interoperate with one another. Connecting these hosts involves two major components: hardware (that is, the physical connections) and software. The software can be run on the same or dissimilar host operating systems, and it is based on standards that define its operation. These standards, referred to as *protocols,* provide the formats for passing packets of data, specify the details of the packet formats, and describe how to handle error conditions. The protocols hide the details of network hardware and permit computers of different hardware types, connected by different physical connections, to communicate, despite their differences. (Protocols are discussed in detail later in this chapter.)

In the strictest sense, the Internet is an internetwork composed of a worldwide collection of networks, routers, gateways, servers, and clients, that use a common set of telecommunications protocols—the IP family—to link them together (see Figure 9.3). The term *client* is often used to refer to a computer on the network

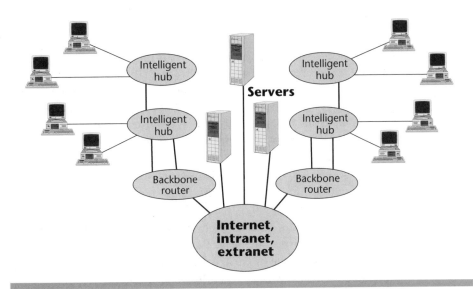

Figure 9.2 Network components

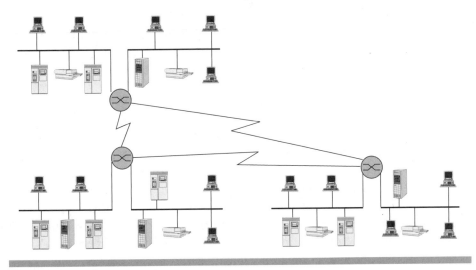

Figure 9.3 An internetwork

that takes advantage of the services offered by a server. It also refers to a user running the client side of a client/server application. The term *server* describes either a
computer or a software-based process that provides services to network users or
Web services to Internet users.

Networks connect servers and clients, allowing the sharing of information and computing resources. Network equipment includes cable and wire, network adapters, hubs, switches, and various other physical connectors. In order for the network to be connected to the Internet, the network must send and retrieve data by using TCP/IP and related protocols. Networks can also be connected to form their own internets: Site-to-site connections are known as *intranets*, internal networks that are generally composed of LANs interconnected by a WAN that uses IP. Connections between partnering organizations, using IP, are known as *extranets*.

The Internet is a complex, highly redundant network of telecommunications circuits connected together with internetworking equipment, including routers, bridges, and switches. In an environment consisting of several network segments with different protocols and architectures, the network needs a device that not only knows the address of each segment but can also determine the best path for sending data and filtering broadcast traffic to the local segment. The Internet moves data by relaying traffic in packets from one computer network to another. If a particular network or computer is down or busy, the network is smart enough to reroute the traffic automatically. This requires computers (that is, routers) that are able to send packets from one network to another. Routers make decisions about how to route the data or packets, they decide which pipe is best, and then they use that best pipe. Routers work at the network layer, Layer 3, of the OSI model, which allows them to switch and route packets across multiple networks. Routers read complex network addressing information in the packet; they can share status and routing information with one another and use this information to bypass slow or malfunctioning connections.

Routing is the main process that the Internet host uses to deliver packets. The Internet uses a hop-by-hop routing model, which means that each host or router that handles a packet examines the destination address in the packet's IP header, computes the next hop that will bring the packet one step closer to its destination, and delivers that packet to the next hop, where the process is repeated. To make this happen, routing tables must match destination addresses with next hops, and routing protocols must determine the content of these tables. Thus, the Internet and the public switched telephone network (PSTN) operate quite differently from one another. The Internet uses packet switching, where there's no dedicated connection and the data is fragmented into packets. Packets can be delivered via different routes over the Internet and reassembled at the ultimate destination. Historically, "back-office" functions such as billing and network management have not been associated with Internet. But the Internet emphasizes flexibility—the capability to route packets around congested or failed points.

Recall from Chapter 5, "The PSTN," that the PSTN uses circuit switching, so a dedicated circuit is set up and taken down for each call. This allows charging based on minutes and circuits used, which, in turn, allows chain-of-supply dealings. The major emphasis of the PSTN is on reliability. So, the Internet and the PSTN have different models and different ways of managing or routing traffic through the network, but they share the same physical foundation in terms of the transport infrastructure, or the types of communication links they use. (Chapter 4, "Establishing Communications Channels," discusses packet switching and circuit switching in detail.)

Internet Protocols

The Internet is a collection of networks that are interconnected logically as a single, large, virtual network. Messages between computers are exchanged by using packet switching. Networks can communicate with one another because they all use an internetworking protocol. Protocols are formal descriptions of messages to be exchanged and of rules to be followed in order for two or more systems to exchange information in a manner that both parties will understand. The following sections examine the Internet's protocols: TCP/IP, User Datagram Protocol (UDP), Internet Control Message Protocol (ICMP), Internet Group Management Protocol (IGMP), Address Resolution Protocol (ARP)/Reverse Address Resolution Protocol (RARP), routing protocols, and network access protocols.

TCP/IP

The IETF has technical responsibility for TCP/IP, which is the most popular and widely used of the internetworking protocols. All information to be transmitted over the Internet is divided into packets that contain a destination address and a sequence number. Packets are relayed through nodes in a computer network, along the best route currently available between the source and destination. Even though the packets may travel along different routes and may arrive out of sequence, the receiving computer is able to reassemble the original message. Packet size is kept relatively small—at 1,500 bytes or less—so that in the event of an error, retransmission is efficient. To manage the traffic routing and packet assembly/disassembly, the networks rely on intelligence from the computers and software that control delivery.

TCP/IP, referred to as the *TCP/IP suite* in Internet standards documents, gets its name from its two most important protocols, TCP and IP, which are used for interoperability among many different types of computers. A major advantage of TCP/IP is that it is a nonproprietary network protocol suite that can connect the hardware and operating systems of many different computers.

TCP   Network applications present data to TCP. TCP divides the data into packets and gives each packet a *sequence number* that is not unique, but which is nonrepeating for a very long time. These packets could represent text, graphics, sound, or video—anything digital that the network can transmit. The sequence numbers help to ensure that the packets can be reassembled correctly at the receiving end. Thus, each packet consists of content, or data, as well as the *protocol header,* the information that the protocol needs to do its work. TCP uses another piece of information to ensure that the data reaches the right application when it arrives at a system: the *port number,* which is within the range 1 to 65,535. Port numbers identify running applications on servers, applications that are waiting for incoming connections from clients. Port numbers identify one listening application from another. Ports 1 to 1,023 are reserved for server applications, although servers can use higher port numbers as well. Numbers between 1 and 1,023 are reserved for "well-known" applications (for example, Web servers run on port 80, FTP runs on port 21). Also, many recent protocols have been assigned well-known port numbers above 1,023. Ports with higher numbers, called "ephemeral" ports, are dynamically assigned to client applications as needed. A client obtains a random ephemeral port when it opens a connection to a well-known server port.

Data to be transmitted by TCP/IP has a port from which it is coming and a port to which it is going, plus an IP source and a destination address. Firewalls can use these addresses to control the flow of information. (Firewalls are discussed in Chapter 11, "Next-Generation Network Services.")

TCP is the protocol for sequenced and reliable data transfer. It breaks the data into pieces and numbers each piece so that the receipt can be verified and the data can be put back in the proper order. TCP provides Layer 4 (transport layer) functionality, and it is responsible for virtual circuit setup, acknowledgments, flow control, and retransmission of lost or damaged data. TCP provides end-to-end, connection-oriented, reliable, virtual circuit service. It uses virtual ports to make connections; ports are used to indicate where information must be delivered in order to reach the appropriate program, and this is how firewalls and application gateways can filter and direct the packets.

IP   IP handles packet forwarding and transporting of datagrams across a network. With packet forwarding, computers can send a packet on to the next appropriate network component, based on the address in the packet's header. IP defines the basic unit of data transfer, the datagram, also referred to as the packet, and it also defines the exact format of all data as it travels across the Internet. IP works like an envelope in the postal service, directing information to its proper destination. With this arrangement, every computer on the Internet has a unique address. (Addressing is discussed later in this chapter.)

IP provides software routines to route and to store and forward data among hosts on the network. IP functions at Layer 3 (the network layer), and it provides several services, including host addressing, error notification, fragmentation and reassembly, routing, and packet timeout. TCP presents the data to IP in order to provide basic host-to-host communication. IP then attaches to the packet, in a protocol header, the address from which the data comes and the address of the system to which it is going.

Under the standards, IP allows a packet size of up to 64,000 bytes, but we don't transmit packets that large because they would cause session timeouts and big congestion problems. Therefore, IP packets are segmented into 1,500-byte-maximum chunks.

IP always does its best to make the delivery to the requested destination host, but if it fails for any reason, it just drops the packet. As such, upper-level protocols should not depend on IP to deliver the packet every time. Because IP provides connectionless, unreliable service and because packets can get lost or arrive out of sequence, or the messages may take more than 1,500 bytes, TCP provides the recovery for these problems.

UDP

Like TCP, UDP is a Layer 4 protocol that operates over IP. UDP provides end-to-end, connectionless, unreliable datagram service. It is well suited for query-response applications, for multicasting, and for use with Voice over IP (VoIP). (VoIP is discussed in Chapter 11.) Because UDP does not request retransmissions, it minimizes what would otherwise be unmanageable delay; the result is that sometimes the quality is not very good. For instance, if you encounter losses or errors associated with a voice packet, the delays that would be associated with retransmitting that packet would render the conversation unintelligible. In VoIP, when you lose packets, you do not request retransmissions. Instead, you hope that the user can recover from the losses by other means. Unlike TCP, UDP does not provide for error correction and sequenced packet delivery; it is up to the application itself to incorporate error correction if required.

ICMP

ICMP provides error handling and control functions. It is tightly integrated with IP. ICMP messages, delivered in IP packets, are used for out-of-band messages related to network operation or misoperation. Because ICMP uses IP, ICMP packet delivery is unreliable. ICMP functions include announcing network errors, announcing network congestion, assisting in troubleshooting, and announcing timeouts.

IGMP

Another Layer 3 protocol is Internet Group Management Protocol (IGMP), whose primary purpose is to allow Internet hosts to participate in multicasting. The IGMP standard describes the basics of multicasting IP traffic, including the format of multicast IP addresses, multicast Ethernet encapsulation, and the concept of a host group (that is, a set of hosts interested in traffic for a particular multicast address). IGMP enables a router to determine which host groups have members on a given network segment, but IGMP does not address the exchange of multicast packets between routers.

ARP and RARP

At Layer 3 you also find ARP/RARP. ARP determines the physical address of a node, given that node's IP address. ARP is the mapping link between IP addresses and the underlying physical (MAC) address. RARP enables a host to discover its own IP address by broadcasting its physical address. When the broadcast occurs, another node on the LAN answers back with the IP address of the requesting node.

Routing Protocols

Routing protocols are protocols that allow routers to communicate with each other. They include Routing Information Protocol (RIP), Interior Gateway Protocol (IGP), Open Shortest Path First (OSPF), Exterior Gateway Protocol (EGP), and Border Gateway Protocol (BGP).

There are several processes involved in router operation. First, the router creates a routing table to gather information from other routers about the optimum paths. As discussed in Chapter 8, "Local Area Networking," the routing tables can be static or dynamic; dynamic routing tables are best because they adapt to changing network conditions. Next, when data is sent from a network host to a router en route to its destination, the router breaks open the data packet and looks at the destination address to determine the most efficient path between two endpoints. To identify the most efficient path, the router uses algorithms to evaluate a number of factors (called *metrics*), including distance and cost. Routing protocols consider all the various metrics involved when computing the best path.

Distance-Vector Versus Link-State Protocols   Two main types of routing protocols are involved in making routing decisions:

- **Distance-vector routing protocols**—These routing protocols require that each router simply inform its neighbors of its routing table. For each network path, the receiving router picks the neighbor advertising the lowest cost, and then the router adds this into its routing table for readvertisement. Common distance-vector routing protocols are RIP, Internetwork Packet Exchange (IPX) RIP, AppleTalk Routing Table Management Protocol (RTMP), and Cisco's Interior Gateway Routing Protocol (IGRP).

- **Link-state routing protocols**—Link-state routing protocols require that each router maintain at least a partial map of the network. When a network link changes state—up to down or vice versa—a notification is flooded throughout the network. All the routers note the change and recompute the routes accordingly. This method is more reliable, easier to debug, and less bandwidth-intensive than distance-vector routing, but it is also more complex and more computer- and memory-intensive. OSPF, Intermediate System to Intermediate System (IS-IS), and Network Link Services Protocol (NLSP) are link-state routing protocols.

Interior and Exterior Routing   *Interior routing* occurs within an *autonomous system,* which is a collection of routers under a single administrative authority that uses a common interior gateway protocol for routing packets. Most of the common routing protocols, such as RIP and OSPF, are interior routing protocols. The autonomous system number is a unique number that identifies an autonomous system in the Internet. Autonomous system numbers are managed and assigned by ARIN (North America), APNIC (Asia-Pacific), and RIPE NCC (Europe). Exterior routing protocols, such as BGP, use autonomous system numbers to uniquely define an autonomous system. The basic routable element is the IP network or subnetwork, or the Classless Interdomain Routing (CIDR) prefix for newer protocols. (CIDR is discussed a little later in the chapter.)

OSPF, which is sanctioned by the IETF and supported by TCP, is intended to become the Internet's preferred interior routing protocol. OSPF is a link-state protocol with a complex set of options and features. Link-state algorithms control the routing process and enable routers to respond quickly to changes in the network. Link-state routing makes use of the Dijkstra algorithm (which determines routes based on path length and is used in OSPF) to determine routes based on the number of hops, the line speed, the amount of traffic, and the cost. Link-state algorithms are more efficient and create less network traffic than do distance-vector algorithms, which can be crucial in environments that involve multiple WAN links.

Exterior routing occurs between autonomous systems and is of concern to service providers and other large or complex networks. Whereas there may be many different interior routing schemes, a single exterior routing scheme manages the global Internet, and it is based on the exterior routing protocol BGP version 4 (BGP-4). The basic routable element is the autonomous system. Routers determine the path for a data packet by calculating the number of hops between internetwork segments. Routers build routing tables and use these tables along with routing algorithms.

Network Access Protocols

Network access protocols operate at Layer 2. They provide the underlying basis for the transport of the IP datagrams. The original network access protocol was Ethernet, but IP can be transported transparently over any underlying network, including Token Ring, FDDI, Fibre Channel, Wireless, X.25, ISDN, Frame Relay, or ATM.

Both Serial Line Internet Protocol (SLIP) and Point-to-Point Protocol (PPP) were designed specifically for IP over point-to-point connections. PPP provides data-link layer functionality for IP over dialup/dedicated links. In other words, whenever you dial in to your ISP, you negotiate a PPP session, and part of what PPP does is to provide a mechanism to identify and authenticate the user that is dialing up.

Internet Addressing

To make the Internet an open communications system, a globally accepted method of identifying computers was needed, and IP acts as the formal addressing mechanism for all Internet messaging.

Each host on the Internet is assigned a unique 32-bit Internet address, called the *IP address,* which is placed in the IP header and which is used to route packets to their destinations. IP addresses are assigned on a per-interface basis, so a host can have several IP addresses if it has several interfaces (note that a single interface can have multiple addresses, too). Therefore, an IP address refers to an interface, not to the host. A basic concept of IP addressing is that some of the bits of the IP address can be used for generalized routing decisions because these bits indicate which network (and possibly which subnet) the interface is a member of. Addressing is performed on the basis of network/subnet and host; routing is performed based on the network/subnet portion of the address only. When a packet reaches its target network, the host portion of the address is then examined for final delivery.

The current generation of IP is called IP version 4 (IPv4). IP addresses have two parts: The first is the network ID and the second is the host ID. Under IPv4, there are five classes, which differ in how many networks and hosts are supported (see Figure 9.4):

- **Class A**—With Class A, there can be a total of 126 networks, and on each of those networks there can be 16,777,214 hosts. Class A address space is largely exhausted, although there is some address space reserved by IANA.

- **Class B**—Class B addresses provide for 16,384 networks and each of which can have 65,534 hosts. Class B space is also largely exhausted, with a few still available, albeit at a very high cost.

- **Class C**—Class C allows 2,097,152 networks, each of which can have 254 hosts.

- **Class D**—Class D belongs to a special aspect of the Internet called the multicast backbone (MBONE). *Singlecast*, or unicast, means going from one transmitter to one receiver. *Multicast* implies moving from one transmitter to multiple receivers. Say, for instance, that you are in San Francisco and you want to do a videoconferencing session that involves three offices located in London. In the unicast mode, you need three separate IP connections to London from the conferencing point in San Francisco. With multi-

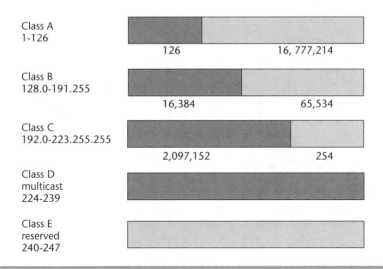

Figure 9.4 IPv4 32-bit addressing

cast, however, you need only one IP connection. A multicast router (mrouter) would enfold your IP packets in special multicast packets and forward those packets on to an mrouter in London; in London that mrouter would remove the IP packets, replicate those packets, and then distribute them to the three locations in London. The MBONE system therefore conserves bandwidth over a distance, relieves congestion on transit links, and makes it possible to address a large population in a single multicast.

■ **Class E**—Class E is reserved address space for experimental purposes.

The digits in an IP address tell you a number of things about the address. For example, in the IP address 124.29.88.7, the first set of digits, 124, is the network ID, and because it falls in the range of numbers for Class A, we know that this is a Class A address. The remaining three sets, 29.88.7, are the host ID. In the address 130.29.88.7, the first two sets, 130.29, comprise the network ID and indicate that this is a Class B address; the second two sets in this address, 88.7, comprise the host ID. Figure 9.5 shows an example of IP addressing.

Network IDs are managed and assigned by ARIN, APNIC, and RIPE NCC. Host IDs are assigned locally by the network administrator. Given a 32-bit address field, we can achieve approximately 4.3 billion different addresses with IPv4. That seems like a lot, but as we began to experience growth in the Internet, we began to worry about the number of addresses left. In the early 1990s, the IETF began to consider the potential of IP address space exhaustion. The result

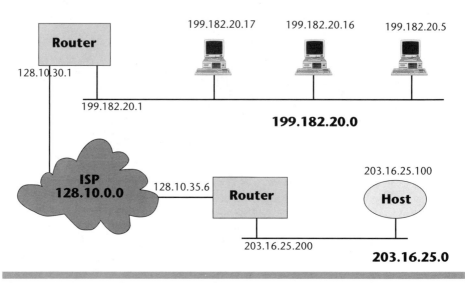

Figure 9.5 An example of IP network addressing

was the implementation of CIDR, which eliminated the old class-based style of addressing. The CIDR address is a 32-bit IP address, but it is classless. The CIDR addressing scheme is hierarchical. Large national and regional service providers are allocated large blocks of contiguous Internet addresses, which they then allocate to other smaller ISPs or directly to organizations. Networks can be broken down into subnetworks, and networks can be combined into supernetworks, as long as they share a common network prefix. Basically, with CIDR a route is no longer an IP address broken down into network and host bits according to its class; instead, the route becomes a combination of an address and a mask. The mask indicates how many bits in the address represent the network prefix. For example, the address 200.200.14.20/23 means that the first 23 bits of the binary form of this address represent the networks. The bits remaining represent the host. In binary form, the prefix 23 would like this: 255.255.254.0. Table 9.1 lists the most commonly used masks represented by the prefix, and the number of host addresses available with a prefix of the type listed. CIDR defines address assignment and aggregation strategies designed to minimize the size of top-level Internet routing tables. The national or regional ISP needs only to advertise its single supernet address, which represent an aggregation of all the subnets within that supernet. Routers in the Internet no longer give any credence to class—it's entirely based on the CIDR prefix. CIDR does require the use of supporting routing protocols, such as RIP version 2, OSPF version 2, Enhanced Interior Gateway Routing Protocol (EIGRP), and BGP-4.

Table 9.1   CIDR Masking Scheme

Mask as Dotted-Decimal Value	Mask as Prefix Value	Number of Hosts
255.255.255.224	/27	32
255.255.255.192	/26	64
255.255.255.128	/25	128
255.255.255.0 (Class C)	/24	256
255.255.254.0	/23	512
255.255.252.0	/22	1,024
255.255.248.0	/21	2,048
255.255.242.0	/20	4,096
255.255.240.0	/19	8,192
255.255.224.0	/18	16,384
255.255.192.0	/17	32,768
255.255.0.0 (Class B)	/16	65,536
255.254.0.0	/15	131,072
255.252.0.0	/14	262,144
255.248.0.0	/13	524,288

Subnetting is a term you may have heard in relationship to addressing. It once referred to the subdivision of a class-based network into subnetworks. Today, it generally refers to the subdivision of a CIDR block into smaller CIDR blocks. Subnetting allows single routing entries to refer either to the larger block or to its individual constituents, and this permits a single general routing entry to be used through most of the Internet, with more specific routes being required only for routers in the subnetted block.

Researchers are predicting that even with CIDR and subnetting in place, we will run out of IPv4 address space by the year 2010. Therefore, several years ago the IETF began developing an expanded version of IP called IPv6 (originally called IPng—for IP Next Generation). IPv6 uses a 128-bit address, which allows a total of 340 billion billion billion billion unique addresses, which equates to approximately

> ### IPv6 Address Allocation and Assignment
> ARIN has published a draft policy document on IPv6 address allocation and assignment that is available at www.arin.net.

70 IP addresses for every square inch of the earth's surface, including oceans. That should hold us for a while and be enough for each and every intelligent appliance, man, woman, child, tire, pet, and curb to have its own IP address. Along with offering a greatly expanded address space, IPv6 also allows increased scalability through multicasting and includes increased Quality of Service (QoS) capabilities. (QoS is discussed in detail in Chapter 10, "Next-Generation Networks.")

The IPv6 specification includes a flow label to support real-time traffic and automated connectivity for plug-and-play use. In addition, IPv6 provides improved security mechanisms. It incorporates Encapsulated Security payload (ESP) for encryption, and it includes an authentication header, to make transactions more secure. Although IPv6 offers many benefits, it requires a major reconfiguration of all the routers out there, and hence we haven't seen the community jump at the migration from IPv4 to IPv6. But in order to meet the demands of the growing population of not just human users but smart machines that are tapping into the Internet, the transition will be necessary. An experimental network called the 6Bone network is being used as an environment for IPv6 research. So far more than 400 networks in more than 40 countries are connected to the 6Bone IPv6 network.

The Domain Name System

The *Domain Name System* (DNS) is a distributed database system that operates on the basis of a hierarchy of names. DNS provides translation between easy-for-humans-to-remember host names (such as www.telecomwebcentral.com or www.lidoorg.com) and the physical IP addresses, which are harder for humans to remember. It identifies a domain's mail servers and a domain's name servers. When you need to contact a particular URL, the host name portion of the URL must be *resolved* to the appropriate IP address. Your Web browser goes to a local name server, maintained either by your ISP, your online service provider, or your company. If the IP address is a local one—that is, it's on the same network as the one you are on—then the name server will be able to resolve that URL with the IP address right away. In this case, the name server sends the true IP address to your computer, and because your Web browser now has the real address of the place you're trying to locate, it contacts that site, and the site sends the information you've requested.

If the local name server determines that the information you have requested is not on the local network, it must get the information from a name server on the Internet. The local name server contacts the root domain server, which contains a list of the top-level domain name servers managed by ICANN. The root domain server tells the local server which top-level domain name server contains the domain specified in the URL. The top-level domain name server then tells the local server which primary name server and secondary name server have the information about the requested URL. The local name server can then contact the primary name server. If the information can't be found in the primary name server, then the local name server contacts the secondary name server. One of those name servers will have the proper information, and it will then pass that information back to the local name server. The local name server sends the information back to your browser, which then uses the IP address to contact the proper site.

Top-Level Domains

For some time, there have been seven generic top-level domains:

.com	commercial
.gov	government
.mil	military
.edu	education
.net	for network operation
.org	nonprofit organizations
.int	international treaty organizations

Seven new top-level domains have been operational since 2001:

.aero	air-transport industry
.biz	businesses
.coop	cooperatives
.info	any use
.museum	museums
.name	individuals
.pro	Accountants, lawyers, and physicians

There are also country code top-level domains. Each of these is a two-letter country code (for example, .au, .ca), and there are 245 country code top-level domains, including a .us domain for the United States. So if you wanted to protect your domain name in the .com domain, for example, you would actually have to register it in 246 domains—.com and then .com with the appropriate two-letter country code after that—and if you really want to get serious about branding, you'd probably want to register another 246 each in the .net, .org, and .biz domains! Of course, very few organizations actually do this.

The Importance of Domain Names

Many new domain names are registered every minute, and it seems that all the simple one- and two-word .com names have already been taken. Therefore, there's a call for new domains to be added. Originally IANA, which was funded by the U.S. government, administrated the DNS. Since 1993, Network Solutions had been the sole provider of direct domain name registration services in the open generic top-level domains, and registration authority over the country code top-level domains has been relegated to the individual countries and bodies within them.

In September 1998 ICANN was formed to take over. ICANN is now introducing competition into the administration of the DNS through two attempts. One is a policy for the accreditation of registrars, and the other is a shared registry system for the .com, .net, and .org domains. In 2001 ICANN operationalized seven new top-level domains, and it must still negotiate with the winning applicants the terms under which they will operate this registry. The future of ICANN is still a bit tenuous; it is a bit political, to say the least.

A story illustrates what value domain names have. There's a small Pacific Islands country, with a population of 10,600 people, known as Tuvalu, and it was assigned the country code .tv. Naturally, .tv is a very appealing domain. It has reference to entertainment, streaming media, and screaming multimedia, and it also has a global context: Once you register something as .tv, you would no longer be able to alter it by appending another country code because it already is a country code. Of course, many entrepreneurs developed an interest in Tuvalu, and many companies approached the country, trying to acquire its domain name; Tuvalu auctioned the name. A company called .tv bought the name for roughly US$1 million quarterly—adjustable for inflation—with a US$50 million cap over 10 years. In addition, Tuvalu holds a 20% stake in the company. This auctioning of the country's domain name produced four times the country's GDP. Needless to say, the island is richly developing its transportation, educational, and health care facilities.

On the .tv domain, some domain names are quite expensive, with bidding starting at US$250,000 for broadband.tv, for instance. On the other hand, some creative and descriptive domains haven't yet been registered, and you'd be able to acquire those for as little as US$50. A lot of money is tied up in domain names, and the process of creating new domains will further challenge identifying the best branding strategy.

▧ The Organization of the Internet

It's important to understand what the Internet infrastructure is composed of and how it's structured in terms of the large variety of players that are represented in the Internet space. It's also important to keep in mind that similarly to the PSTN, the Internet was not originally structured for what we're asking it to do now.

Initially, the Internet was designed to support data communications—bursty, low-speed text data traffic. It was structured to accommodate longer hold times while still facilitating low data volumes, in a cost-effective manner. (That was the introduction of the packet-switching technique, whereby through statistical multiplexing long hold times don't negatively affect the cost structure because you're sharing the channel with other users as well.) The capacities of the links initially dedicated to the Internet were very narrowband: 56Kbps or 64Kbps. The worldwide infrastructure depended on the use of packet switches (that is, routers), servers (that is, repositories for the information), and clients (that is, the user interfaces into the repositories). The Internet was composed of a variety of networks, including both LANs and WANs, with internetworking equipment such as routers and switches designed for interconnection of disparate networks. The Internet relied on TCP/IP to move messages between different subnetworks, and it was not traditionally associated with strong and well-developed operational support systems, unlike the PSTN, where billing systems, provisioning systems, and network management systems are quite extensive, even if they are not integrated.

The traditional Internet relied on the PSTN for subscriber access to the Internet. So the physical framework, the roadways over which a package travels on what we know as the Internet, is the same type of physical infrastructure as the PSTN—it uses the same types of communications, links, and capacities. And in order for users to actually access this public data network, they had to rely on the PSTN. So, two types of access were facilitated: dialup for consumers and small businesses (that is, the range of analog modems, Narrowband ISDN) and dedicated access in the form of leased lines, ISDN Primary Rate Interface (PRI), and dedicated lines based on T-1/E-1 capacities for larger enterprises, and, in some cases, even T-3/E-3.

The Evolution of the POP Architecture

The early Internet point of presence (POP) architecture was quite simple, as illustrated in Figure 9.6. You would have either 56Kbps or 64Kbps lines coming in to access ports on a router. Out of that router, T-1/E-1 trunks would lead to a UNIX host. This UNIX environment was, for most typical users, very difficult to navigate. Until there was an easier way for users to interface—the World Wide Web—the

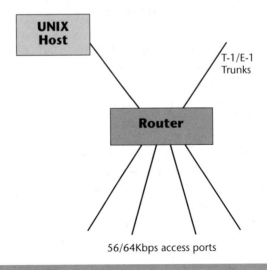

Figure 9.6 POP architecture in the 1980s

Internet was very much the province of academicians, engineers, and computer scientists.

The architecture of the Internet today is significantly different from what it was in the early days. Figure 9.7 shows some of the key components you would find in a higher-level network service provider's (NSP's) or a high-tier ISP's POP today. (Of course, a local service provider with just one POP or one node for access purposes, perhaps to a small community, looks quite different from this.)

First, let's look at the support for the dialup users. Today, we have to facilitate a wide range of speeds; despite our admiration of and desire for broadband access, it's not yet widely available. In the next several years, we should see more activity in terms of local loop modernization to provide broadband access to more users. But for the time being, we have to accommodate a wide range of analog modems that operate at speeds between 14.4Kbps and 56Kbps. Therefore, the first point of entry at the POP requires an analog modem pool of modems that complement the ones that individuals are using. Also, as we add broadband access alternatives, additional access devices are required, for instance, for DSL modems or cable modems. The analog modem pool communicates with a terminal server, and the terminal server establishes a PPP session. PPP does two things: It assigns an IP address to a dialup user's session, and it authenticates that user and authorizes entry. By dynamically allocating an IP address when needed, PPP enables us to reuse IP addresses, helping to mitigate the problem of the growing demand for IP addresses. A user is allocated an address when she dials in for a session; when she

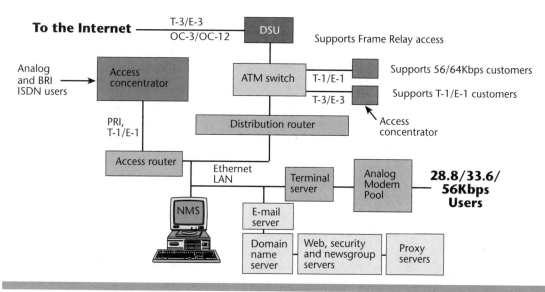

Figure 9.7 POP architecture today

terminates the session, the IP address can be assigned to another user. PPP supports both Password Authentication Protocol (PAP) and Challenge Handshake Authentication Protocol (CHAP) to provide link-level security. PAP uses a two-way handshake for the peer to establish its identity upon link establishment. The peer repeatedly sends the password to the authenticator until verification is acknowledged or the connection is terminated. CHAP uses a three-way handshake to periodically verify the identity of the peer throughout the life of the connection. The server sends to the remote workstation a random token that is encrypted with the user's password and sent back to the server. The server performs a lookup to see if it recognizes the password. If the values match, the authentication is acknowledged; if not, the connection is terminated. A different token is provided each time a remote user dials in, which provides additional robustness.

The terminal server resides on a LAN, which would typically be a Gigabit Ethernet network today. Besides the terminal server, the ISP POP houses a wide range of other servers:

- **E-mail servers**—These servers house the e-mail boxes.

- **Domain name servers**—These servers resolve the uniform resource locaters (URLs) into IP addresses.

- **Web servers**—If the ISP is engaged in a hosting business, it needs a Web server.

- **Security servers**—Security servers engage in encryption, as well as in authentication and certification of users. Not every ISP has a security server. For example, those that want to offer e-commerce services or the ability to set up storefronts must have them. (Security is discussed in detail in Chapter 11.)

- **Newsgroup servers**—Newsgroup servers store the millions of messages that are posted daily, and they are updated frequently throughout the day.

- **Proxy servers**—A proxy server provides firewall functionality, acting as an intermediary for user requests, establishing a connection to the requested resource either at the application layer or at the session or transport layer. Proxy servers provide a means to keep outsiders from directly connecting to a service on an internal network. Proxy servers are also becoming critical in support of edge caching of content. People are constantly becoming less tolerant of lengthy downloads, and information streams (such as video, audio, and multimedia) are becoming more demanding of timely delivery. You want to minimize the number of hops that a user has to go through. For example, you could use a tracing product to see how many hops you've gone through to get to a Web site. You'll see that sometimes you need to go through 17 or 18 hops to get to a site. Because the delay at each hop can be more than 2,000 milliseconds, if you have to make 18 hops when you're trying to use a streaming media tutorial, you will not be satisfied. ISPs can also use proxy servers to cache content locally, which means the information is distributed over one hop rather than over multiple hops, and that greatly improves your streaming media experience. Not all proxy servers support caching, however.

The ISP POP also contains network management systems that the service providers can use to administer passwords and to monitor and control all the network elements in the POP, as well as to remotely diagnose elements outside the POP.

An *access router* filters local traffic. If a user is simply checking his e-mail, working on his Web site, or looking up newsgroups, there's no reason for the user to be sent out over the Internet and then brought back to this particular POP. An access router keeps traffic contained locally in such situations. A distribution router, on the other hand, determines the optimum path to get to the next hop that will bring you one step closer to the destination URL, if it is outside the POP from which you are being served. Typically, in a higher-level ISP, this distribution router will connect into an ATM switch, which enables the ISP to guarantee QoS; this is especially necessary for supporting larger customers on high-speed interfaces and links and for supporting virtual private networks, VoIP, or streaming media applications. The ATM switch, by virtue of its QoS characteristics, enables us to map the packets into the appropriate cells, which guarantee that the proper QoS is administered and delivered. (ATM QoS is discussed further in Chapter 10.) The ATM switch then is front-ended by a data service unit (DSU), the data communications equipment on which the circuit terminates, which performs signal conversion and provides diagnostic capabilities. The network also includes a physical circuit, which, in a larger higher-tier provider, would generally be in the optical carrier levels.

An *access concentrator* can be used to create the appearance of a virtual POP. For instance, if you want your subscribers to believe that they're accessing a local node—that is, to make it appear that you're in the same neighborhood that they are in—you can use an access concentrator. The user dials a local number, thinking that you're located down the street in the business park, when in fact, the user's traffic is being hauled over a dedicated high-speed link to a physical POP located elsewhere in the network. Users' lines terminate on a simple access concentrator, where their traffic is multiplexed over the T-1s or T-3s, E-1s or E-3s, or perhaps ISDN PRI. This gives ISPs the appearance of having a local presence when, in fact, they have none. I talk later in this chapter about the advantages of owning the infrastructure versus renting the infrastructure, but clearly, if you own your infrastructure, backhauling traffic allows you to more cost-effectively serve remote locations. If you're an ISP that's leasing facilities from a telco, then these sorts of links to backhaul traffic from more remote locations will add cost to your overall operations.

You can see that the architecture of the POP has evolved and become incredibly more sophisticated today than it was in the beginning; the architecture has evolved in response to and in preparation for a very wide range of applications.

Internet Challenges and Changes

Despite all its advances over the past couple of decades, the Internet is challenged today. It is still limited in bandwidth at various points. The Internet is composed of some 10,000 service providers. Although some of the really big companies have backbone capacities that are 50Gbps or greater, there are still plenty of small backbones worldwide that have only a maximum of 1.5 or 2Mbps. Overall, the Internet still needs more bandwidth.

One reason the Internet needs more bandwidth is that traffic is increasing at an alarming rate. People are drawn to Web sites that provide pictures of products in order to engage in demonstrations and in order to be able to conduct multimedia communications. Those greater capacities required by these visual objects also demand greater bandwidth. This means that we frequently have bottlenecks at the ISP level, at the backbone level (that is, the NSP level), and at the network access points (NAPs) where backbones interconnect to exchange traffic between providers. These bottlenecks greatly affect our ability to roll out new time-sensitive, loss-sensitive applications, such as Internet telephony, VoIP, VPNs, streaming media, and TV over Internet.

Therefore, we are redefining the Internet as we are redefining the PSTN. In both cases, we're trying to support more real-time traffic flows, real audio, real video, and live media. This requires the introduction of QoS into the Internet. There are really two types of metrics that we loosely refer to as QoS: class of service (CoS) and true QoS. CoS is a prioritization scheme in which you can prioritize streams and thereby facilitate better performance. QoS, however, deals with very strict traffic measurements, where you can specify the latencies end to end (that is, the jitter or variable latencies in the receipt of the packets, the tolerable cell loss, and the mechanism for allocating the bandwidth continuously or on a bursty basis). Thus, QoS is much more stringent than CoS, and what we are currently introducing into the Internet is really more like CoS than QoS.

Techniques such as DiffServ (as discussed in Chapter 10) allow us to prioritize the traffic streams, but they really do not allow us to control the traffic measurements. That is why, as discussed in Chapter 7, "Wide Area Networking," we tend to still rely on ATM within the core: ATM allows the strict control of the traffic measurements, and it therefore enables you to improve performance, quality, reliability, and security. Efforts are under way to develop QoS standards for IP, but we're still a couple years away from clearly defining the best mechanism. In the meantime, we are redesigning the Internet core, moving away from what was a connectionless router environment that offered great flexibility and the ability to work around congestion and failures, but at the expense of delays. We're moving to a connection-oriented environment in which we can predefine the path and more tightly control the latencies, by using techniques such as Frame Relay, ATM, and MPLS, each of which allow you to separate traffic types, prioritize the time-sensitive traffic, and, ultimately, to reduce access costs by eliminating leased-lines connections.

The other main effort in redesigning the Internet core is directed at increasing its capacity, moving from OC-3 and OC-12 (that is, 155Mbps and 622Mbps) at the backbone level to OC-48 (that is, 2.5Gbps) and even OC-192 (that is, 10Gbps). But remember that the bits per second that we can carry per wavelength doubles every year, and the number of wavelengths we can carry per fiber also doubles every year. So, the migration beyond 10Gbps is also under way in the highest class of backbones, and it will continue at a rapid pace.

The emergent generation of Internet infrastructure is quite different from the traditional foundation. First, it's geared for a new set of traffic and application types: high-speed, real-time, and multimedia. It must be able to support and guarantee CoS and QoS. It includes next-generation telephony, which is a new approach to providing basic telephony services, but it uses IP networks. (These types of next-generation network services are discussed in Chapter 11.)

The core of the Internet infrastructure, like the PSTN, will increasingly rely on SDH/SONET, DWDM, and optical networking. It will require the use of ATM, MPLS, and MPλS (Multiprotocol Lambda Switching) networking protocols to ensure proper administration of performance. New generations of IP protocols are being developed to address real-time traffic, CoS, QoS, and security. Distributed network intelligence is being used to share the network functionality.

We are working on providing the capability to rely on multiple broadband access options, not just the PSTN. You may be able to access the Internet on a dial-up basis through the new generation of xDSL facilities, through a cable TV company and a cable modem, through a satellite TV company, via direct broadcast satellites, or through point-to-point microwave solutions such as MMDS and LMDS. (These solutions are discussed in Chapter 13, "Broadband Access Solutions.") For the dedicated environment, largely we're seeing a migration to higher bandwidth (that is, T-1 moving to T-3, E-1 moving to E-3, early adopters and high-bandwidth consumers in the optical carrier levels), and we're seeing increased reliance on Frame Relay and ATM as the access technique.

Service Providers

There is a wide range of service providers in the Internet space. One way they differ is in their coverage areas. Some providers focus on serving a local area, others are regionally based, and others offer national or global coverage. Service providers also vary in the access options that they provide. All ISPs offer plain old telephone service (POTS), and some offer ISDN, xDSL, Frame Relay, ATM, cable modem service, satellite, and wireless as well. Providers also differ in the services that they support. Almost all providers support e-mail (but not necessarily at the higher-tier backbone level). Some also offer FTP hosting, Web hosting, name services, VPNs, VoIP, application hosting, e-commerce, and streaming media. Providers could service a very wide variety of applications, and as a result, there is differentiation on this front as well. Two other important issues are customer service and the number of hops a provider must take in order to get to the main point of interconnection into the Internet.

It is pretty easy to become an ISP: pick up a router, lease a 56Kbps/64Kbps line, and you're in business. This is why there are some 10,000 such providers, of varying sizes and qualities, worldwide. There is a service provider pecking order. Research backbones have the latest technology. Top-tier providers focus on business-class services; lower-tier providers focus on rock-bottom pricing. Consequently, there are large variations in terms of available capacity, the performance you can expect, the topology of the network, the levels of redundancy, the numbers of connections with other operators, and the level of customer service and the extent of its availability (that is, whether it's 24/7 or whether it's a Monday-through-Friday, 9-to-5 type of operation). Ultimately, of course, ISPs vary greatly in terms of price.

Figure 9.8 shows an idealized model of the service provider hierarchy. At the top of the heap are research backbones. For example, Internet 2 replaces what the original Internet was for—the academic network. Some 85% of traffic within the academic domain stays within the academic domain, so there's good reason to have a separate backbone for the universities and educational institutions involved in research and learning. Internet 2 will, over time, contribute to the next commercialized platform. It acts as a testbed for many of the latest and greatest technologies, so the universities stress test Internet 2 to determine how applications perform and which technologies suit which applications or management purposes best. Other very sophisticated technology platforms exist, such as the Abilene Project and the Interplanetary Internet (IPNSIG), the first Internet being constructed in space for purposes of deep space communications. The objective of IPNSIG is to define the architecture and protocols necessary to permit interoperation of the Internet resident on earth with other remotely located internets resident on other planets or spacecraft in transit.

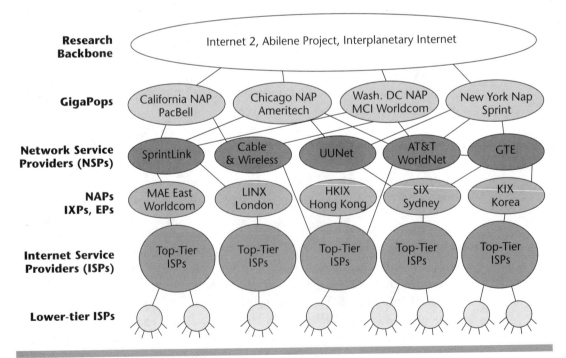

Figure 9.8 Service provider hierarchy

In the commercial realm, the highest tier is the NSP. NSPs are very large backbones, global carriers that own their own infrastructures. The top providers at this level are AT&T, Worldcom, UUnet, Sprint, Verizon, Cable & Wireless, and Qwest. The NSPs can be broken down into three major subsets:

- **National ISPs**—These ISPs have national coverage. They include the incumbent telecom carriers and the new competitive entrants.

- **Regional ISPs**—These ISPs are active regionally throughout a nation, and these service providers own their equipment and lease their lines from the incumbent telco or competitive operator.

- **Retail ISPs**—These ISPs have no investment in the network infrastructure whatsoever. They're basically using their brand name and outsourcing all the infrastructure to perhaps an NSP or a high-tier ISP, but they're building from a known customer database that's loyal and that provides an opportunity to offer a branded ISP service.

These various levels of NSPs interconnect with one another in several ways. First, they can connect at the National Science Foundation-supported NAPs. These NAPs are used to provide connection into the Internet 2 project, largely in the United States. This occurs between the largest of the NSPs as well as the research backbones. Second, there are commercial interconnection and exchange points, which people refer to as NAPs as well, although they are also called metropolitan area exchanges (MAEs) and interconnection and exchange points. These NAPs are typically run by consortiums of ISPs, telcos, entrepreneurs, and others seeking to be in the business of the Internet; these consortiums build public exchange points for traffic between the various Internet backbones. Third, service providers can connect using bilateral arrangements (called *private peering*) between one another to pass traffic over each others' backbones. These NAPs are discussed in more detail in the following section, but for now, suffice it to say that local service providers, the lower-tier ISPs, typically connect to NAPs through the top-tier ISPs, so they are a greater number of hops away from the point of interconnection, which can have a big impact on the performance of time-sensitive applications.

Evaluating Service Providers

The following sections describe some of the important characteristics you should expect in the different levels of service providers.

Evaluating NSPs

NSPs provide at least a national backbone, but it's generally international. Performance depends on the total network capacity, the amount of bandwidth, and the total number of customers contending for that bandwidth. If you divide the total capacity by the number of direct access customers, you get an idea of how much bandwidth is available on average per customer; however, that doesn't take into account the additional traffic that consumer or dialup traffic may add. If you were to perform such an exercise based on your ISP, you'd probably be shocked at how little bandwidth is actually available to each individual user.

The NSPs should operate at the higher speeds, ranging today from OC-3 to OC-48, and looking to move on to OC-192 and beyond. They should have engineered the network such that during peak periods the network has at least 30% to 40% spare bandwidth. They should have nodes in all the major cities. NSPs that own their facilities—that is, facilities-based ISPs—have an added advantage of being able to provide backhauled circuits at no extra charge, whereas those that are leasing facilities from interexchange carriers or telcos incur additional charges to the overall operation. There should be redundancy applied to the circuits, routers, and switches. Most NSPs have at least two redundant paths from each node. Some may have anywhere from three to five redundant paths. An NSP should practice diversity in the local loops and long-haul circuits—that is, it should get them from different carriers so that in the event of a disaster, there is a fallback plan. Facilities-based carriers often offer redundancy, but rarely do they provide diversity. NSPs should have generators at each node. Remember that it doesn't matter how much redundancy you build into your equipment or your circuits if you lose power. You need redundant power, and this is a major differentiator for the very high-tier operators.

NSPs should have implemented BGP in order to filter, or block, any faulty messages from the backbone that can replicate themselves and cause major brownouts or blackouts on the Internet. NSPs should connect to one another through multiple NAPs and interexchange points and also have multiple private peering agreements, again to cover all their bases. They should provide redundant paths to the NAPs as well as to their peers, and they should be able to articulate a very clear reason for their architectural decisions (Why are they using IP routing and connectionless networks? Why does their core consist of ATM? Are they using ATM for its QoS benefits?). They might want to speak to issues of speed, overhead, or QoS, but you want to work with an NSP that actually has a clear-cut architectural reason for its decision.

When comparing backbones, look at the backbone speeds. Look at the underlying transport technology and what that means in terms of QoS. Look at the number of nodes, the number of redundant paths per node, the availability of power backup at each node, the availability of BGP filtering, the number of NAPs or ISPs that they interconnect through, the number of private peering arrangements, and a disclosure of who those peers are. Look at whether performance guarantees are offered, whether you have the potential for any online monitoring, and the access price.

Evaluating ISPs

The top-tier ISPs have the greatest coverage in a region of a particular country. They are associated with multiple high-speed links, generally in the T-1/T-3, E-1/E-3 range, up to perhaps the OC-3 level. They have redundant routers and switches at each node, and they have multiple high-speed connections into their NAPs (and more and more NAPs are becoming discriminating, as discussed later in this chapter, in the section "NAPs"). They require two connections, for example, into the Internet, so you have redundancy, and the larger NAPs may also require that for purposes of transit links, the ISP have arrangements with alternative international providers. Their main focus is to provide high levels of service, to address the business community.

The lower-tier ISPs are generally associated with providing local access—to a mountain village that has a ski community in the winter or to a remote lake where there is summer traffic, or to any other neighborhood. There is generally only one rather low-speed connection, either 56Kbps or 64Kbps, or perhaps up to T-1/E-1, and it leads into a top-tier ISP; these lower-tier ISPs generally do not have direct connections into the NAPs or high-tier ISPs. Lower-tier ISPs focus on offering the lowest prices possible, so they offer the least amount of redundancy of any providers— no power backups and fairly minimal capacities.

As you can see in the idealized model of the Internet shown in Figure 9.9, information flows from a user through a local ISP, through a regional ISP, to a national ISP, through transit ISPs, and back down the hierarchy. Some companies operate on a vertically integrated basis, so they may be represented as local ISPs to their consumers but also offer national backbones to their business customers. Therefore, the relationships can be a little less defined than the figure indicates, but it helps provide a summary view of how this works.

An issue in ISP selection is the level of coverage (How many countries are served? How many cities are served within that country? What's the total number of backbone connections into the countries that it serves?). Another consideration is the number of exchange points you have to go through and what type and number of peering relationships are in practice. You also need to consider the total amount of bandwidth and therefore what the level of oversubscription is if everyone tries to use it at the same time. And you need to consider the transit delays being experienced; ideally we want to see networks evolve to latencies of less than 80 milliseconds, but today 800 to 1,000 milliseconds is much more realistic. Similarly, you want less than 5% packet loss, but today at peak hours you'll see up to 30% or 40% packet loss. Data packets most often are retransmitted to correct for these losses. However, with real-time traffic, such as voice or video, packet retransmission would add too much delay, with the result that conversations can be rendered unintelligible. Again, you need to think about redundancy—the number of lines into the network, the level of network diversity, and the amount of power backup involved.

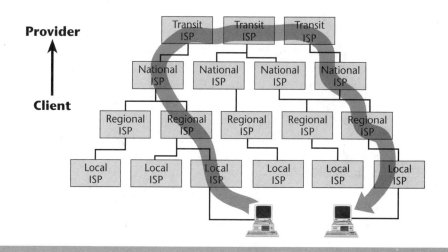

Figure 9.9 Information flow in an idealized model of the Internet

Evaluating Emerging Service Providers

In the past couple years, there have been some exciting developments in niched applications for service providers. This section talks about content delivery networks, application service providers (ASPs), management service providers (MSPs), online service providers (OSPs), and virtual ISPs (VISPs). Each of these serves a different purpose. Some of them have an immediate future, some of them perhaps may last a little bit longer, and some of them are quite unknown.

Content Delivery Networks   Content delivery networks can be structured to support exactly the kind of application you need them to support. For example, you may use Web-delivered training, which is designed to have the types of requirements that streaming media applications have. Content delivery services are becoming essential to the development of e-commerce, making them a requirement for business-class Web sites. They are delivery services that are focused on streaming audio, video, and media, as well as the supporting e-commerce applications. Currently, the major clients for content delivery networks are ISPs and content providers because they stand to reduce their need for bandwidth and get better profit margins on services to customers.

Content delivery and hosting service providers aim to deliver Web-site content to customers faster by storing the content in servers located at the edges of Internet networks, rather than in the network's central location. This reduces the number of hops, thereby reducing the latencies and improving performance. This works because of a combination of technologies, including caching and *load balancing*, which means spreading the content across multiple servers so that at peak periods, you don't overload the server but can still provide access on a balanced basis. Content delivery providers will also use enhanced Internet routing and probably proprietary algorithms that facilitate the administration of QoS. For instance, Enron has a proprietary intelligent call agent that knows how to prioritize streaming content over bursty data applications that may be supported. As another example, IBasis supports VoIP, and when the Internet gets congested, the routing algorithm switches the traffic over to the circuit-switched environment, thereby guaranteeing the high quality that the customers are expecting for the telephony. Also, these content delivery services will be able to deliver content to a user from the nearest servers, or at least from a server located at the edge of the network.

All the changes in the content delivery networks, of course, are driven by the need for faster and faster online transactions. Humans get addicted to speed. We have a physiological speed center in our brain, and each time we complete tasks at a certain pace, we resynchronize that speed center. Consequently, as we've used the Web over the years, improvements in network infrastructure have allowed us to experience faster downloads. Customer loyalty can be increasingly affected by time frames as small as a second.

There are a number of content-delivery providers in the market. Akamai Technologies has more than 4,000 servers and is growing. Digital Island plans to install 8,000 servers by 2002, increasing its current capacity by a factor of 30. Enron recently signed a deal with Blockbuster, and this is an indicator of the importance of the content as part of the overall picture.

ASPs   ASPs have been receiving a great deal of press. There is not really one major business model for ASPs; there's quite a niching opportunity. An ASP is a supplier that makes applications available on a subscription basis. ASPs provide hosting, monitoring, and management of a variety of well-known software applications on a world-class data center infrastructure. A great deal of money is being spent in the ASP arena, and ASPs are increasingly becoming application infrastructure providers (AIPs), which is discussed later in this section.

ASPs are most useful when the majority of an application's users reside outside the enterprise network. The more external touch points there are, the more sense it makes to use an ASP. An ASP is viable for e-commerce, customer relations management, human resources, and even e-mail and listserv applications. An ASP is not really viable for productivity tools, such as word processing or spreadsheets. And an ASP is not really good for financial applications, which benefit from being maintained in-house, because of the more stringent requirements for security and confidentiality of data.

You might want to use an ASP if there's a need for additional bandwidth; if you lack technical resources in-house for reliable 24/7 application support; when you feel that a third party could do the job better; when you need a large and readily available applications inventory; when scalability demands dynamic increases; or when you're seeking performance reliability.

With ASPs, you pay setup fees; on a low-end Web server these fees start at around US$2,000 and on a low-end database server they start at around US$10,000. Setup fees on a high-end Oracle cluster, for instance, could run from US$5,000 for the Web servers to US$40,000 for database servers. These customers are generally ISPs or major international corporations. Ongoing ASP fees also range anywhere from US$2,000 to US$40,000 per month for the software licensing, the applications, and the equipment maintenance, along with perhaps the broadband connectivity. So an ASP paying US$1 million to buy the license for an application may charge its customers between US$200,000 and US$500,000 per year for three years (the typical life span of most of the applications contracts). ASPs that concentrate on small- to medium-size businesses typically offer application hosting in the range of US$200 to US$500 per month, sometimes with an additional US$5 to US$30 per month charge per user for enterprise applications. Thus, ASPs need to invest a lot of money into automating customer setup and maintenance, which then helps them reduce cost to the customer and ensure an attractive margin. Enterprises may not have the resources to realize these types of cost benefits.

Although small and medium-sized businesses may today appear to be the best targets for using ASPs, predictions show that very large enterprise clients will be the most fruitful by 2004. It is likely that large enterprises will use ASPs for e-commerce applications and for internal applications, such as e-mail, data management, office automation, and basic business applications. The emerging "skills drought" may drive larger companies to ASPs as well.

The ASP model comprises no single entity or service. Instead, it's a complex supply chain that includes the following:

- **Independent software vendors (ISVs)**—ISVs develop the applications that the ASPs then put up for sale or for rent.

- **AIPs**—AIPs manage the data center servers, databases, switches, and other gears on which the applications run. It's reminiscent of the gold miner analogy: It wasn't the gold miners who got the gold; it was the guys who sold the picks and shovels. The AINs are the segment of the ASP market that will be seeing the greatest run of success at first.

- **MSPs**—MSPs take over the actual management and monitoring of the network. (They are discussed in more detail later in this section.)

- **NSPs**—NSPs are network access providers.

- **Value-added resellers (VARs)**—VARs deal with distribution and sales.

- ■ **Systems integrators (SIs)**—Like VARs, SIs deal with distribution and sales.

- ■ **E-business infrastructure providers (eBIPs)**—This group saves small businesses time and money with Web-based solutions for human resources, accounting, marketing, group collaboration, and other services. Some of these eBIPs offer their services for free, making money from ads and partnerships with the VARs. Others charge affordable fees that range from $30 to $200 per month. Online business center sites that offer targeted small-business content and community are good partnership candidates for such eBIPs.

ASPs form a complex supply chain. Today, more than 650 companies call themselves ASPs, and a great number of these are telcos. A good resource for information on ASPs is the Application Service Provider Industry Consortium (ASPIC) at www.aspindustry.org.

MSPs MSPs specialize in providing software for network management and for monitoring applications, network performance, and network security. MSPs also take over the actual management and monitoring of the network. They operate similarly to ASPs, in that they use a network to deliver services that are billed to their clients. They differ from ASPs in that they very specifically address network management rather than business process applications. MSPs deliver system management services to IT departments and other customers that manage their own technology assets.

The appeal of the MSP model is that it eliminates the need for companies and individuals to buy, maintain, or upgrade information technology infrastructure management systems, which typically require a major capital expense, are highly technical in terms of the expertise they mandate, and require a considerable investment of time. This model appeals in particular to enterprises that manage e-commerce applications, such as ASPs and ISPs, whose expertise lies in the applications or network infrastructure they provide to customers—not necessarily in their management. It also appeals to small- and medium-size companies that prefer not to invest in large IT staffs. As with the ASP model, using specialists to deploy and maintain complex technology enables companies to focus on their own core competencies and to immediately tap into high-quality expertise as needed. There are variations in the model: some MSPs provide tools and services, whereas others provide services only; and some target corporations, whereas others are designed for consumers.

The MSP Association (www.mspassociation.com) was formed in June 2000, and it aims to be at the forefront of creating new standards for network management and for defining the best practices for the network management market. Its first working group has the job of defining what the whole MSP market looks like. Market analysts expect the demand for MSPs to grow exponentially as an attractive alternative to internally run IT management applications.

OSPs The OSP is a provider that organizes the content for you and provides intuitive user navigation. An example of an OSP is America Online. You can liken an OSP to a department store in a shopping mall in the United States. You enter the mall through strategically placed doors. At that point, you can browse all the different content providers, or shops, in that shopping mall. You may get a little assistance through a directory board, but you must take the initiative to go to each of these locations to determine whether the content you seek is really there. A shopping mall usually has a major tenant, a large department store, that provides its own doors from the parking lot. When you enter through the department store's doors, the department store tries to hold you captive with its content. It has some of everything else you could find in all the individual boutiques throughout the mall, but at the department store, there's a more exclusive or tailored selection. It's been organized into meaningful displays, and assistants are available to guide you through the store to your selected content. So, an ISP is the shopping mall. It gives you access to all the Web sites out there, but you have to use search engines to narrow your search. An OSP, such as America Online, is like the department store, which gives you a more cozy and exclusive space in which to browse the same content.

VISPs The VISP offers outsourced Internet service, running as a branded ISP. It is a turnkey ISP product aimed at affinity groups and mass marketers that want to add Internet access to their other products and services. Services of a VISP could include billing, Web-site maintenance, e-mail and news services, customized browsers, and a help desk. VISPs today include AT&T, Cable & Wireless, GTE, IConnect, and NaviNet. Early customers include Surfree.com and Liberty-Bay.com.

The Service Provider Value Chain

Figure 9.10 is a simplistic diagram of the current value chain, from a technology standpoint. The lower-tier ISP is getting fees, essentially subscription fees and perhaps hosting fees, from a retail end user—and that is the lower-tier ISP's cash flow in. The ISP's cash flow out is the fees that it pays for connection into the higher-tier ISP, as well as the money associated with the links it's leasing from the telecom operator. The higher-tier ISP is getting fees for access in from the lower-tier ISP, and it's also getting subscription fees from higher-end business customers. The higher-tier ISP's outflow is the money it pays to connect into the backbone provider, as well as the money it may be paying for its communication links from a network operator. The backbone provider, then, is getting money from the higher-tier ISPs, as well as from customers that want to host their content—that is, from their Web farms or media servers.

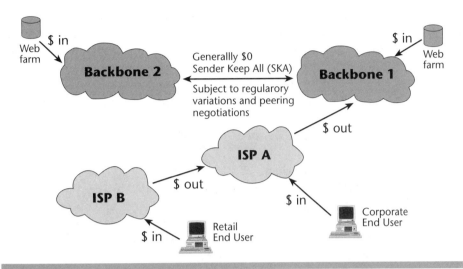

Figure 9.10 The current value chain

Regulatory Decisions

Regulatory decisions could cause some major shifts in the next several years. These decisions will affect who ends up being considered the major backbone provider by virtue of how it regulates this environment. Decisions that are made on unbundling the local loops will have a major impact on the availability of broadband access. The Internet is not going to grow without growth in broadband access, so these decisions play a very important role. Decisions will be made about things such as privacy and whose laws apply in e-commerce. When I buy something in the United Kingdom from the United States, does the U.K. law or U.S. law apply? Further decisions will affect content sensitivity, censorship, and the acceptance of digital signatures as being valid. Interconnection issues need to be decided as well (for example, in Figure 9.10, how moneys are exchanged between the backbone providers).

So, remember that you need to consider more than just the progress and the technology. There are some big human and political issues to think about as well.

The backbones until now have largely practiced Sender Keep All (SKA). Those in an SKA arrangement assume that there is an even exchange of traffic between the two peers, and hence they don't pay each other any money. This is likely to change. The vast majority of content still currently resides in the United States, and that's made some of the U.S. ISPs rather cocky. They tell their overseas colleagues, "If you want a transit link into my backbone, you have to pick up the entire cost of that transit link because basically your people are coming to get our content. There's nothing we really want on your side." One of two things will happen. Either this will become regulated or market forces will take over and we will allow these other countries to say, "We'll develop our own content, and now when your people want to get at it, you can cover the cost of access into *our* backbone."

■ Internet Interconnection and Exchange

As mentioned earlier, NSPs can interconnect at one of several points. First, four NAPs in the United States are partially funded by the National Science Foundation (Ameritech, PacBell, Sprint, and MFS Datanet), and the reason they get some support from the U.S. government is that they also provide interconnection into Internet 2, the academic research backbone. Second, connection can be made via agreements between ISPs (that is, peering). Third, there are commercial interconnection and exchange points, which can be used through private NAPs.

NAPs

Remember that the local service providers typically connect into the NAPs, or exchange points, through top-tier ISPs rather than directly. So what's the definition of a NAP? A *NAP* is the place where NSPs and/or ISPs exchange traffic with their counterparts. It's a public meeting point that houses cables, routers, switches, LANs, data communications equipment, and network management and telecommunications links. NAPs enable the NSPs and top-tier ISPs to exchange Internet traffic without having to send the traffic through a main transit link. This translates to decreased costs associated with the transit links, and it reduces congestion on the transit links.

Figure 9.11 shows the inside of one of the NAPs, Pacific Bell's point in California. On the left are the various ISPs and NSPs that are connecting to the NAP; note the various ISPs and their connection over a DSU into the Pac Bell ATM switch. The ATM switches are redundant and connected by redundant optical carrier levels (OC-3 initially, but they are being upgraded all the time). In addition, there are route servers, which maintain the databases of the appropriate path to take, based not just on the routing algorithm but also on the policy that the ISPs want to observe. In other words, there may be relationships about how traffic is passed between two providers—not just a next-hop or lowest-cost scenario—that determine what the path is. The route servers reside on a LAN, in this case, a fiber-based LAN called Fiber Distributed Data Interface (FDDI). FDDI was the first of the 100Mbps LAN backbones, and today most of these LANs would be Gigabit Ethernet. Resources connect into DSUs that lead to the routes of the selected NSPs.

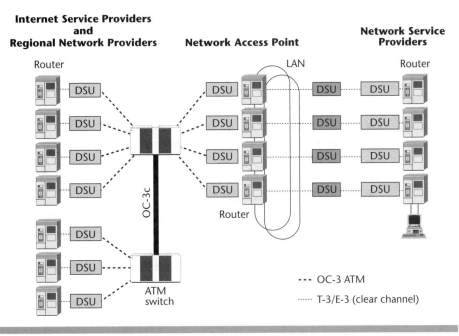

Figure 9.11 The Pacific Bell NAP

Routing arbiters are in place so that if there's dispute about how traffic has been routed, the arbiters can step in and arbitrate the situation.

The NAPs have equipment that's quite similar to what you find inside an Internet POP, which is quite similar to what you find inside a telco POP. This speaks to the convergence between the information types and their supporting infrastructures.

NAPs are becoming more discriminating. For instance, some require that the minimum connections be T-3 or E-3 and that they be redundant as well. That eliminates a lot of the smaller players from connecting to NAPs. If the NAPs were not so discriminating, there would be tremendous congestion at the public exchange points. For any traffic that's time sensitive, such as Internet telephony, VoIP applications, networked interactive games, multimedia, and streaming video, this congestion will cause problems with reliability and predictability. NAPs are also increasing in number; there are about 175 NAPs worldwide today. (For more information on NAPs, go to www.ep.net.)

Besides the four government-funded NAPs in the United States, other NAPs are for profit, and they charge per connection into the switch or router, initially in the US$4,000 to US$6,000 range. The cost varies with the economic times as well as the speed of the connection. And the NAPs, again, demand that you be able to guarantee a level of QoS before you connect at that exchange point.

Despite the fact that NAPs are now becoming more discriminating, they have become a point of congestion. Losses and delays are negatively affecting applications everyone wants to see developed, and therefore other alternatives have been brought about, as discussed in the following sections.

Peering Agreements

An alternative to NAPs is the use of private peering agreements. In a peering solution, operators agree to exchange with one another the same amount of traffic over high-speed lines between their routers so that users on one network can reach addresses on the other. This type of agreement bypasses public congestion points, such as NAPs. It's called *peering* because there's an assumption that the parties are equal in that they have an equal amount of traffic to exchange with one another. That's an important point because it obviously makes a difference in how money is exchanged. This is an issue of concern at the moment and one that many people are studying to determine ultimately whether there has to be a regulatory mechanism or whether market forces will drive it, but in general, with the first generation of peering agreements there was an understanding that peers were equals. Newer agreements often call for charges to be applied when traffic levels exceed what was agreed to in negotiations.

The most obvious benefit of peering is that because two parties agree on working with one another, and therefore exchanging information about the engineering and performance of their networks, the overall performance of the network is increased, including better availability, the ability to administer service-level agreements, and the ability to provide greater security. Major backbone providers are very selective about international peering, where expensive international private line circuits are used to exchange international routes. Buying transit provides the same benefits as peering, but at a higher price. Exchanging traffic between top-tier providers basically means better performance and fewer routers involved. And again, these types of arrangements are critical to seeing the evolution and growth in IP telephony, VoIP, and multimedia.

One problem with peering is that it can be limited. Under peering arrangements, ISPs often can have access only to each other's networks. In other words, I'll agree to work with you, but you can work only with me; I don't want you working with anyone else. Exclusivity types of demands might arise.

Private NAPs

The alternative to NAPs and peering arrangements is to use a private NAP, also called an overnet. Private NAPs are connected directly, via private lines, to the IP

Considerations for the Future

We need to be careful what we consider to be ready for primetime business, especially when it comes to the public Internet, that uncontrolled subcollection of networks that number more than 150,000. For example, one of the U.S. NAPs, MAE East, which handles something like 33% of the world's Internet traffic, for a long time resided in an underground parking garage in an unprotected space. Since that information was published, the problem surely has been resolved, but this was a condition whereby a person who was going in reverse with a very heavy foot could have taken down a third of the Internet.

There's a NAP in California as well: MAE West. MAE West is one of the busiest of the NAPs, connecting points between various NSPs. It's so crowded with equipment that the air conditioning can't keep up at times.

There was an instance not too long ago, in a small Florida ISP, in which a command entry error during router setup redirected 25% of all Internet traffic across a single T-1 link, which caused a two-hour brownout on the global Internet. The ISP hadn't used BGP filtering, but if it had, that message may have been caught and so much of the world's traffic would not have been redirected to what amounted to a local service provider backbone.

Finally, there was a software glitch at Network Solutions, which managed the top-level domain names for the entire Internet. A file containing more than one million Internet addresses got corrupted. Worse yet, a technician ignored the alarm that was issued and allowed the files to be replicated across the Internet, thereby blacking out Web sites for several hours.

So, I very much appreciate the candor of Mike O'Dell, chief scientist for UUnet Technologies, who used to say about the public Internet, "If you're not scared, you just don't understand."

But the Internet is not all bad and scary. The problems described here mainly affect business-class applications, where you need stringent controls. We also see a great many benefits and cost-efficiencies as a result of the public Internet.

backbones of several of the major NSPs or backbone providers. This design means that customers can get access to the major backbones without having to peer at the congested NAPs. The private exchange enables second-tier providers to connect to several first-tier providers, all in one location as well. Examples of private NAPs are InterNAP, Savvis Communications, and Digital Island. Savvis opened a private exchange point in London, and it expects to connect two first-tier ISPs there. Inter-NAP is opening exchanges in London and Amsterdam, and it also has plans for Frankfurt and Paris, expecting to connect with six first-tier ISPs, as well as two major in-country providers. Thus, InterNAP currently has some 50 NAPs that are live or about to open. Both Savvis and InterNAP run exchanges in the United States, and each also claims to get great deals on transit relationships or even to negotiate peering relationships that are unavailable to smaller ISPs.

For more learning resources, quizzes, and discussion forums on concepts related to this chapter, see www.telecomessentials.com/learningcenter.

Part III

Next-Generation Networks

Chapter 10

Next-Generation Networks

This chapter, which explores next-generation networks, is a very important chapter, particularly for those who are looking into the future of these technologies, attempting to make investment decisions, strategic plans, or decisions regarding business development, marketing, or public relations. This chapter covers the essentials of how architectures are shifting and the driving forces and trends behind the new infrastructures. This chapter examines the evolving broadband infrastructure and includes a high-level summary of two popular network architectures: Internet Protocol (IP) networks and Asynchronous Transfer Mode (ATM) networks. It also looks at the broadband architectures, and in doing so, it explores the differences among various Quality of Service (QoS) tactics.

■ The Broadband Evolution

One primary driver toward broadband is the increasing demand for information. Today's key competitive edge is two-fold: It includes both intellectual property (that is, how smart your people are) and the ability to develop and sustain relationships well. To perform well in both these aspects, you need an ongoing stream of the latest information with which to build your knowledge base and, in an attempt to remain competitive and to grow, it is important that you create an infrastructure that encourages fast and effective knowledge exchange.

Another driver toward broadband is the shifting traffic patterns we're now seeing. This chapter looks at which of the traffic types are becoming dominant on the network and what that means to the network characteristics that they call on. Networks are being used more all the time, and we're experiencing rapid technology advances that present us with different strategies and architectures. It becomes increasingly difficult to make a commitment to a set of technologies today because, after all, tomorrow might introduce a vastly improved architecture. Because products and protocols develop so quickly, it is difficult for a given solution to be widely embraced, and without mass appeal, many products and services never have the opportunity to develop in the marketplace.

We're experiencing a wild unleashing of bandwidth, largely driven by developments in both optical networking and wireless communications. We're also seeing a trend toward advanced applications that include high degrees of visualization as well as sensory streams. Finally, convergence is also driving the move to broadband, as industries, devices, and applications find natural synergies in the digital world and merge platforms with one another.

The following sections examine some of these trends in more detail and explore the ways in which they affect next-generation networks.

Communications Traffic Trends

Internet traffic is doubling every 11 months. Along with the increase in the number of users, we're seeing growth of almost 50% per year in the amount of time users are connected; the average connection time is now approaching an hour. Internet-enabled devices, both wired and wireless, will vie more and more for connectivity to the Web; traffic is growing in a number of different dimensions.

We're also seeing a shift from human-to-machine communications to machine-to-machine communications. Today there are some six billion people on earth, only half of whom are served by telephony services. Yet there are 14 billion microprocessors in existence; these smart devices, as part of their intelligence, have communication skills and therefore mandate some network capacity. More and more of the typical business professionals today—many of whom work in the high-tech sector and therefore qualify as early adopters—already have an average of at least five devices (for example, PCs, cell phones, personal digital assistants, MP3 players, pagers, and even clothing). We're looking toward a future of greater numbers of devices communicating with one another, and someday there will be thousands of such devices for each human. As discussed in Chapter 15, "The Broadband Home and HANs," just about everything you can think of is having some kind of intelligence added to it in order to add value to your life. Devices are now beginning to communicate with each other more than people are communicating with each other, and this situation promises to become further exaggerated in the future.

Communications Backbone Trends

The growth and changes in traffic necessitate changes in the network backbone as well. Before the Internet became commercialized in 1995, backbone traffic was growing at a compound rate of about 6% to 10% per year, which was not much different from the traffic growth on the PSTN and in voice communications. But since that commercialization in 1995, traffic has been increasing at a compound annual rate of greater than 100%, and today the average traffic on the Internet's backbones is 1Tbps.

Backbone trends will be further complicated and driven by the advent of advanced applications that consume bandwidth in petabits per second (Pbps)—recall from Chapter 1, "Understanding the Telecommunications Revolution," that 1Pbps is 1,000Tbps. Online virtual reality, for instance, requires 1Pbps to 10Pbps additional capacity on the backbone; 3D holography requires 30Pbps to 70Pbps additional capacity; metacomputing (that is, the harnessing of multiple supercomputers together to compute very significant exercises such as weather prediction and warfare simulation) requires 50Pbps to 200Pbps additional capacity; and Web agents also require an additional capacity of 50Pbps to 200Pbps. The world's first petabits-per-second network was announced by I-21 Future Communications, a subsidiary of Interoute Communications Group, in the year 2000. It will be a fiber system across Europe. When broadband access climbs into the 100Gbps rate, which is projected for later this decade, backbones will require exabits per second (that is, 1 billion Gbps)!

Communications Bandwidth Trends

Technology breakthroughs are having a profound impact on service providers, as demonstrated by the falling prices of intercontinental capacity. The construction cost per 64Kbps has fallen from US$1,400 in 1988 to about US$300 in 1995, to just a couple dollars per line today. Therefore, the market price for intercontinental capacity has rapidly dropped. For example, the market price for a transatlantic 155Mbps link at the start of 1997 was US$20 million; by 1998, it was down to US$10 million; in early 2000 it was down to US$2 million to US$3 million; and in 2001 it had dropped to US$1 million. Another component of the intercontinental capacity equation is the operations, administration, and maintenance (OAM) charges. OAM charges are generally about 3% to 5% of the total cost of the line itself, and traditionally that cost increased if more bandwidth was being exercised over the cable length. But the agreements have recently been restructured such that you are charged OAM costs only based on the cable length, so if the cable allows advanced technologies such as DWDM to be applied, in theory, as you exercise more bandwidth, your OAM charges will be a lower percentage of the line cost. We can expect bandwidth charges to continue to drop.

Tremendous growth is occurring in the wireless realm. Wireless capacity is increasing, the per-minute network costs are falling, and data is comprising more and more of the wireless traffic. Wireless is expected to become the dominant form of Internet communication by the end of the decade. High-speed wireless communications will be the prevailing approach to Web access, as well as between components. When this happens, the "anytime, anywhere" inflection point will move the e-commerce platform of choice from the desktop PC to the palmtop. And satellites are playing a bigger role every year in the broadband Internet and data access market.

The unleashing of bandwidth that we're experiencing is causing us to establish a new relationship with bandwidth, and we're beginning to view it as a commodity. The driving forces behind creating a commodities market for bandwidth are an expected bandwidth capacity surplus and a growing need for risk management. Europe may take center stage in bandwidth trading. In the past two years we've seen the introduction of perhaps 20 different bandwidth exchanges. They use varying strategies, but generally they act as lead generators; there is a portal where buyers and sellers of bandwidth can meet and third parties are available to negotiate deals on their behalf. Some exchanges actually switch minutes based on least-cost routing algorithms or other such proprietary schemes.

Despite talk about the deployment of broadband access media in the local loop, the reality is that it still represents a very small percentage of the total access lines worldwide. The majority of access is still occurring via traditional analog modems. The growth in DSL and cable modems should result in some 40 million to 50 million users worldwide taking advantage of such broadband access options by 2003. But compared to the 1 billion or so subscriber lines that exist, even this is a relatively small percentage. Really large-scale rollouts and large takeoff of broadband access are expected to begin to occur around 2003. As you consider broadband access, it is important to keep in mind that adding broadband access lines puts incredible stress on the core network. Upgrades have to occur in parallel to truly manifest the benefits of broadband networking end-to-end. Remember that there are different stages of development between the access network and the core networks; those access options are discussed in Chapter 13, "Broadband Access Solutions."

Communications Application Trends

Another key trend driving the move to broadband is the changing nature of applications. A whole new generation of business-class services are arising from virtual private networks (VPNs), e-commerce, the capability to handle voice and fax over IP, unified messaging applications, multimedia collaboration, streaming media, the capability to host content or applications, and the capability to cache content on the network edges. All these business-class communications require guaranteed performance, so before they can become fully entrenched as network services, they must provide some level of QoS. What is needed for future networks to support these types of business-class services is discussed later in this chapter.

We're seeing a transition from portables to wearables, such as watches with medical monitors and pagers, eyeglasses with embedded computer displays, belts and watches with embedded computers, rings with universal product code readers and displays, and badges that have Internet connections and tiny teleconferencing cameras. For this trend to really take off, we need a broadband wireless infrastructure and personal area networks (PANs) to locally connect all these smart devices. (This is discussed in Chapter 15.)

We are also evolving to new industry models of information processing and communications. As we move more toward pervasive, or ubiquitous, computing, more and more of our senses—such as smell and taste—will become a part of what we communicate by using a network. Each person will be able to choose the media formats that are conducive to his or her cognitive map and then fully enjoy the realm of sight, sound, smell, and even taste and touch on the network. Visualization will become 3D and life-size, meaning that there will be telepresence. Later this century, we will witness the enhancement and augmentation of our human powers through neural interfaces, bringing about an era, in some 40 years to 50 years, whereby we'll be able to engage in virtuality without the constraint of devices that have to be worn, or enclosed cubicles that have to be entered. Reality will be what you make it!

For these models of information processing to become a reality requires tremendous bandwidth, extremely low latencies (that is, delays) in the network, guaranteed performance (which means administrated QoS), and broadband wireless access as well as PANs.

■ Multimedia Networking Requirements

Today's networks simply were not built for multimedia and, in particular, for applications that involve video communications, multimedia collaboration, and/or interactive-rich media. Curiously, it is through the application of sophisticated computer applications and devices that we have been able to determine what the human information processing model is comprised of: There is a very strong tendency for us to rely on the visual information stream for rapid absorption and longer retention. More than 50% of a human's brain cells are devoted to processing visual information, and combined with the delights of sound, smell, and touch—despite our enormous dependence on the written word—we're very active in processing the cues from the physical world. By changing the cues, we can change the world. Digital-rich media, in every conceivable sort of format—audio, animation, graphic, full-motion video, application, whiteboards, communities, and so on—

will increasingly depend on multimedia. Digital video and digital audio require minimal, predictable delays in packet transmission, which conventional shared-bandwidth, connectionless networks do not offer. (Chapter 4, "Establishing Communications Channels," discusses connectionless networks in detail.) They also require tight controls over losses, yet control of losses is not accounted for in connectionless networks. As more people simultaneously access files from a server, bandwidth becomes a significant issue. Correct timing, synchronization, and video picture quality are compromised if the bandwidth is insufficient.

Two key issues relate to multimedia communications: the nature of digital video and the role of television.

Digital Video

One of the fascinating areas that is driving and motivating the need for broadband access is television. Although television has a tremendous following throughout the world—more than computing or telecommunications—it has remained untouched by the digital revolution, but it is poised to change in the near future. Despite major advances in computing, video, and communications technologies, television has continued to rely on standards that are more than 55 years old. The biggest shortcoming with the existing television standards (that is, National Television Standards Committee [NTSC; used in the North America and Japan], Phase Alternation Line [PAL; used throughout the world], and Systeme Electronique Couleur Avec Memoire [SECAM; used in France and French territories]) is that they are analog systems, in which video signals degrade quickly under adverse conditions. Most of this signal degradation occurs along the path the picture travels from the studio to your TV. Digital TV (DTV) offers numerous advantages over the old analog TV signal, among which is the fact that it is nearly immune to interference and degradation. Another advantage of DTV is the capability to display a much better range of colors. The typical analog television can display around 32,000 colors, whereas the human eye can discriminate 16,000,000 colors. Sophisticated computer monitors and DTVs can display those 16,000,000 colors and more. Most importantly, digital technology will convert television from a mechanism that supports passive viewing to an engaging and interactive sensory experience—an environment in which you choose when, where, and how you engage with the world at your disposal.

People have only so much time and money to spend on electronic goods and services. In many parts of the world, the first thing people seem willing to spend their time and money on involves entertainment. Therefore the television industry, as well as the content, entertainment, and application world, will be increasingly important to how the local loop develops and how this further demands the introduction of home area networking. Of course TV and networks will deliver more than entertainment. They will deliver edutainment and infotainment, too, and the presentation of the information and knowledge you need will be in a format that is palatable and ensures assimilation and retention on a rapid and effective basis. Video and multimedia facilitate our ability to retain information and therefore will become the basis of much information delivery. This will drive the need for more bandwidth not just to the home, but also within the home, to network the range of computing and entertainment systems.

What would be required to carry a digitized stream to today's television? In the U.S. system, NTSC would require approximately 160Mbps, a digitized PAL stream would require about 190Mbps, and high-definition TV (HDTV) would require 1.5Gbps. Videoconferencing requires much less bandwidth than does TV, but it still requires a substantial amount; the H.323 standard from the ITU allows videoconferencing to be carried at bandwidths ranging from 384Kbps to 1.5Mbps. Streaming video requirements vary, depending on the quality: low quality requires 3Mbps, medium quality requires 5Mbps, and high quality requires 7Mbps.

An important driver behind broadband access is content, and much of the content for which people are willing to pay is entertainment oriented. The television industry has yet to undergo the revolution that digital technology has caused in other communications-related industries, and it has yet to capitalize on the potential new revenue-generating services that personal digital manipulation may allow. With the introduction of DTV and the mandate by spectrum management agencies to phase out or decommission analog broadcast, we will need a much greater amount of bandwidth into our homes to feed the new generations of televisions.

In terms of information transfer, television is generally associated with the concept of broadcast or cable delivery of someone else's programming on someone else's timetable. Video is associated with the ability to record, edit, or view programming on demand, according to your own timetable and needs. Multimedia promises to expand the role of video-enabled communications, ultimately effecting a telecultural shift, with the introduction of interactive television.

Video Compression

To make the most of bandwidth, we need to apply compression to video. Full-motion digital video needs as much compression as possible in order to fit on most standard storage devices. Moving Picture Experts Group (MPEG) is a working group of ISO/IEC in charge of the development of standards for coded representation of digital audio and video. It has created the MPEG compression algorithm, which reduces redundant information in images. One distinguishing characteristic of MPEG compression is that it is asymmetric—a lot of work occurs on the compression side and very little occurs on the decompression side. It's off-line versus real-time compression. Off-line allows 80:1 or 400:1 compression ratios, so it takes

80 or 400 times longer to compress than to decompress. It can take as much as an hour to compress one minute of video. The advantage of this asymmetrical approach is that digital movies compressed using MPEG run faster and take up less space. MPEG is hardware dependent.

There are several MPEG standards, in various stages of development and completion, and with different targeted uses. The following are some of the most common MPEG standards:

- **MPEG-1**—MPEG-1 is the standard on which such products as Video CD and MP3 are based. MPEG-1 addresses VHS-quality images with a 1.5Mbps data rate. MPEG-1 can play back from a single-speed CD-ROM player (150Kbps or 1.2Mbps) at 352×240 (that is, quarter screen) at 30 frames per second (fps).

- **MPEG-2**—MPEG-2 is the standard on which such products as DTV set-top boxes and DVD are based, and at this point it is the compression scheme of choice. It addresses DTV- or computer-quality images with a 6Mbps data rate. MPEG-2 offers resolutions of 720×480 and 1280×720 at 30 fps, with full CD-quality audio.

- **MPEG-4**—MPEG-4, an evolution of MPEG-2, features audio, video, and systems layers and offers variable-bit-rate encoding for both narrowband and broadband delivery in a single file. It also uses an object-based compression method, rather than MPEG-2's frame-based compression. MPEG-4 enables objects—such as 2D or 3D video objects, text, graphics, and sound—to be manipulated and made interactive through Web-like hyperlinks and/or multimedia triggers. The best feature of MPEG-4 is that the RealNetworks players, the Microsoft Windows Media Player, and Apple QuickTime all support MPEG-4.

- **MPEG-7**—MPEG-7, which is scheduled for completion in 2001, deals mainly with providing descriptions of multimedia content.

- **MPEG-21**—Today, there are many elements involved in building an infrastructure for the delivery and consumption of multimedia content. There is, however, no big picture to describe how these elements relate to each other. MPEG-21 was created to provide a framework for the all-electronic creation, production, delivery, and trade of content. Within the framework, we can use the other MPEG standards where appropriate. The basic architectural concept in MPEG-21 is the "digital item." Digital items are structured digital objects, including a standard representation and identification, as well as metadata. Basically, a digital item is a combination of resources (for example, videos, audio tracks, images), metadata (such as MPEG-7 descriptors), and structure (describing the relationship between resources).

MPEG-1, MPEG-2, and MPEG-4 are primarily concerned with the coding of audio/visual content, whereas MPEG-7 is concerned with providing descriptions of multimedia content, and MPEG-21 seeks to provide a framework for the all-electronic creation, production, delivery, and trade of content.

MPEG-4 is intended to expand the scope of audio/visual content to include simultaneous use of both stored and real-time components, plus distribution from and to multiple endpoints, but also to enable the reuse of both content and processes. Standards are being proposed as far out as MPEG-21 for specialized applications. Faster compression techniques using fractal geometry and artificial intelligence are being developed and could theoretically achieve compression ratios of 2,500:1. Implemented in silicon, this would enable full-screen, NTSC-quality video that could be deliverable over a LAN, as well as over the traditional PSTN and wireless networks.

Until better compression schemes are developed, most users have standardized on MPEG-2. By applying MPEG-2 encoding to NTSC, we can reduce the bandwidth to 2.7Mbps. Broadcast quality would be reduced to 7.2Mbps, DVD would require 10.8Mbps, and HDTV would come down to 20Mbps. Even so, how many of us have 20Mbps pipes coming into our homes now? Not even a 1.5Mbps connection over DSL or cable modem can come close to carrying a 20Mbps DTV signal. This tells us that broadband access alternatives over time will shift. We will need more fiber, we will need that fiber closer to the home, and we will need much more sophisticated compression techniques that enable us to make use of the even more limited wireless spectrum to carry information. We will also need to move forward with introducing new generations of wireless technologies geared toward the support of multimedia capacities—a combination of intelligent spectrum use and highly effective compression—of course with support for the requisite variable QoS environment and strong security features.

Delay and Jitter

Along with their demands for so much capacity, video and other real-time applications, such as audio and voice, also suffer from delay (that is, latency), and bit errors (that is, missing video elements or synchronization problems or complete loss of the picture) can be fatal. Delay in the network can wreak havoc with video traffic. The delay in a network increases as the number of switches and routers in the network increases. Today, the ITU recommends a maximum delay of 150 milliseconds, and evolving agreements promise packet loss of 1% or less per month and a round-trip latency guarantee of 80 milliseconds. However, the public Internet has as much as 40% packet loss during peak traffic hours and average latencies of 800 to 1,000 milliseconds. Although we really can't control the delay in the public Internet, we can engineer private IP backbones to provide the levels that we're seeking.

Jitter is another impairment that has a big impact on video, voice, and so on. Jitter is introduced when delay does not remain the same throughout a network, so packets arrive at the receiving node at different rates. Video can tolerate a small amount of delay, but when congestion points slow the buffering of images, jitter causes distortion and highly unstable images. Reducing jitter means reducing or avoiding the congestion that occurs in switches and routers, which, in turn, means having as many priority queues as the network QoS levels require.

Television Standards

Given the importance of a new era in television, it is worthwhile establishing some reference points for both analog and digital television standards.

Analog TV Standards

In 1945 the U.S. Federal Communications Commission (FCC) allocated 13 basic VHF television channels, thus standardizing the frequencies and allocating a broadcast bandwidth of 4.5MHz. In 1948 the NTSC was formed to define a national standard for the broadcast signal itself. The standard for black-and-white television was finally set in 1953 (developed primarily by RCA), and was ratified by the Electronics Industries Association (EIA) as the RS-170 specification. Full-time network color broadcasting was introduced in 1964, with an episode of *Bonanza*.

The NTSC color TV specification determines the electronic signals that make up a color TV picture and establishes a method for broadcasting those pictures over the air. NTSC defines a 4:3 horizontal:vertical size ratio, called the *aspect ratio*. This ratio was selected in the 1940s and 1950s, when all picture tubes were round because the almost-square 4:3 ratio made good use of round picture tubes. An NTSC color picture with sound occupies 6MHz of frequency spectrum, enough bandwidth for 2,222 voice-grade telephone lines. To transmit this signal digitally without compression would require about 160Mbps.

The English/German PAL system was developed after NTSC and adopted by the United Kingdom, Western Germany, and The Netherlands in 1967. The PAL system is used today in the United Kingdom, Western Europe (with the exception of France), Asia, Australia, New Zealand, the Middle East, Africa, Asia, and Latin America. Brazil uses a version of PAL called PAL-M. The PAL aspect ratio is also 4:3, and PAL channels occupy 8MHz of spectrum. Uncompressed PAL, digitally transported, would require approximately 200Mbps.

The SECAM system is used in France and the former French colonies, as well as in parts of the Middle East. Russia and the former Soviet-allied countries used a modified form of SECAM. There are two versions of SECAM: SECAM vertical and SECAM horizontal.

The PAL and SECAM standards provide a sharper picture than NTSC, but they display a bit of a flicker because they have a slower frame rate. Programs produced for one system must be converted to be viewed on one of the other systems. The conversion process detracts slightly from in the image quality, and converted video often has a jerky, old-time-movie look.

DTV Standards

DTV represents the growing convergence of broadcasting and computing. Thanks to MPEG-2, studio-quality images can be compressed and transformed into a digital stream. DTV is the next generation of television; its development will improve the audio and video quality of broadcast television, and it will replace the film cameras used in movie production. The difference between analog and digital TV will be profound in terms of picture quality as well as special screen effects, such as multiple-windowed pictures and interactive viewer options. The quality of DTV is almost six times better than what current TV offers, delivering up to 1,080 lines of resolution and CD-quality sound. But the real promise of DTV lies in its huge capacity—the capability to deliver, during a single program, information equivalent to that contained on dozens of CDs. The capacity is so great that wholly new industries will be created to use this digital potential for an entirely new revenue streams. Recognizing that the Web and other Internet services may grow to rival television, it is highly likely that new generations of television system infrastructure design will include this medium as part of the total system—so this is another area where convergence will occur.

Several standards worldwide cover DTV. Advanced Television Systems Committee's (ATSC's) DTV standards include digital high-definition television (HDTV), standard definition television (SDTV), data broadcasting, multichannel surround-sound audio, and satellite direct-to-home broadcasting. On December 24, 1996, the U.S. FCC adopted the major elements of the ATSC DTV standard (Standard A/53). The ATSC DTV standard has since been adopted by the governments of Canada, South Korea, Taiwan, and Argentina.

As shown in Table 10.1, the ATSC high-definition standard includes several basic DTV formats, which are defined by the number of pixels per line, the number of lines per video frame, the frame repetition rate, the aspect ratio, and the frame structure (that is, interlaced or progressive). The ATSC standard recommends that the receiver seamlessly and without loss of video continue to display all these formats in the native format of the television receiver.

One of the biggest issues in television standards involves how DTV images are drawn to the screen. There are two perspectives: those of the broadcast TV world and those of the computer environment. The broadcasters would rather initiate DTV with interlaced scanning, which is used by today's TV sets. Computer companies want progressive scanning DTV signals, similar to those used by computer

Table 10.1 ATSC DTV Standard

Vertical Value	Horizontal Value	Aspect Ratio	Frame Rate	Scanning Sequence
HDTV				
1080	1920	16:9	30, 24	Progressive
1080	1920	16:9	60	Interlaced
720	1280	16:9	60, 30, 24	Progressive
DTV				
480	704	4:3	60, 30, 24	Progressive
480	640	4:3	60, 30, 24	Progressive
SDTV				
480	704	4:3	60	Interlaced
480	640	4:3	60	Interlaced

monitors. The source of the conflict is different historical bandwidth limits. Originally, the NTSC decided that the best way to fit a 525-line video signal into a 6MHz broadcast channel was to break each video frame into two fields, each holding one half of the picture. Interlacing is a technique the camera uses to take two snapshots of a scene within a frame time. During the first scan, it creates one field of video, containing even-numbered lines, and during the second, it creates another, containing the odd-numbered lines. The fields are transmitted sequentially and the receiver reassembles them. This technique makes for reduced flicker and therefore higher brightness on the television receiver for the given frame rate (and bandwidth). Interlacing is rough on small text, but moving images look fine.

Countries in Europe, as well as Australia, use the Digital Video Broadcasting (DVB) standard. Formed in 1993, the DVB Consortium is responsible for recommending technical standards for the delivery of DTV. The DVB Consortium's 300-plus membership includes broadcasters, manufacturers, regulatory bodies, software developers, network operators and others from more than 35 countries. DVB standards are published by the European Telecommunications Standards (ETSI) and there is considerable day-to-day cooperation between the two organizations. ETSI, the Centre for Electrotechnical Standards (CENELEC), and the European

Broadcasting Union (EBU) have formed a joint technical committee to handle the DVB family of standards.

DVB standards are very similar to ATSC standards, including MPEG-2 video compression and packetized transport, but they provide for different audio compression and transmission schemes. The DVB standard has guidelines for a 1,920-pixel-by-1,080-line HDTV format.

At resolutions greater than 1,000 horizontal pixels, more than double that of today's TV sets, DTV receivers are likely to require massive amounts of dynamic random access memory (DRAM) to buffer the frames as they are processed. DTV can require a system to move upwards of 9.5Mbps of data.

At this point, it is not certain which DTV standard will win out, and we may see more than one retain a place. Whichever DTV format is favored, television will soon be fully digital.

■ The Broadband Infrastructure

We are in an era of new, emerging networks that we loosely term *next-generation networks*. Data traffic in these networks is equal to or surpassing voice as the most mission-critical aspect of the network. Remember that when all the traffic is ones and zeros, everything is data, and voice is just another data application. Integration of voice, data, and video without protocol conflicts will greatly simplify the migration of legacy communication systems and network applications to next-generation transport technologies. The huge growth in e-business, extranets, and intranets will also require a convergent infrastructure that offers minimum latencies to ensure the responsiveness that customers need.

Traffic is growing at an alarming rate. More human users, more machine users, and more broadband access are all contributing to the additional traffic. Established carriers and new startups are deploying huge amounts of fiber-optic cable, introducing new possibilities, and optical technology is revolutionizing the network overall. This new era of abundant capacity stimulates development and growth of bandwidth-hungry applications and demands service qualities that can allow control of parameters such as delay, jitter, loss ratio, and throughput. Bandwidth-intensive applications are much more cost-effective when the network provides just-in-time bandwidth management options. Next-generation networks will provide competitive rates because of lower construction outlays and operating costs.

Converging Public Infrastructures

Public infrastructures are converging on a single set of objectives. The PSTN looks to support high-speed multimedia applications, and therefore it also looks to provide high levels of QoS and the ability to guarantee a granular diversification of QoS. The PSTN has traditionally relied on a connection-oriented networking mode as a means of guaranteeing QoS, initially via circuit switching, and now incorporating ATM as well.

The public Internet is also looking to support high-speed multimedia applications, and it must deal with providing QoS guarantees. But we are investigating slightly different options for how to implement this in the Internet than in the PSTN (see Chapter 5, "The PSTN"). Included in the IETF standards are Integrated Services (IntServ), Differentiated Services (DiffServ), and the new panacea, Multiprotocol Label Switching (MPLS), all of which are described later in this chapter.

Broadband Service Requirements

For next-generation networks to succeed, they must offer a unique set of features, including the following:

- **High speed and capacity**—All next-generation networks must offer very high capacities, today measured in Tbps (terabits per second, or 1 trillion bps) and already moving into the range of Pbps (petabits per second, or 1,000Tbps). Higher-bandwidth broadband access (such as 100Gbps) will drive the need for additional core bandwidth, and discussions are beginning about networks providing exabits per second (that is, 1 billion Gbps).

- **Bandwidth on demand**—Next-generation networks must be capable of providing or provisioning bandwidth on demand, as much as is needed, when it is needed—unlike today's static subscription services.

- **Bandwidth reservation**—Next-generation networks must be capable of offering reserved bandwidth, so that when you know you'll need a high-capacity service for streaming media, you can reserve the network resources so that they are guaranteed at the time and place that you need them.

- **Support of isochronous traffic**—Isochronous traffic is timebounded information that must be transferred within a specific timeframe, and as such has a low tolerance for delay and loss.

- **Agnostic platforms**—Agnostic devices support multiple data protocols (for example, IP, Frame Relay, ATM, MPLS) and support multiple traffic types, such as voice, data, and video, so that you can aggregate and administer all traffic at a single point.

- **Support for unicasting and multicasting**—In unicasting, streams from a single origination point go directly to a single destination point. In multicasting, streams from a single origination point flow to multiple destination points. This reduces traffic redundancy by limiting the access to a selected group of users.

■ QoS—As discussed later in this chapter, next-generation networks must provide variable QoS parameters, must ensure that those service levels can be guaranteed, and must ensure that service-level agreements (SLAs) can be honored.

A number of developments have been key to enabling us to deliver on such a set of requirements. One such development is photonics and optical networking. Chapter 12, "Optical Networking," describes the revolution that started with the ability to manufacture glass wires, went further to introduce erbium-doped fiber amplifiers, grew to encompass wavelength division multiplexers and dense wavelength division multiplexers, and is proceeding forward to introduce optical add/drop multiplexers, optical cross-connect switches and routers, and the optical probes and network management devices that are very important for testing networks. We're looking forward to commencing deployment of the end-to-end optical environments in the next three to five years.

A number of broadband access technologies, both wireline and wireless, have been developed to facilitate next-generation networking. Chapter 13 covers these options, which include the twisted-pair xDSL family; hybrid fiber coax alternatives that make use of cable modems; fiber to the curb; fiber to the home; broadband wireless, including direct broadcast satellite, MMDS, LMDS, and Free Space Optics; and innovative new uses of powerline to support high-speed communications. As discussed in Chapter 15, "Wireless Communications," 3G wireless promises up to 2Mbps (but most likely around 384Kbps).

As discussed later in this chapter, multiservice core, edge, and access platforms are being developed. These platforms include integrated access devices (IADs), convergent switches, media gateways, agnostic platforms, and new generations of high-capacity terabits switch routers.

Intelligent networks, which include programmable networking, are potentially a replacement for the capital-intensive PSTN based on circuit switches. Softswitches, media gateways, Signaling System 7 (SS7) gateways, and service-enabling software developments are critical. (These developments are discussed later in this chapter.)

Characteristics of Next-Generation Networks

A next-generation network is a network that is designed for multimedia communications, which implies that it has broadband capacities, multichannel transport with high data rates, low latencies (80 milliseconds or less is the target), low packet loss (less than 5%, with the target being less than 1%), and QoS guarantees.

A next-generation network has a worldwide infrastructure that consists of fast packet-switching techniques, which make maximum use of transport and provide great transmission efficiencies. A next-generation network involves optical networking; today's electronic systems are going to be the bottlenecks to delivering tomorrow's applications, so we will see a replacement of the electronic infrastructure with optical elements that provide end-to-end optical networking.

A next-generation network has a multiservice core, coupled with an intelligent edge. The application of next-generation telephony in the edge environment may replace the existing architectures associated with the PSTN. Next-generation networks will be characterized by intelligent networking, for rapid service delivery and provisioning. They will also have video and multimedia elements, to deliver on the content for which the broadband infrastructure exists. Their access media are broadband in nature and encompass both wired and wireless facilities.

Next-generation networks stand to change how carriers provision applications and services and how customers access them. End-user service delivery from a single platform provides many benefits. It decreases time to market; it simplifies the process of moves, adds, and changes; and it provides a unique connection point for service provisioning and billing. Full-service internetworking between the legacy circuit-switched network and next-generation packet networks is mandatory going forward. Next-generation networks also must be interoperable with new structures that are emerging, which implies that they have to be able to support the most up-to-date transport and switching standards. They also must support advanced traffic management, including full configuration, provisioning, network monitoring, and fault management capabilities. In a next-generation network, it is important to be able to prioritize traffic and to provide dynamic bandwidth allocation for voice, data, and video services; this enables management of delay-tolerant traffic and prioritization of delay-sensitive traffic.

A next-generation network is a high-speed packet- or cell-based network that is capable of transporting and routing a multitude of services, including voice, data, video, and multimedia, and a common platform for applications and services that is accessible to the customer across the entire network, as well as outside the network. The main physical components of the next-generation network are fiber and wireless media, routers, switches, gateways, servers, and edge devices that reside at the customer premise.

Figure 10.1 shows an example of the kind of internetworking that needs to occur in providing access between the legacy PSTN and a next-generation packet-based network. It shows internetworking between the legacy PSTN and the underlying intelligent network, as well as emerging IP-based services. At the endpoints are customers that may be served by traditional plain old telephone service

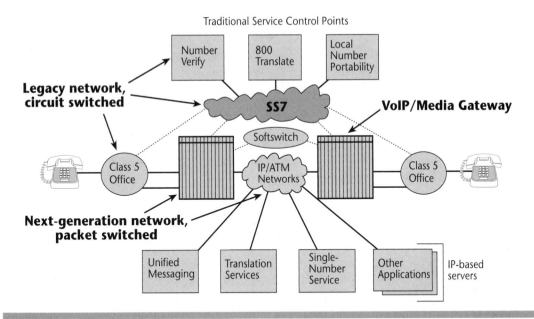

Figure 10.1 Internetworking between the legacy PSTN and a next-generation packet-based network

(POTS). They have access lines into their local exchange. The local exchange, then, has links into the SS7 infrastructure (discussed in Chapter 5), which allows service logic (for example, number verification, translation of toll-free numbers), the support of local number portability, and the provisioning of class services (for example, call waiting and call forwarding); these are the types of services and features that we're accustomed to with the PSTN. The local exchange connects into that intelligence to service the calls that are being requested by the users. The local exchange in a next-generation network also taps into the media gateway switch. The media gateway switch digitizes and packetizes the voice streams and then consults a softswitch, which is a form of intelligence in the network. The softswitch identifies the destination media gateway switch behind the telephone number being requested, and it applies to the packets an IP address that coincides with the destination gateway switch.

The gateway switches also connect into SS7 in order to be able to introduce or support the services that we traditionally associate with voice. Between the media gateway switches then, is the high-speed packet network, which could be an IP backbone, an ATM network, or an MPLS backbone environment. This network could also natively tap into new databases that are being created with advanced services designed specifically for the IP environment.

IP and ATM

IP and ATM are two techniques that are used in next-generation networks. (IP is introduced in Chapter 9, "The Internet: Infrastructure and Service Providers," and ATM is introduced in Chapter 7, "Wide Area Networking.") ATM is used to support a great deal of Internet backbones. Approximately 85% of all IP backbones use ATM in the core.

IP

IP was designed to work in the LAN world. It is a connectionless environment, which means it provides the capability of having information moved between network elements without a preconceived path between the source and destination. In a LAN environment, bandwidth is relatively inexpensive and the deployment, by definition, is over a small geographic area. Because of the small coverage area, transit delay is typically not an issue in a LAN.

In the event of congestion, IP discards packets. Transmission Control Protocol (TCP) retransmits the lost packets, quickly and transparently to the users, and because of the short transit delay, discarded packets are quickly detected, so users don't perceive delays in downloads. But WANs are typically deployed over longer distances than LANs. And in WANs, transit delays become a major issue in two ways: in controlling the QoS and in identifying the loss of packets that may have occurred because of congestion. Also, bandwidth is more expensive in a WAN than in a LAN; you pay for every bit that is sent over a WAN link, so packet discards that create retransmissions can make the expense of retransmission alone significant.

Problems with IP Networks Traditional IP routers were not intended to handle the large-scale type of networking that we are now demanding from IP. In IP router-based networks, the core, like the core in the PSTN, is responsible for providing interconnectivity. But in the IP router network, the core also provides server access and network management to the edge devices on the network periphery.

Because of the increases traffic networks are seeing today, the core network is becoming loaded, and that is resulting in network slowness and unacceptable delays. At the edge of the LAN, a shortage of network capacity, coupled with proliferation of broadcasts and multicasts, is creating significant network problems. When the edge demand exceeds the capacity of the core, queue overruns create capacity overload and lost packets, thereby reducing the availability and reliability of the network. As a result, users are suffering from congestion, inadequate server access, and slow response times.

Traditional IP routers cannot deliver the service quality that is increasingly being demanded. The shortcomings of traditional routers include poor path calculation and slow rerouting. Routers usually use the shortest path metric to calculate their routes, so IP routers send traffic over a shorter path, even if it's congested, instead of over a more desirable, longer, or uncongested path. This is one of the reasons that there is increased use of ATM or MPLS in the core for backbone traffic engineering purposes. Also, in the event of a backbone circuit or router failure, IP routers can take a long time—up to a minute—to calculate the new paths around the failure. This has led to more reliance on the resilient SDH/SONET backbone infrastructure, where there is a backup path—a protect fiber—that can ensure that the data is diverted to the protect fiber within a 50-millisecond timeframe.

Recent introductions of Voice over IP (VoIP) services and streaming media have exposed two other limitations of IP networks: latency and jitter. IP today doesn't provide a way to control latency and jitter. For a packet-based IP network to successfully support voice services, minimum transit delay must be achieved, as must minimum packet loss. High-quality voice demands less than 100 milliseconds for the total one-way latency, including all processing at both ends, which implies digitization, compression, decompression, queuing, playback, and so on, and that must also include the network delay. Voice compression and decompression alone normally take about 30 to 50 milliseconds. Network latency must be tightly controlled to support these services properly. One immediate solution is to increase the amount of available bandwidth. If there's no congestion, there's no problem. And technologies such as Dense Wavelength Division Multiplexing provide relief initially, but history has taught us that throwing bandwidth at a problem does not fix it, so this is a short-term relief measure, but not a long-term solution that addresses the need to differentiate traffic and its requirements on a very granular level. Hence the key to success for large-scale IP networking lies in delivering the flexibility of IP routing with a switched packet-forwarding mechanism that offers the highest possible performance and maximum control: IP switching.

IP Switching   IP switching was designed to speed up increasingly choked networks, by replacing slower, more processing-intensive routers with switches. IP routers that provide connection-oriented services at the IP layer are referred to as *IP switches*. Routers are slower than switches because they must examine multiple packet fields, make substitutions in the packet headers, and compute routes on a packet-by-packet basis, which introduces latency and congestion.

The idea with IP switching is to make a connectionless data technology behave similarly to a circuit-switched network. An IP switch routes the first packet, and then it switches all subsequent packets. The goal is to make intranet and Internet access faster and to enable the deployment of new voice, video, and graphics applications and services. Therefore, IP switching has two objectives: to provide a way for internetworks to scale economically and to provide effective QoS support for IP. In essence, IP switching replaces Layer 3 hops with Layer 2 switching, which leads to good hardware-based forwarding performance.

Even with the advantages of IP switching, IP still doesn't allow us to properly administer all the QoS parameters that are part of traffic definitions, and this is where ATM comes in.

ATM

As discussed in Chapter 7, ATM was created in the WAN environment. It came out of the carrier community as a means by which to reengineer the PSTN for streaming applications. Because ATM comes from the carrier environment, where traffic engineering is essential, it is a connection-oriented technique. It provides a means to establish a predefined path between the source and the destination, which enables greater control of network resources. Overallocation of bandwidth becomes an engineered decision; it offers a deterministic way to respond to changes, on a dynamic basis, to network status. A great benefit of ATM is that it provides for real-time traffic management. It enables policing and traffic shaping; it can monitor (that is, police) the cells and determine, based on congestion, which cell should be dropped (that is, perform traffic shaping).

ATM allows networkwide resource allocation for class of service (CoS) and QoS provisioning. Again, because it is connection-oriented, it looks ahead to the destination point to ensure that each link along the way can deliver on the requested QoS. If it can't, the session is denied. Therefore, ATM also makes possible deterministic transit delay—you can specify and calculate the end-to-end delays, as well as the variations in delays. This is all administered through multiple QoS levels (as described later in this chapter).

Remember from Chapter 7 that a lot of IP takes place over ATM. Because it is connection-oriented, ATM gives service providers the traffic engineering tools they need to manage both QoS and utilization. ATM's virtual circuits control bandwidth allocation on busy backbone routes. In provisioning a network, the service provider can assign each virtual circuit a specific amount of bandwidth and a set of QoS parameters. The provider can then dictate what path each virtual circuit takes. Basing these decisions on overall traffic trends reduces the likelihood of network hot spots and wasted bandwidth, and this is why so many service providers turn to ATM to transport IP traffic. However, the service provider has to deal with two control planes—managing both IP routers and ATM switches. Using ATM virtual circuits to interconnect IP routers leads to scaling problems because every router needs a separate virtual circuit to every other router. As the network grows, the number of routes and virtual circuits can increase exponentially, eventually exceeding the capacity of both switches and routers. Network operators can work around this in one of two ways: either they can forgo a full-mesh architecture or they can move to MPLS, which is discussed later in this chapter.

Table 10.2   IP Versus ATM

Transport	Benefit	Drawback	Services Supported	Packet size	Header
IP	Pervasive at the desktop	No QoS	Data, voice	Variable, 40 bytes to 64,000 bytes	40 bytes
ATM	Multiple service classes	Small cell size that is inefficient for data transport	Data, voice, IP, Frame Relay, X.25, leased lines	Fixed cells, 53 bytes	5 bytes

IP Versus ATM

Table 10.2 is an overview comparison of IP and ATM. An upside of IP is that it is pervasive at the desktop. The downside is that there is no QoS built in. It supports data, voice, and fax. IP packet size is variable. It can be up to 64,000 bytes, but packets are segmented into 1,500-byte frames for transport, and 40 bytes of each packet is for the header information.

The upside of ATM is that it is an architected QoS approach that defines five key service classes (described later in this chapter). The downside is that it uses a small cell size (only 53 bytes, 5 bytes of which is the header information), which means it has a lot of overhead (that is, cell tax), which could be construed as inefficient—for data transport, or for voice transport, or for other traffic types—and this is an issue when bandwidth is constrained and expensive. Remember that ATM was built based on the assumption of gigabits-per-second trunks and generous bandwidth, so the cell tax is less relevant if the prevailing condition is the unleash-

Terabit Switch Routers

Terabit switch routers are relatively new, and they are an emerging class of backbone platform. They will offer, as the name implies, terabits of capacity—the current products range from some 640Gbps to 19.2Tbps—and they will support interfaces that range from OC-3 (that is, 155Mbps) to OC-192 (that is, 10Gbps).

Terabit switch routers are agnostic devices, so they support a wide variety of data traffic types, protocols, and interfaces. They are engineered for short and predictable delays, and they offer robust QoS features as well as multicast support and availability in carrier class, so they will be able to service a wide subscriber base.

Terabit switch routers are being developed to integrate with other network elements, in particular optical switches, and they may communicate by using MPLS. Again, these are the early days for terabit switch routers—at this point the platforms are largely proprietary and vary in how they operate.

ing of abundant bandwidth. ATM supports a wide variety of services, including voice, IP, Frame Relay, X.25, and leased lines.

We don't really have to choose between IP and ATM. At least for the time being, we can use them together quite effectively. IP has become the universal language of computer networking, especially in the desktop environment. IP-based services—including VPNs, e-commerce, outsourced remote access, application hosting, multicasting, and VoIP, along with fax and video over IP—are used in a number of areas. A benefit of IP is that there is a much larger pool of knowledgeable programmers for IP than there is for ATM. However, all these wonderful applications that the programmers are developing for IP tend to require a lot of CoS and QoS, as well as controlled access. IP standards for QoS are in the early development stages. ATM will increasingly be used to switch IP traffic because of its network management, restoration, and reliability capabilities.

■ The Broadband Architecture: Multiservice Networks

Network architectures are definitely in transition. In today's environment, time-division and statistical multiplexers gather customer traffic for additional circuit-based aggregation through a stable hierarchy of edge (that is, local), tandem, and core switching offices in the carrier networks. Overlay networks, such as X.25, Frame Relay, ATM, and the Internet, have been put in place and have created the need to internetwork services, thereby eroding traditional network borders. Then additional access in transport options—including cable, DSL, and wireless—began to be introduced, all joining traditional modems and bringing their own high-density access aggregation devices into the picture. Meanwhile, in the core, SDH/SONET transport has been layered over DWDM, adding capacity and producing a variety of vendor-specific switching, routing, and management options.

Figure 10.2 puts today's networks into a visual context. Residential customers on POTS connect through their first point of access, the Class 5 (that is, local exchange) switch. Some users are serviced by xDSL, and these lines terminate on a DSL access multiplexer (DSLAM). The DSLAM links back to the local exchange for regular voice traffic, which is diverted out over the PSTN, and it also has connections into the packet-based backbone (which could be an IP, an ATM, a Frame Relay, or an MPLS-based core or backbone network) for data traffic.

Some users have dial-in modems that terminate on remote access devices, whereby through digital access cross-connects and routers they use private lines to access their corporate facilities to work with internal LANs and resources. Some customers have optical networks, so they have a series of multiplexers on premise that multiplex suboptical carrier levels up to levels that can be introduced into a SDH/SONET add/drop multiplexer to carry that traffic through the SDH/SONET

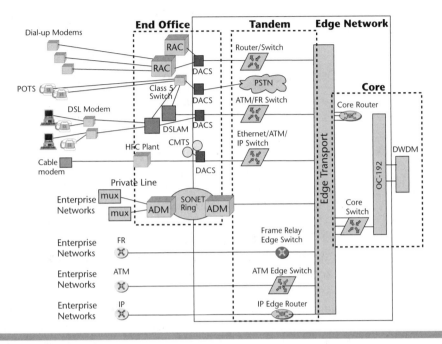

Figure 10.2 Today's networks

ring. Customers also have Frame Relay, ATM, and IP switches and routers that interface into complementary equipment within the carrier network. So between the access and the edge there is a plethora of different equipment, requiring different interfaces, different provisioning, billing and network management systems, and different personnel to handle customer service and technical support and maintenance.

The core network is increasingly becoming optical. Therefore, there is access into the high-speed optical multiplexers via routers or switches. Those optical carrier levels in the SDH/SONET hierarchy are further multiplexed via DWDM systems to take advantage of the inherent bandwidth available in those fibers.

The broadband architecture is an increasingly complicated arena. Many different alternatives in the network have been engineered to support specific voice, data, or video applications, meeting certain performance characteristics and cost characteristics. When we add up all the different platforms and networks that we have, it's quite a costly environment and one that's difficult to maintain and manage cohesively. By building the overlay networks and separating access and transport functions, carriers manage to add capacity and new services without interrupting their existing services. However, the downside of this system is that the new services rarely use the same provisioning management and troubleshooting systems as the old network. These operations and management costs can amount to as much as half of the carrier's total cost to provide a service.

The Three-Tiered Architecture

The broadband architecture has three tiers. The first tier involves the access switches; it is the outer tier, associated with delivering broadband service to a customer. The second tier involves the edge switches. This tier is associated with protocol and data service integration. The third tier, the inner tier, involves the core switches. This tier handles transmission of high-speed packet data throughout the backbone. Figure 10.3 shows the components that comprise these three tiers, and the following sections describe them.

The Outer Tier: The Broadband Access Tier

Access tier devices include legacy network infrastructure devices such as Class 5 local exchanges and digital loop carriers. The access tier also includes DSLAMs, which are designed to concentrate hundreds of DSL access lines onto ATM or IP trunks and then route them to routers or multiservice edge switches.

Also in the access environment are IADs, which provide a point of integration at the customer edge, integrating voice, data, and video networks and supporting broadband access options. Also in the access tier are remote access servers, which

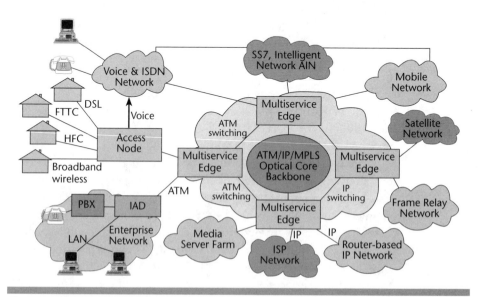

Figure 10.3 A multiservice network

typically provide access to remote users via analog modem or ISDN connections, and which include dialup protocols and access control or authentication schemes. Remote access routers are used to connect remote sites via private lines or public carriers, and they provide protocol conversations between the LAN and the WAN.

The Middle Tier: The Intelligent Edge

The second tier involves the intelligent edge devices. These can include next-generation switches, VoIP gateways, media gateways, trunking gateways, ATM switches, IP routers, IP switches, multiservice agnostic platforms, optical networking equipment, and collaborating servers. This tier is also home to the network management stations that manage all these devices.

The edge devices and the intelligent edge in general handle authentication, authorization, and accounting. They identify the specific levels of performance required and map the proper QoS levels into the packet according to the backbone protocol. The intelligence keeps moving closer and closer to the customer, and it is actually being extended to customer premises equipment. We're trying to get away from an environment where we have a lot of single-purpose networks associated with single-purpose boxes and their own individual access lines (see Figure 10.4). As mentioned previously, there are complexities involved with acquisition, with ongoing maintenance, and with the talent pool to administer and maintain these systems.

The ideal configuration is a multipurpose WAN switch that could facilitate the termination of any type of data protocol, as well as facilitate aggregation at high

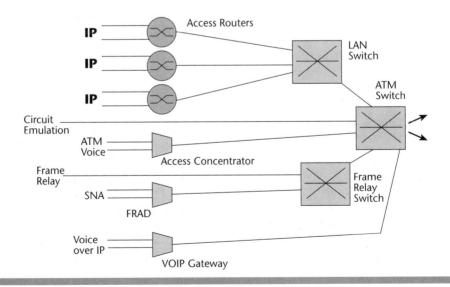

Figure 10.4 Complexities with single-purpose boxes

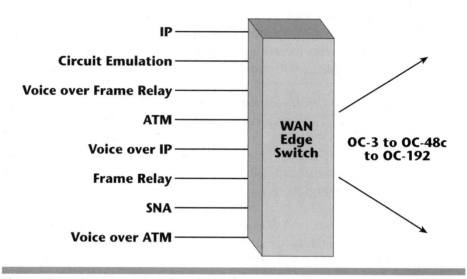

Figure 10.5 Simplicity with multipurpose switches

speeds to the various optical levels (see Figure 10.5). This is what we're striving for with the intelligent edge.

Most equipment manufacturers today produce one of two types of devices for the edge:

- **Access-oriented devices**—These devices include multiservice provisioning platforms (MSPPs), which can handle all the popular data protocols and interfaces, except that they are not designed to be optical aggregators.

- **Transport-oriented devices**—These are optical aggregations systems, and they support a full range of hierarchical aggregation, from DS-3 to OC-48. They offer electrical-to-optical conversion as well. But they don't offer all the data interfaces.

Successful edge devices will have to handle multiprotocol data services as well as multispeed aggregation. Thus, emerging solutions for the intelligent network edge will have to meet three critical objectives. First, there's a need to bridge the bandwidth bottleneck that currently exists between user LANs and the optical core. We have LANs that operate at Gigabit Ethernet, and soon we'll even have 10Gbps Ethernet. We have optical cores that operate at OC-192 (that is, 10Gbps) and are moving beyond that to 40Gbps and 80Gbps. By applying multiple lambdas in a fiber, we can even achieve terabits per second. But our WAN link between the LAN and the optical core is often limited to a link that can handle only 56Kbps to 2Mbps. A severe bottleneck is occurring at the LAN/WAN integration point, and that needs to be resolved. Second, we need to improve the serviceability of the carrier networks; we need to make it easier to define, provision, bill, and manage services and equipment across a converged area. Third, we need to enable converged carrier infrastructures to simplify the carrier networks and to simplify the support of end-user services.

Four new developments promise that equipment providers will soon be able to provide broadband access switches that will address the services providers' bandwidth and serviceability problems:

- **Advanced network processors**—Advanced network processors are programmable and enable the required service function in software. This allows carriers to have the flexibility of "generic cards" instead of having to purchase expensive specialized cards. Some processors will even provide an autodetection feature, automatically detecting the service required. These generic cards can accept any type of native input—TDM connections, IP frames, ATM cells, and so on—and convert that traffic to optically multiplexed flows while maintaining the service requested by each user flow.

- **Advanced computing memory**—Thanks to inexpensive and reliable memory, equipment vendors can now load large volumes of data and software onto individual cards. This is vital to the intensive data collection and computing that is required to support increasingly demanding SLAs. Maintaining user-specific information at the edge makes it easier for the carrier to manage each user's individual service level.

- **High-capacity switching**—High-capacity switching is greatly improving performance by allowing traffic to move at optical speeds without any blocking or buffering. This also allows full protocol processing without affecting the network performance. Thus, using these types of switch fabrics in the edge makes it much easier to allocate and manage capacity.

- **Standardized software support**—Several software vendors, including CrossKeys and Vertel, have been developing standards-based solutions featuring both Telecommunications Management (TMN) and Common Object Request Broker Architecture (CORBA) software. Telcordia has also developed Operations Systems Modifications for the Integration of Network Elements (OSMINE) solutions, which are packages that provide a standard means to integrate new software and hardware systems into the existing regional Bell operating company (RBOC) operations support systems.

The next-generation edge must provide media-agnostic service interworking between multiple access technologies. We have the benefit of multiple options for broadband access, but with that comes the challenge and complication of supporting multiple access techniques. The intelligent edge must also support each converged service, recognizing and properly handling all the voice, data, video, and multimedia traffic. That edge should also be providing an H.323 or perhaps Session Initiation Protocol (SIP) signaling gateway function between the enterprise network and the POTS network. (Chapter 10, "Internet/IP Applications and Services," describes these signaling systems.) By doing so, the edge will provide convergence between the POTS SS7 signaling network and the IP signaling network.

The new edge systems have many things to accomplish. They also need to reduce the human intervention time required to perform simple network tasks. This is key to addressing the people shortage that's affecting all providers. These days it is very difficult to find the appropriate talent and maintain it. Half of the job vacancies in information technology and telecommunications each year go unfilled, and in the United States alone, the number of jobs open is 1.6 million! This is not a minor problem, and the newer the technology, the harder it is to find and maintain knowledgeable and experienced support.

New network designs are promising to facilitate a number of issues—above all to eliminate all the service-specific and hierarchical aggregation layers that reside in today's edge network. All those layers contribute to cost and complexity over time. Figure 10.6 depicts what the next-generation access edge might look like. You can see that we've replaced separate platforms throughout the edge with more integrated environments; for example, we might have softswitches that enable traditional PSTN call telephony-type features, but over packet backbones. Circuit switches are predicted to continue to be present in the network for another 10 years to 20 years, depending on location. Trunking gateways are used to attach multiple media gateways that are putting voice into IP packets to the underlying SS7 network. Remote access concentrators enable remote access for telecommuters and people who need to access remote corporate hosts. New generations of broadband access switches enable the multialternative broadband access environment—cable modems, Frame Relay, DSLs, wireless alternatives, and so on. We want to reduce the edge environment to a simpler set of agnostic, multiplatform, multiprotocol intelligent edge devices.

The main responsibilities of the intelligent edge include broadband access, adaptation of the native traffic to the underlying backbone technique, and concentration of many customer streams onto the bigger pipes within the core. This is the point at which the service attributes will be mapped to QoS mechanisms in order to deliver the requested performance and thereby live up to the SLAs. A major benefit is that it allows rapid and dynamic service provisioning, and it even allows customization for individual users. These service changes can be made without affecting the core, so as new service logic is required, as market segments find demand for new services, we will not necessarily have to reengineer the entire core network to accommodate those changes. Service provisioning is decoupled from service specification and service delivery. The intelligent edge could maintain a policy engine to handle the service provisioning. It could also include features

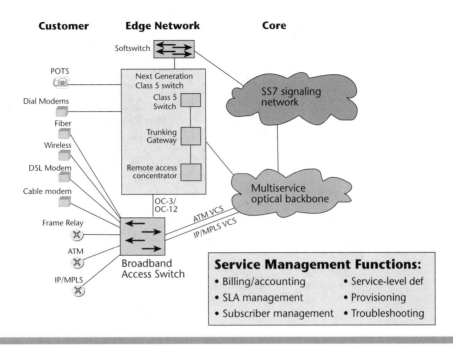

Figure 10.6 The next-generation network edge

such as encryption, key and certificate distribution, tunneling, accounting, address allocation, and QoS administration.

The Inner Tier: The High-Speed Core

The access and edge switches are designed to be scalable, both in port counts and in their capability to deliver multiservice support, and they are evolving to include more and more intelligence and features that would enable policy-based services management. In contrast, core switches are designed to be incredibly big and incredibly fast, but sometimes quite dumb. Their main objective is to transport the traffic as reliably and quickly as possible at the highest available rate.

Thus, in the emerging environment we see a reversal. In the traditional PSTN, the edges served the network core, and the network core had all the intelligence. Now, the network core is serving the edges, and intelligence is being distributed closer and closer to the customer premise (see Figure 10.7).

The Next-Generation Switching Architecture

Next-generation telephony is being introduced into networks, and this is causing a bit of a change in the architecture. In the PSTN, we use traditional Class 5, or local, exchanges and Class 4, or toll, exchanges, that are based on common con-

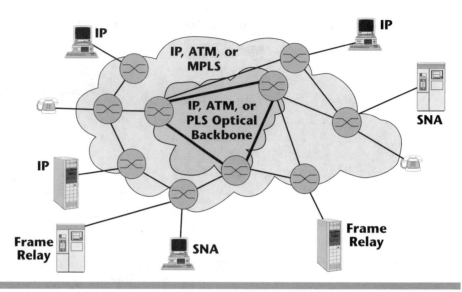

Figure 10.7 The network core serving the edges

trol architecture. This means that intelligence is centralized in proprietary hardware and software.

Another characteristic of the traditional architecture is the use of remote switching modules or digital loop carriers as a means of extending the range of the local exchange as well as shortening the loop length between the subscriber and the access node. Adjunct boxes were used for the provisioning of enhanced services and generally separate data network access altogether. Network operators had to wait for generic software releases from the manufacturers in order to launch new applications and services, which led to long time frames for applications development. Another big issue was the very high up-front costs, somewhere between US$3 million and US$5 million per deployment. In this traditional common control circuit-switched architecture, all the intelligence resided in monolithic switches at the network edge, and then that intelligence was distributed outward to the dumb customer premise equipment.

With next-generation switch architectures, intelligence resides on the network edge, which facilitates distributed control. The core backbone rests on ATM, or IP, or, going forward, MPLS. At the customer premise, the IAD merges the voice and data streams that are coming from various users at the customer premise. A gateway switch provides the Class 5 functionality, with integrated enhanced services and converged network access. Furthermore, switch interfaces with SS7 are accomplished via SS7 gateway switches. This way more applications can be developed more quickly, generating more revenues. Service creation is occurring at the network edge, closer to the customer, which simplifies and speeds the process. This provides the combined benefits of lower cost and faster applications development, and, as an added bonus, the startup cost is around US$100,000.

In the next-generation switch architecture, as all the intelligence is being pushed out to the edges, to the customer premises environment, internetworking is needed between the legacy circuit-switched network and the emerging packet-switched environments. This internetworking is accomplished through a series of gateway switches and signaling system gateways, as well as gateway control mechanisms, called softswitches. This programmable networking approach requires a routing system of softswitches and media gateways that can convert different media and protocol types.

Programmable Networks

Programmable networking is based on separating applications and call control from the switching platform. It requires separating the service logic that activates, controls, bills for, and manages a particular service from the transmission, hardware, or signaling nodes, overall making call functions easier to manage.

Programmable networking gives providers the chance to offer circuit-switched voice and advanced intelligent network services such as caller ID and call waiting. In addition, it supports packet-switched services and applications such as Internet access, e-mail, Web browsing, and e-commerce; and, of course, programmable networking embraces wireless networks. Programmable networking is catching on among carriers, who are seeking to packetize the core of their networks for greater efficiencies, and this is leading to a rise in the sales of softswitches.

Softswitches

The basic appeal of the softswitch architecture is the capability to use converged voice/data transport and to open the PSTN signaling network. Carriers have been buying softswitches primarily for Class 4 tandem replacement and Internet offload. It now seems that for the softswitch market to grow and prosper, the RBOCs, the cable companies, and the foreign service providers will have to decommission their Class 5 local exchanges.

In the next-generation network, call control intelligence is outside the media gateways and is handled by a media gateway controller or a softswitch (also referred to as a call agent). The softswitch implements service logic and controls external trunking gateways, access gateways, and remote access servers. Softswitches can run on commercial computers and operating systems, and they provide open applications programming interfaces. A softswitch is a software-based, distributed switching and control platform that controls the switching and routing of media packets between media gateways across the packet backbone (see Figure 10.8).

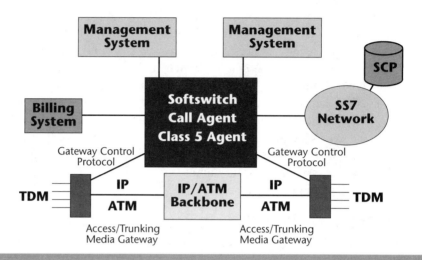

Figure 10.8 The softswitch model

The softswitch controls the voice or data traffic path by signaling between the media gateways that actually transport the traffic. The gateway provides the connection between an IP or ATM network and the traditional circuit-switched network, acting very much like a multiprotocol cross-connect.

The softswitch ensures that a call's or a connection's underlying signaling information is communicated between gateways. This includes information such as automatic number identifiers, billing data, and call triggers. The softswitch architecture has three parts, as shown in Figure 10.9. The switching layer involves the media gateways. The call control layer involves telephony signaling protocols (for example, SIP, MGCP, H.323, SS7), which are discussed shortly. The third layer is the application layer, and this is where services are supported (for example, lifeline services and regulatory issues, such as the ability to perform legal intercept).

Evolving Signaling Standards

Softswitches must communicate with packet switches, VoIP gateways, media gateways, and the SS7 networks. To do so, they have to rely on standardized protocols. A number of different technical specifications, protocols, and standards are used to deliver these services and the desired end functions, some of which are briefly reviewed here; you can find further information on them in Chapter 11, "Next-Generation Network Services."

H.323 version 2 is the ITU standard for IP telephony in the LAN and was used as the basis for several early VoIP gateways. Most VoIP gateways support H.323 and thereby ensure interoperability between different vendors' products.

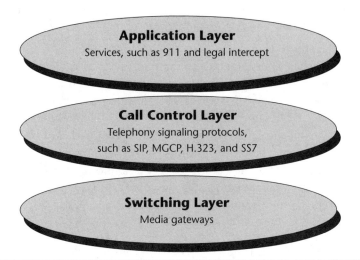

Figure 10.9 Softswitch architecture

Gateway Control Protocol (GCP) is the ITU extension to H.323 to enable IP gateways to work with SS7.

Another ITU standard is Multimedia Gateway Control (MEGACO). This emerging standard describes how the media gateways should behave and function.

SIP, from the IETF, links end devices and IP media gateways. It's a thinner and slightly less robust version of H.323, but it is gaining popularity over H.323. Given the strength of the IETF in Internet-related environments, SIP promises to become quite significant.

Level 3 defined Internet Protocol Device Control (IPDC), and Cisco and Telcordia defined Simple Gateway Control Protocol (SGCP). These two standards have been combined to create the Media Gateway Control Protocol (MGCP), which controls the transport layer and its various media gateways, sending messages about routing priority and quality.

Key Concerns in the Next-Generation Switch Architecture
The key concerns for providers regarding future deployments of the softswitch environment are scalability, reliability, and security. Current products can scale up to a threshold of 200,000 busy-hour call attempts. Class 5 local exchanges are designed to handle more than 1.5 million busy-hour call attempts and they also support more than 3,000 features, whereas softswitches can support perhaps 300 busy-hour call attempts. Clustering software can help to resolve these scalability issues, but this is yet to be demonstrated. There are also issues of reliability and security, in terms of securing the way to interact with intelligence at the customer premises.

Another critical issue that needs to be addressed is the need for softswitches to support the lifeline PSTN services, including 911 or other emergency services and the ability of authorities to wire-tap phone conversations. The problem is not reliability or fault tolerance in the systems; the problem is the complexity of the software required. For example, it takes some 250,000 lines of code just to implement emergency services such as 911. In order to realize the ability to use these applications in the same way as is done on the PSTN, tighter integration between the three layers of the softswitch architecture is required. At this point, we are still trying to determine where the best fit is. It would appear that operators that are new to the environment, who seek to gain access into the local exchange, may be well served by such an architecture. On the other hand, for the incumbent local exchange carriers, the motivation may not be as strong.

QoS

As mentioned throughout this chapter and other chapters, QoS issues play a very important role in the next-generation network. We need to think carefully about how to actually provide for very granulated levels of service, thereby enabling very high performance while simultaneously creating platforms for multitudes of new revenue-generating services.

QoS is the capability to provide different levels of service to differently characterized traffic or traffic flows. It constitutes the basis for offering various classes of service to different segments of end users, which then allows the creation of different pricing tiers that correspond to the different CoS and QoS levels. QoS is essential to the deployment of real-time traffic, such as voice or video services, as well as to the deployment of data services.

QoS includes definitions of the network bandwidth requirements, the user priority control, control of packet or cell loss, and control of delays—both transit delay (which is end-to-end) and traffic delay variations (that is, jitter). Traffic characterizations include definitions of the delay tolerance and elasticity for that application. They can also associate delay tolerance and elasticity with applications and users and potentially even time-of-day, day-of-week scenarios. We have to be able to ensure various levels of service; the availability of bandwidth, end-to-end delay, delay variances, and packet losses that support the application in question; and the relative priority of traffic. Also, QoS is associated with policy admission control and policing of the traffic streams.

There are two ways to implement QoS. *Implicit QoS* means that the application chooses the required QoSs. *Explicit QoS* means that the network manager controls that decision.

There are three main approaches to QoS. The first is an architected approach, and ATM falls under this category. The second is per-flow services, where the QoS is administered per flow, or per session. This includes the reservation protocol that is part of the IETF IntServ specification, as well as MPLS. The third approach is packet labeling, in which each individual packet is labeled with an appropriate QoS or priority mark, and the techniques that use this approach include 802.1p and the IETF DiffServ specification.

The following sections describe various QoS tactics, including ATM QoS, IP QoS, Class-Based Queuing (CBQ), MPLS, Policy-Based Management, COPS, and DEN.

ATM QoS

ATM QoS defines four different service levels (one of which has two variations) that define a series of specific QoS parameters that tailor cells to fit video, data, voice, or mixed media traffic. The following are the four service classes:

- **Constant bit rate (CBR)**—CBR provides a constant, guaranteed rate to real-time applications, such as streaming video, so it is continuous bandwidth. It emulates a circuit-switched approach and is associated with minimum latencies and losses. CBR is the highest class of service that you can get and it's for very demanding applications, such as streaming media, streaming audio, streaming video, and video-on-demand. Initially CBR was to be used for things like voice and videoconferencing, but we have found that in fact in those applications we don't necessarily need the continuous bandwidth. As mentioned previously, much of a voice conversation is silence. If we were to be carrying that voice over CBR service, whenever there was silence, the ATM switches would be stuffing in empty cells to maintain that continuous bandwidth, and of course that's overkill and a waste of network resources.

- **Variable bit rate (VBR)**—VBR has two subsets: real-time (VBR-RT) and nonreal-time (VBR-NRT). VBR provides a fair share of available bandwidth according to a specific allocation policy, so it has a maximum tolerance for latencies and losses. VBR is the highest class of service in the data realm, and it is also an adequate class of service for real-time voice. VBR-RT can be used by native ATM voice with bandwidth compression and silence suppression. So when somebody is silent, VBR-RT makes use of the available bandwidth to carry somebody else's cells, making VBR appropriate for multimedia functions such as videoconferencing. VBR-NRT can be used for data transfer where response time is critical (for example, transaction-processing applications such as airline reservations, banking transactions).

- **Available bit rate (ABR)**—ABR supports VBR data traffic with average and peak traffic parameters (for example, LAN interconnection and internetworking services, LAN emulation, critical data transfer that requires service guarantees). Remote procedure calls, distributed file services, and computer process swapping and paging are examples of applications that would be appropriate for ABR.

■ **Unspecified bit rate (UBR)**—You could call UBR a poor man's ATM. It provides best-effort service. UBR offers no service guarantee, so you would use it for text data, image transfer, messaging, and distributing information that's noncritical, where you don't have to have a set response time or service guarantee.

ATM provides a very well-planned approach to providing QoS. Table 10.3 shows how each service class allows you to define or not define certain parameters. The parameters boil down to two major categories: QoS parameters, including the cell error rate (CER; that is, the percentage of errored cells), cell loss ratio (CLR; that is, the percentage of lost cells), the cell transfer delay (CTD; that is, the delay between the network entry and exit points), the cell delay variation (CDV; that is, the jitter), and cell misinsertion rate (CMR; referring to the number of cells inserted on the wrong connection). The second set of parameters are traffic parameters, including peak cell rate (PCR; which allows you to specify the maximum amount of bandwidth allowed on a connection), sustainable cell rate (SCR; which allows you to specify guaranteed bandwidth during the variable transmissions—used only by VBR), maximum burst size (MBS; allows you to specify the maximum number of cells that will be transmitted at PCR—used only by VBR), cell delay

Table 10.3 ATM classes of service

Parameter	CBR	VBR-NRT	VBR-RT	ABR	UBR
Cell loss ratio	Yes	Yes	Yes	No	No
Cell transfer delay	Yes	Yes	Yes	No	No
Cell delay variation	Yes	Yes	Yes	No	No
Peak cell rate	Yes	Yes	Yes	Yes	Yes
Sustained cell rate	No	Yes	Yes	No	No
Minimum cell rate	No	No	No	Yes	No
Maximum burst size	No	Yes	Yes	No	No
Allowed cell rate	No	No	No	Yes	No

variation tolerance (CDVT; allows you to specify the maximum allowable jitter), minimum cell rate (MCR; allows you to specify the rate in cells per second that the source can transmit—used only in ABR), and allowed cell rate (ACR; works with ABR's feedback mechanism that determines cell rate). As Table 10.3 shows, UBR allows you to define very little, whereas CBR allows you to tightly control most of these parameters.

Depending on the service class, you have the option of defining or not defining certain parameters, and that gives you control over the performance of an application within a service level. The transmission path in a virtual circuit with ATM is comprised of virtual paths and its virtual channels. Think of the virtual channel as being an individual conversation path and the virtual path as a grouping of virtual channels that all share the same QoS requirement. So all CBR streaming video traffic may go over Virtual Path 1. All bursty TCP/IP data traffic may go over Virtual Path 2. All MPEG-2 compressed video traffic may go over Virtual Path 3. Again, what we're doing is organizing all the virtual channels that have the same demands from the network into a common virtual path, thereby simplifying the administration of the QoS and easing the network management process for the carrier. Within the cell structure, the key identifier in the header is which path and which channel is to be taken between any two ATM cells. And those addresses change, depending on what channels were reserved at the time the session was negotiated.

Remember that because it is connection oriented, ATM gives service providers the traffic engineering tools they need to manage both QoS and utilization. In provisioning a network, the service provider can assign each virtual circuit a specific amount of bandwidth and set the QoS parameters. The provider can then dictate what path each virtual circuit takes. However, it does require that the service provider be managing the ATM switches and whatever else is running over that ATM network (for example, IP routers).

IP QoS

There are two IP schemes for QoS: IntServ and DiffServ. The following sections describe each of these schemes in detail.

IntServ   IntServ was the IETF's scheme to introduce QoS support over IP networks. It provides extensions to the best-effort service model to allow control over end-to-end packet delays. In essence, IntServ is a bandwidth reservation technique that builds virtual circuits across the Internet. Applications running in the hosts request bandwidth.

IntServ was introduced first as a setup protocol, used by hosts and routers to signal QoS into the network. It also introduces flowspecs, which are definitions of traffic flow according to traffic and QoS characteristics. Finally, IntServ introduces traffic control, which delivers on QoS by controlling traffic flows within the hosts and routers. IntServ is a per-flow, resource reservation model, requiring Resource Reservation Protocol (RSVP). Its key building blocks include resource reservation and admission control. In IntServ, data transmissions are built around a flow, a uni-directional path with a single recipient. In routing, traditional routers examine packets and determine where to send them and then switch them to output ports. With IntServ, routers must also apply the appropriate queuing policy if packets are part of a flow.

IntServ routers usually use first in, first out (FIFO) queuing. FIFO queuing is fast and easy but can make delay-sensitive applications wait behind long bursts of delay-insensitive data. IntServ uses fair queuing, which ensures that a single flow does not use all the bandwidth and provides minimal guarantees to different flows.

The IntServ model involves a classifier. Packets are mapped to a service class, and, based on their service class, a packet scheduler forwards the packets (see Table 10.4). Admission control determines whether the requested QoS can be delivered, and the setup protocol is RSVP. RSVP relies on router-to-router signaling schemes, which allow IP applications to request priority delay and bandwidth guarantees. Connections are established link by link, and a connection can be denied if a router cannot accept the request (see Figure 10.10). RSVP is particularly well suited for real-time applications and delay-sensitive traffic. RSVP allows applications to reserve router bandwidth. RSVP guaranteed service provides bandwidth guarantees and a reliable upper bound to packet delays. But the resource requirements for running RSVP on a router increase proportionately with the number of separate RSVP reservations. This scalability problem makes using RSVP on the public Internet impractical, so it has largely been left to campus and enterprise-type networks.

Several other protocols are associated with RSVP (see Figure 10.11). Real-Time Transport Protocol (RTP) is for audio, video, and so on. It is based on UDP, to cut down on overhead and latency. RTP is specified as the transport for H.323, and receivers are able to sequence information via the packet headers. Real-Time Control Protocol (RTCP) provides status feedback from senders to receivers. Both RTP and RTCP are standardized by the ITU under H.225. Real-Time Streaming Protocol (RTSP) runs on top of IP Multicast, UDP, RTP, and RTCP.

Table 10.4 IntServ Service Classes

Service Class	Guaranteed Service	Controlled Load Service	Best-Effort Service
End-to-end behavior	Guaranteed maximum delay	Best effort on unloaded net	Best effort only
Intended applications	Real time	Sensitive to congestion	Legacy
ATM mapping	CBR or rtVBR	NRT-VBR or ABR with MCR	UBR or ABR

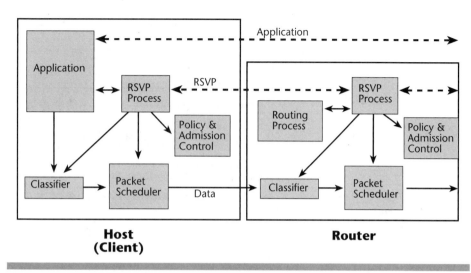

Figure 10.10   RSVP in hosts and routers

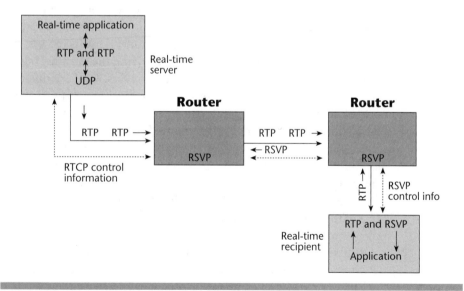

Figure 10.11   RSVP and related protocols

RSVP is simplex (that is, it is a reservation for unidirectional data flow), it is receiver driven (that is, the receiver of data flows initiates and maintains the resource reservation for that flow), and it supports both IPv4 and IPv6. RSVP is not a routing protocol. Again, key issues regarding RSVP include scalability, security, and how to ensure that policy-based decisions can be followed.

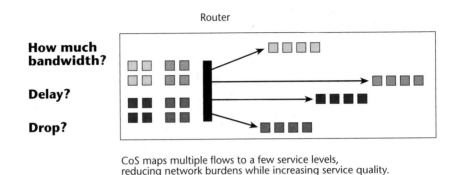

Router

How much bandwidth?

Delay?

Drop?

CoS maps multiple flows to a few service levels,
reducing network burdens while increasing service quality.

Figure 10.12   DiffServ

DiffServ   Today, we concentrate more on DiffServ than on its parent, IntServ. The DiffServ approach to providing QoS in networks uses a small, well-defined set of building blocks from which a variety of services can be built (see Figure 10.12). A small bit pattern in each packet in the IPv4 Type of Service (ToS) octet, or the IPv6 Traffic Class octet, is used to mark a packet to receive a particular forwarding treatment or per-hop behavior at each network node. For this reason, DiffServ is really a CoS model; it differentiates traffic by prioritizing the streams, but it does not allow the specification and control of traffic parameters. DiffServ differentiates traffic by user, service requirements, and other criteria. It then marks the packets so that the network nodes can provide different levels of service via priority queuing or bandwidth allocation, or by choosing dedicated routes for specific traffic flows. DiffServ scheduling and queue management enables routers to act on the IP datagram. Service allocation is controlled by a policy management system. Routers can do four things after receiving an IP datagram: manage a queue, schedule interfaces, select which datagram is the logical choice for discard, and select an outbound interface. Most of the current methods for QoS are based on the first three. QoS routing technologies are still in conceptual stages.

DiffServ evolved from IETF's IntServ. It is a prioritization model, with preferential allocation of resources based on traffic classification. DiffServ uses the IP ToS field to carry information about IP packet service requirements. It classifies traffic by marking the IP header at ingress to the network with flags corresponding to a small number of per-hop behaviors. This DiffServ byte replaces the ToS octet, sorting into queues via the DiffServ flag. Queues then get different treatment in terms of priority, share of bandwidth, or probability of discard. The IETF draft stipulates a Management Information Base for DiffServ, which will make DiffServ-compliant products Simple Network Management Protocol (SNMP) manageable.

CBQ

Another QoS tactic is CBQ, which is based on traffic management algorithms deployed at the WAN edge. CBQ is a fully open, nonproprietary technology that brings bandwidth-controlled CoS to IP network infrastructures. It allows traffic to be prioritized according to IP application type, IP address, protocol type, and other variables. It allocates unused bandwidth more effectively than do other QoS mechanisms, and it uses priority tables to give critical applications the most immediate access to unused bandwidth.

MPLS

A lot of attention is being focused now on the emerging environment MPLS, which was born out of Cisco's tag switching. MPLS was designed with large-scale WANs in mind. MPLS was originally proposed by the IETF in 1997, and core specifications were completed in fall 2000. By plotting static paths through an IP network, MPLS gives service providers the traffic engineering capability they require and it also helps them build a natural foundation for VPNs. Remember that traffic engineering allows service providers to control QoS and optimize network resource use.

Another benefit of MPLS is its potential to unite IP and optical switching under one route-provisioning umbrella. Because IP is a connectionless protocol, it cannot guarantee that network resources will be available. Additionally, IP sends all traffic between the same two points over the same route. During busy periods, therefore, some routes become congested and others remain underused. That's one key difference between MPLS and IP: In MPLS, packets sent between two points can take different paths based on different MPLS labels. Without explicit control over route assignments, the provider has no way to steer excess traffic over less-busy routes. MPLS tags or adds a label to IPv4 or IPv6 packets so that they can be steered over the Internet along predefined routes. MPLS also adds a label identifying the type of traffic, the path, and the destination. This enables routers to assign explicit paths to various classes of traffic. Using these explicit routes, service providers can reserve network resources for high-priority or delay-sensitive flows, distribute traffic to prevent network hot spots, and preprovision backup routes for quick recovery from outages.

As shown in Figure 10.13, an MPLS network is composed of a mesh of label-switching routers (LSRs). These LSRs are MPLS-enabled routers and/or MPLS-enabled ATM switches. As each packet enters the network, an ingress LSR assigns it a label, based on its destination, VPN membership, ToS bits, and other considerations. At each hop, an LSR uses the label to index a forwarding table. The forwarding table assigns each packet a new label and directs the packet to an output port. To promote scaling, labels have only local significance. As a result, all packets with the same label follow the same label-switched path through the network. Service providers can specify explicit routes by configuring them into edge LSRs manually, or

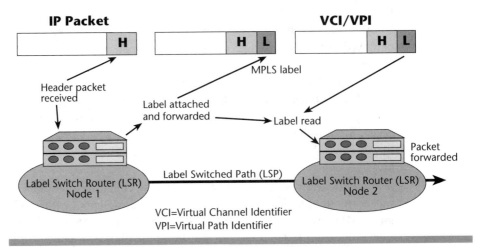

Figure 10.13 MPLS

they can use one of two new signaling protocols. RSVP-TE is RSVP with traffic engineering extensions. The other is the MPLS Label Distribution Protocol (LDP), augmented for constraint-based routing. Most equipment vendors support both.

With MPLS, network operators don't have to use explicit routing—and they probably won't in networks that have plenty of bandwidth. Instead, they can let ingress LSRs use LDP without any constraint-based extensions, to automatically associate labels with paths. With plain LDP, MPLS packets follow the same routes as ordinary routed packets. With MPLS, you can support all applications on an IP network without having to run large subsets of the network with completely different transport mechanisms, routing protocols, and addressing plans.

MPLS offers the advantages of circuit-switching technology—including bandwidth reservation and minimized delay variations, which are very important for voice and video traffic—as well as the advantages of existing best-effort, hop-by-hop routing. It also enables service providers to create VPNs that have the flexibility of IP and the QoS of ATM.

The *MP* part of MPLS means it's multiprotocol—it is an encapsulating protocol that can transport a multitude of other protocols. *LS* indicates that the protocols being transported are encapsulated with a label that is swapped at each hop. A label is a number that uniquely identifies a set of data flows on a particular link or within a particular logical link. The labels, again, are of only local significance. They must change as packets follow a path—hence the *switching* aspect of MPLS.

MPLS can switch a frame from any kind of Layer 2 link to any other kind of Layer 2 link, without depending on any particular control protocol. Compare this to ATM, for example: ATM can switch only to and from ATM and can use only ATM signaling protocols, such as the private network-to-network interface, or Interim Interface Signaling Protocol. MPLS supports three different types of label formats. On ATM hardware, it uses the well-defined Virtual Channel Identifier (VCI) and Virtual Path Identifier (VPI) labels. On Frame Relay hardware, it uses a Data-Link Connection Identifier (DLCI) label. Elsewhere, MPLS uses a new generic label, known as a *shim*, which sits between Layers 2 and 3. Because MPLS allows the creation of new label formats without requiring changes in routing protocols, extending technology to new optical transport and switching could be relatively straightforward.

MPLS has another powerful feature: label stacking. Label stacking enables LSRs to insert an additional label at the front of each labeled packet, creating an encapsulated tunnel that can be shared by multiple label-switched paths. At the end of the tunnel, another LSR pops the label stack, revealing the inner label. An optimization in which the next-to-last LSR peels off the outer label is known in IETF documents as "penultimate hop popping." Whereas ATM has only one level of stacking—virtual channels inside of virtual paths—MPLS supports unlimited stacking. An enterprise could use label stacking to aggregate multiple flows of its own traffic before passing the traffic on to the access provider. The access provider could then aggregate traffic from multiple enterprises before handing it off to the backbone provider, and the backbone provider could aggregate the traffic yet again before passing it off to a wholesale carrier. Service providers could use label stacking to merge hundreds of thousands of label-switched paths into a relatively small number of backbone tunnels between points of presence. Fewer tunnels mean smaller routing tables, and smaller routing tables make it easier for providers to scale the network core.

Before you get too excited about the MPLS evolution, be aware that there are still a number of issues to be resolved between the IETF and the MPLS Forum. For example, they must reconcile MPLS with DiffServ, so that the ToS markings can be transferred from IP headers to MPLS labels and interpreted by LSRs in a standard manner. They must also clarify how MPLS supports VPNs. Right now two models exist—one based on BGP and the other on virtual routers—and which will prevail is unknown. Protocols such as RSVP, OSPF, and IS-IS must be extended in order to realize the full benefit of MPLS.

Major efforts are under way to adapt the control plane of MPLS to direct the routing of optical switches, not just LSRs. This will enable optical switches, LSRs, and regular IP routers to recognize each other and to exchange information. The same routing system can control optical paths in the DWDM core, label-switched paths across the MPLS backbone, and paths involving any IP routers at the edge of the network. So, with MPLS, service providers can simplify their operational procedures, deliver more versatile IP services, and, most importantly to customers, sign meaningful SLAs.

Policy-Based Management, COPS, DEN, and LDAP

A few additional concepts are relevant to QoS: policy-based management, Common Open Policy Services (COPS), Directory Enabled Networking (DEN), and Lightweight Directory Access Protocol (LDAP).

The idea behind policy-based networking is to associate information about individual users, groups, organizational units, entire organizations, and even events (such as the beginning of the accounting department's month-end closing) with various network services, or classes of service. So, on a very granular basis, and on a time-sensitive basis, you can ensure that each user is receiving the QoS needed for the particular application at a specific time and place.

COPS is an IETF query-response-based client/server protocol for supporting policy control. It addresses how servers and clients on a network exchange policy information, and it transmits information between a policy server and its clients, which are policy-aware devices such as switches. The main benefit of COPS is that it creates efficient communication between policy servers and policy-aware devices and increases interoperability among different vendors' systems.

DEN is an industry group formed by Microsoft and Cisco to create a common data format for storing information about users, devices, servers, and applications in a common repository. DEN describes mechanisms that will enable equipment such as switches and routers to access and use directory information to implement policy-based networking. Enterprise directories will eventually be able to represent, as directory objects, all of the following: network elements, such as switches and routers; network services, such as security; class of service; network configurations that implement the network services; and policy services that govern the network services in a coordinated, scalable manner.

QoS and Prevailing Conditions

There's quite a list of potential approaches to implementing QoS. Again, which one makes sense oftentimes depends on what's available and what the prevailing conditions are. At this point, ATM is used most frequently because it offers the strongest capabilities to address traffic engineering and resource utilization. Right now, high hopes are also pinned on MPLS because it does a good job of marrying the best qualities of IP with the best qualities of ATM. But, again, we are in an era of many emerging technologies, so stay tuned. This chapter should give you an appreciation of how many issues there are to understand in the proper administration of the emerging business-class services that promise to generate large revenues.

LDAP is a standard directory server technology for the Internet. LDAP enables retrieval of information from multivendor directories. LDAP 3.0 provides client systems, hubs, switches, and routers, as well as a standard interface to rewrite directory information. Equipment and directory vendors plan to use LDAP for accessing and updating directory information.

For more learning resources, quizzes, and discussion forums on concepts related to this chapter, see www.telecomessentials.com/learningcenter.

Chapter 11

Next-Generation Network Services

This chapter investigates traditional Internet services, as well as new generations of applications and the network platforms that support those applications. It discusses virtual private networks (VPNs), security, various uses of Voice over IP (VoIP) networks, and developments in the streaming media arena and emerging applications.

■ Traditional Internet Applications

Traditional Internet applications are called *elastic applications* because they can work without guarantees of timely delivery. Because they can stretch in the face of greater delay, they can still perform adequately, even when the network faces increased congestion and degradation in performance. The following are the most widely used elastic applications:

- **E-mail**—The most widely used of the Internet applications, generating several gigabytes of traffic per month, is e-mail. Because there is a standardized convention for the e-mail address—*username@domainname*—various companies can interoperate to support electronic messaging.

- **Telnet**—Telnet is one of the original ARPANET applications. It enables remote login to another computer that's running a Telnet server and allows you to run applications present on that computer, with their outputs appearing in the window on your computer.

■ **File Transfer Protocol (FTP)**—FTP allows file transfers to and from remote hosts. That is, you can use FTP to download documents from a remote host onto your local device.

■ **The World Wide Web**—Key aspects that identify the Web are the use of the uniform resource locator (URL) and the use of Hypertext Transfer Protocol (HTTP)—the client/server hypermedia system that enables the multimedia point-and-click interface. HTTP provides hyperlinks to other documents, which are encoded in Hypertext Markup Language (HTML), providing a standardized way of displaying and viewing information contained on servers worldwide. Web browsers are another important part of the Web environment—they interpret the HTML and display it, along with any images, on the user's local computer. The ease of using the Web popularized the use of URLs, which are available for just about any Internet service. (The *URL* is the syntax and semantics of formalized information for location and access of resources via the Internet. URLs are used to locate resources by providing an abstract identification of the resource location.)

So, how are people actually using the Internet? Greenfield Online conducts polls online. In November 2000, Greenfield Online (www.greenfieldonline.com) reported that the Internet was being used as follows:

■ 98% of Internet users went online to check their e-mail.

■ 80% of Internet users were checking for local information, such as movie schedules, weather updates, or traffic reports.

■ 66% of Internet users were looking for a site that provided images and sounds.

■ 66% of Internet users wanted to shop at sites that provided images of the products they were interest in.

■ 53% of Internet users downloaded some form of a large file.

■ 37% of Internet users listened to Internet radio.

This shows that increasingly there is interest in imagery, multimedia, and entertainment-type aspects of the Internet. These are advanced real-time applications that are highly sensitive to timely data delivery. Therefore, any application that includes VoIP, audio streaming, video streaming, or interactive multimedia needs to be addressed by the administration of Quality of Service (QoS). The lack of control over QoS in the public Internet is preventing the deployment of these new applications at a more rapid pace.

Today's flat-rate pricing for Internet access is compatible with the Internet's lack of service differentiation, and it is partially responsible for that structure as well. The main appeal of a flat-rate pricing scheme is its simplicity. It means predictable fees for the users, and it means providers can avoid the administrative time and cost associated with tracking, allocating, and billing for usage. It also gives companies known expectations for payments, facilities planning, and budgeting. However, as QoS emerges within the Internet, the ability to differentiate services will result in differentiated pricing, thereby allowing revenue-generating service levels and packages—and that's extremely important. As we've discussed several times so far in this book, developments in optical networking and in wireless networking are providing more and more bandwidth. Hence, the cost—the cents per minute that you can charge for carrying traffic—is being reduced. If network operators are going to continue to make money in the future, they will need to do so through the administration of value-added services, differentiated performance, and tiered pricing. Therefore, the QoS aspect is very important to the materialization of new revenue-generating services.

Key applications from which service providers are expected to derive revenues include e-commerce, videoconferencing, distance learning and education networks, Webcasting, multiplayer gaming, unified messaging, call centers, interactive voice response, and IP-based centrex systems. Evolving next-generation networks—such as VPNs, VoIP and Packet over IP, streaming audio and video, multimedia collaboration, network caching, application hosting, location-based online services, software downloads, and security services—are introducing a variety of Class of Service (CoS) and QoS differentiators.

■ VPNs

A big driver of interest in VPNs is that customers increasingly need to communicate with people outside their enterprise, not just those inside the enterprise. As mentioned in Chapter 6, "Data Communications Basics," in the 1980s, about 80% of the information that was used within a given address of a business came from within that address. Only 20% was exchanged outside the walls of that location. Today, the relationship has reversed. As much as 80% of information exchanged is with points outside a given business address.

Another reason for interest in VPNs is that customers want to quickly and securely change their access points and needs as changes occur in their businesses. Many strategic alliances and partnerships require companies to exchange messages quickly. Some of these are temporary assignments—for example, a contractor

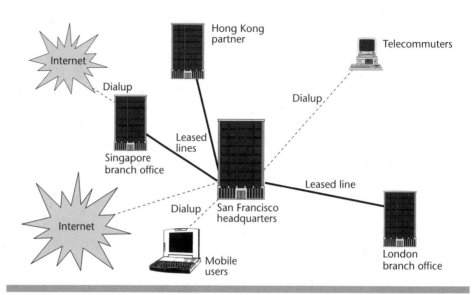

Figure 11.1 An enterprise network based on leased lines

building out a fiber-optic loop or an applications developer building a new billing system—that might last a few months, during which time the individuals involved need to be incorporated into the network. Leased lines are infamous for requiring long waits for provisioning—often 6 months to 18 months! VPNs allow rapid provisioning of capacity where and when needed.

What we see emerging is a requirement for networks that can be very quickly provisioned and changed in relationship to organizational structures. This results in a steady migration of traffic away from the traditional networks, based on leased lines (see Figure 11.1), to public networks. As a result, we're seeing a steady growth in the pseudoprivate realm of the VPN (see Figure 11.2). A *VPN* is a logical network that isolates customer traffic on shared service provider facilities. In other words, the enterprise's traffic is aggregated with the traffic of other companies. VPNs have been around for quite some time—since X.25 closed user groups on the packet-switched network, and with the AT&T Software-Defined Network (SDN) on the circuit-switched networks. A VPN looks like a private network, but it runs across either the public circuit-switched network or public packet-switched data networks. Thus, VPNs are not just a solution within the IP realm—a VPN is a concept, not a specific set of technologies, and it can be deployed over a wide range of network technologies, including circuit-switched networks, X.25, IP, Frame Relay, and ATM.

A VPN uses a shared carrier infrastructure. It can provide additional bandwidth on demand, which is an incredible feat, as compared to the weeks that it normally takes to add bandwidth to dedicated networks. Carriers build VPNs with

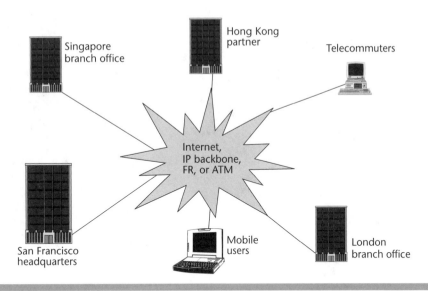

Figure 11.2 An enterprise network using a VPN

advanced survivability and restoration capabilities, as well as network management tools and support, so that QoS can be considered and service-level agreements (SLAs) can be administered and met.

Two basic VPN deployment models exist: customer based and network based. In *customer-based VPNs*, carriers install gateways, routers, and other VPN equipment on the customer premises. This is preferred when customers want to have control over all aspects of security. In *network-based VPNs*, the carrier houses all the necessary equipment at a point of presence (POP) near the customer's location. Customers that want to take advantage of the carrier's VPN economies of scale prefer this type of VPN.

VPN Frameworks

Contemporary VPNs can be described as belonging to one of two categories: the Internet-based VPN and the provisioned VPN.

Internet-Based VPNs

In an *Internet-based VPN* (see Figure 11.3), smaller ISPs provide local access services in defined geographical regions, requiring an enterprise to receive end-to-end services from multiple suppliers. An Internet-based VPN uses encryption to create a form of closed user group, thereby isolating the enterprise traffic and providing acceptable security for the enterprise across the public shared packet network. However, because

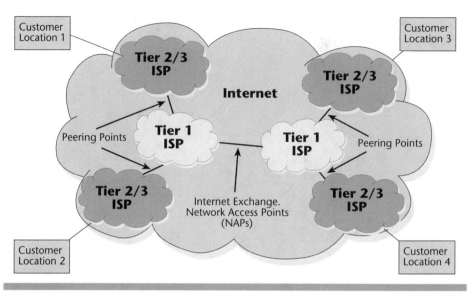

Figure 11.3 An Internet-based VPN

it involves multiple ISPs in the delivery of the VPN, the performance is unpredictable. The biggest problem of having multiple suppliers is the inability to define and meet consistent end-to-end bandwidth or performance objectives.

Figure 11.4 shows what is involved in providing an Internet-based VPN. The customer would have on the premises a wide variety of servers that dish up the corporate content, the finance systems, the customer service systems, and so on. A VPN is responsible for the encapsulation of the information and hence the security aspects. *Remote Authentication Dial-in User Services* (RADIUS), an authentication and access control server, is used for purposes of authenticating whether a user is allowed access into the corporate resources. The RADIUS server connects to a firewall, which is used to determine whether traffic is allowed into or out of the network. The router selects the optimum path for the messages to take, and the circuit physically terminates on a channel service unit/data service unit (CSU/DSU). A private line interfaces with the Internet provider's POP. From that point, the VPN either uses the public Internet that's comprised of multiple ISPs, or it relies on IP backbones provided by a smaller group of providers. Users who are working on mobile devices would have laptops equipped with the client and VPN services necessary for encapsulation and the administration of security.

Provisioned VPNs

VPNs rely on the capability to administer preferential treatment to applications, to users, and so on. The public Internet does not support preferential treatment

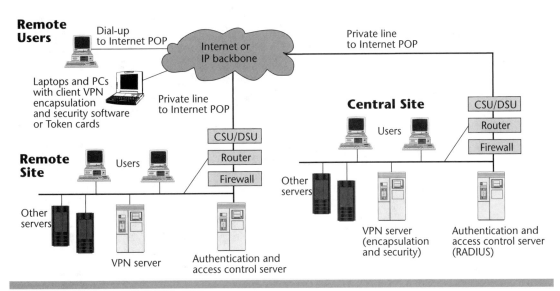

Figure 11.4 The parts of an Internet-based VPN

because it is subject to delay, jitter, and loss; it is therefore unsuitable for next-generation services that require high performance. In most cases, to accommodate business customers that are interested in such advanced services and who demand SLAs, the underlying transport is really Frame Relay or ATM. These Frame Relay and ATM VPNs offer greater levels of QoS and can fulfill the SLAs that customers and vendors agree to. They do, however, require that the customer acquire an integrated access device (IAD) to have on the premises, which can increase the deployment cost significantly. IADs enable the enterprise to aggregate voice, data, and video traffic at the customer edge.

A *provisioned VPN* (see Figure 11.5) is a packet-switched VPN that runs across the service provider's backbone, generally using Frame Relay or ATM. This type of VPN is built on OSI model Layer 2 virtual circuits, such as those used by Frame Relay, ATM, or Multiprotocol Label Switching (MPLS), and it is provisioned based on customer orders. Virtual circuits based on predetermined locations create closed user groups and work well to carve out a VPN in a public shared network, by limiting access and usage to the provisioned VPN community. However, encryption is still required to securely protect the information from theft or modification by intruders.

The provisioned VPN is differentiated from the IP VPN by its ability to support multiple protocols and by the fact that it offers improved performance and management. These VPNs are characterized as having excellent performance and security, but the negative is that a single vendor offers both reach and breadth in terms of service offerings.

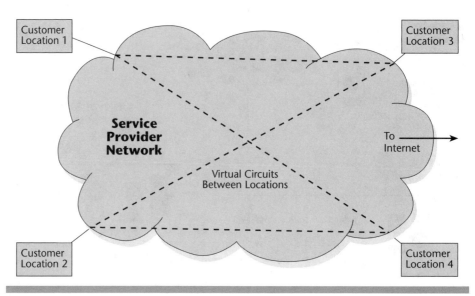

Figure 11.5 A provisioned VPN

Figure 11.6 shows what the equipment would like look at a customer premise in support of a Frame Relay- or an ATM-based VPN. The customer would have an IAD that would allow voice and data to be converged at the customer premise. The IAD would feed into the data communications equipment, over which a circuit would go to the service provider's POP. At the service provider's POP would be a multiservice access device that enables multiple protocols and interfaces to be supported and that provides access into the service provider's core network, which would be based on the use of Frame Relay or ATM. To differentiate Frame Relay- and ATM-based VPNs from Internet-based VPNs, service providers stress that multiple protocols are supported and that they rely on the use of virtual circuits or MPLS labels to facilitate the proper path, thereby ensuring better performance and providing traffic management capabilities.

To further differentiate Frame Relay- or ATM-based VPNs from regular Frame Relay or ATM services, additional functions—such as packet classification and traffic isolation, the capability to handle multiple separate packet-forwarding tables and instances of routing protocols for each customer—reside at the edge.

VPN Applications

A VPN is an architecture, a series of products and software functions that are tied together and tightly calibrated. Managing a VPN entails dealing primarily with two issues: security policies and parameters and making sure that applications function within the latency requirements.

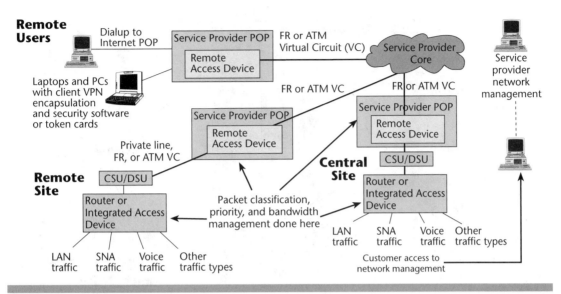

Figure 11.6 A Frame Relay- or ATM-based provisioned VPN

VPN applications provide maximum opportunities to save money and to make money—by substituting leased lines with Internet connectivity, by reducing costs of dialup remote access, and by stimulating new applications, using extranets. These savings can be substantial. According to TeleChoice (www.telechoice.com), in the realm of remote access, savings over customer-owned and maintained systems can range from 30% to 70%; savings over traditional Frame Relay services can range from 20% to 60%; savings over leased lines or private lines can range from 50% to 70%; and savings over international private lines can be up to 90%.

It is important to be able to effectively and easily manage the VPN environment. You need to consider the capability to track the tunnel traffic, the support for policy management, the capability to track QoS, the capability to track security infractions, and the support for public key certificate authorities (CAs).

The one-stop-shopping approach to VPNs—managed VPN services—is designed to lock in users and to reduce costly customer churn, but with this approach, interoperability is very restricted. Managed VPNs provide capabilities such as IP connection and transport services, routers, firewalls, and a VPN box at the customer site. Benefits of this approach include the fact that it involves a single service vendor, SLAs, guaranteed latency and bandwidth, and the security of traffic being confined to one network. Approximately one-third of VPN users opt for such a managed service.

There are three major applications of VPNs—intranets (that is, site-to-site VPNs) remote access, and extranets—which are examined in the following sections.

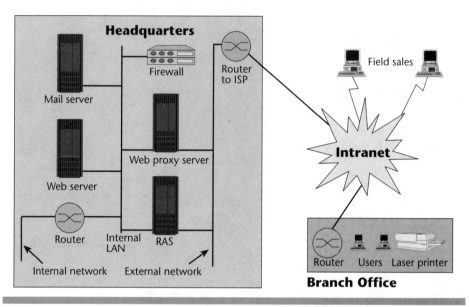

Figure 11.7 An intranet-based VPN

Intranet VPNs

Intranet VPNs are site-to-site connections (see Figure 11.7). The key objective of an intranet VPN is to replace or reduce the use of leased-line networks, traditional routers, and Frame Relay services. The cost savings in moving from private networks to Internet-based VPNs can be very high, in the neighborhood of 50% to 80% per year. Remember that Internet-based VPNs allow less control over the quality and performance of applications than do provisioned VPNs; this is a bit of a deterrent, and many clients still want to consider the Frame Relay- or ATM-based ATMs, which would provide better QoS. The savings might drop a bit, but the cost of a provisioned VPN would be substantially less than the cost of using leased lines.

There are a few key barriers to building out more intranets based on VPNs:

- No standardized approach to encryption
- Variance between vendors' products, which leads to interoperability problems
- Lack of standards regarding public key management
- Inability of today's Internet to provide end-to-end QoS

Remote Access VPNs

The most interesting and immediate VPN solution for most customers is the replacement of remote access servers. VPN remote access implementations can save customers from 30% to 70% over traditional dialup remote access server deployment. Remote access servers provide access to remote users, generally via analog plain old telephone service (POTS) lines, or, perhaps, ISDN connections, including dialup protocols and access control for authentication (administered by the servers). However, a remote access server requires that you maintain racks of modems, the appropriate terminal adapters for ISDN services, or DSL-type modems for DSL services. You also need remote access routers, which connect remote sites via a private line or public carriers and provide protocol conversion between the LANs and WANs. To have an internal implementation of remote access, you have to acquire all these devices, as well as the talent to maintain them.

If an enterprise needs remote access connections outside local calling areas, and/or if it needs encrypted communications, it is generally fairly easy to justify a VPN service over an enterprise-based remote access server. The initial cost of hardware for a VPN approach is about 33% less than the cost of hardware for a traditional dialup remote-access server deployment. The customer also saves on charges for local access circuits, and costly toll and international charges are eliminated.

By virtue of supporting a greater range of customers, a service provider that offers VPN-based remote access is more likely to support a wider variety of broadband access options, including xDSL, cable modems, and broadband wireless. VPN-based remote access also reduces the management and maintenance required with modem banks and remote client dial-in problems. For these reasons, remote access represents the primary application for which customers turn to VPNs. Figure 11.8 shows an example of remote access VPN.

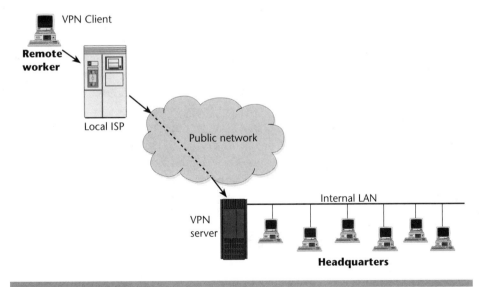

Figure 11.8 A remote-access VPN

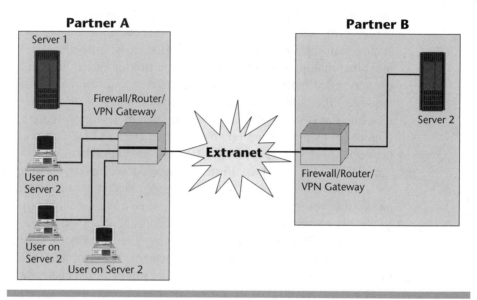

Figure 11.9 An extranet-based VPN

Extranet VPNs

Extranet VPNs allow an external organization to have defined access into an enterprise's internal networks and resources (see Figure 11.9). There are three major categories of extranets: supplier extranets, which focus on speeding communications along the supply chain; distributor extranets, which focus on the demand side and provide great access to information; and peer extranets, which create increased intraindustry competition.

The key applications for extranets include distribution of marketing and product information, online ordering, billing and account history, training policy and standards, inventory management, collaborative research and development, and e-mail, chat, news, and content.

A prime example of an extranet is the Automotive Industry Action Group's Automatic Network Exchange (ANX). This extranet comprises some 50,000 members worldwide. In many ways ANX is producing de facto standards for how extranets should be deployed. Check with ANX (www.anxo.com) for the latest information on how extranets are evolving and how one of the world's largest extranets is performing.

VPN Gateway Functions

The main purpose of the VPN gateways that are required to enable VPNs is to set up and maintain secure logical connections, called *tunnels*, through the Internet. Key functions of VPN gateways include packet encapsulation, authentication, message integrity, encryption, key exchange and key management, as well as firewalling, network address translation, access control, routing, and bandwidth management. The following sections describe these functions in detail.

Tunneling Protocols

Tunneling is a method of encapsulating a data packet within an IP packet so that it can be transmitted securely over the public Internet or a private IP network. The remote ends of the tunnel can be in one of two places: They can both be at the edges of the service provider's network, or one can be at the remote user's PC and the other at the corporate boundary router. Between the two ends of the tunnel, Internet routers route encrypted packets as they do all other IP traffic.

Three key tunneling protocols are needed in VPNs:

- **Point-to-Point Tunneling Protocol (PPTP)**—PPTP was developed by Microsoft, 3Com, and Ascend, and it is included in Windows 95, Windows 98, Windows Me, Windows NT, Windows 2000, and Windows XP. PPTP is a Layer 2 protocol that can work in a non-IP enterprise environment, which is one of its strengths for customers that use multiple protocols rather than using only IP. PPTP provides low packet overhead and good compression, but its weaknesses are on the security front: It does not provide encryption or key management in the published specification, and it essentially relies on the user password to generate keys. But all implementations of PPTP include Microsoft Point-to-Point Encryption (MPPE).

- **Layer 2 Tunneling Protocol (L2TP)**—The IETF promotes L2TP, which is a merger between PPTP and Cisco's Layer 2 Forwarding (L2F) protocol. L2TP is another Layer 2 protocol that can work in a non-IP enterprise environment. L2TP is used primarily by service providers to encapsulate and carry VPN traffic through their backbones. Like PPTP, it does not provide encryption or key management in the published specification (although it does recommend IPSec for encryption and key management).

- **IP Security (IPSec)**—IPSec is an IETF protocol suite that addresses basic data integrity and security. It covers encryption, authentication, and key exchange. IPSec involves a 168-bit encryption key, although the key size can vary, depending on the capabilities of each end of the connection. Recent drafts address encapsulating the secured payload, the key management protocol, and key creation. IPSec emphasizes security by authenticating both ends of the tunnel connection, negotiating the encryption protocol and key for the encrypted session, and encrypting and decrypting the session establishment data. However, IPSec is restricted to IP environments, each user is required to have a well-defined public IP address, and IPSec cannot run on networks that use network address translation.

Benefits and Evolution of VPNs

The main benefit of VPNs as compared to leased lines or Frame Relay is cost savings. VPNs also optimize environments with IP; they have less overhead than Frame Relay, and tunneling protocols may eliminate the need for proprietary encapsulation of protocols. Provisioned VPNs also have the additional benefits of Frame Relay and ATM in the administration of virtual circuits and QoS. VPNs also provide the capability to support dialup access, and greater redundancy is achieved in the network by virtue of meshed nets. Also, VPNs do not necessarily demand a digital fiber infrastructure end-to-end.

VPNs are undergoing an evolution, and various parameters still need to be addressed. Among those are the QoS guarantees. Effective traffic prioritization is at the heart of QoS, and current mechanisms that are available include Differentiated Services (DiffServ), Class-Based Queuing, Common Open Policy Service (COPS), and Multiprotocol Label Switching (MPLS). (These mechanisms are covered in Chapter 10, "Next-Generation Networks.") Other areas of evolution in VPNs are tiering of VPN services (that is, bandwidth tiering and different policy management), the capability to support autoprovisioning, and the emphasis on security.

QoS and security are the two most important considerations in administering VPNs, so uptimes, delays, and SLAs need to be structured. For example, QoS guarantees could be structured to promise 100% premises-to-premises network availability and a maximum latency guarantee of 80 milliseconds. Some vendors offer separate SLAs for dedicated and remote access. For dedicated access, the SLA offers an availability guarantee of 99.9% and a maximum latency guarantee of 125 milliseconds. On remote access SLAs, a busy-free dial availability guarantee of 97% is stipulated, and the latency guarantee specifies an initial modem connection speed of 26.4Kbps at 99%.

■ Security

Security is very important to the proper operation of VPNs. This section describes the available security mechanisms and the anticipated developments in the realm of standards for encryption and key management.

Firewalls

A *firewall* is typically defined as a system or a group of systems that enforces and acts as a control policy between two networks. It can also be defined as a mechanism used to protect a trusted network from an untrusted network—usually while still allowing traffic between the two. All traffic from inside to outside and vice versa must pass through the firewall. Only authorized traffic, as defined by the

Viruses

Virus is a term that's used broadly to refer to a program that is designed to interfere with computers' normal operations. The tab for all computer viruses in 1999 was, shockingly, greater than US$12 billion.

The term *virus* can be used more narrowly to refer to programs that move from one file to another and can be transmitted to other PCs via an infected file. They generally don't seek out the Internet or e-mail to spread.

Another type of virus is the *worm*, such as the Love Bug. Worms make use of a LAN or the Internet (especially via e-mail) to replicate and forward themselves to new users.

Finally, a *Trojan horse* hides within another program or file and then becomes active when someone opens the unwitting host.

A big part of administrating security involves managing viruses. The fact that we can deploy such functionality on a proxy server is very attractive.

local security policy, is allowed to pass through it. The system itself is highly resistant to penetration. A firewall selectively permits or denies network traffic.

There are several variations of firewalls, including these:

- A firewall can use different protocols to separate Internet servers from internal servers.

- Routers can be programmed to define what protocols at the application, network, or transport layer can come in and out of the router—so the router is basically acting as a packet filter.

- Proxy servers can be used to separate the internal network users and services from the public Internet. Additional functions can be included with proxy servers, including address translation, caching, encryption, and virus filtering.

Authentication

Another aspect of security is the authentication of users and access control, which is commonly handled by RADIUS. RADIUS servers are designed to block unauthorized access by remote users. RADIUS provides authentication, authorization, and accounting, and it relies on Challenge Handshake Authentication Protocol (CHAP) to authenticate remote users, which means that there's a back-and-forth dialogue to verify a user's identity. In fact, RADIUS makes use of CHAP, which uses a three-way handshake to periodically verify the identity of the peer throughout the connection. The server sends a random token to the remote workstation. The token is then encrypted, by using the user's password, and sent back to the server. The server performs a lookup to see whether it recognizes the password. If the values match, the authentication is acknowledged; if the values do not match, the connection is terminated. Because a different token is provided each time a remote user dials in, CHAP provides robust authentication.

Encryption

The best way to protect electronic data is to use encryption—that is, to encode data so as to render a document unreadable by all except those who are authorized to have access to it. The content of an original document is referred to as *plain text*. When encryption is applied to the document, the plain text is scrambled, through the use of an algorithm and a variable or a key; the result is called *ciphertext*. The key is a randomly selected string of numbers. Generally, the longer the string, the stronger the security.

There are two major categories of encryption algorithms: symmetric and asymmetric (also called *public key encryption*).

Symmetric Encryption

In symmetric encryption, the sender and the receiver use the same key or machine setup. There are two approaches to encoding data using symmetric encryption: block cipher and streaming cipher. With the block cipher approach, the algorithm encodes text in fixed-bit blocks, using a key whose length is also fixed in length. With the streaming cipher approach, the algorithm encodes the stream of data sequentially, without segmenting it into blocks. Both of these techniques require a secure method of reexchanging keys between the participants.

Symmetric encryption algorithms include the following:

- **Data Encryption Standard (DES)**—DES was developed in the 1970s and is very popular in the banking industry. It is a block cipher that encodes text into fixed-bit blocks, using a 56-bit key. DES is being replaced by the Advanced Encryption Standard (AES).

- **Triple DES (3DES)**—3DES is 168-bit encryption that uses three 56-bit keys. 3DES applies the DES algorithm to a plain text block three times.

- **Rivest Cipher 4 (RC4)**—RC4 is a streaming cipher technique; a stream cipher adds the output of a pseudorandom number generator bit by bit to the sequential bits of the digitized plain text.

- **Blowfish**—Blowfish is a 64-bit block code that has key lengths of 32 bits to 448 bits. Blowfish is used in more than 100 products, and it is viewed as one of the best available algorithms.

- **International Data Encryption Algorithm (IDEA)**—IDEA, developed by ETH Zurich, is free of charge for noncommercial use. It is viewed as a good algorithm and is used in Pretty Good Privacy (PGP) and in Speak Freely, a program that allows encrypted digitized voice to be sent over the Internet.

- **Twofish**—Twofish, developed by Bruce Schneier of Counterpane Internet Security, is very strong, and it was one of the five initial candidates for the AES.

According to the National Institute of Standards and Technology (NIST), it would take 149 trillion years to crack the U.S. government's AES, which uses the Rijndael algorithm and specifies three key lengths—128 bit, 192 bits, and 256 bits. In comparison, DES, which uses a 56-bit key, would take only a matter of hours using a powerful computer, but, of course, this is totally dependent on the speed of the hardware used for cracking the code; a typical desktop PC would require much more than a few hours to crack a 56-bit DES key.

Asymmetric Encryption

Key encryption requires a secure method for exchanging keys between participants. The solution to key distribution came, in 1975, with Diffie and Hellman's public key cryptography scheme. This permits the use of two keys, one of which can be openly published and still permit secure encrypted communications. This scheme later became known as *asymmetric key cryptography*.

Asymmetric cryptography can be used for authentication. After encrypting a signature by using a private key, anyone with access to the public key can verify that the signature belongs to the owner of the private key. As shown in Figure 11.10, the following are the steps in public key encryption:

1. User A hashes the plain text.
2. User A encrypts that hash value with a private key.
3. User A encrypts the plain text with user B's public key.
4. User B decodes the cipher text with the private key.
5. User B decodes the hash value, using User A's public key, thereby confirming the sender's authenticity.
6. User B compares the decrypted hash value with a hash value calculated locally on the just-encrypted plain text, thereby confirming the message's integrity.

Public key management involves the exchange of secrets that both ends use to produce random short-term session keys for authenticating each other. It is a method of encrypting data by using two separate keys or codes. The sender uses a public key that is generally provided as part of a certificate issued by a CA to

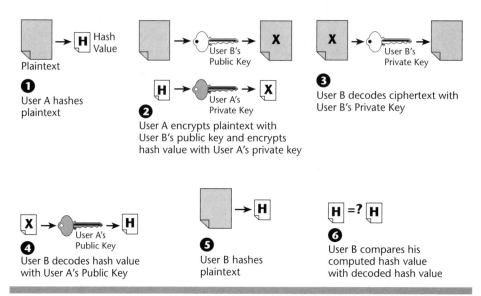

Figure 11.10 Encryption and authentication

scramble data for transmission. The receiver then uses a unique private key to decrypt the data upon receipt. The CA is an entity that, like a bank, is government regulated. It issues certificates that contain data about individuals or enterprises that has been verified to be authentic. In essence, the CA vouches for the authenticity of other parties so that their communications are secured.

Message authentication verifies the integrity of an electronic message and also verifies that an electronic message was sent by a particular entity. Before an outgoing message is encrypted, a cryptographic hash function—which is like an elaborate version of a checksum—is performed on it. The hash function compresses the bits of the plain-text message into a fixed-size digest, or hash value, of 128 or more bits. It is then extremely difficult to alter the plain-text message without altering the hash value.

Message authentication mechanisms include Message Digest-5 (MD5) and Secure Hash Algorithm-1 (SHA-1). MD5 hashes a file of arbitrary lengths into 128-bit value. SHA-1 hashes a file of arbitrary length into 160-bit value; it is more processor intensive but it renders higher security.

Public key management provides a secure method for obtaining a person's or an organization's public key, with sufficient assurance that the key is correct. There are three main public key algorithms: RSA (named for its creators, Rivest, Shamir, and Adelman), Diffie-Hellman, and PGP. RSA is 22 years old, and its security derives from the difficulty of factoring large prime integers. Diffie-Hellman is used mostly for exchanging keys; its security rests on the difficulty of computing discrete algorithms in a finite field, generated by a large prime number. PGP, which is a commercial product sold by Network Associates, was created in 1991. It is one of the most popular public key exchange (PKE) schemes.

Without a functioning universal public key infrastructure, we cannot reliably and easily acquire certificates that contain public keys for persons or organizations we want to communicate with. Standards are emerging, including Public Key Infrastructure (PKI), IETF Public Key Infrastructure X.509 (PKIX), Simple PKI (SPKI), and Public-Key Cryptography Standards (PKCS).

PKI is a system that provides protocols and services for managing public keys in an intranet or an Internet environment—it involves distributing keys in a secure way. PKI secures e-business applications such as private e-mail, purchase orders, and workflow automation. It uses digital certificates and digital signatures to authenticate and encrypt messages and a CA to handle the verification process. It permits the creation of legally verifiable identification objects, and it also dictates an encryption technique to protect data transmitted over the Internet. Trusted PKI suppliers include Entrust and VeriSign. PKI technology is now moving from pilot testing into the real world of e-commerce. Web browsers such as Microsoft Internet Explorer and Netscape Navigator include rudimentary support for PKI by providing an interface into a computer's certificate store, and browsers often include the certificates for some top-level CAs, so that the users can know, incontrovertibly, that the roots are valid and trustworthy.

IKE is the key exchange protocol used by IPSec, in computers that need to negotiate security associations with one another. A security association is a connection between two systems, established for the purpose of securing the packets transmitted across the connection. It supports preshared keys, which is a simplified form of key exchange. It does not require digital certificates. Every node must be linked to every other node by a unique key, and the number of keys needed can grow out of control; for example, 2 devices need 1 key, and 8 devices need 28 keys. New versions of IKE generate new keys through a CA. Legal and political problems will most likely delay widescale use of IKE.

One of the biggest hurdles e-commerce companies face is confirming the identity of the parties involved. Ensuring identity requires an encrypted ID object that can be verified by a third party and accepted by a user's browser. Personal digital IDs contained in the user's browser accomplish this. Historically, these client certificates have been used to control access to resources on a business network, but they can also contain other user information, including identity discount level or customer type. Third parties (that is, CAs) guarantee these types of certificates. The user's browser reads the server certificate, and if it's accepted, the browser generates a symmetric session key, using the server's public key. The server then decrypts the symmetric key, which is then used to encrypt the rest of the transaction. The transaction is then signed, using the user's digital ID, verifying the user's identity and legally binding the user to the transaction.

Digital Certificates

Digital certificates, based on the ANSI X.509 specification, have become a de facto Internet standard for establishing a trusting relationship using technology. Digital certificates are a method for registering user identities with a third party, a CA (such as Entrust, UserTrust, or VeriSign). A digital certificate binds a user to an electronic signature that can be trusted like a written signature and includes authentication, access rights, and verification information. CAs prepare, issue, and manage the digital certificates, and they keep a directory database of user information, verify its accuracy and completeness, and issue the electronic certificates based on that information. A CA signs a certificate, verifying the integrity of the information in it.

By becoming their own digital CAs, service providers can package electronic security with offerings such as VPN and applications services. Vendors that provide the technology required to set up as a CA include Baltimore Technologies (in Ireland), Security Dynamics Technologies, and Xcert.

Server certificates ensure Internet buyers of the identity of the seller's Web site. They contain details about the Web site, such as the domain name of the site and who owns it. Third parties, such as Thawthe in South Africa, then guarantee this information. Sites with server certificates post the CA, and Internet browsers accept their certificates for secure transactions.

There are still many security developments to come and there is a bit of unsettlement in this area. Standards need to be defined and formalized before e-commerce will truly be able to function with the security that it mandates. For now, these are the types of mechanisms that are necessary to ensure that your data remains with you.

■ VoIP

VoIP has been drawing a lot of attention in the past couple years. This section covers the types of applications that are anticipated for VoIP, as well as what network elements are required to make VoIP work and provide similar capabilities to what we're used to from the PSTN.

VoIP Trends and Economics

Although VoIP calling is used for billions of billed minutes each year, it still represents a very small percentage of the market—less than 5% overall. According to Telegeography (www.telegeography.com), 40% of VoIP traffic originates in Asia and terminates in North America or Europe; 30% travels between North America and Latin America; one-third of U.S. international VoIP traffic goes to Mexico, with future volume increases predicted for calling to China, Brazil, and India, and the rest moves among the U.S., Asia Pacific, and Western European regions. It is important to closely examine who will be using this and what carriers or operators will be deploying these technologies. Probe Research (www.proberesearch.com) believes that by 2002, 6% of all voice lines will be VoIP. This is still rather minor, given the fact that some have been saying that VoIP would have replaced circuit-switched calling by now. Piper Jaffray (www.piperjaffray.com) reports that minutes of communication services traveling over IP telephony networks will grow from an anticipated 70 billion minutes and 6% of all the PSTN traffic in the year 2003 to over a trillion minutes by the year 2006. In the United States alone, the PSTN is handling some 3.6 trillion minutes of traffic monthly.

Although VoIP has a very important place in telecommunications, it's important to realize that it is not yet taking over the traditional circuit-switched approach to accommodating voice telephony. The exciting future of VoIP lies in advanced and interesting new applications, an environment where voice is but one of the information streams comprising a rich media application. Many expect that sales of VoIP equipment will grow rapidly in the coming months and years. Part of the reason for this growth is that the network-specific cost for VoIP on dedicated networks is quite a bit lower than the cost of calls on circuit-switched networks—about US 1.1 cents per minute as compared with US 1.7 cents per minute. Using VoIP to carry telephony traffic greatly reduces the cost of the infrastructure for the provider, but at the expense of possibly not being able to maintain QoS. Potential savings are even greater if VoIP is implemented as an adjunct to data network.

Another factor encouraging customers to examine VoIP is the use of shared networks. Because IP emphasizes logical rather than physical connections, it's easier for multiple carriers to coexist on a single network. This encourages cooperative sharing of interconnected networks, structured as anything from sale of wholesale circuits to real-time capacity exchanges. Also, VoIP can reduce the barriers to entry in this competitive data communications world. New companies can enter the market without the huge fixed costs that are normally associated with the traditional circuit-switched network models. Furthermore, because IP telephony will enable new forms of competition, there will be pressure to better align government-controlled prices with underlying service costs. International VoIP services are already priced well below the official rates and some of VoIP's appeal is that it eliminates the access charges interexchange carriers normally have to pay to interconnect to the local exchange carrier. In the United States, these charges range from US 2 cents to US 5 cents per minute.

Advantages of VoIP

The key benefits of VoIP are cost savings associated with toll calls, enhanced voice services, and creative and innovative new applications. The key concerns related to

> **Regulations Related to VoIP**
>
> It's one thing to approach telephony on the Internet such that the incumbent is protected from competition with other voice telephony services on the Internet. But stating that voice on the Internet should not be allowed would be to cut your own throat. All the exciting new applications on the Internet do involve the use of multimedia applications, and voice is part of that overall stream. So, we have to be very careful about what we're regulating—whether it's voice, which is increasingly part of a larger application set, or whether it's traditional voice telephony.

VoIP are voice quality compared to that in today's PSTN; the cost of QoS to ensure the same quality as in the PSTN; security; the current lack of compelling applications; and regulatory issues, such as whether voice will be allowed on the Internet and whether voice will be treated as an altogether different environment—as a converged, integrated application.

VoIP Applications

VoIP includes any set of enabling technologies and infrastructures that digitize voice signals and transmit them in packetized format. Three major network architectures can be used in support of VoIP applications:

- Voice-over intranets, which could be based on leased lines, Frame Relay, ATM, or VPNs
- Voice-over extranets, which could also be based on leased lines, Frame Relay, ATM, or VPNs
- Voice over the public Internet

The following sections discuss some of the key issues related to VoIP applications.

IP Long-Distance Wholesale

So far, the most compelling business case for VoIP has been in IP long-distance wholesale, where there are clear financial benefits and low barriers to entry. Early pioneers in this area include iBasis, ITXC, and Level 3, which predominantly offer IP services to domestic and international carriers, but also offer services to corporations and other service providers. What the customers gain by doing business in this fashion is a reduction in cost associated with carrying their traffic over expensive toll or international transit links.

In IP long-distance wholesale, the voice service levels must match those of the PSTN. End customers of the international carriers expect to perceive the same voice

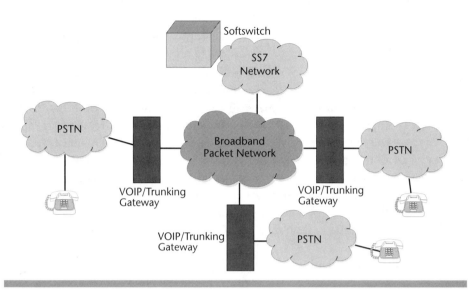

Figure 11.11 A converged long-distance network

quality throughout. How can providers guarantee that when it's almost impossible to control QoS over the public Internet? Even in the case of IP backbones, QoS depends on the underlying architecture used. The solution lies in smart management of packet latency, to ensure circuit-like behavior inside the IP network. For example, iBasis developed a proprietary routing algorithm that monitors performance on the Internet; when it detects that congestion levels may affect the quality of the voice, it switches the calls over to the circuit-switched network, thereby ensuring that customers experience the high quality that they expect end-to-end.

The IP long-distance wholesale environment takes advantage of a converged voice/data backbone by using trunking gateways to leverage the PSTN (see Figure 11.11). This allows support and processing of voice calls. The trunking gateways enable connection of the data network to the PSTN, to support long-haul carrying of the switched calls. In addition, switching services can be added to the data networks through the use of softswitches. (The functions and types of softswitches and gateways that make up the new public network are discussed later in this chapter.)

These are main issues in selecting providers of IP long-distance wholesale:

- **Voice quality versus bandwidth**—How much bandwidth do you use to ensure the best quality?

- **Connecting to the customer**—How many services need to be supported (voice, data, dialup modem, fax, ISDN, xDSL, cable modem)?

- **Maintaining voice quality**—As bandwidth becomes constrained, how do you maintain the voice quality?

IP Telephony

There are two main approaches to IP telephony. First, there's IP telephony over the Internet. Calls made over the public Internet using IP telephony products provide great cost-efficiencies. But the Internet is a large, unmanaged public network, with no reliable service guarantee, so the low costs come at a trade-off. International long-distance consumer calls are the major application of IP telephony over the Internet. Second, the use of private IP telephony networks is rapidly emerging. In this approach, calls are made over private WANs, using IP telephony protocols. The network owner can control how resources are allocated, thereby providing QoS and a managed network. Many private IP telephony networks are being built. They enable an enterprise to take advantage of its investments in the IP infrastructure. Again, because this is a single-owner network, the QoS issues are much easier to contend with; in fact, a single-owner network makes it possible to contend with QoS issues!

Multinational enterprises spend billions of dollars on international voice services each year, so the savings that IP telephony offers is compelling. The cost benefit of running voice services over a private IP network is on the order of 20% or more savings on international long distance, as compared to using traditional voice services. Private IP transport platforms will be increasingly deployed, therefore, as an enterprisewide telephony option.

Recent deployment of IP local exchange products, coupled with low-bandwidth, high-quality voice compression, creates a solid foundation for extending business telephone service to telecommuters at home or on the road. The efficiencies of IP packet technology, coupled with the ITU G.723.1 voice compression standards at 6.4Kbps, enable road warriors and small office/home office workers to have a complete virtual office over a standard 56Kbps Internet modem connection to the office. The really great feature of this environment is that your current location is your office and your IP phone rings wherever you are. However, this requires an IP local exchange—a carrier-class product that resides in the service provider network and provides PBX-like telephony service to multiple business and telecommuter customers. It also requires a softswitch (that is, call-agent software) that's used for purposes of managing call processing functions and administration. Also, end-user services are delivered via IP Ethernet phones or analog telephones that use Ethernet-to-analog adapters.

There are three major categories of IP phones:

- **POTS phone**—The advantage of the POTS phone is high availability and low price. The disadvantage is that it has no feature buttons and the required Ethernet-to-analog adapter is quite costly.
- **Soft phone**—A soft phone is software that runs on the user's PC and graphically resembles a telephone. Its advantage is low price. Its disadvantage is that

it relies on the PC sound card, and it can create volume level problems when you switch between it and other applications that use the PC sound card.

- **IP Ethernet phone**—This device looks and works just like a traditional multiline business display phone, and it plugs into an Ethernet RJ-45 jack. It's priced similarly to PBX phones, at US$300 and up. Emerging "IP phone on a chip" technologies promise dramatically lower prices in the near future.

The evolution of IP telephony will involve many different types of applications, including long-distance wholesale voice services; the support of voice applications for campus or enterprise networks in bringing VoIP to the desktop in the form of new advanced applications that involve converged streams (such as video conferencing or multimedia in the establishment of remote virtual offices); Internet smart phones; IP PBXs; IP centrex service; unified messaging; Internet call waiting; and virtual second-line applications.

VoIP Enhanced Services

Another approach to supporting voice services is to look toward enhanced services. There are two categories of enhanced services:

- **Transaction-oriented services**—These services include Click-N-Call applications, interactive chat, Surf-With-Me, videoconferencing, and varieties of financial transactions.
- **Productivity-enhancing services**—These services include worldwide forwarding, multiparty calling, a visual second line, unified messaging, collaboration, access to online directories, visual assistance, CD-quality sound, personal voice response, and video answering machines.

The key to enhanced services is not cost savings, but cost savings are realized through toll bypass, QoS differentiation, the capability to support remote access, and the capability to create new forms of messaging. Because of the cost savings and features available, the use of enhanced services will grow by leaps and bounds over the next several years.

VoIP is part of a larger trend toward innovative voice-enabled Internet applications and network interactive multimedia. This trend includes various facilities to enhance e-commerce, customer service, converged voice and visual applications, new intelligent agents and various forms of bots, and e-calling campaigns. These sorts of advanced services make it possible to gain greater value from the IP investments that have been made, and at the same time, they create interesting new revenue streams with altogether new businesses.

We'll see VoIP applications increasingly used in a number of ways. VoIP applications will be included on Web-based call centers as automatic call-backs from customer service-based phone numbers entered into a Web page; as multiparty conference calls, with voice links and data sharing, initiated also from a Web page; and in the process of reviewing and paying bills. The key is to blend rich, Internet-based content with a voice service. An example of an emerging application that illustrates such innovation is online gaming. InnoMedia and Sega Enterprises are integrating InnoMedia Internet telephony into Sega Dreamcast game consoles to allow game players worldwide to voice chat with each other while playing games. This device can also be used to cost-effectively place calls in more than 200 countries through InnoSphere, InnoMedia's global network. For example, the rate from the United States to Hong Kong will be US2 cents per minute, from the United States to the United Kingdom it will be US5 cents, and from the United States to Japan, Australia, and most of Europe, it will be US9 cents.

Another example of an interesting new VoIP application is Phonecast, a media network of Internet-sourced audio channels for news, entertainment, and shopping, available to telephones. Created by PhoneRun and WorldCom, Phonecast is modeled after television and radio broadcasting, and it allows callers to create a personal radio station and direct it by using simple voice commands. This is the first of a series of innovative content and service partnerships, assembled to form a comprehensive voice-portal product line.

VoIP Service Categories

There are several main VoIP service categories:

- **Enterprise-based VoIP**—In enterprise-based VoIP, whether for the LAN or WAN, specialized equipment is required at the customer site.

- **IP telephony service providers**—These providers are generally involved in toll-bypass operations. They do not require specialized equipment at the customer site, but they may require additional dialing procedures to gain access to the network. Currently, multistage dialing is one of the problems we still face: You have to dial a seven- or eight-digit number to gain access to your ISP, and then you have to dial a string of digits for the authentication code, and then you have to dial the string of digits corresponding to the number you want to reach. Single-stage dialing will remedy this situation in the very near future.

- **Converged service providers**—These companies will bundle together voice, data, and video services.

- **Consumer VoIP**—Consumer VoIP is generally geared toward consumer connections over the public Internet.

VoIP Network Elements

VoIP may seem like rocket science compared to conversations, but the concept is really quite simple: Convert voice into packets for transmission over a company's TCP/IP network. Two characteristics determine the quality of the VoIP transmission: latency and packet loss. Latency is the time it takes to travel from Point A to Point B. The maximum tolerance for voice latency is about 250 milliseconds, and it's recommended that the delay be less than 150 milliseconds. Small amounts of packet loss introduce pops and clicks that you can work around, but large amounts of packet loss render a conversation unintelligible. With too much packet loss, you would sound like you were saying "Da dop yobla bleep op bop," because little packets with much of your conversation would have been lost in congestion and could not be retransmitted while working within the delay requirements of voice. Hence, packet loss with VoIP can cause big chunks of a conversation to be lost. (We will talk about ways to resolve that a little later in this chapter.)

VoIP gateways have allowed IP telephony applications and new, innovative VoIP applications to move into the mainstream. Other features that have helped the development of VoIP are Internet telephony directory, media gateways, and softswitches, as well as telephony signaling protocols.

VoIP Gateways

VoIP gateways bridge the traditional circuit-switched PSTN and the packet-switched Internet. Gateways overcome the addressing problem. A couple years ago, for two VoIP users to communicate, they had to be using the same software, they had to have sound cards and microphones attached to their PCs, and they had to coordinate a common time during which both would be online in order to engage in a VoIP session. Gateways have made all that unnecessary, and now the only requirement is that you know the user's phone number. Phone-to-PC or PC-to-phone operation requires the use of only one gateway. Phone-to-phone operation requires two gateways, one at each end.

VoIP gateway functionality includes packetizing and compressing voice; enhancing voice quality by applying echo cancellation and silence suppression; dual-tone multifrequency (DTMF) signaling support (that is, touch-tone dialing); routing of voice packets; authentication of users; address management; administration of a network of gateways; and the generation of call detail records that are used to create bills and invoices.

To place a call over a VoIP network, the customer dials the number the same way as on a traditional phone. The edge device, the VoIP gateway, communicates the dialed number to the server, where call-agent software—that is, a softswitch—determines what is the appropriate IP address for that destination call number and returns that IP address to the edge device. The edge device then converts the voice signal to IP format, adds the given address of the destination node, and sends the signal on its way. If enhanced services are required, the softswitch is called back into action to perform the additional functions. (The softswitch is also referred to as a Class 5 agent because it behaves like a local exchange or a Class 5 office.)

There are two primary categories of VoIP gateways:

■ **Gateways based on existing router or remote access concentrator (RAC) platforms**—The key providers here include the traditional data networking vendors, such as 3Com, Cisco, Lucent, and Motorola. As incumbent equipment suppliers to ISPs, the data networking vendors are capturing the largest percentage of these sales. They represented the majority of VoIP gateway sales through 2000 because ISPs were buying gateways at a fast rate based on the significant wholesale opportunity available to larger carriers.

■ **Server-based gateways**—These are designed from the ground up to support VoIP. Key providers of server-based gateways include telecommunications vendors, as well as companies specifically designed for this business; Clarent, Ericsson, Lucent, NetSpeak, Nortel, Nuera, and VocalTec are among the vendors involved. These gateways will overtake router and RAC solutions as incumbent carriers deploy more server-based gateways with extensive call server and signaling capabilities.

More and more merger and acquisition activities will lead to blended solutions, causing the distinction between the different types of gateways to blur. RAC- and router-based gateways will take on more enhanced call-server characteristics as a result. The market segments for the two categories, then, are composed of the following:

■ **Enterprise VoIP gateways**—These gateways are customer premise equipment deployed between a PBX and a WAN device, typically a router, to provide call setup, call routing, and conversion of voice into IP packets and vice versa.

■ **VoIP routers**—Voice cards perform packetization and compression functions and are inserted into a router chassis. The router then directs the packets to their ultimate destination.

■ **IP PBXs**—An IP PBX is an infrastructure of distributed telephony servers that operates in packet-switched mode and offers the benefits of statistical multiplexing and IP routing. We are still in the early days for IP PBXs, although they are beginning to emerge as a viable alternative. A key concern is reliability. (IP PBXs are discussed in more detail later in this chapter.)

■ **Service-provider VoIP gateways**—These are used to aggregate incoming VoIP traffic and route the traffic accordingly. The role is analogous to that of the local exchange. Challenges include the local loop competition among the incumbent carriers, quality concerns, shortage of product, interoperability issues, the lack of hot-swappable and redundant support, and the lack of Network Equipment Building Systems (NEBS) compliance.

- **VoIP access concentrators**—VoIP cards fit into an existing dial access concentrator.

- **SS7 gateways**—SS7 gateways are critical to enabling us to tap into the intelligence services that enhance so much of the telephony activity on the PSTN.

There are many gateway vendors. All gateway vendors share the need for digital signal processors and embedded software solutions that provide for silent suppression, echo cancellation, compression and decompression, DTMF signaling, and packet management. Therefore, another very important part of this equation is the component vendors. Manufacturers of VoIP equipment need to continue to make quality improvements in the underlying technology. This includes addressing interoperability between different gateway vendors' equipment; improving the tradeoffs between cost, function, and quality; and introducing single-stage dialing and the ability to dial from any telephone.

Internet Telephony Directory

An Internet telephony directory is a vital piece of the VoIP puzzle, so this section talks a little bit about the IETF Request for Comment 2916, also known as ENUM services. ENUM services convert telephone numbers into the Internet address information required to support all forms of IP-enabled communication services, including real-time voice, voicemail, fax, remote printing, and unified messaging. In other words, ENUM is a standard for mapping telephone numbers to IP addresses. DNS translates URLs to IP addresses, and EMUM uses the DNS to map a PSTN phone number (based on the E.164 standard) to the appropriate URLs.

ICANN is considering three proposals for the .tel domain. The applicants are NetNumber, which currently runs the Global Internet Telephony Directory (an implementation of ENUM that is used by IP-enabled platforms to convert standard telephone numbers into Internet address information), Number.tel, and Telnic based in the United Kingdom. The ITU is trying to advance an implementation of the IETF ENUM standard under the domain e164.arpa. In this implementation, control of telephone number addressing on the Internet would be distributed to the more than 240 national public network regulatory bodies that administer telephone numbers for the PSTN.

Media Gateways

Media gateways provide seamless interoperability between circuit-switched, or PSTN, networking domains and those of the packet-switched realm (that is, IP, ATM, and Frame Relay networks). They interconnect with the SS7 network and enable the handling of IP services. They're designed to support a variety of telephony signaling protocols. Media gateways are designed to support Class 4, or toll-switch, functions, as well as Class 5, or local exchange, services. They operate in the classic public network environment, where call control is separate from media flow. They support a variety of traffic—including data, voice, fax, and multimedia—over a data backbone. Enhanced applications of media gateways include network conferencing, network-integrated voice response, fax serving, network, and directory services.

As shown in Figure 11.12, media gateways fit between the access and core layers of the network, and they include several categories: VoIP trunking gateways, VoIP access gateways, and network access service devices. They provide service interconnection or intercarrier call handling. The trunking gateways interface between the PSTN and VoIP networks, terminating trunks associated with SS7 control links. These Time Division Multiplexed trunks carry media from an adjacent switch in the traditional circuit-switched network, and the adjacent switch generally belongs to another service provider. (Depending on the agreements between service providers, these are also referred to as cocarrier trunks or feature group D trunks.) The trunking gateways manage a large number of digital virtual circuits. The access gateways provide traditional analog or ISDN interfaces to the VoIP networks; they are devices that terminate PSTN signaling and media, and they connect to PBXs, as well as to traditional circuit switches, such as the Class 5 and Class 4 offices. With network access servers, you can attach a modem to a telephone circuit

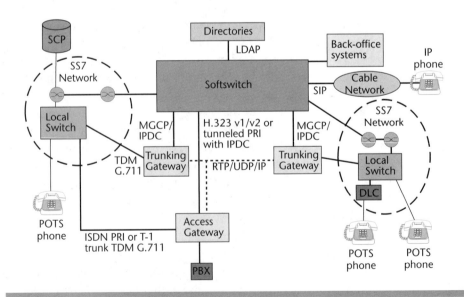

Figure 11.12 VoIP network architecture

and provide data access to the Internet, so that you can attain managed modem service by using cocarrier trunks.

VoIP Softswitches

Call-control intelligence is outside the media gateways and VoIP gateways; it is, instead, handled by a *softswitch,* also referred to as a *media gateway controller* or *call agent.* The softswitch implements the service logic. It controls external trunking gateways, access gateways, and remote access servers. Softswitches run on commercial computers and operating systems, and they provide open application programming interfaces.

A softswitch is a software-based, distributed switching and control platform, and it controls the switching and routing of media packets between media gateways, across the packet backbone. Softswitches provide new tools and technologies to build services in a more productive Internet-based service creation environment. Operators are advised to adopt a "service separation" strategy and to distribute applications throughout the network, avoiding the monolithic closed system that is similar to the circuit-switched environment. We can use application servers to partition enhanced telecommunications services and to determine what interface protocol to select for facilitating interoperability between the softswitches and the applications servers.

The softswitch functionally controls the voice or data traffic path by signaling between media gateways that actually transport the traffic (see Chapter 10). The gateway provides the connection between an IP or ATM network and the traditional circuit-switched network, acting a lot like a multiprotocol cross-connect. The softswitch ensures that a call's or a connection's underlying signaling information—automatic number identifiers, billing data, and call triggers—are communicated between the gateways. Softswitches must reuse intelligent network services through an open and flexible directory interface, so they provide a directory-enabled architecture with access to relational database management systems, and to Lightweight Directory Access Protocol (LDAP) and Transaction Capabilities Applications Part (TCAP) directories. Softswitches also offer programmable back-office features, along with advanced policy-based management of all software components.

The softswitch is a very important element in the new public network. It is what enables the media and trunking gateways to communicate with the underlying infrastructure of the PSTN and thereby to draw on the service logic needed to support telephony activities. In addition, softswitches will be able to reach to new application servers on which new generations of applications have been designed for new versions of enhanced services.

Telephony Signaling Protocols

New generations of signaling and IP telephony control protocols are emerging, and their purpose is to control the communication between the signaling gateway and IP elements. Since the early days of exploring the nature of VoIP and creating devices to enable it, a number of telephony signaling protocols have been considered. Some of the contenders have been H.323, Internet Protocol Device Control (IPDC), Signal Gateway Control Protocol (SGCP), Multimedia Gateway Control Protocol (MGCP), Multimedia Gateway Control (MEGACO), Session Initiation Protocol (SIP), and IP Signaling System 7 (IPS7). Many of those contenders have combined, so this section focuses on the ones that have the strongest presence and potential today.

H.323 The ITU H.323 version 2 specification is based on ISDN standards and limited to point-to-point applications. Version 2 requires multipoint control units (MCUs) to manage multiple sessions. H.323 version 2 provides much of the foundation for exchange of voice and fax messages. The advantage of H.323 is that it is the most mature of the telephony signaling protocols, so many vendors offer it and vendor interoperability is good. On the other hand, H.323 is not as robust as some of the newer entrants, so other protocols on the horizon might eclipse H.323 before too long.

MCGP Bellcore and Level 3 merged their respective SGCP and IPDC specifications into MCGP. In MCGP, softswitches provide the external control and management, so MCGP is becoming a good way to connect an IAD to a gateway.

MEGACO MEGACO is also called H.248 and it is another emerging ITU standard. MEGACO describes how the media gateway should behave and function.

SIP SIP (IETF Request for Comment 2543) is an application-layer control, or signaling protocol, for creating, modifying, and terminating sessions with one or more participants. SIP is used to set up a temporary session, or call, to the server so that the server can execute the necessary enhanced service logic. These sessions may include Internet multimedia conferences, Internet telephony, or multimedia distribution. Linking caller ID to Web page content can link the status of a mobile phone with instant messaging. Members in a session can communicate via multicast or via a mesh of unicast relations, or by a combination of these. This is increasingly popular as the protocol between softswitches and application servers.

LDAP LDAP is the standard directory server technology for the Internet. LDAP enables retrieval of information from multivendor directories. In fact, LDAP 3.0 provides client systems, hubs, switches, routers, and a standard interface to read and write directory information. Directory-oriented services best suited for an LDAP lookup include unified messaging, free phone (that is toll-free number translation), calling name service, and Internet phone number hosting. Remember that as the Internet moves forward, it must connect with the underlying intelligence in the PSTN.

IPS7 The SS7 network acts as the backbone for the advanced intelligent network. SS7 provides access to all the advanced intelligent network features, allows for efficient call setup and teardown, and interconnects thousands of telephony providers under a common signaling network. The capability to communicate with the SS7 network is essential for all service providers. It gives next-generation local exchange carriers access to an existing base of service features, and it ensures that packet-based telephony switching gateways can support key legacy service and signaling features. The interconnection between a legacy circuit switch provider, such as the incumbent local exchange carrier, and a competitive local exchange carrier operated over a packet backbone would include the gateway switch to packetize and digitize the voice coming from the Class 5 office, and the SS7 gateway to provide access into the underlying intelligent network infrastructure. (Chapter 5, "The PSTN," discusses SS7 and next-generation gateway switches in more detail.)

Next-Generation Standards and Interoperability

Next-generation network standards are widely deployed across the globe and are generating billions of dollars in service revenue. Packet-enabled intelligent networks will enhance the revenue stream with new technology to provide intelligent networking services, such as local-number portability, carrier selection, personal numbers, free phone, prepaid call screening, call centers, and voice VPNs. End-to-end, next-generation networks function as seamlessly interoperating wholes; they consist of the legacy-based circuit-switched network, with its underlying SS7 and service logic delivering today's enhanced features, as well as a packet-based network for transport efficiencies that can also be served by new-generation IP servers and enhanced applications, for features we haven't yet thought of.

There are a few key groups to be aware of in the area of standards and interoperability for next-generation networks. There's iNOW!, which stands for Interoperability NOW!, and its members include Ascend, Cisco, Clarent, Dialogic, Natural MicroSystems, and Siemens. These members will interoperate also with Lucent and VocalTec, as well as each other. iNOW! advocates interoperability and certification based on H.323.

The Technical Advisory Committee (TAC), formed by Level 3 Communications, includes 3Com, Alcatel, Ascend, Cisco, Ericsson, Level 3, and others.

The International Softswitch Consortium is focused on enabling softswitch technology and applications on an IP infrastructure. This group advocates interoperability and certification based on H.323, SIP, MGCP, and Real-Time Transfer Protocol (RTP). It is working to develop and promote new standardized interfaces for portable applications, which ride on top of an IP-based softswitch network. The International Softswitch Consortium has more than 68 member companies.

Finally, the Multiservice Switching Forum (MSF) is an open-membership organization committed to developing and promoting implementation agreements for ATM-capable multiservice switching systems. The goal of MSF is to develop multiservice switching with both IP- and ATM-based services, and its founding members are WorldCom, Cisco Systems, Telcordia, AT&T, Alcatel, Lucent, British Telecom, Fujitsu Network Communications, Lucent Technologies, Nortel Networks, Siemens, Telecom Italia, Telia AB, and Qwest.

IP PBXs

IP PBXs are in the very early stages, and they will present some benefits as well as some challenges. Companies can take advantage of IP-based intranets that have been set up between headquarters and remote locations to cost-effectively integrate voice and data traffic. The key strength of IP PBXs is their capability to network over existing IP networks. Because the information is programmed into the phone, phones can be relocated by simply unplugging and moving them. It is also easier to network over existing IP WANs, as long as there is adequate bandwidth to support voice traffic.

Among the challenges to the convergence of IP PBXs is that we expect them to provide high reliability and high availability, which we always require with telephony. Telephony-grade servers are classified as fault tolerant when they achieve 99.99% (that is, four nines) survivability. The standard for most PBX voice systems is 99.999% (that is, five nines), so four nines is quite a bit less than what we're accustomed to. The industry is slowly embracing Windows NT and Windows 2000 for core call processing, but some feel that these products are not reliable enough in their current form. To be fair, research on NT stability and security shows that almost always the problems are a result of poor or improper administrative procedures, not a result of problems in the operating system itself. As NT administrators have gained operational experience, the reliability and security of Windows-based data centers has improved. In summary, customer concerns include security, reliability, survivability, operability, maintainability, and accountability.

Another important issue related to IP PBXs is power distribution. PBXs have internal power distribution plants to support processing memory and internal interface circuit cards. All analog and proprietary digital telephones are line powered by the centralized PBX, using standard unshielded twisted-pair (UTP) wiring. Larger PBXs often have redundant power conversion and distribution elements throughout the cabinet design, and fluctuations in power—such as spikes and surges—are also regulated by the PBXs. Although there are Ethernet switches that can deliver power to the desktop via Category 5 cabling, they are just being introduced, and standards have not yet been developed for this.

Voice quality is another big issue with IP PBXs. The voice quality delivered over an IP PBX has to match that of the PSTN, so VoIP systems will need to meet stringent technical requirements to manage delay and echo, which are affected by the amount of compression and the type of codec used, as well as by the QoS capabilities of the underlying transport network. Voice quality will become a new performance variable, with various levels available and reflected in the pricing of services.

Another issue related to IP PBXs is network QoS. Voice QoS must remain adequate when it shares the network with bandwidth-intensive data applications. Packet loss must be minimized, and latency must be reduced. We still need to figure out how much voice traffic the data network can accept before voice, data, and video start to degrade.

Features and functionality are other issues. PBXs in general have 400 to 500 features, whereas IP phone systems provide only about 100 features.

There are also issues surrounding distance limitations. Fast Ethernet Category 5 cabling is limited to distances of 330 feet (100 meters), whereas PBXs support analog phone extensions over UTP at up to 2 miles (3.5 kilometers) and proprietary digital phones at up to 1 mile (1.5 kilometers).

Another issue is the lack of management systems. Systems designed to accommodate moves, adds, and changes, as well as troubleshooting, need to be developed.

There are also security questions (for example, Will voice over the LAN demand encryption of voice traffic?) and issues related to legacy voice investments (that is, enterprises generally protect investments in their existing equipment). Finally, we face a lack of a really compelling value proposition. However, PBXs are migrating toward a future in which IP-based packet transport will replace circuit-switched Time Division Multiplexing.

This market is poised for major change in the next several years. PBXs are migrating toward telephony server models, in which a nonproprietary platform will perform the call control and feature provisioning. But these are still the early days. Through integration, we will eventually have a much more cost-efficient platform for network services.

The Future of VoIP

VoIP is very important, and it's part of a larger application set that enables the integration of voice, video, data, and images. It is the early days for VoIP as well. Today, VoIP accounts for only a very small amount of global voice traffic. With VoIP we face issues of interoperability, scalability, and the number of features that can be supported. We face issues of whether the incumbents are motivated to replace all Class 5 exchanges with next-generation telephony. IP QoS is still immature, as these are the early days.

■ Multimedia on the Internet: Streaming Media

There's such a wide variety of applications for multimedia on the Internet that we're only just beginning to consider where and how we can use visualization and other sensory information. There are three major categories of multimedia on the Internet: communications applications (including VoIP, video telephony, and video and multimedia conferencing applications), computer applications (including interactive rich media, videomail, and streaming audio, video, and media content), and entertainment applications (including broadcast video, video-on-demand, and network games). This section concentrates on streaming media, and in Chapter 15, "The Broadband Home and HANs," we'll explore the fantastic future of smart devices and sensory networks.

Streaming Media Trends

Most streaming audio and video on the Internet today (for example, music, ads) is entertainment or consumer oriented. Many companies are now also beginning to use streaming media as a business tool. For example, I offer e-learning solutions on a streaming basis.

The appeal of streaming media is evident: Audio and video grab people's attention and can quickly present information that is easy to absorb and retain. Streaming media also allows for novel ways to reach clients, employees, and prospective customers. Audio and video are highly effective in sales and marketing, advertising, corporate communications, motivation, training, instruction, and customer support. Businesses realize gains in revenues and greater efficiencies and decreased costs for information delivery by turning to streaming media. By getting audio and video content in front of an audience, you can charm that audience, but it is costly and can be difficult. Downloading big files is time-consuming. Video file sizes run into the tens of megabytes, and a 5-minute video can be as large as 55MB. Audio files are often several megabytes.

Streaming is the solution to the problem of downloading large media files. Using a streaming media player, such as Apple's QuickTime, Microsoft's Windows Media Player, or RealNetworks's RealAudio and RealVideo, a user can play audio and/or video within seconds after the first bits of the stream hit the user's computer. These players support both live Internet broadcasts and video-on-demand, in which the streaming server keeps a copy of the content so that clients can request it at any time. Millions of people access some form of streaming content—audio or video—every day, and the number of streams available on the Internet is growing phenomenally. With all these people using streaming media and so many streaming media offerings available, streaming search technology is an emerging requirement in next-generation networks.

Streaming Media Applications

There are many applications for streaming media. Streaming media can be used as a novel way to reach and communicate with employees, clients, and partners. And streaming media is becoming more and more necessary where you need to respond to regulations that require a full disclosure or a method for informing a very wide audience. Another key application is virtual roadshows, such as pre-IPO presentations to potential investors. Product demonstrations are a very strong application of streaming media (for example, launches and rollouts of new products, virtual education and training). Some of the key customers for streaming media at this point are entertainment, financial institutions, health care, and education.

With streaming media, the content provider must digitize the content and set up a server that is specific to the client. The provider's total hardware and software costs are typically only in the thousands of dollars per streaming server. All the client needs is the player software, which is free or very inexpensive, and a sound card. Companies that offer Web hosting and streaming media services, however, need to make sure that they address network latencies, bandwidth management, digital rights management, billing systems, ad insertion, player licenses, and storage space. Again, we are in the early stages with streaming media, but it is certainly going to be a very important area.

Streaming Media on the Internet

Streaming media on the Internet today suffers because of restricted bandwidth (which makes the video jerky), poor reliability in the network (resulting in missing frames or dropouts in the audio), a lack of QoS in the network (which causes various types of distortions or artifacts in the video and audio), and packet loss at Internet peering points (ranging up to 40% during peak traffic hours, which is when key problems occur). These factors are being addressed, however; therefore, streaming media has great potential in the business realm.

Businesses have spent billions of dollars on streaming media, and they are expected to spend billions each year in the next several years. Businesses are seeking content conversion or capture, hardware and software infrastructure, network access and transport services, and other services, such as installation and support. Entertainment and consumer-oriented uses of streaming media are also huge. Streaming media is becoming fundamental to the way corporations, as well as individuals, communicate. Software and service providers are addressing three basic problems: delivery, performance monitoring, and content management.

Streaming Media Delivery

Edge caching has gained considerable momentum as a solution to the peering point problem. With edge caching, Web content is duplicated on a machine close to the end user the first time the user requests the content. Subsequent requests for this content, then, are satisfied from the nearby machine. This improves the speed and reliability of access because it avoids the Internet backbone and its peering points. Providers of edge caching include CacheFlow, InfoLibria, Inktomi, Network Appliance, and Novell.

In addition to edge caching, other techniques can be applied, such as hop-by-hop retransmission. This minimizes latency and increases the usefulness of retransmission for real-time broadcasts. With hop-by-hop retransmission, an intermediate device retransmits, so the retransmission travels a shorter path over a fewer number of hops and is therefore less delayed.

Application-layer multicasting is another technique. It ensures that just one stream goes across the backbone whenever possible. It is similar to IP multicasting, but it occurs at the application layer. FastForward Networks provides such solutions.

Streaming Media Performance Monitoring

Streaming content is vulnerable to fluctuations in bandwidth and QoS. The user's experience is closely correlated with metrics such as throughput, jitter, and dropped packets. Streaming applications require performance monitoring systems and services that track such measurements. Key providers in this realm include Mercury Interactive and WebHancer.

Streaming Media Content Management

Content management is another issue that is related to streaming media. Companies that regularly stream content need a system for making the content searchable and navigable by creating metadata that indexes it. Metadata is then stored on an application server, and the video is stored on a video server. Multimedia data search systems are automated software tools that analyze video, comparing each frame to known images and computing image similarity. They also create and index a voice-to-text transcription. Convera Corporation (which is a joint venture between Intel and Excalibur Technologies), Taalee, Virage, and WordWave are key providers of multimedia data search systems.

ISPs will look to offer new types of visually enabled services as a way to make up for reduced connection-fee revenue. Other organizations will look for ways to blend video with Web sites or portals, to improve the way they disseminate information, and to provide enhanced customer interaction. We can expect to see visually enabled call centers, visually enabled help desks, visual virtual meeting rooms, visual chat rooms, and visually enabled e-commerce.

Real-time interactive visual communications have been available for some time, but to date only niche markets (for example, distance learning, telemedicine, and corporate video conferencing) have seen their benefits and adopted their use.

Broadband Internet access with QoS is required for streaming media, and as it becomes more widely available in the near future, we will see many more adopters of this technology. Chapter 10 further discusses the demands of real-time visual streams and related QoS issues.

For more learning resources, quizzes, and discussion forums on concepts related to this chapter, see www.telecomessentials.com/learningcenter.

Chapter 12

Optical Networking

There is little doubt that the recent inventions and developments in optical networking will yield a new, radical perspective on communications. We have yet to witness the type of applications that will be developed as a result of the bandwidth that we are unleashing.

■ Optical Networking Drivers

The performance improvements—in speed, cost, and capacity—of fiber have been fast and furious. The number of bits per second that fiber can carry doubles every nine months for every dollar spent on the technology. The number of bits per second (bps) per lambda (λ), or wavelength, doubles every 12 months. The cost of transmitting a bit of information optically drops by 50% every nine months, and fiber prices, on a per-megabits-per-second basis, are falling by 60% each year. In comparison, the number of transistors on a computer chip doubles only every 18 months. Therefore, over a five-year period, optical technology far outpaces silicon chips and data storage.

Optical equipment has helped to drive down the price of moving a bit of information over long distances to 0.006% of what it was in 1996. If the automotive industry could match that, a BMW could be had for US$2.50 today.

In 2000, network capacity was reported to be doubling every nine months; 2001 statistics suggest that network capacity is doubling every five months. New fiber networks are increasing long-distance transmission capacity incredibly quickly and relatively inexpensively.

What is driving these advancements in optical networking? First, carriers want to boost capacity by orders of magnitude. Dense Wavelength Division Multiplexing (DWDM) enables multiple wavelengths of light to be carried over a single strand of fiber, which allows for the elegant expansion of capacity. We're also now seeing developments in applying Frequency Division Multiplexing (FDM), whereby we can combine more streams of traffic onto the same wavelength, promising a several-fold boost to the carrying capacity of fiber. (DWDM, FDM, and other multiplexing techniques are discussed in Chapter 2, "Telecommunications Technology Fundamentals.") Thus, we can extract more wavelengths, and over each wavelength we can derive more channels, and on each channel we can achieve more bps.

Second, carriers want to slash costs. Advances are being made in eliminating the need for regeneration stations on long-haul networks. Currently, because most optical networks still use electronic repeaters, every 200 miles (320 kilometers) a light signal has to be converted back into an electrical signal in order to be reshaped, resynchronized, and retimed. Then the signal is again converted back into a light pulse. This process alone accounts for about half the cost of optical networking. Provisioning of services needs to occur in minutes. But at this point, a carrier may have to wait six to nine months for an OC-3 (that is, 155Mbps) line to be provisioned. Optical switches will automate the provisioning process while also boosting capacities to handle thousands of wavelengths; that is the promise of end-to-end optical networking.

As described in Chapter 3, "Transmission Media: Characteristics and Applications," today's networks maintain mostly separate electronic connections for voice and data (see Figure 12.1). They achieve reliability in the network by using dual-counter-

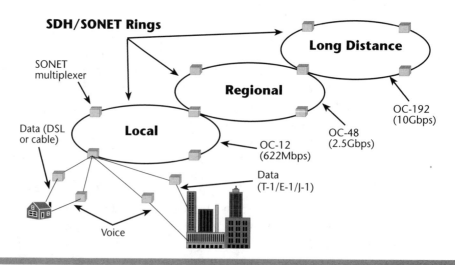

Figure 12.1 An example of today's optical networks

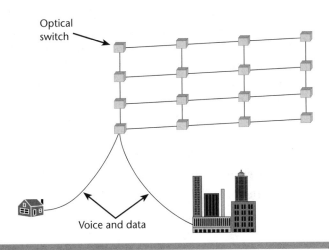

Figure 12.2 An example of tomorrow's optical networks

rotating rings based on the SDH/SONET communications standard (which is discussed in Chapter 5, "The PSTN"). With dual-counter-rotating rings, traffic normally flows in a clockwise direction over the primary fiber. There is also a protect fiber, which is designed to carry traffic in a counterclockwise direction. A SDH/SONET multiplexer aggregates traffic onto the rings. If the primary link is cut, traffic is switched to the protect fiber very quickly—in a matter of 50 milliseconds. This ensures a high degree of network survivability and it is a major strength of SDH/SONET.

Optical networks in the near future will channel all traffic over a single fiber connection and will provide redundancy by using the Internet's mesh of interlocking pathways. When a line breaks, traffic can flow down a number of different pathways. Optical switching will become the foundation for building these types of integrated networks (see Figure 12.2).

■ Components of an End-to-End Optical Network

At this point in the optical networking revolution, we're striving for what will be an end-to-end optical architecture. *End-to-end optical architecture* means that nowhere in the network is the optical signal being converted into an electronic signal. This reduction in the processing of signals would reduce costs and ultimately provide better performance.

No other transmission medium can unlock the same level of available bandwidth as can the visible light spectrum. But today, the electronic equipment acts as the bottleneck. Fibers now can carry terabits per second (Tbps), but they terminate on equipment that, at best, can handle gigabits per second (Gbps). So, before we can unleash the possibilities (and realize the savings) of end-to-end optical networking, we need to replace all the existing electronic equipment with optical equipment, which, of course, will be costly. It will involve not only new hardware but also new skill sets and network management solutions.

Components that comprise an end-to-end optical network include the following:

- Optical-line amplifiers, such as erbium-doped fiber amplifiers (EDFAs)
- Wavelength Division Multiplexing (WDM) equipment
- Optical add/drop multiplexers (OADMs)
- Optical switches

Figure 12.3 shows an example of an optical network that incorporates these components, and the following sections describe these components in detail.

EDFAs

As mentioned in Chapter 2, EDFAs, which were introduced in 1994, were a key innovation in the fiber world. Composed of erbium metal and doped with special atoms, EDFAs are incorporated in optical fiber at periodic intervals, generally 30 to

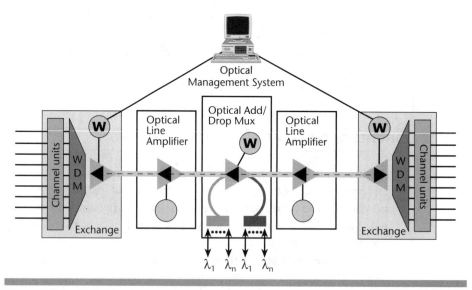

Figure 12.3 Optical network components

60 miles (50 to 100 kilometers), to boost communication signals. The components in an EDFA include an erbium-doped fiber, a laser-pump diode, couplers, and isolators. The light to be amplified is coupled in a section of erbium-doped fiber together with light from a laser-pump diode, normally about 980 nanometers. The EDFA itself operates in the range of 1,550 nanometers. The light from the laser-pump diode boosts the 1,550 nanometers light and is separated on the exit route. An isolator at either end protects the system from unwanted reflections. With EDFAs, an optical signal is amplified without having to undergo any conversions.

Before EDFAs, electronic regenerators had to extract signals, retime them, and then regenerate them. This conversion limited data rates to 2.5Gbps. EDFAs enabled us to quadruple this speed, providing data rates of 10Gbps.

WDM and DWDM

WDM works from the premise that we can spatially separate, or multiplex, different wavelengths of light down a single optical fiber. Current fiber-optic systems use only a fraction of the available bandwidth. They carry just one wavelength, when, in fact, thousands of wavelengths stand to be derived. The data rate supported by each wavelength depends on the type of light source. Today, each wavelength can carry from 2.5Gbps (that is, OC-48) to roughly 10Gbps (that is, OC-192). Some trial systems are operating at 40Gbps (that is, OC-768). In the very near future, we're expecting the delivery of Tbps light sources, and by 2005, we expect to see lasers operating in femtoseconds (that is, 10^{-18}). With speeds in this range, the time between bursts is the same time that light takes to travel one-eighth the width of a human hair.

WDM furnishes separate channels for each service at the full rate. The idea is not to aggregate smaller channels into one larger channel, but to provide a very high-speed channel that can terminate on today's switches and routers that, in fact, support 2.5Gbps interfaces. Systems that support more than 16 wavelengths are referred to as DWDM; you'll see both acronyms—WDM and DWDM—used to describe this network element.

The OC-48 systems today support in the range of 60 to 160 wavelengths. OC-192 systems generally support 8 to 32 wavelengths. Researchers tell us that 320-wavelength systems are on the 2002 horizon.

On top of all this, the potential exists for transmitting thousands of channels—potentially as many as 15,000 wavelengths on a single fiber—with developments such as Bell Labs's "chirped-pulse WDM." The idea of chirped pulse involves a specialized mode-locked laser, which rapidly emits very wide pulses of light. Because each part of a fiber interacts differently with varying frequencies of light, the result of chirped-pulse WDM is unequal dispersion. The pulse is stretched out when it enters the fiber, and data can be put on the discrete frequencies that emerge. You can think of this process in terms of a horse race. When a race starts, horses emerge together from the gate. But because each horse keeps a separate pace, spaces soon develop between the horses. This is the same type of stretching out that happens to the laser light in chirped-pulse WMD.

If we couple the potential for 15,000 wavelengths on one fiber with each of those wavelengths supporting femtobits per second (Fbps), we have an explosion of bandwidth that is like nothing we have known before. As fantastic as all this sounds, we're likely to see even greater achievements; after all, we are still in very early stages of knowledge about what we can achieve with optical networking. Before any real progress can be made, the realm of microphotonics must develop.

DWDM Developments and Considerations

As the number of wavelengths increases and the difference between the wavelengths gets smaller, the need for wavelength stability becomes greater, to ensure that the optical carriers do not bump into each other. To get this stability, you either need network operators maintaining a stock of boards for each wavelength or you need tunable lasers.

If you have 320 wavelengths, you need 320 separate boards, each tuned to the appropriate wavelength. Obviously, for redundancy purposes, you need a backup for each of those boards. And you need this at each location where you have the WDM. So, you can see that a tunable laser that could adopt the behavior of a specific frequency, as needed, would greatly reduce the operating cost and the costs of spare parts and inventory.

Another important development is that DWDM is beginning to be able to address network survivability requirements. DWDM is also now capable of incorporating highly valued SDH/SONET-like capabilities, including monitoring performance, providing protection, and provisioning optical channels. SDH/SONET, as mentioned in Chapter 5, describes the network survivability tactic. The dual-counter-rotating rings provide a protected fiber path over which information can be shunted in the opposite direction if a fiber ring is broken. Until recently, DWDM had no such capability. It was deployed as a point-to-point link; if the fiber was cut, you lost communications between the two DWDM systems. But now we are beginning to see the introduction of those restoration capabilities onto the DWDM platforms, which means that SDH/SONET will have a more limited life in the future. Industry forecasts predict that SONET/SDH has perhaps a 10-year lifespan left, after which the benefits of DWDM will override the reliability factors that we today associate with SDH/SONET. Remember that SDH/SONET is a TDM system, and therefore it cannot take advantage of the capacity gains that DWDM systems provide.

A different consideration emerges as the DWDM systems continue to develop. Because of a combination of nonlinearities and dispersion, most of the fiber currently in place around the world—possibly 95% of it—would have trouble carrying the very fast (Tbps speed and Fbps pulses) signals for long distances in a DWDM system. These impairments that exist in current fiber can lead to crosstalk among the different wavelengths, interference between consecutive pulses on any signal wavelength, and degradation in the overall signal-to-noise ratio. This means that much of the fiber we have deployed over the past two decades will have to be replaced in order to take advantage of the new generation of optical equipment. Fiber solutions exist today, but it will take time and financial resources to deploy them.

Where DWDM Fits in the Network Architecture

The core network was the first place DWDM was deployed because this is where the economics made most sense. Increases in intercity traffic required carriers to expand the capacity of their long-haul pipes. So the response was to deploy these point-to-point links with DWDM. This resolved the bandwidth problem, but it did nothing to address the routing issues. WDM and DWDM currently lack the intelligence to really deliver meshed network configurations, and thus we have a need for optical switches. The main benefit of DWDM in the core is that it reduces deployment costs by eliminating the need for expensive amplifiers. Current DWDM products can operate successfully over about 300 to 450 miles (480 to 725 kilometers), and new developments are promising up to 4,000 miles (6,400 kilometers) without boosting the signal. As mentioned earlier in the chapter, the process of regenerating signals represents as much as half of the overall cost of an optical deployment. Therefore, developments in extending distances are very promising.

Another place DWDM is used is in metropolitan area networks (MANs). MANs are becoming saturated, and network expansion is costly—pulling fiber along existing conduits costs about US$30,000 per mile. But traditional DWDM systems are not well suited to MANs. For one thing, they were designed to work well on point-to-point links, but MAN traffic must be dropped and added frequently. DWDM does not present the same cost justifications in the MAN as it does in the core.

The great savings that comes with DWDM in the MAN is from the reduction in the need for the expensive amplifiers. By definition, a MAN is fairly short, so there is no need for the use of expensive amplifiers. You can spend US$20,000 to US$30,000 or more for an amplifier that is capable of operating over a range of 300 to 450 miles (480 to 725 kilometers). However, runs in MANs are typically no longer than 70 miles (110 kilometers), so these expensive amplifiers are often overkill. As a result, the next generation of MAN products, designed to address the MAN core—that is, metro access and the enterprise networks—are being introduced. Metro core products are used for building citywide rings. Therefore, they generally support longer distances and greater capacity than do metro access products. Metro access products bring fiber closer to the customer, so they reduce deployment costs. Enterprise products address building high-capacity campus networks. In all three of these MAN sectors, the issues are the same: pricing, scalability, access, and flexibility.

As far as pricing and scalability issues go, the lower carrying capacity and distance requirements in the metro area allow providers to reduce costs by using less expensive lasers. The price of a transponder board, which represents 90% of the cost of a laser, can vary by 25%, depending on the quality of the laser. Shorter-distance lasers use less-expensive modulation and amplification techniques. Whereas long-haul lasers are externally modulated, enabling the signal to travel up to 450 miles (725 kilometers), shorter distances may allow direct modulation, where the laser runs only 50 to 60 miles (80 to 100 kilometers) but costs 30% to 40% less than a long-haul laser. But cheaper lasers also mean less capacity. Greater spacing is required between the wavelengths, thereby reducing the number of channels or wavelengths that you can derive by up to 50%.

Additional issues to be considered relative to pricing include the cost of the local loop. Eliminating the active components in the optical network can produce an even more cost-effective network. Thus, passive optical networks (PONs) are used to reduce costs by distributing costs across more endpoints and by replacing expensive OADMs or DWDM nodes with optical splitters and couplers at each fiber connection in the network. Eliminating the active components reduces the distance the signal can travel, so the theoretical range is only about 12 miles (19 kilometers). But the result can be a 10-fold saving as compared to using conventional SDH/SONET equipment, and can be even more as compared to using DWDM systems. PONs (which are covered in more detail in Chapter 13, "Broadband Access Solutions ") are being considered very seriously as a means by which to deliver fiber to the home very cost-effectively.

Two major bandwidth drivers are pushing for delivery of high-speed optics down to the customer premises. First, customers are looking to connect their data centers through high-speed mainframe interfaces, such as ESCON and Fiber Channel. Second, the Internet is generating a huge demand for capacity, and it changes how traffic flows as well. As discussed in Chapter 8, "Local Area Networking," the old 80/20 scenario is reversing. It used to be that 80% of the data generated within a given business address also came from within that business address. Now, 80% of information exchange is outside the local business address. Traffic patterns also shift much more rapidly today than in the past, so they are more difficult to predict.

To meet these new demands, we need a very dynamic network that has the capability to accommodate huge capacity requirements and to change the configuration of that capacity dynamically. Subscribers want to connect at the current speed of their backbone. They want to make a direct connection through MANs and long-haul networks, with the associated protocols. And, of course, they want guaranteed QoS.

IP over DWDM

Today, bandwidth reservation and intelligent IP switches can prioritize voice and video traffic to ensure that high-priority traffic gets the first shot at the underlying bandwidth. New generations of IP-based switches provide the capability to meet QoS commitments. Layer 3/Layer 4 switching services allow the switch to prioritize and guarantee packets, based on predetermined criteria within a switch. Higher-level protocols (such as RSVP) can reserve bandwidth across an entire network. This creates a value proposition for the service provider: The ISP can deliver high bandwidth in a format that users want, for less cost, while approximating the QoS guarantees that the end user expects for high-priority traffic.

As discussed in Chapter 5, the PSTN was not built to be dynamic. It was based on a system of 64Kbps channels, or DS-0s/CEPT-0s, aggregated by time division multiplexers into DS-1/CEPT-1 or DS-3/CEPT-3 facilities that would deliver traffic into cross-connects and switches at the network core. More time division multiplexers were required at the other end to reverse the process and to distribute the DS-0s/CEPT-0s. Time division multiplexers are expensive, and they often require manual configuration, which slows provisioning and further increases costs.

Whereas TDM is reaching its limits in terms of network elements and switching technologies, DWDM is just beginning. But as with any technology that is just beginning, obstacles will be in the way, and in the case of DWDM, the obstacles include management and performance impedance mismatches between networks. The International Telecommunication Union (ITU) has formed a study group that will look into the interoperability standards to ensure that traffic can move between vendor networks despite the underlying differences in the many different vendors' equipment.

Optical OADMs

Next-generation network services must be easily reconfigurable and they must support real-time provisioning. Demultiplexing all the wavelengths at each node is costly, it introduces delay, and it reduces the distance over which a signal can travel. OADMs, as shown in Figure 12.4, work much more inexpensively than demultiplexing all the wavelengths because they simplify the process—they eliminate the costly electronics that are used to convert between light and electricity. Most OADMs use special filters to extract the wavelengths that need to be dropped off at a given location. For most vendors, the wavelength is fixed, so at the time of configuration, the carrier designates the individual wavelengths to be dropped at each location.

Emerging DWDM applications address the growing desire for wavelength-on-demand. Individual wavelengths are assigned either to specific protocols, such as

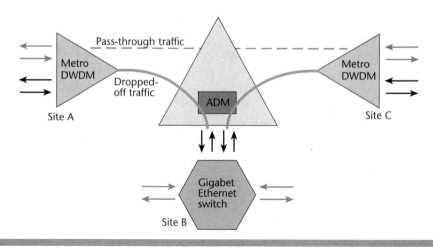

Figure 12.4 Optical add/drop multiplexing

ATM or IP, or to specific customers. Alternatively, some providers might lease an entire dark fiber to each client, and the client would then purchase the customer premises equipment to route different protocols over each individual wavelength. This is opening the door to a whole new way of thinking about providing wavelengths to the long-haul carriers, to the MAN market, and to the customer.

The development of managed wavelength services depends on the development of wavelength changers and optical switches. A *wavelength changer* converts an optical signal to an electronic signal and then sends it to a laser that produces an optical signal at a different wavelength than the original. As you'll see in the next section, optical switches give carriers the capability to provision bandwidth automatically, instead of having to deploy technicians into the field. Optical switches also enable service providers to build mesh optical restoration, which gives them the flexibility of running different kinds of restoration in their networks. Finally, optical switches allow service providers to establish QoS levels associated with restoration.

Optical Switches

Optical switches, sometimes referred to as *optical cross-connects* or *wavelength routers*, are devices that reside at junction points in optical backbones and enable carriers to string together wavelengths to provide end-to-end connections (see Figure 12.5). They link any of several incoming lines to any of several outgoing lines and automatically reroute traffic when a network path fails. Optical switches are the optical version of the general-purpose switching system that provides flexibility

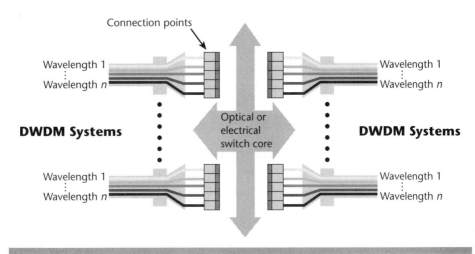

Figure 12.5 An example of an optical switch

and reliability in today's PSTN. Optical switches move transmissions between fiber segments and also enable some network management activities, including optical-layer restoration and reconfiguration, dynamic wavelength management, and automated optical-layer provisioning.

There are three key issues in selecting optical switches:

- **Number of ports**—Carriers are looking for devices that can scale to more than 1,000 ports.

- **Automation**—Carriers want to provision strings of wavelengths from a remote console in real-time.

- **Granularity**—Carriers want the switch to handle small as well as large bandwidths so that they can eliminate multiplexers.

First- and Next-Generation Optical Switches

Two types of optical switches are currently being produced: switches with electrical cores (that is, first-generation optical switches) and switches with optical cores. The electronics in first-generation switches slows their capability to work with the very high rates that the fiber itself can support. The future lies in the pure optical switches, but we still have to fully develop the microphotonics industry; thus, microphotonics is really the next revolutionary technology.

Optical switches fall into two main categories. First, the multiservice provisioning platform (MSPP) enables carriers to get a quick start on offering a full range of services. The MSPP resides either in the carrier's point of presence or at the customer site, and it incorporates DWDM, while also offering customers different grades of IP service, telephony, and other offerings. Second, big switches can be deployed at the carrier's local exchange. These switches act as on-ramps, funneling large volumes of traffic from IP and ATM backbones on and off the optical core.

Challenges in Deploying Optical Switches

Because we are in the early stages with optical switches, we have to deal with issues such as how to quickly provision services, how to accommodate billing, and how to elegantly separate services. In the next three to five years, we should start seeing these more sophisticated elements become available in pure optical form.

Again, with end-to-end optical networking, because transmission rates are reaching the Tbps, Pbps, and even the Ebps (that is, exabits per second) levels, the bottleneck is moving to the network elements. The faster the light pulses are emitted—that is, the faster the data rates on the line get—the more technically challenging it is to handle optical-electrical-optical conversions at line speed. Therefore, to fully take advantage of the capacity that's being created by WDM, fiber networks will need switches that are capable of rerouting light. The good news is that the cost of optical components has decreased by 40% in recent years, and it is expected to continue to drop by 40% to 60% per year.

The biggest problem that converged telcos are now facing is how to accurately forecast what their future bandwidth requirement will be. Transmission speeds are doubling every 12 months, so it is essential that we have infrastructures that are capable of providing a large amount of bandwidth on short notice and at a reasonable cost. Without intelligent optical networking, adding an OC-48 circuit over existing dark fiber can take between six and nine months. To automate provisioning, we need to also address how we can look into a wavelength to determine how to properly act on it.

Optical switches enable improved reliability, improved scalability, and flexible service provisioning. Another major benefit is that they reduce the capital required to add additional capacity, and the overall savings can then be passed on to the customer. Deploying optical networking technology in the metro area can bring the benefits of converged networks down to the customer's premises. The end-to-end optical infrastructure can then support advanced services such as true bandwidth-on-demand.

Optical Switching Fabrics

Optical switching fabrics, such as the following, provide subsystems that connect one wavelength to another:

- **Microelectromechanical system (MEMS) switches**—A MEMS switch uses an array of microscopic mirrors to reflect light from an input port to an output port.

- **Bubble switches**—Similarly to ink-jet printers, bubble switches use heat to create small bubbles in fluid channels that then reflect and direct light.

- **Thermo-optical switches**—With thermo-optical switches, light passing through glass is heated up or cooled down by using electrical coils. The heat alters the refractive index of the glass, bending the light so that it enters one fiber or another.

- **Liquid crystal display (LCD) switches**—LCDs use liquid to bend light.

- **Tunable lasers**—Tunable lasers pump out light at different wavelengths, and they can switch from one wavelength to another very quickly.

Lucent's LambdaRouter is an example of a MEMS switch (see Figure 12.6). It switches lightwaves by using microscopic mirrors. One of these microscopic mirrors is small enough to fit through the eye of a needle. Hence, a LambdaRouter is essentially a switch with 256 ports by 256 ports in a one-square-inch piece of silicon. (Remember how it used to take a multistory building that took up an entire block to house a local exchange switch in the electromechanical era?) The LambdaRouter's 256 ports each start at 40Gbps, which means the LambdaRouter offers a total capacity of nearly 10Tbps. This device can intelligently switch or route the wavelengths without making any optoelectronic conversions. The lightwaves

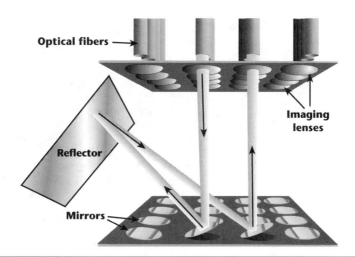

Figure 12.6 A MEMS switch

themselves tell the mirror what bend to make in order to route the light appropriately; they do this by using a digital wrapper, which is the equivalent of a packet header. Lucent's digital wrapper, WaveWrapper, is proprietary, but there are some movements afoot to standardize this intelligence, as discussed later in this chapter, in the section "Managing Optical Networks."

Xros, which was acquired by Nortel, is also focusing on the micromirror technology. The Xros device can scale to 1,024 × 1,024 wavelengths, and it fits in an assembly that's about 10 inches wide by 6 inches tall.

Another approach in optical switches, bubble switches, involves using ink-jet printer technology to switch packets in optical switches. In ink-jet printers, tiny enclosures are filled with gas, and they sit behind the ink in a printer. In front of each enclosure is a minute nozzle. When a character is called for, the gas behind the nozzles that form the letters is heated, and the ink is shot onto the paper. Agilent is applying this technology to optical switches, embedding tiny, liquid-filled cavities in switch fabric (see Figure 12.7). If a packet is supposed to stay on the same network, the liquid remains cool, and the packet passes through unscathed. If a switch is required, the liquid is heated and turns to gas. If the gas has the correct reflective properties and if the cavity is precisely positioned, the light is bounced in the right direction.

Yet another optical switching approach involves thermo-optic switches. Light is passed through glass that is then heated up or cooled down with electrical coils.

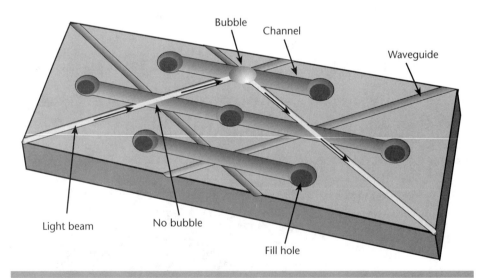

Figure 12.7   A bubble switch

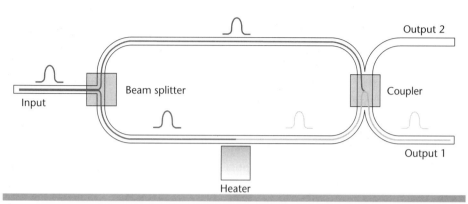

Figure 12.8 A thermo-optic switch

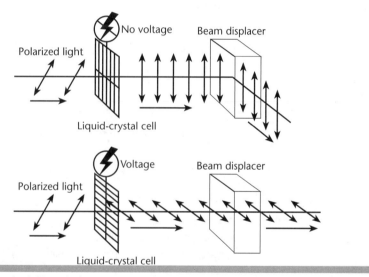

Figure 12.9 An LCD switch

The heat alters the refractive index of the glass, bending the light so that it enters one fiber or another (see Figure 12.8).

An LCD switch, as shown in Figure 12.9, uses liquid to bend light.

There are many issues to address with these evolving types of optical switches. Again, because we are in the early days of these technologies, we have not yet tested each of them, let alone under the full load of the network. We still have to address how well these technologies will scale. Carriers are looking for modular switches that can scale to thousands of ports. Switching speed is another consideration. Routing traffic packet-by-packet will require switching speeds that are measured in nanoseconds.

It is important to remember that we are in the early days. None of these switches have been tested in fully loaded environments, and undoubtedly some will prove to be more fanciful than fruitful.

Other Optical Components

The building blocks of optical networks, the optical components, are critical to the development of optical systems. In addition to the components described so far, the following are some important optical components:

- **Lasers**—Provide light
- **Gratings**—Single out specific wavelengths from a light source
- **Filters**—Read incoming light signals
- **Dispersion compensation modules**—Prevent smudging of light signals
- **Variable attenuators**—Even out the strength of light signals in adjoining wavelengths
- **Passive splitters**—Divert wavelengths into different fibers
- **Amplifiers**—Strengthen attenuated signals

Key issues regarding the optical components part of the optical equation are cost and shortage. Currently, many components are extremely expensive. Also, many vendors have announced big investment in component production facilities. However, demand is likely to exceed supply for some components over the next couple years. Companies that do not yet have contracts for things like fiber-optic cables and fiber components may find themselves unable to obtain these items until the shortages are resolved.

To address the cost and shortage issues, vendors are developing ways of making optical integrated circuits, which are the optical equivalent of electrical integrated circuits. The goal is to consolidate large numbers of separate optical devices into a single chip, customizing them for different applications and drastically reducing costs and improving performance. A wide variety of materials are being used for different applications, including silica, polymer, and rare earths. Each has advantages and disadvantages in terms of the performance of the chip and the ease and cost of manufacturing it. Currently, vendors are producing relatively simple components, such as WDM chips, small switch modules, and passive splitters, but the future has a lot more in store in this arena.

■ IP over Optical Standards

An important part of the optical networking discussion is standards regarding IP over optical. Three standards efforts are working on optical management specifications, addressing the linking of IP services directly to the optical networks that carry data, allowing these networks to take advantage of the routing intelligence now embedded in IP headers:

- ■ **MPλS**—The IETF's Multiprotocol Lambda Switching (MPλS) initiative, supported by Uunet and Cisco Systems, describes an approach to the design of control planes that take advantage of the existing techniques developed for MPLS traffic engineering. The goal is to provide a framework for real-time provisioning of optical channels in automatically switched optical networks, as well as to promote and speed the deployment of a new generation of optical cross-connects. Of course, network management and interoperability in an internetworked environment are also addressed. MPλS uses labels with packet-forwarding information that are attached to IP packets by a label-switching router that sits at the edge of the optical network. This approach also paves the way for the eventual incorporation of DWDM multiplexing capabilities in IP routers.

- ■ **OIF**—The Optical Internetworking Forum (OIF) represents more than 200 companies and was founded by AT&T, Bellcore (now Telcordia), Ciena, Cisco, Hewlett-Packard, US West (now Qwest), Sprint, and Worldcom. The OIF's mission is to foster the development and deployment of interoperable products and services for data switching and routing using optical networking technologies. It is focused on addressing optical internetworking issues.

Of course, given these separate efforts, there is a concern that the existence of several standards could lead to the development of several technologies in this area.

■ Managing Optical Networks

Optical networks have a number of unique management requirements that necessitate new techniques. There are currently no standards for carrying management information in optical networks, so carriers may be forced to retain electrical interfaces so that they can pinpoint faults. There is also currently no way to support error-correcting protocols on optical networks. Carriers still also need electrical interfaces to regenerate the right color light; because there is currently no standard for connecting one shade of blue light to another shade of blue light, for example, carriers must rely on a complete package of transmission equipment and switching from the same vendor.

Adding more wavelengths presents service providers with a new challenge: cost-effectively managing the increasing number of wavelengths to provide fast, reliable services to end customers. Digital wrappers promise to provide network management functions such as optical-layer performance monitoring, error correction, and ring-protection capabilities, on a per-wavelength basis. These digital wrappers are standardized as part of submarine cabling systems, and both the ITU and the OIF have accepted the standard for landline fiber systems. Lucent has also unveiled its proprietary version of the standard, called WaveWrapper, which was developed by Bell Labs. The WaveWrapper works like this:

1. It places a small digital wrapper around each input wavelength. The wrapper carries information, such as restoration signals, what type of traffic is in the wavelength, and where the traffic is headed.

2. As the wavelength moves around the network, the nodes read the header. They scan for originating and terminating details, information about whether it's an IP or ATM signal (or another protocol's signal), and commands such as strong forward error correction.

3. Systems determine the health of the signal, whether it needs to be rerouted, and whether the necessary equipment exists to receive the signal at its intended destination.

Lucent has submitted WaveWrapper as a standard to the ANSI Telecommunications Standards Committee, the OIF, and the ITU.

Remember that with intelligent optical networking, the challenge is to deal with each wavelength individually. It is necessary to understand what is happening on each wavelength in order to route and rearrange a wavelength across different carriers' networks. To understand the wavelength's personality, the wavelength must be monitored, and this capability takes intelligence. Optical network operators will therefore require new tools, including optical channel analyzers, power-balancing techniques, tunable filters, physical restoration techniques, and control plane signaling. An optical probe will be another very important element in the optical equation because it will provide the capability to look into a wavelength to determine its behavior, thereby assuring intelligent end-to-end optical networking, with real-time provisioning capabilities and wavelength management opportunities (see Figure 12.10).

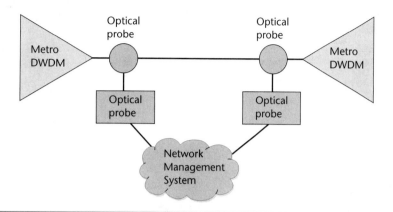

Figure 12.10   Optical probe monitoring

For more learning resources, quizzes, and discussion forums on concepts related to this chapter, see www.telecomessentials.com/learningcenter.

13

Broadband Access Solutions

Broadband access options are very important—they very well may determine how well you're able to grow professionally and personally. The main drivers toward broadband are users' desires to find information that is valuable to them, to be connected, and to experience the multimedia spectacle of the Web.

The global broadband market is predicted to be worth US$580 billion by 2010. In general, the view is that households and small- and medium-size enterprises—rather than the traditional corporate customers—will account for most of that market. Increased economic growth and greater dependence on high-speed networks will lead to higher demand in Europe than in the United States by 2005 and in Asia by 2010. Estimates suggest that there will be 100 million addressable small- and medium-size enterprises globally by that time, with only 14% of those being U.S. based.

What drives a telco to consider deploying broadband access in the first place? One reason is that it may be experiencing slower rates of growth or even a decline in its core business of providing fixed-link telephone services. Also, there's a great deal of competition going on among many alternative networks, and there's an ongoing growth in the demand for nonvoice services.

After a telco decides to deploy broadband access, it has to decide which of the available broadband media options to deploy: twisted-pair (that is, xDSL), coax, fiber, wireless, or one of the emerging options (see Table 13.1). What drives the telco's strategy for deciding which of the options to deploy? One factor is the status of the telco's embedded distribution plant—how old it is, how well it extends into

Table 13.1 Broadband Media Options

Medium	Deployment Examples
Twisted-pair	HDSL, IDSL, SDSL, M/SDSL, ADSL, RADSL, VDSL
Coax	HFC
Fiber	FTTC, FTTH, PONs
Wireless	DBS/DTH, MMDS, LMDS, Free Space Optics, unlicensed bands
Emerging	Powerline, Ethernet-in-the-loop, HomePNA

the neighborhood, and whether it can support the high data rates specified with that broadband access option. Another factor is the services strategy of the network operator: Is it a legacy or new-era services provider? That is, is the telco interested in providing basic telephony and perhaps some specialized traditional low-speed data types of services, such as access to data or ISDN (that is, Is it a legacy provider?), or does the telco aim to deliver IP services, interactive broadband services (for example, Internet access, remote access, teleshopping), and broadcast and interactive video (that is, Is it a new-era provider?)? A third factor is the cost of installing the new distribution system, given the physical footprint realities such as the terrain and environmental conditions. Finally, the telco needs to consider the performance level of the distribution system in terms of the requirements to implement the services strategy. This also deals with the physical footprint realities (for example, broadband wireless may work very well in one area but provide poor performance in another because there are many trees whose leaves act as obstacles to the microwave). This chapter talks about the issues with regard to each of the broadband media.

As discussed in Chapter 10, "Next-Generation Networks," today, broadband network services are predominantly planned as separate overlay networks. When incremental deployment occurs via intelligent edge switches, the result is separate networks for separate services. Integrated access is the key to the cost savings of the converged network architecture.

Chapter 3, "Transmission Media: Characteristics and Applications," discusses each of the transmission media types in detail. This chapter focuses on the important aspects of and considerations in deploying the media types associated with broadband access: xDSL, hybrid fiber coax (HFC; including cable modems and cable TV networks), fiber arrangements that bring fiber to the curb and to the home, the broadband wireless arena, and emerging options, such as Powerline Telecommunications.

The Best Broadband Option for the Footprint

People often want to know what is the best broadband access option. The answer is that there is no best option. What is best for a given situation depends on the footprint reality. Currently, there are multiple options to explore. Across different terrains, across different applications, and across different politics and regulations, one of the options is bound to work and prevail and allow you to enter the broadband era.

■ xDSL

The xDSL technologies—including High-Bit-Rate Digital Subscriber Line (HDSL), ISDN Digital Subscriber Line (IDSL), Single-Line Digital Subscriber Line (SDSL), Multirate Symmetrical Digital Subscriber Line (M/SDSL), Asymmetrical Digital Subscriber Line (ADSL), Rate-Adaptive Digital Subscriber Line (RADSL), and Very-High-Rate Digital Subscriber Line (VDSL)—offer many home users their first taste of broadband, and most users find that once they've tried broadband, they'll never go back. It's exciting how much it can improve your performance, despite it's not being as fast as the data rates we will see in the coming years. According to Cahners In-Stat Group (*Business Communications Review,* July 2001), the world-wide DSL subscriber base is expected to include some 12 million in 2002, 17 million in 2003, and 23 million in 2005.

Bellcore (which is now Telcordia) created DSL as a technique to filter out the incessant background noise on copper wires and to allow clearer connections through the use of electronic intelligence in the form of DSL modems at either end of the twisted-pair line. DSL modems are limited in transmission distance. They generally have a range of up to 3.5 miles (5.5 kilometers), although new specifications are constantly being created to increase the permitted distances. The general rule of thumb with DSL is that the greater the distance, the lower the performance, and the shorter the distance, the greater the data rate you can experience. Another characteristic of DSL to keep in mind is that it is a point-to-point connection—that is, it is always on. So, when you have access into your Internet service provider (ISP) through a DSL line and you've powered up your computer, the connection is on throughout the day. This has security implications—it's very important that you consider some form of firewall and security software to prevent the potential activities of a curious hacker.

DSL provides high-bandwidth transmission over copper twisted-pair. It uses efficient modulation, or line-coding, techniques that enable it to carry more bits in a single cycle (that is, Hz) than older twisted-pair. It uses echo cancellation, which enables full-duplex transmission to occur over a single electrical path, and it relies on frequency splitting to enable you to derive separate voice and data channels from one wire. DSL also retains power in the event of a power failure; if the electricity goes out, you'll lose your high-speed data services, but you will retain your voice services.

Factors that can affect the viability of DSL for a subscriber include the following:

- **Attenuation**—Attenuation is signal loss, and it's a function of frequency. As the frequency increases, the distance the signal can travel decreases, by the square root of the frequency. Higher frequencies lose power more rapidly, thereby limiting the loop length; we have to use the full-frequency spectrum available on the twisted pair to carry the promised data rates; thus, the higher frequencies must be used.

- **Resistance**—As signals are transmitted through wires at very high frequencies, a phenomenon called the *skin effect* occurs. As electricity migrates to the medium's skin, resistance increases because less of the wire is used. This increased resistance weakens the signals. The skin effect is why there are currently no services above 1GHz over wired media.

- **Crosstalk**—When two adjacent wires carry signals, signals from one wire might be able to enter the other wire as a result of electromagnetic radiation—this is called *crosstalk*. Crosstalk increases with increasing frequency, a principal cause of signal degradation at the frequencies required by high-speed services. This affects how many pairs within a cable can be used to deliver DSL service.

- **Phase error**—Phase error introduces bit errors where modulation techniques depend on phase modulation.

- **Loads**—Loaded pairs—which means there are loading coils placed on twisted-pairs for purposes of improving performance over 3.5 miles (5.5 kilometers), when the subscriber is greater than 3.5 miles (5.5 kilometers) away from the access point—cannot be used for DSL.

- **Taps**—Taps are open points on the cable bundle that are left so that technicians will be able to easily splice off a pair to bring additional service to a home or bring service to a new home. These open points cause too much distortion to be used with DSL.

- **Loop carriers**—Loop carriers, or remote concentrators, are not compatible with most of the DSL family. xDSL, therefore, must work around the existing loop carrier systems, or the network operators have to replace older-generation loop carriers with next-generation loop carriers that are designed to work with the DSL modems. Currently only HDSL and IDSL work with existing digital loop carriers. Approximately 30% to 40% of the

Table 13.2 xDSL Characteristics

Characteristic	HDSL	IDSL	SDSL	M/SDSL	ADSL	RADSL	VDSL
Maximum deployment distance	2.2 miles (3.6 km)	3.5 miles (5.5 km)	3.5 miles (5.5 km)	5.5 miles (8.9 km)	3.5 miles (5.5 km)	3.5 miles (5.5 km)	1 mile (1.5 km)
Symmetrical/ Asymmetrical	Symmetrical	Symmetrical	Symmetrical	Symmetrical	Asymmetrical	Symmetrical or asymmetrical	Asymmetrical
Capacity	Up to 2Mbps	Up to 128Kbps	Up to 2Mbps	Up to 2Mbps	ADSL-1: 1.5Mbps to 2Mbps downstream, 16Kbps to 64Kbps upstream; ADSL-2: 6Mbps to 8Mbps downstream, 640Kbps to 840Kbps upstream	600Kbps to 7Mbps downstream, 128Kbps to 1Mbps upstream	Up to 52Mbps downstream, up to 1.5Mbps to 2.3Mbps upstream
Number of twisted-pairs	Two	One	One	One	One	One	One

U.S. population is served by such digital loop carriers, and around the world, remote and rural locations are generally served with digital loop carriers. As a result, certain market territories do not have quick and easy access to DSL. DSL access in those areas will depend on the operator's ability and desire to upgrade the plant.

■ **Other external impairments**—Leakage, impulse noise, narrowband interference, and the general quality of the copper pair can all have an effect on the quality of DSL service.

All these factors together determine whether you will get the kind of service that DSL promises.

The following sections look at each of the DSL family members in turn. Table 13.2 summarizes some of the characteristics of xDSL. Keep in mind that the rates shown in Table 13.2 vary, depending on the loop conditions, crosstalk, impairments, and so on.

HDSL

HDSL is the oldest of the DSL techniques. It has been in full use for over a decade, and it is most commonly used by telcos to provision T-1 or E-1 services. HDSL enables carriers to provision T-1 or E-1 services at a reduced cost because it does not require special repeaters, loop conditioning, or pair selection in order to deliver that service.

HDSL is a symmetrical service, meaning that it gives you equal bandwidth in both directions. Because it is full-duplex, it allows communication in both directions simultaneously. The allocation of bandwidth on HDSL depends on whether

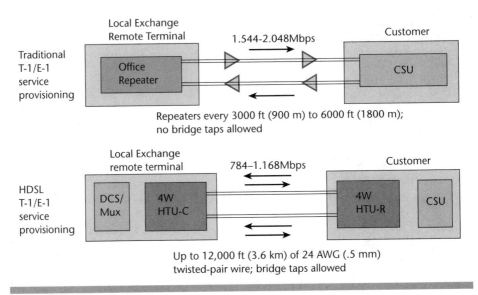

Figure 13.1 Traditional T-1/E-1 versus HDSL provisioning

you are operating on T-1 or E-1 capacities; in the T-1 environment, it offers 784Kbps in each direction, and in the E-1 environment, it offers 1.168Mbps in each direction. HDSL is largely used to provision digital services to business premises. It is standardized under ITU G.991.1 and ADSI T1E1.4, Tech Report 28.

HDSL reduces the cost of provisioning T-1/E-1 because of the way that the bandwidth is delivered (see Figure 13.1). A traditional T-1/E-1 environment makes use of two twisted-pairs. Each pair carries the full data rate, which is 1.5Mbps with T-1 and 2.048Mbps with E-1. Because each pair is carrying such a high data rate, higher frequencies need to be used; as a result, repeaters need to be spaced roughly every 0.5 to 1 mile (900 to 1,800 meters). Furthermore, no bridge taps are allowed in the traditional T-1/E-1 environment.

HDSL modems contain some added intelligence in the form of inverse multiplexers. Because of these multiplexers, each pair carries only half of the data rate. As a result, those bits can ride in the lower range of frequencies, thus extending the distance over which they can flow without the need for a repeater. With HDSL, you need a repeater only at about 2.2 miles (3.6 kilometers). In addition, bridge taps are allowed with HDSL. These factors reduce the cost of provisioning services to customers and allow more customers who are outside the range of the traditional T-1/E-1 environment to enjoy the privileges of this high-bandwidth option. Because taps can be used with HDSL, provisioning can occur rather quickly. Also, HDSL is a good solution for increasing the number of access lines via the digital-loop carrier transport because it is compatible with the existing loop carriers. Key applications of HDSL include replacement of local repeater T-1/E-1 trunks, use as a local Frame Relay option, use in PBX interconnection, and use in general traffic aggregation.

The HDSL2 specification was developed to provide the capacities and symmetry of HDSL to residences. HDSL2 involves the use of a single twisted copper pair for distances up to 2.2 miles (3.6 kilometers). HDSL2 is a symmetrical, full-duplex service that offers up to 768Kbps in each direction. The HDSL2 specification has not yet been fully ratified, and so for the time being various companies (such as ADC Telecommunications, PairGain Technologies, and ADTRAN) are producing products that are proprietary in nature.

Estimates suggest that HDSL will not be an extremely popular environment in the future, but in the short-term, it will continue to be used to provision T-1/E-1 services to businesses at relatively low cost.

IDSL

IDSL is basically ISDN without the telephone switch. It makes use of a DSL access multiplexer (DSLAM), which shunts traffic to a data network, away from the circuit-switched network. IDSL is a full-duplex, symmetrical service, and it offers 128Kbps in each direction. Unlike traditional ISDN, it cannot be channelized. Because it uses the same transmission technology as Basic Rate Interface (BRI) ISDN (that is, 2B1Q line coding), it is compatible with existing loop carriers. The distance limitation on IDSL is 3.5 miles (5.5 kilometers).

Because IDSL offers throughput of only 128Kbps (compared, for example, to the 1.5Mbps throughput that ADSL provides), there's little interest in it, and it is unlikely to have much of a future.

SDSL

SDSL involves a single twisted copper pair that can be up to 3.5 miles (5.5 kilometers) long. It is a symmetrical, full-duplex service. Symmetry can sometimes be very important, depending on the application. If your only goal is to surf the Internet and browse Web sites, then most of the bandwidth you will need is in the downstream direction—from the network to you—in which case solutions such as ADSL are appropriate. But if you're telecommuting or operating in a small office/ home office (SOHO) and you need to do large file or image transfers, or need to engage in videoconferencing, then you need a great deal of bandwidth in the upstream direction as well as in the downstream direction, in which event, symmetrical services are best. So, if your major purpose for wanting broadband access is beyond Internet surfing—for example, to download and upload a lot of data for schoolwork and professional work—then SDSL is probably a better option than

ADSL. It is more costly than asymmetrical options, but it gives you a better performance guarantee.

SDSL also supports multiple data rates—up to T-1 or E-1 rates—so you can subscribe to varying bandwidths, up to 1.5Mbps or 2Mbps. Applications of SDSL include replacement of local repeater T-1/E-1 trunks, use as fractional T-1/E-1, interconnection of PBXs, support of multirate ISDN, support for switched 384Kbps service (and therefore appropriate bandwidth for lower-level videoconferencing), support for local Frame Relay options, traffic aggregation, and high-speed residential service.

M/SDSL

M/SDSL is a descendent of SDSL; it supports changing operating line rates of the transceiver, and thus, the operating distance of the transceiver.

It involves a single twisted copper pair, which can be run up to 5.5 miles (8.9 kilometers), and it provides symmetrical, full-duplex service. M/SDSL offers eight variable line rates, ranging from 64Kbps to 2Mbps. At 5.5 miles (8.9 kilometers), the data rate supported is 64Kbps or 128Kbps; 2Mbps can be enjoyed at distances of 2.8 miles (4.5 kilometers). M/SDSL is designed to provide an autorate plug-and-play configuration, which means it adjusts automatically to the operating distance and line conditions.

ADSL

ADSL was initially introduced in 1993, with the principal driver being the much-anticipated deployment of video-on-demand. However, because of some early issues with video servers, including storage capacity and processing power, video-on-demand was largely abandoned. ADSL has now been identified as the perfect solution for Internet access.

There are two ADSL standards: ADSL-1 and ADSL-2. In the North American and T-carrier countries, ADSL-1 provides 1.5Mbps downstream, and in countries that follow E-carrier, it provides 2Mbps downstream and an upstream channel of up to 64Kbps in both North American and European standards. The distance limitations of ADSL-1 vary depending on the gauge of the wire used, and the range is 2.8 to 3.5 miles (4.5 to 5.5 kilometers).

ADSL-2 is what most of us would really like to get, but there's very little of it in commercial deployment. In T-carrier countries, ADSL-2 provides 6Mbps downstream, and for countries that observe the ITU standards, it provides 8Mbps downstream. ADSL-2 is bidirectional, and the upstream channel provides a range of 640Kbps to 800Kbps. Despite the fact that ADSL-2 is asymmetrical, it would provide sufficient bandwidth in the return channel to support videoconferencing.

As with ADSL-1, the distance ADSL-2 can cover also depends on the gauge of the wire, but it is roughly 1.7 to 2 miles (2.8 to 3.5 kilometers).

ADSL is standardized under ITU G.992.1 and ANSI T1.413, Issue 2. ADSL allows for simultaneous voice and Internet traffic on the same twisted-pair that used to be your phone line. It reserves the bottom 4KHz of spectrum for the voice traffic; filters (known as *splitters*) are used at each end of the copper pair to split the frequency bands. The lower frequencies are sent to the local exchange to switch the voice traffic. The higher frequencies are sent to the DSL modems, and you are generally connected over a packet-switched backbone to your ISP.

Two different modulation schemes are used in ADSL modems—Carrierless Amplitude and Phase Modulation (CAP) and Discrete Multitone Technology (DMT)—which contribute to interoperability problems. CAP relies on the Quadrature Amplitude Modulation (QAM) technique. Its adapters are less expensive than DMT adapters, but CAP is more susceptible to interference. CAP is a single-carrier modulation scheme whereby the bits are spread across the entire frequency spectrum of the twisted-pair. Other devices in the environment (such as CB radios and ham radios) can cause interference, so if those devices are operating while you're transporting information over a CAP-based DSL line, you might experience static on your voice call or corruption in your data bits. The better technique is DMT, which is standardized by ANSI, ETSI, and the ITU. DMT is a multicarrier technique, and its spectrum is divided into 256 4KHz carriers. Variable numbers of bits are put on each carrier, and the portions of the frequency band that suffer interference from other devices don't have any bits put onto them. The result is improved performance. Compared to CAP, DMT is less prone to interference, can carry data over a longer distance, and is marginally more expensive. DMT is the preferred modulation scheme for DSL, but depending on when commitments were made and when rollouts began, some network operators still rely on CAP (for example, in the United States, Qwest ADSL services are CAP based).

Figure 13.2 shows an example of an ADSL environment. At the residence is a splitter that is splitting off the plain old telephone service (POTS) to the telephone instrument, using the bottom 4KHz of spectrum on the twisted-pair; the remainder of the line is left for the ADSL modem and the data communications. At the top of the figure is a business environment that may also be making use of a DSL line to carry the voice and data traffic, on an integrated basis.

In Figure 13.2, numerous DSL lines come in from residential and business premises. Their first point of termination is the DSLAM, which then splits the voice and data traffic, sending the voice traffic through traditional local exchanges onto the PSTN and sending the data traffic through packet-switched backbones onto the appropriate ISP or corporate network. The DSLAMs also convert the DSL traffic into ATM cells, to pass over a backbone that has ATM deployed in the core. DSLAMs are designed to concentrate hundreds of DSL access lines onto ATM or IP

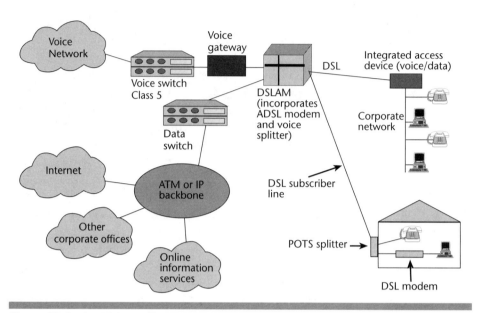

Figure 13.2   An ADSL configuration

trunks and then route them to the ISP. The DSLAMs aggregate dedicated DSL pipes up to the routers or multiservice edge switches. They combine ADSL bit coding and ATM cell switching, and they allow ATM demarcation points to be at the local exchange or at the customer premises.

ADSL Lite and ADSL Heavy

There are variations of ADSL called ADSL Lite and ADSL Heavy.

The Universal ADSL Working Group was established to develop a lower-speed, lower-cost consumer version of ADSL, referred to as splitterless DSL. A range of equipment manufacturers and carriers banded together to provide more strength to the DSL standard, and this standard began to be known as G.Lite, or ADSL Lite. ADSL Lite supports downstream rates of up to 1.5Mbps and upstream rates up to 512Kbps. It can be deployed over distances up to 4.5 miles (7.5 kilometers), depending on the quality of the copper plant.

A benefit associated with ADSL Lite is that no "truck rolls"—that is, physical visits to the home (which cost about US$200 per dispatch)—are required to install the splitters. In reality, however, oftentimes a truck roll is still required for actions such as installing microfilters, which are used between wall jacks and the phones to equalize impedance. As current flows through a wire, a resisting force, called *impedance*, slows it down. In a stable circuit, impedance stays constant and can be dealt with easily. However, because home telephone systems are dynamic—phones continually go on and off hook—the impedance is constantly changing. Shifting impedance disrupts data, and in the absence of a splitter, data is on the same wire as the phone traffic. Basically, installing microfilters helps to facilitate better performance of data.

Reduced powering and computer processing needs are additional benefits of ADSL Lite. Some ADSL Lite modems borrow a portion of their processing power from the host PC's CPU, with the aim of reducing the modem cost. Because ADSL Lite operates at lower rates, the chipsets use less power, which makes it easier to add these modems into other types of equipment and into local exchange racks. ADSL Lite equipment achieves densities four to eight times greater than those of full-rate ADSL, which could become a big issue in achieving high penetration rates in the residential market. The industry is trying to standardize on a single line-coding scheme, G.DMT. However, ADSL Lite may never quite materialize because there is now an equivalent standard, G.Heavy, which is called ADSL Heavy.

ADSL Heavy is a full-rate splitterless system that is now becoming available. ADSL Heavy can support 8Mbps downstream and up to 1Mbps upstream. ADSL Heavy platforms are either available or in development from Alcatel, 3Com, 3Wire, Orckit Communications, and Westell Technologies, and systems are being tested or deployed by Belgacom, Bell South, SBC Communications, Verizon, and Telecom Italia.

Applications of ADSL

The main applications of ADSL are in support of Internet access and remote LAN access. However, Voice over DSL (VoDSL) presents potential opportunities, as does DSL bonding, which is an elegant way to increase bandwidth. The jump from T-1/T-3 to E-1/E-3—from 1.5Mbps to 45Mbps—is rather large. DSL bonding enables you to link together several DSL lines to configure bandwidth between the T-1/T-3 and E-1/E-3 rates. The newest emerging application of ADSL is video-on-demand.

RADSL

RADSL adapts the data rates dynamically, based on changes in line conditions. It can therefore operate over a wide range of loop lengths and conditions, up to a maximum of 3.5 miles (5.5 kilometers). It can also operate with either symmetrical or asymmetrical send and receive channels. The downstream rates range from 600Kbps to 7Mbps, and the upstream rates range from 128Kbps to 1Mbps. Most RADSL devices rely on DMT encoding.

VDSL

VDSL is everyone's dream medium. It relies on a single twisted copper pair, but it operates over extremely short distances. The loop length range is just 1,000 to

VoDSL and Video over DSL

VoDSL is being positioned as the next great thing, particularly for small businesses. One of the most lucrative business lines for a telco is leased lines—the T-1s and E-1s (remember that T-1s offer 1.5Mbps and E-1s offer 2Mbps)—which normally have high pricetags. In the United States, a customer easily pays in the range of US$1,000 to US$1,500 per month for a T-1 access line, and outside the United States the costs of leased lines are even higher. The idea with DSL services is to provide the service to the residential users at a price point that's palatable, which is somewhere in the range of US$50 to US$80 per month. So the telcos had to stop and think. They were afraid they were going to cannibalize their leased-lines business, which is extremely lucrative, by providing the same service offering and same data rates for a fraction of the cost. They backed off to reevaluate their business plans, and they decided that perhaps the best application and marketing for DSL would be for business applications. They decided to let cable modems take the residences because they figured that where the money lies is with the businesses, and so they positioned VoDSL for the business market. Using a single VoDSL connection, service providers would be able to deliver high-speed data access and up to 16 telephone lines. The best target group for this is businesses with 20 to 49 employees. The customer needs an integrated access device that enables the combination of voice and data traffic onto the single DSL line.

Video over DSL is now starting to receive quite a bit of attention as well. DSL was originally developed as a way for the telcos to take on the cable companies, by transporting digitized video over copper wires. The early plans were originally abandoned because of difficulties with server technology, because it was the early days, and because of cost. Telcos are again on a quest to compete with cable companies, by delivering multichannel video to customers and offering bundled packages. Content is the most critical element of success here, but it is leading toward a trend of using Video over DSL, currently ADSL in particular. (VDSL is the preferred technique, but it is still a very early technology and extremely limited in terms of distance. So ADSL is a more appropriate platform for accessing more subscribers.) Early Video over DSL providers include a venture between Blockbuster-Enron, Intertainer, MeTV Network, Pace MicroTechnology, Thirdspace (which is a joint venture between Alcatel and Oracle), and uniView Technologies Corporation. Watch for developments in Video over DSL in the coming year or so, as there is bound to be quite a bit of attention focused there.

5,000 feet (300 to 1,500 meters). At the higher distance, VDSL provides 13Mbps downstream and maybe 1.5Mbps upstream, and at the lower distance, it might be capable of providing up to 52Mbps downstream and around 2.3Mbps upstream.

VDSL is a very high-capacity technology, and its performance degrades rapidly over distances, so it's really meant to be almost a sister technology to fiber-to-the-curb (FTTC), which is discussed later in this chapter, going the very short distance from the curb to the home. (Or in the case of fiber-to-the-building [FTTB] with a multiunit dwelling, VDSL could be run over twisted-pair from the building to each apartment.)

The key applications for VDSL are the next generation of TV—high-definition TV (HDTV), digital TV (DTV), and forms of interactive multimedia Internet access. (See Chapter 10 for more on TV standards.)

VDSL is standardized under the working title ITU G.vdsl, and numerous companies are developing it. Standards efforts are under way in various bodies, including ANSI, the ADSL Forum, the ATM Forum, and the Digital Audio Video Council (DAVIC). Ultimately, the goal of VDSL is to provide less power dissipation, lower costs, and much higher data rates than ADSL provides. VDSL should begin playing a major role within the next three years.

■ HFC

This section covers HFC arrangements, the use of cable modems, and the future of IP telephony over cable. HFC supports a wide range of services, including traditional telephony, broadcast video, and interactive broadband services. It involves the use of fiber in the backbone and in the access network. The fiber termination point (that is, the neighborhood node) can support anywhere from 200 to 2,000 homes, with 200 to 500 homes being the norm. From that neighborhood node, coax (normally 750MHz or 1,000MHz) is run to the home, in a two-way subsplit system.

In countries in which there is a history of cable TV, the cable plants have traditionally operated in one direction, for the broadcast of video programming. To handle a two-way infrastructure, they must be upgraded, and the cost of upgrading is about US$200 to US$600 per customer; companies starting from scratch may have to invest two to three times this amount. Over the past few years, this type of upgrading has been occurring in the existing cable TV infrastructure in the United States. Countries such as the Benelux countries, where there's also a rich history of cable, have also been in upgrade mode. In other parts of the world, new systems are going in with digital two-way capabilities, to support today's interactive services environment.

Figure 13.3 shows the topology of an HFC network. This figure shows a cable TV operator, and on the left side are the headends (that is, where the information is being broadcast from). Increasingly, those headends are tied together by fiber in the backbone. The cable TV operators have also made improvements in the performance of their networks, as well as the costs associated with operating them, by moving away from using coax in the backbone to using a fiber-based backbone. The backbones feed into the neighborhood nodes, or the optical nodes (that is, the access point), and from that point coax goes out to the homes. You can see in this figure that HFC has a shared infrastructure, which is one of the drawbacks of HFC.

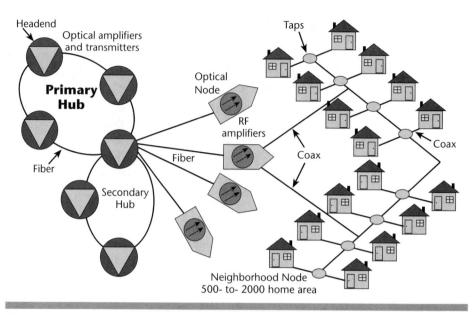

Figure 13.3 The topology of an HFC network

HFC Architectures

The HFC architecture uses a bus topology, meaning that it's a shared access architecture. (Chapter 8, "Local Area Networking," describes bus and other LAN topologies.) It makes use of Frequency Division Multiplexing, to derive individual channels—some of which are dedicated to the support of telephony services, others of which are reserved for analog TV, and still others of which are reserved for future interactive broadband services. There is a bit of a hostile environment represented by this multiple-access coax system, in that the point at which the coax interfaces to TVs or set-top boxes is a point at which noise can be accumulated. The points where the coax connects into set-top boxes or cable-ready TV sets tend to collect noise, so the cable picks up extraneous noise from vacuum cleaners or hair dryers. If every household on the network is running a hair dryer at 6:30 AM, the upstream paths are subjected to this noise, and there will be some performance degradations. Extra signal processing must therefore be added to overcome the impairment in the return channel.

The major concerns with HFC include security, privacy, reliability, and return-path issues, particularly in support of telephony. With twisted-pair, we have a private line to the local exchange. Using a shared coax system to support telephony could raise some privacy issues, so encryption of voice conversations may become very important. Also, HFC faces bandwidth constraints; as more and more homes within the neighborhood make use of their Internet access channel, everyone's downloads and bandwidth become minimized. The problem now surfacing is that cable modems have caught on and there are more subscribers to such services. Whereas a year ago people were experiencing extremely rapid downloads with cable modems, things seem to be slowing down now, which means that more users are subscribing to the services and sharing the facility, which results in lower performance for everyone. Subdividing the nodes, however, can help to alleviate bandwidth constraints, and it can also help to reduce ingress noise. If the service provider continues to subnet, performance can be kept high for the subscribers.

Cable Modems

A cable modem is needed to support high-speed data access over HFC by using the cable TV infrastructure. Cable modems function like special-purpose routers, linking the cable network's Layer 3 to another network or device. Generally this requires an external box with cable and Ethernet connections. Figure 13.4 illustrates cable modem connectivity. On the left side of the figure is a single neighborhood with users attaching to the shared coax system via their cable modems. These various coax trunks, then, come into the headend facility, where they terminate on a cable modem termination system (CMTS). The CMTSs are linked together by accessing a common Ethernet hub, which, in turn, feeds into the IP router, which then develops the optimum path to take over an optical backbone onto the ISP.

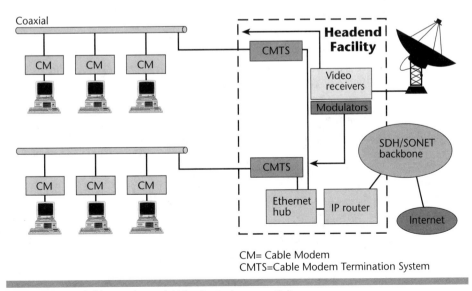

Figure 13.4 Cable modems: LAN-oriented connectivity

CMTS functions include providing QoS, allocating bandwidth, classifying packets, policing packets for Type of Service (ToS) fields, adjusting the ToS fields as needed, performing traffic shaping, forwarding packets, converting and classifying QoS parameters, handling signaling and reserving of backbone QoS, and recording call resource usage.

Cable modems provide downstream data rates of up to 36Mbps, and the downstream rates are generally supported within the frequency band of 42MHz to 750MHz. The downstream channel depends on the QAM technique, because this is what gives it the most bits per second and, hence, the fastest data rates downstream, where rapid downloads are important. Upstream data rates are up to 10Mbps, and the upstream direction operates in the range of 5MHz to 40MHz. As mentioned earlier, this portion of the frequency band is especially subject to noise interference, so it requires modulation techniques such as Quadrature Phase Shift Keying (QPSK) and QAM 16, which transport fewer bits per second than other techniques but which also provide better noise resistance.

Many standards deal with cable modems. CableLabs is an industry leader in creating cable modem standards. Its Multimedia Cable Network Systems (MCNS) includes Data Over Cable Service Interface Specification (DOCSIS), PacketCable, and OpenCable. DAVIC is working on the Digital Video Broadcasting (DVB) standard for the EuroModem specification, which is a set of standards for digital video broadcasting that is supported by the European Cable Communications Association. (Chapter 10 discusses TV standards in more detail.) Another important standard in this area is IEEE 802.14.

DOCSIS uses either QAM 64 or QAM 256 downstream, up to 36Mbps, and it uses QPSK upstream at 2.5Mbps. (See Chapter 6, "Data Communications Basics," for information on modulation schemes such as QAM.) DOCSIS also involves an Ethernet connection to the PC, so data is transferred by using TCP/IP encapsulated in Ethernet frames between the cable modem and headend. DOCSIS includes a baseline privacy specification as well. It relies on the use of both the 40- and 56-bit versions of DES. (See Chapter 11, "Next-Generation Network Services," for more information on security.) DOCSIS is recognized by the ITU specifications and will be formalized under J112.X (where X denotes the region).

At this point CableLabs has certified about 100 modems from more than 36 companies as being DOCSIS 1.0 compliant, and it has qualified CMTSs from 8 vendors as being DOCSIS 1.0 compliant. CableLabs has traditionally focused on data, but DOCSIS 1.1 engineering improvements will facilitate voice. DOCSIS 1.1 was created because of the cable industry's desire for VoIP. DOCSIS 1.1 includes key network technologies, including dynamic QoS, which is very important to VoIP, packet fragmentation, and enhanced security. (QoS is discussed in Chapter 10.) As of mid-2001, no modems or CMTSs had passed the DOCSIS 1.1 certification, but equipment was expected to be certified in 2001. Three types of customer premises products that use DOCSIS 1.1 are expected to emerge: stand-alone cable modems with RJ-11 and Ethernet jacks for both VoIP and Internet-over-cable services; products targeted to the SOHO office market that allow for multiple IP voice and data lines; and Internet appliances (for example, Web tablets) and smart appliances (for example, smart refrigerators).

EuroDOCSIS was created because DOCSIS does not support the European cable standards, which include the 8MHz channels, a 65MHz frequency range for upstream signals, and compliance with Europe's broadcast downstream standard. EuroDOCSIS combines the North American DOCSIS standard with elements of the DVB DAVIC specification that are needed for DOCSIS to work in Europe.

The CableLabs PacketCable 1.0 specification deals with transmitting multifeatured IP phone calls over HFC and allows four independent IP voice channels through a single cable modem.

Another strong standard is the DVB standard advocated by DAVIC. This is the EuroModem specification promoted by the European Cable and Communications Association. It addresses video, audio, data, and voice services, and enables a single multiservice platform that uses ATM as the transport protocol. Standardized as ITU-T J.38 Annex A, it calls for either QAM 64 or QAM 256 downstream, and for QPSK upstream. Some think EuroModem may eventually take as much as 70% of the total European cable modem market. However, interoperability between Euro-Modem and EuroDOCSIS may render the argument moot. At this point EuroDOC-SIS has a major head start over EuroModem. The headway being made with standards, as well as the incredible popularity of cable modems and the advantages of the cable infrastructure, make this a growing market area.

IEEE 802.14 is the Cable TV Media Access Control (MAC) and Physical (PHY) Protocol. It specifies either QAM 64 or QAM 256 downstream, and it specifies QPSK and QAM 16 upstream. For IEEE 802.14, ATM is specified as the MAC from the headend to the cable modems.

Digital Cable TV Devices

Digital cable TV devices present yet another exciting area to watch in the coming years. The goal of the CableLabs OpenCable program is to publish specifications that define digital cable network interfaces, as well as the nature of next-generation cable set-top boxes.

The CableLabs cable modem standard MCNS will be used with OpenCable set-top boxes, with advanced digital video compression circuitry to create terminals that are capable of supporting next-generation video and the entire range of current and future Internet and Web-based applications. The OpenCable effort is seen as the linchpin of the cable industry's digital future. It is processor and operating system independent. Compliant set-tops must allow both high- and low-speed bidirectional

Internet service for both Internet and TV applications, and computer applications must be provided to both the television and the desktop computer through cable. Digital set-top characteristics will include expanded memory, powerful graphics engines, and support for one-way broadcasts (for example, near video-on-demand, Web browsing, Internet e-mail) as well as two-way interactive services (for example, Internet access via TV, high-definition video programming).

Another emerging area for cable TV systems is the cable-based IP telephony environment (see Figure 13.5). Thanks to deregulation and advancements in Class 5 replacement switches and IP telephony, the environment is ripe for cable providers to become competitive local exchange carriers (CLECs) or long-distance carriers. Currently, 90% of cable telephony is supported over circuit-switched networks, and this will likely be the case until late 2001 or 2002. IP telephony over cable, specifically HFC networks, is predicted to grow in the coming years. Circuit-switched telephony services are currently being offered by the likes of AT&T, Cablevision, Comcast, Cox Communications, and MediaOne Group. Operators will be able to offer VoIP or circuit-switched service exclusively or in mixed packages. Keep in mind, though, that VoIP over cable is in early stages of development. (See Chapter 11 for more on VoIP.)

The CableLabs PacketCable working group is leading cable-based IP telephony research efforts. The DOCSIS 1.1 standard addresses real-time applications such as telephony, and it includes critical measures such as dynamic QoS. The key issues in cable-based IP telephony include voice quality and how to guarantee it in terms of

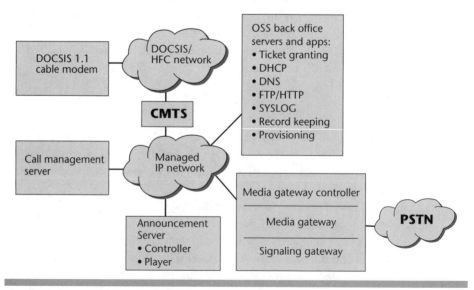

Figure 13.5 Cable-based IP telephony

latency, fidelity, jitter, packet loss, and reliability at the customer end. Other issues are legacy signaling support, data security, scalability, and feature deployment at the service provider's end. Finally, there are a number of provider-specific issues, such as implementation of systems for PSTN gateways and gatekeepers, provisioning, billing, and network maintenance. Implementation of DOCSIS standards will be vital. DOCSIS 1.1 deals with enabling time-sensitive voice and multimedia packets to share in HFC networks with timing-insensitive pure data packets. DOCSIS 1.1 enables a node to recognize a nondata packet and switch to it instantaneously from whatever data packet it is working on. It requires a CMTS at the edge of the cable access network and a DOCSIS 1.1-compliant cable modem at the customer premise. Edge cable CMTSs need the intelligence to isolate traffic flows and to apply policy-based QoS treatments in real-time. Traffic flows need to be isolated by service provider, application, and subscriber so that during times of congestion, flows within the service-level agreement (SLA) are maintained and flows that exceed the SLA are discarded first. Operators then map the DOCSIS-based flows to IP specs such as DiffServ and MPLS, which are discussed in Chapter 10, to manage the handoff to the core network.

Currently, trials for cable-based IP telephony are being conducted by Lucent and High Speed Access Group; Nortel Networks and Adelphia; AT&T, which is working with both Lucent and Motorola; Scientific Atlanta, which is partnering with Net2Phone and Cox Communications; Time-Warner; and Samsung and Videotron in Canada. Cable-based IP telephony considerations include technical architecture, achieving PSTN-level reliability (that is, five nines, or 99.999%), being capable of accommodating the same PSTN-level feature sets, and regulatory issues. Operators face challenges such as how to provide detailed, sophisticated, end-to-end SLAs; how to adjust to the need to do maintenance, which will become more critical; and how to evolve from being broadband video providers to being mission-critical service providers. Stay tuned for developments in the cable-based IP telephony environment in the next couple years.

Fiber

As you've read many times in this book, fiber is an area of rapid evolution. Few other media options promise to offer the capacities of fiber. Where its deployment is possible, fiber is the clear-cut best solution. Fiber can be used on its own or in conjunction with twisted-pair, coax, and wireless to provide broadband access. FTTC is a solution in which fiber is run very close to the home—to the curb—and coax runs from the curb to the home. In addition, all-fiber networks can be used to deliver broadband services. Fiber to the home (FTTH) goes a step further than FTTC—it brings fiber into the residence. In addition, a new generation of technologies, called *passive optical networks* (PONs), promises to dramatically reduce the cost of deploying FTTH.

FTTC

FTTC is also known as *Switched Digital Video* and *Switched Digital Broadband*. In deploying FTTC, the service provider has looked to the future—the capability to support the time-sensitive and high-capacity requirements of interactive multimedia, interactive television, and all the other advanced applications that involve the senses. The FTTC architecture involves laying fiber that offers approximately OC-3 (that is, 155Mbps) bidirectionally from the local exchange to the host digital terminal (HDT). The HDT is involved with traffic supervision and maintenance functions over a number of downstream optical network units (ONUs), also called optical network terminations, which are where the optical-to-electrical conversion takes place. From the HDT to the ONU the downstream rates are up to 52Mbps and the upstream rates are up to 20Mbps. Each ONU serves from 4 homes to 60 homes, and twisted-pair (VDSL or another member of the DSL family) or one of the other media types runs from the ONU to the home.

In provisioning FTTC, some service providers initially laid coax as an underlay because currently the vast majority of content is old analog film archives. In order to run this rich history of entertainment over the digital FTTC network, it is necessary to digitize all that content in order to store it on digital video servers, deliver it digitally over transport, and, at the customer's premise, have digital set-tops that undigitize and decompress the video for viewing over today's sets. In those early stages of digital interactive content, it seemed reasonable to provide coax, with the intention of delivering entertainment or television services and with the thought that if the content becomes digitized to run on an integrated basis over the fiber, that coax could continue to be used for purposes of carrying power. Therefore, some FTTC deployments actually have a second wire, the coax.

The topology of FTTC is a switched star, which means there are dedicated point-to-point connections. It is not a shared infrastructure, so what bandwidth you have is yours and yours only; you have the privacy of having a dedicated link. FTTC security is best addressed with mechanisms that involve encryption, authentication, and public key exchange, but remember that it is more difficult for someone to tap into fiber than to tap into other media. Of course, it can be done, but at great expense, so the often-spoken-of security benefits associated with fiber largely address the difficulty of tapping into the fiber and the improved capability to detect that intrusion (with proper test equipment, you can see when there is a leak in the fiber).

The modulation approach used to integrate the voice, data, and video streams is Time Division Multiplexing (TDM), and the TDM signals are digitally transported over the fiber, backed by ATM-based switching. Remember that ATM pro-

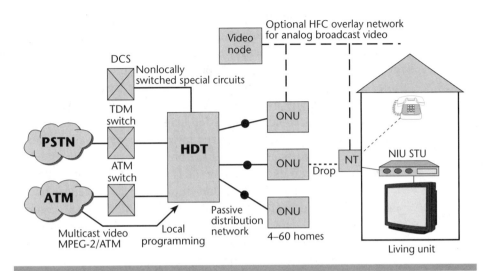

Figure 13.6   An FTTC configuration

vides opportunities for traffic engineering and management and the administration of QoS, which are critical for providing high-quality network services and for being able to meet the SLAs that all providers must have with customers.

Figure 13.6 illustrates an FTTC configuration. At the home, the network termination (NT) splits and controls signals so that the appropriate voice signals go to the telephones, the video programming goes to the set-top boxes, and Internet access is enabled at the PC. A twisted-pair runs to the ONU, and in some cases, a coaxial cable takes a different path onto the headend of the cable TV provider. From the ONU, fibers converge on the HDT, which manages the group of ONUs. From that HDT, private-line traffic can go over the digital cross-connect system (DCS), voice traffic can be switched through the traditional Class 5 offices onto the circuit-switched PSTN, and high-speed multimedia (QoS-sensitive traffic) can go through the ATM switches to the ATM backbone.

The modulation scheme for FTTC was developed by Bellcore (which is now Telcordia) and is standardized by both the ITU and DAVIC. As many as 1,400 channels are possible in this architecture. Why would you want 1,400 channels, when surfing through 50 can present a problem? In public forums worldwide—be they sporting stadiums, concert halls, opera houses, or outdoor venues—video cameras are being placed so that you can participate remotely in more and more functions and also so that you can control your viewing angle. Perhaps you are watching a football game, but you're not interested in the player that the film crew is filming. Instead, you want to zoom in for a better look at the team's mascot. With cameras strategically positioned throughout the stadium, you would be able to take on whatever viewing angle you wanted, but each angle would require its own individual channel. So the availability of thousands of channels has to do with the ultimate control that interactive TV promises. It's not about video-on-demand and getting programming when you want and the ability to stop it; it's about being able to control what you see when you see it, in what language you see it, and who is in it. For example, you might want to watch *Gone With the Wind,* but you don't want to see it with Clark Gable and Vivien Leigh. You would like to see it with Mel Gibson and Joan Chan. In the digitized interactive environment, you would go to the digital thespian bank and deposit the bits you want into the film. You could apply the soundtrack you like and apply the language that's most suitable.

The multichannel FTTC architecture promises to deliver on much more than just broadband access for Web surfing. It allows the ultimate control over the viewing environment. However, as mentioned earlier, it does require that all media streams be digitized, so you need digital video servers at the system headend and digital set-top boxes at the subscriber end. Consequently, this environment has a higher per-subscriber cost than does the simpler HFC environment. But it offers the promise of easier upgrading to interactive broadband, full-service networks; in such an environment, carriers would be better prepared to offer a multitude of new revenue-generating services over the single integrated platform. So, in many ways, FTTC is a solid solution, but it depends to a great extent on the last 1,000 feet (300 meters) being a copper-pair technology that can sustain the data rates to support the applications we're discussing. Of course, this piece of the puzzle is still under development.

FTTH

FTTH is an all-fiber option that provides a minimum of 155Mbps in both directions. As shown in Figure 13.7, it involves fiber from the service node to the optical splitter. From the optical splitter, multiple fibers fan out to terminate on single-home ONUs. So, similarly to FTTC, FTTH is a point-to-point architecture with a dedicated connection from the home to the network, which offers secure transmissions by virtue of the fact that it's challenging to intercept activity on the fiber network. This architecture is definitely suited for broadband service applications and is an integral part of the broadband future we are preparing for.

FTTH also provides a very robust outside plant, meaning extremely low maintenance cost over the lifetime of the system. For many operators of traditional wireline networks, 25% of the cost of operating the network goes to maintenance. Fiber-based networks require considerably less maintenance than do traditional networks, so there are long-term operational savings associated with fiber networks. This is one reason why fiber is such a favored wireline solution. In some parts of the world, fiber already justifies itself economically. However, the cost of deploying FTTH is still quite high (around US$2,500 to US$3,000 per subscriber),

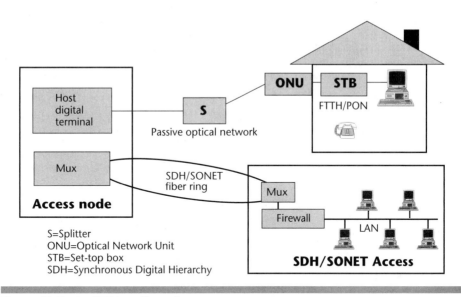

Figure 13.7 An FTTH configuration

but the cost is predicted to drop to US$1,700 or less in the next year or so, and then fiber will begin to compete effectively with some of the other traditional wireline options, such as DSL and HFC. These figures assume new installations, where a big part of this cost is in the construction. This is always the issue with wireline: 80% of the cost of delivering the service is in the construction effort. In wireless, the situation is reversed—the construction is only 20% of the cost. As the cost of deploying fiber drops, FTTH will become an increasingly attractive solution because of the bandwidth and the low noise that it offers.

PONs

The newest fiber option is the PON (see Figure 13.8). A PON allows multiple buildings to share one access line. PONs bundle together multiple wavelengths—up to 32 wavelengths currently—and carry them over a single access line from the carrier's local exchange to a manhole, called a controlled environmental vault (CEV), that is close to a group of customer sites. From the CEV, the wavelengths are broken out, and each one is steered into a different short length of fiber to an individual site. From the customer to the local exchange, each site is given a specific time slot to transmit, using a polling scheme.

A key benefit of PONs is that they extend the use of fiber to business customers. Also, provisioning PONs is comparatively easy because multiple fiber connections can be provisioned from a single connection in one location. PONs also offer bandwidth

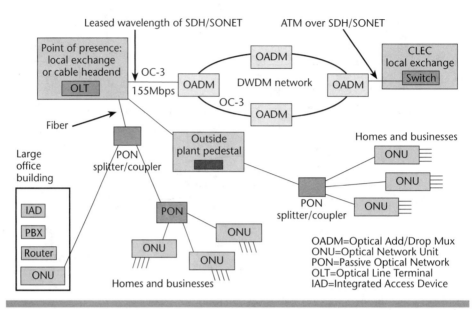

Figure 13.8 A PON configuration

flexibility. Whereas SDH/SONET provides fairly rigid rates, resulting in costly upgrades, PONs allow bandwidth to be allocated quickly. Another benefit of PONs is that they consolidate leased lines. Furthermore, PONs can be configured to give exact increments of bandwidth as needed. The low deployment cost is a big incentive to using PONs and makes them a very attractive alternative to xDSL.

A key issue involved with PONs is that it's a shared-media environment. The upstream bandwidth is divided among a number of users—that is, the fibers that are terminated by ONUs at the customer premises. For example, on a 155Mbps PON link with four splits, each subscriber receives 38.75Mbps, and the more customers you add, the less bandwidth each customer receives. PONs are also subject to distance limitations: According to the Full Service Access Network (FSAN) Coalition specifications, PONs have a theoretical distance limitation of about 12 miles (20 kilometers). The actual distance depends on the power of the laser used to transmit the light and the reduction in power that the light suffers along the way. There is a tradeoff between distance, bandwidth, and the number of sites supported by a single access line into the optical line termination (OLT).

The OLT is a special switch that has a nonblocking architecture. Blocking probability is an important measure of network adequacy. A nonblocking switch ensures that there is always a serving trunk available for each station, so no blocking or contention occurs. The OLT sends traffic downstream to subscribers and handles the upstream traffic as well. Downstream and upstream traffic use different frequencies on the same fiber to avoid interference. Traffic is typically sent in both directions at 155Mbps, although emerging products offer 622Mbps in both directions. Downstream, the OLT either generates light signals on its own or takes SDH/SONET signals from colocated SDH/SONET cross-connects and broadcasts this traffic through one or more outgoing subscriber ports. Upstream, the OLT aggregates traffic from multiple customer sites and uses TDM to ensure that each transmission is sent back to the local exchange over one fiber strand, without interference.

The outside plant includes passive optical splitters placed inside the CEVs. As the light that is broadcast from the OLT hits the splitter, it is deflected onto multiple fiber connections. *Passive* means the splitters don't need any power: They work like a prism, splitting light into the colors of the rainbow, so there is nothing to wear out or to go wrong. Today, splitters feature 2 to 32 branches, and they can be positioned to create PON star, ring, or tree configurations. PON networks terminate on ONUs, whose main function is to take the light coming from the passive splitters, convert it to a specific type of bandwidth—such as 10Mbps or 100Mbps Ethernet, ATM, or T-1/E-1 voice and data—and then to pass it on to routers, PBXs, switches, and other enterprise networking equipment. ONUs can be installed at the customer's data center site, in wiring closets, or in outside plant locations, where the subscribers can connect to the PON via DSL services. This enables carriers to offer PON service under existing DSL tariffs and gives customers the benefit of optical networking without installing new fiber.

PON standards emerged from the FSAN Coalition, which formed in 1995. The coalition decided to use ATM over a simple physical network, with a minimum of moving parts. By 1999 the ITU-T had approved specifications G.983.1 and G.983.2. Current trials of commercial PON equipment include projects sponsored by NTT in Japan; Bell Atlantic, Bell South, Comcast, and SBC in the United States; and Singapore Telecom.

The key issue with PONs is the availability of fiber. As mentioned in Chapter 3, there is a shortage of fiber in access networks. PONs also face distance limitations: Because they are passive—meaning there is no electrical amplification or regeneration of light signals—their distance is limited. Again, shared-media issues affect the actual rates that customers can achieve. Finally, product availability is a problem at this point. But we're still in early stages with PONs, and as the problems are worked out, PONs will be deployed more and more, and the revenue from PON products is expected to skyrocket over the next few years.

■ Wireless Broadband Access Media

Broadband wireless access is increasingly an exciting option, especially because cable modems and DSL aren't available as easily or as widely as we would like. Broadband wireless access provides the opportunity to make use of Direct Broadcast Satellite

(DBS), Multichannel Multipoint Distribution Services (MMDS), Local Multipoint Distribution Service (LMDS), Free Space Optics, and various unlicensed bands, so wireless increasingly offers more options that can operate in a wider range of footprints.

More than 50 million wireless local loops were deployed globally by the end of 1999, and it is likely that within the next couple years, more than half of the new fixed phone lines installed worldwide each year will be wireless. Fixed wireless is a strong contender to fill the gap where existing wiring is not up to the job or where there's no wiring at all. For example, about one in five people in the United States lives in an area that is too remote to receive any type of fast wireline access to the Internet, and this is also the situation in vast parts of Asia-Pacific, Latin America, Europe, and Africa. Furthermore, millions of people work in modest industrial parks that do not have fast access and that are unable to receive DSL connections.

The cost of radio links has been halving every seven years, and the data capacity of these links has been doubling every three years. These factors combined mean that the cost-to-capacity ratio in wireless communications has been dropping by 50% about every two years. As mentioned earlier in the chapter, for wireless links, the construction costs account for approximately 20% of the total installation cost, and equipment accounts for the other 80%.

Wireless systems (see Figure 13.9) often operate in a point-to-multipoint mode. The antenna communicates with several different clients' antennas, usually installed within a well-defined region. Because the air is a shared medium, like

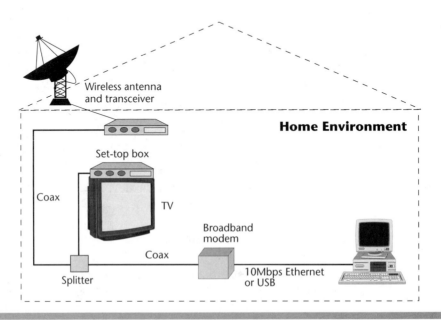

Figure 13.9 A broadband wireless configuration inside a home

cable, the maximum transmission rate that can be provided to any one client decreases as more clients are served. Clients that need the greatest bit rate obtainable from a system (for example, an ISP) may find it advisable to arrange for a point-to-point system.

DBS

One of the first approaches to broadband wireless for Internet access includes the use of DBS, also called Direct to Home (DTH), which uses very-small-aperture terminal (VSAT) technology. (VSATs are discussed in more detail in Chapter 3.) VSATs provide more than 150 digital channels when used in this DBS environment, and DBS was actually the first DTV system to be introduced. As discussed earlier in this chapter, there's a great benefit to offering a large number of channels; besides offering the consumer variety in programming, large numbers of channels means that more channels can be used to deliver advertising content. A great number of advertising dollars were diverted away from cable TV providers when DBS companies came along, because advertisers could reach a wider audience over a larger number of channels to distribute their message.

DBS requires a set-top box that is digital and relies on MPEG-2 as the video compression–decompression scheme (see Figure 13.10). The DBS satellites currently in use are Ku-band systems that operate one-way, providing high-speed downstream service. This means the user must rely on the telephone line or cable connection as the return channel. The new DBS systems that are being planned

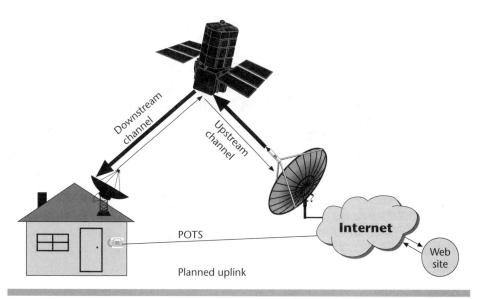

Figure 13.10 DBS

will include Ka-band satellites and will support two-way high-speed data flows. (The frequency allocations for satellite are described in Chapter 3.)

There are approximately 20 million DBS subscribers worldwide today, but they subscribe predominantly for television, and watching two different channels on different devices requires two receivers. So the costs increase steeply as you enable multiparty viewing across different platforms in the home. A number of companies are planning to offer Internet access over two-way satellite connections, including AOL (via its US$1.5 billion stake in Hughes Electronics), Wild Blue, Globalstar, and Star Band (which is a combined effort of Gilat Satellite Networks, Microsoft, Echostar, and ING Furman Selz). More and more people are looking forward to enjoying high-speed Internet access through satellite facilities, particularly in situations where DSL or cable modems are a far cry from current reality.

MMDS

MMDS was first licensed in the 1970s, when it was called Multipoint Distribution Services and was licensed to broadcast one-way 6MHz television channels (see Figure 13.11). In 1996 the U.S. Federal Communications Commission (FCC) expanded the band to cover its present range and to allow for multichannel services. Licensees of these channels can compete directly with cable TV providers, and for this reason, MMDS is sometimes referred to as wireless cable. In 1998 the

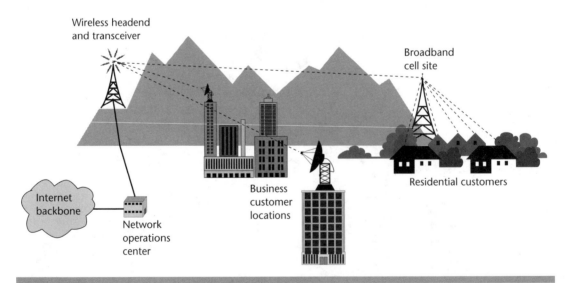

Figure 13.11 MMDS

FCC permitted MMDS providers to offer interactive two-way services for the Internet, requiring upgrades to bidirectional systems.

Today, there are some five million MMDS customers in 90 nations, but as with DBS, they mostly receive just TV service. About one million of these customers receive services from 250 providers in the United States alone. More than three million subscribers to the service in Budapest are also using it for access to the Internet.

MMDS is a digital system that involves terrestrial line-of-sight microwave. It operates in the 2GHz to 3GHz range, and it has a wide coverage area of about 35 miles (55 kilometers). Data throughput ranges from 128Kbps to 10Mbps. Because MMDS is digital, it can support more channels than the analog system, and MMDS supports upward of 150 digital channels. It requires a digital set-top that incorporates MPEG-2 for video compression and decompression. Its long reach and throughput rates make it a good match for residential and rural applications.

A key issue regarding MMDS is regulation. Wide deployment of MMDS service cannot begin until the licensing process is complete. Another issue is that MMDS parts are expensive—it's still a challenge to get price points low enough to compete. It costs around US$1,000 to US$2,000 to install a two-way radio. (In the United States, WorldCom, Sprint, and Pacific Bell have bought rights to offer MMDS.) The biggest problem with MMDS, though, is maintaining line of sight, which is required between the base stations and the subscriber or remote units. Extra transmitters and antennas are needed to overcome obstructions, such as trees and precipitation (remember from Chapter 3 that microwave is very susceptible to distortions caused by moisture), and multipath fading can also cause problems.

Nonlinear deployment is an important concept with MMDS. One emerging technique, Orthogonal Frequency Division Multiplexing (OFDM), promises to improve capacity and performance of wireless systems, including MMDS. OFDM enables more data to be transmitted at higher speeds than over traditional networks, and the signal is strong enough to transmit through some obstacles. By using OFDM, transmitted data is spread over a set of individual frequencies that span a very broad range and is therefore impervious to impairments such as multipath fading and interference. Cisco uses its own version of ODFM that supports up to 22Mbps downstream over a 6MHz channel and up to 18Mbps upstream. As nonlinear deployment options begin to appear, MMDS will be capable of attaining better performance, even in challenging locations and conditions. Another aspect of nonlinear deployment is adaptive antenna techniques. By combining the outputs from multiple antennas, by using sophisticated algorithms, individual beams can be formed at the base station for each user. The algorithms also form nulls in the direction of interferers, further limiting system interference. Because the energy is concentrated into beams, the signal propagates far more effectively than it would if it were radiated in an omnidirectional manner. The end result is that the link budget is increased, further improving cell radius, signal robustness, and the capability to support nonline-of-sight wireless links.

LMDS

LMDS is also known as millimeter, or microwave, technology, and it involves line-of-sight microwave (see Figure 13.12). (LMDS is referred to as *Multipoint Video Distribution Service [MVDS]* and *broadband wireless* access in Europe.) It operates in a much higher frequency band than does MMDS. LMDS operates in a 1.3GHz allocation that falls somewhere in the 10GHz to 45GHz range, depending on where you are in the world. The United States uses 24GHz, 28GHz, 31GHz, 38GHz, and 39GHz. The United Kingdom uses 10GHz, and the rest of Europe uses 25GHz. Carriers in Asia-Pacific are conducting trials in the 24GHz to 26GHz and 38GHz ranges.

A typical LMDS installation has a central base station with an omnidirectional antenna that serves many residences, each of which has a directional dish aimed at the base station. The throughput is about 1.5Gbps downstream and 200Mbps upstream, over shared media. The architecture involves dividing the area surrounding the central base station into sectors. Each sector gets a particular amount of bandwidth that is shared across the subscribers. LMDS tends to operate over microcells of 0.5 to 3 miles (1 to 5 kilometers), serving 5,000 to 10,000 homes. Systems work best if users are within 2 miles (3.5 kilometers) of the base station. LMDS supports two-way symmetrical switched broadband networking, and an

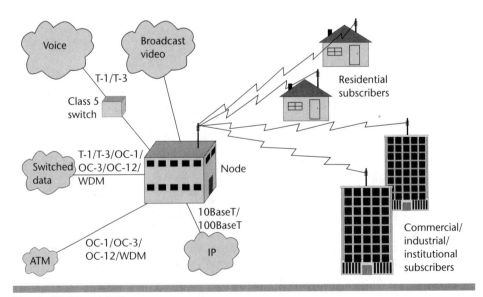

Figure 13.12 LMDS

average system can support around 150 video channels and more than 7,000 64Kbps voice channels.

Some of the key issues with LMDS have to do with licensing and opening up more frequencies for its use, manufacturing issues (radio parts for the higher frequencies are more exacting and more expensive than those for the lower frequencies), rain fade, and a lack of agreement on standards, especially whether LMDS should use Frequency Division Duplexing (FDD) or Time Division Duplexing (TDD). (LMDS, FDD, and TDD are discussed further in Chapter 14, "Wireless Communications.")

LMDS is expected to experience great growth over the next several years because it allows CLECs to offer broadband services to the small- and medium-sized business market much more cost-effectively than can competitors that are banking on fiber networks.

Free Space Optics

Optical wireless, known as Free Space Optics, uses low-powered infrared lasers (see Figure 13.13). There are two categories of Free Space Optics: point-to-point products, which provide high-speed connection between two buildings, and multiple high-speed connections through the air that operate over much shorter distances, either in a point-to-multipoint or meshed architecture. The point-to-point

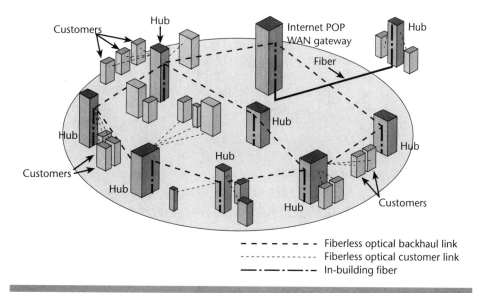

Figure 13.13 Free Space Optics

architectures operate over a range of 1.2 to 2.5 miles (2 to 4 kilometers) and provide throughput of 155Mbps to 10Gbps. The point-to-multipoint architectures operate over a range of 0.5 to 1.2 miles (1 to 2 kilometers) and offer throughput of 155Mbps to 10Gbps. The meshed architectures operate over shorter distances, 650 to 1,500 feet (200 to 450 meters), and offer throughput of around 622Mbps.

The key problem with Free Space Optics is weather, especially fog. Recall from Chapter 3 that as we go up in the electromagnetic spectrum, the wave form becomes smaller, so droplets of moisture can cause interference. It is possible to reduce the impact of bad weather on the link by reducing the range of the link or by deploying redundant (possibly wired) infrastructure. Another problem with Free Space Optics is that buildings actually sway a little bit, so autotracking mechanisms are required, to ensure that the beams stay highly focused on one another.

Another problem can be flying objects, such as birds, which can cause distortion; meshed architecture should be deployed to get better reliability in areas where such flying objects are numerous. However, it has been reported (www.cablefree.co.uk) that birds can in fact see in the infrared section of the EM spectrum and will typically avoid the beam. Nonetheless, it is still possible that they could fly through the beam, and this is likely to disrupt communication for possibly a second or more. But if a reliable protocol such as TCP/IP has been implemented, any lost packets will be retransmitted, making it likely that the overall impact will be negligible from the user's perspective.

Free Space Optics also requires people to take safety precautions. Although the beams involved emit less power than laser pointers, it's wise to be aware that, depending on which frequencies you're operating at, damage can be caused by looking at optical equipment. All persons allowed access should be made aware of the hazardous nature of the laser communication system.

From a market development perspective, there is a strong incentive to get this and other new last-mile broadband access technologies deployed: They potentially decrease the dependence that private network operators and alternative public service providers have on using the incumbents' infrastructure.

Unlicensed Bands

Unlicensed bands can be used to provide broadband access. These bands are known as Industrial, Scientific, and Medical (ISM) radio bands. ISM operates at 900MHz, 2.4GHz, 5.8GHz, and 24GHz in the United States, but spectrum allocations vary around the world. The ITU World Radio Conference defines the world into three regions, and frequency assignments vary between regions (for a complete list see www.itu.int/brterr/faq/ISM.htm). ISM has a range of about 35 miles (55 kilometers) and offers throughput from 128Kbps to 10Mbps over shared media. Traditionally, the lower frequencies have been used for the deployment of wireless LANs.

One benefit of unlicensed bands is that no licenses are required, so there are no up-front costs to obtain a license to use the spectrum in certain bands. But remember that it still may be necessary to obtain a license if that spectrum were to be used to deliver public services. Also, because unlicensed bands operate in the lower frequencies, there is less environmental distortion than with other wireless options. One disadvantage of unlicensed bands is that because the spectrum is unlicensed, interference can occur between providers; this can be a big problem, especially at the lower frequencies.

Several groups are working on standards for unlicensed bands. The IEEE 802.16 Working Group on Broadband Wireless Access Standards is looking into developing standards for unlicensed bands; three of its task groups are working on standards for the bands 10GHz to 66GHz, 2GHz to 11GHz, and 5GHz to 6GHz. The Wireless DSL Consortium wants to develop an open standard that meets the requirements of the marketplace today and that offers a migration path from existing technology to a next-generation standard, perhaps trying to avoid the sorts of problems we're experiencing in planning the move from second-generation digital cellular to third-generation systems, which are discussed in Chapter 14. Another standards group is the OFDM Forum, which was formed by Phillips and Wi-LAN and whose members include Ericsson, Nokia, Samsung, and Sony. This forum wants to foster a single, compatible, global OFDM standard for wireless networks. The forum claims to be vendor-neutral, and it is planning to submit a physical-layer proposal to the 802.16 2–11GHz task group. The Broadband Wireless Internet Forum is another group that's active in this arena, pursuing development of a standard based on Cisco's OFDM technology approach.

■ Emerging Media

New options are beginning to emerge in the broadband access environment, especially outside the United States. HomePNA (Home Phone Networking Alliance), Ethernet local exchange carriers (ELECs), and Powerline Telecommunications (PLT) are three emerging options.

HomePNA

In Korea, where a great amount of broadband access is available, a popular broadband access option is a home area networking technology called HomePNA. HomePNA makes use of the phone wiring in the home to create a LAN. HomePNA can also be used for broadband access in multiple-dwelling units; fiber runs to the building, and then the phone wiring to the apartment units delivers the equivalent of DSL service.

Ethernet-in-the-Loop

Another emerging option is to deploy Ethernet, particularly Gigabit Ethernet and 10Gbps Ethernet, in the local loop. A new service provider category has emerged–the ELEC. Early entrants in this category include Yipes, Telseon, Cogent Communications, Everest Broadband Networks, and Sigma Networks.

PLT

An exciting emerging broadband option is PLT, which is illustrated in Figure 13.14. A patent was recently granted to MediaFusion of Dallas, Texas, which claims to have a technology that would enable up to 4Gbps to be carried over powerline to the home. This option would turn the industry upside-down. The power companies already have dense penetration into nearly every home, so if the PLT option turns out to be viable, the power companies may be able to deliver communication services over the infrastructure that is currently in place.

Some people think that PLT will work, and some believe it will not; companies are beginning to service this space, so we should soon know how well it works. DS2 (Valencia, Spain) produces a chipset that enables high-speed data services to

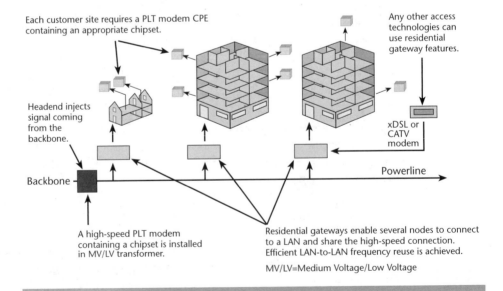

Figure 13.14 PLT

be carried over powerlines at data rates of up to 45Mbps. The proprietary technology can be adapted for use in the LAN or access segments. A high-speed modem (that is, headend), containing the DS2 chipset, is installed in the transformer. Each transformer contains either an Internet router or an ATM concentrator, enabling the link with a large broadband network via either an Internet boundary router or an ATM switch. A telephone operator supplies the broadband core network. Each customer site requires a PLT modem that contains the DS2 chipset. The use of a gateway between the PLT modem and a LAN at the customer premises enables several users to connect and share the high-speed connection, which makes this a useful SOHO option.

PLT is attempting to deliver on a vision that would allow electrical utilities to provide high-speed Internet, voice, and data services to customers of all classes via power transmission and distribution lines. The concept is not new; PLT came to be in the 1920s, although the application then was the protection of power transmission lines, as well as telemetry, remote system control, and voice communication. But as with all broadband strategies, the applications PLT is supporting today include high-speed Internet access, VoIP, video and audio on demand, network games, videoconferencing, in-home LAN connections, and interactive TV. With more than three billion users worldwide, the penetration of the electricity networks is almost ubiquitous, bringing access to a global communications infrastructure within reach of all, without the need for heavy infrastructure costs. Because of differences in the way the electrical grids are designed, Europe and Asia will most likely see PLT before the United States does.

People worldwide are paying close attention to the prospect of the PLT option; imagine what an uproar this has the potential of causing in the telecommunications industry! As in many cases, politics and economics often determine whether a technology finds its way into the marketplace. Regulators generally want to encourage competition and the resulting "price, choice, and quality" benefits arising from it by whatever tools—including technological alternatives—happen to be available. Regulators worldwide would largely welcome some viable and cost-effective way around the last-mile bottleneck.

For more learning resources, quizzes, and discussion forums on concepts related to this chapter, see www.telecomessentials.com/learningcenter.

Chapter 14

Wireless Communications

Most people consider mobility to be one of their most cherished abilities and rights. In fact, what do we take away from those who have been deemed injurious to their fellow humans? Mobility. The freedom afforded by mobility is very precious to humans, indeed.

One area in which we like to exercise our freedom of mobility is at work, and the mobile workforce is growing all the time. Mobile workers, often called road warriors, are people who are away from their primary workplace at least 20% of the time. Today, about one-third of the population fits this category.

Another area in which we want to use our freedom to be mobile is with the Internet. The mobile Internet is already a reality in some places, and it will become more prevalent elsewhere in the near future, as more and more Internet-ready cellular phones and other wireless devices make their way into people's pockets. Eventually, and maybe within just a few years, there will be more mobile Internet devices than PCs connected to the Internet; wireless is predicted to become the dominant form of Internet communication by 2009. These trends, as well as the trend toward portable computing in the form of wearables, contribute to our growing interest in wireless.

We tend to think of wireline facilities as the default and of wireless as something extra that needs to be justified. Wireless has often been justified in situations, such as when wire cannot be physically applied (for example, in a jungle, in a desert, on a mountaintop); when wire cannot be economically justified (for example, when the expense of burying cable is too great); when time is an issue; and when mobility is a factor. The future will see mixed-media approaches (including wireline and wireless solutions), depending on the given situation. For example, we may want to bring fiber as close as possible to an end node, but then to engage in a more mobile lifestyle, we might rely on a wireless link for the last few meters.

The building blocks for the wireless world include cellular and PCS (Personal Communication Services) service providers, cell phone makers, infrastructure companies, handheld computer makers, electronic parts manufacturers, wireless portals, e-commerce companies, movie and music studios, automobile companies, and satellite companies. The wireless world will really have a big impact on transportation. We are reengineering the way vehicles will operate, and things such as traffic management systems, smart cars, smart highways, and navigational systems are very much a part of the telecommunications sector.

Wireless networks will be a very important part of our future. Wireless networks fall into the same domains as wireline networks—wide area networks (WANs), metropolitan area networks (MANs), local area networks (LANs), and personal area networks (PANs)—and are applied in support of mobile (such as cellular and PCS systems), fixed (as in wireless local loop), and broadcast (television) applications.

Wireless has been with us a very long time, in the form of radio, which involves inducing an electrical current at a remote location via the propagation of electromagnetic waves, through space, with the intent of communicating information. This technology is more than 100 years old, so we could turn things around and say that wires can be thought of as private radio spectrum.

The key issues in wireless are technological (for example, standards, bandwidth, performance, spectrum reuse) and political (for example regulation, spectrum allocation). Regulation has a tremendous influence on what is made available, who can use it, and how it's allocated among the various competitive providers. Bandwidth is a huge consideration in anything to do with telecommunications, and in the realm of wireless, *bandwidth* refers to the amount of spectrum available to transport information. *Narrowband wireless* applies a baseband, or single-channel, approach; *wideband wireless* applies a broadband, or channelized, approach. Bandwidth is often limited by regulation, technology, and environmental conditions—in that order.

There are a number of key areas to consider when it comes to the performance of wireless:

- **Path loss**—The path loss in decibels (dB) represents the ratio of the strength of the transmitted signal to the received strength.
- **Multipath**—*Multipath* is the artifact of reflections and echoes. For example, with antenna televisions, there are times when an image has a ghost figura-

tion about it—and that is an echo. Multipath can create secondary and tertiary signals that compete with the primary signal.

- **Fading**—There are a number of propagation characteristics, and they vary with the different frequencies. As a mobile station moves through a cell, the multipath signals abruptly and rapidly add to and subtract from each other. As a result, very good signals are interspersed with very poor signals. This effect is referred to as a *Rayleigh fade* (named after the physicist Lord Rayleigh). The multipath delays can be predicted on a statistical basis, and components can be designed to handle the problem.

- **Interference and noise**—Interference and noise are byproducts of precipitation in the air, metals in the environment, or a variety of other anomalies. Error-correction techniques are needed to fix these problems.

- **Antenna design, position, and orientation**—Antennas are constantly being developed to better deal with the problems of wireless transmissions. Antenna design is as critical as the prevailing radio conditions in which the antennas are operating.

The following sections cover various aspects of wireless communications, including spectrum reuse and the various types of wireless networks—WANs, MANs, LANs, and PANs.

■ Spectrum Reuse

The wireless spectrum is limited—wireless is like having one invisible cable in the sky that the whole world has to share. This is one of the major limitations of wireless, and we need techniques for efficiently using the spectrum that we do have. There are several methods for reusing spectrum.

The first step is to apply space division; you carve up the service area into smaller coverage areas. The key purpose of space division is to reuse frequencies across the coverage areas, or *cells*. The second step is to apply a multiple access technique, to allow the sharing of spectrum by multiple users. After you have delineated the space and combined multiple conversations onto one channel, you can then apply spread spectrum, duplexing, and compression techniques to use the bandwidth even more efficiently.

Space Division

The cellular concept involves subdividing coverage areas. Mobile telephony is not a new invention. It has been around since the early 1950s, but at that time, two things limited its availability to the mass market. First, we were using very high-powered antennas. So, when we relayed a signal, it would have strength over a coverage area of perhaps 100 miles (161 kilometers) in diameter. Second, at that time, the spectrum management agencies issued very few frequencies (perhaps a dozen or two) that could be used for purposes of mobile communications. In a relatively large coverage area of 100 miles (161 kilometers) or so, only 12 channels to 24 channels were available. The majority of these few channels were reserved for critical services, such as police and other emergency services, as well as for those who could afford a body builder to carry those big phones that operated at low frequencies over long stretches.

In the 1970s, two things changed. The first was the advent of the low-power transmitter receiver tower, which reduced the coverage area to a cell size that was only about 8 miles (13 kilometers) in diameter. Second, the regulatory agencies made available large amounts of spectrum for use in support of mobile communications, and depending on where you were in the world, anywhere from 600 to 1,000 channels were made available to service providers.

The cellular architecture depends on cells organized into a reuse pattern. In the traditional analog cellular network, the cellular reuse pattern is $n=7$, and is often depicted as a honeycomb configuration of what are called *seven cells* (see Figure 14.1). The idea of spectrum reuse is that you can reuse frequencies, as long as they are not in adjacent cells. Say that in the honeycomb configuration, 700 channels are available. Each of the cells could make use of 100 of those channels. We could then reuse those 100 channels in the next honeycomb configuration, as long as those channels were not adjacent to one another between cells.

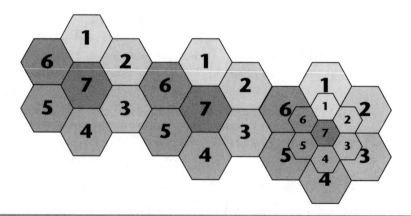

Figure 14.1 Providing channels by subdividing space into cells

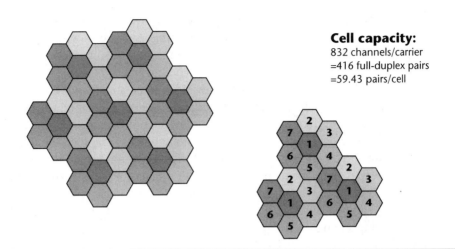

Cell capacity:
832 channels/carrier
=416 full-duplex pairs
=59.43 pairs/cell

Figure 14.2 An AMPS example of a cellular reuse pattern ($n = 7$)

As the density of subscribers increases, the next step is to subdivide the cells into smaller coverage areas, based on accepted reuse patterns. The traditional analog cellular network uses *macrocells* (see Figure 14.2). This network was for fast-moving users, traveling distances of miles on their end-to-end journey. The coverage area was about 8 miles (13 kilometers) in diameter, and the base station power was rather great—generally 10 watts or more. This network offered low deployment costs and a small number of handoffs. Depending on how many channels the spectrum agency gave the region, a cell could support up to about 60 users.

As the demand for use increased, we started to migrate toward a *microcell* architecture. Users of this architecture were assumed to be moving more slowly than those in a macrocell approach; they were, for example, people trapped in a traffic grid, people on golf carts on a golf course, people riding bicycles in Amsterdam, pedestrians anywhere. These users traveled distances of less than 1 mile (1.5 kilometers) end to end. Therefore, there are not as many hand-offs involved with microcells as there are with macrocells. With macrocells and high-speed vehicles, in 1980, when processing power was significantly less than it is today, if you were moving very rapidly through cell boundaries, there would be undue strain on the processing power of the systems, and calls might be dropped. But by the time microcells started to come about, hand-offs were facilitated by more rapid processing. The coverage area of a microcell is about 0.6 miles (1 kilometer) in diameter. Compared to macrocells, this architecture offers better frequency reuse, lower power, and better battery life, as well as smaller subscriber units.

The demand for spectrum is growing beyond what even the microcell design can provide, and so we are now going to the picocell—the tiny cell—architecture.

This approach is for stationary or very slow-moving users—the folks who dash out of a seminar during the conference and go stand by a window so they can conduct a conversation. Users are not traveling great distances, maybe 330 to 1,000 feet (100 to 300 meters) end-to-end. The coverage radius of a picocell is only about 150 feet (46 meters), and because it's such a small coverage area, the base station power is also very small—10 milliwatts or less. Therefore, the picocell design offers even better frequency reuse, even lower power, even smaller subscriber units, and even better, longer battery life than microcells. The picocell architecture does create some concerns in the engineering realm; for example, Tokyo needed to plan how to implement more than 40,000 cells for its Personal Handyphone System (PHS) deployment. There are tradeoffs with the various designs: You can serve greater densities with the picocell design than with other designs, but at the cost of a bigger engineering project.

Multiple Access Techniques

There are three major multiple access techniques: Frequency Division Multiple Access (FDMA), Time Division Multiple Access (TDMA), and Code Division Multiple Access (CDMA). The following sections describe the multiple access techniques that are used to make efficient use of the bandwidth within each cell of the cellular system.

FDMA

FDMA is used in analog cellular systems, and each user is assigned to a different frequency. With FDMA, everybody is speaking at the same time, but each conversation is on a different portion of the frequency band. FDMA is characterized as facilitating what would today be called low capacity—approximately 60 users per cell. Current forecasts suggest that there will be 1.5 billion wireless users worldwide by 2005, and FDMA will not be able to handle the future volume.

The cost of FDMA handsets is low, as these are not smart devices. For example, an FDMA-based device does not know how to search for another frequency that has a better transmission quality associated with it. This approach is inexpensive for the user, but the service operator needs to have a transceiver for each channel, which means the base station cost is high. And because it's an analog technology, FDMA also consumes a great deal of power, and the cost associated with the power consumption is greater than with digital systems.

The advantage of FDMA is that it doesn't need strict clocking devices to enable synchronization between the base stations, as would, for example, TDMA. As Figure 14.3 shows, everybody uses the system at the same time, but each user is working off a different frequency.

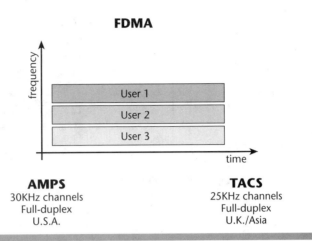

Figure 14.3   FDMA

TDMA

TDMA is used in digital cellular and PCS systems. It is actually a combination of Frequency Division Multiplexing (FDM) and Time Division Multiplexing (TDM). With TDMA, you first divide the available or allocated frequency spectrum into a number of channels. Then, within each channel, you apply TDM to carry multiple users interleaved in time. Therefore, one transceiver can support multiple channels. There are various cellular network standards based on TDMA, including GSM (Global System for Mobile Communications), UWC (Universal Wireless Communications), and JDC (Japanese Digital Cellular). UWC TDMA technology, also referred to as ANSI-136, provides a three-to-one gain in capacity compared to analog technology. Each caller is assigned a specific time slot for transmission. In GSM, eight users per channel are supported. These standards are discussed in further detail later in this chapter.

The digital handsets associated with TDMA are more intelligent than those used with FDMA. For example, they have scanning capabilities, and if the channel you are on is encountering anomalies that are lending themselves to transmission errors, the handset can search for an available channel that provides a better performance.

The key benefits of TDMA are that it offers greater capacity and spectral efficiency than FDMA.

Figure 14.4 shows that in TDMA, everybody is talking on the same frequencies but at different moments in time. The users perceive their conversations as being continuous, even though they are actually getting very rapid samples of that conversation.

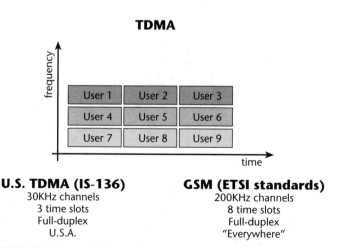

TDMA

frequency ↑

User 1	User 2	User 3
User 4	User 5	User 6
User 7	User 8	User 9

time →

U.S. TDMA (IS-136)
30KHz channels
3 time slots
Full-duplex
U.S.A.

GSM (ETSI standards)
200KHz channels
8 time slots
Full-duplex
"Everywhere"

Figure 14.4 TDMA

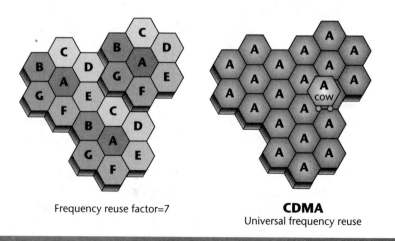

Frequency reuse factor=7

CDMA
Universal frequency reuse

Figure 14.5 CDMA frequency reuse

CDMA

CDMA is a multiple-access technique that is receiving a great deal of attention. In CDMA, everybody is using the same frequency at the same time. This is referred to as *universal frequency reuse* (see Figure 14.5). CDMA provides the ultimate in terms of the density that you can support, and it is possible because each conversation is uniquely encoded. In CDMA, a single spectrum of bandwidth is available for all the users. As Figure 14.6 shows, in CDMA everybody is using the same frequencies at

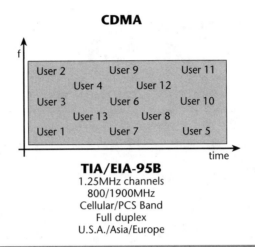

Figure 14.6 CDMA

the same time, but each conversation is uniquely encoded, allowing the transceiver to pick it out from among all the conversations.

There are two generations of CDMA. First-generation CDMA operates in an allocation of 1.25MHz, and the standard specifications for this version basically emanated from Qualcomm. The second generation of CDMA is Wideband CDMA (WCDMA), which operates over allocations of either 5MHz, 10MHz, or 15MHz, and was created by Oki and Interdigital. As is implied by the name, WCDMA can support higher data rates than can first-generation CDMA. Both generations of CDMA use a unique code for each conversation, and both use a spread-spectrum technique. Advantages of WCDMA include its use of a bigger channel than CDMA, which means that it can carry more calls and that those calls can be encoded in longer strings. The longer strings, in turn, mean greater security and better performance.

CDMA is characterized by not requiring any timing coordination, so clocking is not necessary. It offers great reliability because it is highly resistant to interference. CDMA has greatly improved capacity over FDMA and TDMA; the spectral efficiency of CDMA, as standardized in IS-95, is 10 to 20 times greater than that of an analog network. The number of users who can be serviced depends on the location of the users—how many of them are within a given cell and what signal-to-noise ratio the service provider deems acceptable. CDMA allows for two compression ratios for digitized voice, and they're variable according to the channel quality: 13Kbps, which is used to provide near-LAN-line voice qualities (for instance, in support of something like wireless local loop), and 8Kbps, which is used when you want to maximize the use of the spectrum and extend battery life. It is important to

CDMA's Military History

The glamorous movie star Hedy Lamarr and George Antheil held the original patent on CDMA technology. Hedy Lamarr had strong personal sentiments against the war. She had recently escaped from her first husband Fritz Mandl, who was one of Europe's largest armaments manufacturers and selling munitions to Hitler. As his wife, Lamarr was exposed to military technology ideas. Lamarr met George Antheil, who had been at the forefront of experimental music in the 1920s, at a party in Hollywood. Antheil was one of the first people to work with the player piano as an instrument for composed music; his famous *Ballet Mecanique* was written for 12 player pianos, an airplane propeller, and a symphony. Antheil also opposed the Nazis, and it was in this context that Lamarr told Antheil about her idea for a secret communications system that could guide torpedoes to their target without being intercepted by the enemy, by sending messages between transmitter and receiver over multiple radio frequencies in a random pattern. The only problem was how to ensure that the transmitter and receiver would stay in synchronization as they moved through the frequencies. Lamarr thought Antheil could help solve the synchronization problem.

Antheil did come up with a solution: Paper rolls perforated with a pseudorandom pattern would delineate the frequency path. Two rolls with the same pattern would be installed in the transmitter and receiver. If the two rolls were started at the same time, and one stayed at the launch point while the other was launched with the torpedo, you'd maintain the synchronization right on down to where the torpedo hit the ship. Interestingly, Lamarr and Antheil designed their system to use 88 frequencies—exactly the number of keys on a piano—just like the player piano rolls in *Ballet Mecanique*. (There is more to this fascinating story. For a full account, go to www.siriuscomm.com/lamarr.htm.)

Today, we call this technique Frequency Hopping Spread Spectrum (FHSS), and it is one of the ways in which CDMA uniquely encodes its conversations. Along with FHSS, we also now rely on a newer and better technique for transmitting messages securely and with great resistance to noise, Direct Sequence Spread Spectrum (DSSS).

realize that CDMA requires complex power control schemes, and power control is very important in CDMA.

Spread Spectrum Techniques

There are two spread spectrum techniques: FHHS and DSSS. With FHHS, which is the older of the two methods, the frequency hopping varies in a known pattern, and separate error correction must be included (see Figure 14.7). Slow frequency hopping is used to combat fading. Today, we predominantly rely on DSSS, in which each data bit is converted to a series of 10 transmitted bits to 144 transmitted bits,

Power Control Schemes in TDMA and CDMA

The classic example that instructors give their students when talking about wireless is the following: You walk into a TDMA cocktail party, and a group of people stands in a circle. Each person takes a turn at making a comment or answering a question. You can separate the conversations by the moment in time when each individual is speaking.

You walk into a CDMA party, and you feel as though you've walked into the United Nations. There's German in the left-hand corner, Japanese in the right-hand corner, and English in the center. Somebody says a word in your language that you recognize, and you immediately focus your attention there. You're able to filter out the extraneous conversation as noise because you've tuned in on a code that's understandable to you. You can continue to filter out the extraneous conversation, unless another 200 delegates walk in and add their conversations to the overall mix, making it impossible for you to distinguish between the conversations.

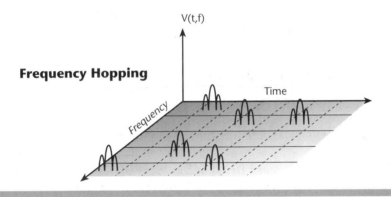

Figure 14.7 FSSS

or chips. DSSS requires greater bandwidth than does FHHS, but this is exactly what makes its performance so good.

Figure 14.8 shows an example of DSSS that uses the Barker Code, which is an 11-bit chipping code. The 1-bits are encoded as a particular sequence of ones and zeros, and the 0-bits are the inverse of that sequence. In the course of a transmission, if a bit is affected by noise and several chips get knocked out, the receiver can determine from the pattern of remaining bits whether a one or a zero got knocked out and recover that information accurately. This is why DSSS provides such good performance and resistance to interference and noise. DSSS also provides great reliability because the DSSS operation generates more bits per second than it starts with, and the resulting signals spread over a wide

Consider an 11-bit chipping code, as follows:

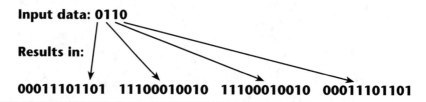

1=11100010010 (Note: a Barker code)
0=00011101101 (the inverse of the 1 bits)

Input data: 0110

Results in:

00011101101   11100010010   11100010010   00011101101

Figure 14.8 A DSSS example

range of frequencies when it is transmitted, minimizing the impact of interference and multipath fading.

Duplexing Techniques

Another way in which the operations of wireless networks differ, and hence also the standards differ, is the *duplexing technique*—the procedure for separating the incoming and outgoing conversations. There are two duplexing techniques:

- **Frequency Division Duplex (FDD)**—FDD is a full-duplex approach. It is used when there is a significant contiguous spectrum allocated and when synchronization between the base stations is not possible. With FDD, each direction (incoming and outgoing) occupies a different portion of the frequency band, and a rather large portion of the spectrum is consumed.

- **Time Division Duplex (TDD)**—TDD is a half-duplex technique—sort of a Ping-Pong approach. Each end of the conversation makes use of the same frequency, but this requires very tight timing coordination, so there's a trade-off. Where spectrum is an issue and where you want to conserve on how you utilize the spectrum, TDD is more efficient than FDD.

Compression Techniques

After you have carved space into cells and applied multiple access techniques within each cell to make better use of the bandwidth available in that area, you need to apply compression to make greater use of the bandwidth within each given channel. Compression is very important because it improves the use of a very precious resource, the communications channel.

Voice compression techniques use voice coders/decors (vocoders), of which there are two general types:

- **High-bit-rate vocoders**—These vocoders are used by PCS, wireless local loops, and wireless office telecommunication systems applications. These vocoders carry voice by using 32-Kbps Adapted-Differential Pulse Code Modulation (ADPCM). A bit rate this high emulates the quality that you achieve on the public switched telephone network (PSTN), and no additional error detection and correction is necessary.

- **Low-bit-rate vocoders**—These vocoders are used in cellular systems that deal with vehicular traffic, where there are large cells and you need to facilitate a large number of conversations. These vocoders reduce the voice to 8Kbps, by using extensive channel coding techniques that help facilitate error correction, such as Line Pulse Coding (LPC), Quantized Code-Excited Linear Predictive (QCELP), or Vector Sum Excited Linear Prediction (VSLEP). GSM uses Regular Pulse Excitation Long-Term Prediction (RPE LTP), which carries digitized voice at 13Kbps, achieving good voice quality.

In the realm of data, unfortunately, there are no set standards for data compression; many techniques exist, and, overall, data compression is underused.

■ Wireless WANs: Cellular Radio and PCS Networks

WANs can be global, national, or regional in scope. Today, they are associated with relatively low data speeds, generally only up to 19.2Kbps; in some locations, VSAT systems provide up to 2Mbps. (VSATs are discussed in Chapter 3, "Transmission Media: Characteristics and Applications.") Third-generation cellular systems are promising to someday be capable of delivering 155Mbps, but that is still quite some time in the future—probably toward the end of this decade. WAN solutions include cellular radio and PCS networks (including analog and digital cellular) and wireless data networks (that is, Cellular Digital Packet Data [CDPD] and packet radio).

Although the history of cellular networks has been rather brief, it has already seen three generations:

- **First generation**—The first generation, which initially debuted in Japan in 1979, is characterized as an analog transmission system.

- **Second generation (2G)**—The second generation introduced digital transmission, and the first of these networks were operational in 1992.

■ **Third generation (3G)**—The third generation, which is now quickly coming upon us, will include digital transmission, but it will also permit per-user and terminal mobility, providing a single mobile communication service, adjusted for broadband applications (including voice, data, and multimedia streams), to be supported at higher data speeds, in the range of 144Kbps to 384Kbps, and even up to 2Mbps in some cases. 3G standards development is occurring in Europe and Asia, but universal deployment seems doubtful at present. There are still a lot of issues to resolve, especially regarding the auctioning process. For instance, in Europe, some countries paid very exorbitant rates for their licenses, and they now have to invest a similar amount in building out 3G networks, which means they face a 15- to 20-year payback period, and that is hard to justify in today's environment.

There is also an intermediate generation—what we call 2.5G—and that's where we currently are and where we are likely to stay for some time. 2.5G offers enhancements to the data services on existing second-generation digital platforms.

Analog Cellular Networks

Analog cellular systems are very quickly on their way out, but you will still hear the terminology related to them, so this section quickly defines some of these terms:

Cellular Versus PCS

Cellular is classified as including both analog and digital networks. Cellular networks started out as being analog, and they migrated to digital infrastructures. Cellular operates in the 800MHz to 900MHz band, depending on where you are in the world. Cellular tends to operate in macrocells, which involve a coverage area of up to 8 miles (12.8 kilometers), and because of the large coverage area, the power use is high, ranging from 0.6 watts to 3 watts.

PCS is a newer introduction than cellular, and it has been digital from the start. It operates in the 1.8GHz to 2GHz band, again depending on where you are in the world. It uses both microcell and picocell architectures, which means the coverage areas are quite small, around 1 mile (1.6 kilometers), and because the coverage area is small, much lower power is used—100 milliwatts or so.

Functionally, cellular and PCS work the same way, they perform the same functions, and they use the same types of network elements. The key differences between them are the frequency at which they operate, the coverage area over which they operate, and the power levels they use.

- **Advanced Mobile Phone System (AMPS)**—AMPS, also known as IS-54, is on the 800MHz band, involves some 832 channels per carrier, and originated in the United States.

- **Total Access Communication Systems (TACS)**—TACS operates in the 900MHz band, offers 1,000 channels, and originated in the United Kingdom.

- **Japanese Total Access Communication Systems (JTACS)**—JTACS works in the 800MHz to 900MHz band, and it originated in Japan.

- **Nordic Mobile Telephone System (NMT)**—The original variation of NMT was 450MHz, offering some 220 channels. NMT had a very large coverage area, thanks to its operation at 450MHz (you could probably travel through half of Scandinavia and still be within one cell), but the power levels are so intense that mobile sets were incredibly heavy. NMT originated in Denmark, Finland, Norway, and Sweden.

Within the cellular radio system there are three key components (see Figure 14.9): a transceiver station, a mobile telephone switching office (MTSO), and the mobile unit (that is, the phone). Each cell needs a base transceiver station—the tower that is transmitting the signals to and from the mobile unit. Each of these base transceiver stations, one per cell, connects to an MTSO. The MTSO then interfaces into the terrestrial local exchanges to complete calls over the PSTN. The connections from the base transceiver stations to the MTSO can be either microwave or

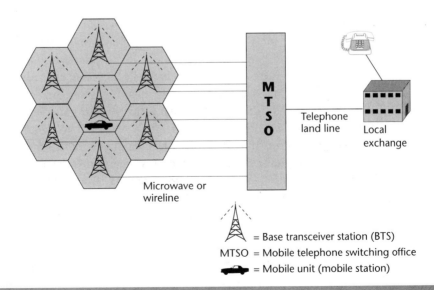

Figure 14.9   The analog cellular architecture

wireline, and then typically from the MTSO to the local exchange there is a wireline facility, but it could also potentially be microwave. (Chapter 3 discussed the various media options in detail.)

When a mobile unit is on, it emits two numbers consistently: the electronic identification number and the actual phone number of the handset. These are picked up by the base transceiver stations, and depending on signal level, they can determine whether you are well within the cell or transitioning out of that cell. If your power levels start to weaken and it appears that you are leaving the cell, an alert is raised that queries the surrounding base transceiver stations to see who's picking up a strong signal coming in, and as you cross the cell perimeter, you are handed over to an adjacent frequency in that incoming cell. You cannot stay on the same frequency between adjacent cells because this creates cochannel interference (that is, interference between cells).

Digital Cellular Networks

Digital cellular radio was introduced to offer a much-needed feature: increased capacity. The growing demand for mobile communications in the late 1980s was well beyond what the analog cellular infrastructure could support. Recall from earlier in the chapter that the basic cell in analog can handle about 60 subscribers; for a number of years, we have expected the number of people using wireless or mobile services to grow exponentially—to an anticipated 1.5 billion people by 2004. So, we realized that we needed to be able to use the existing spectrum more efficiently, and digitalization is the first technique toward that goal. Another reason to switch to digital was to improve security. The industry was suffering from a tremendous amount of toll fraud. Creative thieves would stand on busy street corners, intercepting those electronic identification numbers and phone numbers and then cloning chips; the next month you'd have a bill for US$3,000 to an area you'd never called in your life. Digitizing that ID information meant that we could encrypt it and improve the security. Finally, the digital cellular infrastructure is very closely associated with intelligent networks, and that is what gives you the roaming capability to engage in conversations when you are outside the area of your own service provider.

So with digital cellular architectures, everything remains the same as in the analog architecture. As you can see in Figure 14.10, a base transceiver station services each cell. But because there are more cells to address the increasing capacity (remember that the first technique for spectrum reuse is to break down the coverage areas into smaller chunks), we have more base transceiver stations. Therefore, we need an intermediate device, the *base station controller,* to control a group of base station transceivers. The base station controllers feed into the mobile switching center, which interfaces into the group of databases that enable roaming, bill-

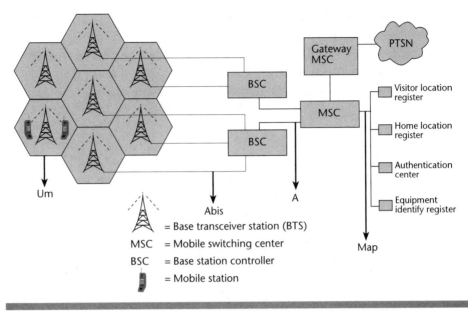

Figure 14.10   The digital cellular architecture

ing, and interconnection, as well as interfacing to a gateway mobile switching center, which passes on the relevant billing information so that the home service provider can produce invoices.

A number of databases are critical to the process of roaming:

- **Home location register**—The home location register provides information about the subscribers in a particular mobile switching center-controlled area.

- **Visitor location register**—The visitor location register stores information about the calls being made by roaming subscribers and periodically forwards information to subscribers' home service providers for billing and other purposes. Each mobile service switching center must have a visitor location register.

- **Authentication center**—The authentication center protects the subscriber from unauthorized access, providing security features including encryption, customer identification, and so on. It is associated with the home location register.

- **Equipment identity register**—The equipment identity register registers the mobile equipment types, and maintains a database of equipment that has been stolen or blacklisted for some reason.

Wireless Data Networks

Wireless data networking methods include CDPD and packet radio. These technologies are not generally part of new deployments today, and the extent to which these methods remain viable depends in large part on the service operators. They are covered here because you'll encounter this language.

CDPD

CDPD is a packet data protocol that is designed to work over AMPS or as a protocol for TDMA. The initial concept of CDPD was publicly introduced in 1992. CDPD was envisioned as a wide area mobile data network that could be deployed as an overlay to existing analog systems, a common standard to take advantage of unused bandwidth in the cellular air link (that is, the wireless connection between the service provider and the mobile subscriber). (Unused bandwidth is a result of silence in conversations, as well as the moments in time when the call is undergoing handover between cells. These periods of no activity can be used to carry data packets and therefore take advantage of the unused bandwidth.) That was the main objective, and large cellular network operators backed it. It is defined by the Wireless Data Forum as a connectionless, multiprotocol network service that provides peer network wireless extension to the Internet. CDPD's greatest advantage is that it was designed to operate as an extension of existing networks, namely IP networks. Any application developed for CDPD can be adapted to run on any IP-based network.

The complete network specification—including architecture, airlink, network interfaces, encryption, authentication, network management, and security—is defined. Throughput is nominally 19.2Kbps, but you should more routinely expect 9.6Kbps. CDPD looks like TCP/IP, which gives it some advantages, but it does require a specialized subscriber unit.

Figure 14.11 shows a CDPD network. A mobile user has a CDPD subscriber device, typically a proprietary modem provided by the network operator. It is an overlay network that goes on top of the existing analog cellular telephone network. Incorporated into the base station are some new elements, including the CDPD mobile database station and a CDPD mobile data intermediate system (that is, a router). The voice calls are switched out over the telco network, and the data traffic is sent over the CDPD router network.

Packet Radio

Packet radio data networks are an offshoot of specialized mobile radio (SMR). They use licensed bandwidth and are built specifically for two-way data, not for voice communications. The data rates supported by packet radio range up to 19.2Kbps, but the norm is 9,600bps. The best applications for packet radio are short sessions,

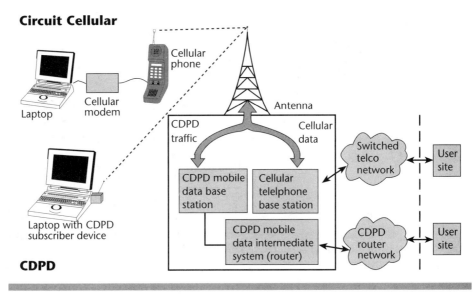

Figure 14.11 CDPD network architecture

as in short message services (SMS), transaction processing, and perhaps e-mail; packet radio is not a solution for bulk file transfers or client/server interactions. The key applications for packet radio include dispatching, order processing, airline reservations, financial services and banking, lottery, remote database access, messaging, point-of-sale, and telemetry.

In the packet radio data network configuration shown in Figure 14.12, the end user has a mobile unit, a laptop, as well as a proprietary packet modem that provides access into the private packet base station. A private packet network is the backbone, and it may interface into public data networks or be used on a private basis, for a company's own enterprise network.

Among the packet data options is Mobitex, which is a trunked radio system based on X.25, originally operated at 8Kbps, and now ranging up to 19.2Kbps. It is available worldwide on various frequencies, and it offers international roaming throughout Europe. It involves a 512-byte packet, and it is a fault-tolerant architecture.

Another packet data option is Advanced Radio Data Information Services (ARDIS), which was originally built by Motorola for IBM. Like Mobitex, ARDIS started out with a slow data rate, 4.8Kbps, and it now ranges up to 19.2Kbps. Generally, it has a coverage radius of 1 to 20 miles (1.6 to 32 kilometers). The base stations emit about 40 watts, and mobile units operate at about 4 watts. ARDIS is a hierarchical network, with 4 hubs, 36 network controllers, and more than 1,200 base stations; it is oriented toward SMS.

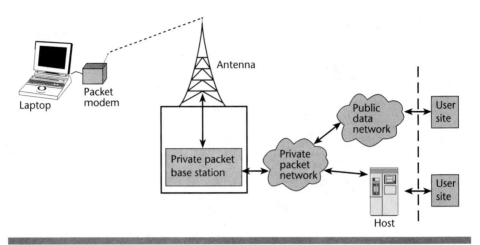

Figure 14.12   Packet radio data network architecture

Cellular and PCS Standards

As mentioned earlier in this chapter, one problem in the wireless realm is that a plethora of standards have been developed and observed worldwide, and that creates interoperability problems. Developments on all the standards fronts are required to address the growing need for data communications and Internet access, as well as the building of a wireless Internet. This section describes the major standards.

GSM

One of the most popular of the digital cellular standards is GSM, which was first deployed in 1992. GSM uses TDMA and FDD, and it is independent of underlying analog systems. GSM networks and networks based on GSM derivatives have been established in more than 170 countries, and GSM involves more than 400 operators, with a user base numbering more than 500 million. In principle, GSM can be implemented in any frequency band. However, there are several bands where GSM terminals are currently available:

- **GSM 900**—This is the first and traditional implementation of GSM, and it operates over 880MHz to 915MHz, paired with 925MHz to 960MHz.

- **GSM 1800**—This band is also referred to as DCS (Digital Cellular System) 1800, and it is the PCS implementation of GSM globally. It operates over 1710MHz to 1785MHz, paired with 1805MHz to 1880MHz.

- **GSM 1900**—This band is also called PCS 1900 and is the North American implementation of GSM. It operates over 1850MHz to 1910MHz, paired with 1930MHz to 1990MHz.

GSM mobile stations transmit on the lower-frequency sub-band, and base stations transmit on the higher-frequency sub-band. Dual-band and triple-band phones are now becoming available, which greatly facilitates roaming between countries that use these different frequency bands.

GSM supports 124 channel pairs with a 200KHz spacing to prevent channel interference and is based on an eight time-slot technique, which means it can support eight callers per channel. Of course, voice is supported, and so is data, but with basic GSM, data rates reach only as high as 9,600bps. Among the features of GSM are international roaming with a single invoice, the capability to handle SMS, which can offset the need for paging by enabling text messages up to 160 alphanumeric characters in length to be sent to and from a GSM phone, and an external system such as e-mail, paging, and voicemail systems. It also offers message-handling services in support of the X.400 standard, which was quite important when we were using largely proprietary e-mail systems. Now with the ubiquitous addressing scheme afforded by the Internet, it's not as important, but remember that GSM evolved quite some time ago. GSM also supports Group 3 fax and, very importantly, it provisions a subscriber identity module (SIM) card, which is a smart card that defines the accounting and personal details of your service. The SIM card can be used in any GSM handset to activate service, so it can help you roam on a global basis and still be able to maintain service. You simply rent a handset tuned to the frequencies of the country you're visiting and use your SIM card to authorize the services and ensure that accounting occurs to the proper address.

GSM offers spectrum utilization that is much better than in the analog environment, the capability to improve security by applying encryption to the digital bitstreams, and authentication and fraud prevention via SIMs.

A variety of voice compression devices—both half-rate coders and enhanced full-rate coders where voice quality is the preeminent concern—are being developed so that we can use GSM to make more efficient use of the available spectrum. Another area of development is the capability to create closed user groups and to engage in group calls. GSM is working on offering a number of important 2.5G data services. There are currently more than 80 items being covered in the various working groups, and the following sections highlight just a few of the most important developments.

HSCSD High-Speed Circuit-Switched Data (HSCSD) makes use of the existing circuit-switched equipment, but via software upgrades. This enables you to grab several time slots, which increases the overall data rate you, as a single user, experience. HSCSD is a high-speed transmission technology that enables users to send and retrieve data over GSM networks at transmission speeds between 28.8Kbps and 43.2Kbps (but the norm is generally around 28.8Kbps) by enabling the concurrent usage of up to four traffic channels of a GSM network. The key applications for

HSCSD are those in which an end-to-end circuit is important, including applications such as large file transfers, remote access, the delivery of multimedia information, mobile navigation, and mobile video.

GPRS The 2.5G technology General Packet Radio Services (GPRS) is receiving a lot of press right now, especially because it's a prerequisite for enabling the mobile Internet. GPRS makes it possible for users to make telephone calls and to transmit data at the same time. (For example, with a GPRS phone, you will be able to simultaneously make calls and receive e-mail massages.) The main benefits of GPRS are that it reserves radio resources only when there is data to send and it reduces reliance on traditional circuit-switched network elements. Also, GPRS introduces IP to GSM networks.

GPRS is an always-on nonvoice value-added service that allows information to be sent and received across a mobile telephone network. It supplements today's circuit-switched data services and SMS. It is a packet-switched solution, so it works by overlaying a packet-based air interface on the eight time slots that are used for GSM transmission. Obviously, this requires that network operators install new hardware, but when they do, they can offer their subscribers transmission speeds of up to 115Kbps.

However, achieving the theoretical maximum GPRS data transmission speed of 115Kbps would require a single user taking over all eight time slots without any error protection. It seems unlikely that service providers would allow all eight time slots to be allocated to a single user. In addition, the initial GPRS terminals are expected be severely limited, supporting only one, two, or three time slots each. Therefore, the stated theoretical maximum GPRS speeds should be compared against the reality of constraints in the networks and terminals.

Adding GPRS to a GSM network requires several additions to the network. First, two core modules—the gateway GPRS service node (GGSN) and the serving GPRS service node (SGSN)—must be added. The GGSN acts as a gateway between the GPRS network and public data networks, such as IP and X.25 networks. GGSNs also connect to other GPRS networks to facilitate GPRS roaming. The SGSN provides packet routing to and from the SGSN service area for all users in that service area. It sends queries to home location registers (HLRs) to obtain profile data of GPRS subscribers. SGSNs detect new GPRS mobile subscribers in a given service area, process registration of new mobile subscribers, and keep a record of their location inside a given area. Therefore, the SGSN performs mobility management functions such as mobile subscriber attach/detach and location management. The SGSN is connected to the base-station subsystem via a Frame Relay connection to the packet control units (PCUs) in the base station controller.

The GGSN acts as a gateway between the GPRS network and public data networks, such as IP and X.25 networks. GGSNs also connect to other GPRS networks to facilitate GPRS roaming. GGSNs maintain routing information that is used to properly tunnel the protocol data units (PDUs) to the SGSNs that service particular mobile subscribers. Additional functions include network and subscriber screening and address mapping. One or more GGSNs may be provided to support multiple SGSNs.

To add GPRS to a GSM network, other changes need to take place as well, including the addition of PCUs (often hosted in the base station subsystems), mobility management to locate the GPRS mobile station, a new air interface for packet traffic, new security features such as ciphering, and new GPRS-specific signaling.

The best-suited and most popular applications for GPRS are Internet e-mail, corporate e-mail, and other information services, such as qualitative services, job dispatch, remote LAN access, file transfer, Web browsing, still images, moving images, chat, home automation, document sharing/collaborative working, and audio.

GPRS is not the only service designed to be deployed on GSM-based mobile networks. The IS-136 TDMA standard, which is popular in North and South America (and which is discussed earlier in this chapter), also supports GPRS.

EDGE   Enhanced Data rates for Global Evolution (EDGE) is an enhanced version of GPRS. It combines digital TDMA and GSM, and it is anticipated that we will be able to use EDGE to reach 85% of the world by using dual-mode handsets that are backward compatible with older TDMA schemes. EDGE offers anywhere from 48Kbps to 69.2Kbps per time slot on an aggregated basis, up to 384Kbps.

The GSM Association (GSMA), European Telecommunications Standards Institute (ETSI), Third Generation Partnership Project (3GPP) and UWC have agreed on EDGE as a standard. EDGE has strong endorsement because both TDMA and GSM operators can deploy it. Additionally, EDGE can be deployed in multiple spectrum bands and serve as the path to UMTS (W/CDMA) technology. TDMA operators have the option of deploying a GSM/GPRS/EDGE overlay existing in parallel to their TDMA networks at both 850MHz and 1900MHz. Eventually, we will see the convergence of TDMA and the more specialized variation of GSM. (GSM and GPRS are discussed earlier in this chapter.)

UWC

UWC, also known as ANSI-136, is the dominant technology in the Americas, with approximately 70 million worldwide users as of mid-2001, and 150 million users anticipated by 2005.

UWC uses TDMA and TDD schemes, and it offers a total of six time slots (two per user). Because it employs TDD, a time slot is required for each end of the conversation, resulting in the capability to carry three conversations per channel.

UWC operates in the 800MHz frequency band, uses AMPS for signaling to reserve resources, and transfers speech in digital form; therefore, it is a digital overlay that is interoperable with the analog AMPS infrastructure. TDMA can now support a tenfold increase over AMPS capacity by using microcell and hierarchical cell engineering. In terms of data capabilities, the IS-136 standards that exist today, and those that are soon to be introduced, include the following:

- IS-136 currently allows data rates up to 30Kbps.
- IS-136+ will provide 43.2Kbps to 64Kbps.
- IS-136 HS (high-speed) will range from 384Kbps to 2Mbps. It is looking toward the same sorts of data rates that 3G promises. It uses the Eight Phase Shift Keying modulation scheme and GPRS for packet data, and it also supports EDGE.

One of the main UWC developments is UWC-136, an advancement of the IS-136 standard that uses EDGE technology. The International Telecommunication Union (ITU) has endorsed UWC-136 technology.

TIA/EIA IS-95

The TIA/EIA IS-95 standard, also known as CDMA, makes use of the spread-spectrum technologies discussed earlier in the chapter. It operates in the 800MHz and 1,900MHz frequency bands but can work on other frequency bands as well, depending on the country's standards; it's simply a matter of engineering the appropriate radio frequency on the front end. It is full-duplex (that is, it is FDD): 1.25MHz for the forward direction, and 1.25MHz for the reverse direction. cdmaOne is the CDMA Development Group's (CDG's) name for cellular carriers that use 2G CDMA technology (IS-95), and it offers a data rate range of 9.6Kbps to 14.4Kbps. The first commercial cdmaOne network was launched in 1995. Today, there are more than 71 million subscribers to CDMA networks worldwide. It is used in the United States, Asia, and Europe. In the CDMA arena, we are seeing these developments:

- **IS-95A**—The initial data-friendly revision to the cdmaOne protocol falls under the TIA/EIA-95-A standard and is commonly called IS-95A. This revision provided for low-rate data services up to 14.4Kbps by using a CDPD overlay.
- **IS-95B**—IS-95B adds a data capability of up to 115Kbps. This can be considered to be IS-95's 2.5G solution. This upgrade allows for code or channel aggregation to provide data rates of 64Kbps to 115Kbps. To achieve 115Kbps, up to eight CDMA traffic channels offering 14.4Kbps need to be aggregated. IS-95B also offers improvements in soft hand-offs and inter-frequency hard hand-offs.

- **IS-95 HDR**—Qualcomm's IS-95 HDR (high data rate) promises a 2.4Mbps data rate in a standard 1.25MHz CDMA voice channel (using Qualcomm technology). It includes enhanced data capabilities, and it is optimized for IP packets and Internet access.

3G Mobile Systems and Beyond

Data service is expected to rise sharply as a traffic stream on wireless networks. However, the allotted wireless spectrum and the compression techniques we know today really won't allow us to make use of the existing wireless infrastructure as if it were a wireless Internet. Visual traffic will play a very demanding role in the future of telecom networks, and the problems this traffic poses are magnified many times over with wireless media.

The future demands a new generation of infrastructure—the third generation (3G), the broadband wireless realm. When you think about 3G, it's important to keep a number of things in mind. First, 3G is under development. Do not expect large-scale implementations to occur until 2003 or so; that's when 3G handsets are expected to become available in numbers that matter. Second, it is not yet certain that 3G networks will actually be implemented and installed. Although auctions have occurred and companies have acquired licenses, many have paid very large sums for those licenses and now face the prospect of having to invest just as much into the actual infrastructure because 3G requires a wholly new generation of equipment. It's not an upgrade from existing platforms, so it will require new investments to be made in the variety of network elements that will serve 3G. The bottom line is that we don't know how quickly we can expect to engage in the services and features of 3G, but we will begin to see rollouts, at least on a trial basis, between late 2001 and 2003. For wide-scale availability of broadband data rates (that is, 2Mbps), 2008 is most likely, although 3G technology can begin ramping up commercial customers by the end of 2003 if spectrum is identified by the end of 2001.

Keep in mind that while we argue the lifetime of 3G, the labs are already in development on 4G and 5G. At any point in time, new technologies are being developed and operating in labs that will emerge commercially within five to seven years. The result is that between the time of the vision and the time of the implementation, enough changes will have occurred to render the solution somewhat outdated, yet the formalization of the new and improved version is still too far off to be viable. So, let's examine the goal of 3G, and then compare 4G and 5G expectations.

3G

3G is designed for high-speed multimedia data and voice (see Figure 14.13). Its goals include high-quality audio and video and advanced global roaming, which

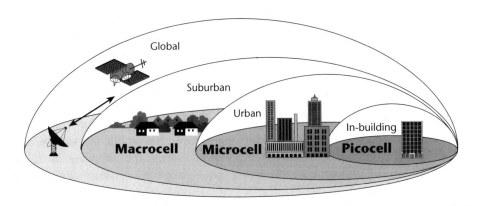

Figure 14.13 A vision of 3G networks

means being able to go anywhere and be automatically handed off to whatever wireless system is available.

The following are some of 3G's objectives:

- Support for messaging, Internet access, and high-speed multimedia
- Improved throughput and QoS support
- Improved voice quality
- Improved battery life
- Support for fixed applications and a broad range of mobility scenarios
- Support for position-location services
- Support for all current value-added voice services
- Ease of operations and maintenance
- Coexistence with current infrastructures, including backward compatibility, ease of migration or overlay, interoperability and handoffs, the need for bandwidth on demand, improving authentication and encryption methodologies to support mobile commerce (m-commerce), and moving toward supporting higher bandwidths over greater allocations (that is, 5MHz to 20MHz)

The 3G frequencies for IMT-2000 are identified by the ITU. The bands 1,885MHz to 2,025MHz and 2,110MHz to 2,200MHz are intended for use, on a worldwide basis, by administrations that want to implement International Mobile Telecommunications 2000 (IMT-2000). Such use does not preclude the use of these bands by other services to which they are allocated. Terrestrial IMT-2000 services will operate in the FDD mode in the bands 1,920MHz to 1,980MHz paired with 2,110MHz to 2,170MHz with mobile stations transmitting in the lower sub-band and base stations transmitting in the upper sub-band. The bands 1,885MHz to 1,920MHz and 2,010MHz to 2,025MHz are unpaired for TDD operation.

3G Standards 3G is defined by the ITU under the International Mobile Telecommunications 2000 (IMT-2000) global framework. In 1992 the ITU World Radio Conference identified 230MHz, in the 2GHz band, on a worldwide basis for IMT-2000, including both satellite and terrestrial components. As a strategic priority of ITU, IMT-2000 provides a framework for worldwide wireless access by linking the diverse system of terrestrial- and/or satellite-based networks. It will exploit the potential synergy between the digital mobile telecommunications technologies and those systems for fixed wireless access (FWA)/wireless access systems (WAS).

IMT-2000 services include the following:

- **Voice**—IMT-2000 promises to offer end-to-end store-and-forwarding of messages, which implies a data rate of 8Kbps to 64Kbps.

- **Audio service**—Audio service, including telemetry and signaling, should be available at 8Kbps to 64Kbps or 64Kbps to 384Kbps.

- **Text**—Text, including messaging, paging, and e-mail services, is expected to be offered at 8Kbps to 64Kbps.

- **Image services**—Image services, which would support fax and other still images, should be provided at 8Kbps to 64Kbps.

- **Video**—IMT-2000's video services are expected to support video telephony, video mail, teleshopping, and so on, at 64Kbps to 1,920Kbps.

The IMT-2000 terrestrial standard consists of a set of radio interfaces that enable performance optimization in a wide range of radio operating environments (see Table 14.1):

- **WCDMA**—This interface is also referred to as the Universal Terrestrial Radio Access (UTRA) Frequency Division Duplex (FDD) UMTS. FDD operations require paired uplink and downlink spectrum segments. The radio access scheme is direct-sequence WCDMA.

- **Cdma2000**—This radio interface is also called CDMA MC (multicarrier), and it operates in FDD. The radio interface uses CDMA technology and is a wideband spread-spectrum system. It provides a 3G evolution for systems using the current TIA/EIA-95-B family of standards. Radio frequency channel bandwidths of 1.25MHz and 3.75MHz are supported at this time, but the specification can be extended to bandwidths up to 15MHz.

Table 14.1 IMT-2000 Radio Interfaces

Interface	Technology	Technique	ITU Designation
WCDMA (UMTS, UTRA FDD)	CDMA	Direct sequence	IMT DS
Cdma2000 (1X and 3X)	CDMA	Multicarrier	IMT MC
UTRA TDD and TD-SCDMA	CDMA	Time code	IMT TC
UWC-136/EDGE	TDMA	Single carrier	IMT SC
DECT	FDMA/TDMA	Frequency time	IMT FT

- **UTRA TDD**—This radio interface uses a direct-sequence CDMA radio access scheme. There are two versions: UTRA Time Division Duplex (TDD), which uses 5MHz bandwidth, and TD-SCDMA, which uses 1.6MHz bandwidth. TDD systems can operate within unpaired spectrum segments.

- **UWC-136**—This radio interface was developed with the objective of maximum commonality between TIA/EIA-136 and GSM GPRS. UWC-136 enables the TIA/EIA-136 technology to evolve to 3G capabilities. This is done by enhancing the voice and data capabilities of the 30KHz channels, adding a 200KHz carrier for high-speed data (384Kbps) for high-mobility applications, and adding a 1.6MHz carrier for very high-speed data (2Mbps) for low-mobility applications.

- **DECT**—This radio interface uses an FDMA/TDMA scheme, and it is defined by a set of ETSI standards.

IMT-2000 satellite interfaces cover LEO, MEO, and GEO orbits as well as those specifically aimed at maximizing the commonality between terrestrial and satellite interfaces.

Universal Mobile Telephone Systems (UMTS, a WCDMA approach) is part of ETSI's Advanced Communications Technologies and Services (ACTS) program. ETSI standardization groups have been involved in defining the access method to use in sharing the new UMTS spectrum. The major objective of UMTS is personal mobility, and the vision is that any UMTS user will be able to approach any fixed or mobile UMTS terminal, register his or her presence, and then access services, such as telephony, data, and video, over this terminal. Any calls made to an international mobile user number will make use of UMTS mobility management features to find the user at the terminal of registration.

UMTS aims to remove any distinctions between mobile and fixed networking and will support the ITU's UPT concept, which means personal mobility across many different networks. Each user is issued a unique UPT number, and each UPT number has a unique user profile associated with it. By manipulating these profiles, the user can specify individual terminals for call delivery and call origination and also access advanced services such as call screening and call forwarding. UPT supports SS7 integration.

UMTS, then, defines both narrowband (that is, 2Mbps) and broadband (over 100Mbps, in the 60GHz band) types of services. Additional ETSI programs have developed Mobile Broadband System (MBS), which uses spectrum in the 40GHz to 60GHz bands, to provide data rates greater than 155Mbps. MBS aims to marry the mobile environment with intelligent networks and WCDMA, and it also promises support for multimedia, improved voice quality, improved security, interoperability, international roaming, and support for technological evolution in general. This is a combining of the mobile environment and intelligent networks. UMTS network architecture involves the development of additional intelligent networking functional entities, which will reside at nodes within the network and communicate with each other, by using sophisticated signaling protocols to deliver advanced telephony features, such as freephone and televoting, as well as some core mobility functions.

The ETSI standardization groups have been involved in defining the access methods to be used in sharing the new spectrum, and they have settled on WCDMA, which is standardized under IS-665 (OKI/Interdigital Wideband CDMA) and is the airlink technology of choice. There will be a single WCDMA standard with three modes: Direct-Sequence FDD (DS-FDD), which employs a single wideband carrier; Multicarrier FDD (MC-FDD), which involves multiple 1.25MHz carriers; and TDD for unpaired frequency bands.

The ETSI strategy is to evolve the core UMTS network from the current GSM technology. Phase 2+, or 2.5G, acts as a pre-UMTS system, and more advanced capabilities can be added in microcell or picocell environments as we evolve. The use of dual-mode or multimode handsets should enable users to move from pre-UMTS systems to the full 3G capability. UMTS support for data will probably be based on GPRS. Data speeds will range from 100Kbps, for a pre-UMTS GSM-based system, up to 2Mbps, for the new 3G radio access networks; again, the goal is to provide 155Mbps soon, sometime between 2008 and 2010.

Cdma2000 is a 3G technology for increasing data transmission rates for existing CDMA (cdmaOne) network operators, and it is a common name for ITU's IMT 2000 CDMA MC. There are several levels of Cdma2000. Cdma2000 1X is a 3G technology that offers a two-times increase in voice capacity and provides up to

307Kbps packet data on a single (1.25MHz, or 1X) carrier in new or existing spectrum. Cdma2000 1XEV is an evolution of Cdma2000 1X. 1XEV-DO (data only) uses a separate 1.25MHz carrier for data and offers peak packet data rate of 2.4Mbps. 1xEV-DV (data voice) integrates voice and data on the same carrier. Phase 2 of these standards promises the integration of voice and data at up to 4.8Mbps. Cdma2000 3X is a 3G technology that offers voice and data on a 5MHz carrier (or three times [3X] the 1.25MHz carrier).

Many standards and technologies are being considered, and there is no global agreement on what the standard for 3G should be, so, again, we are violating the promise of being able to engage in open standards on a global basis.

3G Technology Data Rates Figure 14.14 tracks where CDMA, GSM, TDMA, and mixed approaches stand in terms of the data rates they support in 2G, 2.5G, and 3G.

Barriers to 3G A main barrier to 3G is that there is a lot of competition in this arena, with many different standards being advocated. Also, there is already an installed base, and we need to protect our investment there. Another barrier to 3G is that many nations suffer from the syndrome of "not invented here" pride. There is also some basic fear about whether there is truly market demand for the services that 3G will want to promote. Also, different nations have different priorities

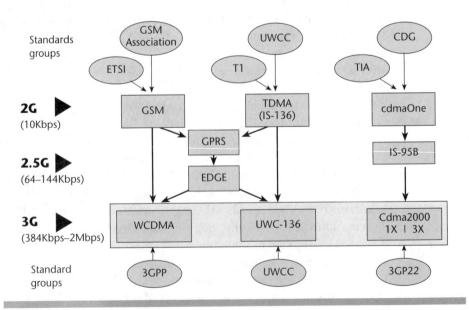

Figure 14.14 3G technology evolution

in terms of frequency allocations. Finally, the issues of cost and coverage are barriers to 3G.

4G and 5G Visions

Although we haven't even made it to 3G yet, at least a few parties are already advocating a vision for 4G and 5G technologies. The 4G vision is to be capable of supporting data rates of 5Mbps to 80Mbps, averaging around 20Mbps. It's a combination of Orthogonal Frequency Division Multiplexing and EDGE technologies. The features to be supported include streaming audio and video; the capability for asymmetric network access; adaptive modulation or coding schemes; dynamic packet assignment; and the use of smart adaptive antennas. It is important to consider even the generations beyond 3G, so that as you assess the future, you are considering the full range of options.

Mobile Internet

It is wise to be careful in how you interpret the use of the Internet on a wireless basis. Although in the wireline Internet we are striving for more bandwidth-intensive applications (such as voice, video, and streaming media), we need to have different expectations of the mobile Internet. We are not going to be able to Web surf visually, engaging in high-quality interactive multimedia, on a wireless basis for quite a few years. Yes, we will have the ability to access text-based information, so in the near term, the wireless Internet will be extremely usable as a messaging platform. But if you promise customers that they are going to get the mobile Internet, you may find yourself regretting having stated that, because if their experience has been a PC-based experience, their mobile Internet experience will not come close to what they're used to. On the other hand, in places such as Japan, where the PC penetrations are lower, the mobile experience is like a very first engagement with the Internet, and the users' perception will be much different.

A single device will not be suitable for all mobile Internet activities. People will use a variety of devices to connect to the Internet, depending on where they are going and for how long, and depending on what they need to do.

The main applications of mobile Internet are expected to be messaging, entertainment, wireless gaming, real-time financial data, online banking, travel information and reservations, geographical information, and location-based services. M-commerce is seen as potentially being a revolutionary new approach to using wireless. It is expected that in the next several years, more than a billion handsets, personal digital assistants, and Internet appliances equipped with wireless capabilities will be in use. The number of mobile devices connected to the Internet is expected to exceed the number of connected PCs in a very few years; couple this with the fact that the majority of the global households do not have a PC, and there is a potential m-commerce market worth double-digit billions.

WAP and i-mode

A student in France asked me if I know what WAP stands for, and then he proceeded to tell me with a smile: "wrong approach to portability." It's a good example of how lack of compelling applications and a difficult user interface can diminish the potential of a new technology. Indeed, this seems to be the case, and let's examine why. Wireless Application Protocol (WAP) is an enabling technology, a set of rules, for transforming Internet information so that it can be displayed on the necessarily small screen of a mobile telephone or other portable device. It enables a standard way of transmitting real-time content, which allows mobile phones to browse the Internet. WAP must strip down much of the information that we today enjoy on the Internet—most of the images and multimedia—to just the bare essential text-based information, and therein may lie some of WAP's limitations. Some of its other drawbacks are slow transmission speeds, difficulty related to inputting Web and e-mail addresses by using a 12-digit phone pad, and a scarcity of sites that use Wireless Markup Language (WML) rather than HTML as a basis.

This is how WAP gets you on the Web:

1. A person with a WAP-enabled cell phone types the address of the Web site on the phone's screen, using a keypad, a stylus, or another interface.

2. The microbrowser sends the request over the airwaves as a digital signal.

3. A cell phone transmission tower picks up the signal and relays it by landline to a server operated by the wireless network.

4. The server, which contains a software filter called a WAP gateway, is then linked to the Internet. The WAP gateway software finds the Web page requested by the cell phone user.

5. The coding software converts the Web page from HTML to WML, which is optimized for text-only displays because it is a compact binary form for transmission over the air. This enables greater compression of data that is optimized for long latency and low bandwidth. The WAP gateway then prepares the document for wireless transmission.

6. The WML document is transmitted to the user's cell phone. The device's microbrowser receives the signal and presents the text on the phone's small screen.

Whether WAP succeeds depends on its services and features, as well as the population for which it is targeted. To date it has been seen as a bit of a failure because it involves an entirely new language (WML), slow operating speeds, difficult user interfaces, and a capability to duplicate only parts of existing Web sites. Many believe that m-commerce will be the force to drive growth in the mobile sector, and according to some estimates, the growth of m-commerce will outstrip e-commerce within three years. These estimates are based on the success of one early entrant that has been very popular: DoCoMo's i-mode system in Japan, which currently has about 20 million users. i-mode is very much like WAP, except that it uses a proprietary protocol. People who have never owned a PC before are capable of enjoying the benefits of e-mail, and of buying things on the Internet, by using i-mode.

The key to i-mode's popularity has been Japan's love of the mobile phone. Cellular phone users in Japan number some 49 million, whereas PC users total between 3 million and 4 million. Another interesting reality of i-mode is that 50% of the users are in their twenties, 30% are in their teens, and most of the rest are in their thirties. The major revenue producer for i-mode is the capability to download the day's cartoon character. So i-mode is not trying to make today's wireline Internet applications available on a wireless basis. Instead, it is an entirely new set of services, tailored specifically for the mobile or location-based market, and it is based on the youth culture. The use of i-mode is now being considered in parts of the world other than Japan, including the United States.

Mobile Applications

The mobile Internet, like its wired sibling, is a composition of infrastructure and applications. The full-service wireless networks will support a range of mobile services, including mobile entertainment, mobile Internet, mobile commerce, and mobile location-based services. M-commerce needs to develop quickly, because it is required in order to provide effective delivery of electronic commerce into the consumer's hand, anywhere, by using wireless technology. The success of mobile entertainment, mobile location-based services, and mobile Internet depend on the ability to conduct secure financial transactions. M-commerce has the power to transform the mobile phone into a mobile wallet. Already, major companies have begun to establish partnerships with banks, ticket agencies, and top brands to take advantage of the retail outlet in the consumer's hand.

One of the main requirements for m-commerce content is ease of use. Another consideration is how personal the content is; successful content has an electronically adjustable skin, if you will, to meet the inexhaustible demand for customization. One eagerly anticipated m-commerce application is the personal finance manager, which integrates all the aspects of your finances, including bank records, work expenses, and electronic purse expenditures.

M-commerce transactions are very important because doing finances is more compelling than monitoring them. A successful system will let you pay your bills while sitting on the bus, shuffle your shares while taking a break from work, or book your plane tickets while walking down the street.

Among other mobile applications, mobile entertainment is expected to grow, with GSM WAP or GPRS-based technology being used to deliver mobile games, mobile betting, mobile music, and mobile cartoons/icons. Mobile music will offer a wide array of possibilities, including MP3 music and artist or music clips, and the downloadable ringtone musique. Mobile betting is often considered an early example of m-commerce, with large segments of the population likely to participate. Japanese networks today offer the capability to download cartoons/icons (a major revenue producer for DoCoMo's i-mode system), and will soon be seen in GSM with WAP/GPRS capability.

Geography is very important in content development, and location-based online services promise to be a very big business. The position of a handheld device is instantly identifiable because the radio signals it emits can be tracked from cellular towers and triangulated, yielding locations nearly as accurate as those of global positioning system (GPS) receivers. The triangulation calculation yields the location of the transmitting phone, and the first derivative of location yields speed, which could be used to deduce traffic jams, road construction locations, and other roadside events. Bus stations could broadcast schedules to nearby pedestrians. Trains could become online shopping malls. Automobiles could locate the nearest restaurant, give directions to the nearest filling station that sells your brand of gasoline, or locate the nearest police station, hospital, parking lot, or movie theater. Broadband compasses could allow users to access pictures and information about landmarks. So a very wide range of everyday communication services could potentially be developed.

The geography factor also means that content can be tailored to where the user is—weather forecasts, restaurant locations with table availability and instant reservations, parking spaces, fast food delivery, dating services with prerecorded video profiles, and e-mail or voice mail exchanges. Any service where physical proximity is important can add value to the new devices.

Mobile consumers want convenience and they want novelty, and because a cell phone conversation provides a very important piece of information—the user's location—every business will need physical latitude, longitude, and elevation coordinates to sell merchandise to these moving targets. Therefore, Internet push technology may experience a revival. Once they are wired, mobile consumers offer endless new moneymaking possibilities. Unfortunately, we currently lack the business models and technology needed to realize this dream, but creative partnerships will see that the m-commerce marketplace materializes. Many such partnerships have already formed: Microsoft MSN Mobile and Ericsson, IBM and Nokia, HP and Nokia, Oracle and Telia, Sun Microsystems and NTT DoCoMo, and Yahoo! Mobile Services and Sprint. Toyota is launching My Car Universe, which is being created in partnership with Intel, Hewlett Packard, and Compaq. It would be difficult for any one supplier to carry through the entire chain, which requires cus-

A View into the Wireless Future

What might life look like in the wireless future—say, in 2008? In the next few years, companies plan to introduce handheld devices that could perform a wide variety of tasks, and this scenario involves a few people conducting their daily activities.

A university student, waiting at the bus stop, uses his digital companion to find out whether the bus is running on time. On the bus, a woman's device beeps an alert. She's been bidding for a collectible phone booth; someone has just outbid her, so she quickly sends in a higher bid.

A set of twins on the same bus are playing a networked game with an Internet friend who lives halfway around the globe.

Meanwhile, a woman riding along in a limo is using her device to check her stock portfolio because her news service just sent her a flash on merger rumors.

In a taxi nearby, a matchmaker service on a man's device beeps a proximity alert. A single woman who shares his taste in movies is close by. The man finds the woman, thanks to GPS location services, and starts a conversation. He used his digital companion to identify the closest flower shop and orders flowers for her, and as they walk by, the shop owner meets them at the door with a smile. Another wireless service helps him find a nearby Thai restaurant. Over lunch, they review the local movie reviews and schedules, then book tickets to a movie later that evening.

Meanwhile, outside the Thai restaurant, a teen walks down the street, bouncing to the beat of the latest music releases he downloaded to his wireless device earlier that morning.

After a long and leisurely lunch, the man and woman consult their digital companions, clearing their schedules so they can spend the rest of the day together.

tomer premises equipment, transport, and content, but creative partnerships bundling several of these together will produce the revenue streams that tomorrow's infrastructures promise.

■ Wireless MANs

There's an increasing interest in the application of wireless technologies to MANs, particularly in line with wireless local loop deployments, delivery of Internet access and high-speed video transmissions, and the new role of wireless competitive local exchange carriers (CLECs).

The range of MANs is up to 30 miles (50 kilometers). The configuration can be point-to-point or multipoint. The data rates for MANs are low to medium; 9,600 bps up to 128Kbps is typical—but in some arrangements, such as with the use of VSAT, up to 512Kbps may be feasible. Wireless LANs make use of both the licensed (800MHz to 935MHz range) and unlicensed (2.4GHz) bands. The technologies used to facilitate wireless MANs include microwave, infrared laser, and spread spectrum solutions.

Wireless Local Loop Applications

You can think of wireless local loop as an application. It doesn't speak to a particular technology. Various wireless alternatives can be deployed in order to activate the equivalent of the twisted-pair local-loop subscriber line. There are two major categories of wireless local loop:

- **Fixed wireless local loop**—Fixed wireless local loop involves a stationary installation. The main purpose is to dramatically reduce the cost of installing and maintaining the local loop plant, or subscriber lines. Distance in fixed wireless local loop is cost-insensitive, which is one of the advantages of this deployment. It is particularly used to provide the last mile/kilometer of connection, and the key advantage of the fixed-type category is that it uses a fixed antenna location, so it's relatively easy to use for traffic engineering, and it makes use of AC power.

- **Mobile wireless local loop**—Mobile wireless local loop involves the use of cellular telephone or cordless technology, along with satellites. This approach enables subscriber mobility, so you could use it as a replacement for a fixed line when you're in your home, but you could also move outside those boundaries and use it as a mobile line. The advantage is that you get greater roaming capability, but then you face a challenge in terms of traffic engineering, and the infrastructure design is more difficult than that of fixed wireless local loop.

Key applications for wireless local loop include addressing the needs of remote, rural, or isolated regions. It is also useful where rapid deployment is required. Wireline facilities require a minimum of 9 months for deployment, and many times it's 12 to 18 months, whereas with wireless techniques, deployment times are only 3 to 6 months. Another application for wireless local loop is for industrial or commercial sites, where there may be a need for temporary setups. Emergency and disaster relief are also greatly facilitated with wireless local loop systems—for example, where there's been a hurricane, an earthquake, or another major disaster that disables the land-based facilities. Other potential applications include data collection and telemetry, surveillance, security, pay phones, and kiosks.

One thing to bear in mind is that as you go forward, whatever technology you consider should be looking forward to handling nonvoice traffic. As mentioned many times throughout this book, the major type of traffic growth is in the area of data, and increasingly it will also include more complex objects, such as images and full-motion video. So be sure to account for this data traffic as you're choosing a long-term solution.

Wireless Local Loop Options

Cellular, PCS, Local Multipoint Distribution Service (LMDS), Multichannel Multipoint Distribution Service (MMDS), and Direct Broadcast Satellite (DBS) are the main options in wireless local loop technologies:

- **Cellular**—Cellular is the best option in a rural area or an area that is not densely populated, where large distances separate subscribers. In this environment, you need the advantages of a large cell size and, hence, the cellular architecture serves well.

- **PCS**—PCS is best for metro areas that are densely populated because it works at a high frequency over a small coverage area, so the frequencies can be reused more frequently and can address growing metropolitan populations.

- **LMDS**—LMDS is not really intended to support mobile applications, but it is seen as being a good alternative for supporting very-high bandwidth, and it's aimed at both voice and high-speed data access. The key concern with LMDS is that it operates in a very high portion of the microwave frequency band, making it easily obstructed and suffers great distortions in the face of adverse environmental or weather conditions.

  LMDS is terrestrial line-of-sight microwave, but it operates in the 10GHz to 45GHz range, depending on where in the world you are. A large frequency allocation of 1.3GHz operates in smaller microcells of 0.5 to 3 miles (1 to 5 kilometers), and within each system, it has the capability to serve 5,000 to 10,000 homes. Key applications of LMDS are wireless local loop, high-quality telephony, Internet access, two-way video, and security and energy management systems. LMDS promises downstream rates in the range of 51Mbps to 155Mbps and a return link of 1.5Mbps. But remember that the key issues here include frequency stability, interference from foliage, and rain fade. It appears that the first market for this service will be the business realm, rather than consumers.

- **MMDS**—MMDS involves terrestrial line-of-sight microwave. Because it is microwave, it does suffer from environmental interferences. But because it operates in the lower part of the frequency band, the 2GHz to 3GHz range, it is more tolerant of adverse conditions than its colleagues that operate at the higher bands (including LMDS). Again, operating at lower frequencies also means that it can have a larger range of coverage, and we're looking at a coverage cell of some 30 miles (50 kilometers).

MMDS can support up to 33 analog channels and more than 100 digital channels for purposes of digital TV. An MMDS set-top uses MPEG-2 for video compression–decompression and MPEG-2 carries entertainment-quality video, at 6Mbps. MMDS is also referred to as wireless cable TV because it competes with cable television. It is one technique for providing fixed wireless access to the Internet, as well as two-way data services.

■ **DBS**—DBS includes products such as Hughes DirectPC. This is not the same thing as Direct TV; DBS involves a different dish, a 21-inch dish. It provides for 400Kbps downstream from the Internet, and the reverse channel is the telephone subscriber line. DBS involves costs of around US$300 to US$500 for the equipment and a monthly charge of up to $40 per month. Hughes also recently announced DirectDSL, which offers ADSL downstream data rates. DBS can do well at delivering bulk volumes of data because of the high-speed downstream channel, and it should also eventually be capable of supporting multimedia. In the next year, new DBS systems will be making a significant difference. For example, AOL has a US $1.5 billion stake in Hughes Electronics (with two-way service planned for 2002), Wild Blue (formerly iSky; due to launch in 2002), Globalstart, and StarBand (a joint project of Gilat Satellite, Microsoft, Echostar and ING Furman Selz) are all moving in the DBS arena.

■ **DirecTV Duo**—DirecTV Duo combines digital video programming and Internet access. In the next year or so we can expect to see several two-way interactive satellite systems being introduced that involve some very interesting partnerships.

Broadband capabilities at the local loop need to be supported by wireless alternatives, as well as by wireline. One option is to implement a point-to-multipoint topology that makes use of broadband technologies operating in the megabits per second range. Such a system would be capable of supporting Internet access as well as providing for VoIP. An advantage here is the greatly reduced cost for consumer traffic, and, ultimately, also for more interesting applications such as where voice becomes part of a greater set of applications that include data and multimedia.

Wireless CLECs play a big role in this arena, and the key issue is speed of deployment. Another important issue is the ability to deploy what are viewed as high-bandwidth data services for businesses on a reduced-cost basis. The wireless CLECs look to provide data rates of 56Kbps up to 45Mbps, which are normally associated with private-line alternatives. A popular band for this is 38GHz, but the actual spectrum allocation varies, depending on where you are in the world.

Again, the wireless CLECs are business-oriented. They promise to lower the installation time and cost as compared to wire or fiber alternatives, and some of them will extend their offering to include wired facilities. But keep your eye on this space as there are continually new developments in broadband wireless, including the use of Free Space Optics, which is covered in Chapter 13, "Broadband Access Solutions."

Wireless LANs

LANs are important in two areas: in wireless office telecommunication systems (which are essentially cordless telephony as adjuncts to the on-premise PBXs) and in the use of wireless LANs (which employ either spread-spectrum or infrared technology).

The idea behind wireless LANs is augmentation, not replacement, of wired LANs and telephone systems. So, there may be issues with asbestos walls, or oak paneling, or ancient marble that's a pity to break into, that require some alternative to wire. Wireless LANs operate over a small range, about 1 to 330 feet (0.3 to 100 meters), so it's a microcellular architecture. Wireless LANs typically support what we'd call medium speeds today, ranging from 1Mbps to 11Mbps, although emerging standards, such as 802.11a, promise to increase those data rates to 40Mbps. The architecture of a wireless LAN in shown in Figure 14.15.

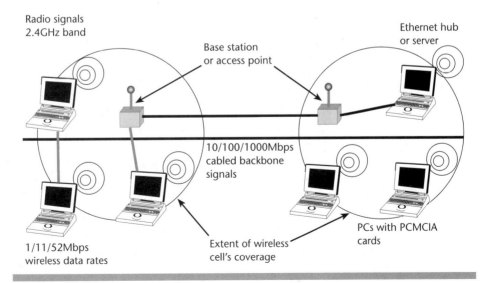

Figure 14.15 Wireless LAN architecture

Primary benefits of wireless LANs are that they reduce costs, particularly from the standpoint of moves, adds, and changes, in situations in which you need to dynamically reorganize where people and their devices reside. Wireless LANs also simplify the installation process, speed deployment, and enable mobility, so they facilitate low-cost installations, temporary arrangements, the working around environmental hazards or preserving historic buildings, and disaster recovery. All these applications are well suited for the consideration of a wireless LAN.

Wireless LANs can be implemented as infrared systems or as unlicensed narrowband microwave and spread spectrum that operate in the Industrial, Scientific, and Medical (ISM) band (900MHz and 2400MHz), as specified in ETSI 300.328.

IEEE 802.11 represents the first standard for wireless LAN products from an internationally recognized, independent organization, the IEEE. The 802.11 standard provides MAC (Media Access Control) and PHY (Physical Layer) functionality for wireless connectivity of fixed, portable, and moving stations moving at pedestrian and vehicular speeds within a local area. Specific features of 802.11 include support of asynchronous and time-bounded delivery service, accommodation of transmission rates of 1Mbps and 2Mbps, support of most market applications, multicast (including broadcast) services, network management services, and registration and authentication services. The target environments for use of 802.11 include inside buildings—such as offices, banks, shops, malls, hospitals, manufacturing plants, and residences—and outdoor areas—such as parking lots, campuses, building complexes, and outdoor plants. New high-speed extensions include 802.11a, which will support up to 40Mbps in the 5GHz band, and 802.11b, which will support 11Mbps in the 2.4GHz band, by using DSSS.

HIPERLAN is the European Community's standard for wireless LANs. A committee set up by the ETSI designed it. The designed standard was aimed to be as close as possible in performance to wireline LANs such as Ethernet. A bit rate of 23.529Mbps was provided for each channel, and the five existing channels occupy 150MHz of bandwidth, in either the 5.15MHz to 5.30GHz range or the 17.1MHz to 17.2GHz range. At the lower frequencies, it has power up to 1 watt, and at the higher frequency band, it has power up to 100 milliwatts. It offers a range of three channels to five channels, with a little over 23Mbps for each channel. At 150 feet (46 meters) it can support 20Mbps. At 2,500 feet (762 meters), the data rates drop to 1Mbps. In the 17GHz band, 100Mbps to 150Mbps is possible. Time-bounded, or isochronous, services are defined for HIPERLAN and use distributed control, which is essentially a physical- and data-link-layer definition.

The Unlicensed National Information Infrastructure (UNII) band, originally called SUPERNet (Shared Unlicensed Personal Radio Networks), was originally proposed by WINForum and Apple. It's an allocation of some 300MHz, largely in the 5GHz to 6GHz bands, and it somewhat overlaps with the HIPERLAN standard.

A number of 10 Mbps+wireless LAN products are in development, including RadioLAN, Clarion, Aironet, the 802.11 high-speed extensions, and HIPERLAN 2, 3, and 4. There's also exploration at the 60GHz ISM band.

Wireless PANs

As we continue to distribute intelligence into smaller and smaller devices and everyday accessories, the area domain of the network is reduced, until it rests upon our very selves, in the form of PANs. Many approaches to PAN are under investigation and development, including the use of our own human energy fields to create a low-power network to provide connectivity between the badge-based computers, smart wearables, and implants that are on or in the person.

A wireless PAN is a network that serves a single person or a small workgroup. Limited distance, limited throughput, low volume, and peripheral sharing are characteristics of PANs. Today, PANs are generally used to transfer data between a laptop or PDA, or a desktop machine or server, to a printer. They also provide support for virtual docking stations, peripheral sharing, and ad hoc infrared links. Future applications will grow to embrace wearables and will rely on human energy fields to power badge-based computers. At the moment, wireless PANs largely use infrared links, but that will change as intelligence begins to migrate onto and into the human.

The main PAN standards today, as discussed in the following sections, include Infrared Data Association (IrDA), Bluetooth, and HomeRF. Technologies such as Bluetooth and HomeRF are expected to be deployed in dual-mode smart phones that we'll be able to use to download e-mail and Web data while on the road and then exchange that data with a laptop or desktop machine in the office.

IrDA

The IrDA standard is sometimes referred to as point-and-squirt because it allows you to point your notebook at a printer and squirt the document via the air, rather than requiring a cable. IrDA operates at 115.2Kbps but is moving toward 4Mbps, 10Mbps, and 20Mbps rates. Low cost, low power, and high noise immunity are characteristics of IrDA, which is standard on many notebooks and printers.

Bluetooth

Of great interest at the moment is a standard called Bluetooth, which was the joint effort of 3Com, Ericsson, IBM, Intel, Lucent, Microsoft, Motorola, Nokia, and Toshiba. It involves a very low-cost chip, ideally at US$5. (That's not to say it's there already. We're still probably more in the US$10 to US$20 range, but the idea is to get it down to about US$5 a chip and embed it in everything around you.) Bluetooth would give each device a short-range wireless capability. It operates over a 100-foot (30-meter) coverage area, so it's a technology that would allow personal digital assistants, laptops, cell phones, and any intelligent appliance embedded with such a chip to communicate and be linked wirelessly. We're looking at supporting 1Mbps by using FHSS in the 2.4GHz band. One synchronous channel can be configured either asymmetrically or symmetrically. With asymmetric arrangements, you get 721Kbps downstream and 57.6Kbps upstream; with symmetrical arrangements, you get 432.6Kbps in each direction. Bluetooth also offers up to three asynchronous channels, at 64Kbps each.

Bluetooth standards include authentication, encryption, forward error correction, and automatic request for retransmission. More than 2,000 manufacturers have joined the movement. Bluetooth is an important standard, particularly to the realm of pervasive computing, and, again, this emphasizes the inevitable requirement for a wireless home area network (HAN) between your other options that you'll need for high-speed entertainment and computing networks. (Chapter 15 "The Broadband Home and HANs," discusses HANs.)

HomeRF

The HomeRF standard was developed by the HomeRF Working Group, which was founded in 1998 by Compaq, IBM, Hewlett Packard, and others. It uses Shared Wireless Access Protocol (SWAP) and provides an open standard for short-range transmission of digital voice and data between mobile devices. It transmits in the 2.4GHz band and uses a frequency hopping technique. Up to 127 devices can be addressed within a range of 150 feet (46 meters), and HomeRF supports a data rate of 1Mbps to 2Mbps.

For more learning resources, quizzes, and discussion forums on concepts related to this chapter, see www.telecomessentials.com/learningcenter.

Chapter 15

The Broadband Home and HANs

This chapter is devoted to an entirely new domain in networking: the broadband home and home area networking. As intelligence has become more affordable and miniature, it has found its way into everyday objects, affecting our lifestyles and our homes.

■ The Broadband Home

Consider the top technological advances over the past 100 years—developments in airplanes, antibiotics, television, computers, the Internet. In this context, the housing industry today is where the auto industry was in the 1950s. Although the technological revolution has affected most aspects of our lives, our homes have been left behind. But that will change with the introduction of intelligent appliances that work together to complete tasks; for example, self-cleaning surfaces will make life easier power-generating fuel cells will save money and visual reminders will help protect you and your family.

As broadband access alternatives are deployed, an interesting phenomenon occurs. The bottleneck shifts from the local loop to the inside of the home. As you bring in more broadband services to the home—your smart house—you require a networking solution within the home to distribute that information among the various devices that will be making use of it and among the various settings within the home where you might want to access the network and its services. This network domain is referred to as the home area network (HAN).

The Smart House

Ideally, the smart house will use computers to assist its inhabitants in living a safe, healthy, and happy life. The smart house is not yet a perfected reality, but the age of robotics might make that happen. For the time being, the smart house allows you to integrate and manage your home, your work, your learning, and your leisure activities. The smart house can take over many home management tasks, performing them automatically, and actually learning from them. And, most importantly, the details of the smart house are transparent—you can't see how it's actually working and doing what it does.

Who can benefit from such an infrastructure? Well, certainly people who want to make the most intelligent use possible of their time, people who appreciate convenience, people who care about saving energy, people who care about security, people who care about their health, and people with functional limitations, including those who are physically disabled, aging, or extremely busy.

The smart house supports its inhabitants in many ways. It can wake you in the morning at a specified desired time. It can make sure your shower is at what you consider the ideal water temperature. It can ensure that you leave on time for work, school, or social engagements.

The smart house can also provide you with information as needed. It can handle routine daily information, such as keeping schedules, providing music, and video-tracking a person moving around the premises. It can do special assignments, such as handling to-do lists, home management information, and disaster planning (as well as management of those disaster plans). It can help in the area of nutrition and health management by working with you to plan and prepare good meals. For instance, it might look at your nutritional requirements and health needs, preferences, and interests, and then explore menu possibilities for you. It could also assist in determining the availability of ingredients by procuring the required ingredients, organizing the necessary cooking resources, and synchronizing multiple tasks, including preparation. It could also help manage food by managing purchasing schedules to match your nutritional requirements and planned activities, as well as take advantage of bargains. The smart house could also assist in food storage by maintaining inventory control, managing leftovers, and dealing with waste.

When you embed intelligence into a device, you create an interesting new opportunity for business. That device has to have a reason for being, and it has to have a reason to continue evolving so that you will spend more money and time on it. To address this challenge, device manufacturers are beginning to bundle content and applications with their smart appliances. For instance, a smart toaster might have the capability to, on a community basis with other toasters in your neighborhood, bid on bread over the Internet, achieving a greater discount for you and all your neighbors.

The smart house also provides a communications infrastructure for its inhabitants, so it can support telephony, television, radio, and intelligent appliances that chat with each other, along with Web browsing, online banking, and education. It supports communications between the house and family and other household members, friends, the community, coworkers, service providers, and emergency services.

The smart house can help with household chores, and it can look after your things. By providing security, it can help keep out intruders, protect the inhabitants from unwanted interruptions, monitor a range of smart devices within and outside the home, and provide outsiders access to your home when and where needed. It can protect you from harm. For example, if you leave the stove on, LCDs can display the offending burner to warn you. Or the house could alert you if the roof has sprung a leak or if there is mold growing in the ducts.

The smart house can also manage energy; with electrochromic windows each kilowatt of energy used to darken the window saves 30 kilowatts of air conditioning. This feature is especially important because managing energy will be increasingly important. According to the U.S. Energy Information Administration, 22 trillion kilowatt hours of electricity will be needed for the world by 2020, representing a 75% increase over existing kilowatt hour levels.

A smart house can help ensure that you are educated by bringing you information that's pertinent to your professional profile or to your educational plan. And it can certainly help make sure that you have some fun—for example, by preparing your entertainment menu for the day.

In a smart house, anything can be automated. You can call the house from your car to fill the hot tub. You can time outside lights based on longitude and latitude so that they're precisely aligned to turn off and on with sunrise and sunset. Intelligent appliances can learn from your purchasing habits and build intelligence to keep you informed and to care for you. In essence, all these smart things that become automated will be self-aware and self-managing. As the smart house becomes a reality, homes will begin to take on personalities of their own, and you just may have to learn to live with them!

Intelligent Appliances

So, what goes into a smart house? A variety of infrastructures are involved in the smart house, including sensors, fiber optics, and solar energy. One key aspect of a smart house is smart components, such as doors, windows, drapes, elevators, security systems, heating and ventilation, sprinklers, hot tubs, and showers. Smart components can also be found in furniture—for example, smart beds, drawers, cupboards, medicine cabinets, wall screens, tables, and breakfast trays. (I'm not making these up; these are actually examples of items that exist today!) Intelligent appliances are a great new area of smart components; in the near future, you are likely to encounter smart refrigerators, ovens, alarm clocks, washers, dryers, books, cameras, TVs, entertainment system, and picture frames, among a multitude of other things.

The smart house has many human-centered interfaces that support multimedia, multimodal, and multisensory information flows. The smart house obviously requires telecommunications services in the form of broadband access, for which xDSL, coaxial cable, hybrid fiber cable, broadband wireless, Powerline Telecommunications, or Gigabit Ethernet could be used.

A critical component of the smart house is the HAN, which, as discussed later in this chapter, provides the invisible infrastructure that links together all the smart things in the house. It enables control of those devices from anywhere, and it enables control of devices either individually or in groups. One day, a home will have computing networks that supply every room of the house with automation and data. Analysts predict that over the next several years, an increasing number of households will become totally interconnected, with a HAN joining their communications, entertainment, and domestic appliance equipment. In the broadband era, bandwidth starts at home!

When the network is in place, the dynamics of the home begin to change, and this means that computer accessories need to be built into everything that you normally associate with the home. So, for example, today we have many manufacturers of kitchen environments. Whirlpool, Telia, and General Electric are among those producing smart refrigerators, smart alarm clocks, smart coffee pots, and smart microwaves—all of which talk to each other. If you set your alarm clock for 6:00 AM, it knows that it needs to tell the coffee pot to make coffee for 6:45 AM. If you get a call from the airline reservation system at 3:00 AM, the message goes to your alarm clock, telling it that flights tomorrow morning are being delayed by an hour. Because the alarm knows you want it to, it can set itself to wake you an hour later than planned. And, of course, it contacts the coffee pot, requesting that it reset itself as well. Smart microwaves today are Internet connected, and they can go out actively throughout the day to seek new recipes that are known to be appealing to you; they provide these to you, along with an assessment of your pantry inventory at home that tells whether you have the needed ingredients for the new recipes.

ICL and Electrolux were two of the first companies to introduce smart refrigerators. These smart appliances have volume-based sensors that can tell when an item is running low and thereby put the item on your shopping list or automatically place an order online. They have scanners that can read bar codes, so that they can place items on a shopping list. They have LCDs that can enable you to Web surf or conduct communications or messaging activities through that panel as well, saving on space in the kitchen. And very soon, these smart refrigerators will have artificial noses—sniffers that will be able to determine the freshness of your foodstuffs based on smell. If your milk carton is full and has been sitting there for two weeks, the refrigerator can take a quick sniff and determine that the milk is sour and discourage you from consuming it—and it can order you a fresh carton at the same time. A smart refrigerator can also have a display monitor on the outside door that allows you to surf the Web from the kitchen, looking for recipes, investigating pricing, engaging in communications, and using different types of applications.

All sorts of low-cost smart tablets are being created—intelligent appliances that are not full-scale PCs, but which are slimmed-down versions that allow you to Web surf and take care of some rudimentary tasks such as scheduling and messaging. Such tablets are now being built into kitchen cabinetry, again to conserve on space. Some are designed for just collecting recipes and depicting cooking preparations or panels that are designed to control the various home systems. Several appliance manufacturers are introducing Internet appliances that replace all those little sticky yellow papers that you to stick on your fridge to leave messages for family members and to remind yourself what to get at the store and to do different activities. Now all this information can be very neatly contained in one very smart, attractive device that even alerts you to the fact that important messages have been left.

Intelligence is being built into doors so that if a painter is trying to come in to paint your living room when you're at work, when the painter rings the doorbell, you can see a view of him so you can decide to let him in by remotely activating the door. You could continue to track the painter's activities throughout the home by using remote eyes. Of course, those remote eyes would also facilitate communication among families and friends; for example, grandparents could observe their grandchildren at play with their parents.

Wide-panel TV screens are expected to become available within two or three years, and they may even reach a price point that many of us find realistic. These TVs introduce a new window to the world that involves not just entertainment information, but a platform for gathering educational and other resources. Interactive wide-panel components are also being introduced onto mobile platforms, which enable you to progress throughout the home, viewing information as you go.

You might at first think a wired breakfast tray seems odd, but the first thing many of us do in the morning is check our e-mail, so now furniture is being developed that incorporates keyboards and screens into other everyday functions such as dining. Coffee tables have been designed such that when you open the lid, you have a full-scale PC, complete with a high-resolution screen and all the input/output devices you might need.

Within five years we're expecting marvelous new equipment that's specifically designed to act as a medical assistant. For example, sensors will be built into toothbrushes so that as you brush your teeth, your mirror will display your temperature, heart rate, blood pressure, cholesterol count, and so on, and make recommendations for menus or exercises. Sensors that can measure electrolyte levels are small enough to fit into a toothbrush. Now we're working on sensors that will be able to measure protein levels, aiding in the ongoing maintenance of cardiac ailments. Other developments will also contribute to this hospital-at-home. For instance, smart socks are being developed; they are fiber-optic-cabled socks for people who have diabetes or spinal cord injuries and who suffer from ulceration in their feet. The smart socks will detect whether there are weak spots and where they might be occurring in the feet, proactively managing the condition. There's also a suggestion that a melanoma monitor might become part of a normal shower installation, and every time you take a shower, the monitor will take an image so that over time it can compare the images and determine whether there are any changes in the size, coloring, or texture of any spots you may have.

Another combination of a smart piece of furniture and a health care device is the smart bed. This bed would monitor your vital statistics while you sleep, and in the morning it would provide you with a summary of how you performed through-out the night, perhaps including the fact that you tossed and turned at least ten times and therefore might need to do some stress-reducing exercises. Your virtual personal trainer (a Web agent) would then appear to facilitate a round of such exercises for you. Stuffed toy pets are being developed for the elderly. They can monitor vital signs, and if something's awry, they initiate communication with whomever has been designated to be informed of any changes in health status.

Soon, when you get up in the morning, there will be hundreds of little sensors that will all be engaged in somehow managing some part of your life—and most likely reporting on it! The privacy implications of pervasive computing are huge, and it seems that the best advice is to assume that there is no privacy any longer and protect your personal data with forethought.

■ HANs

Smart devices need channels over which to communicate, so the more intelligent appliances and accessories you have in the home, the greater the likelihood that they need a network—a HAN—over which to exchange information in order to realize value. The emergence of intelligent appliances also opens up an entirely new level of market involvement. It creates a new outlet for knowledge, content, and information services that can be offered by online experts and service provid-ers. The appliance acts as a vehicle for stimulating interest in activities that benefit from using the appliance. In essence, the appliance becomes a part of a collabora-tive system that satisfies a much higher human need. Basically, a smart device needs a reason to exist, and that reason is a continually developing set of applica-tions and services with which to better your life. So it's important to look beyond the last mile, at what technologies apply in HANs and why.

Pervasive Computing

As we distribute intelligence across a wider range of devices, we are experiencing *pervasive computing* or *ubiquitous computing*. Much of this pervasive computing will occur in smart homes, but much of it will occur elsewhere, too—devices being pioneered include smart clothing and smart tracking devices.

As we miniaturize intelligence, we can place it on mobile platforms, but today we still have to hold and manipulate small keys or a stylus on the device. Wouldn't it make much more sense to simply embed the computing and communications tool set into the clothing or into accessories like your jewelry or your belt or your glasses? Work is going on in all these areas right now, as well as in areas such as smart food, smart wrappers, smart medical needles, and smart cars.

Another fascinating idea is smart tattoos, which are smart dermal implants. Instead of having to inject insulin, a diabetic could get a tattoo every so often that contains insulin within it. A medical office can monitor the tattoo remotely, and if it sees that the person's insulin level is dropping, it can send a little message over the network that causes the correct amount of insulin to be dispensed. A backpack traveler who's going on a year-long mission of viewing the world could get a smart tattoo that contains vaccines that can be administered as she gets to certain countries.

Of course, the new developments make yet more new developments necessary. Many cars today are equipped to access the Internet through built-in panels. To help people drive safely while Web surfing in their vehicles, we need smart highways: A series of scanners and sensors are placed along roadways to guide vehicles, and wireless capabilities, radar built into the vehicles, allows distances to be calculated and therefore collisions to be predicted and cars to automatically brake when needed.

Devices are getting smaller and more powerful all the time, and they're getting physically closer to our bodies, as well. For example, if I tell you we have a smart telephone available, you would naturally think that it should know how to route the call based on the number dialed over what will be the most cost-effective carrier. But a really smart telephone would be able to tap into your brain waves. It would be able to detect that you're in beta wave form, which implies heavy thought process, and as a result, it should divert the call to a messaging system because if it rang, it would disrupt you at doing something that seems to be more important at the moment. MIT labs is working on another level of smart-affective computing, giving the computer the capability to sense and understand your state of mind. One MIT project involves an electromyogram. With it, when you're clenching your jaw, for instance, your cheek turns a bright red, and that alerts the computer to the fact that there's a problem occurring. Your friendly machine can now stop and work with you to resolve the frustration.

If we embed intelligence into our clothing and accessories, and even use it on our bodies, we create yet another frontier for networking: the personal area network (PAN), which surrounds an individual and provides networking between badge-based computers and other input/output devices in the form of accessories. These PANs are already being created in labs.

(continued on next page)

(continued)

Other emerging areas in the Age of Intelligence are tagging human beings (for example, children, diplomats who are at risk of being kidnapped), artificial intelligence, and artificial life. Humans' weakest point is our physiology. No matter how smart or wealthy a person is, a knife wound or a bullet in a strategic spot can kill him. So if we're going to explore the frontiers that the universe presents us with, one of our accomplishments will need to be breaking the light barrier, and a carbon-based being will not be able to accomplish that; therefore, we're looking at building a new form of intelligence that will be the electronic and photonic equivalent of today's humans. Recently, we've seen the introduction of single-purpose robots that can mow a lawn or vacuum a home. Within 10 years, we will begin to see multifunctional robots that will become assistants in our everyday life.

I could spend many more pages talking about the myriad new areas of research and discovery. Suffice it to say, though, that we're somewhere near the beginning of a great journey, and we're really only starting to see the possibilities and what we need to do to make those possibilities a reality.

The HAN Market, Applications, and Elements

Broadband deployments are accelerating. As of the middle of 2001, something on the order of 10 million to 12 million broadband developments had been implemented worldwide. In the next several years, the number of broadband deployments is expected to reach the 40 million mark. Traditionally these broadband deployments have focused on core networks and on the last mile, the local loop. But the last mile is really only half of the broadband solution. Simplicity and user-friendliness are driving rapid penetration of intelligence into all the various home elements. The HAN—which is the last 328 feet (100 meters)—will complete the broadband access solution. Therefore, we can expect to see the global market for home networking equipment rise substantially. Experts say that the home data and entertainment networking market, as well as the connectivity services market, will be worth billions of dollars. Connectivity products will offer additional voice management, home monitoring, and new entertainment services. The service provider will begin to move its area of domain into the home, offering broadband access along with home area networking technology, smart appliances, and bundled applications.

We will be developing quite a complex HAN infrastructure, which might include the components shown in Figure 15.1. The product range includes transceivers or communications interfaces, network interface cards for the various devices participating on the network, gateways, servers, sensors, controllers, and

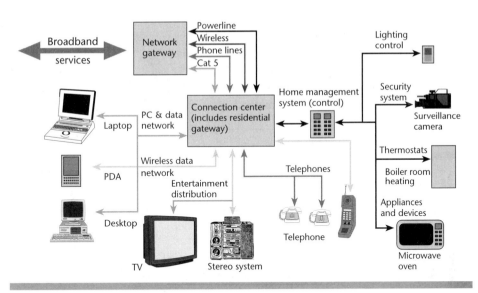

Figure 15.1 Home networking elements

some form of an operating system. A variety of broadband services—including DSL, hybrid arrangements, fiber, and wireless—will be possible. Those services will terminate on the home network gateway. From that network gateway you will connect into some form of a communications hub, a residential gateway device that can split the signals and deliver them to the proper receiver. From this residential gateway you'll have several different networks. You'll have the automation and control network on which reside the various sensors that help automate the home to make your life easier and happier. Through that gateway you'll also have access to *mobility networks*—wireless networks that allow you to roam within the range of your home and the outdoor area surrounding it. You'll have the very high-speed computer and entertainment networks that may be required for purposes of professional or leisure activities.

Computer interconnection is a major application of HANs. It allows access to the Internet, as well as the connection and communication of multiple PCs with various peripherals and communications and entertainment devices. This computer connection requires very high-speed networks. Generally, homes with two or more computers are considered to be prime candidates for this type of HAN, and in the United States there are about 17 million such homes. Industry analysts project that HANs for communications and entertainment will find their way into more than 6 million U.S. households by 2003. So controlling the home—including management of lights, appliances, climate control systems, and surveillance cameras—will be a huge market for HANs.

Types of HANs

Let's take a look at the technologies that can be applied in HANs. Again, remember that the home network is likely to become a layered network, just like the enterprise network, where there's a need for backbone networks, mobility networks, control networks, and wired networks, each of which is best served by one or another alternative. The success of HANs depends on standard products that are operable with a variety of physical infrastructures, so we'll see the use of voice-grade telephony wiring, electric powerlines, wireless, and fiber, among other techniques. By far, currently, the greatest penetration is of the phone-line approach, followed by wireless, and then by the powerlines approach. We expect to see growth in the wireless and powerlines areas in the very near future.

HANs over Phone Lines

Phone lines can be used in HANs, and a big interest group here is the Home Phone Networking Alliance (HomePNA), described in Chapter 13, "Broadband Access Solutions," which continues to grow the home networking market and whose membership is continually expanding. Today, HomePNA consists of more than 150 companies, 25% of which are outside the United States. HomePNA has specified products that have up to 10Mbps capacity. According to the HomePNA, home area networking is very important for the customer because it enables broadband Internet distribution, shared broadband access via a multitude of devices in the home, low-cost IP telephony, and streaming audio throughout the house. HomePNA (www.homepna.com) expects that by 2003, killer applications will include video distribution, e-commerce that's integrated via television and the Internet, and next-generation peer-to-peer applications.

Another standards group is involved with home networking over phone lines: The ITU's Question 4/Study Group 15 is working on the standard G.pnt for phone network transceivers.

The advantages associated with the phone-line approach include the fact that current products can use phone lines to interconnect PCs and peripherals for shared Internet access. A disadvantage is that because phone jacks do not offer sufficient network access points to support pervasive computing within the home, the phone-line approach cannot serve as a long-term backbone solution. Figure 15.2 shows an example of a HAN over phone lines.

HANs over Powerlines

Numerous standards address home networking over powerlines (see Chapter 13). X10 Ltd.'s standard X10 controls appliances over electric powerlines in the home and publishes the specifications of transmitting devices. Manufacturers of home appliances can design and embed X10 transmitters in them, and the receiving and control devices are made by X10 itself.

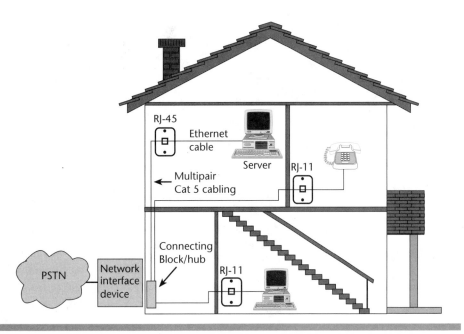

Figure 15.2 A HAN over phone lines

Another standard involves the use of Orthogonal Frequency Division Multiplexing (OFDM), and several companies are pursuing this approach. CEBus, based on Electronic Industries Association (EIA) 600, also opens the home networking standard to multiple alternatives, including power lines. And the International Power Line Communications Forum (IPCF), based in the United Kingdom, is working to make powerline communications products interoperable.

The main advantage of the powerline approach is that it's an ideal architecture for data networks because the majority of devices must already connect to a power source in order to operate in the first place. The main disadvantage is that your flexibility is dependent on the availability and placement of those power sources. Figure 15.3 shows an example of a powerline HAN.

Wireless HANs

A multitude of standards address wireless HANs:

- IEEE 802.11 originally supported 1Mbps to 2Mbps, in the 2.4GHz range. The IEEE has since published two supplements to this 802.11 standard: 802.11a (40Mbps in the 5.8GHz band) and 802.11b (11Mbps in the 2.4GHz band).

- The HomeRF Working Group uses the Shared Wireless Access Protocol (SWAP) and frequency hopping. The SWAP system can operate either as an

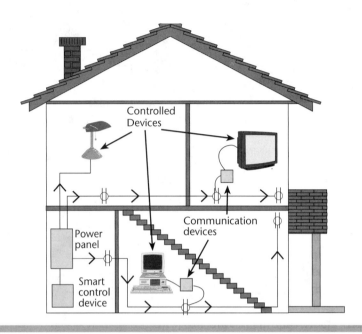

Figure 15.3 A powerline HAN

ad hoc network or as a managed network under the control of a connection point.

■ The Bluetooth Consortium deals with networks that operate over very short ranges (about 100 feet, or 30 meters), but an increasing number of devices are being created to work in these ranges; approximately 2,500 manufacturers have signed up to incorporate Bluetooth in their products, so this is likely to be a very important step in the growth of wireless.

■ The Wireless LAN Interoperability Forum promotes OpenAir, which also makes use of frequency hopping.

■ The European Telecommunications Standards Institute has broadband radio access networks (BRANs), which follows the HIPERLAN standard and uses a technique called Gaussian frequency shift key (GFSK) as its access technique.

■ Digital Enhanced Cordless Telecommunications (DECT) uses GFSK.

■ ShareWave (that is, Proxim) is also working on wireless standards.

There are numerous HAN standards, which is sometimes good and sometimes bad. Clearly, there can be lots of interoperability issues involved here. (Chapter 14, "Wireless Communications," describes wireless communication, including standards, in more detail.) Figure 15.4 shows an example of a wireless HAN.

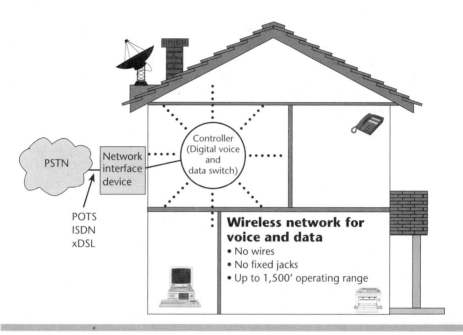

Figure 15.4 A wireless HAN

The main advantage of wireless is that you have an untethered solution for devices that need mobility in communications. I adore my wireless LAN, specifically for that reason: I can take my work where I want it, within my grounds, and not worry about being near a phone jack or even a power connection.

The disadvantage of wireless HANs is that, generally, wireless has limited bandwidth. Wireless also has unresolved security issues, network infringement issues, interference from other wireless sources, and comparatively high costs. (These issues are discussed in Chapter 13.)

Control Networks

Control networks are typically low-speed powerline networks. The most widely used technologies for home automation and control purposes are based on three standards:

- **Echelon Corporation's LonWorks**—LonWorks is an open standard under EIA 709. More than 4,000 developers worldwide are working on hardware, software, and integrated systems for the LonWorks platform. The protocol is now embedded in silicon neuron chips from Cypress Semiconductor, Toshiba America, and other companies. Dozens of manufacturers are incorporating these chips into their modules for controlling household electrical equipment.

■ **X10**—As mentioned earlier in the chapter, X10 is a communications protocol for remote control of electrical devices and communications (off, on, and dim functions) over standard household AC powerline wiring. X10 publishes the specs, manufacturers can embed the transmitters into their appliances, and X10 manufactures and sells the receiving and control devices.

■ **CEBus**—CEBus, as discussed earlier in the chapter, is based on EIA 600 and is an open standard that specifies the technology and the parameters for communication by using powerlines, Category 5 twisted-pair, coax, wireless, and infrared.

Advantages of control networks include the fact that there are existing product solutions and well-established industry standards. Control networks also have relatively low cost and simple implementation. The disadvantage is that these networks are not designed to support real-time, high-bandwidth, or mobility requirements, so the value proposition of stand-alone applications does not offer the right incentives for the mainstream market to consume the products.

Wired Networks

Wired networks include universal serial bus (USB), Category 5 or 10BaseT wiring, and the IEEE's 1394 Firewire. Benefits are that wired network standards are reliable and robust. The drawbacks of wired networks are that penetrating the mass market requires a "no new wires" technology. These solutions, therefore, will primarily extend only to new homes that are making use of structured wiring and perhaps to the technophile hobbyist and professional home user market.

HAN Gateways and Servers

A HAN needs a system for identifying data and routing it to its destination, and this implies the need for gateways and servers. Coactive Network supplies a home telemetry gateway. It supports LonWorks currently, and future releases will also support X10 and connect to multiple media types, including both powerline and wireless. Rebel.com provides a product called NetWinder, which is a Linux-based server.

Planning for the Future

When considering HANs, you must plan for the future. You need to plan and install an infrastructure that's designed to address today's needs, and you also need to understand that tomorrow you'll need to support much more advanced applications and a greater range of devices. It's a good idea to stay away from permanent equipment that will soon become obsolete. You should try not to choose products that limit your ability to change or to upgrade in the future, and you should try to ensure that the infrastructure stays invisible.

You should consider a number of other points going forward, as more and more intelligence surrounds you and becomes self-aware in an attempt to serve you even better:

- Who's in control in the smart house?
- Does the house's behavior act consistently with the image you would like to project?
- Does the house now have a personality of its own?
- What happens when the power goes off? More importantly, what happens when the house crashes? Do you get locked in forever?

Of course, these and many other issues will be resolved in time. Security will be quite important to all this, and while I won't claim that security solutions abound, there has been significant progress in the areas of encryption, authentication, and key exchange. There is much additional development being done in this area, including the use of biometrics. We are now in the early stages with HANs.

For more learning resources, quizzes, and discussion forums on concepts related to this chapter, see www.telecomessentials.com/learningcenter.

Glossary

Numerals

10Base2   Thin coax Ethernet cable.

10Base5   Thick coax Ethernet cable.

10BaseFL   2 strands of multimode optical fiber Ethernet cable.

10BaseT   2-pair UTP Ethernet cable.

100BaseFX   2 strands of multimode optical-fiber Fast Ethernet cable.

100BaseT2   2-pair Cat 3 UTP Fast Ethernet cable.

100BaseT4   4-pair Cat 3 UTP Fast Ethernet cable.

100BaseTX   2-pair Cat 5 UTP Fast Ethernet cable.

1000BaseCX   Coax patch cable Gigabit Ethernet cable.

1000BaseLX   Long-wavelength single-mode optical-fiber Gigabit Ethernet cable.

1000BaseSX   Short-wavelength multimode optical-fiber Gigabit Ethernet cable.

1000BaseT   4-pair Cat 5 or Cat 5e UTP Gigabit Ethernet cable.

1000BaseTX   2-pair Cat 6 (currently a TIA draft proposal) Gigabit Ethernet cable.

23B+D   The North American and Japanese infrastructure for PRI, which provides twenty-three 64Kbps B-channels for information and one 64Kbps D-channel for signaling and additional packet data.

2B1Q   A single-carrier modulation scheme that provides for 2 bits/Hz and is used in ISDN, HDSL, and IDSL.

2G (second-generation) wireless   The second generation of wireless communication, which introduced digital transmission and includes digital cellular and PCS systems, such as TDMA (ANSI-136), GSM, and IS-95.

2.5G (2.5-generation) wireless   The generation of wireless communication between 2G and 3G, which offers enhancements to the data services on existing second-generation digital platforms. 2.5G can support faster data rates, ranging from 64Kbps to 384Kbps, depending on the standard and the technology.

3DES (Triple DES)   168-bit encryption that uses three 56-bit keys. 3DES applies the DES algorithm to a plaintext block three times.

3G (third-generation) wireless   The third generation of wireless communication, which will include digital transmission; however, it also permits per-user and terminal mobility by providing a single mobile communication service, adjusted for broadband applications (including voice, data, and multimedia streams), that will support higher data speeds, 2Mbps, with the objective of ultimately supporting up to 155Mbps.

30B+D   The ITU infrastructure for PRI, which provides thirty 64Kbps channels and one 64Kbps D-channel.

6bone   An experimental network that is being used as an environment for IPv6 research. So far more than 400 networks in more than 40 countries are connected to the 6bone network.

A

A (access) link   A link that interconnects an STP with either an SSP or an SCP. The SSP and SCP, collectively, are referred to as the *signaling endpoints*. A message sent to and from the SSPs or SCPs first goes to its home STP, which in turn processes or routes the message.

ABR (available bit rate)   One of the ATM service classes. ABR supports VBR data traffic with average and peak traffic parameters (for example, LAN interconnection and internetworking services, LAN emulation, critical data transfer that requires service guarantees). Remote procedure calls, distributed file services, and computer process swapping and paging are examples of applications that would be appropriate for ABR.

access charge   A cost assessed to interexchange carriers for access to the local exchange network.

access concentrator   A device that can be used to concentrate local subscriber lines and multiplex them over high-speed transport to another point in the network, creating a virtual POP.

access line   The connection from the customer to the local telephone company for access to the public switched telephone network, also known as the local loop; can also refer to the connection between the serving toll exchange and the serving office of the interexchange carrier used to access public switched network transport services.

ACK (acknowledge character)   A transmission control character transmitted by a station as an affirmative response to the station with which a connection has been set up. An acknowledge character may also be used as an accuracy control character.

adaptive equalization   Line equalization, sometimes known as impedance equalization, used for optimizing signal transmission to adapt to changing line characteristics.

adaptive routing   Routing that automatically adjusts to network changes such as traffic pattern changes or failures.

address   (1) A coded representation of the destination of data, as well as of its source. Multiple terminals on one communications line, for example, must each have a unique address. (2) A group of digits that makes up a telephone number. Also known as the called number. (3) In software, a location that can be specifically referred to in a program. (4) A name, label, or number that identifies a location in storage, a device in a network, or any other data source.

address signals   Signals that carry information that has to do with the number dialed, which essentially consists of country codes, city codes, area codes, prefixes, and the subscriber number.

ADM (add/drop multiplexer)   A device that facilitates easy dropping and adding of payload by converting one or more lower-level signals, such as T-1 or E-1 signals, to and from one of the optical carrier levels.

administrative domain   A collection of hosts, routers, and networks governed by a single administrative authority.

ADPCM (Adaptive Differential Pulse Code Modulation)   An encoding technique, standardized by the ITU-T, that allows analog voice signals to be carried on a 32Kbps digital channel. The voice input is samples at 8KHz with 4 bits used to describe the difference between adjacent samples.

ADSL (Asymmetrical Digital Subscriber Line)   A technology for supporting high bandwidth over conventional twisted-pair local loop lines that enables subscribers to access multimedia-based applications such as video-on-demand. ADSL-1 supports a downstream channel of 1. 5Mbps (North America) or 2Mbps (Europe), with an upstream channel of 64Kbps. ADSL-2 supports a downstream channel of 6Mbps (North America) or 8Mbps (Europe) and an upstream channel of 640Kbps.

AES (Advanced Encryption Standard)   An encryption algorithm for securing sensitive but unclassified material by U.S. government agencies. It may eventually become the de facto encryption standard for commercial transactions in the private sector. Uses the Rijndael algorithm to specify three key lengths—128 bits, 192 bits, and 256 bits.

agent   Software that processes queries and sends responses on behalf of an application.

agnostic device   A device that supports multiple data protocols (for example, IP, Frame Relay, ATM, MPLS) and supports multiple traffic types, such as voice, data, and video.

AIN (advanced intelligent network)   The second generation of intelligent networks, pioneered by Bellcore (which is now Telcordia). A service-independent network architecture that enables carriers to create and uniformly support telecom services and features via a common architectural platform, with the objective of allowing for rapid creation of customizable telecommunication services.

AIP (application infrastructure provider)   A provider that manages the data center servers, databases, switches, and other gears on which the applications run.

A-law encoding   Encoding, according to ITU-T Recommendation G.711, that is used with European 30-channel PCM systems that comply with ITU-T Recommendation G.732. Employs nonuniform quantization to obtain the desired compression characteristic.

alerting signals   The ringing tones, the busy tones, and any specific busy alerts that are used to indicate network congestion or unavailability.

alternate mark inversion   A digital signaling method in which the signal carrying the binary value alternates between positive and negative polarities; zero and one values are represented by the signal amplitude at either polarity; no-value "spaces" are at zero amplitude. Also called bipolar.

alternate routing   The routing of a call or message over a substitute route when an established route has failed, is busy, or is otherwise unavailable for immediate use.

AM (amplitude modulation)   Varying of a carrier signal's strength (amplitude) depending on whether the information being transmitted is a 1 or a 0 bit.

ambient noise   Communications interference that is present in a signal path at all times.

amplifier   A device that boosts an attenuated signal back up to its original power level so that it can continue to make its way across the network.

amplitude   A measure of the height of the wave, which indicates the strength of the signal.

AMPS (Advanced Mobile Phone System)   A standard for analog telephony that is deployed widely in the U.S.

analog   A signal that varies continuously (e.g., sound waves), along two parameters: amplitude (strength) and frequency (tone). The unit of measurement is the Hertz, or cycle per second.

analog loopback   A technique for testing transmission equipment and devices that isolates faults to the analog signal receiving or transmitting circuitry, where a device, such as a modem, echoes back a received (test) signal that is then compared with the original signal.

ANI (automatic number identification)   A feature, often associated with SS7, that passes a caller's telephone number over the network to the receiver so that the caller can be identified. Also referred to as caller ID.

ANSI (American National Standards Institute)   A standards-forming body affiliated with the ISO that develops U.S. standards for transmission codes, protocols, media, and high-level languages, among other things.

ANSI X12   A U.S. standard for electronic data interchange.

answer signal   A supervisory signal (usually in the form of a closed loop) from the called telephone to the exchange and back to the calling telephone (usually in the form of a reverse battery) when the called number answers.

API (application programming interface)   A set of routines that an application program uses to request and carry out low-level services performed by the operating system.

AppleTalk   Apple Computer's set of specifications for connecting computers and other devices to share information over LANs. It describes network hardware, software, and protocols and lets an assortment of Mac and non-Mac devices communicate over a variety of transceivers and communications media.

application   (1) Software with which the user interacts. (2) The use to which a system is put; for example, e-mail, videoconferencing, high-speed data access, and network management.

application layer   Layer 7 of the OSI model, which enables users to transfer files, send mail, and perform other functions that involve interaction with the network components and services.

application-layer multicasting   A technique which ensures that just one stream goes across the backbone whenever possible.

application program   A software program that contains no I/O coding (except in the form of macro instructions that transfer control to the supervisory programs) and is usually unique to one type of application.

architecture   The physical interrelationship between the components of a computer or a network.

area code   A three-digit code designating a toll center that is not in the NPA of the calling party.

area code restriction   The capability of switching equipment to selectively identify three-digit area codes and to either permit or deny passage of long-distance calls to those specific area codes.

ARQ (automatic repeat request)   An error-control technique that requires retransmission of a data block that contains detected errors. A special form, called "go-back-n," allows multiple blocks to be acknowledged with a single response. "Stop and wait" requires an acknowledgment after each block.

artificial intelligence   The capability of a computer to perform functions that are associated with human logic such as reasoning, learning, and self-improvement.

AS (autonomous system)   A collection of TCP/IP gateways and networks that fall under one administrative entity and cooperate closely to propagate network reachability (and routing) information among themselves, using an interior gateway protocol.

ASCII (American Standard Code for Information Interchange)   The code developed by ANSI for information interchange among data processing systems, data communication systems, and associated equipment. The ASCII character set consists of 7-bit coded characters (8 bits including the parity bit), providing 128 possible characters. The ASCII character set consists of 34 control codes and 94 text characters, including the letters of the alphabet in both upper- and lowercase, the 10 digits, and a number of special characters.

ASP (application service provider)   A supplier that makes applications available on a subscription basis.

aspect ratio   The horizontal:vertical size ratio used for television. Traditional television has an aspect ratio of 4:3, and new DTV standards include a 16:9 aspect ratio, which more closely resembles human vision.

asynchronous   (1) Occurring without a regular or predictable time relationship to a specified event. (2) In data communication, a method of transmission in which the bits representing a character are preceded by a start bit and followed by a stop bit, which are used to separate the characters and to synchronize the receiving with the transmitting station. It does not use a regular time relationship between the sending and receiving devices.

asynchronous transmission   A transmission in which each information character, or sometimes each word or small block, is individually synchronized, usually by the use of start and stop elements. Also called start-stop transmission.

ATM (Asynchronous Transfer Mode)   An international packet-switching standard that uses a cell-based approach, in which each packet of information features a uniform cell size of 53 bytes. ATM is a high-bandwidth, fast packet-switching and multiplexing technique that allows the seamless end-to-end transmission of voice, data, image, and video traffic. It's a high-capacity, low-latency switching fabric that's adaptable for multiservice and multirate connections and offers an architected approach to Quality of Service.

ATM adaptation layer   The ATM layer that is responsible for the adaptation of the information of the higher layer to the ATM cells. It is composed of two layers, the Segmentation and Reassembly sublayer and Convergence sublayer. ATM Adaptation Layer 1 supports CBR voice and video network services. ATM Adaptation Layer 2 supports VBR voice and video network services. ATM Adaptation Layer 3 supports VBR connection oriented data services. ATM Adaptation Layer 4 supports VBR connectionless oriented data services. ATM Adaptation Layer 5 supports connectionless variable bit rate data (e.g., IP or signaling) over ATM.

ATM layer   The layer that performs four main functions: multiplexing and demultiplexing of cells of different connections; translation at ATM switches and cross-connects; cell header extraction or addition before or after cell is delivered to or from the adaptation layer; and flow control.

ATM physical layer   A layer composed of two sublayers: Physical Medium, which supports pure medium-dependent functions, and Transmission Convergence, which converts the ATM cell stream into bits to be transported over the physical medium.

ATM reassembly   Restructuring of data units from information contained in cells.

ATM segmentation   Parsing of the information units of the higher layers into ATM cells.

ATSC (Advanced Television Systems Committee)   An organization that establishes voluntary technical standards for advanced television systems, including DTV.

attenuation   A decrease in the power of a received signal due to loss through lines, equipment, or other transmission devices. Usually measured in decibels.

audible ringing tone   A tone received by the calling telephone indicating that the called telephone is being rung (formerly called ringback tone).

audio frequencies   Frequencies that correspond to those that can be heard by the human ear (usually 30Hz to 20,000Hz).

AUI (attachment unit interface)   The connector used to attach a device to an Ethernet transceiver.

authentication   Any technique that enables the receiver to automatically identify and reject messages that have been altered deliberately or by channel errors. Also can be used to provide positive identification of the sender of a message.

B

B (bidirectional) frame   The part of the MPEG video compression process in which both past and future pictures/frames are used as references. B frames typically result in the most compression.

B/D link (bridge/diagonal link)   A link that interconnects two mated pairs of STP. It carries signaling messages beyond the initial point of entry to the signaling network, toward the intended destination.

backbone   A central network that connects several other, usually lower-bandwidth, networks so that those networks can pass data to each other. The backbone network is usually composed of a high-capacity communications medium, such as fiber optic or microwave.

backplane   The board that contains a bus.

backup   The provision of facilities, logical or physical, to speed the process of restart and recovery following failure.

backup copy   A copy of information, usually on a floppy disk, zip disk, or CD-ROM, that is kept and can be used if the original information is lost or unintentionally destroyed.

bandpass filter   A circuit that is designed to allow a single band of frequencies to pass, neither of the cut-off frequencies being zero or infinity.

bandwidth   The range of frequencies, expressed in Hertz, that can pass over a given transmission channel. Also, the difference between the lowest and highest frequency carried. The bandwidth determines the rate at which information can be transmitted through a circuit. The greater the bandwidth, the more bits per second that can be carried.

bandwidth exchange   An organization or a facility that functions as an exchange where bandwidth is the commodity. Some exchanges act to bring together buyers and sellers of bandwidth, and facilitate contract negotiations and transactions; other exchanges actually switch traffic in real-time based on changes in bandwidth prices throughout the course of the day.

bandwidth-on-demand   A concept in wide area networking in which the user can access additional WAN bandwidth as the application warrants. It enables users to pay for only the bandwidth they use, when they use it.

Barker Code   An 11-bit chipping code. The one-bits are encoded as a particular sequence of 1s and 0s, and the zero-bits are the inverse of that sequence.

base station controller   An intermediate device in the cellular system that controls a group of base-station transceivers,

baseband signaling   Transmission of a digital or analog signal at its original frequencies (that is, a signal in its original form, not changed by modulation).

batch processing   A processing method in which a program or programs process data with little or no operator interaction.

baud   A unit of signaling speed.

Baudot code   A data code that uses a 5-bit structure that was used on vintage teleprinters (e.g., Telex).

beacon frame   A frame sent by a Token Ring adapter indicating that it has detected a serious problem. An adapter sending such frames is said to be beaconing.

BECN (Backward Explicit Congestion Notification)   A bit in the Frame Relay header that the network uses to inform the transmitter of network congestion.

BER (bit error rate)   In data communications testing, the ratio between the total number of bits transmitted in a given message and the number of bits in that message received in error. A measure of the quality of a data transmission, usually expressed as number referred to a power of 10 (e.g., 1 bit error in 10^5 bits transmitted, or 1 in 100,000).

best-effort QoS   QoS that is not guaranteed but that is as good as possible under the circumstances.

beta test   The stage at which a new product is tested under actual usage conditions.

BGP (Border Gateway Protocol)   A gateway protocol that allows routers to communicate with each other. BGP is an exterior routing protocol used between autonomous systems and is of concern to service providers and other large or complex organizations.

binary   A base-two system of numbers; the binary digits are 0 and 1.

bipolar   The predominant signaling method used for digital transmission services, such as DDS and T1, in which the signal carrying the binary values successfully alternates between positive and negative polarities. One values are represented by the signal amplitude at either polarity, and no-value "spaces" are at zero amplitude.

bit   The smallest unit of information in a digital device. In binary notation, either the characters 0 or 1.

bit duration   The time it takes one encoded bit to pass a point on the transmission medium. In serial communications, a relative unit of time measurement used for comparison of delay times, where the data rate of a transmission channel can vary.

bit errors   Missing video elements or synchronization problems or complete loss of the picture.

bitmap   A pixel-by-pixel description of an image. Each pixel is a separate element.

bit-oriented protocol   A communications protocol or transmission procedure in which control information in encoded in fields of one or more bits.

bit rate   The speed at which bits are transmitted, usually expressed in bps.

blocking   A network is said to be blocking if there are connection sets that will prevent some additional desired connections from being set up between unused ports, even with rearrangement of existing connections.

Blowfish   A 64-bit block code that has key lengths of 32 to 448 bits. Blowfish is used in more than 100 products, and it is viewed as one of the best available algorithms.

Bluetooth   A very low-cost chip that gives a device a short-range wireless capability. Personal digital assistants, laptops, cell phones, and any other intelligent appliance embedded with a Bluetooth chip are capable of communicating and linking with each other wirelessly.

BNC connector   A locking type of connector. Thinnet, a form of Ethernet, uses BNC connectors.

board   The circuit card on which integrated circuits are mounted.

bps (bits per second)   A measure of the amount of transmission capacity available. For example, a 10Gbps backbone can support 10 billion bits per second. Bytes are used as a measure of storage, so a 10GB hard drive is not the same thing as a 10Gbps communications link. Abbreviated as Kbps for thousands of bits per second; Mbps for millions of bits per second; Gbps for billions of bits per second; Tbps for trillions of bits per second; Pbps for 1,000Tbps; and Ebps for 1 billion Gbps.

BRI (Basic Rate Interface)   In ISDN, the interface to the basic rate, which is 2B+D: two 64Kbps information-carrying channels plus one 16Kbps signaling channel. Also called Basic Rate Access (BRA).

bridge   An attaching device that connects two LAN segments to allow the transfer of information from one LAN segment to the other. Bridges operate by filtering packets according to their destination addresses. Most bridges automatically learn where these addresses are located and, thus, are called learning bridges. A bridge works at OSI Layer 2 and is transparent to upper-layer devices and protocols.

broadband   (1) A multichannel, high-bandwidth transmission line. (2) According to the ITU-T, any transmission rate over 2Mbps. (3) Typically, the technology of CATV transmission, as applied to data communications; employs coaxial cable as the transmission medium and radio frequency carrier signals in the 5MHz to 1,000MHz range.

Broadband ISDN   A standard that was envisioned for use with advanced applications. SDH/ SONET and ATM were both born out of the Broadband ISDN standard and a desire to be able to deliver advanced applications.

broadcast   A transmission to multiple receiving locations simultaneously. A broadcast can be made, for example, over a multipoint line to all terminals that share the line, or over a radio or television channel to all receivers tuned to that channel.

broadcast storm   A pathological network condition in which an increasing and insupportable number of broadcast packets are generated.

brouter   A device that can transparently bridge protocols as well as route them. It is a hybrid of a bridge and a router.

brownout operation   An operation in response to heavy demand, in which main system voltages are lowered and power is not lost but reduced. Although conventional networking equipment is relatively immune to brownouts, the computer controlling the system is very sensitive to voltage variations and could fail under these conditions. Most equipment today has the capability to cope with these reductions, or a heavy-duty power supply can be furnished. A UPS can be installed to ensure continued service during prolonged outages and to regulate power.

BSC (binary synchronous communications)   A half-duplex, character-oriented data communications protocol originated by IBM in 1964. It includes control character and procedures for controlling the establishment of a valid connection and the transfer of data. Also called bisync.

buffer   A storage device that is used to compensate for a difference in rate of data flow, or time of occurrence events, when transmitting data from device to another.

buffered network   A real-time store-and-forward message-switching network, with computers at the switching points, which act as buffers for the packets.

buffered repeater   A hybrid device halfway between a repeater and a bridge. Entire packets are received and retransmitted (as with a bridge) but no address filtering is implemented (as with a repeater).

bundled   A pricing strategy in which a service provider or manufacturer includes all products—hardware, software, services, training, and the like—in a single price.

burst   In data communications, a sequence of signals counted as one unit in accordance with some specific criterion or measure.

burst switching   A switching method to switch digitized voice and data characters in an integrated fashion.

bus   (1) A physical transmission path or channel. Typically an electric connection, with one or more conductors, wherein all attached devices receive all transmissions at the same time. (2) A LAN topology, such as used in Ethernet and the token bus, where all network nodes listen to all transmissions, selecting certain ones based on address identification. Involves some type of contention-control mechanism for accessing the bus transmission medium.

bus topology   A network architecture in which all the nodes are connected to a shared cable.

bypass   To establish a communication link without using the facilities of the local exchange carrier (that is, the telephone company).

byte   The amount of storage required to represent one alphanumeric character, or 8 bits. Bytes are used as a measure of storage, as in a 2GB hard drive. This is different from the measurement for transmission capacity, which is expressed in bits per second (for example, a 10Gbps backbone).

C

C-band   A portion of the electromagnetic spectrum, approximately 4GHz to 6GHz, that is used primarily for satellite and microwave transmission.

C (cross) link   A link that interconnects mated STPs.

CA (certificate authority)   A trusted third-party organization that issues digital certificates used to create digital signatures and public-private key pairs. The CA guarantees that the individual granted the unique certificate is, in fact, who he or she claims to be.

cable modem   A device designed to operate over cable TV networks to provide high-speed access to the Internet.

call processing   A sequence of operations performed by a switching system from the acceptance of an incoming call through the final disposition of the call.

campus network   A network that connects LANs from multiple departments in a single building or campus. Campus networks are local area networks, while they may span several miles, they do not include wide area network services.

CAP (carrierless amplitude phase) modulation   A single-carrier modulation scheme used in early deployments of ADSL.

carrier frequency   The frequency of the carrier wave that is modulated to transmit signals.

carrier system   A means of obtaining a number of channels over a single path by modulating each channel on a different carrier frequency and demodulating at the receiving point to restore the signals to their original frequency.

Category 1 UTP   An EIA/TIA 586 standard for commercial building telecommunications wiring. This old-style UTP telephone cable is unsuitable for data transmission.

Category 2 UTP   An EIA/TIA 586 standard of cable that can be used for data rates up to 4Mbps.

Category 3 UTP   An EIA/TIA 586 standard of cable that can be used for data rates up to 10Mbps. This is the minimum cable requirement for 10BaseT.

Category 4 UTP   An EIA/TIA 586 standard of cable that can be used as the lowest grade UTP, acceptable for data rates up to 16Mbps (Token Ring).

Category 5 UTP   An EIA/TIA 586 standard which specifies of cable that can be used for data rates up to 100Mbps.

CATV (community antenna television)   Signals that can be received at a selected site by sensitive, directional antennas and then transmitted to subscribers via a cable network. Additional channels, not normally available in that area, can also be transmitted. Traditional analog CATV is based on RF transmission, generally using 75-ohm coaxial cable as the transmission medium. CATV offers multiple frequency-divided channels, allowing mixed transmissions to be carried simultaneously.

CBQ (Class-Based Queuing)   A fully open, nonproprietary technology that brings bandwidth-controlled CoS to IP network infrastructures. It allows traffic to be prioritized according to IP application type, IP address, protocol type, and other variables. It allocates unused bandwidth more effectively than other QoS mechanisms do, and it uses priority tables to give critical applications the most immediate access to unused bandwidth.

CBR (constant bit rate)   The highest ATM service class. CBR provides a constant, guaranteed rate to real-time applications such as streaming video, providing continuous bandwidth. It emulates a circuit-switched approach and it is associated with minimum latencies and losses.

CC7 (Common-Channel Signaling System 7)   An ITU-T specified signaling protocol used in high-speed digital networks to provide communication between intelligent network nodes.

CCIS (Common-Channel Interoffice Signaling)   An electronic means of signaling between any two switching systems independent of the voice path. The use of CCIS makes possible new customer services, versatile network features, more flexible call routing, and faster connections.

CCITT (Comité Consultatif International de Téléphonie et de Télégraphie)   An advisory committee to the ITU whose recommendations covering telecommunications have international influence among engineers, manufacturers, and administrators. It is now known as the ITU-T.

CDDI (Copper-Distributed Data Interface)   A version of FDDI that runs on UTP cabling rather than on fiber-optic cable.

CDMA (Code Division Multiple Access)   A digital cellular technology that uses spread-spectrum techniques. With CDMA, every channel uses the full available spectrum and individual conversations are encoded with a pseudorandom digital sequence or frequency-hopping schedule.

CDPD (Cellular Digital Packet Data)   A North American standard for transferring packet data over cellular phone channels.

CD-ROM (compact disc-read only memory)   A storage device that is used in computer systems and typically contains multimedia information.

cell   A fixed-length packet.

cell relay   A form of packet transmission used by ATM networks. Cell relay transmits 53 octet fixed-length packets over a packet-switched network. Because the cells are tiny and of fixed length, they can be processed and switched at very high speeds. ATM makes it possible to use a single transmission scheme for voice, data, and video traffic on LANs and WANs.

cellular   A communication service in which voice or data is transmitted by radio frequencies. The service area is divided into cells, each served by a transmitter. The cells are connected to a mobile switching exchange, which is connected to the worldwide telephone network.

CELP (Code-Excited Linear Prediction)   A vector-quantization-based compression scheme for speech. CELP can compress speech down to 4.8Kbps. There is also a low-end variant called LPC.

centrex   A local exchange carrier service in which switching occurs at a local exchange rather than at customer-owned PBXs. The telephone company owns and manages all the communications equipment.

CEPT (Commission of European Post and Telecommunications)   An organization formed by the European PTTs for the discussion of operational and tariff matters. CEPT-0 (or E-0) is the basic increment, and it operates at 64Kbps. CEPT-1 is a 2.048Mbps 32-channel circuit; CEPT-2 is an 8.488Mbps 128-channel circuit; CEPT-3 is a 34.368Mbps 512-channel circuit; CEPT-4 is a 139.246Mbps 2,048-channel circuit; CEPT-5 is a 565.148Mbps 8,192-channel circuit.

channel   The logical conversation path. It is the frequency band, time slot, or wavelength (also referred to as lambda) over which a given conversation flows.

channel bank   Equipment typically used in a telephone exchange that performs multiplexing of lower speed, digital channels into a higher speed composite channel. The channel bank also detects and transmits signaling information for each channel and transmits framing information so that time slots allocated to each channel can be identified by the receiver.

channel capacity   The maximum data traffic that can be handled by the channel.

CHAP (Challenge Handshake Authentication Protocol)   A protocol that uses a three-way handshake to periodically verify the identity of the peer throughout the life of the connection. The server sends to the remote workstation a random token that is encrypted with the user's password and sent back to the server. The server performs a lookup to see if it recognizes the password. If the values match, the authentication is acknowledged; if not, the connection is terminated. A different token is provided each time a remote user dials in, which provides additional robustness.

chirped-pulse WDM   A Bell Labs system in which a specialized mode-locked laser rapidly emits very wide pulses of light. Because each part of a fiber interacts differently with varying frequencies of light, the result of chirped-pulse WDM is unequal dispersion. The pulse is stretched out when it enters the fiber, and data can be put on the discrete frequencies that emerge.

CIDR (Classless Interdomain Routing)   An IP addressing scheme that replaces the older system based on Classes A, B, and C. With CIDR, a single IP address can be used to designate many unique IP addresses. The CIDR addressing scheme is hierarchical. Large national and regional service providers are allocated large blocks of contiguous Internet addresses, which they then allocate to other smaller ISPs or directly to organizations. Networks can be divided into subnetworks, and networks can be combined into supernetworks, as long as they share a common network prefix.

CIR (committed information rate)   The amount of bandwidth that a user can expect from a Frame Relay carrier on a particular virtual circuit.

circuit   The physical path that runs between two or more points that can be used for two-way communication or to perform another specific function.

circuit grade   The data-carrying capability of a circuit; the grades of circuit are broadband, voice, subvoice, and telegraph.

circuit switching   The temporary direct connection of two or more channels between two or more points in order to provide the user with exclusive use of an open channel with which to exchange information. A discrete circuit path is set up between the incoming and outgoing lines, in contrast to message switching and packet switching, in which no such physical path is established.

cladding   In fiber-optic cable, a colored, low-refractive index material that surrounds the core and provides optical insulation and protection to the core.

clear-forward/clear-back signal   A signal transmitted from one end of a subscriber line or trunk, in the forward/backward direction, to indicate at the other end that the established connection should be disconnected. Also called disconnect signal.

CLEC (competitive local exchange carrier)   A telephone company that competes with an ILEC. CLECs in the United States today focus mainly on delivering dial tone to business customers.

client   A computer that requests network or application services from a server. A client has only one user; a server is shared by many users.

client/server model   The model of interaction in a distributed system in which a program at one site sends a request to a program at another site and awaits a response. The requesting program is called a client; the program satisfying the request is called the server.

clocking   The use of clock pulses to control synchronization of data and control characters.

closed user group   A group of users in a network who are permitted to communicate with each other but not with users outside the group.

cluster   Two or more terminals connected to a single point or node.

cluster controller   A device that handles the remote communications processing for multiple (usually dumb) terminals or workstations.

CMIP (Common Management Information Protocol)   The OSI management information protocol for network management. CMIP is an alternative to SNMP. It is not widely implemented.

CMISE (Common Management Information Services)   A service interface created and standardized by ISO for managing heterogeneous networks.

CMTS (cable modem termination system)   A device on which coax trunks terminate. CMTSs are linked together by accessing a common Ethernet hub, which, in turn, feeds into the IP router, which then develops the optimum path to take over an optical backbone onto the ISP.

CO (central office)   The physical location where local service providers terminate subscriber lines and locate the switching equipment which interconnects those lines. CO is used as a term in North America; elsewhere in the world, it is also referred to as a local exchange or Class 5 office.

coax (coaxial cable)   A transmission medium consisting of one (sometimes more) central wire conductor, surrounded by a dielectric insulator, and encased in either a wire mesh or extruded metal sheathing. There are many varieties, depending on the degree of EMI shielding afforded, voltages, and frequencies accommodated.

code   The conventions that specify how data may be presented in a particular system.

code character   A set of conventional elements established by the code to enable the transmission of a written character (letter, figure, punctuation sign, arithmetical sign, and so on) or the control of a particular function (spacing, shift, line-feed, carriage return, phase corrections, and so on).

codec (coder-decoder)   A device used to convert analog signals, such as speech, music, or television, to digital form for transmission over a digital medium, and back again to the original analog form. One codec is required at each end of the channel.

coding scheme   A pattern of bits that are used to represent the characters in a character set, as well as carriage returns and other keyboard functions. Examples of coding schemes are ASCII, EBCDIC, and Unicode.

collision   Overlapping transmissions that interfere with one another. A collision occurs when two or more devices attempt to transmit at or about the same instant.

collision domain   A small cluster in a LAN where collisions occur. Collision domains are used to reduce collisions throughout a network.

command   A signal or group of signals that cause a computer to execute an operation or series of operations.

command-driven   Programs requiring that the task to be performed be described in a special language with strict adherence to syntax.

common-battery signaling   A method by which supervisory and telephone address information is sent to an exchange by depressing and releasing the switch on the cradle of the handset.

common carrier   An organization in the business of providing regulated telephone, telegraph, telex, and data communications services.

common control   An automatic switching arrangement in which the control equipment necessary for the establishment of connections is shared and is associated with a given call only during the period required to accomplished the control function.

communication adapter   A hardware feature that permits telecommunication lines to be attached to the processor.

communication line   A physical link (wire, telephone circuit, microwave, satellite) that is used to transmit data between computers and/or remote devices.

communications controller   (1) A hardware device that lets you attach either communication lines, ASCII devices, or a local area network to the processing unit. (2) A dedicated device with special processing capabilities for organizing and checking data and handling information traffic to and from many remote terminals or computers, including functions such as message switching. Also called communications processor.

communications satellite   A satellite designed to act as a telecommunications radio relay and usually positioned in geosynchronous orbit 23,000 miles (35,800 kilometers) above the equator so that it appears from earth to be stationary.

compander   The combination of a compressor at one point in a communications path for reducing the volume range of signals, followed by an expander at another point for restoring the original volume range. Designed to improve the ratio of the signal to the interference entering in the path between the compressor and expandor.

compression   The application of any several techniques that reduce the number of bits required to represent information in data transmission or storage, thereby conserving bandwidth and/or memory.

compressor   An electronic device that compresses the volume range of a signal.

concatenation   The linking of transmission channels (phone lines, coaxial cable, optical fiber) end-to-end. Also refers to the linking of SONET STS-1 frames in order to carry a broadband information stream.

concentrator   A device that connects a number of circuits that are not all used at once to a smaller group of circuits for economical transmission. A telephone concentrator achieves the reduction with a circuit switching mechanism. In data communications it refers to a multiport repeater or hub that brings together the connections from multiple network nodes. Concentrators have moved past their origins as wire concentration centers and often include bridging, routing, and management devices.

conditioning   A procedure for making transmission impairments of a circuit lie within certain specified limits and typically used on telephone lines leased for data transmission to improve the possible transmission speed. Two types are used: C conditioning and D conditioning. Also called line conditioning.

configuration   The devices and programs that make up a system, subsystem, or network. The term configuration may refer to a hardware configuration or a software configuration.

configure   To describe to the system the devices and optional features installed on the system and describe their utilization.

connect time   The amount of time that a circuit, typically in a circuit-switched environment, is in use.

connectionless network   A network that treats each packet or datagram as a separate entity that contains the source and destination address. Connectionless services can drop packets or deliver them out of sequence, based on encountering various network conditions, such as congestion or outages.

connection-oriented network   A network in which the connection setup is performed before information transfer occurs. The path is conceived at the outset, and after the path is determined, all the subsequent information follows the same path to the destination. In a connection-oriented network, there can be some delay up front, while the connection is being set up; but because the path is predetermined, there is no delay at intermediate nodes in this type of network after the connection is set up.

connectivity   A term used to describe the physical interconnections of multiple devices/computers/networks employing similar or different technology and/or architecture together to accomplish effective communication between and among connected members involving data exchange and/or resource sharing.

content delivery network   A network with delivery services that are structured specifically for a client that are focused on streaming audio, video, and media, as well as the supporting e-commerce applications.

contention   A method of line control in which the terminals request permission to transmit. If the channel in question is free, transmission proceeds; if it is not free, the terminal will have to wait until it becomes free. A computer can build up a queue of contention requests; this queue can be organized in a prearranged sequence or in the sequence in which requests are made.

control character   A character that is inserted into a data stream for signaling the receiving station to perform a function to identify the structure of the message. Newer protocols use bit-oriented control procedures.

control station   The station in a point-to-point or multipoint network that controls the sending and receiving of data. A station that can poll or address tributary stations.

control unit   Circuitry or a device that is used to coordinate and control the operation of one or more I/O or storage devices and to synchronize the operation of such devices with the operation of the computer system as a whole.

controlled access unit   A managed MAU or a managed multiport siring hub for Token Ring networks.

conversion   The process of changing from one method to another; may refer to changing processing methods, data, or systems.

COPS (Common Open Policy Services)   An IETF query-response–based client/server protocol for supporting policy control. It addresses how servers and clients on a network exchange policy information, and it transmits information between a policy server and its clients, which are policy-aware devices such as switches.

core   The central part of a network.

CoS (Class of Service)   A categorization of subscribers or traffic according to priority levels. Network resources are allocated based on the CoS.

CPE (customer premises equipment)   Equipment that is located at the customer premise that is owned and managed by the customer.

CRC (cyclic redundancy check)   A powerful error-detecting technique. By using a polynomial, a series of two 8-bit block-check characters are generated that represent the entire block of data. The block-check characters are incorporated into the transmission frame, and then checked at the receiving end.

crossbar switch   A switch that has a crosspoint for each input output pair, and only one contact pair needs to be closed to establish an input to output connection.

crosstalk   Interference or an unwanted signal from one transmission circuit detected on another, usually parallel, circuit.

CSMA (Carrier Sense Multiple Access)   A LAN access technique in which multiple stations connected to the same channel are able to sense transmission activity on that channel and to defer the initiation of transmission while the channel is active. Similar to contention access.

CSMA/CA (Carrier Sense Multiple Access/Collision Avoidance)   A scheme for controlling network traffic that enables any of multiple nodes to send information over a shared network cable if the cable is free. It avoids collisions by having all nodes signal their intention to transmit before transmitting. If two nodes send intentions to transmit messages at the same time, both nodes wait for random amounts of time before trying again.

CSMA/CD (Carrier Sense Multiple Access/Collision Detection)   A LAN protocol that is a refinement of CSMA in which stations are able to detect the interference caused by simultaneous transmissions by two or more stations (collisions) and to retransmit colliding messages in an orderly manner.

CSU (channel service unit)   A component of customer premises equipment (CPE) used to terminate a digital circuit, such as a leased line or T-1/E-1 facility, at the customer site. Performs certain line-conditioning functions and responds to loopback commands from the local exchange. Also, ensures proper ones density in a transmitted bitstream, and performs bipolar violation correction.

CTS (clear to send)   A control circuit that indicates to the data terminal equipment that data can or cannot be transmitted.

customization   The process of designing or configuring a device, installation or network, to meet the requirements of particular users.

cutover   The physical changing of lines from one system to another, usually at the time of a new system installation.

CVSD (Continuous Variable Slope Delta Modulation)   A speech encoding and digitizing technique that uses 1 bit to describe the change in the slope of the curve between two samples, rather than the absolute change between the samples.

CXR (carrier)   A signal of known characteristics (for example, frequency) that is altered (modulated) to transmit information.

cycle   One complete repetition of a regularly repeating electronic function. The number of cycles per second, measured in Hertz (Hz), is called the frequency.

D

DAMA (demand assigned multiple access)   A system for allocation of communication satellite time to earth stations as the need arises.

dark fiber   Fiber-optic cable that has been installed but is not lit—that is, there are no active light sources.

data center   The computer-equipped, central location within an organization. The data center processes and converts information to a desired form such as reports or other types of management information records.

data circuit   A communications facility that enables transmission of information in digital form.

data communication   The transmission and reception of data between computers and/or remote devices according to appropriate protocols.

data compression and coding   Techniques used to reduce bandwidth requirements for transmission of information over a particular communication link. May also be used in noncommunications applications, such as data storage and retrieval.

data exchange   The use of data by more than one program or system.

data line privacy   Critical system extension lines, such devices as facsimile machines and computer terminals, are very sensitive to extraneous noise. Data privacy prohibits activities that would insert tones on the station line while the line is in use. Data lines can then be connected through the PBX without danger of losing data through interference.

data link   (1) The equipment and rules (protocol) used for sending and receiving data. (2) Any serial data communication transmission path, generally between two adjacent nodes or devices and without any intermediate switching nodes.

data-link layer   OSI Layer 2, which defines how data is packetized and transmitted to and from each network device. It is divided into two sublayers: medium access control and logical link control.

data management   Provision of access to data, monitoring or storage of data, and control of input/output devices.

data PBX   A switch that enables a user on an attached circuit to select from other circuits, usually one at a time and on a contention basis, for the purpose of establishing a through connection. A data PBX is distinguished from a PBX in that data transmission, and not voice, is supported.

data rate   The speed at which a channel carries data, measured in bits per second (bps).

data service   A digital service offered for data communications at subscriber locations.

data set   An infrequently used term for modem.

data-switching exchange   The equipment installed at a single location to provide switching functions, such as circuit switching, message switching, and packet switching.

data system   A system for the storage and retrieval of data, its transmission to terminals, and controls to provide adequate protection and ensure proper usage.

data transmission   The movement of information from one location to another by means of some form of communication media.

datagram   A message of fixed maximum length, sent without network provided facilities for assuring its accuracy, delivery, or correct sequencing with respect to related messages, that carries the full destination address used for routing.

dB (decibel)   A unit for measuring relative strength of a signal parameter such as power or voltage. The number of decibels is 10 times the logarithm (base 10) of the ratio of the power of two signals, or ratio of the power of one signal to a reference level.

DBS (Direct Broadcast Satellite)   A satellite system that can transmit digital TV signals directly to individual homes.

DCE (data communications equipment)   Equipment that provides an interface between the DTE and the transmission channel (that is, between the carrier's networks). It establishes, maintains, and terminates a connection between the DTE and the transmission channel and is responsible for ensuring that the signal that comes out of the DTE is compatible with the requirements of the transmission channel.

DCLEC (data-competitive local-exchange carrier)   A company that is specifically focused on supporting data services in the local loop (for example, providers that offer DSL services to end users).

DCS (digital cross-connect system)   A device that enables the reconfiguration of a digital network in response to congestion or failure in the network, as well as on-demand reconfiguration. DCSs add, drop, and/or switch payload as necessary across multiple links.

DDS (digital data service)   A digital transmission service that supports speeds up to 56Kbps/64Kbps.

dedicated line   An end-to-end communications line used exclusively by one organization. Also called a dedicated circuit.

delay distortion   The change in a signal from the transmitting end to the receiving end resulting from the tendency of some frequency components within a channel to take longer to be propagated than others.

delta modulation   A method of representing a speech wave form (or other analog signal) in which successive bits represent increments of the wave form. The increment size is not necessarily constant. Produces digitized voice at 56Kbps.

demodulation   The process of recovering data from a modulated carrier wave. The reverse of modulation.

DEN (Directory Enabled Networking)   An industry group formed by Microsoft and Cisco to create a common data format for storing information about users, devices, servers, and applications in a common repository. DEN describes mechanisms that enable equipment, such as switches and routers, to access and use directory information to implement policy-based networking.

DES (Data Encryption Standard)   A cryptographic algorithm designed by the National Bureau of Standards (now the National Institute of Standards and Technology) to encipher and decipher data using a 56-bit key. As a secret-key, symmetric system, it requires the exchange of secret encryption keys between users.

diagnostics   Software routines or microcode used to check equipment malfunctions or to pinpoint faulty components.

dial tone   A signal, generated by a service circuit within the local exchange or PBX, that is sent to an operator or user as an audible indication that the switch is ready to receive dialing digits.

dialup   The process of, or the equipment or facilities involved in, establishing a temporary connection via the switched telephone network.

dialup line   A circuit that is established by a switched circuit connection; generally refers to the public telephone network.

DID (direct inward dialing)   Incoming calls from the exchange network can be completed to specific station lines without attendant assistance. Also called direct dialing in (DDI).

Diffie-Hellman   A public-key algorithm used mostly for exchanging keys; its security rests on the difficulty of computing discrete algorithms in a finite field, generated by a large prime number.

DiffServ (Differentiated Services)   An approach to providing QoS in networks that use a small, well-defined set of building blocks from which a variety of services can be built. DiffServ evolved from IETF's IntServ. It is a prioritization model, with preferential allocation of resources based on traffic classification.

digital   Communications procedures, techniques, and equipment whereby information is encoded as either binary 1 or 0; the representation of information in discrete binary form, discontinuous in time, as opposed to the analog representation of information in variable, but continuous, wave forms.

digital certificate   A method for registering user identities with a third party, a CA. A digital certificate binds a user to an electronic signature that can be trusted like a written signature and includes authentication, access rights, and verification information.

digital loopback   A technique for testing the digital processing circuitry of a communications device. It can be installed locally, or remotely, via a telecommunications circuit; the device being tested will echo back a received test message, after first decoding and then reencoding it, the results of which are compared with the original message.

digital network   A network that incorporates both digital switching and digital transmission.

digital signal   A discrete or discontinuous signal, one whose various states are identified with discrete levels or values.

digital switching   The process of establishing and maintaining a connection, under stored program control, where binary-encoded information is routed between an input and an output port. Generally, a virtual circuit is derived from a series of time slots (time-division multiplexing), which is more efficient than requiring dedicated physical circuits for the period of time that connections are set up.

Dijkstra algorithm   An algorithm that determines routes based on path length; it is used in OSPF.

directory service   A service that provides a white pages-like directory of the users and resources located on an enterprise network. Instead of having to know a device's or user's specific network address, a directory service provides an English-like listing for a user. The directory is being standardized collaboratively by the ITU (X.500 standards) and ISO.

distance-vector routing   Routing in which a router is only aware of routers that are directly connected to it. Each router sends its routing table to each of its neighbors; they in turn merge this routing table with their own.

distortion   The modification of the wave form or shape of a signal caused by an outside interference or by imperfections of the transmission system. Most forms of distortion are the result of the varying responses of the transmission system to the different frequency components of the transmission signal.

distributed computing environment   An architecture in which portions of the applications and the data are broken up and distributed among the server and client computers.

distributed database   An application in which there are many clients as well as many servers. All databases at remote and local sites are treated as if they were one database. The data dictionary is crucial in mapping where all the data resides.

distributed data processing   Data processing in which some or all of the processing, storage and control functions, in addition to input/output functions, are situated in different places and connected by transmission facilities.

distributed system   A corporate system that can function independently from the host to provide local processing capabilities that meet end-user requirements, yet can connect into the host network for file transfer, access to other applications, and host-specific functions.

distribution frame   A structure (typically wall-mounted) for terminating telephone wiring, usually the permanent wires from, or at, the telephone exchange, where cross-connections are readily made to extensions. Also called connector block, distribution block, MDF, or IDF.

DLC (digital loop carrier)   A type of concentrator, also called a remote concentrator or remote terminal. Traditional DLCs are not interoperable with some of the new DSL offerings, including ADSL and SDSL.

DLCI (data-link connection identifier)   An identifier in a Frame Relay header that specifies the Layer 2 virtual circuit.

DLI (data-line interface)   The point at which a data line is connected to a telephone system.

DMT (Discrete Multitone)   A multicarrier modulation scheme used in ADSL.

DNS (Domain Name System)   A set of protocols and databases that translates between Web site names and physical IP addresses in the Internet or in any TCP/IP based internet.

downlink   The portion of a satellite circuit extending from the satellite to the earth station.

download   To load software into the nodes of a network from one node over the network media.

downstream   The direction of transmission flow from the source toward the user.

downtime   The total time a system is out of service due to equipment failure.

DPNSS (Digital Private Network Signaling System)   The European standard for common channel signaling between PBXs.

DQDB (distributed queue dual bus)   The media access method of the IEEE 802.6 standard for metropolitan area networks.

drop   A connection point between a communicating device and a communications network.

DS (Digital Signal) level   The increments of the PDH hierarchy (North American standard). DS-0 is a single channel with a capacity of 64Kbps; DS-1 is 24 DS-0 channels multiplexed into one 1.544Mbps T-1 digital trunk; DS-1C is a 3.152Mbps digital signal carried on a T-1 C facility; DS-2 is a 6.312Mbps digital signal carried over 96 DS-0 channels on a T-3 facility; DS-3 is a 44.736Mbps digital signal carried over 672 DS-0 channels on a T-3 facility; DS-4 is a 274.176Mbps digital signal carried over 4032 DS-0 channels on a T-4 facility.

DSI (digital speech interpolation)   A system of digitized speech in which the speech can be cut into slices such that no bits are transmitted when a person is silent. As soon as speech begins, bits flow again.

DSL (Digital Subscriber Line)   A family of broadband technologies that use sophisticated modulation schemes to pack data onto copper wires. They are sometimes referred to as last-mile technologies because they are used only for connections from a telephone switching station to a home or office, not between switching stations.

DSL bonding   The process of linking together several DSL lines to configure bandwidth in between the T-1/T-3 and E-1/E-3 rates.

DSLAM (DSL access multiplexer)   A device at a phone company's central location that links many customer DSL connections to a single high-speed ATM line.

DSSS (Direct Sequence Spread Spectrum)   A spread spectrum technique in which each data bit is converted to a series of 10 to 144 transmitted bits or chips.

DSU (digital or data service unit)   A synchronous serial data interface that buffers and controls the flow of data between a digital terminal and the CSU attached to a digital communications facility, converting between incompatible digital formats. DSUs can be considered as modem replacements in digital networks.

DTE (data-terminating equipment)   Equipment (including any type of computer terminal, including PCs, as well as printers, hosts, front-end processors, multiplexers, and LAN interconnection devices such as routers) that transmits data between two points without error. Its main responsibilities are to transmit and receive information and to perform error control. The DTE generally supports the end-user applications program, data files, and databases.

DTH (direct to home)   A satellite system that can transmit digital TV signals directly to individual homes.

DTMF (dual-tone multifrequency) signaling   The basis for operation of pushbutton telephone sets. A method of signaling in which a matrix combination of two frequencies, each from a group of four, is used to transmit numerical address information. The two groups of four frequencies are (a) 697Hz, 770Hz, 852Hz, and 941Hz, and (b) 1209Hz, 1336Hz, 1477Hz, and 1633Hz.

DTV (digital TV)   Television sent over a digital network. It is nearly immune to interference and degradation, and it can display a much better range of colors than can analog television.

duplex   Communications in which data can be transmitted between two stations in both directions at the same time, with the use of a four-wire circuit. Same as full-duplex.

duplex circuit   A four-wire circuit used for transmission in both directions at the same time. It can be called *full-duplex* to distinguish it from *half-duplex*.

duplex signaling   A signaling system that occupies the same cable pair as the voice path, yet does not require filters.

duplex transmission   Simultaneous, two-way, independent transmission. Also called full-duplex transmission.

duplexing technique   A procedure for separating the incoming and outgoing conversations.

DVB (Digital Video Broadcasting Group)   A European organization that has authored many specifications for satellite and cable broadcasting of digital signals.

DWDM (Dense Wavelength Division Multiplexing)   An optical technology used to increase bandwidth over existing fiber-optic backbones. DWDM works by combining and transmitting multiple signals simultaneously at different wavelengths on the same fiber. In effect, one fiber is transformed into multiple virtual fibers.

dynamic routing   Routing that automatically adjusts to network topology or traffic changes.

E

E.164   The ITU-T's international public telecommunication numbering plan for the PSTN.

E-carrier   A time-division multiplexed, digital transmission facility, operating at an aggregate data rate of 2.048Mbps and above. E-carrier is a PCM system that uses 64Kbps for a voice channel. E-0 is the basic increment of the PDH hierarchy; it is a single channel with a capacity of 64Kbps. In E-1, 32 channels are multiplexed into one 2.048Mbps E-1 digital channel, also referred to as G.703; 30 channels are used for information, and 2 channels are reserved for signaling and control. Other

E-carrier levels are E-2 (8.488Mbps over 128 channels), E-3 (34.368Mbps over 512 channels), E-4 (139.246Mbps over 2,048 channels), and E-5 (565.148Mbps over 8,192 channels).

e-commerce (electronic commerce)   The secure exchange of funds, executed over a network, for goods and services exchanged between parties.

E (extended) link   A link that provides enhanced reliability by providing a set of links from the SSP to a second STP pair.

E&M signaling   A signaling arrangement that uses separate paths for signaling and voice signals. The M lead (derived from "mouth") transmits ground or battery to the distant end of the circuit, while incoming signals are received as either a grounded or open condition on the E (derived from "ear") lead.

EBCDIC (Extended Binary-Coded Decimal Interchange Code)   A character set that consists of 8-bit code characters and is widely used for exchanging data between computer systems. It has 256 possible combinations: 17 are used for control purposes; 96 are used for text characters; and the remaining code combinations are unassigned.

eBIP (e-business infrastructure provider)   A provider that saves small businesses time and money with Web-based solutions for human resources, accounting, marketing, group collaboration, and other services.

Ebps (exabits per second)   One billion Gbps.

echo   A wave that has been reflected or otherwise returned with sufficient magnitude and delay for it to be perceived as a wave distinct from that directly transmitted.

echo cancellation   A process that allows full-duplex transmission to occur over a single electrical path. It relies on frequency splitting to derive separate voice and data channels from one wire. This feature is necessary for voice transmission but often interferes with data transmission.

EDFA (erbium-doped fiber amplifier)   An optical amplifier. Erbium is injected into fiber, and as a light pulse passes through the erbium, it is amplified, thus, it does not have to be stopped and processed as an electrical signal. The introduction of EDFAs opened up the opportunity to make use of fiber-optic systems operating at 10Gbps.

edge   The network boundary between the customer and the core or central network.

edge device   A device that can pass packets between a legacy type of network such as an Ethernet network and an ATM network, using data-link layer and network layer information. An edge device does not have responsibility for gathering network routing information, but simply uses the routing information it finds in the network layer using the route distribution protocol.

EDGE (Enhanced Data rates for Global Evolution)   An enhanced version of GPRS that combines digital TDMA and GSM to provide 48Kbps to 69.2Kbps per time slot on an aggregated basis, up to 384Kbps.

edge caching   A system in which Web content is duplicated on a machine close to the end user the first time the user requests the content. Subsequent requests for this content, then, are satisfied from the nearby machine. This improves the speed and reliability of access because it avoids the Internet backbone and its peering points.

EDI (electronic data interchange)   The asynchronous exchange from computer to computer of intercompany business documents (such as purchase orders, bills of lading, and invoices) and information. EDI can be accomplished through OSI standards or through proprietary products.

EGP (Exterior Gateway Protocol)   A routing protocol that is used to exchange network reachability information among organizational networks. EGP indicates whether a network is reachable; it does not weight that decision. EGP has largely been replaced by BGP-4.

EIA (Electronic Industries Association)   A U.S. organization that develops standards in the areas of electrical and electronic products and components.

EIA interface   A standardized set of signals characteristics (time duration, voltage, and current) specified by the Electronic Industries Association.

elastic application   A traditional Internet application that can work without guarantees of timely delivery. Because it can stretch in the face of greater delay, it can still perform adequately, even when the network faces increased congestion and degradation in performance.

ELEC (Ethernet Local Exchange Carrier)   A competitive provider that specializes in providing Ethernet solutions in the local loop and metro area.

electromagnetic spectrum   The electromagnetic waves that can propagate through free space that are created when electrons move. It ranges from extremely low-frequency radio waves of 30 Hz—with a wavelength of nearly the earth's diameter—to high-frequency cosmic rays of more than 10 million trillion Hz—with wavelengths smaller than the nucleus of an atom. The electromagnetic spectrum is depicted as a logarithmic progression: the scale increases by multiples of 10, so that the higher regions encompass a greater span of frequencies than the lower regions. The greater the span of frequencies, the greater the bandwidth of the media operating over that portion of the electromagnetic spectrum.

electronic tandem networking   Operating of two or more switching systems in parallel.

e-mail (electronic mail)   An application that enables users to send and receive messages and files over their computer networks.

EMI (electromagnetic interference)   The noise on data transmission lines that reduces data integrity. Motors, machines, and other generators of electromagnetic radiation cause it. Shielding can reduce EMI.

emulate   To imitate one system with another, so that the imitating system accepts the same data, executes the same computer programs, and achieves the same result as the imitated system.

encapsulation   The process of encasing one protocol into another protocol's format. Also called tunneling.

encryption   The process of coding data so that a specific code or key is required to restore the original data. Encryption is typically applied for secure data transmission or to prevent unauthorized reception of broadcast material. Sometimes referred to as scrambling.

end office   The first point of access to the PSTN, or the point at which the subscriber loop terminates. Also referred to as Class 5 office, local exchange, central office, and serving office.

end-to-end optical architecture   A network in which the optical signal never needs to be converted to an electronic signal.

ENUM   A protocol that is the result of work of the IETF's Telephone Number Mapping working group. The charter of this working group was to define a DNS-based architecture and protocols for mapping a telephone number to a uniform resource identifier (URI) which can be used to contact a resource associated with that number.

enterprise network A network that connects the computer resources throughout a company and supports a wide variety of the company's applications.

enterprise wiring hub A hub that not only connects the PCs on a LAN, it also provides the flexibility to perform a number of network functions that can benefit network administrators and network users in general.

equalization The introduction of components to an analog circuit by a modem to compensate for signal attenuation and delay distortion. Generally, the higher the transmission rate, the greater the need for equalization.

ERL (echo return loss) Attenuation of echo currents in one direction caused by telephone circuits operating in the other direction.

error In data communications, any unwanted change in the original contents of a transmission.

error burst A concentration of errors within a short period of time as compared with the average incidence of errors. Retransmission is the normal correction procedure in the event of an error burst.

error control A process of handling errors that includes the detection and correction of errors.

error-correction code A code that incorporates sufficient additional signal elements to enable the nature of some or all of the errors to be indicated and corrected entirely at receiving end.

error rate The ratio of the amount of data incorrectly received to the total amount of data transmitted.

ESCON (Enterprise Systems Connection) A proprietary optical networking system.

ESP (Encapsulated Security Payload) A security system in which IP datagram data is encrypted.

ESS (electronic switching system) A system that uses computer-like operations to switch telephone calls.

Ethernet A baseband LAN specification invented by Xerox Corp. and jointly developed by Xerox, Intel, and DEC. Ethernet networks operate at 10/100/1000Mbps by using CSMA/CD running over thick or thin coaxial, twisted-pair, or fiber-optic cable. Standards are being developed for 10Gbps Ethernet as well. Ethernet is defined in IEEE 802.3.

ETSI (European Telecommunication Standards Institute) A telecommunications standardization organization.

even parity check (odd parity check) A test of whether the number of digits in a group of binary digits is even (even parity check) or odd (odd parity check).

exchange The assembly of equipment in a communications system that controls the connection of incoming and outgoing lines and includes the necessary signaling and supervisory functions. Different exchanges, or switches, can be co-sited to perform different functions, for example, local exchange/central office, tandem exchange, toll/trunk/transit exchange, and so on.

extranet A network between partnering organizations.

extranet VPN A VPN that allows an external organization to have defined access into an enterprise's internal networks and resources.

F

F (fully associated) link   A link that directly connects to signaling endpoints, generally SSPs.

facility   (1) Any or all of the physical elements of a plan used to provide communications services. (2) A component of an operating system. (3) A transmission path between two or more points, provided by a common carrier.

fading   A phenomenon, generally of microwave or radio transmission, where atmospheric, electromagnetic, or gravitational influences cause a signal to be deflected or diverted away from the target receiver. The reduction in intensity of the power of a received signal.

Fast Ethernet   A standard for high-speed Ethernet that has a rate of 100Mbps.

fast packet switching   A packet processing technology that has streamlined protocol handling, including Frame Relay and ATM.

fault   A condition that causes any physical component of a system to fail to perform in acceptable fashion.

fault tolerance   The capability of a program or system to operate properly even if a failure occurs.

FCC (Federal Communications Commission)   A regulatory agency established by the Communications Act of 1934, charged with regulating all electrical and radio communications in the United States.

FDD (Frequency Division Duplexing)   A full-duplex technique that it is used when there is a significant contiguous spectrum allocated and when synchronization between the base stations is not possible. Each direction (incoming and outgoing) occupies a different portion of the frequency band, and a rather large portion of the spectrum is consumed.

FDDI (Fiber Distributed Data Interface)   A 100Mbps, fiber-based token-passing ANSI standard. It consists of dual fiber-optic counter-rotating rings, each capable of supporting 100Mbps data rates. FDDI is defined for fiber-optic cable, but it has a twisted-pair alternative called CDDI. FDDI II is an enhanced version of FDDI that supports isochronous transmission (for voice and video) as well as the packet-oriented (both asynchronous and synchronous) traffic handling of FDDI.

FDM (Frequency-Division Multiplexing)   A technique of dividing the bandwidth of a communications line into multiple smaller units of bandwidth, each of which supports an independent information stream.

FDMA (Frequency Division Multiple Access)   A multiple access technique used in analog cellular systems, in which each user is assigned to a different frequency.

FECN (forward explicit congestion notification)   A bit in the Frame Relay header by which the network can inform the receiver of network congestion.

femtosecond   0.000000000000001 (that is, 10^{-15}) second.

FEP (front-end processor)   A dedicated communications system that intercepts and handles activity for the host. It may perform line control, message handling, code conversion, and error control, as well as such application functions as control and operation of special-purpose terminals.

FHHS (Frequency Hopping Spread Spectrum)   A spread spectrum technique in which the frequency hopping varies in a known pattern, and separate error correction must be included.

fiber-optic waveguides   Thin filaments of glass through which a light beam can be transmitted for long distances by means of multiple internal reflections. Occasionally, other transparent materials, such as plastic, are used.

fiber optics   A technology that uses light as digital information carrier. Fiber-optic cables (light guides) are a direct replacement for coaxial cables and twisted-wire pairs. The glass-based transmission facilities occupy far less physical volume, yet provide a tremendous amount of transmission capacity, which is a major advantage in crowded underground ducts. The fibers are immune to electrical interference, which is another advantage. Also called lightwave communications, photonics, or, simply, fiber.

Fibre Channel   A high-speed interface, standardized by ANSI, that supports up to 800Mbps over 6.2 miles (10 kilometers) of fiber.

FIFO (first in, first out)   A queuing technique in which the next item to be retrieved is the item that has been in the queue for the longest time. This ensures that cells remain in the correct sequence.

file server   In local networks, a station dedicated to providing file and mass data storage services to the other stations on the network.

filter   To selectively forward data, based on criteria specified by the network manager.

firewall   A system designed to prevent unauthorized access to or from a private network. Firewalls can be implemented in both hardware and software, or a combination of both.

fixed wireless local loop   A stationary installation that dramatically cuts down on the cost of installing and maintaining the local loop. It uses a fixed antenna location, so it's relatively easy to engineer.

flat network   A network that is constructed by using bridges or Layer 2 LAN switches. This type of network is easy to configure, and it promises better performance than hierarchical networks; it offers higher throughput and therefore also lower latencies. However, the scalability of a flat network is limited, and a flat network is subject to broadcast storms.

flat rate   A fixed cost for service. Additional charges may be applied for additional services or usage if so specified.

flow control   A system that uses buffering and other mechanisms, such as controls that turn a device on and off, to prevent data loss during transmission.

FM (frequency modulation)   One of three ways of modifying a sine wave signal to carry digital bits. The sine wave or "carrier" has its frequency modified in accordance with the information to be transmitted. The frequency function of the modulated wave may be continuous or discontinuous.

forward channel   The communications path that carries voice or data from the call initiator to the network.

forward error correction   A system that uses redundant information in received data to permit the receiver to correct transmission errors.

four-wire circuit   A circuit that contains two pairs of wire (or their logical equivalent) for simultaneous (i.e., full-duplex) two-way transmission. Two pairs of conductors, one for the inbound channel and one for the outbound channel, are connected to the station equipment.

fractional T-1/E-1   T-1/E-1 lines that have apportioned bandwidth for separate transmission channels (DS-0/64Kbps subchannels), generally in increments of four channels.

fragmentation   The process of splitting a packet into pieces when it is larger than the MTU it must transmit.

frame   (1) In data transmission, the sequence of contiguous bits bracketed by and including beginning and ending flag sequences. (2) In a TDM system, a repetitive group of signals resulting from a signal sampling of all channels, including any additional signals for synchronizing and other required system information.

frame bandwidth allocation   The sum of the committed information rates associated with all the PVCs for a specific customer.

Frame Relay   A packet-switch technology that is simpler and more powerful than the X.25 standard. Frame Relay provides a multiplexed channel between a router and a T-1/E-1 nodal processor. It increases bandwidth utilization while reducing overall equipment costs. The standard addresses data communications speeds up to 45Mbps.

framing   A control procedure used with multiplexed digital channels, such as T1 carriers, in which bits are inserted so that the receiver can identify the time slots that are allocated to such subchannel; framing bits may also carry alarm signals indicating specific alarm conditions.

Free Space Optics   An optical wireless networking option that uses low-powered infrared lasers. There are two options in Free Space Optics: point-to-point products, used to provide high-speed connection between two buildings, and multiple high-speed connections through the air that operate over much shorter distances, either in a point-to-multipoint or meshed architecture.

frequency   An expression of how frequently a periodic (repetitious) wave form or signal regenerates itself at a given amplitude. It can be expressed in hertz (Hz), kilohertz (KHz), megahertz (MHz), and so on.

FSK (frequency shift keying)   A method of modulation that uses two different frequencies to distinguish between a mark (digital 1) and a space (digital 0) when transmitting on an analog line. Used in modems operating at 1,200bps or slower.

FTAM (File Transfer Access and Management)   An ISO standard that describes how to create, delete, read, and change file attributes as well as transfer and access (at file or record level) files stored at remote sites. It is an application-layer protocol.

FTP (File Transfer Protocol)   A protocol that enables a TCP/IP user on any computer to get files from another computer, or to send files to another computer. Usually implemented as application-level programs, FTP uses the Telnet and TCP protocols. The server side requires a client to supply a login identifier and password before it will honor requests.

FTTC (fiber-to-the-curb)   A system in which fiber cable extends from a switching office to a curb.

FTTH (fiber-to-the-home)   A system in which fiber cable extends from a switching office to the subscriber's house.

full-duplex   A communication system or equipment that is capable of transmission simultaneously in both directions.

full-motion video   Moving images that the human eye perceives as being fully realistic. While there are no defined standards, full-motion video is frequently referred to as VHS-quality. Frame rates range from 24 frames per second in motion pictures, 25 frames per second in the PAL system, and 30 frames per second in the NTSC system.

FX (foreign exchange) line   A line that makes a toll call appear to be a local call.

G

gateway   A device or program (that is, hardware or software) that connects two different networks that use different protocols and translates between these protocols, allowing devices on the two networks to communicate with each other.

gateway daemon   A program that runs under BSD UNIX on a gateway to allow the gateway to collect information from within one autonomous system using RIP, HELLO, or other IGPs, and to advertise routes to another autonomous system using the EGP.

Gateway-to-Gateway Protocol   The original IGP used by Internet core gateways (i.e., by routers).

GB (gigabyte)   1 billion bytes, or 1,000MB.

GEO (geosynchronous orbit)   A circular orbit with a 24-hour orbital period approximately 22,300 miles (36,000 kilometers) above the earth's equator. Because satellites in this orbit appear stationary relative to the earth's surface, GEO is especially useful for communications satellites transmitting to fixed earth stations.

GHz (gigahertz)   1 billion cycles per second.

Gigabit Ethernet   An Ethernet standard, introduced in 1997, that supports 1,000Mbps.

global information infrastructure   A vision of individual national information infrastructures joined together to form an international network.

GPRS (General Packet Radio Service)   An always-on nonvoice value-added service that enables information to be sent and received across a mobile telephone network via GSM phones.

grooming   The process of selectively removing channels from a digital facility for routing to a designated remote location via another digital facility. Grooming basically allows you to drop and add payload flexibly.

ground circuit   (1) A circuit in which energy is carried one way over a metallic path and returned through the earth. (2) A circuit connected to earth at one or more points.

ground start   A signaling method whereby one station detects that a circuit is grounded at the other end.

ground station   An assemblage of communications equipment, including signal generator, transmitter, receiver, and antenna, that receives (and usually transmits) signals to/from a communications satellite. Also called earth station.

Group 3 fax   An ITU-T standard for encoding an image and transmitting it over dial-up lines.

Group 4 fax   An ITU-T standard for encoding an image and transmitting it over ISDN or other wideband digitized services.

GSM (Global System for Mobile Communications)   A European standard for 2G wireless digital communications, it is globally implemented and supports both voice and data communications. It operates in three frequency bands: GSM 900 (900MHz); DCS 1800 (1.8GHz); and PCS 1900 (1.9GHz). New GSM data standards include HSCSD, GPRS, and EDGE, and are referred to as 2.5G.

H

H.323   An ITU standard that defines how audiovisual conferencing data is transmitted across networks. In theory, H.323 should enable users to participate in the same conference even though they are using different videoconferencing equipment.

H-channel   A class of high-speed ISDN channels. H-0 is 384Kbps, H-11 is 1.536Mbps, and H-12 is 1.920Mbps.

half-duplex   Communications in which data can be transmitted between two stations in both directions, but only one direction at a time.

HAN (home area network)   A broadband network in a smart house that connects the various smart devices.

handoff   The transfer of duplex signaling as a mobile terminal passes to an adjacent cell in a cellular radio network.

handshake   The exchange of predetermined signals for control when a connection is established between two modems or other devices.

haptic interface   An interface that enables virtual touch.

hard wired   (1) Referring to a communications link, whether remote phone line or local cable, that permanently connects two nodes, stations, or devices. (2) Descriptive of electronic circuitry that performs fixed logical operations by virtue of unalterable circuit layout, rather than under computer or stored-program control.

hardware   The physical equipment, as opposed to programs or procedures of a computer system.

harmonic distortion   A wave form distortion, usually caused by the nonlinear frequency response of a transmission.

hash function   The process of producing hash values for accessing data or for security. A hash value (or simply hash) is a number generated from a string of text. The hash is substantially smaller than the text itself, and is generated by a formula in such a way that it is extremely unlikely that some other text will produce the same hash value.

HCSD (high-speed circuit-switched data)   A standard for transferring high-speed data over aggregated GSM channels; provides data rates up to 64Kbps.

HDLC (High-Level Data Link Control)   A form of communications line control that uses a specified series of bits rather than control characters to control data transmission over a communication line. A bit-oriented protocol developed by the ISO.

HDSL (High-Bit-Rate DSL)   A symmetrical service that can be deployed over a distance of about 2.2 miles (3.6 kilometers). HDSL is deployed over two twisted-pair cables, and it affords equal bandwidth in both directions (i.e., it is symmetrical). HDSL2 provides symmetrical capacities of up to 1.5Mbps or 2Mbps over a single twisted-pair cable.

HDTV (high-definition television)   A television format for which several competing standards exist but which normally require a screen aspect ratio of 16:9 (versus 4:3 with current TVs) and which is capable of reproducing at least four times more detail than is the existing broadcasting system.

headend   The control center of a cable TV network.

header   The initial portion of a message or file, which contains statistic and control information.

HELLO   The protocol used by a group of cooperative, trusting packet switches to allow them to discover minimal delay routes.

heuristic   An exploratory method of problem solving in which solutions are arrived at by an interactive, self-learning method.

hexadecimal   A system of numbers in base 16; hexadecimal digits range from 0 (zero) through 9 (nine) and A (10) through F (15). Each hexadecimal digit is represented by 4 binary bits.

HFC (hybrid fiber coax)   A networking arrangement that supports a wide range of services, including traditional telephony, broadcast video, and interactive broadband services. It involves the use of fiber in the backbone and in the access network. The fiber terminates at a neighborhood node, and from that neighborhood node, coax (normally 750MHz or 1,000MHz) is run to the home, in a two-way subsplit system.

hierarchical routing   Routing that is based on a hierarchical addressing scheme. Most TCP/IP routing is based on a two-level hierarchy in which an IP address is divided into a network portion and a host portion. Routers use only the network portion until the datagram reaches a router that can deliver it directly. Subnetting introduces additional levels of hierarchical routing.

high frequency   The portion of electromagnetic spectrum, typically used in shortwave radio applications; frequencies approximately in the 3MHz to 30MHz range.

HIPPI (High Performance Parallel Interface)   A gigabit-per-second OSI Layer 1 and 2 interface standardized by ANSI. HIPP5 supports 800Mbps up to 82 feet (25 meters) using a 32-bit parallel copper connector, and can be extended up to several miles/kilometers by using fiber-optic technology. A higher speed option uses 64 parallel lines to support operation at up to 1.6Gbps.

holding time   The length of time a communication channel is in use for each transmission. Includes both message tone and operating time. Also called connect time.

HomeRF   An open standard for short-range transmission of digital voice and data between mobile devices.

hop   A unit of network distance. In particular, the number of hops between a source and a destination is the number of nodes between them (e.g., number of routers between hosts on the Internet).

hop-by-hop retransmission   A system in which an intermediate device retransmits, so the retransmission travels a shorter path over a fewer number of hops and is therefore less delayed.

horizontal distribution frame   A hub for terminating cables run on a floor.

host   An end user computer system that connects to a network. Hosts range in size from personal computers to supercomputers.

host interface   The link between a communications processor or network and a host computer.

host system   (1) The computing system to which a network is connected and with which other devices can communicate. (2) The primary or controlling computer in a network.

howler tone   The tone that alerts a subscriber when the telephone is off the hook.

HSCSD (High-Speed Circuit-Switched Data)   A high-speed transmission technology that enables users to send and retrieve data over GSM networks at transmission speeds between 28.8Kbps and 43.2Kbps (but the norm is generally around 28.8Kbps) by enabling the concurrent usage of up to four traffic channels of a GSM network.

HSSI (high-speed serial interface)   A physical-layer interface between a DTE, such as a high-speed router or similar device, and a DCE, such as a DS-3 (45Mbps) or SDH/SONET OC-1 DSU.

HTML (Hypertext Markup Language)   A document standard that defines a simple logical structure including titles, heading, paragraphs, lists, forms, tables, and mathematical equations, as well as a language to specify hypertext links.

HTTP (Hypertext Transfer Protocol)   The standard mechanism used on the World Wide Web for the transfer of documents between server and client systems.

hub   A device that extends the maximum physical length of a network by cleaning and retransmitting signals among network segments. A hub provides the central connecting point in a star network topology. Also called a multiport repeater.

Huffman encoding   A particular statistical encoding technique for lossless compression. Statistical encoding is an entropy-encoding method. The Huffman algorithm calculates the frequency of occurrence of each octet for a given portion of data stream. It then determines the minimum number of bits to allocate to each character and assigns an optimal code accordingly. The codes are stored in a codebook. This technique is used in sound, still, and moving image compression.

hybrid circuit   A circuit that has four sets of terminals arranged in two pairs designed so that there is high loss between the two sets of terminals of a pair when the terminals of the other pair are suitably terminated. Commonly used to couple four-wire circuits to two-wire circuits.

hybrid network   A network composed of both public and private facilities.

Hz (Hertz)   A unit of electromagnetic frequency that is equal to one cycle per second.

I

ICANN (Internet Corporation for Assigned Names and Numbers)   A nonprofit corporation that was formed in 1998 to take over work previously done by the U.S. government in managing the domain name and root server systems.

ICMP (Internet Control Message Protocol)   An integral part of the Internet Protocol that handles error and control messages. Specifically, routers and hosts use ICMP to send reports of problems about datagrams back to the original source that sent the datagram. ICMP also includes an echo request/reply used to test whether a destination is reachable and responding.

ICP (Internet content provider)   A service provider that specializes in providing content, rather than infrastructure.

IDEA (International Data Encryption Algorithm)   An algorithm developed by ETH Zurich that is free of charge for noncommercial use. It is viewed as a good algorithm and is used in PGP and in Speak Freely, a program that allows encrypted digitized voice to be sent over the Internet.

IDF (intermediate distribution frame)   A frame that has distributing blocks on both sides, permitting the interconnection of telephone circuitry.

IDSL (ISDN DSL)   A transmission medium that has a maximum loop length of 3.4 miles (5.5 kilometers), and it is deployed as a single twisted-pair cable that offers 128Kbps in each direction.

IEEE (Institute of Electrical and Electronics Engineers)   A scientific, engineering, and educational society that develops and publishes standards in a variety of electrical engineering and computer-related areas. IEEE membership is open to any dues-paying individual. IEEE is responsible for 802 LAN standards.

IETF (Internet Engineering Task Force)   A nonprofit organization that produces the standards used in TCP/IP and the Internet.

I-frame (intracoded frame)   A frame that is not reconstructed from another frame. An I-frame is also a reference frame; it serves as a reference to construct other frames.

IFRB (International Frequency Registration Board)   A board within the ITU that is responsible for the maintenance of an international list of radio frequency usage and the allocation of new frequencies.

IGMP (Internet Group Membership Protocol)   A protocol that allows Internet hosts to participate in multicasting. It describes the basics of multicasting IP traffic, including the format of multicast IP addresses, multicast Ethernet encapsulation, and the concept of a host group (that is, a set of hosts interested in traffic for a particular multicast address).

IGP (interior gateway protocol)   Any protocol that is used to propagate network reachability and routing information within an autonomous system. RIP and IGRP are examples.

IGRP (Interior Gateway Routing Protocol)   A proprietary network protocol, developed by Cisco Systems, designed to work on autonomous systems. IGRP is a distance-vector routing protocol, which means that each router sends all or a portion of its routing table in a routing message update at regular intervals to each of its neighboring routers.

IKE (Internet Key Exchange)   The key exchange protocol used by IPSec. It supports pre-shared keys, which is a simplified form of key exchange. It does not require digital certificates.

ILEC (incumbent local exchange carrier)   A telephone company that was providing local service in the United States when the Telecommunications Act of 1996 was enacted. For most residents in the United States, this would be one of the four "baby Bells"—Qwest, SBC, BellSouth, and Verizon.

immersion   In virtual reality, refers to the user's subjective sensation of being inside the virtual world, and not observing it from an outside perspective.

i-mode   A proprietary protocol for transforming Internet information so that it can be displayed on the small screen of a mobile telephone or other portable device. i-mode is used in Japan and is also called DoCoMo (which means "anywhere").

IMT-2000 (International Mobile Telecommunications 2000)　An evolving standard for third-generation mobile communications, enabling personal mobility and converging mobile and fixed networks.

IMUN (International Mobile User Number)　A number used to dial a subscriber in third-generation mobile networks.

IN (intelligent network)　An architecture for providing advances services in telecommunications networks.

in-band management　A system in which management information is communicated across the network.

induction coil　An apparatus for obtaining intermittent high voltage consisting of a primary coil through which the direct current flows, an interrupter, and a secondary coil of a larger number of turns in which the high voltage is induced.

information infrastructure　High-speed communications networks capable of carrying voice, data, text, image, and video (multimedia) information in an interactive mode serving an enterprise computing architecture.

information path　The functional route by which information is routed.

information signals　Signals that are associated with activating and delivering various enhanced features, such as call waiting.

information systems network　A network of multiple operating-level systems and one management-oriented system (centered around planning, control, and measurement processes). The network retrieves data from databases and synthesizes the data into meaningful information to support the organization.

information technology　A broad term that describes the computer hardware, software, and networking industry, including telecommunications and audiovisual equipment.

infrared　The frequency range in the electromagnetic spectrum than is higher than radio frequencies but below the range of visible light.

infrastructure　The underlying structure or framework of the telecommunications system (for example, switching, multiplexing, and transmission systems) that allows for the transmission of voice, video, and data.

input queue　A holding area for packets that come to the input port more quickly than the router can process them.

Integrated IS-IS　A routing protocol that combines routing for TCP/IP and OSI protocols. It is a superset of IS-IS, the OSI routing technology that combines the functionality of both OSPF and IS-IS.

interactive　A term that describes the mode of transaction with a particular information service. An interactive service allows for both input and output. It is sometimes referred to as two-way, as opposed to a one-way, service.

interactive processing　A processing method in which each operator action causes a response from the program or system.

interconnected systems   Systems that are linked together in local and/or remote networks. The exchange of data between systems in a network is through standard channels or through communications lines. Communication between interconnected systems normally occurs without manual intervention; it is provided by combined hardware and software supporting the interconnection.

interconnection   The interworking of two separate networks, including wireline and wireless. Interconnection is used to refer both to the technical interface and to the commercial arrangements between two network operators providing service.

interface   A boundary between two pieces of equipment across which all signals that pass are carefully defined. The definition includes the connector signal levels, impedance, timing, sequence of operation, and the meaning of signals.

interior routing   Routing that occurs within an autonomous system.

international business service   A satellite-based service at up to 8Mbps. Services include data, fax, digital voice, and video- and audioconferencing.

international gateway   A device that connects calls between different countries.

international number   Digits that have to be dialed after the international prefix to call a subscriber in another country; that is, the country code followed by the subscriber's national number.

Internet   Physically, a collection of packet-switching networks interconnected by routers along with protocols that allow them to function logically as a single, large, virtual network. Internet with a capital *I* refers to the worldwide Internet consisting of large national and regional backbone networks, local Internet service providers, and IP networks.

Internet 2   A network that replaces what the original Internet was for—the academic network. Internet 2 acts as a testbed for many of the latest and greatest technologies. The universities stress-test Internet 2 to determine how applications perform and which technologies suit which applications or management purposes best.

Internet-based VPN   A VPN that is comprised of multiple ISPs that provide local access services in defined geographical regions. Because it requires an enterprise to receive end-to-end services from multiple suppliers, performance is difficult to control and guarantee.

interoffice channels   A portion of a leased circuit between IXC exchanges.

interoffice trunk   A direct trunk between local exchanges (Class 5 offices), or between tandem, toll, or international exchanges. Also called interexchange trunk.

interoperability   The ability to exchange information in a network that contains computers and additional devices that have dissimilar operating systems or protocols.

intranet VPN   A site-to-site connection whose key objective is to replace or reduce the use of leased-line networks, traditional routers, and Frame Relay services.

IntServ (Integrated Services)   The IETF's scheme to introduce QoS support over IP networks. It provides extensions to the best-effort service model to allow control over end-to-end packet delays. IntServ is a per-flow, resource reservation model, requiring RSVP. Its key building blocks include resource reservation and admission control.

intranet   A network based on TCP/IP protocols (an internet) that belongs to an organization and is accessible only by the organization's members, employees, or others with authorization.

Inverse ARP An extension to the ARP protocol that permits a station to request a protocol address (e.g., an IP address) given a hardware address (e.g., a Frame Relay DLCI).

inverse multiplexer A device that spreads a high-bandwidth information stream over multiple lower-speed transmission channels (e.g., a 1.5Mbps signal transmitted over twenty-four 64Kbps channels of a T-1).

I/O (input/output) (1) A device or channel that may be involved in an input process, and, at a different time, in an output process. (2) A device whose parts can be performing an input process and an output process at the same time. (3) Pertains to either input or output, or both.

IP (Internet Protocol) The protocol that specifies the exact format of all data as it travels through a TCP/IP network. In addition, IP performs the routing functions and selects the transmission path on which data will be sent. As part of these two functions, IP also provides a mechanism for dealing with unreliable data, specifying the manner in which network nodes will process data, specifying how and when to generate error messages, and specifying when to discard unreliable data.

IP address The 32-bit address assigned to hosts that want to participate in a TCP/IP internet. IP addresses are the abstraction of physical hardware addresses just as an internet is an abstraction of physical networks. Actually assigned to the interconnection of a host to a physical network, an IP address consists of a network portion and a host portion. The partition makes routing efficient.

IP backbone A packet-switching network interconnected by routers along with protocols that allow them to function logically as a single, large, virtual network. IP backbones are operated by individual service providers, unlike the Internet, which is comprised of more than 10,000 service providers.

IP datagram The basic unit of information passed across a TCP/IP internet. An IP datagram is to an internet as a hardware packet is to a physical network. It contains a source and destination address along with data.

IP forwarding The process of forwarding internet packets from one network to another.

IP fragmentation A multibridge feature that handles packet size mismatch problems between FDDI and Ethernet endpoints. The maximum FDDI packet size is 4,500 bytes. The maximum Ethernet packet size is 1,548 bytes. Messages that are longer than 1,548 bytes must be fragmented into smaller packets to allow them to enter the Ethernet network.

IP long-distance wholesale VoIP service providers that offer IP services to domestic and international carriers, corporations, and service providers to carry their traffic, particularly international transit.

IP Multicast A protocol for transmitting IP datagrams from one source to many destinations in a LAN or WAN.

IP PBX A new-generation PBX that uses packet-switching technology and offers an attractive platform for the integration of voice and data in the enterprise.

IP switch A switch that replaces slower, more processing-intensive routers. An IP router that provides connection-oriented services at the IP layer.

IP telephony The use of the Internet or a private IP network for telephony.

IPDC (Internet Protocol Device Control)   A specification that creates flexible management of media gateway devices.

IPNSIG (Interplanetary Internet)   A network project that defines the architecture and protocols necessary to permit interoperation of the Internet resident on earth with other remotely located internets resident on other planets or spacecraft in transit.

IPSec (IP Security)   A set of protocols developed by the IETF to support secure exchange of packets at the IP layer. IPSec has been deployed widely to implement VPNs.

IPS7 (IP Signaling System 7)   A signaling protocol that works with SS7.

IPv4 (Internet Protocol version 4)   The current generation of IP, in which an IP address has two parts: The first is the network ID and the second is the host ID. Under IPv4, there are five classes (Class A through Class E), which differ in how many networks and hosts are supported.

IPv6 (Internet Protocol version 6)   An IP addressing scheme that uses a 128-bit address, which allows a total of 340 billion billion billion billion unique addresses. IPv6 offers many benefits, but it requires a major reconfiguration of all the routers out there, and hence we haven't seen the community jump at the migration from IPv4 to IPv6. Also called IPng (IP Next Generation).

IPX (Internetwork Packet Exchange)   The Novell equivalent of IP. It is used to route NetWare packets between LANs. IPX does not guarantee the delivery of messages; NetWare's SPX protocol handles that task.

IrDA (Infrared Data Association)   A short-range wireless technology that allows connection between devices using infrared links instead of wired cabling.

IRP (Interdomain Routing Protocol)   A descendent of BGP that is being considered by ISO as the basis for an inter AD routing protocol standard.

ISC (international switching center)   An exchange used to switch traffic between different countries over international circuits.

ISDN (Integrated Services Digital Network)   A circuit-switched digital subscriber line service; an access technology. ISDN is part of the physical layer of the OSI reference model. ITU-T I.430 defines a 144Kbps Basic Rate Interface (BRI), and ITU-T I.431 defines a Primary Rate Interface (PRI) of 1.544Mbps in North America and Japan and of 2.048Mbps in Europe.

IS-IS (Intermediate System to Intermediate System)   The OSI's emerging IS-IS protocol uses a link state algorithm to provide routing services for TCP/IP and OSI. It determines the best path for TCP/IP and OSI packets through the network, and keeps routers informed of the status of the network and the systems available.

ISM (Industrial, Scientific, and Medical)   Unlicensed radio bands that operate at 900MHz, 2.4GHz, and 5.8GHz.

ISO (International Organization for Standardization)   An organization established to promote the development of standards to facilitate the international exchange of goods and services, and to develop mutual cooperation in areas of intellectual, scientific, technological, and economic activity.

ISO Ethernet   An isochronous Ethernet standard designed to provide an efficient way of sharing normal Ethernet and isochronous traffic on a single twisted-pair cable, in a local area environment.

ISOC (Internet Society)   A nongovernmental, nonprofit organization dedicated to maintaining and enhancing the Internet. Through its committees, such as the Internet Advisory Board and the IETF, ISOC is responsible for developing and approving new Internet standards and protocols.

isochronous   A descriptor signifying enabling network characteristics. This includes the ability to simultaneously transport disparate data types (voice, video, and data), across the same circuit. It also includes the capability to dynamically allocate bandwidth as the application warrants.

isochronous data stream   A nonpacketized data transmission. A circuit-switched, fixed rate, continuous data stream, such as voice, video, or real-time sensor data.

IS-54   TIA's Interim Specification 54, also called NADC and Digital AMPS, and updated by IS-136. It is a TDMA-based wireless network that operates at 800MHz.

IS-95   TIA's Interim Specification 95. A spread-spectrum wireless network, operating in the 800MHz range, using a CDMA/FDD scheme.

IS-136   TIA's Interim Specification 136. An updated TDMA-based standard that updates IS-54. Provides 3x spectral efficiency over analog AMPS systems.

ISV (independent software vendor)   A vendor that develops the applications that the ASPs then put up for sale or for rent.

ITU (International Telecommunication Union)   A telecommunications agency of the United Nations, established to provide standardized communications procedures and practices including frequency allocation and radio regulations on a worldwide basis. Parent group of the ITU-T (telecommunications), ITU-R (radio), and ITU-D (developing nations).

IXC (interexchange carrier)   A long-distance telephone company that offers circuit-switched, leased-line, or packet-switched service.

J

jack   A device used generally for terminating the permanent wiring of a circuit, access to which is obtained by the insertion of a plug.

J-carrier   The Japanese standard of the PDH, a time-division multiplexed, digital transmission system. J-carrier is a PCM system that uses a 64Kbps per channel as the basis of the hierarchy. Higher levels reflect aggregation of the 64Kbps channels. J-1 is a 1.544Mbps 24-channel communications circuit; J-2 is a 6.312Mbps 96-channel communications circuit; J-3 is a 32.064Mbps 501-channel communications circuit; J-4 is a 97.728Mbps 1,527-channel communications circuit; and J-5 is a 397.200Mbps communications circuit.

jitter   The slight movement of a transmission signal in time or phase that can introduce errors and loss of synchronization for high-speed synchronous communications.

JPEG (Joint Pictures Expert Group)   An international standard used primarily for still image compression.

JTACS (Japanese Total Access Communication Systems)   A Japanese wireless system that operates in the 800MHz to 900MHz band.

jumper   A patch cable or wire used to establish a circuit, often temporarily, for testing or diagnostics.

K

Ka-band   The portion of the electromagnetic spectrum allotted for satellite transmission; frequencies are approximately in the 20GHz to 30GHz range.

Kbps (kilobits per second)   1,000 bits per second.

KHz (kilohertz)   1,000 cycles per second.

Ku-band   The portion of the electromagnetic spectrum being used increasingly for satellite communications. Frequencies are approximately in the 12GHz to 14GHz range.

L

L2TP (Layer 2 Tunneling Protocol)   A Layer 2 protocol that can work in a non-IP enterprise environment. L2TP is used primarily by service providers to encapsulate and carry VPN traffic through their backbones.

LAN (local area network)   (1) A system for linking terminals, programs, storage, and graphic devices at multiple workstations over relatively small geographic areas. (2) A network that is limited to a small area, for example the premises of an office building or plant.

LANE (LAN Emulation)   An ATM Forum standard for emulating a LAN across an ATM network.

LAPB (Link Access Protocol Balanced)   A modified form of HDLC that the ITU-T chose as the link-level protocol for X.25 networks. LAPB provides for the reliable transfer of a packet from a host to an X.25 packet switch, which then forwards the packet on to its destination.

laser (light amplification by simulated emission of radiation)   A device that converts electrical energy into radiant energy in the visible or infrared parts of the spectrum, emitting light with a small spectral bandwidth. Lasers are widely used in fiber-optic communications, particularly as sources for long-haul links.

LATA (Local Access and Transport Area)   Geographic regions within the United States that define areas within which the Bell operating companies (BOCs) can offer exchange and exchange access services (local calling, private lines, and so on).

latency   The delay associated with the time it takes a packet to travel from entry point to exit point.

layer   In the OSI reference model, a collection of related network-processing functions that comprise one level of a hierarchy of functions.

L-band   The portion of the electromagnetic spectrum commonly used in satellite and microwave applications. L-band operates in the 390MHz to 1550MHz range, and it supports various mobile and fixed applications.

LCD (liquid crystal display)   A graphic display on a terminal screen using an electroluminescent technology to form symbols or shapes.

LDAP (Lightweight Directory Access Protocol)   The standard directory server technology for the Internet. LDAP allows retrieval of information from multivendor directories.

LDP (Label Distribution Protocol)   An MPLS signaling protocol.

leased line   A communication channel contracted for exclusive use from a common carrier, frequently referred to as a private line.

LEC (local exchange carrier)   The incumbent local telephone company. There was originally no competition among LECs, but as soon as competition in the local loop picked up, LECs were segmented into ILECs, CLECs, and DCLECs.

LED (light-emitting diode)   A semiconductor junction diode that emits radiant energy and is used as a light source for fiber-optics communications, particularly for short-haul links. Also used in alphanumeric displays in electronic telephones and calculators.

LEO (low earth-orbit) satellite   A satellite that orbits at about 400 to 1,000 miles (640 to 1,600 kilometers) above the earth.

lightwave communications   A term sometimes used in place of *optical communications* to avoid confusion with visual information and image transmission, such as facsimile or television.

limited-distance modem   A device that translates digital signals into analog signals (and vise versa) for transfers over limited distances; some operate at higher speeds than modems that are designed for use over analog telephone facilities.

line   (1) The communications path between two or more points, including a satellite or microwave channel, also referred to as the transmission line. (2) In data communication, a circuit connecting two or more devices. (3) The transmission path from nonswitching subscriber terminal to a switching system.

line hit   Electrical interference that causes the introduction of undesirable signals on a circuit.

line of sight   (1) A characteristic of some open-air transmission technologies (such as microwave, infrared, and open-air laser-type transmissions) in which the path between a transmitter and a receiver must be clear and unobstructed . (2) A clear, open-air, direct transmission path that is free of obstructions such as buildings but may in some cases be impeded by adverse weather or environmental conditions.

line speed   The maximum data rate that can be reliably transmitted over a line.

link   (1) A physical circuit between two points. (2) A conceptual (or virtual) circuit between two users of a packet switched (or other) network that allows them to communicate, even when different paths are used.

link redundancy level   The ratio of actual number of paths to the minimum number of paths required to connect all nodes of a network.

link state   A state in which each router is aware of the topology of the entire network. Each router sends out information about the links that the router has to all other routers on the network. The final routing table is based upon the shortest path to each destination. Most new routing protocols are based on this algorithm.

link-state protocol   A generic class of routing protocols in which information about the status of the entire network is propagated to every node and used in routing decisions. OSPF, IS-IS, and NLSP are link-state routing protocols.

LLC (logical link control)   A protocol developed by the IEEE 802, common to all of its local network standards, for data link-level transmission control. The upper sublayer of the IEEE Layer 2 (OSI) protocol that complements the MAC protocol (IEEE 802.2). LLC 1 is a minimal function LLC that supports connectionless link layer service. LLC 2 supports connection-oriented data link service.

LMDS (Local Multipoint Distribution Service)   A technique for supplying broadband access via a point-to-point microwave digital system. Referred to as Multipoint Video Distribution service in Europe, it operates over a very large frequency allocation, a 1.3GHz band that's generally located somewhere in the range of 28GHz to 45GHz, depending on the country. It is a popular technique for deploying wireless local loop.

LMI (local management interface)   A Frame Relay specification for the method of exchanging status information between the user (e.g., bridge or router) and the network.

loading   Adding loading coils to a transmission line to minimize amplitude distortion.

loading coil   An induction device used in local loops, generally those exceeding 3.4 miles (5.5 kilometers) in length, that compensates for the wire capacitance and serves to boost voice-grade frequencies. They are often removed for new generation, high-speed, local loop data services, because they can distort data signals at higher frequencies than those used for voice.

local   Pertains to a device that is connected directly to the computer without using a WAN communication line.

local exchange   The switching center in which subscribers' lines terminate. The exchange has access to the other exchanges and to national trunk networks. Also called central office, end office, serving office, and Class 5 office.

local exchange trunk   A trunk between the CPE and the local exchange. Also referred to as central office trunk.

local loop   A line connecting a customers' telephone equipment with the local telephone company exchange. Often referred to as a subscriber line, an access line, or the last mile.

local number portability   A service that enables you to keep your own telephone number when you move to a new location.

local service area   The area within which the telephone operating company uses local rates for calling charge.

LocalTalk   Apple Computer's proprietary 230.4Kbps baseband CSMA/CA network protocol.

location-based online services   Services provided over a wireless infrastructure that are based on the location of the user. The location of the user can be determined by global positioning systems (GPS) or by cellular networks. Radio signals emitted from cellular phones can be tracked from cellular towers and triangulated, yielding locations nearly as accurate as those from a GPS receiver.

logical address   An address that is used to identify the communications program by "name" to the protocol stack with which you are working. No matter where your program is put in the network, your logical address will remain the same, even though your physical address may change.

long-haul   Long-distance, describing (primarily) telephone circuits that cross out of the local exchange.

loop   (1) A local circuit between an exchange and subscriber CPE, either residential (single line telephone) or business (PBX). Also called subscriber loop, local line, and local loop. (2) In programming, a sequence of computer instructions that repeats itself until a predetermined count or other test is satisfied.

loop back   A diagnostic procedure used for transmission devices; a test message is sent to a device being tested, which then sends the message back to the originator for comparison with the original transmission. Loop-back testing may be performed within a locally attached device or conducted remotely over a communications circuit.

loop circuit   The circuit connecting the subscriber's equipment with the local exchange switch. Also called metallic circuit and local loop.

loop signaling systems   Any of the three methods of transmitting signaling information over the metallic loop formed by the trunk conductors and the terminating equipment bridges. Transmission of the loop signals can be accomplished by (a) opening and closing the DC path around the loop, (b) reversing the voltage polarity, or (c) varying the value of the equipment resistance.

loop start   The most commonly used method of signaling an off-hook condition between an analog phone set and a switch, whereby picking up the receiver closes a wire loop, allowing DC current to flow, which is detected by a PBX or local exchange and interpreted as a request for service.

loss   A decrease in energy of signal power in transmission along the circuit as a result of the resistance of impedance of the circuit or equipment.

lossless compression   In data compression, the process by which the information is recovered without any alteration after the decompression stage. This technique is used for computer-based data or programs. It may also be required in certain multimedia applications where the accuracy of the information is essential, such as in medical imaging. Lossless compression is also called bit-preserving or reversible compression. Examples of lossless compression include run-length encoding or Huffman encoding.

lossy compression   In data compression, the case in which the decompressed information is different from the original uncompressed information. This mode is suitable for most continuous media, such as sound and motion video, as well as for many images. That the decompressed information is different from the original in lossy compression does not imply that the perceptual response of an observer is different. Also called irreversible compression.

low frequency   Generally indicates frequencies between 30KHz and 300KHz.

low-level language   A programming language in which instructions have a 1-to-1 relationship with machine code.

LPC (linear predictive coding)   A vector-quantization-based compression scheme for speech. It can compress speech down to 2.4Kbps.

LSR (label-switching router)   An MPLS-enabled router and/or MPLS-enabled ATM switch. As each packet enters the network, an ingress LSR assigns it a label, based on its destination, VPN membership, ToS bits, and other considerations. At each hop, an LSR uses the label to index a forwarding table.

M

MAC (Media Access Control)   The part of OSI Layer 2, it describes how devices share access to the network. Token Ring, Ethernet, and FDDI are MAC layer specifications. Wiring hubs primarily deal with MAC layer equipment.

MAE (metropolitan area exchange)   An interconnection and exchange point where public Internet backbones meet and exchange traffic. Also called a NAP.

MAN (metropolitan area network)   A network spanning a geographical distance of up to a 62-mile (100-kilometer) diameter; a citywide network.

managed object   A data processing or data communications resource that may be managed through the use of an OSI Management protocol. The resource itself need not be an OSI resource. A managed object may be a physical item of equipment, a software component, some abstract collection of information, or any combination of the three.

MAPI (Messaging Application Programming Interface)   A messaging API from Microsoft. It consists of two components: Simple MAPI and Extended MAPI. Simple MAPI provides hooks to various messaging systems, so developers can create message-enabled applications by writing those applications to Simple MAPI , rather than developing those hooks themselves. Extended MAPI is platform specific to Windows.

mapping   In network operations, the logical association of one set of values, such as addresses on one network, with quantities or values of another set, such as devices on a second network (e.g., name-address mapping, internet work-route mapping).

mark   The signal (communications channel state) corresponding to a binary 1.

marker   A wired-logic control circuit that, among other functions, tests, selects, and establishes paths through a switching state(s) in response to external signals.

matrix   (1) An arrangement of elements (numbers, characters, dots, diodes, wires, and so on) in perpendicular rows. (2) In switch technology, the portion of a switch architecture where input leads and output leads meet, any pair of which can be connected to establish a through circuit. Also called a switching matrix.

MAU (media attachment unit)   A transceiver that connects to the AUI port of an Ethernet interface card and provides attachments to some type of data communications medium.

MB (megabyte)   1,048,576 bytes; usually referred to as one million bytes.

mbone (multicase backbone)   An experiment to upgrade the Internet to handle live multimedia messages. With mbone, a single packet can have multiple destinations and isn't split up until the last possible moment. This means that it can pass through several routers before it needs to be divided to reach its final destinations. This leads to much more efficient transmission and also ensures that packets reach multiple destinations at roughly the same time.

Mbps (megabits per second)   1,048,576 bits per second; usually referred to as one million bits per second.

MBS (mobile broadband services)   Very high bit-rate services (100Mbps+) over wireless channels.

m-commerce (mobile commerce)   Financial transactions that occur on mobile devices.

MCU (multipoint control unit)   A device that supports multiparty video conferencing between several individual circuit videoconferencing systems. The MCU acts as a videoconference hub.

MD5 (Message Digest-5)   An algorithm, created in 1991, that is used to create digital signatures. It is intended for use with 32-bit machines. It is a one-way hash function, meaning that it converts a message into a fixed string of digits called a message digest.

MDF (main distribution frame)   A structure containing all of the necessary power and test equipment to support terminal strip connections and wiring arrangements that connect outside and inside telephone exchange circuitry.

measured rate   A message rate structure that includes payment for a specified number of calls within a defined area, plus a charge for additional calls.

media filter   A filter used in Token Ring lobe wiring to convert STP-only adapter cards to UTP wiring.

media gateway   A device that provides seamless interoperability between circuit-switched, or PSTN, networking domains and those of the packet-switched realm (that is, IP, ATM, and Frame Relay networks). It interconnects with the SS7 network and enables the handling of IP services.

medium   (1) The material on which data is recorded; for example, magnetic tape or floppy disk. (2) Any material substance that is, or can be, used for the propagation of signals, usually in the form of modulated radio, light, or acoustic waves, from one point to another, such as optical fiber, cable, wire, dielectric slab, water, air, or free space.

medium frequency   Frequencies in the range between 300KHz and 3MHz.

mega   One million.

MEGACO (Multimedia Gateway Control)   An emerging ITU standard that describes how the media gateway should behave and function. Also called H.248.

memory   Area of computer system that accepts, holds, and provides access to information.

menu   A displayed list of items from which you can make a selection.

menu-driven   A set of instructions that was a list of commands and available options. The user only has to select the desired option; compare to command driven.

MEO (middle earth orbit) satellite   A satellite that orbits at an elevation of about 6,200 to 9,400 miles (9,900 to 15,000 kilometers) above the earth.

mesh   A topology in which nodes are connected in an unconstrained way which may contain loops. A fully connected mesh has every pair of nodes directly connected.

message   An arbitrary amount of information whose beginning and end are defined. In data communications, a message consists of a header, a body, and a trailer.

message authentication   Authentication that verifies the integrity of an electronic message and also verifies that an electronic message was sent by a particular entity.

message format   Rules for the placement of such portions of a message as message heading, address, text, end-of-message indication, and error-detecting bits.

message numbering   Identification of each message within a communications system by the assignment of a sequential number.

message switching   A technique that transfers messages between points not directly connected. The switching facility receives messages, stores them in queues for each destination point, and retransmits them when a facility becomes available. Synonymous with store-and-forward.

message unit   A unit of measure for charging local calls that details the length of call, distance called, and time of day.

metric   Information that a routing algorithm uses to determine the best path to the destination. Some examples of the metrics include path length, destination, next-hop associations, reliability, delay, bandwidth, load, and communication cost.

metro access product   A MAN product that brings fiber closer to the customer, to reduce deployment costs.

metro core product   A MAN product that is used in building citywide rings.

MGCP (Multimedia Gateway Control Protocol)   A combination of the SGCP and IPDC specifications. In this protocol, softswitches provide the external control and management, making MCGP a good way to connect an IAD to a gateway.

MHz (megahertz)   A unit of frequency equal to one million cycles per second.

MIB (Management Information Base)   The specification for how data is stored, monitored, and managed in an SNMP device. MIB I and MIB II are revisions of the database used on TCP/IP networks.

micro   One millionth.

microsecond   One millionth of a second.

microwave   (1) The portion of the electromagnetic spectrum ranging between 1GHz and 100GHz. (2) High-frequency transmission signals and equipment that employ microwave frequencies, including line-of-sight open-air microwave transmission and satellite communications.

MIDI (Musical Instrument Digital Interface)   A standard for defining the way of coding all the elements of musical scores, such as sequences of notes, timing conditions, and the instrument that is to play each note.

milli   One thousandth.

millisecond   One thousandth of a second.

MIME (multipurpose Internet mail extensions)   An Internet standard that enables a message to contain textual, binary, or arbitrarily formatted data. An advantage of MIME is that it encodes the data into an SMTP-compatible format.

MMDS (Multichannel Multipoint Distribution Service)   A technique for supplying broadband access via a point-to-point microwave digital system. It operates in the 2GHz to 3GHz band and can cover a fairly large area (approximately 30 miles [48 kilometers]). It provides great capacity in that it enables 150 channels. Also called wireless cable.

mobile earth station   A radio transmitter and/or receiver situated on a ship, vehicle, or aircraft, or in a briefcase, and used for satellite communications.

mobile wireless local loop   A last-mile solution that uses cellular telephone or cordless technology, along with satellites. This approach enables subscriber mobility, so you could use it as a replacement for a fixed line when you're in your home, but you could also move outside those boundaries and use it as a mobile line.

mobility network   A wireless network that allows you to roam within the range of your home and the outdoor area surrounding it.

modal dispersion   The tendency of light to travel in a wavelike motion, rather than a straight line. The greater the level of wave fluctuations, the greater the dispersion of the signal and the associated degradation of performance.

modem (modulator-demodulator)   A conversion device installed at each end of an analog communications line. The modem at the transmitting end modulates digital signals locally from a computer or terminal; the modem at the receiving end demodulates the incoming signal, converting it back to its original (i.e., digital) format, and passes it to the destination business machine.

modular   A design technique that permits a design or system to be assembled from interchangeable components; permits the system or device to be expanded or modified simply by adding another module.

modulation   The process of converting voice or data signals for transmission over a network. Also called line coding.

modulation division multiplexing   A mutliplexing methods in which the signals that modulate the optical carriers are mutliplexed.

modulator   A device that converts a signal (voice or other) into a form that can be transmitted.

module   A hardware or software component that is discrete and identifiable.

monitor   (1) A software tool used to supervise, control, or verify the operations of a systems. (2) A device used to display computer-generated information.

MPEG (Motion Picture Experts Group)   The ISO standards body responsible for the MPEG international video compression standards. MPEG-1 addresses VHS-quality images with a 1Mbps to 2Mbps data rate. MPEG-1 can play back from a single-speed CD-ROM player (150Kbps, or 1.2Mbps) at 352×240 (that is, quarter screen) at 30 frames per second (fps). MPEG-2, which at this point is the compression scheme of choice, addresses DTV—or computer-quality—images with a 6Mbps data rate. MPEG-2 offers resolutions of 720×480 and 1280×720 at 30 fps, with full CD-quality audio. MPEG-3 will address HDTV-quality images, at data rates up to 60Mbps. MPEG-4, an evolution of MPEG-2, features audio, video, and systems layers, and offers variable-bit-rate encoding for both narrowband and broadband delivery in a single file. It also uses an object-based compression method, rather than MPEG-2's frame-based compression. MPEG-4 allows objects—such as 2D or 3D video objects, text, graphics, and sound—to be manipulated and made interactive through Web-like hyperlinks and/or multimedia triggers.

MPLS (Multiprotocol Label Switching)   An IETF initiative that integrates Layer 2 information about network links (bandwidth, latency, utilization) into Layer 3 (IP) within a particular autonomous system in order to simplify and improve IP-packet exchange. MPLS gives network operators a great deal of flexibility to divert and route traffic around link failures, congestion, and bottlenecks.

MPλS (Multiprotocol Lambda Switching)   A variation of MPLS in which specific wavelengths serve in place of labels as unique identifiers. The specified wavelengths, like the labels, make it possible for routers and switches to perform necessary functions automatically, without having to extract instructions regarding those functions from IP addresses or other packet information.

MPOA (Multiprotocol over ATM)   An ATM Forum standard to link a number of local networks across an ATM backbone catering to many different network protocols.

mrouter (multicast router)   A router that enfolds IP packets in special multicast packets and forwards them on toward their destination.

MSAU (multistation access unit)   A device that enables workstations on a LAN to be cabled in a star configuration. Also known as a Token Ring hub.

MSP (management service provider)   A provider that takes over the actual management and monitoring of the network.

MSPP (multiservice provisioning platform)   An access-oriented device that can handle all the popular data protocols and interfaces, except that they are not designed to be optical aggregators.

MSU (modem sharing unit)   A device that permits two or more terminals to share a single modem.

MTBF (mean time between failures)   The average length of time for which the system, or a component of the system, works without fault.

MTS (mobile telephone service)   A telephone service provided between mobile stations and the public switch telephone network; radio transmission provides the equivalent of a local loop.

MTSO (mobile telephone switching office)   A component in the cellular radio system that links the base transceiver stations with the terrestrial local exchanges to complete calls over the PSTN.

MTTR (mean time to repair)   The average time required to perform corrective maintenance on a failed device.

MTU (maximum transmission unit)   The maximum packet size that can be transmitted over a LAN or an internet.

mu-law encoding   Encoding according to ITU-T recommendation G.711, used with 24-channel PCM systems in the United States and Japan. It is similar to a-law encoding, but the two differ in the size of the quantizing intervals.

multicarrier modulation   A modulation scheme that uses and aggregates a certain amount of bandwidth and then subdivides it into subbands. Each subband is encoded by using a single-carrier technique, and bit streams from the subbands are bonded together at the receiver.

multicasting   Simultaneous distribution of data to a defined subset of all receive points in a network. The subset may be redefined for each transmission and range from one to all receive points.

multichannel   Pertaining to broadcasting media capable of carrying multiple different television and radio channels.

multidrop   A communications arrangement in which multiple devices share a common transmission channel, although only one may transmit at a time.

multimedia   The presentation of more than one medium, typically images, sound, and text in an interactive environment.

multimode fiber   A fiber-optic cable with a core diameter large enough to allow light to travel on different paths, supporting propagation to multiple nodes.

multiple access technique   A method that enables sharing of spectrum by multiple users. FDMA, TDMA, and CDMA are examples of multiple access techniques.

multiple trunk groups   Indicates that the switching system is capable of being equipped for more than one group of trunk circuits.

multiplex   To interleave or simultaneously transmit two or more messages on a single channel.

multiplexer   A device that enables more than one signal to be sent simultaneously over one physical channel. It combines inputs from two or more terminals, computer ports, or other multiplexers, and transmits the combined datastream over a single high-speed channel. At the receiving end, the high-speed channel is demultiplexed, either by another multiplexer or by software. Sometimes called a mux.

multipoint   Pertaining or referring to a communications line to which three or more stations are connected. It implies that the line physically extends from one station to another until all are connected.

multipoint network   In data communication, a configuration in which more than two terminal installations are connected to a single port.

multiprocessing   The simultaneous execution of two or more computer programs.

mux   *See* multiplexer.

N

NACK or NAK (negative acknowledgment)   A message that says there was an error in transmission and the previous block needs to be re-sent before anything else can happen.

NADC (North American Digital Cellular)   A TIA standard that is specified as IS-54 and was adopted in 1992. It has since been updated, and it is now called IS-136. It uses TDMA and TDD schemes, and it offers a total of three time slots. It operates on the 800MHz frequency band, uses AMPS for signaling to reserve resources, and transfers speech in digital form; therefore, it is a digital overlay that is interoperable with analog AMPS infrastructure. UWC-136, an advancement of the U.S. TDMA (IS-136) standard, uses EDGE technology.

nailed-up connection   A slang term for a permanent, dedicated path through a switch; often used for lengthy, regular data transmission going through a PBX.

name resolution   The process of mapping a name into a corresponding address. The domain name system provides a mechanism for naming computers in which programs use remote name servers to resolve machine names into IP addresses for those machines.

nanosecond   One billionth of a second.

NAP (network access point)   The point where backbones interconnect to exchange traffic between providers. Bottlenecks at NAPs greatly affect the ability to roll out new time-sensitive, loss-sensitive applications, such as Internet telephony, VoIP, VPNs, streaming media, and TV over Internet.

narrowband   A service occupying low bandwidth (64Kbps or below).

narrowcast   Transmission of specific programming to predetermined users of a telecommunications network. Only some users of the network are receiving the same information.

NCP (Network Control Program)   A program that resides in a communications controller that controls the operation of the communications controller.

near-end crosstalk   Unwanted energy transferred from one circuit usually to an adjoining circuit. It occurs at the end of the transmission link where the signal source is located, with the absorbed energy usually propagated in the opposite direction of the absorbing channel's normal current flow. Usually caused by high-frequency or unbalanced signals and insufficient shielding.

NetBIOS (Network Basic Input/Output System)   A session-layer interface that is widely used in PC networks.

NetBIOS extended user interface   A transport-layer protocol designed to support NetBIOS over 802.2 LANs.

network   (1) A collection of devices connected by communication lines for data processing or information interchange. (2) A series of points connected by communications channels. (3) A network of telephone lines normally used for dialed telephone calls. (4) A group of computers and peripherals that are interconnected so that they can communicate with each other.

network address translation   An Internet standard that enables a LAN to use one set of IP addresses for internal traffic and a second set of addresses for external traffic. A NAT box located where the LAN meets the Internet makes all necessary IP address translations.

network architecture   The philosophy and organizational concept for enabling communications between data processing equipment at multiple locations. The network architecture specifies the processors and terminals, and defines the protocols and software that must be used to accomplish accurate data communications.

network control   In a network, the establishment, authorization, and maintenance of logical and physical connections between stations and applications, plus the synchronization, routing, integrity, and recovery of data transmitted during the established connections.

network layer   In the OSI model, the logical network entity that services the transport layer. It is responsible for ensuring that data passed to it from the transport layer is routed and delivered through the network.

network node   A point on the network where communications lines interface. Thus, a network node might be a PBX, a local exchange, a multiplexer, a modem, a host computer, or one of several other devices.

network redundancy   Including in communication pathway additional links in order to connect all nodes.

network topology   The physical and logical relationship of nodes in a network; the schematic arrangement of the link and nodes of a network, typically either a star, ring, tree, or bus topology, or some hybrid combination thereof.

networking   Communication between stations in a network.

next-generation gateway switch   A switch that is designed to support a wide variety of traffic—data, voice, fax, multimedia, and other emerging sensory forms—over a data backbone. It provides seamless interoperability between the circuits that network the PSTN and packet-switching networks.

next-generation network   A high-speed packet- or cell-based network that's capable of transporting and routing a multitude of services, including voice, data, video, and multimedia. It is a common platform for applications and services that the customer can assess across the entire network, as well as outside the network.

NIC (network interface card)   A component that connects a station to a network (e.g., LAN). Also called a network adapter card.

NIOD (Network Inward/Outward Dialing)   A system that provides the capability for dialing both ways between a toll network and a local network.

N-ISDN (Narrowband ISDN)   A network architecture and set of standards introduced in 1983 for an all-digital network. It was intended to provide end-to-end digital service using the public telephone networks worldwide and, therefore, to provide high-quality, error-free transmission.

NIST (National Institute of Standards and Technology)   A group that prior to 1988, was called the National Bureau of Standards.

NLSP (NetWare Link Services Protocol)   A link-state protocol that offers low network overhead and fast convergence.

NMC (network management center)   A center used for control of a network. May provide traffic analysis, call detail recording, configuration control, fault detection and diagnostics, and maintenance.

NMT (Nordic Mobile Telephone System)   A Scandinavian wireless system that originally operated at 450MHz, offered around 220 channels, and had a very large coverage area.

node   Any device on a network that can independently send or receive information and that has a network address; also the point at which the device is linked to the network.

noise   Unwanted electrical signals, introduced by circuit components or natural disturbances, that tend to degrade the performance of a communications channel.

nonblocking   Describes a switch where a through traffic path exists for each attached station. Generically, a switch or switching environment designed to never experience a busy condition due to traffic volume.

nonswitched line   In data communication, a permanent connection between computers or devices that does not have to be established by dialing.

nonvolatile storage   A storage medium whose contents are not lost when the power is removed.

NPA (numbering plan area)   A geographic subdivision of the territory covered by a national or integrated numbering plan. An NPA is identified by a distinctive area code.

NRZ (nonreturn to zero)   A digital signaling technique in which the signal is at a constant level for the duration of time.

NSP (network service provider)   A very large, global backbone carrier that owns its own infrastructures (for example, AT&T, WorldCom, UUnet, Sprint, Verizon, Cable & Wireless, and Qwest).

NTSC (National Television Systems Committee)   A television broadcasting system that uses 525 picture lines and a 60Hz field frequency. It was developed by the committee, and is used primarily in the United States, Canada, Mexico, and Japan. *See also* PAL and SECAM.

NTU (network terminating unit)   The part of the network equipment that connects directly to the data terminal equipment.

null attached   The operation of an FDDI concentrator without being attached to the backbone network. This configuration establishes a small, autonomous, single-ring FDDI network consisting of a limited number of directly connected single attached stations.

NXX   The current exchange numbering plan, in which N is any digit from 2 to 9 and X is any digit from 0 to 9.

O

OADM (optical add/drop multiplexer)   An optical multiplexing device that uses special filters to extract the wavelengths that need to be dropped off at a given location. It eliminates the costly electronics that are used to convert between light and electricity in a nonoptical multiplexer.

OC-1 to OC-48 (Optical Carrier-1 to Optical Carrier-48)   OC-1 is the base optical carrier transmission speed of 51.840Mbps. To calculate OC-2 to OC-48 speeds, simply multiply the OC-1 base by the desired magnitude. Common OC levels include OC-1 (51Mbps), OC-3 (155Mbps), OC-12 (622Mbps), OC-48 (2.5Gbps), OC-192 (10Gbps), and OC-768 (40Gbps).

octet   8-bit byte. Used instead of *byte* when talking about packet services.

OFDM (Orthogonal Frequency Division Multiplexing)   A multicarrier modulation scheme that broadcasts on many frequencies, reducing interference from collisions with walls and objects.

off-hook   A state in which a telephone set is in use (that is, the handset is removed from its cradle).

off-line   (1) Pertaining to equipment or devices not under direct control of the central processing unit. (2) Used to describe terminal equipment that is not connected to a transmission line. (3) Not controlled directly by or communicating with a computer.

offload   To move data or programs out of storage.

OGT (outgoing trunk)   A one-way trunk that carries only outgoing traffic.

OLT (optical line termination)   A switch that sends traffic downstream to subscribers and that also handles the upstream traffic.

one-way trunk   A trunk between a switch (that is, a PBX) and an exchange, or between exchanges, where traffic originates from only one end.

ones density rule   A principle which says that if you transmit more than 15 zeros in a row, the network may lose synchronization, which means transmission errors could occur.

on-hook   A state in which a telephone set is not in use (that is, the handset is resting in the cradle).

online   (1) Being controlled directly by or directly communicating with a computer. (2) Connected to a computer so that data can pass to or from the computer without human intervention. (3) Directly in the line loop.

online services   Computer functions offered to end users not owning a host computer; includes time sharing, archival storage, and prepared software programs.

ONP (Open Network Provision)   A pan-European standard ensuring the provision of the network infrastructure by European telecommunications administrations to users and competitive service providers on terms equal to those for the administrations themselves.

ONU (optical network unit)   A device in which optical-to-electrical conversions takes place.

open system   A system that facilitates multivendor, multitechnology integration based on publicly available standards for subsystem interaction. Three characteristics of an open system are portability, scalability, and interoperability.

optical carrier   Specifications defining line speeds and transmission encoding and multiplexing methods for the SDH/SONET fiber-optic backbone network.

optical fiber   Any filament, or fiber, made of dielectric materials, that is used to transmit laser- or LED-generated light signals, usually for digital communications. An optical fiber consists of a core, which carries the signal, and cladding, a substance with a slightly higher refractive index than the core, which surrounds the core and serves to reflect the light signal back into it. Also called lightguide or fiber optic.

optical switch   A device that resides at a junction point in an optical backbone and enables carriers to string together wavelengths to provide end-to-end connections. It links any of several incoming lines to any of several outgoing lines and automatically reroutes traffic when a network path fails. Sometimes referred to as an optical cross-connect or a wavelength router.

OPX (off-premises extension)   A telephone extension located other than where the main switch is.

OSI (Open Systems Interconnection) model   A seven-layer logical network architecture that is used for the definition of network protocol standards to enable an OSI compatible computer or device to communicate with any other OSI-complaint computer or device for a meaningful exchange of information. Layer 7, the application layer, is responsible for exchanging information between the programs that are running on a computer and other services on a network. Layer 6, the presentation layer, formats information so that a software application can read it. Layer 5, the session layer, supports connections between sessions and handles administrative tasks and security. Layer 4, the transport layer, corrects transmission errors and ensures that the information is delivered reliably. Layer 3, the network layer, identifies computers on a network and determines how to direct information transfer over that network. Layer 2, the data-link layer, groups data into containers to prepare that data for transfer over a network. Layer 1, the physical layer, defines how a transmission medium connects to a computer, as well as how electrical or optical information is transferred on the transmission medium.

OSP (online service provider)   A provider that organizes online content and provides intuitive user navigation.

OSPF (Open Shortest Path First)   A routing protocol, used on TCP/IP networks, in which routers maintain an internal map of the network and exchange information about the current state of each network link. OSPF's features include least-cost routing, multipath routing, and load balancing.

OTDR (optical time domain reflectometer)   A device that can be used in fiber networks to detect potential leaks that could be the result of unwanted intrusion.

out-of-band management   A system which management data is communicated through a link, outside the network, typically through a modem or some other serial connection.

out-of-band signaling   Signaling in which the conversation and the signaling take place over different paths. A separate digital channel (called a signaling link) is created, where messages are exchanged between network elements at 56Kbps or 64Kbps. Out-of-band signals run no danger of interference from speech or data, which allows signaling to take place during the conversation. However, the out-of-band signal needs extra bandwidth and extra electronics to handle the signaling band.

output   Data that has been processed.

overflow   Excess traffic, on a particular route, that is offered to another (alternate) route.

overlay network   A high-performance digital network that interconnects with the main public network but which has its own lines, exchanges, and, often, a separate international gateway.

overnet   A PNAP.

override   To seize a circuit even though the circuit is already occupied.

P

PABX (private automatic branch exchange)   Another term for a PBX.

packet   A group of binary digits, including data and call control signals, that is switched as a composite whole. The data, call control signals, and error control information are arranged in a specific format. Also called block, frame, cell, or datagram.

packet loss   A problem that occurs when there is congestion at the packet switches or routers. It can considerably degrade real-time applications.

packet overhead   A measure of the ratio of the total packet bits occupied by control information to the number of bits of data, usually expressed as a percent.

packet radio   A data network that uses licensed bandwidth and which is specifically built for two-way data, not for voice communications.

packet-switched network   A network consisting of a series of interconnected switches that route individual packets of data over one of several redundant routes. Packet-switched networks include X.25, Frame Relay, IP, and ATM.

packet switching   A method of transmitting messages through a communication network, in which long messages are subdivided into short packets. Each packet contains the data and a destination address and is passed from source to destination through intermediate nodes. At each node, the packet is received, stored briefly, and then passed on to the next node. The packets are then reassembled into the original message at the receiving end.

PAD (packet assembler/disassembler)   A protocol conversion device that accepts characters in a serial data stream and converts them into packets to send across a packet-switched network (e.g., X.25 network).

PAL (Phase Alternate Line)   The color television broadcasting system developed in West Germany and the United Kingdom that uses 625 picture lines and a 50Hz field frequency. *See also* NTSC and SECAM.

PAM (pulse amplitude modulation)   A form of modulation in which the amplitude of the pulse carrier is varied in accordance with successive samples of the modulating signal.

PAN (personal area network)   A network that surrounds an individual and provides networking between badge-based computers and other input/output devices.

PAP (Password Authentication Protocol)   A protocol that uses a two-way handshake for the peer to establish its identity upon link establishment. The peer repeatedly sends the password to the authenticator until verification is acknowledged or the connection is terminated.

parallel transmission   The simultaneous transmission of all the bids making up a character or byte, either over separate channels, or on different carrier frequencies on the same channel.

parity   The state of being even-numbered or odd-numbered. A parity bit is a binary digit appended to a group of binary digits to make the sum of the digits either all odd (odd parity) or all even (even parity).

parity check   A procedure in which the addition of noninformation bits are added to data to make the number of ones in a grouping of bits either always even or always odd. This procedure allows detection of bit groupings that contain single errors. It can be applied to characters, blocks, or any specific bit grouping. Also called VRC.

password   A word or set of characters that must be given to satisfy security needs.

patch panel   A passive wiring device that facilitates manual patching of end users onto ports on one or more network hubs.

path   (1) In a network, any route between any two nodes. (2) The route traversed by the information exchanged between two attaching devices in a network.

Pbps (petabits per second)   1,000Tbps.

PBX (private branch exchange)   A telephone switch located on a customer's premises that primarily establishes voice-grade circuits between individual users (extensions) and the switched telephone network. Typically, the PBX also provides switching within a customer's premises and usually offers numerous other enhanced features, such as least-cost routing and call-detail recording. Also called a PABX.

PCM (Pulse Code Modulation)   A scheme used to convert an analog voice signal into a digital bitstream for transmission. Digital transmission technique that involves sampling of an analog information signal at regular time intervals and coding, the measured amplitude into a series of binary values, which are transmitted by modulation of a pulsed, or intermittent, carrier. A common method of speech digitizing by using 8-bit code words, or samples, and a sampling rate of 8,000 times per second.

PCS (Personal Communication Services)   A digital service that operates in the 1.8GHz to 2GHz band and uses both microcell and picocell architectures.

PDC (Personal Digital Cellular)   Also known as Japanese Digital Cellular (JDC), a 2G standard for digital wireless communications deployed widely in Japan.

PDH (Plesiochronous Digital Hierarchy)   The first generation of digital hierarchy, defining the available digital transmission rates and number of channels. It is used by telecommunications operators and implemented according to three standards: T-carrier in North America, E-carrier in ITU-T countries, and J-carrier in Japan. PDH is defined by the ITU-T in its G.703 standard.

PDN (public data network)   A packet-switching network (e.g., X.25, Frame Relay, Internet, IP backbones) that is designed to provide low error-rate data transmission.

PDU (protocol data unit)   The OSI term for a packet.

peer-to-peer   The interaction by which computers and other network devices communicate with each other as equals and on their own initiative (as opposed to a host/terminal environment).

peering agreement   An arrangement in which operators agree to exchange with one another the same amount of traffic over high-speed lines between their routers so that users on one network can reach addresses on the other.

performance   A major factor on which the total productivity of a system depends. Performance is largely determined by a combination of several other factors: throughput, latencies, response time, and availability.

pervasive computing   An environment in which computers are taken out of stand-alone boxes to which we are tied and put into ordinary things, in everyday objects around us. Also called ubiquitous computing.

P-frame (predicted frame)   In MPEG terminology, a frame that is only reconstructed from preceding reference frames. It can also be a reference frame, as it serves to reconstruct other frames in some instances.

PGP (Pretty Good Privacy)   A technique for encrypting messages. PGP is one of the most common ways to protect messages on the Internet because it is effective, easy to use, and free. PGP is based on the public-key method, which uses two keys: a public key that you disseminate to anyone from whom you want to receive a message and a private key that you use to decrypt messages that you receive.

phantom circuit   A third voice circuit that is superimposed on two 2-wire voice circuits.

phase   The angle of a wave form at a given moment.

phased-array antenna   A small, flat antenna that is steered electronically. It provides great agility and fast tracking, as well as the ability to form multiple antenna beams simultaneously. The beam is electrically pointed by adjusting the phases of the individual transmitters. This allows for very fast and precise steering of the communications beam, which is very important for high-bandwidth communication because the data rate is inversely proportional to the angular offset.

phase jitter   A random distortion of signal lengths caused by the rapid fluctuation of the frequency of the transmitted signal. Phase jitter interferes with interpretation of information by changing the timing.

PHS (Personal Handyphone System)   A Japanese standard for 2G PCS wireless networks.

physical address   The address of the physical communications device in a system.

physical interface   The definition of the number of pins in the connector, the number of wires in the cable, and what signal is being carried over which of the pins and over which of the wires, to ensure that the information is being viewed compatibly.

physical layer   Layer 1 of the OSI model. Defines the electrical, optical, mechanical, and procedural characteristics of the interface.

ping (packet Internet groper)   The name of a program used with TCP/IP internets to test reachability of destinations by sending them an ICMP echo request and waiting for a reply.

pixel (picture element)   In computer graphics, the smallest element of a display space that can be independently assigned color and intensity.

PKE (public key encryption)   A message authentication mechanism that is part of most Web browsers.

PKI (public key infrastructure)   A process that secures e-business applications such as private e-mail, purchase orders, and workflow automation. It uses digital certificates and digital signatures to authenticate and encrypt messages and a certificate authority to handle the verification process.

plant   The physical equipment of a telephone network that provides communications services.

plotter   A device that converts computer output into drawings on paper or displays the output on display-type terminals instead of printing a listing.

PLP (Packet Layer Protocol)   A standard in the network layer of X.25.

PM (phase modulation)   A way of modifying a sine wave signal to make it carry information. The sine wave, or carrier, has its phase changed in accordance with the information to be transmitted.

PNAP (private network access point)   A private point of access to the Internet, also called a peering point, that bypasses public NAPs.

point-to-point line   A circuit that connects two points directly, where there are generally no intermediate processing nodes, although there could be switching facilities. Synonymous with two-point and always on.

policy-based management   A system in which you can associate information about individual users, groups, organizational units, and entire organizations, as well as events (such as the beginning of the accounting department's month-end closing), with various network services or classes of service.

polling   A host-system–controlled method for determining whether each of the stations on a communication line has data to send.

PON (passive optical network)   A network in which one access line is shared among multiple buildings. Optical splitters and couplers are used at each fiber connection in the network.

POP (point of presence)   The physical access location into a network.

port   A point of access into a communications switch, a computer, a network, or other electronic device; the physical or electrical interface through which one gains access; the interface between a process and a communications or transmission facility.

port number   A number in the range 1 to 65,535 that identifies a port. The port number does not represent a physical port, such as the serial port to which a modem or a mouse might be attached; instead, it is more like a regional memory address.

port speed   The maximum signaling rate on a digital access line.

POTS (plain old telephone service)   The standard analog telephone service that most homes use.

PPP (Point-to-Point Protocol)   A successor to SLIP, this protocol provides router-to-router and host-to-network connections over synchronous and asynchronous circuits.

PPTP (Point-to-Point Tunneling Protocol)   A Layer 2 protocol that can work in a non-IP enterprise environment, which is one of its strengths for customers who use multiple protocols rather than using only IP. PPTP provides low packet overhead and good compression, but its weaknesses are on the security front.

presentation layer   Layer 6 in the OSI model that provides services to the application layer, enabling it to interpret the data exchanged, as well as to structure data messages to be transmitted in a specific display and control format.

preventive maintenance   The routine checking of components to keep the system functioning.

PRI (Primary Rate Interface)   A bundle of ISDN circuits, primarily a PBX interface. The United States and Japan use 23B+D, and the ITU uses 30B+D. Also called Primary Rate Access (PRA).

primary station   On a point-to-point communication line, the station that gains control of the line first. On a multipoint line, the station controlling communications.

private key   The decryption (reception) or encryption (signature) component of an asymmetric key set.

private line   The channel equipment furnished to a customer as a unit for exclusive use, generally with no access to or from the public switched telephone network. Also called leased line.

private network   A network based on leased lines or other facilities that provide telecommunication services, within an organization or within a closed user group, as a complement or as a substitute to the public network.

protocol   A set of rules that govern network communications. Low-level protocols define transmission rates, data encoding schemes, physical interfaces, network addressing schemes, and the method by which nods contend for the chance to transmit data over the network. High-level protocols define functions such as printing and file sharing.

protocol header   Information in a packet that the protocol needs in order to do its work.

protocol stack (or protocol suite)   A collection of protocols that computers use to exchange information.

provisioned VPN   A packet-switched VPN that runs across the service provider's backbone, generally using Frame Relay or ATM.

Proxy ARP (Proxy Address Resolution Protocol)   The technique in which one machine, usually a router, answers ARP requests intended for another by supplying its own physical address. By pretending to be another machine, the router accepts responsibility for routing packets to it. The purpose of proxy ARP is to allow a site to use a single IP network address with multiple physical networks.

proxy server   A server that provides firewall functionality, acting as an intermediary for user requests, establishing a connection to the requested resource either at the application layer or at the session or transport layer.

PSK (phase-shift keying)   A modulation technique for transmitting digital information to analog whereby that information is conveyed as varying phases of a carrier signal.

PSTN (public switched telephone network)   The complete traditional public telephone system, including telephones, local and interexchange trunks, transport equipment, and exchanges.

PTO (public telecommunications operator)   An incumbent carrier in places other than the United States.

PT&T (postal, telegraph, and telephone) organization   Usually a governmental department that acts as its nation's common carrier.

public key   A device that is used by algorithms that encrypt and decrypt using asymmetric yet mathematically linked keys. Each security module is assigned a pair of keys: The encryption key is "public" and does not require distribution by secure means. The decryption or "private" key cannot be discovered through knowledge of the public key or its underlying algorithm. Public key algorithms can apply to one or more of the following: key distribution, encryption, authentication, or digital signature.

pulse   A momentary, sharp alteration in the current or voltage produced in a circuit to operate a switch or relay which can be detected by a logic circuit; a sharp rise and fall of finite duration.

punchdown block   A common termination point in the wiring closet for wires going out to the individual offices and wall sockets.

push technology   A program that updates news, weather, or other selected information on a computer user's desktop interface through periodic and generally unobtrusive transmission over the World Wide Web.

PVC (permanent virtual circuit)   A defined path that provides essentially a dedicated private line between users in a packet switching network. The network is aware of a fixed association between two stations, permanent logical channel numbers are assigned exclusively to the permanent circuit, and devices do not require permission to transmit to each other.

PWM (pulse width modulation)   The process of encoding information based on variations of the duration of carrier pulses. Also known as pulse duration modulation (PDM).

Px64   The ITU-T H.320 standard for interoperability in video conferencing over ISDN.

Q

QAM (Quadrature Amplitude Modulation)   A single-carrier scheme that modulates both the amplitude and phase to yield higher spectral efficiency. Various levels of QAM exist, and they are referred to as QAM nn, where nn indicates the number of states per Hertz. The number of bits per symbol time is k, where $2^k = nn$. So, 4 bits/Hz is equivalent to QAM 16, 6 bits/Hz is equivalent to QAM 64, and 8 bits/Hz is equivalent to QAM 256.

QoS (Quality of Service)   In networking, a concept by which applications may indicate their specific requirements to the network, before they actually start transmitting information data. *Implicit QoS* means that the application chooses the required levels of QoS. *Explicit QoS* means that the network manager controls that decision.

QPSK (Quadrature Phase Shift Keying)   A single-carrier modulation scheme that supports 2 bits per symbol time. Equivalent to QAM 4.

Q.Sig   The ECMA standard for common-channel signaling between PBXs.

quantization noise   Signal errors caused by the process of digitizing a continuously variable slope.

query   A request for information entered while the computer system is processing.

queue   An ordered accumulation of data or transactions stored for later processing.

queuing   The process whereby communications calls, processing requests, processes, and so on are stacked or held so that they can be worked with in sequence.

R

radio channel   The frequency band allocated to a service provider or transmitter.

radio wave   An electromagnetic wave of frequencies between approximately 20KHz and 3GHz.

RADIUS (Remote Authentication Dial-in User Services)   An authentication and access control server that is used for purposes of authenticating whether a user is allowed access into the corporate resources.

RADSL (Rate-Adaptive DSL)   A symmetrical or asymmetrical transmission medium that has a maximum loop length of 18,000 feet (5.5 kilometers) and is deployed as a single twisted-pair cable. It adapts the data rate dynamically, based on any changes that may be occurring in the line conditions and based on the loop length. With RADSL, the rates can vary widely, from 600Kbps to 7Mbps downstream and from 128Kbps to 1Mbps upstream.

RAM (random-access memory)   A type of computer memory that can be accessed randomly; that is, any byte of memory can be accessed without touching the preceding bytes.

RARP (Reverse Address Resolution Protocol)   The TCP/IP protocol that a diskless machine uses at startup to find its address. The machine broadcasts a request that contains its physical hardware address and a server responds by sending the machine its IP address.

RBOC (regional Bell operating company)   One of several independent telephone companies created from the break-up of AT&T.

RC4 (Rivest Cipher 4)   A streaming cipher technique; a stream cipher adds the output of a pseudorandom number generator bit by bit to the sequential bits of the digitized plain text.

redundancy   (1) The portion of the total information contained in a message that can be eliminated without loss in essential information. (2) The provision of duplicate, backup equipment to immediately take over the function of equipment that fails. (3) In a database, the storage of the same data item or group of items in two or more files.

redundancy check   An automatic or a programmed check based on the systematic insertion of components or characters used especially for checking purposes.

regenerative repeater   (1) A repeater used in telegraph applications to retime and retransmit the received signal impulses and restore them to their original strength. These repeaters are speed-and-code sensitive and are intended for use with standard speeds and codes. (2) A repeater used in PCM or digital circuits that detects, retimes, and reconstructs the bits transmitted. (3) A LAN interconnect relay device that copies electrical signals from one LAN to another. Also called a regenerator.

register   The first unit in the assembly of common control equipment in an automatic exchange. The register receives address information in the form of dial pulses or DTMF signals and stores it for possible conversion or translation.

reliability   The measure of a network's availability. Often measured in terms of the number of nines; for example, "five nines" reliability means that the network is available 99.999% of the time.

remote   Pertains to a computer or device that is connected to another computer or device over a communication line.

remote access   Communications with a computer or PBX in one location from a device that is physically removed from the location of the computer.

remote access server   A server that provides network access to remote users, generally via analog POTS lines, or perhaps ISDN connections, including dialup protocols and access control for authentication.

remote access software   Sometimes called remote control software, a program that is a superset of the asynchronous communications software market. It allows a PC to have complete control over another PC at a different site.

remote data concentration   A communications processor that is used for multiplexing data from low-speed lines or terminals onto one or more high-speed lines.

remote maintenance   A feature or service in which a service technician can dial into a system and be connected to the system and can be connected to the system processor to run diagnostics and perform system administration.

remote monitoring MIB   The MIB that enables any SNMP management console to extract information from a protocol analyzer running RMON.

repeater   (1) In analog transmission, equipment that receives a pulse train, amplifies it, and retimes it for retransmission. (2) In digital transmission, equipment that receives a pulse train, reconstructs it, retimes it, and then amplifies the signal for retransmission. (3) In fiber optics, a device that decodes a low-power light signal, converts it to electrical energy, and then retransmits it via an LED or laser-generating light source, often including, some form of signal amplification.

resale carrier   A company that redistributes the services of another common carrier and retails the services to the public.

reverse channel   A simultaneous data path in the reverse direction over a half-duplex facility. Normally it is used for positive/negative acknowledgments of previously received data blocks.

RF (radio frequency)   A frequency that is much higher than the audio frequencies but below the infrared frequencies; usually, above 20KHz.

ring   (1) A ring-shaped contact of a plug, usually positioned between, but insulated from the tip and sleeve. (2) An audible alerting signal on a telephone line. (3) A network topology in which stations are connected to one another in a closed logical circle, with access to the medium passing sequentially from one station to the next by means of polling from a master station or by passing an access token from one station to another; also called a loop.

ring in   A connection on a Token Ring MAU used to tie multiple MAUs into a larger ring.

ring out   A connection on a Token Ring MAU used to tie multiple MAUs into larger ring.

ringing signal   Any AC or DC signal transmitted over a line or trunk for the purpose of alerting a party at the distant end of an incoming call. The signal can operate a visual or sound-producing device.

RIP (Routing Information Protocol)   A routing protocol used on TCP/IP networks that distributes the addresses of reachable networks and metrics reflecting the degree of difficulty involved in reaching particular networks form particular locations.

RJ-11   A standard four-wire modular connector used with telephones.

RJ-45   An eight-wire modular connector used with UTP.

RO (receive only)   (1) A printer terminal without a keyboard for data entry. (2) A satellite earth station capable of receiving, but not of transmitting, a signal.

robot   An easily reprogrammable, computer-controlled device that can physically manipulate its surroundings.

rotary dial calling   A system that accepts dialing from conventional rotary dial sets that generate pulses.

router   A device that connects two LAN segments, which use similar or different architectures, at the OSI network layer, Layer 3. The router determines the most efficient route for passing data through an internet. Those packets that contain a network address different from the originating PC's address are forwarded onto an adjoining network. Multiprotocol routers can handle this job for two or more protocols simultaneously.

routing algorithm   A formula that uses metrics (such as path length, destination, next-hop associations, reliability, delay, bandwidth, load, and communication cost) to determine the best path to the destination.

routing protocol   A protocol that enables routers to communicate with each other. Routing protocols include RIP, IGP, OSPF, EGP, and BGP.

routing table   A database that tells the router how to send packets to various destinations.

RPC (remote procedure call)   A system that enables an application programmer to distribute programs between computer systems interconnected with a network. RPC development tools eliminate the need for in depth knowledge of diverse network protocols and computing platforms, enabling a programmer to concentrate on developing the application itself.

RS-232-C   A technical specification published by the EIA that establishes mechanical and electrical interface requirements between DTE and DCE, employing serial binary data interchange and operating at speeds up to 19.2Kbps.

RS-366-A   An EIA standard for interfaces between DTE and automatic calling equipment for data communication.

RS-422-A   An EIA specification for electrical characteristics of balanced voltage digital interface circuits.

RS-423-A   An EIA specification for electrical characteristics of unbalanced-voltage digital interface circuits.

RS-449   An EIA specification for general-purpose, 37-position and 9-position interface for DTE and DCE, employing serial binary data interchange and operating at speeds up to 2Mbps.

RSA (Rivest, Shamir, and Adelman)   A public key algorithm whose security derives from the difficulty of factoring large prime integers.

RSVP (Reservation Resource Protocol) A protocol that enables an internet to support specified levels of QoS. By using RSVP, an application is capable of reserving resources along a route from source to destination. RSVP-enabled routers then schedule and prioritize packets to fulfill the QoS.

RTCP (Real-Time Control Protocol) An ITU protocol that provides status feedback from senders to receivers.

RTP (Real-Time Transport Protocol) An Internet protocol for transmitting real-time data such as audio and video. RTP itself does not guarantee real-time delivery of data, but it does provide mechanisms for the sending and receiving applications to support streaming data.

RTSP (Real-Time Streaming Protocol) A protocol that runs on top of IP multicasting, UDP, RTP, and RTCP.

S

sampling A statistical procedure whereby generalizations are drawn from a relatively small number of observations.

satellite communications The use of orbiting satellites to relay transmissions from one earth station to another, or to multiple earth stations.

scattering Causing of lightwave signal loss in optical fiber transmission; diffusion of a light beam caused by microscopic variations in the material density of the transmission medium.

SCP (service control point) A centralized node that contains service logic for the management of the call.

scrambler A coding device that is applied to a digital channel to produce an apparently random bit sequence. A corresponding device is used to decode the channel (i.e., the coding is reversible).

SDH (Synchronous Digital Hierarchy) An ITU-T standard for digital broadband communications.

SDLC (Synchronous Data Link Control) An IBM data-link layer protocol associated with SNA. In contrast to BSC, SDLC provides for full-duplex transmission and is more efficient.

SDSL (Symmetrical [or Single-Line] DSL) A symmetrical service that has a maximum loop length of 18,000 feet (5.5 kilometers) and is deployed as a single twisted-pair cable. It can be deployed in various capacities, in multiples of 64Kbps, up to a maximum of 2Mbps in each direction.

SDTV (standard definition television) A DTV format that provides a picture quality similar to that of DVD. SDTV and HDTV are the two categories of display formats for DTV transmissions, which are becoming the television standard.

SECAM (Systeme Electronique Couleur Avec Memoire) A TV system used in France and the former French colonies, as well as in parts of the Middle East. Russia and the former Soviet-allied countries used a modified form of SECAM. There are two versions of SECAM: SECAM vertical and SECAM horizontal. *See also* PAL and NTSC.

secondary channel A low-speed channel established on a four-wire circuit over which diagnostics or control information is passed. User data is passed on the primary, high-speed channels of the circuit.

security   The protection of information against unauthorized access or use.

segmentation and reassembly sublayer   A sublayer of the AAL that supports mapping between variable length data units and ATM cells.

selective ringing   A system that has the capability of ringing only the desired subscriber's telephone on a multiparty line. Ringers turned to one of five possible frequencies are used to achieve this effect.

server   A processor that provides a specific service to the network. A routing server connects nodes and network of like architectures, a gateway server connects nodes and networks of different architectures, and so on.

server-based network   A network in which one computer is the repository (that is, the *server*) and the other computers request information from and store information on the server.

session   A period of time in which an end user engages in dialog with an interactive computer system.

session layer   Layer 5 of the OSI model. It manages a logical connection between two communication points.

set-top box   A locally powered piece of cable equipment that resides in the subscriber's home and provides tuning, descrambling, and pay-per-view capabilities.

SHA-1 (Secure Hash Algorithm-1)   A message authentication mechanism that hashes a file of arbitrary length into a 160-bit value; it is more processor intensive, but renders higher security.

SHF (superhigh frequency)   Frequencies from 3GHz to 30GHz.

shielded cable   A cable in which the signal carrying wire is enclosed by an outer sheath to reduce the effects of electromagnetic interference on the signals. The shielding also reduces the effect of these signals on nearby electrical components and helps to prevent electronic eavesdropping.

ships-in-the-night routing   An approach to routing multiple protocols by which each protocol is routed based on a separate routing mechanism. For example, IP routed via OSPF and CLNP routed via IS-IS might be used to handle the routing for both IP and CLNP.

sideband   The frequency band on either the upper or lower side of the carrier frequency band within which the frequencies produced by the process of modulation fall. Various modulation techniques make use of one or both of the sidebands, some of which also suppress the carrier frequency.

signal   A physical, time-dependent energy value used for the purpose of conveying information through a transmission line.

signaling   The process by which a caller or equipment on the transmitting end of a line informs a particular party or equipment at the receiving end that a message is to be communicated.

SIM (subscriber identity module) card   A smart card that defines the accounting and personal details of a service and can be used in any GSM handset to activate service.

simplex   Pertaining to the capability to transmit in one direction only.

simplex circuit   A circuit that permits the transmission of signals in one specified direction only.

single-attached station   A station connected to an FDDI network over a single fiber pair using a concentrator as the DAS. Single-attached stations can only be attached to one ring.

These stations are less expensive than dual-attached stations, but are less reliable because the optics, electronics, and the physical link must all be operational for the SAS to connect to the network.

single-carrier modulation A modulation scheme in which a single channel occupies the entire bandwidth.

SIP (Session Initiation Protocol) An application-layer control or signaling protocol for creating, modifying, and terminating sessions with one or more participants.

skin effect An occurence where as electricity migrates to the medium's skin, resistance increases because less of the wire is used.

SLA (service-level agreement) A contract between an ASP and the end user that stipulates and commits the ASP to a required level of service. An SLA should contain a specified level of service, support options, enforcement or penalty provisions for services not provided, a guaranteed level of system performance as relates to downtime or uptime, a specified level of customer support and what software or hardware will be provided and for what fee.

sleeve The third contacting part of a telephone plug, preceded in the location by the tip, and ring.

SLIP (Serial Line Internet Protocol) A minimal character-oriented protocol that provides basic IP encapsulation over dedicated or dialup asynchronous lines. Largely replaced by PPP.

smart card A credit-card–sized device with imbedded processors that provide a means of secure electronic storage. A smart card can be programmed to decrypt messages, to verify messages and digital signatures, and to create digital signatures for outgoing messages.

smart house A home in which broadband services connect various intelligent devices, such as smart appliances.

SMDS (Switched Multimegabit Data Service) A high-speed, packet-switched, datagram-based WAN networking technology that is offered by some telephone companies. It operates from 1.544Mbps to 44.736Mbps.

SMP (Simple Management Protocol) An SNMP extension that includes security features, bulk retrieval, manager-to-manager communication, better definition of managed objects, improved error handling, and configurable exception reporting while running over protocols other than UDP, and requiring less memory for implementation.

SMS (short message service) A system that enables text messages up to 160 alphanumeric characters in length to be sent to and from a GSM phone and to an external system such as e-mail, paging, and voicemail systems.

SMTP (Simple Mail Transfer Protocol) The message transport protocol used by TCP/IP networks, such as Internet and other UNIX-based network systems, for the exchange of electronic messages.

SNA (Systems Network Architecture) (1) IBM's standardized relationship between its VTAM and the NCP. (2) SNA specifies how products connect and communicate with one another in a network. SNA is a design for a total data communication system, encompassing every part of the communication network from the user's application program at the central site to the terminal at a remote location possible hundreds of miles away. SNA itself is not a system; it is an architecture. The purpose of SNA is to define uniform formats and protocols for data communication networks.

SNMP (Simple Network Management Protocol)   A standard low-level protocol that is used to monitor and manage nodes on a network. SNMP consists of agent software, which runs on the managed device, and manager software, which resides on a central system that polls the agents. SNMP is an alternative to CMIP.

SNMPv2 (Simple Network Management Protocol version 2)   A revision of SNMP that includes additional security features, the capability to transfer a large chunk of data at once, and the capability to communicate between SNMP management stations.

SNR (signal-to-noise ratio)   The relative power of a signal compared to the power of noise on a line, expressed in decibels (dB). As the ratio decreases, it becomes more difficult to distinguish between information and interference.

socket   An interface to the transport layer that consists of a group of functions that can be called from a program written in C. The calls that make up sockets are system calls, that is, they are direct calls to an operating system. Sockets permit an application program to access the services provided by TCP and UDP.

software   Computer instructions that perform common function for all users as well as specific applications for particular user needs.

softswitch   A device that implements service logic to control external trunking gateways, access gateways, and remote access servers. Softswitches run on commercial computers and operating systems, and they provide open applications programming interfaces. Also called a call agent or a media gateway controller.

solid-state device   Electronic pathways made of solid materials (e.g., chips and bubble memories).

SONET (Synchronous Optical Network)   The ANSI standard, incorporated into the SDH standard, defines a line rate hierarchy and frame formats for use with high-speed optical-fiber transmission systems (50.84Mbps to 2.488Gbps).

source route bridging   A bridging protocol supported by the 802.5 Token Ring standard. With source routing, the sending station is responsible for providing routing information for messages that cross multiple network segments. The sending station acquires routing information by first issuing a command to find the location of a particular destination. When the message is sent, the source station specifies the route to use by using the routing information field of the frame.

source routing transparent   The combination of source routing and transparent bridging in the same device.

SP (service provider)   A generic term for providers of different types of services.

space division   The carving up of a cellular service area into smaller coverage areas.

space-division switching   A method for switching circuits in which each connection through the switch takes a physically separate path.

spanning tree   A loop-free subset of a network's topology.

Spanning Tree Protocol   A protocol for complex bridge configurations defined by IEEE 802.1D. This protocol ensures that a complex bridge configuration has no loops; that is, there is one and only one possible patch from any particular end point to any other.

S-PCS (Satellite Personal Communications System)   A system that uses satellites to provide ubiquitous mobile communications.

SPE (synchronous payload envelope)   The payload portion of an STS or STM frame.

spectral efficiency   A measure of the number of digital bits that can be encoded in a single cycle of a wave form.

splitter   A filter used at each end of a copper pair to split the frequency bands.

spooling   Temporarily storing input and output data streams on disk or tapes files until the processor is ready.

spread spectrum technique   A technique by which a signal is transmitted in a bandwidth considerably greater than the frequency content of the original information. FHHS and DSSS are examples of spread-spectrum techniques.

SPX (Sequenced Packet Exchange)   The NetWare communications protocol used for interprocess communications. It guarantees that an entire message arrives intact and uses the NetWare IPX protocols as its delivery mechanism.

S/S (Start/Stop) signaling   A form of asynchronous communication line control that uses start elements and stop elements to control the transfer of data over a communication line. Each group of signals representing a character is preceded by a start signal and followed by a stop element.

SS7 (Signaling System 7)   A telecommunications protocol defined by the ITU as a way to offload PSTN data traffic congestion onto a wireless or wireline digital broadband network. SS7 architecture is set up in a way so that any node could exchange signaling with any other SS7-capable node, not just signaling between switches that are directly connected.

SS7 gateway   A device that allows an interface between circuit-switched networks (with their powerful SS7 infrastructure) and the emerging packet-switched networks that need to be able to handle the more traditional type of voice communications on a more cost-effective basis.

SSP (service-switching point)   A switch that originates or terminates a call.

ST connector   A type of connector used on optical-fiber cable, using a twist and lock coupling similar to the BNC connector that is used with Thinnet.

star   A network topology in which nodes are connected to a single central hub rather than to each other, forming a star-shaped configuration. If the hub is an intelligent device that controls the nodes' access to the network, the star topology is called active; when the hub is only a wiring connector, it's called passive.

static routing   Routing in which the routes are manually entered into the routing table.

station   A computer or device that can send and receive data over a communication line.

statistical multiplexer   A multiplexer that uses the idle time of connected devices to carry data traffic from active devices.

STDM (Statistical Time Division Multiplexing)   A method of TDM in which time slots on a shared medium are allocated on demand.

stop bit   In asynchronous transmission, the quiescent state following the transmission of a character; usually required to be at least 1-, 1.5-, or 2-bit times long.

stop element   The last bit of a character in asynchronous serial transmission, used to ensure recognition of the next start element.

store-and-forward   A technique that involves accepting a message or packet on a communications pathway retaining it in memory, and retransmitting it to the next station. Synonymous with message switching.

STM (Synchronous Transmission Module)   The basic building block of SDH. STM-1 consists of 9 rows of 270 bytes each. The first 9 columns contain the section and line overhead for all STS-3s. The remaining 261 columns contain the combined envelope capacity of the component STS-1s. STM levels include STM-0, STM-1, STM-4, STM-16, STM-64, and STM-256.

STP (service transfer point)   A switch that is responsible for translating the SS7 messages and then routing those messages between the appropriate network nodes and databases.

STP (shielded twisted-pair)   Two insulated wires in a cable wrapped with metallic braid or foil to prevent interference and to provide noise-free transmission.

streaming media   Data that is transferred so that it can be processed as a steady and continuous stream. Streaming technologies are becoming increasingly important with the growth of the Internet, because most users do not have fast enough access to download large multimedia files quickly. With streaming media, the client browser or plug-in can start displaying the data before the entire file has been transmitted.

STS (Synchronous Transport Signal)   The basic building block of SONET. The basic building block signaling rate for a SONET transmission medium is STS-1, which is 51.8 million bits per second. The signal is composed of 8000 frames per second, with 810 8-bit bytes per frame (8 bits/byte × 810 bytes/frame × 8000 frames/sec = 51.840Mbps). A SONET STS-1 frame contains more than 30 times the data of a T-1 frame. Other STS rates are STS-3, STS-12, STS-48, STS-192, and STS-768.

subnet mask   A configuration feature of a router that is used to select the portion of a 32-bit TCP/IP node address that refers to the LAN and to select the portion that refers to the node on the LAN.

subnetting   A technique used to impose a hierarchy on IP addresses that supports a form of area routing.

subrate   Transmission speeds below DS-0/64Kbps.

subsystem   A part of a system that does defined functions.

subvoice grade channel   A channel with bandwidth narrower than that of voice grade channels. Such channels are usually subchannels of a voice grade line.

supervision   The process of detecting a change of state between idle and busy conditions on a circuit.

supervisory signal   A signal that handles the on-hook/off-hook condition.

SVC (switched virtual circuit)   A virtual connection that is set up on a call-by-call basis.

switched digital access   A dialup option in which facilities are allocated based on demand, rather than being associated with a specific customer all the time.

switched line   A temporary connection between computers or devices that is established by dialing.

switching   Establishing of transmission path from a particular inlet to a particular outlet of a group of such inlets and outlets.

switching center   A location that terminates multiple circuits and is capable of interconnecting circuits or transferring traffic between circuits.

switching system   A device that connects two transmission lines together.

switchhook   A switch on a telephone set that is associated with the structure supporting the receiver or handset and is often used to signal the switching equipment or an attendant during a call.

switchover   A switch to an alternative component that happens when a failure occurs in the equipment.

symmetric encryption   Encryption in which the sender and the receiver use the same key or machine setup.

synchronization   The process of adjusting a receiving terminal's clock to match the clock of the transmitting terminal.

synchronous   (1) Having a constant time interval between successive bits, characters, or events. Synchronous transmission uses no extra information (such as the start and stop bits in asynchronous transmission) to identify the beginning and end of characters and thus is faster and more efficient than asynchronous transmission. The timing is achieved by transmitting sync characters prior to data. Usually, synchronization can be achieved in two- or three-character times. (2) Occurring with a regular or predictable time relationship. In data transmission, the time of occurrence of each signal representing a bit is related to a fixed time frame.

synchronous communications   High-speed transmission of contiguous groups of characters in which the stream of monitored and read bits uses a clock rate to transfer the characters over a communication line.

synchronous network   A network in which all the communications links are synchronized to a common clock.

Synchronous TDM (Time Division Multiplexing)   A method of TDM in which time slots on a shared transmission line are assigned on a fixed, predetermined basis.

synchronous transmission   In data communication, a method of transmission in which the sending and receiving of characters is controlled by timing signals. The sending and receiving terminals are operating continuously in step with each other.

synchronous transport module level *n*   One of the elements that comprise the SDH signal hierarchy. STM-1 defines the basic building block corresponding to a data rate of 155.52Mbps and a frame structure of 2,430 bytes every 125 microseconds.

synchronous transport signal level *n*   One of the elements that comprises the SONET signal hierarchy. STS-1 defines the basic building block corresponding to a data rate of 51.84Mbps and a frame structure of 810 bytes every 125 microseconds.

system   A computer and its associated devices and programs.

system test   A complete simulation of an actual running configuration for purposes of ensuring the adequacy of the configuration.

T

TA (terminal adapter)   A protocol converter that connects a non-ISDN device to the ISDN network.

TACS (Total Access Communications System)   A standard for analog telephony that was deployed widely in Europe before GSM became the most popular approach.

T-carrier   The North American standard of the PDH, a time-division multiplexed, digital transmission system. T-carrier is a PCM system that uses 64Kbps per channel as the basis of the hierarchy. Higher levels reflect aggregation of the 64Kbps channels. T-1 is a 1.544Mbps 24-channel communications circuit; T-2 is a 6.312Mbps 96-channel communications circuit; T-3 is a 44.736Mbps 672-channel communications circuit; T-4 is a 274.176Mbps 4,032-channel communications circuit.

tandem   (1) The connection of networks or circuits in series (i.e., the connection of the output of one circuit to the input of another). (2) An intermediate switch used in a tandem network, which connects only to other switches instead of customers.

tandem data circuit   A data circuit that contains two or more pieces of DCE in series.

tandem switch   Also called a junction exchange or a tandem office, a switch that is used to connect local exchanges throughout the metropolitan area.

tap   An open point on a cable bundle that is left so that technicians can easily splice off a pair to bring additional service to a home or to bring service to a new home.

tariff   The published rate for the use of a specific unit of equipment, facility, or type of service provided by a communications common carrier; also, the vehicle by which the regulating agencies approve or disapprove such facilities or services.

TASI (Time-Assignment Speech Interpolation)   Specialized switching equipment that connects a party to an idle circuit while speech is taking place, but disconnects the party when speech stops, so that a different party can use the same circuit. During the periods of heavy traffic, TASI can improve line efficiency by 45% to 80%.

Tbps (terabits per second)   Trillions of bits per second.

TCAP (Transaction Capabilities Applications Part)   A system that supports intelligent network service by enabling the exchange of noncircuit-related information between different signaling points (that is, network nodes).

TCP/IP (Transmission Control Protocol/Internet Protocol)   The most widely used internetworking protocol. Ensures that packets of data are delivered to their destinations in sequence in which they were transmitted. TCP roughly corresponds to Layer 4 of the OSI model. It provides reliable transmission of data. IP corresponds to Layer 3 (the network layer) of the OSI model and provides connectionless datagram service.

TDD (Time Division Duplexing)   A half-duplex technique in which each end of the conversation makes use of the same frequency.

TDM (Time Division Multiplexing)   A means of obtaining a number of channels over a single path by dividing the path into a number of time slots and assigning each channel its own intermittently repeated time slot. At the receiving end, each time-separated channel is reassembled.

TDMA (Time Division Multiple Access)   A multiple-access technique in which you first divide the available or allocated frequency spectrum into a number of channels. Then, within each channel you apply TDM to carry multiple users interleaved in time.

telco   A telephone company.

telecommunication lines   Telephone and other communication pathways that are used to transmit information from one location to another.

telecommunications   Any process that permits the passage of information from a sender to one or more receivers in any usable form (printed copy, fixed or moving pictures, visible or audible signals, and so on) by means of any electromagnetic system (electrical transmission by wire, radio, optical transmission, waveguides, and so on).

Telecommunications Technology Committee   A body that creates telecommunications standards that are followed in Japan.

teledensity   The number of main telephone lines per 100 inhabitants.

telephone channel   A transmission path designed for the transmission of representing human speech or other telephone communication (e.g., fax) requiring the same bandwidth. The bandwidth of an analog telephone channel is 4,000Hz.

telephony   A generic term describing voice telecommunications.

Telnet   The TCP/IP site protocol that supports a remote login capability.

tera   One trillion.

Terabit switch router   An emerging class of backbone platform that supports Tbps capacity. This type of router is agnostic, and it involves short and predictable delay, robust QoS features, multicast support, and carrier class-availability.

terminal   (1) A point at which information can enter or leave a communication network. (2) Any device capable of sending and/or receiving information over a communication channel. (3) Same as work station.

terminal multiplexer   A device that permits two or more terminals to share one cable as a data transmission path.

terminal server   A device that connects terminals to a network that is typically running Ethernet.

ThickNet (thick Ethernet cable)   Coaxial cable with electrical characteristics that meet the 10Base5 specification for Ethernet networks. It enables a signal to be carried as far as 1,640 feet (500 meters) before requiring a repeater. Also called 10Base5 cable.

ThinNet (thin Ethernet cable)   Coaxial cable with electrical characteristics that meet the 10Base2 specification for Ethernet networks. It enables a signal to be carried as far as 607 feet (185 meters) before requiring a repeater. Also called 10Base2 cable or Cheapernet.

throughput   The useful information processed or communicated during a specific time period; expressed in bits per second or packets per second.

TIA (Telecommunications Industry Association)   An organization that recommends standards for telecommunication.

time-division switching   A switching method for a TDM channel that requires the shifting of data from one slot to another in the TDM frame. The slot question can carry a bit, byte, or, in principle, any other unit of data.

timeout   A set time period for waiting before a terminal system performs some action. Typical uses include a poll release (when a terminal is disconnected if the time-out period elapses before keying resumes), or in access timeout (when a terminal on a local area network using a CSMA/CD access method is prevented from transmitting for a specified time period after a collision occurs).

time-slot interchange   The interchange of time slots within a TDM frame.

Time to Live   A field in an IP datagram that is decremented by each router in order to guarantee that datagrams do not circulate on the Internet forever.

time transparency   The absence of delay and delay jitter through an ATM network thus allowing high-speed transportation of real-time services.

tip   The contacting part at the end of a telephone plug or the top spring of a jack. The conductors associated with these contracts. The other contact is called a ring.

token   A small, 8-bit word that is circulated in a unidirectional fashion among the devices on the network.

token passing   A network access method that uses a special bit pattern called a token that gives permission to nodes to transmit data, one node at a time. Each node is allowed to transmit a message only when it has the token. If a node has no messages to transmit when it receives the token, it passes the token to the next node.

Token Ring   A networked ring of devices that passes a special bit pattern called a token from node to node to determine which device can transmit data on the network. Operates at either 4Mbps or 16Mbps.

toll center   The exchange that is responsible for establishing and completing national, long-distance communications. Also called the Class 4 office, transit switch, toll office, or trunk exchange.

tone signaling   Transmission of supervisory, address, and alerting signals over a telephone circuit by means of tones.

tone-to-dial-pulse conversion   A system of converting DTMF signals to dial pulse signals when the trunks associated with outgoing trunk calls are not equipped to receive tone signals. Auxiliary dial pulse conversion equipment is not necessary.

topology   The connectivity among a group of nodes. Physical topology relates to how devices are cabled. Logical topology refers to how nodes actually interact.

trace packet   In packet switching, a packet that functions as a normal packet but causes a report of each stage of its process to be sent to the network control center.

traffic   (1) Messages sent and received over a communications channel. (2) A quantitative measurement of the total messages and their length, expressed in 100 call seconds or other units.

traffic flow   A measure of the density of traffic.

transaction   An item of business. The handling of customer orders and billing are examples of transactions.

transaction processing   In batch or remote batch processing, the processing of a job or job step-in interactive processing, an exchange between a terminal and another device that does a particular action; for example, the entry of a customer's deposit and the updating of the customer's balance.

transceiver A device that connects a host interface to a local area network.

transducer A device for converting signals from one form to another, such as a microphone or a receiver.

transmission line A connection over which data devices communicate. There are five main types of transmission lines: circuits, channels, lines, trunks, and virtual circuits.

transmission medium A physical pathway that connects computers, other devices, and people on a network. Transmission media can be either wireline (e.g., twisted-pair, fiber) or wireless (e.g., satellite, microwave).

transfer rate The speed at which information can be sent across a bus or communications link.

translational bridge A bridge that may connect two different MAC layers (e.g., 802.3 and FDDI).

transmission Information that is sent in the form of electrical signals over electric wires, waveguides, or radio.

transmission speed The rate at which information is passed through communications lines, generally measured in bits per second (bps).

transmit To send information from one location to another.

transparent bridging A system in which the bridge functions as a node on each of the connected networks, and its presence in the communications path between nodes is transparent. Communications proceeds as if the nodes were on the same network.

transponder The receiver, transmitter, and antenna equipment that together forms a single repeater channel on a satellite.

transport layer Layer 4 of the OSI model, providing reliable, transparent transfer of data between endpoints.

tree A type of bus network topology in which the medium branches at certain points along its length to connect stations or clusters of stations; also called a branching bus.

troubleshooting Monitoring and testing the performance of a network to detect and fix problems.

trunk A circuit that is configured to support the calling loads generated by a group of users; the transmission facility that ties together switching systems.

tunneling The encapsulation of one protocol within another. Tunneling is often used to transport a LAN protocol across a backbone network that does not support the LAN protocol.

turnkey system A complete communications system, including hardware and software, assembled and installed by a vendor, and sold as a total package.

twisted-pair cable A cable that consists of two insulated wires twisted around each other (and sometimes wrapped in additional insulation to help shield their signals from electromagnetic noise). Twisted-pair cable is often used in telephone wires; it also serves as the transmission medium in some LANs.

two-wire circuit A circuit formed by two conductors insulated from each other that can be used as either a one-way transmission path, a half-duplex path, or a duplex path.

Twofish   A very strong encryption algorithm that was one of the five initial candidates for the AES.

type approval   An administrative procedure of technical tests and vetting applied to items of telecommunication equipment before they can be sold or interconnected with the public network. Also known as *homologation*.

U

UBR (unspecified bit rate)   An ATM service class that provides best-effort service. UBR offers no service guarantee, so you would use it for text data, image transfer, messaging, and distributing information that's noncritical, where you don't have to have a set response time or service guarantee.

UDP (User Datagram Protocol)   A minimal-functionality transport-layer protocol in the TCP/IP protocol suite.

UHF (ultrahigh frequency)   The portion of the electromagnetic spectrum that ranges from about 300MHz to about 3GHz and includes television and cellular radio frequencies.

UMTS (Universal Mobile Telecommunications System)   An evolving European standard for 3G mobile communications. The convergence of mobile and fixed networks, as well as terrestrial wireless and satellite-based networks.

unicasting   Sending streams from a single origination point directly to a single destination point.

Unicode   A coding scheme that assigns 16 bits per character (that is, 2^{16}), which translates to more than 65,000 possible characters.

uniform-spectrum random noise   Noise distributed over the spectrum in such a way that the power-per-unit bandwidth is constant. Also called white noise.

UNII (Unlicensed National Information Infrastructure)   Unlicensed radio bands that operate at 5.2GHz.

UNIX   A multiuser, open operating system developed by Bell Laboratories.

unlicensed bands   Radio bands that can be used to provide broadband access, without the need for obtaining a license. Networks that use unlicensed bands have a range of about 35 miles (55 kilometers) and offer throughput from 128Kbps to 10Mbps over shared media.

unshielded cable   A cable in which the signal carrying wire or circuit is not shielded to keep out electromagnetic noise that can potentially damage the data stream.

UPS (uninterruptible power supply)   A device that usually includes in an inverter, drawing its power from batteries, which generates an extremely "well-behaved" AC power signal for a PBX or other equipment. If a particularly heavy demand is anticipated, the system can be coupled with an auxiliary generator that is started when commercial power is interrupted.

upstream   The direction of transmission flow away from the user.

UPT (Universal Personal Telephony)   An evolving ITU-R standard for the provision of personal mobility across many different kinds of fixed and mobile networks.

UTP (unshielded twisted-pair cable)   A twisted-pair cable in which the two insulated wires that twist around each other are not surrounded by additional insulation.

UWC (Universal Wireless Communications)   Also called NADC, a wireless standard specified as IS-54 that was adopted in 1992. It has since been updated, and it is now called IS-136. It uses TDMA and TDD schemes.

V

V.11   An ITU-T standard that describes electrical characteristics for balanced double-current interchange circuits for general use with integrated circuit equipment.

V.21   An ITU-T standard that describes 300bps modems for use in the PSTN.

V.24   ITU-T definitions for interchange circuits between data terminal equipment and data circuit-terminating equipment.

V.25   An ITU-T standard that describes automatic calling and/or answering equipment on the general switched network.

V.29   An ITU-T standard that describes 9,600bps modems for use in the PSTN.

V.35   An ITU-T standard that describes data transmission at 56Kbps that uses balanced transmission methods through a 34-pin physical interface.

VAD (voice activity detection)   A technique that reduces the amount of information needed to re-create the voice at the destination end by removing silent periods and redundant information found in human speech; this also helps with compression.

validation   An attempt to find errors by executing a program in a given environment.

value-added carrier   A company that sells services of a value-added network. It can be a PTT, or a subsidiary, or an independent company.

value-added service   A communications facility that uses communications common carrier networks for transmission and that provides enhanced extra data features with separate equipment; such extra features, including store-and-forward message switching, terminal interfacing, and host interfacing, are common.

VAN (value-added network) services   Telecommunication services provided over public or private networks which, in some way, add value to the basic carriage, usually through the applications of computerized intelligence, for instance, reservation systems, bulletin boards, information services.

VAR (value-added reseller)   A provider that deals with distribution and sales.

VBR (variable bit rate)   An ATM service class for network traffic that is typically from bursty data transfer applications, such as client/server and LAN to LAN interconnection. VBR offers guaranteed service delivery. VBR-RT (real-time) is designed for real-time voice and videoconferencing applications, and VBR-NRT (nonreal-time) is for mission-critical data applications.

VC (virtual circuit)   A logical connection established through a packet network, over which packets are routed, mimicking to some extent the behavior of a dedicated physical connection.

VC (virtual container)   A data structure designed for the transport and switching of sub-STM-0 network services such as CEPT-1. All network services below E-3 are mapped into VCs, and VCs are multiplexed into the SPE of an STM-1.

VCI (virtual channel identifier)   In ATM, the part of a cell header that identifies the channel associated with the cell.

VDSL (Very-High-Bit-Rate DSL)   A transmission medium that provides a maximum span of about 5,000 feet (1,500 meters) over a single twisted-pair cable. Over this distance, you can get up to a rate of 13Mbps downstream, and if you shorten the distance to 1,000 feet (300 meters), you can get up to 52Mbps downstream, which would be enough capacity to facilitate tomorrow's digital TVs. VDSL gives you 1.5Mbps to 2.3Mbps upstream.

VDT (video dial tone)   A U.S. term defining the capability of a network access provider to offer video access and carriage directly to or from subscribers.

vertical blanking interval   Unused lines in each field of a TV signal. Some of these lines may be used for captions and specialized signal and cable service.

VF (voice frequency)   Any frequency within the part of the audio frequency range that is essential for the transmission of speech of commercial quality; that is, 250Hz to 3,400Hz. Also called telephone frequency.

VHF (very high frequency)   The portion of the electromagnetic spectrum with frequencies between about 30MHz and 300MHz. Operating band for radio and television channels.

video signal   A signal comprising frequencies normally required to transmit moving image information.

videoconferencing   A two-way communication between two or more parties that involves the exchange of images as well as voice. The images may or may not be in full motion.

videotelephony   Interactive communication between two-parties involving the transmission and reception of images, as well as voice. The degree to which the images are in full motion depends upon the level of data compression used, as well as the available bandwidth.

videotext   A public or private telecommunication service that offers interactive browsing of a menu of textual and graphical information. The most widely used public videotex service is France Telecom's service, offered via Minitel terminals.

virtual channel   In ATM, the specific conversation path over which the cells from a given conversation flow from one ATM switch to another.

virtual circuit   A series of logical, rather than physical, connections between sending and receiving devices. With a virtual circuit, two hosts can communicate as though they have a dedicated connection, although the packets may be taking very different routes to arrive at their destination.

VISP (virtual Internet service provider)   A provider that offers outsourced Internet service, running as a branded ISP. It is a turnkey ISP product aimed at affinity groups and mass marketers that want to add Internet access to their other products and services.

VLAN (virtual local area network)   A network of computers that behave as if they are connected to the same wire even though they may actually be physically located on different segments of a LAN. VLANs are configured through software rather than hardware, which makes them extremely flexible. A big advantage of VLANs is that when a computer is physically moved to another location, it can stay on the same VLAN without any hardware reconfiguration.

VLF (very low frequency)   Frequencies below 30KHz.

VoATM (Voice over ATM)   A technology for transporting integrated digital voice, video, and data over ATM networks.

vocoders (voice coder/decoder)   A device used for compression of voice traffic. High-bit-rate vocoders are used by PCS, wireless local loops, and wireless office telecommunication systems applications. Low-bit-rate vocoders are used in cellular systems that deal with vehicular traffic, where there are large cells and a need to facilitate a large number of conversations.

VOD (video-on-demand)   A service whereby a subscriber can order and (almost) immediately view films and other entertainment from a television set. In "true" video-on-demand, the film can be paused, rewound, or fast-forwarded. In "near" video-on-demand these functions are not possible.

VoDSL (Voice over DSL)   A technology for delivering voice transmissions over DSL lines. VoDSL enables service providers to deliver high-speed data access and up to 16 telephone lines over 1 DSL line.

VoFR (Voice over Frame Relay)   A technology for transporting integrated digital voice, video, and data over Frame Relay networks.

voice digitization   Conversion of an analog voice into digital symbols for storage or transmission.

voice grade   A telecommunications link with a bandwidth (about 4KHz) appropriate to an audio telephone line.

voice-grade channel   A channel with a frequency range of 4KHz. Also referred to as a telephone channel.

voice recognition   A technology that allows spoken words in the form of human voice to provide input to a computer.

voice synthesis   Computer-generated sounds that simulate the human voice.

VoIP (Voice over IP)   A technology for transporting integrated digital voice, video, and data over IP networks.

VoIP gateway   A device that bridges the traditional circuit-switched PSTN and the packet-switched Internet.

volatile storage   Memory that loses its contents when electrical power is removed.

VP (virtual path)   A generic term for a collection of virtual channels that have the same endpoint.

VPI (virtual path identifier)   In ATM, the portion of a cell header that identifies the virtual path to which the cell belongs. Virtual paths are defined to permit groups of virtual channels to be manipulated as if they were a single channel.

VPN (virtual private network)   A software-defined network offered by telephone carriers for voice and data communications among multiple sites. The VPN provides the appearance of a private line network, except that it makes use of the public switched network rather than physically dedicated leased lines. In *customer-based VPNs,* carriers install gateways, routers, and other VPN equipment on the customer premises. This is preferred when customers want to have control over all aspects of security. In *network-based VPNs,* the carrier houses all the necessary equipment at a point-of-presence (POP) near the customer's location. Customers that want to take advantage of the carrier's VPN economies of scale prefer this type of VPN.

VPN gateway A device that enables VPNs to set up and maintain secure tunnels through the Internet.

VR (virtual reality) A computer-based application that provides a human-computer interface such that the computer and its devices create a sensory environment called the virtual world. The sensory environment is dynamically controlled by actions of the individual so that the environment appears real.

VRC (vertical redundancy check) An error-checking method that uses a parity bit for each character.

VSAT (very-small-aperture terminal) An earth station with a small antenna, usually 0.6 meters or less.

VT (virtual tributary) A data structure designed for the transport and switching of sub-STS-1 network services such as DS-1, DS-1C, and DS-2. All network services below DS-3 are mapped into VTs, and VTs are multiplexed into the SPE of an STS-1.

W

WAN (wide area network) A group of computer networks connected over long distances, often by telephone lines and satellite transmission.

WAP (Wireless Application Protocol) A protocol for transforming Internet information so that it can be displayed on the small screen of a mobile telephone or other portable device.

WARC (World Administrative Radio Conference) A regular meeting of global authorities to decide on spectrum allocation.

wave form A curve that shows the shape of a wave at any given time.

waveguide A transmission path in which a system of boundaries guides electromagnetic energy. The most common of these are hollow metallic conducting tubes (microwave communications) or rods of dielectric material.

wavelength The distance between two consecutive maxima or minima of the wave form.

wavelength changer A device that converts an optical signal to an electronic signal and then sends the signal to a laser that produces an optical signal at a different wavelength than the original.

wavelength division switching Switching in which input information is used to modulate a light source that has a unique wavelength for each input. All the optical energy is combined and then split, so it can be distributed to all the output channels.

WCDMA (Wideband CDMA) A multiple-access technique that operates over allocations of either 5MHz, 10MHz, or 15MHz. WCDMA can support higher data rates than first-generation CDMA.

WDM (Wavelength Division Multiplexing) The multiplexing of signals by transmitting them at different wavelengths through the same fiber.

wearables Smart devices that are small enough to be worn on the human body and are able to be networked.

wideband Refers to the range of speeds between narrowband and broadband, typically ranging between $n \times 64$Kbps up to 45Mbps.

wideband channel   A channel that is wider in bandwidth than a voice-grade channel.

wireless   A generic term for mobile communications services such as cellular, radiopaging, or PCS, that do not use wireline networks for direct access to the subscriber.

wireless local loop   A technology that uses low-power radio transmission, cellular radio and/or cordless telephony, as an alternative to local loops for accessing the switched telephone network.

wiring closet   A location in a building where building wiring terminates and where equipment (e.g., hub electronics) is placed.

WML (Wireless Markup Language)   A markup language that is used in the WAP environment.

workstation   A device that lets you transmit information to or receive information from a computer, or both, as needed to perform a job; for example, a display station or a printer.

world numbering plan   An ITU-T numbering plan, E.164, that divides the world into nine zones. Each zone is allocated a number that forms the first digit of the country code for every country in that zone. The zones are follows: (1) North America (including Hawaii and Caribbean islands, except Cuba), (2) Africa, (3 and 4) Europe, (5) South America and Cuba, (6) South Pacific (Australasia), (7) Russia, (8) North Pacific (Eastern Asia), and (9) Asia and the Middle East. There is also a spare code (0), which is available for future use.

WWW (World Wide Web)   An Internet application that uses hypertext links between remote network servers for accessing and displaying multimedia information.

X

X.3   An ITU-T standard that defines the basic functionality of an asynchronous PAD usually used in conjunction with ITU-T standards X.28 and X.29.

X.21   An ITU-T recommendation that defines a general purpose physical interface between a DTE and DCE for full duplex synchronous operation on circuit switched or packet-switched data networks.

X.25   A standard that defines the interface between DTE and DCE for equipment operating in the packet mode on public data networks. It also defines a link control protocol.

X.75   A standard for connecting X.25 networks, developed by the ITU-T

X.121   The ITU-T standard for the addressing plan used with X.25 PDNs.

X.400   A standard for electronic mail exchange; developed by the ITU-T.

X.500   The family of protocols that define the operation of the ITU-T/ISO directory service.

X.509   The ITU-T/OSI recommendation for a directory authentication framework.

Index

LIDO Telecommunications Essentials® e-Learning

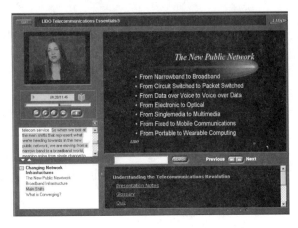

Part I—Communications Fundamentals

Part II—Data Networking and the Internet

Part III—Next-Generation Networks

Lillian Goleniewski's innovative new e-Learning series includes:

- Twenty-two hours of dynamic video lectures
- Simultaneous word-for-word transcript
- Synchronized slide show
- Search capability
- Comprehensive notes and diagrams
- Clickable links to related resources
- An online learning center

Previous customers have said:

"This is an excellent 'starter course' for new people in the industry and an outstanding 'refresher course' for those already in the industry."
—*Keith Holdt, Senior Consultant, IBM*

"Excellent content, knowledge of the issues, and ability to communicate key areas."
—*Justin Forsell, Head of Legal Affairs, BT Japan*

"Covered many technical areas while still being clear and engaging."
—*Alexandra Rehak, Manager Asia Pacific, Motorola*

For more information, or to order, please visit www.telecomessentials.com, or send an email to info@lidoorg.com.

Lido Telecommunications Essentials® is the registered trademark of The Lido Organization, Inc.

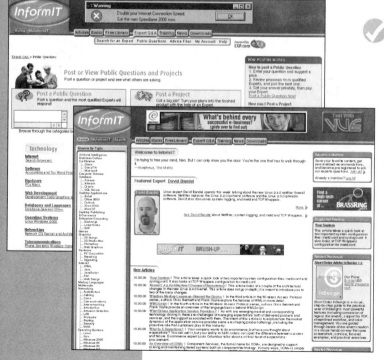